PERSPECTIVES ON POLITICAL COMMUNICATION

A Case Approach

LAUREN COHEN BELL

Randolph-Macon College

JOAN L. CONNERS

Randolph-Macon College

THEODORE F. SHECKELS

Randolph-Macon College

PEARSON

2200

Boston   New York   San Francisco
Mexico City   Montreal   Toronto   London   Madrid   Munich   Paris
Hong Kong   Singapore   Tokyo   Cape Town   Sydney

Acquisitions Editor: *Jeanne Zalesky*
Series Editorial Assistant: *Brian Mickelson*
Marketing Manager: *Suzan Czajkowski*
Production Supervisor: *Karen Mason*
Editorial Production Service: *Nesbitt Graphics, Inc.*
Composition Buyer: *Linda Cox*
Manufacturing Buyer: *JoAnne Sweeney*
Electronic Composition: *Nesbitt Graphics, Inc.*
Cover Administrator: *Kristina Mose-Libon*

Library of Congress Cataloging-in-Publication Data
Bell, Lauren Cohen
Perspectives on political communication : a case approach / Lauren Cohen Bell, Joan L. Conners, Theodore F. Sheckels.—1st ed.
p. cm.
Includes bibliographical references and index.
ISBN 0-205-50887-1 (alk. paper)   ISBN-13: 978-0-205-50887-7
1. Communication in politics—United States—Case studies. 2. Communication in public administration—United States—Case studies. I. Conners, Joan L. II. Sheckels, Theodore F. III. Title.
JA85.2.U6B45 2007
320.97301'4—dc22

2007027925

Printed in the United States of America

10   9   8   7   6   5   4   3   2   1   11   10   09   08   07

CONTENTS

CHAPTER SIX

CHAPTER SEVEN

CHAPTER EIGHT

CHAPTER NINE

Case Five: 2006 Midterm Elections   160

CHAPTER TEN

Case Six: Ronald Reagan's 1981 Inaugural Address   190

CHAPTER SIXTEEN

Case Twelve: The Gay-Lesbian Rights Movement   328

CHAPTER SEVENTEEN

Case Thirteen: Politics in Popular Culture   352

CHAPTER EIGHTEEN

PREFACE

We wrote this book because we believe that the case study approach offers significant benefits over the traditional approach to teaching political communication, especially to undergraduate students. With real-world stories to learn from and distinct perspectives of analysis, students will gain a more comprehensive view of political communication.

THE CASE STUDY APPROACH

Case studies offer students something tangible, something real. Our experiences teaching this material to our students demonstrates that they typically remember the "stories," and then they remember the theoretical and practical elements of the class discussion. Moreover, an important corollary benefit of the case study approach is that it permits a focus on *how* we analyze political communication. Dealing with the *how* in a thoughtful, comprehensive way is necessary to empower students to become critical consumers of political communication, not only learners who know about concepts, theories, and studies.

MULTIDISCIPLINARY PERSPECTIVES

The question of *how* to analyze political communication, however, is a tricky one, for there is no single answer. Our experience as three colleagues who share an interest in American politics and political communication has demonstrated this fact to us repeatedly. Although we frequently identify the same things as important features of an election campaign, for example, and may ultimately reach similar conclusions about that campaign, we arrive at our assessments using different processes because we come from three rather different traditions.

One author is a political scientist, trained to use empirical methods to study American government. Another author is a mass communication scholar, trained in journalism and mass communication more broadly to combine theory and empirical investigation to discern what different types of media do. The other author is a rhetorician, trained in various kinds of criticism and how they can be used to illuminate the ways that "texts" work.

We believe strongly that students will benefit by studying political communication through all three of these lenses. Doing so gives them a repertoire of approaches to choose among when considering the cases in this textbook and when applying what they have learned to other moments in political communication. Furthermore, by using different approaches students will understand diverse political topics more fully than they would have with only a single approach. Finally, because each of the authors offers in the introductory chapters a guide to *how* we examine the cases considered in this text, students will be able to approach their reading of the cases with a solid understanding of what each perspective entails.

OVERVIEW

This book represents the juxtaposition and synthesis of three complementary perspectives on important cases in political communication. Three introductory chapters present, in turn, the political science, rhetorical, and mass communication perspectives and yield to thirteen case studies. In each case study, the authors take turns, suggesting to students what each perspective might highlight if considering the case followed by a summary that integrates and compares the themes highlighted by each perspective.

Chapter 1 explains our approach to students. Chapters 2, 3, and 4 offer snapshots of the three perspectives. In these chapters, we do not try to offer complete courses on our separate subjects. Rather, we offer an overview of the concepts that we think are the most important to an understanding of how we approach thinking about political communication. We try to address the needs of undergraduates as well as to present what we believe are the core concepts in our fields. As scholars, we do not see ourselves as necessarily traditional, but we do see our undergraduate audience as needing a strong, somewhat traditional foundation before moving forward. There are points in the book where we do push, and we hope that those who really want to push can further our commentary.

We each adapt and refine these concepts in later chapters. Chapters 5 through 17 are the case studies. Our goal is not to assemble the three perspectives into a complete analysis; instead, our goal is to present insights, drawn from three disciplinary perspectives, that lead to a fuller discussion of the particular case—and cases like it.

WHY THESE CASES?

Each case study chapter offers an overview of the case, our separate responses to it, and some concluding thoughts. We selected cases based on our sense of what political communication courses typically cover. We know from looking at many such courses that there is no such thing as *the* "political communication" course. However, most classes spend a great deal of time looking at election campaigns. (In fact, many do nothing but look at election campaigns.) As a result, we devote five chapters to elections—three to presidential elections and two to statewide races. In choosing the elections to feature we considered the topics we wanted the five chapters to collectively discuss. For example, we knew that we wanted to write about negative advertising, so we selected the 1988 presidential campaign; because we also wanted to talk about presidential debates that made a difference, we selected the 2000 presidential campaign. The 2004 presidential campaign gave us the opportunity to talk about advertising sponsored by sources other than the candidates as well as the impact of emerging technologies, such as the Internet, on the conduct of campaigns. Our consideration of the 1998 Minnesota gubernatorial campaign enabled us to talk about such matters as celebrity politicians and third parties—not to mention Jesse Ventura, whose campaign and governorship are interesting in and of themselves. Finally, we wanted to apply each of our perspectives to as current a campaign as possible. For that reason, we include a case focused on the crucial U.S. Senate races in 2006. This case, broader than the others dealing with elections, allowed us to talk about the common elements in an election year while noting that different campaign dynamics operate in different states and races.

In addition to elections, political communication courses frequently explore presidential communication. So, in Chapters 10, 11, and 12 we focus on different aspects of the presidency. Chapter 10 deals with a presidential inaugural address as an example of a presidential speech that sets forth one president's philosophy of governing. The inaugural we selected—Ronald Reagan's in 1981—is especially interesting because of how Reagan took advantage of his vista from the Capitol's west side and because Iran was simultaneously releasing Americans long held hostage in the U.S. embassy in Tehran. Chapter 11 offers insights into another presidential genre— the apology, with an analysis of former President Bill Clinton's *mea culpa* in the Monica Lewinsky scandal. Chapter 12 deals with crisis and war rhetoric, with a focus on George W. Bush's comments on terrorism, Afghanistan, and Iraq.

Despite the relative paucity of research in the communication discipline on the legislative and judicial branches of the federal government, many courses give some consideration to communication in these institutions. Chapters 13 and 14 offer examples of congressional communication. Chapter 13 focuses on the famous Supreme Court confirmation hearing for Clarence Thomas, which featured graphic accusations of sexual harassment directed at the nominee, and Chapter 14 analyzes a flamboyant, nonstop, 24-hour-long Senate debate.

We devote only one chapter, Chapter 15, to the judicial branch since the judiciary communicates less with the public than do the other branches. We focus on the primary method of external communication used by the high court—the decision it renders and the accompanying concurring and dissenting opinions. We chose *Texas v. Johnson* (1989) because it exemplified these forms of communication.

Other topics, including social movements and popular culture, also find their way into political communication courses. We offer a look at social movements because there are many in the communication field, especially among the rhetoricians, who have a strong research interest in the subject, and chose the Gay-Lesbian Rights Movement as our case because it has been identified by many commentators as this generation's most important civil rights battle. We include a case study of popular culture because students engage with popular culture on a regular basis and because popular culture is becoming increasingly important in politics.

THE DESIGN OF THE CASE STUDY CHAPTERS

For each case study chapter, we first offer some background information as well as a generous amount of "text" from the case. We use the primary text so that students can interact with the real political communication event, not analyses of it. Then, we offer separate political science, rhetorical, and mass communication perspectives on the case. Each of us highlights the matters that we would bring into a conversation on the case in question. Sometimes our focus is very much on the text or type of communication discussed at the outset of the chapter; in other instances, we explore beyond the precipitating event to bring in material that we think helps to put the case in context. We quite consciously return to ideas introduced in Chapters 2, 3, and 4, because we want students to see how these ideas might be used in practice to illuminate a moment in politics.

Finally, at the end of each case study chapter we offer additional, similar cases students might explore. For each additional case we suggest, we offer students a way into the case—usually a reference to the relevant "text" and, in many cases, a reference to some explanatory material.

THE CHOICES WE MADE

All books involve choices. Besides choosing certain topics and not others, and certain cases and not others, we also had to choose what to offer the student by way of an overview of our perspective and what aspects to highlight case by case. These were not easy choices. Books can be written about each of the perspectives, and here we had only thirty or so pages. Plus each case invited many observations and we had space for only a handful each. How did we choose?

The same philosophy that informed our earlier chapters on our individual perspectives informed our choices as we framed our commentaries on the different cases. We wanted to expose students to certain fundamental matters. At the same time, we did occasionally want to push the discussion beyond the usual insights a political commentator might offer and toward what innovative critics and scholars might say. We hope we achieved a balance between what is essential for students to know and what students might want to ponder. We know that our colleagues will add their own insights to the exploration of the cases when they teach their courses, which will further enrich the students' analyses.

We chose to maintain our three distinct voices throughout this book. We did so because we discerned that, in our voices, there was not only a difference in academic persona but also a disciplinary distinction and the different voices will identify for the reader the perspective he or she is reading. Genuine criticism is informed by the speaker's voice and we tried to keep the commentary authentic.

Finally, we chose to steer a middle path between citing the relevant literature as we would if we were writing a scholarly essay and offering only our own critical reflections with few citations. Students need to know that a wealth of theory and research undergirds the conversation we are inviting them into, and they need to know what some of the crucial work is. The middle course we take in this text sends an important message about the considerable body of work that provides the intellectual foundation for what we do with political communication events.

We hope that faculty members who choose to ask undergraduates to read and use this textbook understand and appreciate why we proceeded with this unique approach. We also hope that, in the spirit of looking at case studies and then amassing insights from different perspectives on them, our colleagues will join us in encouraging students to continue to explore additional cases. Ultimately, we hope that the structure and content of this textbook will encourage lively and thoughtful discussions in political communication classes—and beyond.

ACKNOWLEDGMENTS

None of our three separate perspectives would have been enough to sustain this textbook on its own, and none of us would have been able to complete this project without the dedication of each of our coauthors. We were also aided by the excellent suggestions made by the reviewers selected for this text by our editors at Allyn & Bacon as well as by these editors' shrewd commentary. We thank the reviewers—Eric Brown, Canyon College; Ferald J. Bryan, Northern Illinois University; J. Thomas Failla, Iona College; Bertram W. Gross, Marshall University; Stephen A. Klien, Augustana College; Brad Mello, Trinity University, Washington, DC; and Zizi Papacharissi, Temple University—and our editors—Karon Bowers and Jeanne Zalesky—for their assistance. We also thank Susan Timberlake, faculty secretary at Randolph-Macon College, for her assistance with the clerical and technical aspects of preparing the manuscript drafts.

LCB

JLC

TFS

ABOUT THE AUTHORS

Lauren Cohen Bell, a native of Ohio, is Associate Professor of Political Science at Randolph-Macon College. She holds a B.A. from the College of Wooster and an M.A. and Ph.D. from the Carl Albert Congressional Research and Studies Center at the University of Oklahoma. She is the author of *Warring Factions: Interest Groups, Money, and the New Politics of Senate Confirmation* (2002) and *The U.S. Congress: A Simulation for Students* (2005) as well as articles in journals such as *The Journal of Politics, Political Research Quarterly, The Journal of Legislative Studies, The Journal of Public Administration Research and Theory*, and *Judicature*. During 2006–2007, she served as a U.S. Supreme Court Fellow at the U.S. Sentencing Commission in Washington, DC. At Randolph-Macon, she has codirected the Honors Program and serves as Pre-Law Advisor.

Joan L. Conners, a native of Wisconsin, is Associate Professor of Communication at Randolph-Macon College. She holds a B.A. and M.A. from Marquette University and a Ph.D. from the University of Minnesota—Twin Cities. She has published essays in *PS: Political Science and Politics, American Behavioral Scientist, Communication Research Trends, Harvard International Journal of Press/Politics*, and *Media Studies Journal*. She also has contributed to *Race/Gender/Media: Considering Diversity Across Audiences, Content, and Producers* (2004) as well as the following forthcoming volumes: *Common Sense: Intelligence as Presented on Popular Television* and *Women, Wellness, and the Media*. She was a media consultant in the Midwest and advises student publications at Randolph-Macon.

Theodore F. Sheckels, a native of Washington, DC, is Professor of English and Communication at Randolph-Macon College. He holds a B.S. from Duquesne University and an M.A. and Ph.D. from Pennsylvania State University. He is the author of *When Congress Debates: A Bakhtinian Paradigm* (2000) and *Maryland Politics and Political Communication, 1950–2005* (2006). He is the co-editor of *Readings in Political Communication* (2007), and he has published articles in *Communication Quarterly, Southern Journal of Communication, The Howard Journal of Communications, Argumentation and Advocacy*, and *Rhetoric and Public Affairs*. He has also published widely on Canadian, Australian, and South African literature. At Randolph-Macon, he chairs the communication studies program and coaches the college's debating teams.

■ ■ ■ ■ ■

CHAPTER 1

INTRODUCTION

Open any American government or introduction to political science textbook, and you'll often find that the first chapter contains a definition of the word *politics*. It is far less common to open a political communication textbook to find that the first chapter is focused on the definition of *politics*. Yet that is precisely what a reader will find in this text. As we set out to write this book, we realized that although the political science and communication disciplines both are essential to the development of a full understanding of political communication, too few textbooks in either discipline provide sufficient instruction in both areas. This text is our attempt to contribute to the body of scholarship in political communication by bringing together the varied disciplinary interests that inform the study of the subject. In Chapters 2 through 4, we present three different perspectives on political communication—that of political science, that of rhetoric, and that of mass communication. In the case study chapters that follow (Chapters 5 through 17), we offer, in turn, what each of these three different disciplinary approaches has to say about the chosen case. At the end of each chapter is a brief summary that helps to integrate the three different perspectives.

The three disciplinary perspectives presented in this text have different primary concerns. Among other matters, political science is concerned with power—how it is distributed among levels of government, among the institutions within each level, among political parties, and between the governing and the governed. Even though various governmental and social structures create the illusion that these power distributions are set, they are nonetheless dynamic. Power shifts do occur. Communication is both a means to effect these shifts and a way to reflect what the new distributions of power might be. Political scientists study political communication with an eye to discerning where power rests—and how it got there.

Rhetoric is concerned with texts. These days, the word *text* is defined broadly to include the spoken, the written, the visual, and the simply enacted. In all of these cases, rhetoric is concerned with how an individual or a group uses various means to persuade an audience. When no one is directing the "text," rhetoric is concerned with the effect it has and how it achieved that effect. Rhetoric then tends to look more closely at communication per se than political science. Both are concerned with effects, but political science is looking for larger effects than rhetoric is. However, when a text's immediate effect is dramatic, the political scientist and the rhetorician may be shining their searchlights on much the same area. Even in this case, the political scientist would probably say more about the effect itself; the rhetorician more about how, in the text, the effect was achieved.

Political science also tends to rely heavily on quantitative, empirical data in offering its conclusions. Rhetoric, on the other hand, is more of a critical endeavor. It reads texts closely; it offers reasonable conjectures as to how the texts affect those who are reading, listening, or seeing them. Mass communication tends to be more like political science than rhetoric in how it analyzes communication insofar as empirical analysis is used more frequently than is normative critical analysis.

Mass communication is concerned with the media through which communication reaches its various audiences. Scholars of mass communication are acutely aware that the media chosen will affect the message. Furthermore, mass communication scholars recognize that the mass media industry, for various reasons, can affect the messages these audiences receive. Sometimes the industry may be aware of the effects it has; sometimes it is not. Students of mass communication, like rhetoricians, are concerned with how a communicator has chosen to get his or her message across. But whereas the rhetorician is concerned with smaller elements such as words and specific visual images, the mass communication scholar is concerned with the medium chosen, how its characteristics may alter the message, and what effect the message may have on an audience. The mass communication scholar is also concerned with how the message is broadcast to larger audiences and how the message might change further based on such mundane matters as the timing of the broadcast and such serious matters as the political bias of the media entity involved. As previously noted, in addressing these concerns, mass communication is more likely to offer data than not.

Typically, a student of political communication learns from a member of one group—a political scientist, a rhetorician, or a scholar of mass communication—and never has the opportunity to learn what others might say. Regrettably, faculty sometimes fall into the same trap—they know their own disciplinary perspective but have only a vague idea about the perspective of others with a similarly keen interest in the subject. We have designed this textbook to avoid the unfortunate tendency for students to receive only part of the picture.

Integrating the three approaches is necessary to understand fully the communication surrounding political events. For example, consider the tearing down of the wall that separated West and East Berlin in 1989. The political scientist would consider the event as signaling a tremendous change in the international power balance between the United States and the former Soviet Union. He or she would look at the communication surrounding the event for the purpose of attaining a more nuanced view of what was happening with regard to global power. The rhetorician might look at any speeches delivered in celebration of the event, as well as any that tried to explain it away. But the rhetorician would also be interested in the message those who participated in tearing down the Berlin Wall were sending by their very action. The mass communication scholar would immediately look at how the event was covered by media in the United States and abroad. He or she would ask how the coverage might be altering the message that was being received. In this case, the rhetorician would zero in on the most public texts; the political scientist would root out less public ones that might reveal the "real" state of affairs, and the mass communication scholar would focus on media coverage and how people came to understand the event and the communication about it because of that coverage.

WHY STUDY POLITICAL COMMUNICATION?

Even more fundamental than how political communication is studied is the question of why one would want to study it in the first place. Many people have a negative image of politics. This is not surprising. Candidates for public office often seem willing to say anything to get elected, and politicians, during campaigns or once they've entered public service, are frequently criticized for offering more style than substance.

There are, of course, candidates and officeholders who fail to live up to citizens' expectations, but for every such person, there are many others who are genuinely trying to accomplish the important task of governing a group of people who have joined together in some kind of community—whether a city, a county, a state, or a nation. Governing involves making sure that the day-to-day services we depend on are working, but governing also includes identifying and solving new or unexpected problems. Our health, our prosperity, and our security depend on how those who govern us define and solve problems, and how well.

Communication plays a vital role in what these politicians do. Communication is essential to be elected into a position of public trust. Once in office, public officials communicate with each other about their communities' problems. They also communicate to and with citizens: they rally us to support certain courses of action, they inform us of government action and the rationales behind it, and they help us to understand complex public policy questions and solutions. Elected officials also sometimes communicate in subtle ways about who they are or what government does, without being aware that they are sending messages.

At the same time, the public doesn't just sit back and receive political messages. Those who govern are engaged in politics, and, at least in democratic societies, so are those who are governed. Citizens read newspapers; we watch television news programs; we visit Internet sites. We discuss issues with our friends and neighbors, and we share our opinions on public questions with those who hold positions of responsibility. Periodically, we express our views at the ballot box by casting a vote for one candidate or another. All of these activities are part of the vital two-way communication between those who govern and those who are governed. Even when citizens are on the receiving end of political information, the receipt of information is not a passive activity. Whether we are conscious of doing so or not, we interpret that information as we receive it. We often do so in consort with others—family members, coworkers, neighbors—and we are frequently guided in the process of assimilating political messages by people whose judgment we've come to trust as well as by the media that are delivering the messages to us. As a result, it is often the case that the information we say we possess ends up being different from the message that the sender thought he or she sent.

What those who govern do is political communication; what we do is political communication. By engaging in this process, we—those governing and those governed—are directing the affairs of the communities in which we live. This communication is vital: our lives as citizens are tied up in it. It is essential to study and understand the ways in which political messages are sent and received so that we can recognize how our lives are shaped by these messages and so that we can better affect the process of governing. Finally, because political communication is not perfect, we also study it so that we can devise ways of improving it.

WHY STUDY POLITICAL COMMUNICATION USING CASE STUDIES?

Although the preceding section has offered a general explanation for why studying political communication is important, many of the points we've raised are best illustrated through real-world examples. This is why we've opted to present our discussion of political communication through case studies; the cases included in this text offer extended examples that uncover the complexity of political communication. No situation we might have chosen—whether an election or a presidential speech or a famous Supreme Court decision—is simple, if one really looks at it. A case study provides enough material so that one can begin to understand the nuances of the political messages that comprise the case.

Case studies also move the study of political communication from the theoretical to the very real. The situations presented in Chapters 5 through 17 actually occurred. The words that the cases reproduce were actually uttered; the visual images that the cases reference were actually sent out over the airwaves. When the study of political communication sticks to theoretical level, the subject may seem cut-and-dried: an election campaign has a certain number of phases; a State of the Union address represents presidential agenda setting; a Senate debate follows certain rules and conventions. These all could be listed, memorized, and repeated. But real cases show how complicated political communication can be. The complexity arises both because politics and communication are dynamic—always changing—and because there are real people involved. These people know and care little about what theorists or researchers have concluded to be generally true. They may act contrary to theory. Case studies alert students of political communication to both the dynamics and the idiosyncrasies of transmitting political messages.

The case studies that we have included in this textbook are drawn from the set of topics typically discussed in a political communication course; the number of cases per topic is intended to reflect the emphases one often finds in such courses. Because many political communication courses emphasize election campaign communication the most, with the presidency a frequent secondary emphasis, we likewise offer multiple cases for analysis in these areas. Other topics such as the legislature, the judiciary, and social movements are sometimes addressed but usually not at length. Popular culture is sometimes brought in, when election campaigns or the presidency are being discussed. In this textbook, we make a systematic effort to provide case studies in all of these areas, not only because they offer additional insights into the ways in which citizens and politicians communicate but also because they offer alternative ways of thinking about political messages than do the elections and presidency case studies.

There are certainly other election campaigns, other presidential addresses, other legislative hearings or debates, other court decisions, and other social movements that we could have selected for inclusion in this text. We chose ones that we think serve as good introductions to the fundamental tenets of political communication. Others that we think are rich examples are listed at the end of each case study chapter. Students who wish to extend their understanding of the subject discussed in each individual case can do so by taking a look at some of these other suggested cases and by studying them with an eye toward understanding them from the variety of perspectives through which we present the cases in the text.

CASE STUDIES FROM A MULTIDISCIPLINARY PERSPECTIVE

As you proceed through this text, it might be useful to consider each perspective on each case as a searchlight. In some chapters, the three searchlights will illuminate some of the same aspects of the case and the lights will overlap. In other cases, the three searchlights will illuminate rather different aspects. Regardless of the way in which the perspectives do or don't overlap in each case, it is important to remember that the three emphases presented in this text are not in competition with each other—one need not choose which perspective to consider. Instead, the perspectives complement each other. Together, they offer a fuller understanding of both political communication and the moments in public affairs that the communication surrounds. By looking at different aspects of an event, the perspectives may highlight the differences in emphases of each approach. The occasional tension among the perspectives is just as useful to the student of political communication as those times when the three approaches reach the same conclusion about an event.

CONCLUSION

The study this textbook invites students to participate in is an important one—important to students with a specific interest in political communication, to be sure, but also important to citizens of a representative democracy. We believe that the case study approach and the particular case studies we include are a more engaging way to learn about political communication than a more traditional approach. We also believe that the multidisciplinary perspectives are illuminating. They focus on different aspects of the same phenomenon and, regardless of which disciplinary tradition one comes from, they offer the chance to embrace the other perspectives and to see where their concerns and questions lead. It is our hope that, through the approach taken in this book, students will attune themselves to all three disciplinary perspectives and will gain the fullest understanding possible of important theories and practices of political communication.

CHAPTER 2

A POLITICAL SCIENCE PERSPECTIVE

In 1994, the Health Insurance Industry of America (HIAA) opposed pending legislation in Congress to reform the nation's health care and insurance systems. The organization launched a series of advertisements, which came to be known as the "Harry and Louise" ads. These ads featured a fictional married couple ("Harry" and "Louise") discussing the dire consequences of the reform proposals. At the end of each commercial, the group included a phone number that citizens could call to get more information and to be connected to the office of their member of Congress in order to tell them to vote against the pending reforms. According to industry estimates, more than 800,000 people called.[1] The plan worked; the bill failed. More important, however, the ads aired long before the text of the bill had been written; the HIAA had successfully taken advantage of people's ignorance and fear of change to promote their own objectives.

This chapter offers an overview of the importance of communication to the conduct of government business. More specifically, it discusses the political history of and governmental constraints on political communication, the symbolic and substantive uses of political communication, and, finally, how understanding political communication allows political scientists and others to evaluate critically the actions of government and governmental actors. Every study of politics or political science is at some level a study of political communication, since communication is essential to understanding the political world. As the Harry and Louise example makes clear, political communication can have real consequences for the content and success or failure of public policies. At the same time, and as the next two chapters will make even more clear, the act of communicating between and among individuals is an inherently political act. Communication creates meaning, enlightens or obfuscates reality, and shapes power relationships in government and in society as a whole.

This chapter, as well as many of the political science sections of subsequent chapters, also provides the constitutional and political context for many of the events that comprise the case studies in this text.

---

[1]Cohen, Lauren M., "Lacking a Theory of Policy Effects—The 1994 Health Care Debate in Media Context." Paper presented at the 1995 meeting of the Media, Government, and Public Policy Section of the Association for Education in Journalism and Mass Communication. Syracuse, New York.

POLITICAL SCIENCE AND POLITICAL COMMUNICATION

Political communication—which at its most basic level might be thought of as a message about government, politics, or power, however transmitted—pervades societies worldwide. Messages about politics are everywhere—on television, in newspapers and magazines, in music, in conversations among friends, in literature, in the physical structures of buildings, in art, on people's lapel pins, in advertisements, and in houses of worship. When the U.S. president makes a public speech, he is often communicating his vision for the country's future course. Both the citizen who sends a letter to his or her representatives in Congress, and the interest group that files an *amicus curiae* brief with the U.S. Supreme Court are engaging in political communication. Even those who engage in terrorism or other political violence do so to send a message—to communicate—to their targets. In short, there is literally nothing that takes place in politics that does not involve communication, and, clearly, communication and politics are inseparably intertwined.

Political scientists study political communication as a part of their broader study of power relationships in society; the ways in which political messages are communicated affect how the public perceives proposed policy changes and prospective public leaders and how incumbent public officials evaluate policies, size up one another, and ultimately are evaluated by the public.

Political scientists who study political communication borrow their methods from such diverse fields as journalism, rhetoric, mass communication, political science, psychology, education, philosophy, sociology, and gender and ethnic studies. The methodologies that are brought to bear on the study of political communication by political scientists are varied. Political scientists use both quantitative—mathematical—methods and qualitative—experiential—research methodologies as appropriate to their project or object of study. Among the common methodologies are textual analyses, including content analysis, observational studies of politicians and their communication activities, and the quantitative analysis of data gathered in the course of study. Although some political scientists study political communication as their life's work, others consider the content of political messages as essential for understanding other phenomena that they are studying more closely. In that sense, political communication is both a narrowly focused *subfield* of the discipline as well as a ubiquitous *subtheme* of political science.

Political communication can be used to educate and to improve the quality of government actions, but it can also be used to manipulate the outcomes of political contests. Political scientist R. Douglas Arnold's conception of the American electorate as consisting of two separate publics—the attentive public and the inattentive public—offers some perspective on the education-manipulation dichotomy inherent in political communication. The attentive public is composed primarily of political elites, people who are well educated about politics, who are active participants in the democratic process, and who are interested in learning about pending policy and political decisions. Individuals in the attentive public follow both electoral and institutional politics closely and compose the majority of voters and political activists in the United States. In contrast, the inattentive public pays little attention to politics. For the most part, people in the inattentive public know and care little about elections and governance, except when a trusted third party provides them with information that suggests that their economic or social well-being is threatened. Such trusted third parties can be celebrities, athletes, prominent community leaders, spokespersons for groups with which an individual identifies, and even the media. Whether or not the third party is actually trustworthy or is telling the whole story is not important; what matters is only that an individual who usually pays little attention to politics trusts the source.

When members of the inattentive public receive political information that indicates that there is the possibility that they will suffer a negative consequence, they may begin to participate in the political process. Thus, the content of political messages is important. Political communication between and among political elites in the attentive public is generally educational and informative in nature, because these individuals have sufficient substantive information to make their own reasoned judgments about politics. In contrast, individuals in the mass or inattentive public can be easily swayed by misleading information.

Communication targeted at these different audiences has been around since the very beginning of the American republic. For example, the Federalist Papers—a series of newspaper editorials published in New York newspapers to urge ratification of the Constitution—were aimed at political elites who would be called on to vote whether or not New York should assent to the Constitution. On the other hand, early

Former Secretary of State Madeline Albright visits The Oprah Winfrey Show *in 2001 to raise awareness of international sex trafficking.*

political newspapers frequently distorted facts or offered normative assessments designed to sway the opinions of nonelites to support or oppose the actions taken by early American governing coalitions. The next section of this chapter offers a brief overview of the ways in which communication both shaped and continues to be shaped by the U.S. Constitution.

COMMUNICATION AND THE CONSTITUTION

The United States system of government started with a letter written by the delegates to the Second Continental Congress to England's King George III. That letter, better known as the Declaration of Independence, expressed the American colonists' grievances against the British throne and announced that the colonies were prepared to defend themselves as an independent, sovereign nation. It was not a military act that started the Revolutionary War, but instead an act of communication between the colonists and their rulers.

Such has always been the power of communication. This power was recognized, and indeed, was institutionalized by the Framers of the American system of government. For scholars of American politics, the Constitution of the United States is a touchstone for framing contemporary questions. When considering the intertwined nature of communication and politics, the Constitution again provides a useful point of departure. For example, Article I, Section 5 obliges the Congress to keep a journal of its proceedings and Section 6 references speeches and debates during legislative sessions. Article II, Section 1 mandates the presidential oath of office, and Section 2 requires the president to deliver to the Congress "information on the state of the union" at regular intervals. Each of these sections imposes an obligation on members of the government to communicate with one another and to ensure that the public is able to review the actions of their government by reading accounts of its activity.

The most significant provision of the Constitution to the contemporary study of political communication is, of course, the First Amendment, which reads:

> Congress shall make no law respecting an establishment of religion, or prohibiting the free
> exercise thereof; or abridging the freedom of speech, or of the press; or the right of the
> people peaceably to assemble, and to petition the Government for a redress of grievances.

Added to the Constitution as part of the Bill of Rights in 1791, the First Amendment establishes protections for speech, press, assembly, and—through its defense of religious freedom—protections for freedom of conscience. The Framers of the Constitution were ardent believers in the essentialness of free communication, between and among citizens and between and among citizens and their government. Writing to future President John Tyler in 1804, then-President Thomas Jefferson wrote of the young American republic: "No experiment can be more interesting than that we are now trying, and which we trust will end in establishing the fact, that man may be governed by reason and truth. Our first object should therefore be, to leave open to him all the avenues to truth. The most effectual hitherto found, is the freedom of the press."[2] British political philosopher John Stuart Mill echoed this sentiment in *On Liberty*, in which he noted that permitting free expression of ideas was the only way to prevent either political or religious tyranny, regardless of the accuracy or reasonableness of the messages expressed.

Law Professor Thomas Emerson more explicitly linked the articulation of political ideas with the practice of government when he described the centrality of freedom of expression to the conduct of democracy in *The System of Freedom of Expression* (1970). Emerson noted that there are four main purposes for free expression relative to the functioning of democracy: first, free expression helps individuals to achieve self-fulfillment. Next, free expression allows for the advancement of knowledge and the discovery of truth. Third, free expression "is essential to provide for participation in decision making by all members of society."[3] Because this comment gets at the core of the linkages between politics and communication that are studied by political scientists, it is worth considering Emerson's explication on this point:

> Once one accepts the premise of the Declaration of Independence—that governments 'derive their just powers from the consent of the governed'—it follows that the governed must, in order to exercise their right of consent, have full freedom of expression both in forming individual judgments and in forming the common judgments.[4]

Finally, Emerson notes that communication is necessary for achieving consensus and, thus, increasing the stability of communities.

Although political scientists and others have long recognized the need for the free articulation and exchange of ideas for democratic principles to be translated into action, as it was originally understood the First Amendment amounted to little more than a protection from prior censorship by the government. The First Amendment was understood to prohibit the Congress from enacting laws forbidding the utterance or printing of ideas but, at least initially, the First Amendment was not interpreted to prohibit the punishment of ideas deemed offensive by the Congress. Indeed, in 1798, the Federalist Congress passed and then-President John Adams signed into law the Alien and Sedition Acts, which punished the publication or articulation of any antigovernment epithet. Nominally aimed at protecting the fragile new government from dangerous ("seditious") antigovernment speech, the acts imposed significant penalties on political speech that was deemed offensive by those in power and was used as the basis of several federal prosecutions. Although the acts were eventually repealed, the precedent was set that the government could in fact limit free expression to protect the national interest.

---

[2]Letter to John Tyler, June 28, 1804. Reprinted in Merrill D. Peterson, ed., *The Political Writings of Thomas Jefferson*. Monticello Monograph Series: Thomas Jefferson Memorial Foundation.

[3]Emerson, Thomas I. *The System of Freedom of Expression* (New York: Random House, 1970), 6.

[4]Ibid, 7.

The disconnect between the liberty promised in the First Amendment and the punishment of expression led to significant legal and political conflict concerning issues relating to free expression and political communication throughout the course of American history. It was not until World War I that the Supreme Court began to clarify the limits on free speech. In *Schenck v. U.S.* (1919), the Supreme Court ruled that the Espionage Act of 1917, which made it a crime to interfere with the draft or the prosecution of the U.S. part of World War I, was constitutional. The appellant in that case had been convicted under the federal statute of distributing antidraft and antiwar leaflets in violation of the law. By upholding the Espionage Act's limits on free expression during wartime, the Court set the precedent that in times of national conflict or in the face of threats to national security, the expression of political opinions could be limited if they created a "clear and present danger" of fostering undesirable consequences that Congress is empowered to prevent.[5]

After the Bill of Rights was incorporated by the Supreme Court and applied to all states during the 1930s,[6] the Supreme Court's First Amendment decisions applied nationwide. The Court also began to interpret federal and state statutes in the area of free speech generally, and political communication, specifically. For example, in the 1967 case *New York Times v. Sullivan*, the Supreme Court declared that public officials could not sue newspapers for libel or defamation of character, unless the newspapers had published false information, with a reckless disregard for the truth or falsehood of the content of the speech. This was a victory for advocates of unfettered political speech because it ensured that the media could scrutinize the conduct of public officials. In 1989, the Supreme Court protected the rights of private citizens to comment critically on the conduct of government in *Texas v. Johnson*, a so-called speech-plus-action case involving the question of whether a state could prohibit flag burning.

As the Supreme Court's majority opinions in late twentieth century cases relating to the First Amendment make clear, today the First Amendment is interpreted broadly to protect the rights of the public and the press to comment on the activities of the government.

COMMUNICATION IN POLITICS—CAMPAIGNS

Another Supreme Court decision, this one in the 1976 case *Buckley v. Valeo*, not only reinforced the essential role of free speech to the conduct of politics and governance, but also expanded the kinds of activities protected as acts of "speech." In its decision in that case, the Supreme Court ruled that the Congress could not, under the First Amendment, limit or prohibit candidates for public office from spending money to promote their own candidacies, noting: "The Act's expenditure ceilings impose direct

[5]*Schenck v. United States* 249 U.S. 47 (1919).

[6]Until the 1930s, the First Amendment and the rest of the Bill of Rights applied only to the federal government, a point that was articulated in the U.S. Supreme Court's decision in *Barron v. Baltimore* in 1833. However, each state had its own provisions to protect freedom of speech and the press.

and substantial restraints on the quantity of political speech."[7] In addition, the Court noted that "[t]he First Amendment denies government the power to determine that spending to promote one's political views is wasteful, excessive, or unwise."[8] The Court's decision in *Buckley v. Valeo* recognized that without the ability to communicate with voters and to convince them of their credentials, politicians could not adequately participate in the electoral process.

Free and fair elections are a prerequisite for representative democracy. And for candidates seeking public office, nothing is more important than improving name recognition and "getting the message out" to prospective voters. Although the Court's decision in *Buckley* has been challenged as promoting the interests of wealthy, self-financing candidates and permitting wealthy interest groups to hijack the electoral process by campaigning independently for the candidate of their choice, most observers agree that the ability to raise and spend sizable sums of money is essential in national and most statewide elections.

Money is crucial because as communications technologies have evolved, so too have the costs associated with campaigning for political office. According to U.S. presidency scholars Stephen Wayne and Clyde Wilcox, candidates for national political office now spend more time in television studios taping advertisements and interviews than they spend on the campaign trail making public appearances. Every serious candidate hires a communication specialist—or more than one—to be responsible for promoting the candidate in the media and at the grass roots. This is increasingly true even in smaller-scale state and local races. Especially when elections are being held for important state or local offices, candidates will turn to professional campaign managers and staff to help them be successful. During the campaign, the communications staff is responsible for testing prospective advertisements and speech themes with focus groups of citizens, for coordinating the design, ordering, and distribution of the candidate's printed materials, and for seeking out opportunities for the candidate to appear in public or to receive free media coverage. These communications specialists also cultivate relationships with members of relevant media outlets. Because of their centrality to the success of the campaign, in many cases staff salaries consume significant campaign resources.

Other areas of significant expenditure include hiring companies or individuals to conduct scientific polls and the costs associated with renting or purchasing the computing technology necessary to assist with targeting voters for direct mail and telephone solicitations.[9] Robert Lorch, a political scientist at the University of Colorado at Colorado Springs, reports that a candidate for the Washington State Senate spent more than $280,000 to be reelected to his Senate seat; the candidate described his campaign budget as looking roughly as follows:

- 30 percent for direct mail promotion (includes printing and postage)
- 23 percent for consultant services such as polling

[7]*Buckley v. Valeo* 424 U.S. 1 (1976).
[8]Ibid.
[9]Ibid., 92.

- 15 percent for administrative items including campaign staff salaries, phones, rent, and the like
- 10 percent for miscellaneous
- 10 percent for TV and radio
- 6 percent for contributions and
- 6 percent for fundraising.[10]

As this list demonstrates, many campaign expenditures relate to candidates' efforts to inform voters of their candidacies and to their efforts to ensure that voters know something about their policy positions. The extent to which campaigns focus on any given method of communication varies, but all campaigns use or attempt to use signs, buttons, stickers, bumper stickers, direct mail, telephone calls, face-to-face meetings with the candidates, debates, television advertising, and campaign rallies to introduce the candidate to the voters and to help voters learn about the candidate's issue positions.

Of course, campaign costs increase concomitantly with the number of these tactics a candidate wishes to employ and increase substantially when a candidate chooses to use television advertising to promote his or her candidacy. A single television advertisement on a national network can cost hundreds of thousands of dollars. Even in smaller local markets, television airtime can cost several hundreds of dollars per minute. Lorch writes: "Candidates for important offices may commit half their campaign budget for media expenditures and it is extremely important to know how and where to spend it."[11] Indeed, during the 2004 presidential elections, TNS Media Intelligence/Campaign Media Analysis Group[12] estimated that total media expenditures across all national, state, and local elections approached $1.5 billion. Expenditures on television advertisements in the presidential elections alone were estimated at $546.6 million, including independent expenditures by politically active groups.[13] By way of comparison, two decades earlier, in 1984, presidential candidates Ronald Reagan and Walter Mondale spent a combined estimated $50 million on television advertisements, although that figure does not include independent expenditures.[14]

In addition to employing static forms of communication, such as two-dimensional signs, posters, buttons, and bumper stickers, as well as passive forms of communication such as radio and television advertising, most candidates for public

---

[10]Ibid.

[11]Lorch, Robert S., *State and Local Politics: The Great Entanglement*, 6th ed. (Upper Saddle River, NJ: Prentice Hall, 2001), 89.

[12]According to its website, http://www.tmsmi-cmag.com: "TNSMI/Campaign Media Analysis Group is the leading provider of advertising tracking and analysis of political, public affairs and issue advocacy advertising. A TNS Media Intelligence/CMR company, TNSMI/CMAG provides customized media analysis services to national trade associations, foundations, Fortune 100 companies, national media organizations, academia and hundreds of national, statewide and local political campaigns."

[13]TNSMI-CMAG news release. Available online at http://www.tns-mi.com/news/11012004.htm. Accessed June 29, 2005.

[14]Edwin Diamond and Adrian Marin, "Spots," *The American Behavioral Scientist* (March/April, 1989), p. 382.

office seek out opportunities to appear in person at events to meet one-on-one with prospective voters. They also participate in candidate forums and debates designed to showcase their substantive policy proposals. The first broadcast presidential debate occurred in May 1948, the evening before the Oregon Republican primary election,[15] and since then debates have become staples of every presidential primary and general election and of most elections to important federal and statewide offices. Although debates are in theory designed to offer insights into candidates' abilities to think on their feet, there is little that happens that is not scripted. Indeed, a 1988 *New York Times* op–ed piece offered these words of wisdom from Republican campaign strategist Eddie Mahe: "You don't try any line or any thought or any theme that hasn't been pre-tested. The thing you have to avoid is the snap response that becomes a disaster. If you haven't said it before, don't say it now."[16] Moreover, just as with any other form of campaign communication, debates are carefully managed by a candidates' handlers, who offer focus-group-tested advice about how the candidate should dress, how he or she should smile, what he or she should (or should not) say, and who try to manipulate reporters' coverage of the debates immediately after they are over.

Candidates' campaign communication choices are a function of several different things, including the candidate's personality and preferences, the resources the candidate has available to him or her, the kind of media market that the district or state is in, and the geographic and demographic makeup of the member's constituency. Congressional scholar Richard Fenno, for example, found that members of Congress perceive their constituencies in a variety of ways; they not only see the political boundaries that are drawn to separate their district from the others in their state, but they further subdivide the constituents in the district into those likely to vote for them against a candidate of the opposing political party, those who will vote for them when they are running against other candidates from their own parties (for example, in a contested primary election), and those whom they know personally.[17]

Members of Congress emphasize different things in their campaign communications depending on the constituency group that is being targeted. Moreover, Fenno discovered through his research that incumbent members of Congress practiced multiple styles of "presentation of self" when they went back to their home districts. Some members of Congress were most comfortable meeting one-on-one with constituents; these members tended to come from very homogenous districts with small populations, and their constituents tended to expect their representative in Congress to know them personally and to interact with them. In contrast, other members of Congress represented diverse constituencies with changing demographic profiles, and therefore they could not rely on personal relationships to assure them of

---

[15]Oreskes, Michael, "Eye Bounce? Tactical Smile? Some Pointers for Debates," *New York Times*, September 19, 1988, p. A16.

[16]Ibid., A16.

[17]Fenno, Richard. "U.S. House Members in their Districts: An Exploration," *American Political Science Review* (1977): 71.

reelection. Instead, they relied on small group meetings in which they could demonstrate their objective qualifications for office.[18]

COMMUNICATION AND POLITICS—GOVERNING

Candidates spend so much of their campaign resources on communicating with prospective voters because they know that the content and frequency of the messages voters get about them can affect the outcome on Election Day. Indeed, even after the election night victory parties end and campaign headquarters are abandoned, communication remains essential to the conduct of public business. Without the ability to communicate among themselves and with the people they represent, elected officials would not be able to work together to make good public policy decisions. How well these officials communicate—and how truthfully—affects the quality of their decision making and determines how the public—both the attentive and inattentive public—will respond to the work of the government. The remainder of this section considers how the three primary institutions of American national government—the President of the United States, the United States Congress, and the federal judiciary—employ a variety of communication techniques to govern.

The President

The president is the only elected official capable of commanding a national audience on short notice. When the president wishes to address the nation on matters of national concern, his press staff works with the news and program directors of the major national media outlets to secure airtime for a live broadcast. Although Americans frequently grumble about the president preempting their favorite television shows, the president uses his power of the "bully pulpit" to communicate important information and to promote his view of national and international issues.

One of the most visible forms of presidential political communication is the president's annual State of the Union Address. As noted above, the Constitution requires the president to inform the Congress at regular intervals of the state of the union. Initially, presidents delivered the address in person, but President Thomas Jefferson discontinued the practice, believing it to be too similar to the British tradition of the "speech from the throne," delivered annually by the king or queen (or his or her representative). Until 1913, when President Woodrow Wilson reinstated the tradition of delivering the speech in person to a joint session of Congress, presidents delivered an annual message to the Congress in writing to fulfill the requirements of Article II.[19] Between 1913 and 1933, presidents varied in their approaches; some presidents delivered their addresses in writing and others appeared in person. Since

---

[18]Ibid.

[19]The American Presidency Project, http://www.presidency.ucsb.edu/sou.php. Accessed on June 19, 2005.

1933, however, virtually all State of the Union addresses have been delivered by presidents in person.

The State of the Union Address was first televised in 1947, although it was not common for households to have at least one television set until the mid-1950s. In the last half century, however, viewership has increased commensurately with the increasing prevalence of televisions in people's homes. The United States Department of State estimates that 43.4 million people around the world watched President George W. Bush's 2004 State of the Union Address.[20]

The size of the audience for the annual State of the Union Address makes it an incredibly important speech for sitting presidents. More than any other speechmaking opportunity, presidents view their State of the Union addresses as the opportunity to appear presidential. They use the opportunity of appearing before a joint session of the Congress, the heads of the executive branch's cabinet-level department (with the exception of whichever cabinet secretary has been selected to not attend the speech to allow for the continuation of the American governmental system in the event of a catastrophe), the Supreme Court of the United States, and a worldwide audience to highlight their achievements over the past year and to promote their agenda for the coming year. Because no other government official is able to command the same degree of attention in a single appearance, the president is able to capitalize on the State of the Union Address each year to gain attention and support for his policy initiatives. Indeed, presidents routinely receive a "bounce" in the polls following the delivery of their State of the Union Addresses.[21]

In addition to his ability to preempt local and national programming for scheduled and unscheduled speeches to the public, the president has also become the focal point of media attention. But the relationship between the president and the press is symbiotic. The president requires the media to disseminate his message to the large and diverse American audience. But the media recognize that the president is an important national figure and that the presence of a story focusing on the White House during their broadcasts encourages people to watch. Therefore both the permanent White House press staff and the national news staffs of the major broadcast and cable networks work to meet each others' needs. Mark Hertsgaard, in his book *On Bended Knee: The Press and the Reagan Presidency*, offers examples of how members of the press work together with the president and his staff to disseminate the message the president wants the public to hear. He also describes how, during the Reagan Administration, the president and his staff catered to reporters' needs. The White House press corps was given significant access to the president and his staff, and the president and his staff worked to conform to the networks' deadlines. In return, Hertsgaard asserts that Reagan received better press coverage than any other modern president.[22]

[20]United States Department of State, http://usinfo.state.gov/dhr/Archive/2005/Jan/28-505175.html. Accessed on June 19, 2005.

[21]http://www.cbsnews.com/stories/2003/01/29/opinion/lynch/main538360.shtml

[22]Hertsgaard, Mark, *On Bended Knee: The Press and the Reagan Presidency* (New York: Farrar, Strauss, and Giroux, 1988).

Beyond scripted speeches, presidents communicate daily with a plethora of important interests. These interests may include members of the other branches of government or leaders of U.S. states or foreign nations. They may meet one-on-one and discuss matters of mutual concern with the head of state of another country, which requires them to be very good interpersonal communicators. Or they may be the keynote speaker at a fund-raising event for their political party and deliver prepared remarks on matters of political strategy. Many of these presidential communication moments are captured for posterity and reprinted in both the *Weekly Compilation of Presidential Documents* and the *Public Papers of the Presidents* (which today are now also available in electronic format from the National Archives and the Government Printing Office). In this way, the president's messages are preserved and made available to the public and to researchers who wish to analyze his policies or his communication more fully. Reviewing the president's words in these volumes allows for an individual to draw his or her own conclusions about the content of the speech; there is no media "spin" included in the texts.

Volumes such as the *Weekly Compilation of Presidential Documents* and the *Public Papers of the Presidents* have become vital to the impartial analysis of presidential communication. If Hertsgaard is correct that the media offer very little by way of substantive critique of presidential ideas in order to continue to have access to the White House, this has implications for the public's ability to evaluate the performance of its leaders and to act to encourage them to change policy directions. Because the majority of the public is inattentive and will not take the time to learn about important political issues and options for addressing them, the intertwined nature of the press and the president contributes to keeping the public less than fully informed about politics and governance.

The Congress

Of course presidents are not the only ones who use communication to their advantage in campaigning and governing. Although members of Congress do not have the ability to command media attention in the same way that presidents do, members of Congress have considerable communication resources at their disposal. Every congressional office has a press staffer as well as interns or junior staff members to assist with office communications. In addition, members of Congress generate thousands of pages of letters, speeches, "talking points," and transcripts as they engage in their responsibilities: lawmaking, representation, oversight of the president and the executive branch, and legitimation of the American political system.

There is, of course, a relationship between members' activities while in Washington and the ways in which they communicate these activities to their constituents; as noted earlier, members engage in "presentation of self " through their communication of their Washington behaviors to their constituents back in their home states and districts. Because members of Congress enjoy significant perquisites of office, such as travel to and from their home state or district and the right to send large quantities of mail to their constituents without charge, they are able to keep their activities and plans at the forefront of constituents' minds. In fact, many of the advantages that are enjoyed by incumbent members of Congress as they pursue reelection result from members' communication advantages over their opponents.

Congress as an institution keeps excellent records of the communication that occurs in the legislative process. *The Congressional Record*, which has been maintained under various names and in various formats since the very first Congress, provides a transcript of members' statements on the floor of the House and Senate. Because it is a record of the Congress's daily business, it also includes measures introduced, votes cast, and lists of nominations received and acted on. Members of Congress may also submit documents from external sources, such as letters they receive from interest groups or constituents in support of their position, to the *Record*. In this way, the *Congressional Record* also provides a snapshot of the communication between members of Congress and the constituents and interests they represent.

In addition to recording the transcripts of floor debates in each chamber, congressional committees keep detailed records of their proceedings. Stenographers record the proceedings of committee hearings and markups (although the markup transcripts are generally kept for the exclusive use of the committee members and their staffs and are not usually made available to the public), and copies of the hearing transcripts are printed by the Government Printing Office (GPO) and made available to the public. The proliferation of online government and private information web-sites, such as the GPO online and LexisNexis, allow interested members of the public to have access to the transcripts as well as the reports that are prepared by the committees after they have acted to vote a bill to the full House or Senate for additional action. These committee reports provide a summary of the legislation, a detailed discussion of the committee's actions to process the bill or resolution, and the opinions of the members of the committee concerning why it should or should not be passed by the full chamber. These reports offer members of Congress who do not serve on the committee a chance to learn about the issue and to understand the concerns their colleagues raised and addressed during the committee stage of the legislative process.

As the preceding paragraph suggests, Congress generates thousands of pages of transcripts of its debates and activities each year. Anyone who has worked on Capitol Hill will attest to the tremendous volume of paper that is circulated through congressional offices, even in an e-mail and web-based information age. In addition to official committee and chamber transcripts, members of Congress deluge each other with "Dear Colleague" letters—letters written from one member of Congress to his or her colleagues to encourage them to support a pending piece of legislation or to participate in some activity of importance to the letter writer. And, of course, members of Congress receive thousands of letters from their constituents in a given congressional session. These letters offer constituents' opinions, seek members' assistance with cutting through bureaucratic red tape, and make routine requests of the services provided by congressional offices, such as tickets for White House and Capitol tours, flag requests (individuals can request that their member of Congress procure for them a flag that has flown over the U.S. Capitol), and general travel assistance for visiting Washington, DC. Although the widespread use of congressional web pages now means that many of these requests are made via web forms, congressional offices still receive huge quantities of U.S. mail. In fact, some members of Congress, especially senators from large states or "celebrity" members of Congress are allocated additional low-level staff members to assist them with managing the volume of mail their offices receive.

Communication between constituents and the members of Congress who represent them, as well as between and among members within the institution, is essential in Congress. In 1995, the then-new Republican leadership launched an initiative to improve congressional communication with the public. The centerpiece of this initiative was a comprehensive website, http://thomas.loc.gov, which was launched to provide public access to the full text of proposed and passed laws, the *Congressional Record*, and lists of roll call votes. In addition, the Thomas website (named for Thomas Jefferson, who founded the Library of Congress, which hosts the website) offers links to a variety of legislative and executive branch agencies, as well as links to other important government information on the World Wide Web. Although the website requires the public to be active in seeking out information about the Congress, the fact that it was launched and is maintained demonstrates the continued congressional commitment to offering the information necessary for people to make informed choices about policy proposals.

The Thomas site is not the only source for information about the Congress that attentive and interested individuals can use to learn more about what their elected representatives are doing. C-SPAN (Cable-Satellite Public Affairs Network) and

Industry leaders and members of Congress rally outside the U.S. Capitol in October 2003.

C-SPAN2 provide cable and satellite subscribers the opportunity to watch the House and Senate, respectively, in action. The two networks provide television coverage of congressional debates and selected hearings. In addition, when the Congress is not in session, the two networks offer coverage of selected political events (such as fundraising dinners) and of the debates in both the British and Canadian parliaments.

C-SPAN has played an important role in the development of congressional communication. Before having cameras in the chambers, members of Congress had few incentives to put on a show. The vast majority of members do not attend floor sessions, but instead monitor activity on the floor of the House or Senate by way of closed-circuit television from their offices. This allows them to keep track of what is happening, but also to work on other things. Once cameras were installed in the chambers, the incentive structures for members of Congress changed; although they recognize that it is primarily political elites who watch the floor debates, the presence of cameras meant that their audience was much larger than 434 colleagues in the House or 99 colleagues in the Senate.

Former Speaker of the House Newt Gingrich took advantage of this long before he ever became Speaker. As he worked his way up through the leadership ranks, Gingrich launched a strategy of using the House's "one-minute" speeches (where members can go to the House floor and speak for literally one minute on any topic of their choosing) to rail against the incumbent Democrats. As part of his speechmaking, Gingrich would from time to time gesture theatrically as he railed against his "colleagues across the aisle." Dismayed by the negative coverage the Democrats were receiving, Democratic Speaker of the House Tom Foley (Washington) ordered C-SPAN to begin panning the chamber with its cameras in May 1984; when the cameras began to move from their fixed position, which had focused on Representative Gingrich, viewers became aware that there was literally no one else in the room besides Gingrich, a handful of clerks, and a presiding officer. What had appeared to be a courageous and principled stand against members of the opposing party was revealed to be little more than political grandstanding. In the end, however, the Democratic leadership's image was also tarnished, as Republicans accused them of tricking the Republicans; the Democrats had not told their colleagues that the cameras now freely roved the chamber.[23]

The Federal Judiciary

As the two preceding sections have demonstrated, the president and Congress have multiple avenues for communicating internally with their staff members and externally with their constituents in the public. The third branch of American national government, the judicial branch, uses considerably fewer methods of communication. Nevertheless, the quality of communication that is produced by judges in

[23]Steven Frantzich and John Sullivan, *The C-SPAN Revolution* (Norman, OK: University of Oklahoma Press, 1996), 51–53.

the federal courts is substantially higher than that of their executive or legislative counterparts.

Because federal judges do not stand for election, they do not have traditional constituents. They also do not actively seek out media coverage of their activities in the same way the president does, and they do not have a need to share their proceedings with the public through television programming, the way the U.S. Congress does. As a result, there is substantially less public communication that occurs in judicial proceedings as compared with legislative or executive ones. To be sure, judges must pay attention to signals and cues from a number of external actors, including state and federal legislators and executives, interest groups, and even the public. But judges, who under the Constitution are appointed for terms of good behavior (essentially lifetime terms) and who are insulated politically from the whims of public opinion, are not required to be responsive to each and every voice that seeks redress through the federal courts. Especially at the United States Supreme Court, where the justices have the ability to select which cases they wish to hear, the justices do not take a position on all matters brought to them.

However, federal judges (state judges in most states, too) are not fully insulated from the public. Members of the public, generally acting through interest groups or other politically active secondary groups, can file *amicus curiae*—friend of the court—briefs in support of their preferred position in a pending judicial proceeding. These briefs highlight the groups' concerns about pending cases, attempt to inform the justices of matters of concern about which they may not already be aware, and discuss the consequences of a decision in each direction. Recently, research by political scientists who study the federal courts has demonstrated that these briefs can affect the rates at which the justices on the Supreme Court agree to hear cases. Studies have demonstrated that the briefs are signals to the judges that the case is potentially significant. In addition, who files the brief can be an important signal. In cases where the Solicitor General of the United States—the federal government's chief attorney—files an *amicus curiae* brief, the message that is communicated to the justices is that the executive branch, or quite possibly the president himself, has a vested interest in the case. This type of communication is perhaps subtler than a future Speaker of the House calling his political opponents antidemocratic and unpatriotic, but it is no less powerful when it comes to helping to secure the outcomes that are sought. The solicitor general's success rate at convincing the Supreme Court both to agree to hear a case in the first place and then to decide the case in the way preferred by the government is substantially higher than that of other rank-and-file attorneys.

Although the form and method of communication between judges and their constituents is typically far less dramatic than the communication that occurs between and among actors in the other two branches of American national government, federal judges are the only political actors who fully explain and justify their actions. In every case that is decided, the decision is announced in writing and is supported by an opinion putting the decision into context. Like other forms of political communication, these opinions are primarily accessible only to political elites—not because members of the mass public cannot easily obtain them (indeed, the Supreme

Court, like the other branches of government, also maintains an easily navigable website at http://www.supremecourtus.gov, as does the rest of the federal judiciary at http://www.uscourts.gov)—but instead because the opinions are written in technical, legal language. They also make extensive use of lengthy footnotes and references to previous decisions of other courts. Thus, a person who wishes to understand fully the content of the Court's opinion likely needs significant training in judicial or legal studies.

The opinions written by judges are the primary method through which these members of the government communicate with their constituents. The Chief Justice of the United States also issues a report to the United States Congress every year. Known as the *Year-End Report on the Federal Judiciary*, the Chief Justice uses the report as an opportunity to communicate his concerns about caseload, staffing, funding, and other issues important to the federal courts. It is the way in which the chief justice formally communicates to the Congress, and beyond, the technical and managerial issues related to the administration of justice in the United States. In the year-end report, the chief justice will also make recommendations to the Congress concerning ways in which Congress can help alleviate the workload and financial pressures facing the courts, through such activities as authorizing new judgeships, filling vacancies on the federal bench, and increasing court budgets and judges' salaries.

Internally, the justices communicate with one another through the use of hand-written, typed, faxed, or e-mailed memoranda, or they communicate face-to-face with one another during their conferences. These meetings take place several times per week and are used to determine which cases the Court will hear or, after the Court has heard a case, how the case will be decided and who will write the majority opinion. Only the justices—no legal or clerical support staff—are permitted into the conference room, so relatively little is known about the patterns of communication in these conferences. However, studies of the papers of former justices that are now available in public libraries and at the National Archives shed some light on the ways in which the justices communicate with each other. It is clear that the Supreme Court operates in similar ways to other forms of policy-making committees, with vote trading and bargaining occurring behind the scenes. By extension, it is likely that this is the pattern of interaction among judges in collegial courts at all levels of the federal judiciary and within the states.

Some Concluding Thoughts on Communication and Governing

The preceding section demonstrates how important it is for elected or appointed officials in the government to have the means to communicate both internally with their colleagues and externally with those who will be affected by the products of the policy-making process. Different political actors have different methods of communicating throughout the policy process. The president, because he is one person, and is perceived to be the head of the U.S. national government, capitalizes on the power of the media to engage in agenda setting with the Congress and to shore up political support within the mass public. Congress, the most open of the three branches of American national government, permits gavel-to-gavel coverage of its activities to be broadcast on C-SPAN and C-SPAN2, allowing those who are interested unfettered and unmediated access to information about the work of their representatives. Judges in the federal judiciary communicate primarily through the opinions they release in the cases they have heard.

Regardless of the form of communication that is used, without the ability to disseminate their messages widely, public officials could not engage meaningfully in the central function they must perform: representing the will of the American people. At the same time, as the preceding section has demonstrated, the institutions of government maintain an extraordinary level of control over the messages that are transmitted beyond the walls of the institutions of government. The media work closely with the president, the congressional leadership has significant influence over the camera work of the networks that cover the Congress, and the federal judiciary can write multiple drafts of opinions until what the public is permitted to read says no more and no less than what the judges want them to know.

CONSTRUCTING POLITICAL MEANING

As we have seen thus far, political messages are essential to relationships both within and between governments. But the ways in which political messages are presented matter greatly to how they are perceived. As the example of Newt Gingrich and the C-SPAN cameras in the previous section demonstrated, messages take on different meanings depending on the context within which they are presented. The public reacted to Gingrich as a courageous champion of political principle when it thought he was standing up in front of hundreds of his political opponents and challenging them on serious philosophical and political grounds; he appeared to be much less courageous when it was clear he was speaking to an empty room.

Thus, it is not enough to simply recognize the centrality of public communication with elected and appointed officials, or for these officials to be able to communicate with one another. The public rarely has firsthand access to political information. What most of us know about politics we know because we have seen, heard, or read someone else's account of it. To understand fully the importance of political communication, it is crucial also to understand *how* political actors communicate with one another.

Much of what is communicated in politics is less about the substantive information being conveyed and more about trying to influence what the listener does with the information. In his 1922 text *Public Opinion*, Walter Lippman observed that "[i]f someone digs up yellow dirt that looks like gold, he will for a time act exactly as if he had found gold. The way in which the world is imagined determines at any particular moment what men will do."[24] The notion of the way the world is imagined

---

[24]Walter Lippman, *Public Opinion* (New York: Harcourt Brace and Company, 1922), 6.

leading to action is a critical one for understanding the ways in which political communication is essential to the conduct of politics. Political scientist Murray Edelman has documented the extent to which political communication can be used to persuade the public to believe political messages that may not be fully accurate. In *The Symbolic Uses of Politics*, Edelman explains that it is less important what a message says and more important how people are encouraged to perceive the message. The public wants to know that its elected and appointed representatives are hard at work; it is less concerned about just what those officials are doing. This is especially true for members of the inattentive public, who may have the sense that they ought to get something in return for paying their taxes, but who may not have a strong sense of just what they should be getting. Edelman identifies several examples of symbolic policies, designed to engender warm feelings in the hearts and minds of the public, but that really have little substantive import. As he notes, however, in American politics today, how a person feels about government often matters more to his or her voting behaviors than what, if anything, of substance the government has done for him or her. The way political decisions are packaged and presented by politicians, through the media, is crucial for shaping people's feelings of goodwill.

The idea that the way that a message is communicated affects how it is received was more fully articulated by Marshall McLuhan, the source for the often-quoted maxim "the medium is the message."[25] McLuhan's point is that if a person hears political information on a talk radio program, he or she will respond to the message differently than if he or she sees a story on the same topic on a television program. In McLuhan's view, the visual messages will take priority for viewers, while the aural messages will be paramount for radio listeners.

A good example of McLuhan's theory operating in practice is veteran *60 Minutes* correspondent Leslie Stahl's experience covering President Ronald Reagan. In her public reminiscences on her years covering the White House for CBS, Stahl frequently recounts her tale of covering President Reagan's reelection bid in 1984. In a piece for *60 Minutes*, Stahl focused on the disparity between Reagan's rhetoric on programs for the elderly and people with special needs and the reality of his administration's budget cuts in areas affecting these same populations. Stahl was proud of the piece, which she considered a hard-hitting news story about Reagan's incongruent behavior. But when the piece aired, Stahl's explanation of the budget cuts was played over top of video images of President Reagan visiting an elder care facility and meeting with several elderly people who seemed genuinely happy to welcome him as a visitor. After the story aired, Stahl was contacted by the Reagan press team, which thanked her for her story. As she tells it, the president's staff told her: "Nobody heard what you said." In the 1984 presidential election, Reagan won by a landslide.

The significance of Stahl's story has been debated over the last two decades, with some observers claiming this demonstrates the power of the visual over other

[25]Marshall McLuhan, *Understanding Media: The Extensions of Man* (New York: McGraw Hill, 1964).

methods of communicating information and other observers claiming it simply reinforces the image of Ronald Reagan as having an extraordinary ability to connect with the public. Nevertheless, McLuhan's theory that the medium is the message seems to have been borne out in this instance. The way that people perceive the political world will determine their political choices.

Not all individuals are equally susceptible to misleading political images or messages. Returning to the notion of attentive versus inattentive publics, individuals in the attentive public have substantially more information about politics and possess a greater desire to acquire information about politics than do their counterparts in the inattentive public. This probably makes them less likely to be swayed to incorrect impressions of public policies or policy proposals. At the same time, the symbolic uses of political communication that Edelman, McLuhan, and others describe likely have a greater influence on people who know less about politics. For their part, politicians know that they are operating in a political environment that includes both political elites and nonelites. The trick for them is to target their communication to both groups, or at least not to alienate the political elites as they attempt to sway less well-informed citizens to see the political universe in a particular way. How successfully the country's elected and appointed officials are able to do this depends in large part on their ability to master the skills of rhetoric and mass communication.

Political meaning is also frequently constructed through the conduct and interpretation of poll data, one of the most central feedback mechanisms through which the public communicates with elected and appointed public officials. Polls are now taken on an almost daily basis, especially during the last few weeks of the congressional and presidential campaigns. The mass media have a special role to play in mediating the communication between constituents and their leaders, since the polls are often conducted by one of the major media organizations for use in their print and electronic news coverage. As will be discussed more fully in later chapters, polling has developed into a precise statistical science, but one that is not completely accessible to those who are not social scientists. As a result, poll data can be manipulated by pundits and candidates. Moreover, studies have demonstrated that polls that suggest that an election will go in a particular direction may affect voter turnout, as those who anticipate being on the losing side may be less activated to head to the polls. The collection and reporting of polling data is among the most significant ways in which the content and method of communicating political information constructs political meaning for citizens.

THE REST OF THE BOOK

It has been said that politics is often a zero-sum game; when one person or group gains a benefit from the government, it is at the expense of some other person or group. Political communication often determines who wins and who loses, and therefore it is essential to understand both the content and context of these messages.

My goal in my sections of the analyses that follow is to explore the linkages between the medium, the message, and the consequences for governance. For the most part, however, my sections of the case studies will provide the essential framework and context to enable the student of political communication to assess the cases in their political context, while offering limited commentary on the content of the messages themselves.

CHAPTER 3

A RHETORICAL PERSPECTIVE

One assuming a rhetorical perspective would look closely at "texts," whether speeches or advertisements or debates or social movements. The general goal would be to discern how these texts work. One would not just look, however. One would be guided by a framework that allows focus on whichever aspects of the texts seem most crucial in understanding the political communication that is occurring. This chapter introduces you to that framework.

Rhetoric was once at the center of a young person's educational program. Then, for various reasons, it faded; and people began using the term *rhetoric* negatively, suggesting empty words and maybe even misleading ones. Words spoken in politics were sometimes labeled "just rhetoric" or "mere rhetoric." Lately, rhetoric has again assumed an important place in education. As it has, *rhetoric* has become defined, as it was in Classical antiquity, as the art of persuasion. But now, those teaching—and learning—rhetoric think of persuasion as something much broader than speeches such as those given in a public forum as in Classical Greece or Rome. A speech can of course persuade, but so can a pamphlet or a televised advertisement or symbolic action taken by a group of demonstrators. A knowledge of rhetoric can help one succeed in these different persuasive situations. It can also help one analyze what transpires in them with an eye toward understanding how the attempt to persuade succeeded or failed. Furthermore, these texts do more than just persuade. They may actually help constitute who we—those delivering messages and those receiving them—think we are as a community or as a people.

This chapter is not a comprehensive survey of rhetoric. Nor is it a thorough introduction to "rhetorical criticism," the academic term for the analysis of communication (in whatever form) to see if and how it persuaded audiences or constituted a community. Rather, it is an introduction to those concepts in rhetoric and rhetorical criticism that illuminate political communication especially well.

When we engage in rhetorical criticism, we do not just assess the success of a speech or a text or a symbolic act based on our instincts. Rather, we use various lenses through which to view the attempts at persuasion. This chapter briefly introduces a variety of such lenses and periodically demonstrates precisely how the lenses would be used to study political communication. The case study chapters of this textbook use these lenses at greater length. This chapter, then, provides what you need to know to grasp what the rhetorical perspective brings to our multiperspective discussion of varied political communication cases. The case studies show the rhetorical perspective, as well as the other two perspectives, "at work."

THE RHETORICAL TRIANGLE

A useful starting point for a discussion of rhetorical criticism is what has been termed "the rhetorical triangle." The three points of the triangle are the *rhetor*, the *audience*, and the *artifact*. These are the three basic elements in any communication situation. Each one will be discussed at length in the pages that follow, but a preliminary word about each will be useful.

The rhetor was traditionally the speaker. But the rhetor can also be the writer. Those who study political communication know, however, that frequently several people are behind communication artifacts. So, critics need to consider speechwriters, Congressional staffers, legal clerks, advertising campaign designers and copywriters, and others under the term "rhetor." In political communication, although critics may well speak as if a single actor were the one doing the persuasion (e.g., Senator Hillary Clinton used a particular strategy in arguing for expanded government-sponsored health care), critics and those in training to be critics need to be aware that the rhetor is frequently several people, some barely visible in the background.

The artifact was traditionally the speech. But the artifact could, as already noted, also be any number of different types of written documents. It could also be an advertisement, which mixes words and visual images; or a memorial dedicated to an important civic leader or event, which is almost entirely visual; or even a carefully orchestrated protest demonstration.

The audience was traditionally out there in front of the rhetor, easy to see. But now the audience could be sitting at a kitchen table reading or in a recliner watching television. Perhaps, way back, the audience for political communication was more homogenous than it is today. All along, however, there were times when the audience members were asked to set aside their individual concerns and become a "people" with broader concerns and, perhaps, greater objectivity.

So, the fundamental terms of the rhetor, the artifact, and the audience are not as simple as might seem initially to be the case. Not surprisingly, then, a good deal of theorizing has been focused on all three down through the ages. And, as the section following our discussions of the three elements in the triangle will suggest, rhetor, audience, and artifact—and the interactions among them—exist in a number of contexts.

THE RHETOR

Ethos

Aristotle observed in his *Rhetoric* that audiences are persuaded by three means, logos, pathos, and ethos. Logos is the substantive information and argumentation the rhetor provides; pathos is the emotional appeal he or she might make. Ethos is the persuasive appeal a rhetor makes based on who the audience believes he or she is. Eighteenth-century Scottish rhetorician George Campbell classified these beliefs into two categories, intelligence and character. More recent researchers have revised "intelligence" to "competence," a broader concept, and have added a third category, dynamism. Thus, before a rhetor speaks or is read, the audience members have in their minds a sense of whether he or she is competent, of good character, and likely to be dynamic. The rhetor's performance can affect this "antecedent ethos." Research tells us, for example, that if a speech or text is well-organized, then the rhetor's ethos will rise on the competence dimension. A similar rise would occur if he or she talks about the research that underpins the artifact's ideas. Should the rhetor mention (without bragging) his or her good deeds or should he or she admit as possibly valid arguments that go against his or her personal interest, then the rhetor's ethos on the character dimension will likely rise.[1]

Debates between or among presidential candidates illustrate well how the dynamics of ethos work. Before a debate, the candidates are thought to be good or not-so-good debaters. And, of course, their "people" try to manipulate this predebate assessment, which is really a measure of the competence dimension of *ethos*, so as to lower the expectations for their candidates and increase those for their opponents. The debate itself can boost ethos or lower it. In 2000, for example, Al Gore's tendency to stretch the truth about what he had done lowered his ethos on the character dimension. And in both 2000 and 2004, George W. Bush's stronger than anticipated performance arguably raised his ethos on the competence dimension.[2] Which dimension will prove more crucial seems to vary from election to election. In 1960, a rather young John F. Kennedy needed to enhance his perceived competence; in 1984, an aging incumbent Ronald Reagan needed a similar boost. Al Gore in 2000 and John Kerry in 2004 needed help on the character dimension, because both men were thought to be somewhat wooden and too willing to say whatever it took to win votes going into their debates against Bush.

Eloquence

Research also suggests that the excellent delivery of a speech can enhance one's ethos. Surprisingly, however, this excellence—a major component of what has been traditionally termed "eloquence"—has not always been something rhetoricians have stressed. The Classical rhetoricians had very mixed feelings, it seems, about its importance. Too often, in more modern times, eloquence has been treated either with

---

[1]A useful review of research on ethos is found in James C. McCroskey, *An Introduction to Rhetorical Communication*, 8th ed. (Englewood Cliffs, NJ: Prentice-Hall, 2002), 83–102.

[2]For a discussion of ethos in the 2000 presidential debates, see Theodore F. Sheckels and Lauren Cohen Bell, "Character versus Competence: Evidence from the 2000 Presidential Debates and Elections," in Lynda Lee Kaid, et al., eds., *The Millennium Election: Communication in the 2000 Campaign* (Lanham, MD: Rowman & Littlefield, 2003): 59–71. Our unpublished research on the 2004 debates and elections confirms the findings in 2000.

disdain because it could distract from the logic of a speech/text or with indifference because it was just the window dressing.

In the eighteenth century, a group of rhetoricians did devote a great deal of attention to eloquence. Unfortunately, these rhetoricians, who made up what historians of rhetoric refer to as "the elocutionary movement," turned the study of eloquence into a pseudo science. For example, they prescribed exactly—mathematically—how various gestures ought to be used to evoke particular effects. Much twentieth-century research on nonverbal communication covers much the same ground; however, the quality of the research is, not surprisingly, much better. As a result, rhetorical critics can suggest how such matters as volume, pace, pitch, pauses, eye contact, and gestures can be used by a rhetor to enhance his or her efforts to persuade.

A course in nonverbal communication would be required to equip a rhetorical critic to offer detailed commentary on delivery, but even one without specialized training can comment on the strength of President Franklin D. Roosevelt's delivery—at a time when America needed strength—as well as the problems with high pitch and singsong delivery sometimes exhibited by President Jimmy Carter, and the mismatch between the natural, folksy style of President Lyndon B. Johnson and high-styled speeches that were scripted for him by President John F. Kennedy's speechwriter Theodore Sorenson. One can watch

Texas Governor Ann Richards uses wit and charm to command the attention of her audience at the Democratic National Convention.

President Bill Clinton deliver a speech and observe how he uses his body to suggest openness and his eyes to suggest sincerity. And one can watch and listen to President Ronald Reagan—a master of pausing, pausing that made many rhetorical moments in his presidency effective and memorable. His training as an actor, perhaps, taught him such timing.

Stylization

Both the United States and the world have seen many successful rhetors, many whose words or ways of using words remain memorable. Russian literary critic Mikhail Bakhtin observed that all words and phrases have been used before, and he argued that these words and phrases, when used anew, entail all these previous uses. Most often, rhetor and audience are entirely unaware of these echoes. However, a rhetor can make conscious use of this phenomenon by deliberately echoing a previous successful rhetor's way of speaking. Should a rhetor do this, then that previous speaker or writer can be said to be "speaking through" the rhetor's words. In a sense, both the rhetor and the previous one who is evoked speak together. Bakhtin termed this phenomenon "stylization."[3]

A rhetor would, of course, wish to "stylize" his or her artifact only if the echoed voice enhances his or her effort. Early in the Johnson administration, the president may well have been "stylizing" the assassinated John F. Kennedy—to lend the authority of the fallen leader to the political agenda that Kennedy and Johnson shared. Since Kennedy's high style did not fit the slow-speaking Texan Johnson well, this "stylization" led to some awkwardness. Nonetheless, the evocation of Kennedy may have helped Johnson achieve his political goals.

Kennedy was certainly one of the most memorable public speakers of the latter half of the twentieth century—memorable in the United States and abroad. An interesting use of the "stylization" of Kennedy can be seen overseas in South Africa. Two of Kennedy's most memorable addresses were his 1961 inaugural and his 1963 "I Am a Berliner" address delivered within sight of the wall that separated Communist East Berlin from democratic West Berlin. In 1996, while serving as deputy president of South Africa, future President Thabo Mbeki delivered his "I Am an African" address; in it, he evoked both of Kennedy's famous speeches. Why? Mbeki was, arguably, trying to signal that the new South African Constitution would establish a "Camelot"-like era much as Kennedy's inaugural did. He was also arguably signaling that South Africa intended to play a major role in African affairs the way Kennedy's addresses signaled that the United States, under his leadership, intended to play a major role in global ones. Mbeki also uses the respect that his audience had for the Kennedy name to add a persuasive aura to his speech.

[3]See Mikhail Bakhtin, *Problems of Dostoevsky's Poetics*, Caryl Emerson, ed. (Minneapolis: University of Minnesota Press, 1984).

And the Rhetor Is?

Rhetorical critics tend to analyze texts. But before they dig in, they need to consider where these texts come from. Public address scholars have alerted critics to the need to not say "Nixon said" or "Bush said" too quickly. Before a speech or a position paper or an advertisement can be examined as an artifact, the critic needs to consider its genesis. Doing so results in more accurate criticism. In addition, it provides some fascinating insights into political communication that otherwise might be missed.

For example, we know that President Richard M. Nixon used multiple speech writers. He set them up in competition with each other and then chose the speech he liked. So, in a sense, the rhetor varied from Nixon speech to Nixon speech. Late in the Nixon administration, speechwriter Patrick Buchanan became the very frequent "winner"; thus, late, the rhetor was arguably just as much Buchanan as Nixon. Buchanan's role became especially noteworthy because, years later, he ran for the Republican presidential nomination and delivered some rather caustic speeches.[4]

President Jimmy Carter also asked several people to sketch out what they thought he should say. In one case, Carter combined contributions by hawkish National Security Advisor Zbigniew Brezinski with ones by more dovish Secretary of State Cyrus Vance, resulting in a Carter speech that was contradictory in tone if not in its very ideas. Carter affixed his name to the speech by delivering it: the speech, for good or ill, was his speech. Nonetheless, our knowing the speech's provenance deepens our critical understanding of it.

Questions then can be profitably asked about speechwriting. They can also be asked about advertising. Robert Schrum, for example, has played a major role crafting television advertising for many Democrats—presidential candidates, Senate candidates, gubernatorial candidates. If one were to examine his (and his associates') advertisements, one would note striking similarities. Thus, to what extent is the rhetor behind an advertisement (in the 2004 presidential race) John Kerry or Robert Schrum? Yes, Kerry—or at least his "people"—approved the ad, but can one accurately say, "In his recent TV spot, Kerry argued"?

THE AUDIENCE

Pathos

As previously noted, Classical rhetoricians suggested that there were three fundamental routes to persuasion: logos, pathos, and ethos. We associated ethos with the rhetor, since it is an appeal he or she has based on the audience's assessment of his or her competence, character, and dynamism. We will associate logos with the artifact itself, since it contains the substance of the arguments being offered. Pathos is best associated with the audience, since pathos refers to the ways the rhetor tries to evoke

---

[4]Several excellent discussions of presidential speechwriting are in Kurt Ritter and Martin J. Medhurst, eds., *Presidential Speech-Writing* (College Station, TX: Texas A & M University Press, 2003).

the emotions or the passions of the audience in an attempt to persuade them. This pathetic appeal is, of course, made through the arguments the rhetor offers, so pathos arguably belongs under the heading "The Artifact" as well as under "The Audience." We place it here to stress the audience-focused nature of pathos.

Pathos, as a route to persuasion, has been valued differently through the ages. Before Plato and Aristotle, there were teachers of rhetoric known collectively as "the sophists." These teachers tended to emphasize emotional appeals, and, since these teachers taught skills without paying much attention to whether those skills were used for good or ill, Plato, Aristotle, and others were very suspicious about pathos. They talked about it, but they seemed to be backing away from it as they spoke. Thus, it is surprising that Aristotle devoted so many pages in his *Rhetoric* detailing fourteen emotions a rhetor might evoke. In the eighteenth century, rhetorician George Campbell discusses emotions as fully. For Campbell, pathos was an important means to move the will of the audience. A rhetor, according to Campbell, could do so by either recalling emotional scenes from the audience's memory or using his or her imagination to create such scenes. These scenes would be especially evocative if they exhibited qualities such as plausibility, intensity, proximity in time and place, and personal importance to the audience—what later communication theorists would term *salience*.

In the twentieth century, rhetorician Chaim Perelman reiterated Campbell's ideas in his concept of "presence": In order for pathos to have "presence," the appeal must have urgency, duration, proximity, magnitude, and severity. Also in the twentieth century, European rhetoricians such as Ernesto Grassi and Michel Meyer have argued strongly that, since human beings are both rational and emotional, rhetorical practice that recognizes both dimensions is essential. Their approach is not as methodical as Aristotle's or Campbell's or Perelman's, but it points to a similar rhetorical practice—one that does not shy away from evoking human emotions as an avenue to persuasion.

Following their philosophy, the rhetorical critic would not apologetically identify instances of emotional appeals being made to an audience. Rather, that critic would examine how they work. President Lyndon Johnson's 1965 address to Congress on behalf of the Voting Rights Act was heavily emotional. So were President George W. Bush's several speeches after the terrorist attack on September 11, 2001.[5] To the extent that these addresses persuaded, they did so heavily because they evoked emotions ranging from pity and outrage to fear and anger. The speeches evoked such emotions by offering moving anecdotes, evoking visual images, and using sensory language as well as words that in our culture prompt a quick visceral response. In his discussion of "presence," Perelman notes these as well as rhetorical techniques such as repetition and accumulation and more stylistic ones such as metaphor and analogy as means to bring an idea before an audience—making it "present"—and evoke a strong emotional response to it.

---

[5]See John M. Murphy, "'Our Mission and Our Moment': George W. Bush and September 11th," *Rhetoric and Public Affairs* 6 (2004): 607–32.

Audience Analysis

A rhetor, of course, needs to know what emotional appeals will work with what audiences. More broadly, a rhetor needs to know what appeals, whether they be logical, emotional, or ethical, will work with what audiences. Thus, rhetoricians have offered both insights into how different audiences might be reached (e.g., old versus young, male versus female, rich versus poor) and heuristic procedures for analyzing an audience. A heuristic procedure is a systematic way of discovering. So, rather than simply telling rhetors to "think about" their audiences, rhetoricians have suggested *how* one might do that thinking. In the eighteenth century, for example, George Campbell suggested that rhetors ask about their audiences' education, moral beliefs, habits, occupations, politics, religious affiliations, and geographical locations. To that list, we might add public policy concerns.

The rhetorical critic can ask what a rhetor assumed about his or her audience and, perhaps more interestingly, whether the assumptions were accurate or not. Consider, for example, the 1992 and 2004 presidential elections. In 1992, Democrat Bill Clinton, Republican George H. W. Bush, and independent Ross Perot arguably made different audience assumptions. Clinton accurately guessed that any morality-based concerns that voters might have about his personal life would be trumped by their anxiety about the economy. In 2004, George W. Bush and John Kerry clearly made different audience assumptions, with Bush discerning and Kerry missing how much moral values had come to the fore.

Identification

Audience analysis helps a rhetor create a powerfully persuasive bond between himself/herself and the audience. Twentieth-century rhetorician Kenneth Burke terms this bond "identification." As Burke sees persuasion, this "identification" is the crucial element in whether a rhetor succeeds or not. The rhetor's goal should be to become so closely bonded with the audience that rhetor and audience can be said to be "consubstantial."

The 1992 presidential campaign once again is illustrative. George H. W. Bush, because he had the aura of the incumbent and also because of his personality, seemed aloof from the voters. In fact, on several occasions, he inadvertently demonstrated that he could not identify with them. He fumbled when asked the grocery store price for common purchases, and during one of the campaign debates, he came across as not being able to grasp an average voter's economic anxiety. Clinton and Gore, on the other hand, connected. Emblematic of their ability to achieve identification and consubstantiality was the bus tour they undertook while the Republican National Convention was under way. They did not utter memorable words; rather, their symbolic action of traveling from town to town to meet and connect with the people caused people to see the Democratic candidates as future leaders who knew the people's concerns and felt the people's pain. Clinton/Gore achieved identification; Bush/Quayle did not.

Particular versus Universal; Second Persona

Plato in the Classical era, David Hume in the eighteenth century, and Chaim Perelman in the twentieth century all posited that there is an audience out there before the rhetor that transcends all of the demographic particulars one might cite after a comprehensive audience analysis. This audience is not the sum of all of the people in it; rather, it is something greater, something achieved when the people set aside many of their personal concerns and try to respond to a message as the citizenry or as thinking men and women.

These rhetoricians were speaking to potential audience members—encouraging them to play that greater role. However, these rhetoricians were also suggesting to the rhetor that he or she might nudge an audience in that "enlightened" direction. A classic illustration is Senator John F. Kennedy's 1960 address to the Houston Ministerial Association. Kennedy, as a Roman Catholic candidate for the presidency, was experiencing considerable anti-Catholic prejudice in certain parts of the nation. He chose to talk specifically about the role his religious affiliation would play in his prospective presidency before a southern, protestant group. He trusted that, as ministers, they would be willing to put any prejudices aside; and he brilliantly urged them to assess his arguments from what Perelman would term a "universal" perspective. Kennedy's ability to get this particular audience to embrace a greater role is credited with defusing the "religion issue" in the 1960 election.[6]

These rhetoricians all point to a "greater" role an audience might assume prompted by the rhetor's work. Edwin Black, in a 1970 essay in the *Quarterly Journal of Speech*, argued that rhetors may almost always create an implied audience just as they create a voice or persona for themselves. Black termed this audience "the second persona." Kennedy clearly created such a persona for his audience in 1960, but, Black suggests, speakers always do so. "Universal," then, would be an apt description of only one such construct.[7] Many candidates, for example, try through their rhetoric to create an audience dissatisfied with Washington, DC. This particular second persona might be termed "the ignored."

Constitutive Rhetoric

Black's focus was very much what individual speech "texts" might do. However, there can be an accumulation of texts—spoken and written—that can create an audience that never before existed in quite that way. Maurice Charland's account of separatist *Québécois* rhetoric is, perhaps, the classic study of discourse that defined an audience.[8] But similar rhetorical phenomena are more common than one might think.

---

[6]This point about Kennedy's speech is made by James L. Golden, et al., *The Rhetoric of Western Thought: From the Mediterranean World to the Global Setting*, 8th ed. (Dubuque, IA: Kendall/Hunt, 2004), 334–35.

[7]Edwin Black, "The Second Persona," *Quarterly Journal of Speech* 56 (1970): 109–19.

[8]"Constitutive Rhetoric: The Case of the *People Québécois*," *Quarterly Journal of Speech* 73 (1987): 133–50 .

For example, antiwar discourse during the Vietnam era may have played a major role in constituting a large antiwar audience or, today, pro-"family values" discourse may be playing a major role in constituting a powerful constituency in the American electorate.

THE ARTIFACT

Rhetoricians and rhetorical critics alike have been drawn to the text, whether a speech or a pamphlet or an advertisement. Thus, there is much that needs to be reviewed on this topic. This commentary has focused on the content, the small-scale organization, the large-scale organization, and the style of the text or artifact.

The Content

The content rhetoricians have focused on has been the substantive matter that makes up the logical arguments the rhetor is offering to persuade the audience, what Classical rhetoricians termed "logos." Classical rhetoricians divided this matter into two categories, artistic and inartistic. The artistic derived from the problem under consideration—how it was defined, what caused it, what effects it had, what it was like, what it was unlike, and so on. To help a would-be rhetor discover and work up the artistic arguments he or she might offer, theorists suggested the different places they might look, not literal places but categories. Thus, "definitions" would be such a place. The theorists developed heuristic lists of these places—called *topoi* in Greek and *topica* in Latin from the words for "places." In addition to these heuristics, Classical theorists offered heuristic lists of lines of argument that a rhetor might pursue. These lists incorporated the topoi or topica, but also contained what seem more like strategies. For example, among the many lines of arguments offered by Aristotle were turning the tables and pointing out conflicting facts in an opponent's argument or previous mistakes he or she had made.

The "inartistic," the most important example of which was authoritative testimony, was undervalued in Classical antiquity. In the eighteenth century, perhaps because the culture, influenced by numerous advances in science, appreciated evidence more, the inartistic (i.e., not created by the rhetor but rather just located and used) received more attention. Campbell, for example, offered a heuristic for assessing authoritative testimony that would be useful even today.

From Campbell and the eighteenth-century philosopher David Hume onward, the artistic versus inartistic distinction has faded. Rhetoricians have offered various heuristic lists to aid the rhetor in finding the logical "stuff" of his or her argument. Campbell and Hume talked about "moral reasoning" and listed experience, testimony, analogy, and probability as the chief topoi. Twentieth-century American rhetorician Richard Weaver listed definition, cause–effect, similarities–dissimilarities, circumstances, and testimony—a rather "Classical" set. Twentieth-century rhetorician Perelman offered two lists: one of types of argument termed *reciprocity, transitivity, sacrifice, waste,* and *direction*; another, perhaps more useful one of categories of what he called "quasi-logical argumentation" such as definition, appeals to the real (success, causality, classification), and attempts to establish the real (example, illustration, analogy, model). Perhaps the most useful of the many strategies Perelman lists is "dissociation," where a rhetor resolves what seems like cognitive dissonance by dissociating appearance from reality, theory from practice, the letter of the law from the spirit of the law, and so forth.

Any of these lists, as well as Perelman's concept of disassociation, might be used by the rhetorical critic as a lens through which to see a political communication artifact. For example, President John F. Kennedy's speech to the nation about the presence of Soviet missiles in Cuba might be examined using Weaver's list. It would be instructive to see what kinds of proof Kennedy offered as he inched the nation very close to nuclear war. Testimony, including visual evidence, played a role, but so did material drawn from other topoi. What precise mixture did Kennedy use and why? That would be the rhetorical critic's question. Or an antiwar presidential candidate's words during either the 2004 or 2008 election might be examined using the concept of disassociation. How successfully did these candidates separate the seemingly connected matters of supporting the war and supporting American troops in order to explain votes that would, at first glance, seem inconsistent? Were they able to argue that they supported our troops while opposing the war?

All of these approaches are in line with what Aristotle did in his *Rhetoric*, a suggestion of how influential Aristotle's work has been. A rather different approach to logos is suggested by the work of Bakhtin. Bakhtin believed that discourse can be placed on a continuum between uniphonic and polyphonic. Uniphonic discourse has little resonance, virtually no richness. It is the voice of the authoritarian government or of the scientist. Polyphonic discourse, on the other hand, contains within it many other voices—quoted, referred to, alluded to, stylized. In Bakhtin's view, the more polyphonic, the better.

A rhetorical critic can use Bakhtin's concept as a lens to see what other voices a rhetor enters into his or her discourse. In the U.S. House of Representatives' debate on the impeachment of President Bill Clinton, those speaking on the two sides chose differently when it came to incorporating other voices. Both sides heavily quoted or referred to the Founding Fathers. They implicitly and explicitly argued over what these sources meant. They similarly both brought in the voices of former President Gerald R. Ford and defeated 1996 Republican presidential candidate Robert Dole, offering what they said as testimony evidence for their different positions. Those speaking against impeachment, however, also brought in the voice of the American people, either referring to it or quoting constituents, much more frequently than did those speaking in favor. Implicit in this example of how Bakhtin's concept could be applied is the notion that rhetors choose which voices to admit and do so strategically. Those supporting the president were adamant that American voters saw the impeachment as an exercise in partisan politics by the Republicans and wanted those elected to serve the nation in Congress to "move on" and do the people's "true" business.[9]

Two other Classical concepts might be useful in examining the logical argumentation in a text—the concept of "stasis" and the concept of "presumption."

Simply put, *stasis* refers to the point on which a particular argument turns. President John Quincy Adams, who was also a nineteenth-century rhetorician, suggested that stasis frequently will be a question of definition, a question of quantity, or a question of quality. Consider the House impeachment debate in light of Adams's take on stasis. Clinton's offense, based on consensus, was lying to a grand jury while under oath. Some argued that Clinton's offense was minimal, especially since the testimony was about a civil lawsuit referencing his actions before being elected president; some argued it was an affront to our legal system. They, therefore, disagreed as to whether it was "big" enough to be what the Founding Fathers had in mind when they included the impeachment provisions in the U.S. Constitution. The stasis, then, seemed to be a question of quantity. Of what significance is identifying the stasis? Doing so allows the critic to pinpoint attempts at persuasion that misidentify the crucial point and therefore fail. Much of the moral wailing about Clinton's sexual behavior in the Oval Office would seem to fall into that category: it made the president look bad; however, it wasn't relevant to the point on which the impeachment verdict turned. Another example: When, in 1988, Democratic presidential candidate Michael Dukakis responded to George H. W. Bush attack ads that questioned Dukakis's competence by running spots suggesting that Bush and his "people" would say anything to win the election, a critic could argue Dukakis missed the "stasis" or the point on which the argument turned—whether he was competent—and, therefore, ran response ads that failed to adequately respond. Viewers could agree with the anti-Bush message in the Dukakis response spots and still think the Democrat lacked the competence to serve as president.

Presumption refers to the position that is presumed to be true. In our courts, we presume that the accused is innocent; in our legislatures, we typically presume that current laws and policies are doing what they are supposed to do. Those rhetors who wish to overcome presumption are said to have the burden of proof. Guilt must be proved; a problem requiring legislative remedy must be demonstrated. If presumption is with a rhetor, his or her job is easier than if it is not. If it is not, then the rhetor can either offer persuasive arguments and evidence to overcome presumption or try to shift presumption. In discussions of torture as a technique to extract vital intelligence from terrorists, those defending torture would ordinarily be compelled to mount a persuasive case to overcome the American presumption against torture. However, some used the charged atmosphere after September 11, 2001, to shift presumption so that it favored whatever was necessary to combat further terrorism.

---

[9]For a full discussion of stylization in this debate, see Theodore F. Sheckels, *When Congress Debates: A Bakhtinian Paradigm* (Westport, CT: Praeger, 2000), 123–39.

Small-Scale Organization

What a rhetor says is, of course, crucial, but so is how he or she organizes that information. Rhetoricians who have discussed how to organize arguments so that they are full and persuasive have looked at the matter close up, examining how the individual argument is structured, and from a distance, examining how the entire text is put together. Both of these dimensions of organization are crucial.

Aristotle, in his *Logic*, suggested that arguments be arranged in syllogisms. As he saw the matter, there were three types: categorical, hypothetical, and disjunctive. The first is probably the most familiar sort—something like

> All men are mortal. (major premise);
> Socrates is a man. (minor premise);
> Therefore, Socrates is mortal. (conclusion).

The second type would begin with an "if" statement; the third, with an "either/or" one. *Logic*, however, was written for realms of knowledge such as science, in which there can be certainty. Aristotle's *Rhetoric* covered realms in which there can only be probability, and, in that realm, arguments were presented in what Aristotle called "enthymemes," not syllogisms.

Aristotle is not as clear as he might have been about the enthymeme. It seems, however, to be both an abbreviated form of the three types of syllogism as well as an abbreviated form of structures for arguing using a sign relationship (low voter turnout is a sign of civic disengagement), example(s) (Johnson's negative ads in 1964 demonstrated the effectiveness of "going negative"), and probability (Those who use negative ads are likely to experience a backlash; therefore . . .).

The word "abbreviated" must be explained. Aristotle correctly observed that public speakers do not speak in anything like syllogisms. What a speaker says in an enthymeme might well be transformed into syllogism, but, if so, there would usually be elements missing that the speaker assumed the audience would fill in when constructing that syllogism. Some enthymemes would not readily adapt to a syllogistic form—at least the three forms that we usually think of (categorical, hypothetical, disjunctive). But even in these cases, there would be considerable filling in of missing elements taking place on the part of the person or people trying to assemble the more complete argument. Those commenting on the enthymeme in more recent times have observed that its abbreviated nature may be a strength, not a weakness. It may be a strength because audience members, insofar as they complete the arguments, become coauthors of them. Rhetorical critics then might well look at arguments offered in political speeches to ascertain to what extent the audience has had to coauthor them. And what is true of speeches is even truer of advertisements: advertisements are, because of time limitations, almost always enthymemes that require audience involvement if the message is to be grasped. Kathleen Hall Jamieson, in her book *Dirty Politics*, cites this process as adding to the effectiveness of negative campaign ads: audiences buy them because they, to an extent, coauthor them.

In the late Renaissance and eighteenth century, many commentators argued that both the syllogism and the enthymeme were inadequate ways of describing how arguments truly work. Descartes, Hume, and Campbell critiqued the syllogism/ enthymeme in this manner. A viable alternative, however, was not devised until the twentieth century. Then, logician Stephen Toulmin did the pioneering work.

Toulmin offers a new model. Rhetors make "claims"; to support these claims, they offer "grounds." Rules of reasoning allow one to make the jump from "grounds" to "claims," and Toulmin terms these rules "warrants." Some warrants require proof; Toulmin refers to that proof as "backing." And arguments can be qualified by citing circumstances under which the claim would be invalid. Toulmin terms these "rebuttals." Arguments can be qualified by the language used to express one's degree of certainty. Toulmin calls this dimension the argument's "modality."

Toulmin is attuned to the fact that argumentation varies from field to field—for example, from aesthetic judgments in the fine arts to management decisions in business.[10] However, he nonetheless believes that he can offer valid general observations about how arguments are structured. To fully grasp the utility of Toulmin's model, one has to go beyond the basics outlined here and understand what he has to say about the different types of claims a rhetor might make and the different types of warrants that can transport one logically from "grounds" to those claims.

It is beyond the scope of this book to address Toulmin's approach in detail. In a nutshell, he names four types of claims: designative, definitive, evaluative, and advocative. He further names three types of warrants: substantive (cause, sign, generalization, parallel case, analogy, classification); authority; and motivational. Only certain kinds of warrants are possible for certain kinds of claims, so if one makes a designative claim, one can use all types of substantive warrants and authority warrants, but not motivational, but, if one makes an evaluative claim, one can use authority warrants and motivational warrants, but only certain varieties of substantive warrants (generalization, parallel case, analogy, and classification).

Toulmin's model can be used to test arguments offered in political discourse. For example, we might find claims without grounds or claims and grounds without expressed or even strongly implied warrants. These would be weak arguments and, therefore, might not persuade an audience. A rhetorical critic can also use Toulmin's model to identify the kinds of warrants offered in a given artifact. For example, it is interesting to know what kinds of warrants President Dwight D. Eisenhower offers in his 1957 speech ordering federal troops into Arkansas to integrate the public schools in Little Rock. Eisenhower did not want to seem fully responsible for this action because it was not one endorsed by some of his core Republican supporters and Southern Democrats, whose votes in Congress he had often counted on,. Thus, to place responsibility more on the law and the courts than on himself he used authoritative warrants heavily. Eisenhower thereby pleased African Americans and even

---

[10]The textbook authored by Toulmin, together with Richard Rieke and Allan Janik, *An Introduction to Reasoning*, considers the particular dimensions of argumentation in law, science, the arts, management, and ethics.

progressive Democrats with his claims, but escaped the negative political consequences among groups that were politically important to him.

Large-Scale Organization

Classical rhetoricians divided discourse into three categories, depending on the place
and purpose of the speech: forensic for the courtroom; deliberative for the legislating
assembly; epideictic for praising and blaming in the Greco-Roman equivalent of the
public square. Eighteenth-century American rhetorician John Witherspoon divided
discourse into four categories, also tied to purpose: informative, demonstrative, persuasive, and entertaining. This categorizing work is a useful reminder to the critic
that a speech is not just a speech. Rather, a critic must discern what kind of speech (or
text) it is and critique it as such.

More useful than these general categories, however, is the late twentieth-
century work on genres by Karlyn Kohrs Campbell and Kathleen Hall Jamieson.
In their study *Deeds Done in Words*, they defined several genres of presidential
public address, such as the inaugural address, the state of the union address, the
war declaration, and the farewell. Their definitions were based on how the genre
has been used through the years. Some were more fixed than others, suggesting
that some genres are stable and others evolving. Using their definitions, one can
assess the extent to which a new speech in the genre conforms to or departs from
the norm. Some departures are successful and may redefine the genre. The departures, however, are more often failures. Using the definition of the inaugural
(a rather stable genre), one can see why Jimmy Carter's in 1977 was not especially
memorable: he made it too personal for such a highly ritualistic occasion. Using
the definition of the pardon, one can see why Gerald Ford's pardon of Richard
Nixon was so poorly received. Pardons need to be timely—and perceived that way
by the audience, and Ford's was, in a number of ways, offered at the wrong time.[11]

Campbell and Jamieson define genres by listing characteristics. At times, there
is a sense in their study that speeches must also proceed in a particular pattern. Many
other rhetoricians have suggested patterns that a rhetor should follow to maximize his
or her effectiveness. The Classical pattern was proem (attention-getting introduction), statement (bald presentation of what speech will argue), argument (full presentation with appropriate proof), and epilogue (emotional call for action), with,
perhaps, some anticipatory refutation inserted. In the eighteenth century, we see the
beginnings of psychology in philosophers' attempts to define the different faculties
of the mind. Rhetoricians then tied the patterns they advocated to these faculties with
Campbell, for instance, arguing that a rhetor needed to take an audience through

---

[11]These observations are from Karlyn Kohrs Campbell and Kathleen Hall Jamieson, *Deeds Done in
Words: Presidential Rhetoric and the Genres of Governance* (Chicago: University of Chicago Press,
1990).

President Ronald Reagan enacts all of the rituals surrounding the State of the Union Address.

steps of instruction, imagination, passion, and will.[12] All of these patterns presuppose that a text must have a clear order that systematically leads the audience to the point where they are so persuaded that they might act. Without necessarily tying one's analysis to any of these patterns per se, the rhetorical critic could see if and how well a political speech does so. Many speeches that have fallen flat have done so because they either lacked a discernible order or skipped—or largely skipped—a step. George W. Bush's 2004 State of the Union Address, for example, listed many policies he wanted Congress to adopt to address a range of domestic problems. Bush, however, did not spend much time on establishing what the problems are, thereby, arguably, leaving the policy recommendations weakly justified.

Campbell also noted how effective a narrative organization is. In the twentieth century, rhetorician Walter Fisher pushed this idea farther, creating a narrative theory of argumentation. If narratives rang true—Fisher argued—and were made meaningful to auditors or readers, they could be a very effective structure for an entire speech or a very effective element to include in a speech organized along other lines.[13] President

[12]A very similar sequence was suggested by twentieth-century public speaking instructor Alan Monroe and is known as "Monroe's motivated sequence." If following it, a rhetor, after identifying a problem and proposing a solution, would try to visualize for the audience what "the world" will look like if either there is no solution or the proposed solution is adopted.

[13]See, among Fisher's several treatments of the subject, his *Human Communication as Narration: Toward a Philosophy of Reason, Value, and Action* (Columbia: University of South Carolina Press, 1987).

Ronald Reagan, for example, frequently sprinkled narratives into his speeches. In his 1982 State of the Union Address, for example, he tells the story of Lenny Skutnik, an average man who became a hero by jumping into the icy Potomac River to try to save the lives of passengers aboard a Air Florida jet that crashed. And in his 1984 tribute to the men who lost their lives on D-Day, 1944, he interweaves many of their stories.[14]

Narratives in general can be powerful, as Reagan's speeches repeatedly demonstrated. Certain narratives may have more power than others. Twentieth-century rhetorician Kenneth Burke suggests that much rhetoric purges communal guilt by stories of mortification or stories of scapegoating that an audience can share. In Burke's terms, Franklin Delano Roosevelt helped Americans overcome the personal guilt they felt in the economic hard times of the early 1930s by scapegoating "big business" in his 1932 inaugural address. President Richard Nixon and Vice President Spiro T. Agnew tried to help Americans deal with a sense that the nation was falling into chaos in the late 1960s by scapegoating outside agitators, the liberal press, and even liberal college professors. Whereas Roosevelt's strategy arguably worked, Nixon's and Agnew's may not have—at least with some audiences. Even less successful was President Jimmy Carter's attempt to purge Americans' guilt over their excessive consumption of fossil fuel—and a more general lackadaisical attitude—by mortification, not scapegoating. In July 1979, Americans were not ready to be redeemed by mortification.

Narratives with mythic overtones can also be especially effective. The source of the myth might be Classical lore or the Bible, but it could just as easily be popular culture—for example, the six-part "Star Wars" saga. Reagan's call to defeat the "evil empire" of the Soviet Union evoked the first "Star Wars" films. And different nations may have different national myths. In the United States, one powerful mythic story is the conquering of the frontier. John F. Kennedy evoked that myth—in general when he labeled his administration's program "the new frontier" and in particular when he advocated an aggressive American space program in an address to Congress on May 15, 1961.

Finally, any structures—whether narrative or not—in which the audience can participate have special power. The audience can participate whenever the structure is sufficiently set up so that the audience knows what the next step is. Then, when the rhetor takes it, the audience takes it with him or her and feels "good," feels smart. If the audience feels this way, then it is much more likely to accede to whatever the rhetor is arguing for. Kenneth Burke notes this persuasive power that form has—if rhetor and audience can become consubstantial as author—in *The Philosophy of Literary Form*. The principle applies to political texts as well as to literary ones. For example, in 1964, Minnesota Senator Hubert H. Humphrey delivered one of the most memorable vice presidential acceptance speeches ever at that year's Democratic National Convention. He told those assembled at the Convention Hall in Atlantic

---

[14]Kathleen Hall Jamieson noted how important storytelling was to Reagan's rhetorical success in *Eloquence in an Electronic Age: The Transformation of Political Speechmaking* (New York: Oxford University Press, 1988), 118–64.

City, New Jersey, that President Lyndon Johnson had done this and that. After each acclaim, Humphrey added, "but not Senator Goldwater." After a while, the audience joined Humphrey in saying, "but not Senator Goldwater." And, then, Humphrey let the crowd say it alone. Humphrey could have implied anything about the Republican presidential candidate. It would not have mattered; the audience was so consubstantial with Humphrey that they would have joyfully agreed.

Style

Classical rhetoricians talked in terms of high, middle, and low style. The Sophists seemed to prefer the high. Plato and Aristotle, who came on the Greek scene next, exhibited their distrust of the Sophists by advising against the high style, except for ceremonial speeches. Roman rhetorician Cicero, who also spoke frequently as a member of the Senate, preferred the high—so much so that the dominance of the high style in the early Renaissance was known as "Ciceronianism."

The high style featured elaborately structured sentences containing a great deal of parallel structure and repetition. Classical and Renaissance rhetoricians offered lists of the ways such sentences might be structured. By the time Renaissance theorists George Puttenham and Henry Peacham were done, these lists were lengthy: more than a hundred "schemes," all with "fancy" Latin names such as *anaphora, anadiplosis*, and *asyndeton*—just to mention three of the As.

Most rhetorical critics know many of these names, but they use them sparingly in analyzing texts. Six of the hundred-plus are especially useful to know. Two are keyed to repetition within a sentence. If one offers a sequence of phrases or clauses that all begin with the same words, the scheme is called *anaphora*; if one offers a sequence of phrases or clauses that all end with the same words, the scheme is called *epistrophe*. Winston Churchill's famous "We shall fight on the beaches, we shall fight on the landing grounds, we shall fight in the fields and in the streets ..." is an example of the former. Malcolm X's recitation of black men's involvement in American wars, all followed by "You bled" is an example of the latter.

When the phrases or clauses are set against each other (often with words such as "not" or "but not"), the scheme is called *antithesis*. John Kennedy's "ask not what your country can do for you—ask what you can do for your country" from his inaugural address is an example. Should the phrases or clauses be linked with conjunctions, even where a comma would suffice, the scheme is called *polysyndeton*; if there are no conjunctions at all, the scheme is *asyndeton*. Both of these schemes seem to suggest that the lists go on beyond the elements uttered or written. Finally, if phrases or clauses are chained in such a way that the last word of one element becomes the first word in the next, the scheme is called *anadiplosis*. Zbigniew Brzezinski's analysis of totalitarianism—"isolation breeds insecurity; insecurity breeds suspicion and fear; suspicion and fear breed violence"—is an example of *anadiplosis*.[15]

---

[15] I am indebted for these examples to Edward P. J. Corbett and Robert J. Connors, *Classical Rhetoric for the Modern Student*, 4th ed. (New York: Oxford University Press, 1999).

That these examples are drawn from twentieth-century political or historical figures should suggest that the high style is still with us. It is, however, used more in speeches on either highly ritualized occasions, such as inaugurals, or highly emotional ones, such as speeches rallying a nation to fight a war or to continue to do so. That the high style is so limited is perhaps because rhetoricians since the late Renaissance have advocated a less ornate style. Ronald Reagan's very effective style was very much in line with nineteenth-century rhetorician John Witherspoon's advice that one use a middle style: he (or his speechwriters) used Classical schemes, but they also used such common vocabulary that the schemes did not draw attention to themselves the way they did in many speeches penned by Theodore Sorenson for John F. Kennedy.

There has been very little research on the effect a scheme or a style might have. Even absent empirical proof, rhetorical critics often suggest how the rhetor's choices help him or her achieve the persuasive effects desired. The same is true of the smaller units, the words, the rhetor uses. And several theorists have talked about language in ways that are useful to the critic.

Early twentieth-century rhetorician I. A. Richards noted that some words refer to things but that others simply reflect the rhetor's emotional state. He thus distinguishes between the symbolic and emotive uses of language. Richard Weaver called the critic's attention to the "god" terms and the "devil" terms that are present—sometimes unnoticed—in much political communication. Semiotics noted that there are "signs" that have both a denotation and a connotation, the latter involving the rhetor's—and potentially the audience's—emotional response to whatever the topic might be. In all of these treatments of language, there is a common thread—that more lurks in language than might be apparent if one were to read a text solely for its meaning. For example, both Lyndon Johnson's and Richard Nixon's defenses of their policies in Vietnam reveal negative attitudes toward those who, in their judgment, were questioning America's resolve or morality in pursuing combat operations in that nation.

Kenneth Burke also talked about words. He noted that some have meaning insofar as they posit a "dialectical" relationship. Thus, "rational" has little meaning outside a dialectic relationship with "irrational," "freedom" outside a dialectic relationship with whatever term one might posit as its opposite. Burke here is reflecting a strain in contemporary thought that runs from linguist Ferdinand de Saussure through structuralism to postmodern thinker Jacques Derrida. The rhetorical critic need not "deconstruct" a text exhaustively the way followers of Derrida have; however, the critic does need to be aware that what is negated often hides behind what is said. Every evocation of safety or security in post-9/11 speaking or writing, for example, has power only insofar as the opposites of safety and security are in the audience's minds. Thus, in the 2004 presidential campaign, George W. Bush's emphasis on safety and security was so powerfully evocative.

Burke also argued that the words a rhetor uses are not neutral but, rather, reveal how he or she sees the concept under discussion. Thus, if legislators talking about social security refer to it, in turn, as a "government program," a "retirement system," or a "promise to working Americans," their words suggest that they see social security in very different ways. Burke refers to these as "terministic screens." Frequently, the words in political discourse reveal the screens or filters through which the rhetors see the world. President George W. Bush's words in conjunction with the American attacks on both the Taliban regime in Afghanistan and Sadam Hussein's in Iraq are revealing. He seemed to see the world before him in terms of "good guys" and "bad [or evil] guys." The former, like sheriffs in the American Wild West, seemed authorized to bring in the latter "dead or alive." Similar to the "terministic screen" is Michael Calvin McGee's concept of the "ideograph." Ideographs are value- and emotion-laden concepts such as liberty, freedom of speech, the right to bear arms, and private property.[16] Such ideographs can be readily evoked by a rhetor and can bring to an argument an entity far more resonant and potent than just a word or a phrase. They entail an ideology, which becomes attached to an argument a rhetor might make.

The Visual

Crucial in the analysis of an increasing number of "texts" is the visual dimension. It is both an element of style insofar as it adds to the discourse; and it is a substantive part of a text, if not the "text" in its entirety.

Rhetorical critics have looked at the "biopics" presidential candidates now routinely develop, at the political conventions' spatial designs, at editorial cartoons covering candidates or elected officials, and at campaign advertising. All have visual dimensions that play a significant role in persuasion. For example, Ronald Reagan's "Morning in America" ads in his 1980 campaign were highly effective because of the positive images of the nation they depicted. These various artifacts mix words and visuals, and, typically, neither dimension—nor their interaction—can be overlooked by a critic attempting to discern the artifact's meaning(s).

Rhetoricians have also looked at public memory sites, such as memorials, where the visual may well dominate the verbal. Carole Blair's work is especially useful insofar as she models a procedure that "reads" the sites themselves (i.e., what the memorial visually and sometimes verbally "says") in addition to the context into which the memorial has been placed. This context includes any structures that may be nearby as well as any experiences that visitors to the memorial might have experienced before seeing the site under examination. Blair's examination of the Astronaut's Memorial in Cape Canaveral, Florida, for example, analyzes the complex design and what its several meanings might be, but it also argues that those visiting the memorial don't "get" these messages because they have just been to both Disney World and the Kennedy Space Center Visitors Center where they have received

---

[16]See Michael Calvin McGee, "The 'Ideograph': A Link between Rhetoric and Ideology," *Quarterly Journal of Speech* 66 (1980): 1–16.

Maya Lin's design and tourists visiting the Vietnam Veterans Memorial together create a memorial site that rhetorical critics might study.

a contradictory message about man's technological capacity and achievement.[17] The nation is full of memorials rife with overt and subtle political meaning: Mount Rushmore in South Dakota, the Civil Rights Memorial in Alabama, and the Vietnam Veterans and World War II Memorials in Washington, DC. These and others can be profitably analyzed as ever-changing sites.

Public sites other than memorials might also be examined. For example, the U.S. Capitol sends many messages. As an obvious example, it signals that we have a bicameral legislature—the Senate to the north; the House of Representatives to the south, with a large domed space uniting the two. Its physical location on a hill also signals its powerful position. Contrast it to Australia's capitol in Canberra. It is built into a hill so that visitors can walk across it on top of the debating legislators below. Australia is signaling its belief that the people are superior to those elected to govern.

CONTEXTS

Rhetor, audience, and artifact are the basic elements in a text, but texts do not exist in a vacuum. They exist in a range of contexts. These contexts are as simple as the situation in which they perform a role and the medium they are in. The contexts are as

[17]See Carole Blair and Neil Michel, "Commemorating in the Theme Park Zone: Reading the Astronauts' Memorial," *At the Intersection: Cultural Studies and Rhetorical Studies*, Thomas Rostack, ed. (New York: Guilford, 1999), 29–83.

broad as any social movements they may be part of or any episteme they may reflect or challenge.

Speech Acts

Both European rhetorician Jurgen Habermas and American rhetorician Douglas Ehninger have based some of their thoughts about language on "speech act" theory. Basically, this theory posits that discourse *does* something as well as conveys meaning. Habermas thus categorizes speech acts as "imperatives," "constatives," "regulatives," "expressives," and "communicatives." Ehninger lists speech acts' functions as instructing, advising, providing reasons, and persuading. Their work is worth noting because sometimes a speech's effect has more to do with what it *does* than what it says. What it does, of course, is not always evident if one examines just the words that were uttered. One needs to see the act situated in its full context.

For example, in the midst of the urban rioting that followed the assassination of Dr. Martin Luther King, Jr., in April 1968, Maryland Governor Spiro T. Agnew summoned handpicked "moderate" black leaders to an auditorium in Baltimore. He proceeded to lecture them about their failure to prevent incendiary voices from prevailing in their communities. His text was, in many ways, a plea for reasonable men and women, white and black, to work together. However, the very act—lecturing after officially summoning in the midst of an urban crisis that called for conciliatory, not confrontational, language—is what dominated the audience's response and led to more than two-thirds of them walking out on the governor before he was finished.[18]

The Rhetorical Situation

How discourse may act in one way or another can be discerned only if the discourse is situated. A useful way to understand that situation was suggested by Lloyd Bitzer in a 1968 essay in *Philosophy and Rhetoric*. In it, Bitzer defined the "rhetorical situation" as consisting of exigence, audience, and constraints. The latter two elements are easy to grasp, although, as the earlier discussion of the audience would suggest, they are richer concepts than might initially seem to be the case. "Exigence" is the less familiar concept. It refers to a sense, shared by rhetor and audience, that something needs to be done. Discourse responds to this "exigence" by pointing to a "something." Without this sense of "exigence," a speech can fall flat: well-conceived, well-delivered, but without any effect.

Related to "exigence" are two other similar rhetorical concepts that have been the subject of considerable theorizing, *kairos* and decorum. Both suggest that there is a proper moment—a ripe moment—for discourse on a given subject. President Jimmy Carter's speech on the nation's energy crisis (referred to earlier) may have failed because it was delivered at the wrong moment. On the other hand, President

---

[18]See Theodore F. Sheckels, *Maryland Politics and Political Communication, 1950–2006* (Lanham, MD: Lexington Books, 2006).

Lyndon Johnson's speech to Congress shortly after President John F. Kennedy's assassination may have exhibited *kairos* insofar as it seized the moment in calling for the immediate passage of the civil rights legislation the fallen president had campaigned for.

The Political Context

This last example suggests that a critic needs to know what the political context is for a given speech. Traditional rhetorical criticism, like the so-called New Criticism that dominated literary studies well into the 1960s, tended to examine artifacts removed from their contexts. This tendency led to some very rich readings of important public speeches; however, it also may have kept the critics from extracting from these speeches' contexts clues that, if attended to, would alter those readings. Both political communication and public address scholars are now much more attentive to context.

Martin J. Medhurst has made the Eisenhower presidency his special study. Earlier critics had "read" Eisenhower's noteworthy farewell address as a somewhat surprising warning about the growing power of "the military and industrial complex." They were, perhaps, led to such a reading by their consideration of the speech's genre, for farewell addresses have frequently offered warnings. Medhurst, however, puts the speech in the context of the 1960 presidential election and what Eisenhower feared would be the direction, especially in foreign affairs, of the Kennedy presidency. Medhurst's reading deemphasizes "the military and industrial complex" segment of the address and, instead, sees the speech as the outgoing president's last attempt to steer his successor in a moderate direction.[19]

The Medium

Canadian theorist Marshall McLuhan called our attention in the 1960s to the importance of the medium in which a message is sent. Although his distinction between "hot" media, which require much audience participation to complete the message, and "cool" media, which use more sensory channels and therefore do not require much participation, may no longer be useful, rhetoricians and communication researchers agree with Kathleen Hall Jamieson that "Television has changed public discourse dramatically," shifting it from 'impassioned appeals' to "a cooler, more conversational art."[20] The "coolness" of television, for example, whether in McLuhan's sense or Jamieson's, may partially explain why, during the 1960

---

[19]See Martin J. Medhurst, "Reconceptualizing Rhetorical History: Eisenhower's Farewell Address," *Quarterly Journal of Speech*, 80 (1994): 195–28.

[20]Kathleen Hall Jamieson, *Eloquence in an Electronic Age: The Transformation of Political Speechmaking* (New York: Oxford University Press, 1988) 44.

presidential debates, radio listeners seemed to respond positively to Richard Nixon, while television viewers seemed to respond positively to John Kennedy.[21] Kennedy's style, both how he appeared and how he spoke, suited the television medium. More recently, the failure of 2004 Democratic presidential candidate Howard Dean's fiery "screaming" at a postprimary rally of his supporters in Iowa to come across well when televised may be explained by noting, in McLuhan's terms, that the campaign rally is "hot," but television medium, "cool." Whereas the more participating rally audience simply cheered, the less participating television audience felt uncomfortable sitting on the couch.

In local and state elections (as well as in some presidential primaries), campaigning is a person-to-person affair, but most campaigns heavily use various media. Once in office, public officials also use various media, and over the past decades, those media have expanded and changed. As will be discussed more fully in Chapter 4, the medium a political communicator chooses to use can be ignored by the critic only at the risk of not fully understanding what's going on.

Social Movements

Rhetorical critics have considered artifacts that can be pinpointed, be they a speech, a pamphlet, or a war memorial. These critics have also broadened their perspective and examined social movements, such as the Civil Rights Movement of the 1960s or the Green Movement of more recent times. Arthur Smith has offered a useful lens through which to examine such movements by pointing to the communication strategies that seem to characterize them: vilification, objectification, mythication, and legitimation. Smith suggests that movements move loosely through phases dominated, in turn, by these different strategies. John W. Bowers, Donovan J. Ochs, and Richard J. Jensen have offered a different progressive scheme, its phases consisting of petition of the establishment, promulgation, solidification, polarization, nonviolent resistance, and escalation into confrontation.[22] Robert Scott and Donald Smith have suggested a different set of phases that may characterize both a movement as a whole and individual pieces of discourse within it. According to Scott and Smith, the rhetoric focuses on the people's figurative death. Then, it suggests that rebirth is possible, that those in the movement have the determination to fight, that those opposed do not, and that those in the movement are united and, therefore, strong.

Social movements, then, are both a subject for criticism and a context in which particular "texts" should be considered. One can, for example, study the American Civil Rights Movement. However, if one chooses to study only King's classic "I Have

---

[21]A useful review of the research on media and Kennedy-Nixon debates is David L. Vancil and Sue D. Pendell, "The Myth of Viewer–Listener Discrepancy in the First Kennedy–Nixon Debates," *Central States Speech Journal*, 39 (1987): 16–27.

[22]See *The Rhetoric of Agitation and Control*, 2nd ed. (Prospect Heights, IL: Waveland Press, 1993).

Antinuclear demonstrators rally, thereby participating in one of the recurring communication tools used by American social movements.

a Dream" speech, one needs to situate it in the context of the movement to understand the address fully.

The Episteme

The context that social movements provide is small compared to that explored by French theorist Michel Foucault. Foucault argued that a given era permits certain messages to be delivered and attempts to silence others. This process is not necessarily a conscious one; rather, those messages in line with the era's dominant philosophy or "episteme" find voice, whereas those that run contrary to it are pushed aside. Discourse seems to produce the episteme; however, once the episteme is dominant, it regulates discourse. So, for example, if an era is dominated by the belief that human reason can address and solve problems, communication that exhibits rationality in its contents and structure would be "permitted," whereas communication that seemed irrational would be suppressed.

"Suppressed," however, does not mean these messages that run contrary to the dominant episteme aren't heard or read at all. Foucault referred to the episteme as an era's "discursive formation," suggesting that the dominant philosophy, especially the epistemology, gives form to an era's discourse. He terms those deviant messages "counter-discursive." Such messages, Foucault argued, are important in shifting humankind from one era or episteme to another.

Foucault's thinking has inspired critics to look for the "counter-discursive" in an era. It might be found in the utterances of "fringe groups," whether they are on the "right" fringe or the "left." It is usually found in close conjunction with people who are in a "power-down" position in society. Thus, much early political communication by women was "counter-discursive." It challenged not only the prevailing political order but, in many ways, also how politics and political arguments should be conducted. Similar communication can be found in the many protest movements of the 1960s and 1970s as well as in the campaigns of "fringe" political candidates.

Against the Patriarchy

Historically, many "power-down" groups have found a voice—immigrants and workers in the late-nineteenth and early-twentieth centuries; African Americans during and after the heyday of the Civil Rights Movement; gays and lesbians today. However, probably the most successful "counter-discursive" voice has been the feminist one. This voice has not only demanded to be heard in the "man's world" of traditional American politics, but also it has insisted that discourse be conducted on different terms.

Many have written about feminist epistemology and feminist politics—and how the former affects how the latter is conducted. They suggest that a feminist perspective is characterized by being holistic, by emphasizing process, by finding knowledge through consensus instead of consulting or yielding to those with authority within a hierarchy, by believing that such knowledge is approximate not absolute, and by stressing cooperation rather than competition.[23] One needs to be careful not to fall prey to essentialism here—to reduce all discourse considered "feminist" to a set of characteristics alleged to arise from the essence of being gendered female. However, it seems quite often true that the socialization of women will result in discourse that exhibits some if not all of these traits.

The 1994 debate in the U.S. Senate over the retirement rank of Admiral Frank B. Kelso exhibits this feminist perspective well. Kelso had been "in charge" when a convention of Naval aviators occurred in Las Vegas. That convention featured excessive drinking, pornography, and sexual assault—all seemingly condoned by the U.S. Navy as an opportunity for the men "to blow off steam." The seven women in the U.S. Senate joined together to argue that Kelso should retire as a two-star admiral, not a four-star one, because he was "in charge" and failed to stop and adequately investigate the convention. The women worked together in conducting what they knew would be an unsuccessful fight; they refused to accept the recommendations of all those in authority (including the powerful Senate Armed Services Committee) who had recommended the higher rank; and they refused to focus just on the convention

[23]For a useful summary presentation of this perspective, see Karen A. Foss, Sonja K. Foss, and Cindy L. Griffin, *Feminist Rhetorical Tradition* (Thousand Oaks, CA: Sage, 1999).

but looked at the treatment of women in the military as a whole and in government service as a whole.[24] They then exhibited a feminist style.

Double-Voiced Discourse; The Carnivalesque

Russian literary critic Mikhail Bakhtin also provided the critic with some tools to analyze that which Foucault would label "counter-discursive." In his book on novelist Dostoevsky, Bakhtin talked about double-voiced discourse; and in his book on the Renaissance French satirist Rabelais, Bakhtin talked about "the carnivalesque."[25]

Univocal discourse is straightforward. It is on one-level; there is no subtext. However, far richer is double-voiced discourse, which features both the surface text and the subsurface subtext. If the subtext supports the text, then Bakhtin terms the communication "unidirectional." Far more interesting, however, is the situation in which the subtext goes in a different (not necessarily opposite) direction.

Such is the case in the debate over Kelso. On the surface, the women were arguing for a two-star retirement rank for the admiral. However, beneath the surface, they were arguing that sexual discrimination, sexual harassment, and even sexual assault were widespread in the military. They were arguing that the same was true in other government agencies and government institutions. They even implicitly indicted the U.S. Senate, where Anita Hill, testifying against Supreme Court nominee Clarence Thomas, was treated poorly by interrogating male Senators *and* where the seven women Senators standing together against Kelso were being treated poorly by some of their colleagues off and on the Senate floor. On the surface, they made an argument they knew they could not win; beneath the surface, they made a much broader one that, although not strictly speaking germane, they wanted heard.

They also exhibited what Bakhtin terms "the carnivalesque" as they rallied, joined by female colleagues from the House, against those with power in the Senate who had tried to silence their protest against a four-star retirement for Kelso. In his book on Rabelais, Bakhtin dissects the medieval carnival as an explosion of irreverence directed against the higher social classes on the part of the peasants. Thus, authority figures of all sorts—secular and spiritual—were parodied, often in grossly physical terms. Political communication rarely features anything exactly like the medieval carnival. Nonetheless, any event that defies authority and celebrates that defiance possesses a similar rhetorical energy. Many filibusters or near-filibusters do so, as a minority—often in a frolicsome way—delays—defies—majority rule. So did the disruptive demonstrations at the national political conventions that party officials have gone out of their way to silence—so that the carnivalesque energy not distract the television audience from the chosen candidate's message.

---

[24]For a discussion of this debate, see Sheckels, *When Congress Debates*, 51–66.

[25]Mikhail Bakhtin, *Rabelais and His World*, trans. Helene Iswolsky (Bloomington, IN: Indiana University Press, 1984).

Other "Power-Down" Groups

The double-voiced discourse and "the carnivalesque" that Bakhtin talks about are available as rhetorical strategies to any "power-down" groups. Many such groups, such as women's groups in earlier eras, have been compelled to conduct political business in the language and form of the "power-up" group. Increasingly, however, such groups have either used their own language and forms or mixed them with those of the dominant group.

As a result, the rhetorical critic needs to know something about African American rhetoric, Latino/Latina rhetoric, and Native America rhetoric, for example, if he or she is to deal intelligently with political speaking and writing in the United States today. In the House of Representatives' debate on the impeachment of Bill Clinton, for example, many African American members chose to use elements of black rhetoric in defense of the president.[26] So has the Reverend Jesse Jackson at several past Democratic National Conventions. The rhetorical critic runs the risk of making very superficial comments on style unless he or she makes a concerted effort to know this and other traditionally "power-down" ways of presenting the speaker/writer, conceiving of one's audience, and putting together one's text. The critic needs to ask why African Americans who supported Clinton on the floor of the House of Representatives were using the language of a "power-down" group.

BEYOND RHETORIC PER SE

Rhetorical critics have traditionally used their analytical skills to unpack a text—to see in it what might not be evident at first hearing or first reading. In so doing, rhetorical critics have worked much as literary critics have. Meanwhile, those using research methods traditionally associated with the social sciences have also delved into political texts. Although rhetorical critics should not abandon their theory-driven ways of probing an artifact, they should be alert to some of the ways analytical procedures drawn from the social science tradition can deepen their understanding of a text. And, sometimes, rhetorical criticism and empirical research can proceed nicely, hand-in-hand.

Researchers frequently look at a body of communication systematically in order to categorize its content. For example, in the 1998 Maryland gubernatorial election, incumbent Democrat Parris Glendening launched a barrage of attack ads (authored by Robert Schrum and his advertising associates) against opponent Ellen Sauerbrey. These ads seemingly worked. It would be valuable to know what kinds of appeals were offered in these ads. A researcher would devise a list of possible positive and negative appeals. Having examined the ads, this researcher might, for example, come up with two lists of adjectives (e.g., "crusading" and "committed" and others in the positive column; "bigoted" and "narrow-minded" and others in the

---

[26]See Sheckels, *When Congress Debates*, 123–39.

negative). Or, maybe this researcher might come up with a list of policy areas—affirmative action, abortion rights, environmental protection, and so on. Either way, once a list was ready, this researcher (perhaps in conjunction with others) would count in order to see what appeals Glendening's ads made.[27]

It is undoubtedly better to use a scheme for studying content that has been developed and tested by others—as long as that scheme truly serves one's needs. For example, William L. Benoit has developed and used a scheme based on a political utterance's functions. The scheme, which is relatively simple, asks a critic/coder to determine whether the utterance acclaims, attacks, or defends.[28] More elaborate are the multiple schemes developed by Lynda Lee Kaid and Anne Johnston to study the "videostyle" of political advertising. They've developed a list of "Verbal Components" and "Nonverbal Components" as well as a list of "Production Components," such as length, format, production style, production techniques, camera angle, and camera shot. For each, there are subcategories. Their research has led to lists of what they argue is the "Incumbent Videostyle" and the "Challenger Videostyle."[29] The Glendening ads, for example, could be content analyzed to see if they exhibit this "Incumbent videostyle," just as Sauerbrey's ads could be examined to see if they exhibit the "challenger videostyle."

Focused less on content and almost entirely on style is the procedure Roderick P. Hart has developed over several decades. He has developed and refined a dictionary-based computer program known as DICTION. It analyzes a political speaker's verbal style and offers numerical ratings in categories such as activity, optimism, certainty, realism, and commonality. Hart initially applied the procedure to American presidents. For example, he finds that Jimmy Carter used two distinctively different verbal styles, both of which could be taken to ineffective lecturing/preaching extremes.[30] More recently in *Campaign Talk*, he has applied it to the communication from various groups—candidates, media, voters—who talk during an election. He discovered that these groups talk differently. For example, the media are much less optimistic than the other studied groups.[31]

The rhetorical critic will continue to proceed as in the past. Based on theory, he or she will use various critical lenses to discern what may be true of the rhetor, the audience, the artifact, and the various contexts in which the rhetor-artifact-audience

---

[27]For an analysis of these ads, see Theodore F. Sheckels, "Narrative Coherence and Antecedent Ethos in the Rhetoric of Attack Advertising: A Case Study of the Glendening vs. Sauerbrey Campaign," *Rhetoric and Public Affairs*, 5 (2002): 459–81.

[28]For example, William L. Benoit, *Seeing Spots: A Functional Analysis of Presidential Television Advertising, 1952–1996* (Westport, CT: Praeger, 1999).

[29]Lynda Lee Kaid and Anne Johnston, *Videostyle in Presidential Campaigns: Styles and Content of Televised Political Advertising* (Westport, CT: Praeger, 2001).

[30]Roderick P. Hart, *Verbal Style and the Presidency: A Computer-Based Analysis* (Orlando, FL: Academic Press, 1984).

[31]Roderick P. Hart, *Campaign Talk: Why Elections Are Good for Us* (Princeton, NJ: Princeton University Press, 2000).

communication occurs. This procedure, however, could occasionally be enriched by borrowing some approaches pioneered by political communication researchers working more in the social science tradition.

CONCLUSION

The rhetorical perspective on political communication has as its goal the illumination of whatever communication event has been chosen for analysis. Traditionally, the perspective has focused on the rhetor, the audience, and the artifact. Traditionally, much more attention has been focused on the artifact than the other two. Lately, however, the rhetorical perspective has broadened. It is attentive to the various contexts in which political communication occurs, and it considers not just speech or text but also highly visual "texts" as well as symbolic acts and large-scale movements.

In the case study chapters that follow, the rhetorical perspective will offer insight into a wide range of communication activities. In each chapter, different rhetorical approaches will be used. In fact, one of the purposes of this book is to demonstrate the utility—the power—of a variety of approaches. In each case, the critic has chosen the lens or lenses that he or she thinks will best illuminate the activity in question. The use of other lenses is, of course, possible. In fact, one of the delights of rhetorical criticism, when it is conducted communally as in a seminar, is that different critics will indeed choose to look at a political communication event through different lenses and see different things. Once those varied insights are shared, the critics/researchers know far more about what they have studied than what a single perspective would have shown them.

CHAPTER 4

A MASS COMMUNICATION PERSPECTIVE

When we hear "mass communication" or "mass media" mentioned, some of us think primarily of news, others think solely of television entertainment, and still others think of persuasive messages of advertising. All of these different factors compose mass communication. The focus on mass communication in the following case studies will be the role of mass media with regard to politics, its relationship with politics, and the potential influence media may have in elections and other political events.

Charles Wright's *Mass Communication: A Sociological Perspective* (1959) offered three characteristics to define *mass communication*:

> 1) It is directed toward relatively large, heterogeneous, and anonymous audiences. 2) Messages are transmitted publicly, are often timed to reach most audience members simultaneously, and are transient in character. 3) The communicator tends to be or operates within a complex organization that may involve great expense.[1]

In what ways has mass communication and our conceptualization of it changed? Although this historic definition stills applies to some types of media, mass communication has evolved, and this categorization no longer fits. The nature of the audience has changed for many media messages, which challenges Wright's first characteristic. For example, we still find major media reaching millions of people, but we now see narrowcasting of messages, in specialty publications as well as on the Internet, in which media no longer attempt to reach large or heterogeneous audiences. One look at the variety and volume of magazines on the stands in any bookstore demonstrates this specialization of audiences. Market research aids the media in "getting to know" their audiences to the point that we are not so anonymous anymore. Internet shopping tracks our purchases and recommends additional products, digital cable records what programs we watch when, and online news tracks where we click and how long we remain on one web page versus another.

The transmission and status of media messages, Wright's second characteristic, has also evolved. Although television traditionally provides messages to audiences simultaneously, time shifting of messages is now possible, thanks to VCRs and DVRs.

[1]Charles Wright, *Mass Communication: A Sociological Perspective*. (New York: Random House, 1959), 15.

We can also delay and store messages that were once fleeting. Internet news archives provide greater permanence of messages than we have had in the past.

The organizational and financial elements of Wright's third characteristic of mass communication still exist within much mass media today. Media conglomerates continue to expand, with fewer companies owning more and more of diverse media resources. However, no longer does everyone need to be part of a complex organization with vast financial resources to be part of mass media. For example, blogging and streaming online video allow individuals to quickly and cheaply disseminate messages to a potentially vast audience.

The traditional channels of mass communication were considered to be broadcast (radio, television) and print (newspaper, magazine, books). Film was often closely associated with broadcast, in part due to the evolution of broadcast technology from early film production. Political communication, whether originated by media organizations or by political candidates or government officials, may use a variety of these channels for different purposes and with differing approaches. For example, a political candidate may purchase television airtime to broadcast an advertisement in the midst of a campaign; for print media, that candidate may buy space to publish a print advertisement with a similar message or perhaps write a letter to the editor that argues the same points. The approach and decisions taken to convey a similar message vary from one medium to another.

Although these traditional channels of mass communication are those most often used and studied in political communication, media convergence is now blurring the distinctions and perhaps changing further the definition of *mass communication*. These different channels, or platforms, for information or entertainment are no longer mutually exclusive categories. In newsrooms, convergence may mean creating the same product for listening, reading, and viewing audiences. Some newspapers, such as the *Ventura County Star*, the *Seattle Post-Intelligencer*, and the *Denver Post*, are also getting involved in podcasting to provide portable news and entertainment. Media ownership may also contribute to such convergence, as resources may be shared between various news organizations, such as newspaper and TV outlets and their corresponding or collaborative websites. Political campaigns can now offer their messages directly to voters by communicating via email or their own campaign website. These approaches offer politicians and organizations the opportunity to skip the potential filtering or gatekeeping by the news media that may alter or reduce an intended message. These examples demonstrate the continuing evolution of how we define mass communication.

MASS MEDIA AND POLITICAL CAMPAIGNS

Presidential elections occur every four years, U.S. Senate races every six years, and House of Representatives elections every two years. When we consider gubernatorial and other state-level elections, local elections, ballot initiatives, there is always an election occurring or being planned. At the presidential level, possible contenders become the focus of media coverage and speculation years before Election Day. Regardless of the level of the race, political campaigns cannot deny either the potential influence the mass media have in elections or the possible opportunities mass media present for campaigns.

Issues of Campaign Coverage

News coverage is considered by political campaigns to be "free media" (compared to paid media in the form of advertising) or perhaps "earned media" (if considered a legitimate candidate, the media will cover him or her). And although the news media convey from political campaigns to voters through print and broadcast news, they do much more than that in their attention to political elections. News media can provide context for campaign messages, sometimes even against the wishes of political candidates. For example, "ad watches" conducted by news media provide truth-testing of the assertions made in political advertisements. Much news coverage of campaigns explores the campaign process, not just the campaign events in which the same message may be repeated from one audience to another.

Although the organization of this section on campaigns implies a clearly defined line between campaign coverage and political advertising, that distinction is blurred in many campaigns. One approach many news organizations use that focuses attention on strategy of the campaign (and perhaps away from issues) is the use of an ad watch, a review and critique of recently released political advertisings.

There are also other potential intermedia effects between news and advertising in agenda setting, in terms of prioritizing issues of importance that might affect public discourse and media attention. In some cases the key phrases from political advertising are repeated in news coverage, reinforcing a candidate's message beyond the ads themselves. The advertising sponsored by the Swift Boat Veterans for Truth against John Kerry in 2004 is one example of a well-funded advertising campaign that received considerable news coverage and increased attention toward the organization's subsequent advertising.

Much campaign coverage sounds similar to sports lingo, as in who is leading the pack in the horse race, who is trailing, or who is making a serious run from the end and could surprise everyone. Even the analysis following political debates often frames the event as "who won and who lost," with headlines containing further references to the competition. This type of coverage is the media process of *kingmaking*, or identifying the serious contenders in an election. Some suggest the mass media have replaced political parties in the historic role of winnowing down the field of candidates to the "serious contenders." This type of coverage may influence campaign fund-raising and, potentially, voters, but there may also be economic reasons for the news media to narrow down the field for coverage. Covering two or three front-runner candidates can be considerably less expensive than covering a field of eight candidates with individual reporters or broadcast news crews.

A primary aspect of the horse race and kingmaking coverage is the media's attention on public opinion polls during campaigns. Polls can determine the nature of

Although overall coverage of conventions has declined, news organizations still invest considerable resources to cover presidential conventions.

campaign coverage, because the front-runners garner more prominence than the rest of the pack. We often see poll results in the final weeks of a campaign, but reporting on the horse race during a campaign may also occur when there isn't much "new news" to report about the political candidates. After particular political events the news media attention will again be focused on poll results, when, for example, the presidential nominee selects a running mate for vice president. Polls also highlight predictable convention bumps, increases in the favorable attitude toward the presidential candidate whose political convention just concluded. In *Polling and the Public*, Herbert Asher acknowledges how pervasive polls have become in contemporary politics, and how polls may not be completely accurate in predicting the electorate, as we saw in the 2000 presidential election turmoil.[2]

A common criticism of political campaign coverage, particularly at the presidential level, is the concern of *pack journalism*, that the reporters covering the campaign offer homogeneity in their news stories of the candidates and campaign. First discussed in Tim Crouse's focus on the 1972 presidential election in *The Boys on the Bus*, it suggests that news routines often result in reporters covering the same

[2]Herbert Asher, *Polling and the Public: What Every Citizen Should Know* (Washington, DC: CQ Press, 2004).

events in the same ways as each other.[3] Although reporters often desire a "scoop" or exclusive story to stand out from the competition, the pack mentality often discourages them from going out on their own to report news that others are not covering. Crouse suggests that in some cases editors may reinforce the pack mentality by exploring who else is covering the same story or angle on the campaign, and discouraging some stories that are not garnering enough attention from other media.

Other common criticisms of campaign coverage relate to the media focus on the negative aspects of the campaign and their intrusion into the private lives of political candidates. Thomas Patterson's research in *Out of Order* found that the more positive candidate coverage in the presidential election coverage from 1960 to 1976 shifted to more negative candidate coverage starting with the 1980 presidential election.[4] This "media as critic" includes coverage of campaign events, as well as the candidates' personalities, issue positions, and campaign strategies. Negative media coverage may be found to be reserved primarily for the serious contenders as part of vetting their potential for elected office, whereas the underdog in a campaign may receive less coverage but it is more likely to be neutral or positive attention.

Other Campaign Media: Political Advertising, Debates, Cyberspace

Much of our exposure to campaign messages comes from sources beyond print or broadcast news, including political advertisements, televised political debates, and the ever-expanding arena of online resources to reach potential voters. Although it might be safe to conclude that these venues convey potentially different messages, involve different media-based decisions, and have different consequences from "mainstream news," they have become (or, in the case of cyberspace, are becoming) institutions of messages over which political campaigns may have more direct control than they do over news coverage.

Political advertising often consumes the largest portion of campaign budgets, especially at the federal level. We see, hear, or read advertisements introducing the candidate and why he or she is running for office, discussing particular issues of top concern to the candidates, and contrasting candidates on issues, background, and even personal qualities. A common approach taken in mass communication research on political advertising is to make the distinction between image advertising and issue advertising. Issue advertising introduces or discusses policy positions of a candidate and may include retrospective references ("what I've done on the environment") as well as prospective references ("what I will do on the environment if I'm elected"). Image advertising conveys personal qualities of the candidate to create particular emotions, positive as well as negative, in voters but contains little discussion of policy. One noteworthy approach in this type of analysis is Lynda Lee Kaid and Anne Johnston's videostyle, which examines

---

[3]Tim Crouse, *The Boys on the Bus* (New York: Ballantine Books, 1973).

[4]Thomas Patterson, *Out of Order* (New York: Knopf, 1993).

political advertising for its verbal and nonverbal content, as well as for its video production qualities.[5] They found that the majority of presidential advertising since Eisenhower's first paid television ads in 1952 deal with issues, not personal qualities or image. While a common criticism of campaign advertising is that it lacks substance and focuses instead on image, this research suggests that the focus of the campaign is on issues rather than image. Given the visual content of most political advertisements, some aspects of candidate image are conveyed indirectly by the video clips used as well as by the quotes or sound bites offered. And the more attention-getting advertisements—those that garner free replay by media—often focus on some image aspect of the candidate rather than a substantive discussion of policy. The focus on issues in political advertising continues at state-level races as well.

As campaign coverage has been found to be more negative in recent elections than in the past, so has political advertising. Darrell West reports that from 1952 to 2004, 56 percent of presidential advertisements were predominantly negative, with the greatest increase taking place in the 1980s (83 percent of advertisements in 1988 were negative), but the trend of negativity continues today, with 82 percent of presidential ads in 2004 being assessed as negative.[6] Most attack ads do not involve a political candidate directly attacking his or her opponent; rather, the harshest advertisements are sponsored by political action committees or interest groups rather than by a candidate directly. This has become a common way for negative messages to reach potential voters without damaging the image of or support for the candidate. When used directly by a candidate, however, "going negative" has been identified as a common strategy for a trailing challenger in an election, as well as being quite common in close races. West's *Air Wars* raises a number of concerns regarding the role of political advertising in campaigns, one being the strategic manipulation that occurs in advertising from visual editing to taking information out of context. Manipulation also occurs in campaigns when one candidate is able to control the agenda of issues or qualities an opponent must address, rather than discuss his or her own agenda or concerns.

Political debates may also be subject to some degree of manipulation, but not in the same way as advertising. Appearing to be spontaneous interchanges between candidates, debates are controlled in format and are highly rehearsed by the candidates, and what tends to garner media attention is what was not predicted. They do, however, offer the voter the opportunity to contrast opposing candidates beyond what advertising or campaign coverage can offer. The televised presidential debates broadcast since 1960 have little in common with the historic debates we might consider, such as those between Abraham Lincoln and Stephen Douglas in 1858. Today's political debates involve considerable negotiation with the campaigns and a number of decisions regarding media attention and coverage. Although the debate itself is typically broadcast live and is followed by postdebate analysis with various pundits

[5]Lynda Lee Kaid and Anne Johnston, *Videostyle in Presidential Elections: Style and Content of Televised Political Advertising* (Westport, CT: Praeger, 2001).

[6]Darrell M. West, *Air Wars: Television Advertising in Election Campaigns, 1952–2004*, 4th ed. (Washington, DC: CQ Press, 2005).

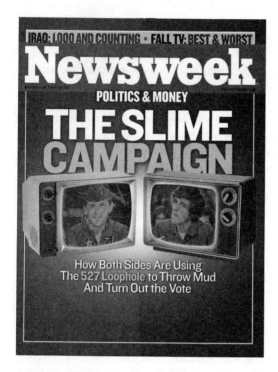

This Newsweek cover reflects the negativity of the political advertising in the 2004 presidential election.

or spin doctors from the campaigns, news attention precedes the debate as well. For example, the debate process is the focus of many news stories, insofar as who gets to debate and who may be excluded, what will be the debate format, and which format may favor which political candidate.

The hype surrounding political debates, from the news media as well as political campaigns, may affect audiences for such events. The first presidential debate of 2004 was watched live by more than 62 million viewers, but audiences dwindled for the subsequent two presidential and one vice presidential debates, ranging from 43 to 51 million, according to the Commission on Presidential Debates.[7] This compares to 1960 and the first series of televised debates, between John F. Kennedy and Richard M. Nixon, with audiences ranging from 60 to 66 million viewers. Not only has the population of the United States increased since 1960, so has the number of alternatives to the traditional networks of ABC, CBS, and NBC, which might explain why debate viewership hasn't increased over time.

Do debates influence voters? Much research suggests political debates reinforce the decisions made by voters who have already made up their minds but is not very influential on undecided voters. However, viewers of debates may become more interested in a campaign, may gain information about the candidate and campaign,

[7]Commission on Presidential Debates. "2004 Debates." http://www.debates.org/pages/his_2004.html.

and therefore may be able to discuss the campaign with others. Research by James Lemert has examined the influence of the postdebate analysis, or what he calls the "news verdict" about the outcome of the debates.[8] The media coverage following a political debate may be more influential than the debate itself, as the press and pundits provide interpretations of the debate. One compelling example of the influence of postdebate analysis is Frederick Steeper's analysis of the second debate in 1976 between Gerald Ford and Jimmy Carter.[9] Steeper found that most viewers surveyed immediately following the debate, in which Ford twice insisted that Eastern Europeans were not under Soviet domination, thought Ford had won the debate, while those surveyed the day after the debate, and plenty of media commentary about Ford's gaffe and why he lost the debate, thought Carter won the debate.

While campaigns certainly use additional message vehicles (e.g., direct mail, phone calls to voters), the area of growing attention in mass communication studies is the use and influence of cyberspace in campaigns and elections. It is too early to predict the potential scope of the use of the Internet in campaigns and elections, but we have already seen considerable change in how campaigns, candidates, media, voters, and interest groups can communicate. Gary Selnow predicted in his 1998 book *Electronic Whistle Stops: The Impact of the Internet on American Politics* that the Internet would be essential to campaigns, perhaps equaling the importance of traditional media.[10] Since the first use of campaign websites for political office in the mid-1990s, we have witnessed the explosion of online vendors of campaign fund-raising (and the success of candidates such as Howard Dean in raising campaign money online in 2004), the use of an online primary (in Arizona's Democratic primary in 2000), and the use of the Internet to mobilize supporters offline, as in Meetup groups in 2004 and social-networking sites such as MySpace and Facebook in 2006 races. Campaign websites have become mainstream, as have e-mails to supporters and weblogs ("blogs") by campaigns themselves or about the campaign from outsiders. Continuing the negative campaign issues we have witnessed in campaign coverage as well as in political advertising, online attacks are used as well. Political candidates have been found to be willing to do as much attacking of opponents online, through either news releases or online ads, as they do in television advertisements.[11]

Although the majority of campaign activities may take advantage of the Internet, those who study mass communication also consider issues of access to such technologies. The theory of diffusion of innovations predicts that new resources such as the

---

[8]James B. Lemert, "Do Televised Presidential Debates Help Inform Voters?" *Journal of Broadcasting & Electronic Media*, 37 (1993): 83–94.

[9]Frederick T. Steeper, "Public response to Gerald Ford's Statements on Eastern Europe in the Second Debate." In George F. Bishop, Robert G. Meadow, & Marilyn Jackson-Beeck, eds., *The Presidential Debates: Media, Electoral and Policy Perspectives* (New York: Praeger, 1978).

[10]Gary Selnow, *Electronic Whistle Stops: The Impact of the Internet on American Politics* (Westport, CT: Praeger, 1998).

[11]Robert Wicks and Boubacar Souley, "Going Negative: Candidate Usage of Internet Web Sites During the 2000 Presidential Campaign," *Journalism and Mass Communication Quarterly* 80 (2003): 128–44.

Internet will be adopted by different groups of consumers at different rates, with innovators being the first to try a new development and laggards trailing far behind at the end of the adoption curve. And although access to the Internet has increased substantially, it still does not reach all potential voters, particularly older and lower-income publics. Additionally, the concept of the "digital divide" reinforces the distinction between the technology and information "haves" and "have nots." Public access to the Internet may lead to this divide shrinking, but there will still be segments of the population who have limited exposure to any online campaign information from candidates or other sources. The Internet may provide the potential for information overload of users, given the number of resources available, but there remains a portion of the public who may find themselves in an information vacuum or excluded from developments regarding online voting or other political involvement.

Traditional media have also been influenced by growing developments in online resources, providing their own Internet news sites with additional story information, streaming video footage, and photographs. They have also witnessed additional competition in covering news events from the "blogosphere." For example, in 2004, blogs kept attention on Dan Rather's report for CBS News regarding President Bush's National Guard service and questioned the authenticity of the story. Three CBS News executives were fired as an outcome of the discredited report. Although we could debate whether bloggers should be considered journalists or not, they have

Dan Rather appears on The Chris Matthews Show *after leaving CBS News following the 2004 elections. Political programs on cable television offer an alternative to traditional news.*

shown their potential to influence the news agenda and they provide additional sources of information for the public beyond mainstream media. Case studies on the 2004 and 2006 elections in particular will further discuss the potential influence and opportunities of blogs in political campaigns.

BEYOND ELECTIONS: NEWS MEDIA AND POLITICS

Although many of the case studies in this book focus on elections and the various communication vehicles discussed earlier, the relationship between mass media and political actors continues beyond electoral events. Other areas of research and discussion about news media involve objectivity, newsworthiness of events, the relationship between reporters and government officials, and reporters' coverage of the courts.

Reporter Objectivity: Expectations and Challenges

Underlying much criticism of contemporary news media is an expectation of reporter objectivity. We want reporters to provide us news of the day in an unbiased manner—to favor neither side in an argument, but simply to provide the facts and let us make up our own minds on the issue. Objectivity should be a goal reporters strive for, but it is an unrealistic expectation, because it requires reporters to interpret events without any influence from their prior experiences. How a story is covered, how a lead or headline is written, and even how a photograph is framed involve an interpretation of events. Although it might be unintentional, bias may creep into these interpretations. What many newsrooms use as more realistic goals are balance and fairness and that a story will provide quotes from both sides of the issue. Achieving these goals is typically examined in mass communication research by coding or assessing each paragraph or sentence of a news story as favorable (toward a particular side or person), neutral, or unfavorable and then totaling those assessments, with each favorable statement or paragraph canceling out an unfavorable one.

A number of models of mass media exist conceptually that reflect different expectations in the news media's role regarding objectivity. Leighley identifies a number of approaches to objectivity that may aid in understanding different expectations of the mass media.[12] For example, the "reporters of objective fact" model holds that media play a small role in communication between government and the public, only to disseminate information. The "neutral adversary" role reflects the watchdog role of the media, as the media exist to monitor government officials. Both of these are in contrast to the "profit-seeker model," as nearly all U.S. media are privately owned businesses whose goal is to make money.

The goal of reporter objectivity itself grew out of economic motivations, according to Lance Bennett's research; in order to attract the largest possible reader-

---

[12]Jan E. Leighley, *Mass Media and Politics: A Social Science Perspective* (Boston: Houghton-Mifflin Company, 2004).

ship, newspapers in the early 1900s worked to avoid overtly political slants in their reporting.[13] Bennett concludes that this approach may have in fact increased bias, in reporters' greater reliance on government officials as sources in news stories. Some would suggest government officials, and perhaps a small handful of other experts, compose a "Golden Rolodex" for the news media.[14] News routines and deadline pressure increase the temptation to rely on a small group of spokespeople and pundits for a quote or sound bite on the issue of the day.

As stated above, the U.S. media are businesses, profit-making ventures. Ownership and revenues play key influences in media operations, and even though many operations attempt to keep their "salesroom" separate from their "newsroom," we continue to see the potential to influence news content and decision making. Despite such goals, the growing trend in media concentration raises concerns of decision making in newsrooms, marketing the news, and possible conflicts between business practices and newsroom routines. In the first edition of Ben Bagdikian's *The Media Monopoly* in 1983, he identified fifty companies that controlled the majority of mass media in the United States.[15] With each edition of his book, that number has dwindled, with fewer companies owning more and more of the media. In Bagdikian's revised version, *The New Media Monopoly* in 2004, that list has dwindled to five companies controlling the majority of U.S. mass media.[16] Although media concentration may not directly challenge goals toward objectivity in the newsroom, added pressures may exist to remain competitive and cost-effective in the news beyond traditional news routines.

Another area of routines and expectations used by reporters is the evaluation of news events on the basis of newsworthiness. When reporters are assigned to cover one story over another, or an editor is filtering through wire stories from the Associated Press to decide what to include in the newspaper, news values are being used to make those decisions. The more criteria for newsworthiness a potential story has, the more likely it is to be covered by a reporter and included in a newscast or newspaper. Melvin Mencher identifies seven key news values in *Basic Media Writing*[17]:

1. *Timeliness*: The more recently something occurred, the more likely the media are to cover it, especially in the era of 24-hour broadcast and instantaneous online news updates.
2. *Proximity*: The closer in geographic distance an event is to one's news audience, the more likely it is to be covered by the news media. This may be due in part to convenience, based on whether the story is easy to get to and cover or not.

---

[13]W. Lance Bennett, *News: The Politics of Illusion*, 6th ed. (New York: Pearson/Longman, 2004).

[14]For political campaigns, however, a Golden Rolodex is considered to be the list of supporters who can be contacted to make major campaign contributions.

[15]Ben Bagdikian, *The Media Monopoly* (Boston: Beacon Press, 1983).

[16]Ben Bagdikian, *The New Media Monopoly* (Boston: Beacon Press, 2004).

[17]Melvin Mencher, *Basic Media Writing*, 6th ed. (Boston: McGraw-Hill, 1999).

3. *Conflict*: A clash between people, organizations, or institutions is at the heart of many news stories. A story that people are coexisting peacefully is newsworthy only if they've been fighting for years.
4. *Impact*: The significance or importance of a story is the primary factor in impact. The more people who might be affected by an event, the more newsworthy it is.
5. *Prominence*: If well-known people are involved in the story—celebrities, politicians, and so forth—the more likely it is to be covered, even if other criteria are not met. So a DUI arrest of an elected official may be newsworthy because of the "who" of the story alone.
6. *Currency*: If a story is of current interest to the public, it may be more likely to be included in a newscast or newspaper. This criterion reflects audience interest more than the others, but given issues of agenda setting, perhaps the media do influence what events or issues the public discuss.
7. *Uniqueness*: Stories that are out of the ordinary in some way may be covered for uniqueness alone. Also referred to as human-interest stories, this would be the "man bites dog" story versus the "dog bites man" story in the news. Often the bizarre nature of the event drives media attention to the story.

Sometimes stories are deemed newsworthy based on the above criteria, but the events have been structured by organizations for the primary purpose of gaining news attention; Daniel J. Boorstin has termed such events "pseudo-events."[18] They might be considered primarily media events rather than simply events that the media chose to cover. Although Boorstin first discussed the notion of pseudo-events in the early 1960s, the concept still applies today to many news-related events, including those involved in politics. Boorstin discussed four characteristics of an event that would qualify it as a pseudo-event: (1) the event is not spontaneous but rather "planned, planted, or incited,"[19] (2) the event occurs primarily for the purpose of gaining news attention, (3) asking "what does it mean?" about a situation or event is ambiguous, and (4) a self-fulfilling prophecy may occur or be intended to occur. For example, if a political candidate refers to herself as "a citizen, not a career politician," that may be the label attached to her by others as well. Many events look like news and sound like news, but when we explore further their potential newsworthiness, we may conclude that they are pseudo-events with little purpose beyond media coverage.

Reporters' Relationship with Government Officials

We know that much of the time spent between officials and the media occurs during political campaigns, but these relationships persist outside of the election arena as well. Every member of the U.S. Congress has at least one staff member dedicated to media affairs activities. Most news organizations have their own Washington news bureau or are affiliated with one through syndication agreements.

---

[18]Daniel Boorstin, *The Image: A Guide to Pseudo-Events in America*, reissue ed. (New York: Vintage, 1992).
[19]Ibid., 11.

Doris Graber articulates four functions media perform for government officials that demonstrate a number of different relationships between the two institutions:

1. Media inform government officials about current events,
2. Media keep government officials attuned to major concerns of the public,
3. Media allow government officials to convey their message to the public as well as to other political elites, and
4. Media allow government officials to remain in public view, and therefore on constant display.[20]

These functions demonstrate the variety of roles mass media play in their relationship with government officials. What varies in these functions is who controls the "message," the information being disseminated. In the first two examples, media control the message, whereas in the third and fourth functions, government representatives have the upper hand in controlling content to some degree. These functions also demonstrate the distinction, described next, of journalists as watchdogs over government and journalists as lapdogs of government.

Journalists as Watchdogs.   In this conceptualization of the relationship between news media and government officials, news media serve as a watchdog over government, checking the accuracy of people's statements and "barking" to alert the public to issues of concern. This is an adversarial relationship between the two parties, perhaps reflected in officials refusing to comment or be interviewed for a news story and reporters investigating what they perceive to be "wrongdoing" by officials (a technique made famous in the twentieth century by *Washington Post* reporters Bob Woodward and Carl Bernstein's investigation of Watergate). Expectations of a watchdog role of the media have roots in the consideration of the press as the Fourth Estate by the nineteenth-century historian Thomas Carlyle.[21] The first three estates come from pre-Revolutionary France: the aristocracy, the clergy, and the bourgeoisie. The press as the Fourth Estate serves to watch for the wrongdoing of the other three. In American politics, the three branches of government provide checks and balances on each other, and the news media may provide outside monitoring of all three: executive, legislative, and judicial.

Journalists as Lapdogs.   The opposite perspective of news media, rather than one of journalists "guarding" the public, is the news media serving at the will of government officials (rather than of the people or of the companies owning the media). Officials and institutions are interested in using the news media to get their messages out, to convey information to the public or other stakeholders. In contrast to purchasing advertising time or space to provide a message to the public, access through the news

---

[20]Doris Graber, *Mass Media and American Politics*, 7th ed. (Washington, DC: Congressional Quarterly Press, 2006).

[21]Thomas Carlyle, *On Heroes: Hero Worship and the Heroic in History* (Boston: Ginn, 1901).

media is perceived to be "free media" and may be perceived as being more legitimate as part of news than pure persuasion affiliated with advertising. This use of the media to convey interested parties' messages leads to this lapdog image of the media, in which reporters may do the bidding of government (or big business, for that matter). Examples include covering a press conference or following up on a lead (often "leaked" from an unnamed government official). In some cases, these may be considered to be "trial balloons" intentionally provided by government offices to test potential responses to an idea or issue. Another example of news media being used as a conduit to convey information directly from the government to the public is the use of a press release as the basis for a news story. Although this is a common routine, because press releases provide basic facts of a story and invite follow up by a reporter, many news organizations repeat information verbatim from press releases. Video news releases are commonly provided to television news organizations by government offices as well as by corporations, and often the news broadcast fails to attribute the source of such footage. These approaches run counter to enterprise reporting, in which a reporter develops story ideas on his or her own, rather than have them provided (and perhaps already packaged) by a news source.

Rather than watchdog or lapdog, could it be a codependent relationship? One additional interpretation of the relationship between the news media and officials is the "junkyard dog." Sabato suggests we saw the lapdog role of the media primarily from 1941 to 1966, the watchdog role from 1966 to 1974, and then a shift to what he calls the junkyard dog role from 1974 to the present.[22] The junkyard dog exemplifies the reporter as aggressive and intrusive and suggests that gossip may be perceived as newsworthy. Others may suggest society needs a watchdog for the watchdog; that is, we need someone to serve that role over the mass media. Such formal structures exist with the Federal Communications Commission's (FCC) oversight of broadcast content and licensing. An informal structure to monitor the mass media and bring to light inconsistencies and inaccuracies has developed in weblogs or blogs. Such blogs may be operated by news-savvy individuals or organizations with an interest in the accuracy and fairness of news coverage. While these sites do not have the official power of the FCC, they can bring attention to issues within news coverage to the reading and viewing public.

The watchdog and the lapdog perspectives may be seen as the extremes of a continuum; somewhere in between lies the day-to-day relationship between news media and government. Some may expect antagonism between watchdog reporters and government officials, but that would be counterproductive for reporters trying to get information from or access to those government officials. Likewise, officials need news media for the reasons identified earlier, to get messages disseminated and perhaps for visibility as well. It may best be understood as a codependent relationship: news media need government officials to do their job and report on the news about government, and officials rely on access to the public and other groups via the news media. Both parties are motivated to continue the mutually beneficial relationship, to "give" on some days in order to "take" on others.

---

[22]Larry Sabato, *Feeding Frenzy: Attack Journalism and American Politics* (New York: Free Press, 1991).

Media Coverage of Courts

Compared to attention given to the executive and legislative branches of government, news coverage of the judiciary trails considerably. Doris Graber's analysis of 2003–2004 evening network news coverage[23] found the Supreme Court received an average of 10.4% of total network airtime dedicated to the presidency, Congress, and the Court. Attention to the presidency dominated, with 52.5% of network coverage of the three branches, followed by coverage of Congress, with 37%.

When the Court's decisions are newsworthy, news stories may quote from the decision in the case and interview attorneys or clients tied to the case under decision. Experts who may be tracking particular cases may also be sources for interpretation of Court decisions. However, few Court decisions merit news media attention. Graber cites a report that in 1998, newspapers covered just 11% of the Court's decisions, while television news covered less than 8% of the cases.[24]

Reporters face a number of challenges in covering the Supreme Court. Decisions handed down by the Supreme Court are not given via press conference by any of the justices, but rather are presented as written opinion. And although the Court's press office provides some reference materials to reporters, they do not provide interpretation of opinions. The structure of Supreme Court opinions also presents a challenge, because multiple decisions may be handed down on the same day. Reporters are often left to read and interpret lengthy opinions to meet tight news deadlines. Graber points out that much coverage of lower level courts is imprecise or possibly inaccurate. This may be the result of a shortage of skilled legal reporters and reporting of court processes by journalists who are unfamiliar with the law (although this is less likely with reporters covering the Supreme Court).

A Supreme Court case that merits media attention typically is covered when the petition is submitted, when oral arguments are heard, and when the decision by the Court has been issued.[25] Beyond covering the case as initially presented to the Court (although oral arguments cannot be recorded or videotaped to aid in broadcast coverage) and the decision reached by the Court, the majority of media attention occurs prior to a justice becoming a member of the Supreme Court. Justices proceed through nomination and then a Senate Judiciary Committee hearing before the full Senate vote, which requires a majority for confirmation. Media scrutiny is high once a nominee is announced, and it even precedes the announcement with speculation from pundits about who might be on the president's "short list" of nominees and how qualified those potential nominees are. Interest groups who support or oppose the nominee may vie for media attention by holding press conferences, staging protests, and even producing television advertisements. As key issues that may confront the justice are identified, and perhaps past rulings are researched, spokespeople from

---

[23]Doris Graber.

[24]Graber.

[25]V. James Strickler and Richard Davis, "The Supreme Court and the Press." In *Media Power Media Politics*, edited by M. J. Rozell (Lanham, MD: Rowman and Littlefield, 2003), 45–73.

interest groups and other organizations related to those issues are often interviewed for news reports.

The First Amendment and Press Regulations

Another way in which the mass media has a relationship with the Court that is unique compared with the other branches of government is the direct impact Court decisions have regarding the First Amendment rights of the press. When assessing various aspects of political communication, one mass communication focus may concentrate on legal and ethical implications or issues of particular media content, as well as regulation involving the mass media.

The First Amendment guarantees that "Congress shall make no law . . . abridging the freedom of speech or of the press." Although not everyone may appreciate what the news media report, in particular a political candidate who received what he or she perceives as unflattering coverage, the First Amendment protects the rights of those in the press to do their job.

There are a number of regulations that reinforce the freedom of the press and enable reporters to effectively cover entities from political candidates to elected officials to government agencies. For example, the Freedom of Information Act (FOI) allows reporters (as well as private individuals and interest groups) to request access to records and files closed to the public. There are many exemptions to what will be made available in an FOI request, but reporters have the potential to gain access to information that otherwise would not be available to them. *Shield laws* exist in more than thirty states and serve as another protection for the news media by protecting journalists from being forced to testify in court, turn over their notes or recordings, or identify confidential sources. Although we may consider *defamation* law as offering protection to private citizens who may be the focus of news media attention, the Court's definition of libel and slander offers a number of defenses to the news media. The one most consistent with our expectations of reporters is that they tell the truth; if unflattering but true information is published about an individual, there are no grounds for defamation. The information published must be knowingly false, or published with reckless disregard whether it was false or not, to meet that criterion in a libel case. Decisions regarding *prior restraint* have reinforced the news media's right to publish information without censorship from the government. Such laws, however, do not prevent the media from facing criminal or civil penalties that result from publishing news stories.

The primary focus of the First Amendment in political communication is on news media content. Although product advertising is regulated, primarily regarding the accuracy of the claims made, political advertising faces no comparable requirements or enforcement by government agencies such as the Federal Trade Commission. Candidates who feel an attack advertisement against them is inaccurate and potentially defamatory do have recourse in the court system to sue, but these cases will not typically reach a court hearing until after an election has concluded. In some state-level races, as well as through proposals by organizations such as the Alliance

Reporters embedded with troops in Iraq face restrictions on coverage by the military, but technology such as videophones allow them to provide extensive and rapid coverage.

for Better Campaigns, candidates agree to refrain from particular negative campaign tactics, particularly in advertising, as a form of self-regulation.

MASS COMMUNICATION RESEARCH AND POLITICAL COMMUNICATION

The earlier sections of this chapter introduced a number of factors regarding the variety of content considered to constitute mass communication, as well as issues and decisions of the media and politics inside and outside of elections. This final section reviews some key areas of research regarding the potential effects of mass media in political campaigns and theories related to media impact.

Media Effects and Politics

Given the hundreds of millions of dollars currently spent on the media-related aspects of political campaigns, we could easily conclude that the media have an influence and move on to our next subject. However, mass communication research has encompassed a variety of aspects of media content and potential effects that merit further consideration. The media may not affect all people in the same way all of the time, but they do have the potential to influence some of the electorate in their knowledge, attitudes, and potentially behavior. These three effects may be steps in the process of media influence; voters may first become aware of candidates and gain knowledge about them, then develop and shape attitudes about the candidates, which may lead to their vote choice and ultimate behavior in casting their vote on Election Day.

Regarding *knowledge*, we might consider this to be political learning, or voter education. Research does suggest considerable potential for voter learning from campaign messages and the media. For example, in Patterson's research on the impact of campaign events on voters' learning from the 2000 campaign, he identified three key times of greatest voter learning: the primary season, the presidential conventions, and the presidential debates.[26] Learning during these three periods accounted for 80 percent of what voters learned during the campaign. Sotirovic and McLeod identify a number of conclusions research has made regarding political learning from the mass media based on different sources or content.[27] For example, reading a newspaper has a greater effect on knowledge than watching television news, except for the audience who is less informed. The viewing of entertainment programs has a negative effect on knowledge, but attention to talk shows (e.g., *Larry King Live, Rush Limbaugh*) can increase knowledge.

Voters' *attitudes* and perceptions may also be influenced by campaign media. Beyond gaining information regarding a candidate such as his or her background or issue positions, voters have the potential to develop attitudes regarding the candidate, and both positive and negative perceptions may be formed.

Regarding the effects of political advertising specifically, Kaid summarizes a number of patterns found in both survey and experimental research that confirms that exposure to campaign advertising can influence evaluations of a candidate.[28] She also acknowledges that such patterns vary by viewer predispositions, the production techniques of the advertisements, and the channel of exposure between television advertisements and more recently created Internet advertisements.

The negativity of contemporary political campaigns has raised concerns regarding the impact of such campaign content on political cynicism. As described by Perloff, the process toward cynicism is: "The more people watch television news, the less interested they are in politics and the less efficacious they feel—that is, the less they feel they can influence what goes on in government."[29] The impact of negative advertising on attitudes is mixed, with some voters finding negative information to be as believable as positive information in a campaign, whereas others report a backlash effect in increasing negative attitudes toward the candidate who sponsored the attack ad.

[26]Thomas Patterson, *The Vanishing Voter* (New York: Knopf, 2002).

[27]Mira Sotirovic and Jack McLeod, "Knowledge as Understanding: The Information Processing Approach to Political Learning." In *Handbook of Political Communication Research*, edited by Lynda Lee Kaid, (Mahwah, NJ: Lawrence Erlbaum Associates, 2004), 357–94.

[28]Lynda Lee Kaid. "Political Advertising." In *Handbook of Political Communication Research*, edited by Lynda Lee Kaid (Mahwah, NJ: Lawrence Erlbaum Associates, 2004), 155–202.

[29]Richard Perloff, *Political Communication: Politics, Press, and Public in America* (Mahwah, NJ: Lawrence Erlbaum Associates, 1997), 340.

Finally, voter *behavior*, considered to be mobilization or turnout, is perhaps the most desired effect from a campaign's perspective. Although it might be desirable to have potential voters know many things about the candidate and have clear or accurate perceptions of the candidate, it does not count in the final tally if those prospective voters do not actually vote.

Some may conclude that negative advertising may demobilize the electorate, but research has not found a consistent pattern regarding mobilizing or demobilizing effects of negative campaign advertising.[30]

There are also other behavioral outcomes to consider, perhaps precursors to voting. For example, Patterson's Vanishing Voter project found that voters' interest in the campaign, discussions with others, and attention to other media coverage increased following exposure to the presidential debates in 2000.[31] Other desirable behavior of potential supporters also includes volunteering and donating to the campaign, although the potential connections between media exposure and these types of activities has not been explored to the degree that other types of political behavior have been.

Although the preceding discussion suggests the potential effects the mass media may have, it does not conclude that there are pervasive or powerful effects on voters. However, even a 1 percent change in vote choice based on media content may be enough to influence the outcome of close elections. In *Political Campaign Communication: Principles and Practices*, Judith Trent and Robert Friedenberg identify a number of principles of campaign communication based on mass media research. Many of them acknowledge the potential influence the mass media may have on aspects of electoral politics, in that the media bring attention to candidates and provide information that may affect perceptions. They also conclude that "the contemporary candidate needs the mass media, in part because voters have expectations regarding the media's role in providing information about the candidate and the campaign" and that "[t]he media have tremendous power in determining which news events, which candidates, and which issues are to be covered in any given day."[32] Their conclusions also reflect the potential influence of the media not on voters, but on how it has changed how candidates run for office and, potentially, the electoral process itself.

Mass Communication Theories

Other theories can be explored in the context of political communication regarding the mass media, but three of the most prominent and often-discussed theories are agenda setting, framing, and priming. These three theories also intersect in that they examine what issues the news media emphasize (agenda setting), how those issues

---

[30]Richard R. Lau, Lee Sigelman, and Ivy Brown, "The Effects of Negative Political Campaigns: A Meta-Analytic Assessment." Paper presented at the Annual Meeting of the American Political Science Association, Washington, D.C., 2005.

[31]Thomas Patterson. *The Vanishing Voter*.

[32]Judith Trent and Robert Friedenberg, *Political Campaign Communication: Principles and Practices*, 5th ed. (Lanham, MD: Rowman and Littlefield, 2004), 141.

are reported (framing), and the effects of this reporting (priming).[33] One example of such intersections can be found in West's research, in which he reviews a number of ways in which advertising may influence voters, including learning about candidates, agenda setting of issues, and priming and defusing various aspects of issues in voters' minds.[34]

Agenda Setting.   A succinct description of *agenda setting* comes from Bernard Cohen's *The Press and Foreign Policy*. It states that the media "may not be successful much of the time in telling people what to think, but it is stunningly successful in telling its readers what to think about."[35] One method to study agenda setting is to track news media attention to issues based on the amount of coverage as well as the prominence of the coverage by content analysis and then compare those findings with the ranking by the public in survey research of the perceived importance of those same issues. Maxwell McCombs and Donald Shaw first examined how the media set the agenda during the 1968 presidential campaign. They found a strong relationship between the salience and importance of issues to undecided voters[36] and the amount of space devoted to those issues in news media before the election.

Agenda-setting effects may be more prominent for those with less political interest and involvement, those who are political independents, and media consumers with less education. Additionally, issues with which people may not have personal experience (foreign policy, for example) may be more influenced by the media agenda than those with which individuals may have personal experience or interpersonal sources of information (e.g., inflation, unemployment) that supersede the media as a source of information.

In addition to studying the connection between the media agenda and the public agenda, research has also explored what factors influence the media agenda, referred to as *agenda building*. Richard Perloff identifies a number of factors that may influence the media agenda in his book *Political Communication: Politics, Press, and Public in America*.[37] News sources, such as those from government offices and other organizations, may be influential in building the news agenda, news values within a newsroom, public opinion on what issues may have widespread appeal, and elite media influences such as the *New York Times*, whose decisions about what to cover and what not to cover have the potential to influence other media.

---

[33]David Weaver, Maxwell McComb, and Donald Shaw, "Agenda-Setting Research: Issues, Attributes, and Influences." In *Handbook of Political Communication Research*. Lynda Lee Kaid, ed. (Mahwah, NJ: Lawrence Erlbaum Associates, 2004).

[34]Darrell West.

[35]Bernard C. Cohen. *The Press and Foreign Policy*. (Princeton, NJ: Princeton University Press, 1963), 13.

[36]Maxwell McCombs and Donald Shaw, "The Agenda-Setting Function of Mass Media," *Public Opinion Quarterly* 36 (1972):1766–87. Undecided voters composed the sample of this pioneering study and were chosen based on the assumption that they may be more receptive to campaign information as they had not already made their vote choice.

[37]Richard Perloff.

Framing. Following the decision by the news media about what issues and events to cover, *framing* considers issues at the next level: how to cover the issue or event. Framing considers how the media, citizens, and policy makers interpret and organize issues. Robert Entman said, "...to frame is to *select some aspects of a perceived reality and make them more salient in a communication text, in such as way as to promote a particular problem definition, causal interpretation, moral evaluation and/or treatment recommendation* for the item described"[38] (original italics).

Framing research has taken a number of approaches to studying news frames, such as issue versus strategy framing in the 2004 campaign coverage,[39] or comparing U.S. and Chinese media coverage of SARS with news frames of economic consequences, responsibility, human interest, and conflict.[40]

In addition to examining news frames, researchers have also studied the effects of framing on media audiences. Shanto Iyengar identified episodic and thematic news frames in television news: episodic frames addressing concrete events and personalities, often with visual descriptions, and thematic frames presenting an event in a broader context with explanations.[41] His research found that episodic framing, with a focus on individual cases and stories, resulted in viewers blaming problems on individuals, but that thematic framing, with a focus on the context and the history of an issue or story, resulted in voters blaming problems on social or political institutions. Beyond the impact of types of news frames themselves, framing effects have also been studied for their potential interaction with individual differences and values.[42]

Priming. The study of *priming* in the mass media explores how news coverage makes "certain issues or attributes more salient and more likely to be accessed in forming opinions."[43] Priming research examines the consequences of agenda setting on public opinion. With a twist on Cohen's definition of agenda setting earlier, Lars

---

[38]Robert M. Entman, "Framing: Toward Clarification of a Fractured Paradigm." *Journal of Communication* 43.4 (1993): 52.

[39]Paul D'Angelo, Matthew Calderone, and Anthony Territola, "Strategy and Issue Framing: An Exploratory Analysis of Topics and Frames in Campaign 2004 Print News," *Atlantic Journal of Communication.* 13.4 (2005): 199–219.

[40]Catherine A. Luther and Xiang Zhou, "Within the Boundaries of Politics: News Framing of SARS in China and the United States," *Journalism and Mass Communication Quarterly*, 82.4 (2005): 857–872.

[41]Shanto Iyengar, *Is Anyone Responsible? How Television Frames Political Issues* (Chicago: University of Chicago Press, 1991).

[42]See, for example, Fuyuan Shen and Heidi Hatfield Edwards "Economic individualism, Humanitarianism, and Welfare Reform: A Value-Based Account of Framing Effects," *Journal of Communication*, 55.4 (2005): 795–809.

[43]David Weaver, Maxwell McCombs, and Donald Shaw, "Agenda-Setting Research: Issues, Attributes, and Influences." In *Handbook of Political Communication Research.* Lynda Lee Kaid, ed. (Mahwah, NJ: Lawrence Erlbaum Associates, 2004), 264.

Willnat suggests that priming and agenda setting are linked to each other, because priming provides "a better understanding of how the mass media not only tell us 'what to think about' but also 'what to think.'"[44]

The more recent or prominent media attention on some issues makes them more salient, and people may draw on them to make judgments or express opinions. In the political arena, the salience of particular issues owing to media attention can influence the criteria that voters use to judge candidates or current political leaders. Experimental research by Shanto Iyengar and Donald Kinder in *News That Matters* explored the effects on viewers' evaluation of the president caused by agenda setting of television news. They found that viewers who were shown more stories about a particular issue (e.g., defense, economic problems, pollution) considered that issue more heavily when evaluating the president's performance. They found similar patterns in election decisions: "... the priorities that are uppermost in voters' minds as they go the polls to select a president or a representative appear to be powerfully shaped by the last-minute preoccupations of television news."[45] They also found that viewers who are more politically involved can be primed by the media just as much as those who are uninterested in politics.

Although most researchers may contemplate priming effects of news media, other media have been examined and found to have the potential to make salient particular issues that are then used for subsequent evaluations. For example, television crime dramas were found to prime concerns about crime as well as viewers' evaluation of the president.[46] This study suggests the "power" to prime opinions comes not only from news sources, but even from entertainment. One can also see how political advertising could work to make salient particular issues in voters' minds that may be considered when making their decision to vote for one candidate or against another.

MASS COMMUNICATION APPROACH TO CASE STUDIES

The goal of the mass communication perspective in this book is to discuss issues that help us understand why the media "do what they do." This involves what factors shape media content, how media are used for different purposes, and what are the implications of the mass media's role in the political communication process.

---

[44]Lars Willnat, "Agenda Setting and Priming: Conceptual Links and Differences." In *Communication and Democracy: Exploring the Intellectual Frontiers in Agenda-Setting Theory*, Maxwell McCombs, Donald Shaw, and David Weaver, eds. (Mahwah, NJ: Erlbaum, 1997), 53.

[45]Shanto Iyengar and Donald Kinder, *News That Matters* (Chicago: University of Chicago Press, 1987), 110.

[46]R. A. Holbrook and Timothy G. Hill, "Agenda Setting and Priming in Prime Time Television: Crime Dramas as Political Cues," *Political Communication*, 22.3 (2005): 277–95.

In the subsequent case studies, the mass communication perspective will discuss the media-related decisions made, as well as their possible consequences. These decisions and consequences may involve message production from a media organization, message creation from a political campaign or institution, as well as message influence on varying audiences. We will consider issues in the relationships among the mass media, the political actor (candidate, elected official, government office), and the public. We will explore mass communication theories and structural factors of the mass media relevant to these cases as well.

CHAPTER 5

CASE ONE: THE 1988 PRESIDENTIAL ELECTION

THE CASE

In 1988, several Democrats sought their party's presidential nomination. As the primary season evolved, most either ran into difficulties or failed to "catch fire," leaving Massachusetts Governor Michael Dukakis as the presumptive nominee. The mid-July convention was upbeat, giving Dukakis quite a "bounce." After the convention, he was ahead in the polls by 18 percent over presumed Republican nominee Vice President George H. W. Bush.

Bush—it was said—would have to deliver "the speech of his life" at the August Republican convention to overcome this lead. He delivered an excellent address, one that culminated a well-executed convention. Thanks to his postconvention "bounce," the candidates were in a dead heat in mid-September polls.

Kathleen Hall Jamieson reports in *Packaging the Presidency* that focus groups arranged by Republican pollster Robert Teeter in May showed that voters really knew very little about either Dukakis or Bush. The conventions, as successful as they were, seemed to change that situation little. As a result, both candidates had the opportunity in the early weeks of the general election campaign to define themselves and define their opponents. The Dukakis campaign was experiencing management problems at that point. Therefore, the Bush campaign was able to dominate the airwaves with advertisements that depicted Bush as a compassionate, grandfatherly figure and Dukakis as a liberal menace.

Three negative advertisements were dominant. One targeted Dukakis's environmental record by suggesting that a polluted Boston Harbor was the fault of his Massachusetts administration. It perhaps weakened Dukakis's support from those concerned with environmental issues. The two advertisements that more significantly damaged Dukakis, however, called into question how strong he was on crime and on defense. These two advertisements, usually referred to as the "Revolving Door" ad and the "Tank" ad, are the focus of this chapter's case.

Advertisements do not exist in a vacuum. Part of the context for the "Revolving Door" ad was another advertisement financed by a political action committee (PAC) called the National Security Political Action Committee. That PAC ad has come to be known as the "Willie Horton ad."

"Willie Horton"

The advertisement consists of eleven frames. Each frame includes a picture and a relatively small number of words:

> Frame One: Side-by-side pictures of Bush and Dukakis, the latter photograph not very flattering. The text says "Bush & Dukakis on Crime."
>
> Frame Two: The picture of Bush. The text says "Supports Death Penalty."
>
> Frame Three: The picture of Dukakis. The text says "Opposes Death Penalty."
>
> Frame Four: The picture of Dukakis. The text says "Allowed Murderers to Have Weekend Passes."
>
> Frame Five: A very unflattering picture of an African American male. No text.
>
> Frame Six: The same picture with the text saying "Willie Horton."
>
> Frame Seven: The picture shows Horton, on the street, presumably being arrested by a police officer. The text says "Horton Received 10 Weekend Passes From Prison."
>
> Frame Eight: Same picture. The text says, on separate lines, "Kidnapping" and "Stabbing."
>
> Frame Nine: Same picture. The text says, on separate lines, "Kidnapping," "Stabbing," and "Raping."
>
> Frame Ten: The picture of Dukakis again. The text says "Weekend Prison Passes."
>
> Frame Eleven: The picture of Dukakis. The text adds "Dukakis on Crime" underneath "Weekend Prison Passes."

The script offers a slightly fuller version of the story relayed by the captions:

Bush and Dukakis on crime. Bush supports the death penalty for first-degree murderers. Dukakis not only opposes the death penalty, he allowed first-degree murderers to have weekend passes from prison. One was Willie Horton, who murdered a boy in a robbery, stabbing him nineteen times. Despite a life sentence, Horton received ten weekend passes from prison. Horton fled, kidnapping a young couple, stabbing the man and repeatedly raping his girlfriend. Weekend prison passes. Dukakis on crime.

"Revolving Door"

This advertisement features stark black-and-white photography. It opens with prison scenes; then it shifts to a parade of menacing-looking criminals (played by Republican campaign workers) circling through a revolving gate. The deliberately poor-quality photography makes the men look dark, ethnic. The only one who looks into the camera seems darker than the others.

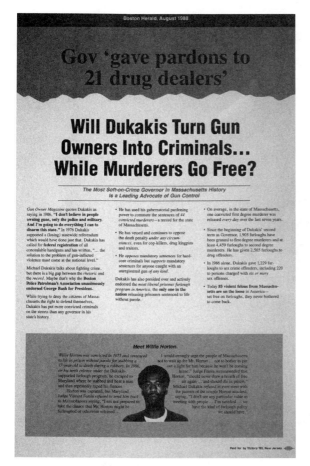

A later 1998 ad reminds viewers of the message they had received from the earlier "Willie Horton" ad.

The announcer reads the following as the audience watches the men process:

As Governor, Michael Dukakis vetoed mandatory sentences for drug dealers. He vetoed the death penalty. His revolving door prison policy gave weekend furloughs to first-degree murderers not eligible for parole. While out, many committed crimes like kidnapping and rape. And many are still at large. Now Michael Dukakis says he wants to do for America what he's done for Massachusetts. America can't afford that risk.

When the announcer mentions that parolees had committed crimes, "268 escaped" is flashed on the screen.

"Tank"

Michael Dukakis's campaign staged an event designed—we imagine—to suggest his familiarity with defense. He rode an M1 tank at a Michigan General Dynamics plant. The Bush campaign used the film of the event as the visual component of the "Tank ad."

A Michael Dukakis photo op is used against him in a 1988 attack ad.

Dukakis looks silly, smiling beneath his combat helmet, driving the tank in circles. The announcer reads the following text:

> Michael Dukakis has opposed virtually every defense system we developed. He opposed four missile systems, including the Pershing Two Missile deployment. Dukakis opposed the Stealth bomber and a ground emergency warning system against nuclear attack. He even criticized our rescue mission to Grenada and our strike against Libya. And now he wants to be our commander-in-chief. America can't afford that risk.

As the audience watches the tank circle and listens to this script, a litany of weapons Dukakis allegedly opposed appears on the screen, superimposed on the picture.

Dukakis Responses

The Dukakis campaign was slow to respond to these negative advertisements. A first response used *cinema verité* techniques to depict Bush's supposed "handlers" discussing how they were using information they knew to be false about Dukakis to "sell" Bush. The ad concluded by saying, "They'd like to sell you a package. Wouldn't you rather choose a president?"

Somewhat later, the Dukakis campaign launched an advertisement that refuted the combined "Willie Horton"–"Revolving Door" ad by noting, "George Bush talks a lot about prison furloughs. But he won't tell you that the Massachusetts program was started by a Republican and stopped by Mike Dukakis." Then, the ad talks about a program that furloughed "thousands of drug kingpins . . . from federal prison" while Bush "led the war on drugs." The ad then shows the picture of one who "raped and murdered" and the picture of his victim, noted as being the "pregnant mother of two."

THE POLITICAL SCIENCE PERSPECTIVE

A good deal of what political scientists study relates to elections. Modern political science has evolved into a highly quantitative discipline, and elections provide a nearly endless supply of data. There are polls to analyze and votes to count, trends to uncover, and results to predict. Presidential elections in particular receive significant attention from scholars. Although U.S. presidents are formally selected by the electoral college, which in theory could select a president other than the one preferred by a majority of voters, for all practical purposes the popular vote in every state determines who is elected president. Although this may from time to time lead to presidents elected by the Electoral College who did not receive a majority of the popular vote (for example, in 2000), such instances are rare. Thus, because they are the mechanism for the selection of the U.S. president, the public face of the American political system, these elections have a clear and essential purpose.

But presidential elections also have other practical and symbolic functions. They remind the public of the importance of civic engagement through voting. They raise important matters of public concern for discussion and debate. And, they provide a quadrennial reminder that, in the United States, governmental power is not held indefinitely and indiscriminately by any one individual. In these ways, presidential elections serve to connect the people with their government, and scholars of American presidential elections have sought to understand these connections using the myriad methodological approaches available to them.

In 1988, these scholars found themselves with even more than usual to talk about. For the first time since 1968, there was no incumbent president in the race. Then-president Ronald Reagan was enormously popular with both Republicans and Democrats, leading to speculation about how his popularity would affect the presidential election. Reagan was working hard in support of his vice president's bid for the White House. With no incumbent president on the ballot, though, the 1988 election was a presidential "open seat" election, which meant more competition in both parties' primaries and more uncertainty about the ultimate election outcome than is usual for presidential elections.

Campaign '88

American presidents are expected to fulfill two separate and distinct roles: to be both the head of government (similar to a prime minister in parliamentary systems) and the head of state, the country's recognized leader in international affairs. As the head of government, presidents are expected to monitor domestic policies and suggest changes that would be in the national interest; as the head of state, presidents are expected to engage in foreign policy leadership.

Presidency scholar Aaron Wildavsky articulated this dual role for the American president in a 1969 essay.[1] His thesis was that presidents are more successful in foreign policy than they are in domestic policy because the American public possesses little knowledge of foreign affairs and is therefore willing to defer to the president. But the public has strong opinions when it comes to domestic affairs. Thus, with a few exceptions, presidential elections tend to focus on domestic policy concerns, especially—as was the case in 1988—when there is no significant foreign policy crisis at the forefront of the electorate's collective consciousness.

The "two presidencies" duality should have leveled the playing field in 1988. Vice President George H. W. Bush had significant prior experience as the director of the Central Intelligence Agency, but he was not known for his domestic policy prowess. Massachusetts Governor Michael Dukakis had served as chief executive of a state with a heterogeneous population and with a multiplicity of industries, issues, and concerns, but had little foreign policy experience. Moreover, while the election pitted an incumbent vice president against the governor of a small state, who was known to few outside his home state at the outset of the election, the absence of a specific foreign policy crisis meant that Governor Dukakis could argue from his position of strength—domestic politics. In fact, heading into the summer before the election, Dukakis enjoyed a lead in the public opinion polls.[2]

At the same time, the Bush campaign held a number of advantages over the Dukakis camp. For one thing, Bush was the sitting vice president and had been a real contender for the Republican nomination in 1980. His campaign had more sophisticated technology to help them internally,[3] while externally the media tended to present Vice President George H. W. Bush more favorably than they presented the Democrats' candidate, Michael Dukakis.[4] However, following the Republican National Convention, Vice President Bush enjoyed the advantage, and for much of the crucial 60-day period before the November election, the two candidates were in a virtual dead heat.

Symbols in the 1988 Presidential Election Campaign

The two campaigns adopted different strategies as a way to distinguish their candidates from each other. Indeed, the themes of Campaign '88 that were pursued by each of the major-party candidates highlighted the dual nature of the American presi-

---

[1]Aaron, Wildavsky, "The Two Presidencies." In A. Wildavsky (ed.), *The Presidency* (Boston: Little, Brown, 1969), 230–243.

[2]Joel, Lieske, "Cultural Issues and Images in the 1988 Presidential Campaign: Why the Democrats Lost. Again!" *PS: Political Science and Politics* 24 (1991): 2.

[3]Jeffrey Rothfeder, "Democrats strive to Beat the Bush High-Tech Advantage. (Michael Dukakis' campaign)," *PC Week* 55(2) (September 19, 1988): 5n.38.

[4]Bruce Buchanan, "Presidential Campaign Quality: What the Variance Implies," *Presidential Studies Quarterly* 29.4 (December 1999): 798.

dency. Vice President Bush's campaign emphasized his foreign policy prowess, both before and after serving as President Reagan's second-in-command. The campaign also sought to minimize Governor Dukakis's claims of superior skill at understanding domestic policy priorities, particularly issues of public safety. For his part, Dukakis focused on his successes as the chief executive of a very diverse state.

Not only were the campaign themes different, the two campaigns were also markedly different in tone. In contrast to the generally positive tone of the campaigns that outgoing President Ronald Reagan had run in 1980 and (to a lesser extent) in 1984, the Bush campaign strategy was to "go negative," opting to run a very negative campaign best remembered for its ads that portrayed the Democratic nominee, Michael Dukakis, as a soft-on-crime Massachusetts liberal who would be unable to keep the public safe from domestic or foreign attack. For example, both the "Willie Horton" and the "Revolving Door" ads preyed on the public's fear of domestic crime. Dukakis was unable to convince voters that he would be tough on crime and criminals. It was not only the highly effective "Revolving Door" prison ads that were run by the Bush campaign that concerned voters. During the second presidential debate, Dukakis—long an opponent of the death penalty—was asked if he would support capital punishment if his own wife were raped and murdered. His answer—that he did not support the death penalty because he did not think it was a deterrent to criminal activity—seemed to lack the will to punish violent criminals even if someone in his own family were murdered and reinforced the "soft-on-crime" image that the Bush campaign had been attempting to convey about Dukakis.[5]

Likewise, Dukakis's participation in the staged media event at the Michigan General Dynamics Plant, in which he rode in circles in a tank, did not help his image as a foreign policy and defense neophyte, especially when the images from the event found their way into the Bush Campaign's advertisements. Political scientist Paul Peterson notes: "The Michael-Dukakis-in-a-tank picture has been credited as being one of the most effective of the negative advertisements of the 1988 presidential campaign, simply because Republicans scored heavily by denouncing Democrats as being soft on defense."[6]

The Dukakis campaign adopted a strategy of nonresponse, rather than resort to the same techniques of the Bush campaign's negative attacks. The Dukakis campaign's strategy was to try to emphasize the positive features of their candidate, and, in fact, Dukakis himself stated that he would not engage in negative campaigning.[7] This strategy also likely worked against him, as some voters likely perceived his lack of response to Bush's attack ads either as tacit affirmation that their content was accurate or as a separate symbol of Dukakis's weakness.

[5]See the transcript of the second presidential debate, available online from the Commission on Presidential Debates: http://www.debates.org/pages/trans88b.html.

[6]See Paul E. Peterson, "The Rise and Fall of Special Interest Politics," *Political Science Quarterly* 105(4) (1990).

[7]See William G. Mayer, "In Defense of Negative Campaigning," *Political Science Quarterly* 111 (1996): 3.

One of the most important symbols of the 1988 campaign, although one that was not discussed very openly or explicitly during the contest, was the appeal to latent racial tensions by the Bush campaign, and especially by its independent supporters. Both the "Willie Horton" and "Revolving Door" ads preyed on white voters' fear of crime. As political scientists David Sears, Nicholas Valentino, and Sharmaine Cheleden wrote in a 1999 assessment: "The Republican nominee, George Bush, prominently featured an attack on the record of the ultimate Democratic nominee, Michael Dukakis, on issues of 'law and order.' His frequent use of the 'revolving door' commercial, portraying a series of racially ambiguous convicts being released from prison, and his occasional allusion to the 'Willie Horton' case served to prime whites' racial attitudes."[8]

The Republicans were not alone in using race as a cue to encourage voters to cast ballots in favor of their preferred candidate, with the Democrats courting the votes of racial minorities even as Bush allies were engaging in thinly veiled race appeals to white voters. This strategy may have cost the Dukakis campaign the election, because its appeals to minority voters served to reinforce the racial appeals being used by the Republicans to discourage voters from voting in favor of Dukakis. As political scientist Joel Lieske has explained:

> It can be argued that the Democratic Convention helped sow the seeds for Dukakis's defeat because it resurrected negative racial, ethnic, and cultural stereotypes for the two groups, white ethnics and white Southerners, whom the Dukakis-Bentsen team was supposedly designed, at least in theory, to attract. Stereotypic cues that may have negatively influenced these two groups include . . . [t]he attention lavished on Jesse Jackson, a controversial civil rights leader, by liberal Democrats and the media during the first three days of the convention. As a champion of the black race and an exponent of racial confrontation, Jackson infuriates many white southerners and northern white ethnics. . . . This hostility can be seen, for example, in the low thermometer ratings he received from these two groups in the 1988 National Election Study, the lowest received by any Democratic candidate for President.[9]

In general, the 1988 election was fraught with symbolism, although that symbolism was used far more advantageously by the Republicans than by the Democrats. With images from the Bush campaign's "Revolving Door" ad in their minds, voters came to believe that Dukakis was soft on crime. The unspoken but evident racial component of much of the two campaigns' strategies served to reinforce existing negative stereotypes of racial and ethnic minorities and in that way undermined the

---

[8]See David O. Sears, Nicholas A. Valentino, and Sharmaine V. Cheleden, "Long Term Continuities in the Politics of Race." Paper prepared for presentation at the 1999 Annual Meeting of the American Political Science Association, Atlanta, Georgia.

[9]Joel Lieske, "Cultural Issues and Images in the 1988 Presidential Campaign: Why the Democrats Lost. Again!" *PS: Political Science and Politics* 24(2) (1991): 182.

ability of the Dukakis campaign to connect with many of the groups that would have been essential if he were to win the presidency.

Winners and Losers

Another reason that political scientists, who are concerned with understanding power relationships, study elections is that elections provide clear winners and losers, and in 1988, George H. W. Bush was the decisive winner. His margin of victory in the popular vote—54 percent to 46 percent—was substantial, but was nothing compared with the 411 electoral college votes (to Dukakis's 129) that he received.

Numerous studies in both the political science and the political communication literatures, some of which were discussed earlier, have offered explanations for Bush's victory. Some of these studies have pointed to factors that political scientists have long known to be responsible for shaping election outcomes: in times of peace and prosperity, the public is frequently reluctant to "rock the boat" by voting out an incumbent or changing the partisan demography of the White House. Everett Carll Ladd, an expert on polling and public opinion, pointed to the public's expressions of satisfaction with the quality of their social and economic fortunes during President Ronald Reagan's second term to explain why other scholars who have looked at the 1988 election have reached different conclusions. For example, another study, which used the 1988 National Election Studies (NES) data, found that voters in 1988 saw their votes less as a way to promote policy change and more as a way to cheer on the candidate they liked better.[10]

Still other studies have pointed to the superior use of images and symbols by the Bush campaign to challenge everything from Dukakis's record on crime and punishment to his environmentalism and patriotism. With many Reagan campaign veterans on his side, Bush was able to mount an effective strategy of negative campaign advertisements that capitalized on the power of vivid images to produce desired effects in the voters' minds.

Conclusion

Political scientists and communication scholars had much to analyze after Campaign '88 was over. The race pitted two highly qualified candidates against each other and gave voters the opportunity to weigh whether domestic affairs or foreign affairs were more important to them. In the end, however, voters' choices on Election Day were less about the substance and relative importance of the domestic and foreign policy issues confronting the country and more about the ways in which they had been primed to think about each of the candidates. The power of images and of negative campaigning was certainly reinforced by the outcome. In addition, the extent to

---

[10]See K. Kan, and C. C. Yang, "On Expressive Voting: Evidence from the 1988 U.S. Presidential Election," *Public Choice* 108.3 (August 2001): 295(18).

which lingering racial and ethnic stereotypes likely affected the election outcome led to a significant number of postelection assessments based on the issue of race.

THE RHETORICAL PERSPECTIVE

The trajectory of a presidential campaign typically takes the ultimately successful party nominees through a preprimary surfacing phase and then the primaries themselves. In the course of these two phases, the public gets to know who these nominees are. At least that's the way the process is supposed to work. However, if the field is crowded, if the primary season is becoming condensed, and if only a relatively small segment of the public is paying attention, a nominee may enter the general election period (traditionally beginning on Labor Day) without a clear identity in the prospective voters' minds. This is indeed what happened to Michael Dukakis in 1988.

George H. W. Bush's story was somewhat different. He had served as vice president for 8 years in the shadow of President Ronald Reagan. Although the Bush campaign wanted voters to think of Bush as "Reagan II" to some extent, that campaign knew that voters needed more information.

Candidate Advertising and Ethos

Aristotle, back in Classical antiquity, noted how important ethos is in persuading an audience—more important than either logos or pathos. *Ethos* is the appeal a rhetor makes based on who the audience believes him or her to be. Is the candidate thought to be competent? Is the candidate thought to have an upstanding character? Is the candidate dynamic? A candidate's arguments and the emotional appeals he or she might make are filtered through the audience's responses to these questions about the candidate's ethos.

On Labor Day, 1988, many prospective voters could not offer much more than vague answers. This situation offers the candidate two opportunities: first, to define himself or herself for these voters; second, to define his or her opponent for these voters.

Televised advertising offers presidential candidates a quick way to take advantage of these opportunities. The Bush campaign did an excellent job of helping voters form a positive ethos for Bush and a negative ethos for Dukakis. That excellent job, however, left a bad taste in many people's mouths.

The Bush campaign offered what are termed "image ads," depicting him interacting with world leaders as well as with (presumably) his grandchildren. He looked competent; he also looked as if he possessed both warmth and what have come to be termed "family values." These Bush ads were not controversial.

What were controversial were the negative ads that did considerable damage to Dukakis's ethos. Kathleen Hall Jamieson in *Dirty Politics* suggests that such ads work rhetorically by evoking emotions, inviting viewers to create false arguments, and fixing associations in their minds between the attacked candidate and negatively perceived events or people.[11] The Bush "Revolving Door" ad and the PAC "Willie Horton" ad both evoked fear. The ads suggested that dangerous criminals were roaming the streets and committing heinous crimes. Negative ads often use visual distortion to make their point almost subliminally. Thus, candidates being attacked are shown in grainy black-and-white, and actions are presented in a degree of slow-motion. In "Revolving Door" and "Willie Horton," it is not Dukakis who is visually distorted but the "criminals."

Thus distorted, the visual image acquires extra fear-invoking power. Unfortunately, many Americans see crime in racial terms. They believe African American men are more likely to be armed robbers, murderers, and rapists than white men; and these Americans are therefore more fearful of a black criminal on furlough than a white. Interestingly, of all the men walking around the "revolving door," only one is possibly African American. However, Willie Horton was black. Either because viewers were reading the "Willie Horton" ad onto the "Revolving Door" ad or because viewers see crime through a racist lens, they saw the threatening criminals in both ads as predominantly black. The fear the ads evoked then had a pronounced racist quality.

Ads cannot, in 30 seconds, present full arguments. In Classical terms, they present enthymemes. Viewers fill in the blanks; viewers complete the arguments. Those who design ads may, in fact, be counting on this process and setting things up on the screen and in an ad's text so that viewers complete arguments that are false. In "Revolving Door," for example, the text tells viewers that "many" furloughed first-degree murderers "committed crimes like kidnapping and rape." At that point, "268 escaped" appears on the screen. Viewers conclude that 268 first-degree murderers escaped *while on weekend furlough.* As Jamieson notes in *Packaging the Presidency,* only four did over a 10-year period. Viewers conclude that a large number kidnapped and raped after escaping, when, in reality, only one—Willie Horton—did so.[12] Viewers then construct a frightening picture that they associate with Michael Dukakis, a picture not in line with the facts.

The Boston Harbor ad associates Dukakis with a visually distorted picture of a polluted waterway. Similarly, in 1992, a Bush ad tries to associate Bill Clinton with a visually distorted picture of environmental damage in his home state of Arkansas. The visual distortions were so extreme that the ad became dubbed "Nuclear Winter." Back in 1968, a Nixon campaign advertisement tried to connect his Democratic opponent, Hubert H. Humphrey, with crime, civil unrest, and immoral behavior rampant in America. These associations are the rhetorical norm in attack ads. In the eyes of most, the "Willie Horton" and "Revolving Door" ads exceeded the norm insofar as they played off race-based fears.

The "Tank" ad associated Dukakis the candidate with Dukakis the silly, grinning "boy" riding a tank in pointless circles. The unspoken message is that

[11]Kathleen Hall Jamieson, *Dirty Politics: Deception, Distraction, and Democracy* (New York: Oxford University Press, 1992). See especially Ch. 2, "Tactics of Attack."

[12]Kathleen Hall Jamieson, *Packaging the Presidency: A History and Criticism of Presidential Campaign Advertising,* 3rd ed. (New York: Oxford University Press, 1996): 471.

Americans should not want this latter Dukakis serving as commander-in-chief. In general, Republican candidates for president are thought to be more competent on foreign affairs, especially those involving the military, whereas Democratic candidates are thought to be more competent on domestic matters. The "Tank" ad plays off the viewers' assumption that Dukakis, as a Democrat and a governor, might be weak on defense issues. The litany of defense expenditures or military operations he opposed are offered as proof that he is weak, but, in an illogical way, the visual image validates the unstated claim that Dukakis's opposition was wrong or silly. The argument that viewers construct is circular: Dukakis's positions prove that the visual image is correct, and the visual image proves that Dukakis's positions were silly or wrong. Viewers receive no information to help them assess whether Dukakis's positions on defense issues had any merit: they couldn't have merit—the ad "says" just look at Dukakis and you can see that.

Dukakis's Weak Response

Bush's advertising—both positive and negative—dominated the post–Labor Day period. Both candidates had the opportunity to define both their own ethos and that of their opponent, but only the Bush campaign acted on the opportunity. Why? Part of the answer is found in Dukakis's reluctance to engage in negative campaigning; part of the answer is found in the disarray that characterized the Dukakis campaign during this crucial period. Either way, the Dukakis campaign did not act when the moment was ripe. In Classical rhetorical terms, the moment exhibited *kairos*. By the time the Dukakis campaigned responded, *kairos* had arguably faded.

Delaying seems to have hurt Dukakis. Samuel Popkin, in *The Reasoning Voter*, argues that the electorate takes many shortcuts in arriving at its voting decision. One such shortcut is generalizing from the competency the campaigner demonstrates to his or her likely competence as an elected official.[13] The Dukakis campaign did not project competence at this point. Voters may have generalized to broader conclusions about Dukakis. Popkin's reasoning would suggest as much. So would Richard Petty and John Cacioppo's "Elaboration Likelihood Model," which would suggest that voters would take a nonreflective peripheral route in a case such as this one, relying on consistency between Dukakis as inept campaigner and Dukakis as inept president and not really thinking the matter through.[14] Therefore, Dukakis's ethos probably suffered a two-part "hit"—hit by the negative ads and hit by the failure to act.

That failure to act finally ended when the Dukakis campaign counterattacked with the "Handlers" ad and with the ad alleging that Bush, as leader of the federal war on drug trafficking, had a worse furlough record than that of the Massachusetts governor. These ads work rhetorically much as the Bush ads had. They exhibit visual

[13]Samuel L. Popkin, *The Reasoning Voter: Communication and Persuasion in Presidential Campaigns*, 2nd ed. (Chicago: University of Chicago Press, 1994): 61–63.

[14]For theory, see Richard E. Petty and John T. Cacioppo, *Communication and Persuasion: Central and Peripheral Routes to Attitude Change* (New York: Springer-Verlag, 1986).

distortions; they appeal to fear—fear of sleazy political operatives in the first and fear of criminals in the second. The ads also try to get viewers to create arguments.

In the case of "Handlers," the argument—that the Bush campaign will say anything, positive or negative, to get elected, even outright lie—was evidently too buried in the ad's text. Voters reportedly found the ad puzzling. In the case of the ad attacking Bush for furloughing more dangerous criminals, the argument leaves the claim implicit in "Willie Horton" and "Revolving Door" largely unchallenged. The ad calls on the viewer to construct a comparison between the Bush record and the Dukakis record. Even if the viewer concludes that the former is worse, he or she still has granted that Dukakis has a worrisome record. The ad initially tells viewers that a Republican governor initiated the weekend furlough program in Massachusetts and that Dukakis ended it. Thus, the ad initially accuses the PAC "Willie Horton," the Bush campaign "Revolving Door," and several PAC follow-up ads of lying. These early seconds in the ad—a critic might suggest—get lost in the comparative argument viewers create. The ad's concluding line stating that Bush had "taken a furlough from the truth" does not succeed in refocusing viewers on how the ad initially directly refutes the anti-Dukakis ads.

When Michael Dukakis took to the podium at the 1988 Democratic National Convention, his ethos was high, and his successful acceptance speech increased it. However, that ethos was largely unformed. The Bush campaign seized the opportunity to help voters form that ethos along negative lines while also assisting them in creating a positive one for the vice president. Dukakis never recovered from the Bush campaign's action and his own campaign's inaction.

Conclusion

The crucial texts that a rhetorician would look at from the 1988 presidential election are the televised advertising "spots." They were crucial because who both candidates were was not "set" in the minds of voters. The Bush campaign helped improve his ethos in the voters' eyes through the positive advertising it used; more important, both the Bush campaign and a PAC helped weaken Dukakis's ethos through some of the most memorable attack ads in the history of campaigning. These ads heavily relied on disturbing visual images, associating these in voters' minds with Dukakis. Dukakis's failure to respond quickly and effectively further hurt his ethos.

THE MASS COMMUNICATION PERSPECTIVE

From a mass communication perspective, the political advertising of the 1988 presidential campaign is important for several reasons. First, it raises the issue of advertising sponsorship—are campaigns paying for the advertisements, or are outside groups? Second, concerns regarding the effects of negative political advertisements arose in the midst of the attacks on Michael Dukakis. Finally, the media attention on the political advertising in 1988 might have contributed to the potential effects of these advertisements, and changes in news reporting occurred as a result of the 1988 campaign coverage of political advertisements.

Sponsorship of Political Advertisements

Although we might associate the influence of independent organizations in negative advertising with the Swift Boat Veterans for Truth in the 2004 election, such advertising activity has consistently occurred in past political campaigns. The 1988 "Willie Horton" ad was not sponsored by the Bush campaign itself, but rather by Americans for Bush, a subsidiary of the National Security Political Action Committee (NSPAC).

The "Willie Horton" ad first aired on cable television in September 1988 and had a limited airing. However, broadcast and print news media brought broader public attention to the controversial ad and its allegations. The advertisement was controversial not only for its content, but also for allegations that it was not completely independent of the Bush campaign, because Bush campaign manager Lee Atwater had discussed the Horton case previously[15] and that one of the advertisement's creators was a former employee of Roger Ailes, who at the time was Bush's campaign media consultant (and went on to be the founder of Fox News). However, the allegations of connections to the campaign were investigated by the Federal Election Commission and dismissed.[16]

Impact of Negative Advertisements

West also suggests not just a connection in the coverage between these two ads, but also in their impact with regard to priming voters' opinions. The media attention surrounding the "Willie Horton" ad and his crime spree while on furlough from prison primed the audience to consider those factors when Bush's "Revolving Door" ad followed. Horton was not mentioned in this ad, but it was assumed that viewers would make that connection themselves.

Besides the potential priming effects of the "Willie Horton" ad on attitudes regarding the "Revolving Door" ad, agenda setting effects of these political advertisements existed as well. In *Air Wars: Television Advertising in Election Campaigns, 1952–2004*, Darrell West found that among voters who had not seen the "Revolving Door" ad, 5 percent identified crime and law and order as the most important problems facing the country, while 12 percent of those who saw the "Revolving Door" ad ranked crime as the most important problem.[17] West found the strongest

---

[15]Although Lee Atwater may have mentioned the Willie Horton case while he was Bush's campaign manager before the advertisement was produced, the Horton case was reportedly first mentioned during the Democratic primary elections by Al Gore, who was also seeking the nomination for president.

[16]Albert L. May, "Swift Boat Vets in 2004: Press Coverage of an Independent Campaign," *First Amendment Law Review* 4 (2005): 66–106.

[17]Darrell M. West, *Air Wars: Television Advertising in Election Campaigns, 1952–2004*, 4th ed. (Washington, DC: CQ Press, 2005).

agenda-setting effect with women, which could be explained by the focus on the crime of rape addressed in the Willie Horton ad. West acknowledges the potential overlap in advertising effects between these two similarly themed ads. The messages differed, and the ads were sponsored by different organizations (one by the Bush campaign, the other by NSPAC), but viewers may not have distinguished between the two, especially when addressing survey questions about them, because both ads address Dukakis's lack of toughness on crime.

The "Revolving Door" ad was also part of a study of the effects of political advertising in 1988. Kaid, Leland, and Whitney showed college students a series of advertisements[18]; some students saw three advertisements from the Bush campaign (two positive ads, and the negative "Revolving Door" ad), some students saw three advertisements from the Dukakis campaign (again, two positive ads, and one negative advertisement, one of the positive advertisements being Dukakis's "Crime" ad that responded to the weak-on-crime attacks from the "Willie Horton" and "Revolving Door" ads), and some students saw both Bush and Dukakis's advertisements. They describe the Dukakis "Crime" ad as "an attempt to answer the furlough ad with a positive rebuttal ad" (p. 294) and cite research that finds rebuttals can offset the impact of a negative advertisement and that voters believe attacks on one's political record is fair, but that personal attacks are not fair. "This helps explain why Bush's attack on Dukakis's record (furlough) was more effective than Dukakis's attack on Quayle (personal)" (p. 294) in their research findings.

News Coverage of Negative Advertisements

Regarding media discussion of these advertisements, West says, "The same ad can have very different consequences depending on the manner in which an opponent responds, the way a journalist reports the ad, the number of times the sport of broadcast, or the disposition of the viewer." The "Willie Horton" advertisement[19] was followed shortly by the "Revolving Door" ad, which was sponsored by the Bush campaign itself. In *Air Wars: Television Advertising in Election Campaigns, 1952–2004*, Darrell West reports the news attention to these ads from CBS News. CBS aired a report about Willie Horton on September 22, 1988, after the airing of the NSPAC ad. CBS News then covered the "Revolving Door" ad when it was broadcast on October 7, 1988. CBS News followed with another story on October 20, detailing Horton's crime record as well as supplying background on Bush's "Revolving Door" ad. Finally on October 24 and 25, Democratic opponents appeared on the news (including vice presidential candidate Lloyd Bentsen and former Democratic primary candidate Jesse Jackson) claiming Bush's ad implied racism with the furloughed African American criminal attacking a white female victim.

---

[18]Lynda Lee Kaid, Chris M. Leland, and Susan Whitney, "The Impact of Televised Political Ads: Evoking Viewer Responses in the 1988 Presidential Campaign," *Southern Communication Journal* 57 (1992): 285–295.

[19]West, 16.

Unlike the 1964 "Daisy Girl" ad, which was immediately condemned and taken off the air, the "Revolving Door" ad continued to be broadcast in news reports about the negativity of the campaign, providing the Bush campaign free airtime by replaying the ad. Although the news reports might have analyzed the advertisements or critiqued the content, viewers saw the advertisement itself over and over. When an inconsistency exists between the visual elements (the ad) and the verbal elements (critique and analysis in news reports), media audiences tend to rely on the visual over the verbal. Richard Perloff's research also summarizes a number of criticisms raised about these political ads, in that Bush's ad was misleading, that both ads capitalized on voters' lack of understanding about furlough programs, and that they reinforced racial stereotyping by associating Dukakis's policy with an African American raping a white woman.[20]

The 1988 "Willie Horton" and "Revolving Door" ads also had an impact on the news media. Journalists felt they had been manipulated by the campaigns regarding these ads, and critics assessed most reporting on the political ads as discussing strategy rather than evaluating the accuracy of the assertions made. In the aftermath of the 1988 advertisements, *Washington Post* columnist David Broder argued that journalists needed to police the 1990 midterm election ads for their truthfulness and that the ads should not be replayed as part of a news report about the ads, as had often been done in 1988.[21] What followed in the 1990 elections was the rise of "ad watches," by both print and broadcast news outlets. Reporters would confirm the facts and assertions made in the advertisements in such ad watches or "truth boxes," as well as point out discrepancies, inconsistencies, and misstatements made in the ads. While this truth-testing mechanism gave reporters the opportunity to scrutinize ads more critically, it also provided the campaigns with at least a partial free replay of the advertisement under question as part of the analysis. One study found that by the 1992 presidential election cycle, 40 percent of stories on political advertising published in the *Los Angeles Times*, *Chicago Tribune*, and *New York Times* were ad watches.[22] Such advertising scrutiny by the press confirmed the watchdog role of the media in elections, in this case monitoring the claims made by political campaigns, rather than by elected officials or government offices when outside of the election cycle.

Conclusion

The "Willie Horton" and "Revolving Door" ads of the 1988 presidential campaign are memorable not only for their degree of negativity, but also for their consequences. The combination of these two advertisements demonstrated the potential priming effects of political messages: voters associated the Willie Horton case with the

---

[20]Richard M. Perloff, *Political Communication: Politics, Press, and Public in America* (Mahwah, NJ: Erlbaum, 1998).

[21]Judith S. Trent and Robert V. Friedenberg, *Political Campaign Communication: Principles and Practices*, 5th ed. (Lanham, MD: Rowman & Littlefield, 2004).

[22]Chris Glowacki, Thomas J. Johnson, and Kristine E. Kranenberg, "Use of Newspaper Political Adwatches from 1988–2000," *Newspaper Research Journal 25* (2004): 40–54.

"Revolving Door" ad without any mention of him in the advertisement. Agenda-setting effects were also found, in that these crime-related advertisements caused voters to express more concern about crime and what Michael Dukakis might do on issues of crime if he was elected president. Finally, one development in the news media following the hype surrounding these ads in 1988 was the more consistent and balanced use of ad watches by reporters covering future political campaigns.

CONCLUSION

Political scientists, rhetoricians, and media analysts do not always gravitate to the same dimension of a political campaign. When they do, as was the case in 1988, their doing so says something: that a single dimension was clearly dominant. Thus, we can conclude that the negative advertising launched against Michael Dukakis was such a clearly dominant dimension. It is no wonder then that many decried the dominance of negative advertising in the wake of 1988—and that many used such advertising in campaigns that followed.

But even when a single dimension dominates, people can draw out of it different conclusions. The political scientist sees the negative adverting as a distraction from a campaign that ought to have seen American voters deciding what was more important to them, domestic issues or foreign ones. Unfortunately, that distraction tapped—and brought to the surface—ugly racial stereotypes that still affect American political discourse. The rhetorician accepts the negative ads as the campaign's dominant "text" and explores how they work, finding that they offer voters powerful visual associations for the attacked candidate. The mass communication analyst also accepts the ads as the dominant media messages. However, this analyst is primarily interested in the effects that ads have in priming and agenda setting for the duration of the campaign and in inspiring "ad watches" for future elections.

━━━

ADDITIONAL CASES

Some of the issues we've raised about the 1988 presidential elections could be further explored by considering the following:

- **The 1964 presidential election between Lyndon B. Johnson and Barry M. Goldwater**
  A good starting point would be Chapter 5, "1964: Goldwater vs. Goldwater" in Kathleen Hall Jamieson, *Packaging the Presidency: A History and Criticism of Presidential Campaign Advertising*, 3rd ed. (New York: Oxford University Press, 1996), 169–220.

(continued)

■ ■ ■ ■ ■

ADDITIONAL CASES   CONTINUED

- **The 1968 presidential election between Hubert H. Humphrey and Richard M. Nixon**
  A good starting point would be Chapter 6, "1968: The Competing Pasts of Nixon and Humphrey" (pp. 221–75) in Jamieson's *Packaging the Presidency*.

- **The 2000 U.S. Senate race in New York between Hillary Clinton and Rick Lazio**
  A good starting point would be Grant C. Cos and Brian J. Snee, "'New York, New York': Being and Creating Identity in the 2000 New York State Senate Race," *American Behavioral Scientist* 44 (2001): 2014–29.

- **The 2004 U.S. Senate race in South Dakota between Tom Daschle and John Thune**
  A good starting point would be Terry Robertson, "A Perfect Storm: A Case Study Analysis of the Defeat of Tom Daschle by John Thune in the 2004 South Dakota Senate Race," *American Behavioral Scientist* 49 (2005): 326–42.

- **The 2005 Virginia gubernatorial race between Tim Kaine and Jerry Kilgore**
  A good starting point would be two newspaper articles: Robert Barnes, "Ads May Hurt Kilgore More Than They Help," *Washington Post* (October 30, 2005): A11; Michael D. Shear, "Democrat Kaine Wins in Virginia," *Washington Post* (November 9, 2005): A1.

CHAPTER 6

CASE TWO:
THE 1998 MINNESOTA
GUBERNATORIAL ELECTION

THE CASE

"We shocked the world!" These were Jesse Ventura's words the night he won the election for Minnesota Governor on November 4, 1998.

Before serving as Minnesota's thirty-eighth governor, Ventura was a former U.S. Navy Seal who served in Vietnam, a former professional wrestler ("The Body"), a former actor (featured in the film *Predator*, with another future governor, Arnold Schwarzenegger), and former mayor of Twin Cities suburb Brooklyn Park.

Ventura beat Minnesota Attorney General Hubert "Skip" Humphrey III, the Democratic-Farm-Labor candidate (and son of former Vice President Hubert Humphrey), and Republican Norm Coleman, mayor of St. Paul, who went on to win Minnesota's U.S. Senate seat in 2002. Ventura won with 37 percent of the vote, compared to 34 percent for Coleman and 28 percent for Humphrey.

However, the day before the election, one poll showed Coleman leading with 36 percent, and Ventura tied with Humphrey at 29 percent. So, how did Ventura do it?

The 1998 Minnesota Gubernatorial election had a turnout of more than 60 percent and many votes were cast by first time voters. Minnesota allows same-day voter registration, so a late push to mobilize potential voters may have aided Ventura's victory. Only five other states allow same-day registration of voters: Maine, New Hampshire, Idaho, Wisconsin, and Wyoming.

The 60 percent turnout is considerably higher than Minnesota's typical rate of 53 percent. It was reportedly one of the nicest election days in terms of weather Minnesota had seen in years. Ventura was successful in motivating unlikely voters to turn out at the polls, as one exit poll reported 28 percent of Ventura voters said they would not have voted at all had he not been on the ballot for governor.

Another unique aspect of politics in Minnesota is the political party system. While they may align closely with the Democratic and Republican parties, in Minnesota they are the Democratic-Farm-Labor (DFL) party and the Independent Republican (IR) party. Jesse Ventura ran as a Reform Party candidate, the same party that brought voters Ross Perot in 1992, whom 24 percent of Minnesotans voted for in that election.

The political climate in 1998 may have contributed to Ventura's win, as voters may have been "turned off" to traditional politics and politicians. This was the first election cycle following the Clinton-Lewinsky scandal, when public opinion about the institution of the presidency was declining, when Clinton faced possible impeachment, and when First Lady Hillary Clinton declared that the scandal was based on accusations of a "vast right-wing conspiracy." Hillary Clinton campaigned for Skip Humphrey the week before Election Day, referring to Ventura's campaign as a "carnival sideshow." Ventura responded with his own attack, saying, "It seems to me, rather than being concerned about Minnesota politics, Hillary should be more concerned about leaving Bill home alone."

Ventura also promoted an antipolitician perspective during his campaign. Not only did he run outside the norm as candidate for the Reform Party, but also he singled himself out apart from the other gubernatorial candidates in his campaign. For example, one of Ventura's radio ads stated, "When the other guys were cashing government checks, he was in the Navy getting dirty and wet" (set to the tune from the theme of the film *Shaft*) and concludes, "Well, they try to tell you he can't win, but we'll vote our conscience and we'll vote him in."

Ventura's position in debates against Humphrey and Coleman also took an antipolitician stance; he often differentiated himself from both of his opponents simultaneously. Although he was critiqued as being short on details, Ventura was also praised for his commonsense approach in his responses. Attending the Governor's Economic Summit in September 1998, which had invited only Humphrey and Coleman to participate,[1] Ventura arrived in a camouflage jacket, black jeans, combat boots, and his Australian Outback hat from his role in the movie *Predator*. His initial comment to the suit-clad audience: "You're going to find me a little different from the other candidates."

Money is a powerful force in many political campaigns, but it is not an explanation for Ventura's win in Minnesota. Campaign finance laws in the state limited campaign spending by the major party candidates to between $2.1 and $2.3 million in order to receive public money for their campaigns. This allowed Ventura not to trail too severely in campaign spending; some reports suggest Ventura's campaign had only one paid staff member and spent only $600,000 in the campaign, most of it on advertising late in the campaign. However, these campaign-spending limits did not apply to party support for a candidate, which was over $5 million for the Coleman campaign from the Republican Party and $3 million for Humphrey's campaign from the Democrats. Ventura received little more than $30,000 from the Reform Party.

Jesse Ventura's campaign was also nontraditional in that he did not begin airing any advertisements until just 3 weeks before Election Day, and the first ad was on the radio because he could not afford television advertising. One of his rare, late television advertisements featured the Jesse Ventura action figure and told viewers, "You can make Jesse battle special interest groups!" Children are shown playing with the

---

[1]A *Star Tribune* report from September 19, 1998, explains that Roger Moe, Skip Humphrey's running mate as lieutenant governor, was filling in for Humphrey and gave a portion of his time to Ventura to speak.

Jess Ventura celebrates his unexpected victory for Minnesota governor on election night 1998.

Ventura action figure against Evil Special Interest Man and Lobbyist Man. The advertisement proved so popular that Jesse Ventura and his wife, Terry, established Ventura for Minnesota, a nonprofit organization to license Ventura's likeness, and raised more than $100,000, which they donated to Minnesota charities.[2]

Whether it was public appearances, comments made during debates, or infrequent political advertisements, Jesse Ventura was able to capture the public's attention and prospective voters' antipolitical sentiments, and found himself in the Governor's mansion in 1999. Seen on Minnesota cars within a week after his victory: a bumper sticker reading "Our governor can beat up your governor."

THE POLITICAL SCIENCE PERSPECTIVE

Jesse Ventura's assessment—that his victory "shocked the world"—was perhaps the most astute observation anyone made concerning his election. Few people outside Minnesota even knew that Ventura had been seeking the post of governor, and many who did know likely assumed it was another of Ventura's infamous publicity stunts. After all, Ventura was well known for his flamboyant attire and color commentary as an athlete-turned-"analyst" on the professional wrestling circuit. After his wrestling career ended, Ventura moved on to acting, although the majority of his acting jobs were small parts in movies that did not achieve much critical or financial success.

Although Jesse Ventura's campaign and subsequent victory were the fodder for countless jokes, celebrity candidates are not unusual in American politics. University of Wisconsin political scientist David Canon, in his book *Athletes, Actors, and*

---

[2]Bill Hillsman, *Run the Other Way: Fixing the Two-Party System, One Campaign at a Time* (New York: Free Press, 2004).

Astronauts: Political Amateurs in Congress,[3] notes that well-known political amateurs (individuals who have not previously run for or served in elective office) can make formidable challengers to professional politicians. This is because celebrity candidates do not need to expend scarce campaign resources trying to establish or increase name recognition. Moreover, the public often makes the assumption that candidates who have had previous career success in a very visible field, such as acting or college or professional athletics, possess the kind of work ethic and ability to be successful in politics, another highly visible career path. Such assumptions may be explained by *schema theories* of how people organize information. These theories posit that when people hear, see, or otherwise are confronted with new information, they will seek to assimilate this new information using as little analytical energy as possible.[4] Thus, when confronted with a situation that creates cognitive dissonance—a retired professional wrestler as governor of a large Midwestern state?—people look for cues within their existing stores of knowledge to help them make sense of the situation. Success and fame in one aspect of a person's life might be a cue that he or she is a "winner," a "team player," or a "hard worker" or simply that he or she is known and liked by others and therefore worthy of receiving one's vote.

Celebrity candidates have advantages that frequently other political amateurs do not. Not only do celebrity candidates have significant name recognition within the public long before they decide to run for office, they also have experience with the kinds of public relations activities that are involved with campaigning for public office. They may be wealthy enough to contribute sizable sums to their own campaign chests. Celebrity candidates and their families are accustomed to the public scrutiny and lack of privacy that a run for public office often entails.

Successful celebrity candidates for public office have included not only actor-turned-President Ronald Reagan, but also John Glenn (former astronaut and U.S. Senator from Ohio), Fred Grandy ("Gopher" from the 80s television show *Love Boat* and former Member of Congress from Iowa), the late Sonny Bono (former singer/television personality and Member of Congress from California), Steve Largent (wide receiver for the Seattle Seahawks and former Member of Congress), Clint Eastwood (actor and former Mayor of Carmel, California), and Ventura's *Predator* co-star, Arnold Schwarzenegger, the current governor of California, among others. Comedian Al Franken has indicated that he may run for the U.S. Senate from Ventura's home state of Minnesota in 2008, and rumors circulated across the Commonwealth of Virginia that actor Ben Affleck might seek the Democratic nomination for U.S. Senator and run against incumbent Republican George Allen in 2006. (Whether Affleck had ever intended to do so or not, he ultimately was not a candidate in either the 2006 Virginia Senate primary or general elections.)

---

[3]David T. Canon, *Athletes, Actors, and Astronauts: Political Amateurs in Congress* (Chicago: University of Chicago Press, 1990).

[4]For an explanation of the application of schema theory to political science, see Pamela Johnston Conover, and Stanley Feldman, "How People Organize the Political World: A Schematic Model," *American Journal of Political Science* 28 (1984): 95–126.

Sonny Bono takes the oath of office for House of Representatives in 1995 from House Speaker Newt Gingrich.

Despite his celebrity status, Ventura was not completely without prior political experience when he decided to run for governor, having previously served four years as the mayor of Minneapolis/St. Paul suburb Brooklyn Park. Nevertheless, without the backing of either of the two major political parties, prior experience running for statewide elective office, and the kind of extensive campaign apparatus typical of a gubernatorial campaign, Ventura would have been at a disadvantage regardless of who his opponent was. Adding to the list of factors that made a Ventura victory unlikely was that he was running against two formidable opponents. His Democratic opponent, Hubert "Skip" Humphrey III, is the son of a former U.S. vice president; the Humphreys are something of a Minnesota political dynasty. In addition, the Republican challenger, Norm Coleman, had previously sought and won election to the mayorship of St. Paul, one of Minnesota's "Twin Cities," with a population vastly larger than that of Brooklyn Park.

Ventura As Symbol

Although Humphrey tried to portray himself as the "regular guy" in the gubernatorial race, Ventura won the election because a plurality of voters found him easier to relate to than either of his opponents. Ironically, instead of the flamboyant professional wrestler, voters saw Ventura as a plainspoken, common man, someone who was more concerned with doing what made sense than he was with attacking his opponents or burnishing his party credentials. As one newspaper account stated, "A TV ad that aired several days ago positions Ventura as 'a card-carrying union member. A military veteran. And a volunteer football coach. In other words, one of us.'"[5] His imposing physical size, parodied in the "Action Figure" television ad run by his campaign, suggested to voters that he would have the strength to fight for their interests against the entrenched political parties and special interests. As voters sought to make sense of Ventura's candidacy, Ventura was speaking to them in commonsense terms, meeting the voters where *they* were, and talking about himself and the issues, rather than simply bashing his opponents. In short, the combination of his plainspokenness, physical size, and down-to-earth personality worked to turn Ventura into a symbol of populist renewal and an agent for positive change, which resonated with Minnesota voters. Ventura won in part because he did not create the kind of political spectacle that is typical of most statewide or national campaigns; instead, he appealed to voters by being a regular guy.

Additional Explanatory Factors

Not only did Jesse Ventura's natural populist tendencies mobilize new and disenfranchised voters, several additional factors helped to propel him to win the 1998 Minnesota gubernatorial election. The Ventura campaign was aided in its task of translating public interest in Ventura into votes by several additional factors, including same-day registration, diminished expectations, and public discontent with partisan bickering at both the state and national levels.

Same-day voter registration allows individuals to register to vote when they go to the polls to cast a vote in an election. States that have adopted same-day registration have done so in an effort to increase voter turnout. In states without same-day registration, voters must be registered to vote days or weeks ahead of any election in which they intend to vote. A citizen who misses the deadline—which often is 30 days before Election Day—will not be permitted to vote. Preregistration of this sort not only prevents some people from voting (such as those who move to a new area inside the 30-day preelection window), but it may also have the effect of suppressing turnout among third-party or independent voters, since they may be unable to vote in partisan primaries or may believe that their votes will not matter.

On the other hand, same-day registration can provide opportunities to participate in elections for voters who might not have been paying attention to an upcoming election a month beforehand. According to government professor Howard J. Gold, writing in a 2002 article in *Polity*, same-day registration has the effect of "enabling last-minute voters, who are disproportionately young and politically inexperienced, to vote."[6]

Because same-day voter registration means that, until the polls close, literally everyone of voting age in a particular jurisdiction is a potential voter, the playing

[5]Patricia Lopez Baden, "'This is not politics as usual'; Ventura's adman says that's the point of a humorous new TV spot featuring an action figure of the candidate." *Minneapolis Star-Tribune*, October 28, 1998, B3.

[6]Howard J. Gold, "Third-Party Voting in Gubernatorial Elections: A Study of Angus King of Maine and Jesse Ventura of Minnesota." *Polity* 35.2 (Winter 2002): 270–71.

field is leveled somewhat for third-party or independent candidates. Instead of using the 30 days preceding an election to try to change the minds of registered party voters, third-party and independent candidates can work right up until the moment of the election to bring new voters to the polls. This is precisely what Ventura did. In the 1998 election, according to Gold,

> over 330,000 voters, or about 16 percent of the electorate, registered on Election Day. And about 60 percent of Minnesotans voted in the 1998 election, a figure significantly higher than the 1998 national average of 36 percent. According to a Coleman campaign operative, 100,000 new voters voted in Minnesota that day, with 80 percent of them supporting Ventura.[7]

An article in the October 30, 1998, edition of the *Minneapolis Star Tribune*—just a few days before the election—recounted how Ventura was appealing to first-time and disenfranchised voters: "It's funny. I wasn't even remotely interested in the election until I went to a party last Sunday," said Eric Sharbo, a salesman at Rudy Luther's Burnsville Volkswagen. "Everybody there was talking about Jesse Ventura. I decided right there, I've got to figure out this governor's race. I haven't voted for years. I'm not impressed with Norm, and I'm not impressed with a big family name. So Jesse may well get my vote."[8]

Ventura benefited as well from diminished expectations. Because no one expected him to win, the two major party candidates spent much of their time pointing out each other's shortcomings, rather than paying attention to the support that Ventura was quietly building. While Humphrey and Coleman attacked each other, Ventura campaigned generally free from the kind of scrutiny the major party candidates were applying to each other. Pundits and Humphrey and Coleman campaign staffers also had diminished expectations about the likely consequences of the Ventura campaign's decision to focus on young people and those who felt disenfranchised from politics. Consistent with what is known about voting demographics, the assumption was that the people Ventura targeted would simply fail to show up on Election Day—when the votes were counted; however, it became apparent just how much the Ventura voters had been underestimated.

Finally, working against both Humphrey and Coleman was the public's general dissatisfaction with partisan politics. The 1998 election took place in the shadow of questions about whether Bill Clinton should be impeached, with partisan voices on both sides of the question reaching fever pitches as the campaigns entered their final stages. Although Ventura was nominally a Reform Party candidate, he received virtually no support from Reform Party founder H. Ross Perot and was thus able to campaign without any significant partisan baggage. In addition to the allegations of

---

[7]Gold, 271.

[8]Bob Von Stenberg, "As Vote Nears, Voters Are All over the Road; From Governor to County Boards, Minnesota's Political Races Couldn't Find Issues to Rev up the Electorate," *Minneapolis Star Tribune*. October 28, 1998, A1.

perjury, questions remained about the impropriety of campaign funds raised by both of the two major parties during the 1996 presidential election cycle. Ventura, the only candidate who refused to accept funds from special interest groups, was largely beyond reproach for his campaign's financial conduct.

Conclusion

Ventura was able to overcome what should have been a position of significant weakness by taking advantage of structural features of the Minnesota electoral system, public discontent with career politicians, and partisan bickering at both the state and national levels to be elected governor of Minnesota in 1998. Although he was a celebrity candidate who was known for his flamboyant antics inside the professional wrestling ring, Ventura took an "of-the-people" approach to his campaign and came to symbolize, even embody, the public's desire for an alternative to traditional partisan politics.

THE RHETORICAL PERSPECTIVE

Voting data might explain why Jesse Ventura won the 1998 gubernatorial election. The turnout was unusually high, with many of the voters being first-time voters; evidently, many of these novices went to the polls just to vote for Ventura. The *real* question, however, is not why Ventura won, but how he got in a position to win. The voters Ventura pulled to the polls would not have made any difference if he was not also making a significant dent among those who would ordinarily vote for either the DFL or Republican candidate.[9]

Third-Party Candidates and Voter Attitudes

Third-party candidates ordinarily must overcome one of two audience attitudes to be competitive. First, they must show that they can win; second, they must convince voters that a vote cast for them is not "wasted." Overcoming the first necessarily overcomes the second, but the second alone can be overcome if they can convince voters that a vote for a third-party candidate "sends a message" worth sending.

Few candidates have been able to surmount these twin attitudes. However, historically, party affiliation has been far stronger than it is today. The number of voters self-identifying as "independent" is at a record high, and there are indications that some demographic groups that once were solidly in a particular party's camp are not reliably so anymore. An example is the Catholic vote, once reliably Democratic.

[9]For a more quantitative study of the question "why," see Howard J. Gold, "Third-Party Voting in Gubernatorial Elections: A Study of Angus King of Maine and Jesse Ventura of Minnesota," *Polity* 35.2 (2002): 265–83.

What is true nationally is also true in Minnesota, where the media often refer to the "old DFL" with a tone that suggests that the party's glory years were long ago and that today's DFL candidates, such as "Skip" Humphrey, are not the giants of old, such as Skip's father, former U.S. Senator and Vice President Hubert H. Humphrey. In addition, Minnesota—it might be argued—has always exhibited a pronounced independent streak. Before the Democratic Party and Farmer Labor Party merged in the 1940s, they both fielded candidates along with what was called the Independent Republican Party. This historic mix is neither the simple two-party system found in most states nor a state-level mirror of the national situation.

Political history, then, of the nation or of only Minnesota, offers a partial explanation for Jesse Ventura's success. However, rhetorical criticism also helps to explain what many called a surprising outcome in the 1998 election.

AUDIENCE ANALYSIS

Audience analysis is a keystone in rhetoric: one is not likely to persuade if one does not know who one is trying to sway. It would not have required a political genius to determine in 1998 that potential Minnesota voters (i.e., the audience Ventura's campaign addressed) were not as characterized by party loyalty as Minnesotans who had sent the likes of Hubert Humphrey and Walter Mondale to Washington back in the middle of the century. Skip Humphrey was not his father, and he was also not the DFL insiders' choice. That choice had been beaten in the primary by Humphrey.[10] Knowing that party loyalty, especially on the DFL side, was weak, however, would only tell a potential persuader—a potential candidate—that there was a possibility of success. That persuader/candidate would also need to know what attitudes he might tap to get voters to act in a nonparty manner.

Jesse Ventura posited that Minnesota voters were, in sufficient numbers, turned off by politics as usual. Whether the scandals of the Clinton administration had turned off prospective voters is difficult to say. They may have been turned off by both Clinton's behavior in office and the very partisan rhetoric of many Republicans who were leading the charge to impeach and convict the president. Historically, voters have not required a great deal of evidence to turn antipolitical. Thus, many candidates for federal office have run "against Washington" and against "politics as usual." Voters respond to such an approach because they seem to believe, almost intuitively, that there is something wrong with politics. Eisenhower was elected in 1952 to clean up what his campaign had termed "the mess" in Washington. Carter in 1976, Reagan in 1980, Clinton in 1992, and Bush in 2000 in different ways persuaded voters by distancing themselves from the center of politics, as if there were necessarily something unsavory there. Ventura's campaign took a similar tack and was perhaps aided in doing so by the "moralistic culture" in Minnesota,

---

[10]The lack of strong DFL support for Humphrey is one of the causes of the Ventura victory cited by Jacob Lentz in *Electing Jesse Ventura: A Third-Party Success Story* (Boulder, CO: Lynne Rienner Publishers, 2002).

a culture that does not tolerate either the faintest scent of scandal or the slightest deviation from full service on the part of its elected officials.[11]

Creating an Audience to Appeal To

Some of Ventura's appeals were "low"—not in the sense of being negative, but in the sense of being farcical. His Jesse Ventura "Action Figure" ad, for instance, was not an example of high-minded political discourse. The lowness is evidence of the Ventura campaign's carnivalesque quality. More about that in a minute. The lowness also runs contrary to what one might think would be the nature of Ventura's rhetoric in appealing to what Chaim Perelman termed "the universal audience."

Perleman in *The New Rhetoric* speaks of "the universal audience" in philosophical terms, citing Kant, Sartre, and the like.[12] As he puts it, "the universal audience" is to "the particular" much as true ideas are the shadowy images we are stuck with on the wall of Plato's cave. One might expect, for example, "the universal audience" to be cited as what Democrats and Republicans both appealed to when they pushed aside partisan concerns and crafted a way to "save" Medicare. They undoubtedly used rhetoric that sounded high-principled, noble. This is not the kind of rhetoric Ventura used; he was nonetheless trying to appeal to an audience that wanted government to work for the people, that wanted politics pushed aside and problems addressed and solved, that wanted "Evil Special Interest Man" and "Lobbyist Man" defeated because they did not stand for what was "good." The Ventura campaign, as irreverent as it was, did succeed rhetorically because it tried to transform the partisan "particular audience" that often gets involved in electoral politics into "the universal audience" that wants "good" government.

Perelman implies that this "universal audience" is superior to the particular one that might be before a rhetor. Black's concept of "second persona" is more general and also applicable here. Black posits that all rhetorical performances create an audience just as they create the rhetor who is before that audience. Ventura clearly creates a persona for himself. This would be what Black terms "first persona." Ventura also creates an audience that he wants the people who are receiving his message to become. This is what Black would term "second persona."[13]

The Carnivalesque

Bakhtin highlights the irreverent when defining the "carnivalesque" in his study of Rabelais. In the Middle Ages, those who were in power-down positions in society used carnival to rudely and crudely mock those in power. Rabelaisian satire, according to

---

[11]For a full discussion of how this "culture" may have affected the race, see Virginia Gray and Wyman Spano, "The Irresistible Force Meets the Immovable Object: Minnesota's Moralistic Culture Confronts Jesse Ventura," *Daedalus* 129.3 (2000): 221–26.

[12]See Chaim Perelman and Lucie Olbrechts-Tyteca, *The New Rhetoric: A Treatise on Argumentation*, trans. John Wilkinson and Purcell Weaver (Notre Dame, IN: University of Notre Dame Press, 1969), 26–40.

[13]Edwin Black, "The Second Persona," *Quarterly Journal of Speech*, 56 (1970): 109–119.

Bakhtin, does much the same thing. Those who have applied the concept of the "carnivalesque" to nonliterary topics, such as political communication, have deemphasized the rude and crude—although sometimes they are present—and have pointed to moments when those who are "power-down" defy those in control and celebrate—sometimes with comic touches—the fact that they are so defying. Filibusters in the U.S. Senate are often classic "carnivalesque" moments, as are disruptive demonstrations by social activists designed to stop a building from being razed or a war from being fought. The 1968 demonstrations in Chicago's Grant Park directed against the Vietnam War and the presidency of Lyndon Johnson were "carnivalesque." More recently, marches and demonstrations against the World Trade Organization have exhibited the "carnivalesque."

Oddly, the body plays a major role in classic "carnivalesque," and Jesse Ventura's wrestling moniker was "The Body." But this is not just a coincidence, for the Ventura campaign foregrounds the body in a number of ways. The Jesse Ventura action figure was muscular. Ventura's radio ad positioned him "in the Navy getting dirty and wet." He was bodily manifest, whereas Humphrey and Coleman "were cashing government checks." The radio ad played Isaac Hayes' theme music to the motion picture *Shaft*, which featured Richard Roundtree as black detective John Shaft, who, although not as muscular as "The Body," was nonetheless a very physical hero. Ventura associated himself aurally with this action hero, and when he attended (uninvited) the Governor's Economic Summit in September 1998, he dressed as action hero, not businessman or politician.

The "carnivalesque" in politics rarely succeeds in achieving immediate goals; after all, those behind it are "power-down." However, the "carnivalesque" can often rally people for the next fight. Ventura's "carnivalesque" antics rallied enough people by Election Day that he did not have to wait for a better day; he won then and there. There were enough people in his audience who felt "power-down" because government was wasting time and just not attending to their needs that Ventura secured 37 percent of the vote and won. Name recognition may have given Ventura an initial boost in the campaign; however, it was ultimately the votes of the discontented "little guys" that gave Ventura his plurality.[14]

Scapegoating

One other rhetorical theory explains Ventura's success. Kenneth Burke posits that the goal of persuasion—the goal of rhetoric—is identification between the rhetor and the audience. If the rhetor is effective, rhetor and audience become so identified with each other that they become one, become consubstantial. The goal can be accomplished in several ways. One of the more powerful ways is by scapegoating a person or a group. The scapegoat becomes responsible for all that's wrong, and the rhetor and the audience unite against this scapegoat and achieve a kind of redemption by purging the scapegoat from their midst. Often, as one may suspect based on how the

---

[14]For a brief, popular discussion of these dynamics, see David Beiler, "The Body Politic Registers a Protest: Jesse Ventura's Stunning Victory in Minnesota as More than a Fluke," *Campaigns and Elections* 20.1 (1999): 34–42.

scapegoat figure functions in myth and literature, the person or group chosen is not as responsible for what's wrong as the rhetor claims.

Ventura scapegoated those who had held political office and those who sought such office through the usual political means. They, regardless of political party, were responsible for what was wrong. And voters needed to purge them from their midst by not electing them. Is the indictment offered by this rhetoric fair? Probably not: there are good politicians as well as bad ones. But the argument did not hold sway because of its *logos*. No one asked Ventura for examples as evidence; no one rushed to provide counterexamples as counterevidence. The argument was effective because of its emotional appeal. And that appeal was a vague one: "Things" are wrong; politicians are at fault; let's purge them from our midst. Ventura's campaign then enacted a scapegoating ritual.

The Ventura campaign may not have "shocked the world," but it certainly did put others around the nation on notice. Someone, if he or she shrewdly analyzed the voters as discontented with the norm, could appeal to them as a "universal audience" that desired responsive, scandal-free government. That shrewd politician could use irreverent rhetorical moves such as staging the "carnivalesque" against those in power and, then, playing on the voters' emotions, scapegoat them out of office. In an era of declining party loyalty and discontent with those in government, Jesse Ventura may have written a rhetorical script that other political outsiders might follow.

Conclusion

The Ventura campaign seems to have done a shrewd job of audience analysis in the 1998 Minnesota gubernatorial campaign: the campaign discerned that party loyalty had weakened, that Minnesotans were independent-minded as well as moralistic, and that they were turned off to "politics as usual." The Ventura campaign also encouraged voters to act as a principled "universal audience" that believed that politics could and should be in service of the "good." The campaign further rallied voters through both its carnivalesque energy and its scapegoating of traditional politicians. Both the audience analysis and the choices of rallying strategies proved surprisingly effective.

THE MASS COMMUNICATION PERSPECTIVE

The Ventura campaign differed in several ways from previous state-level races. This section will discuss a few issues related to media aspects of Ventura's campaign: the news coverage his campaign received, the political advertising and financial resources to pay for the ads, and the campaign's use of the Internet.

News Coverage of Ventura's Campaign

One news report in the *Star Tribune*, on October 23, 1998, just two weeks before Election Day, tested Ventura's viability to be governor. Before an in-depth assessment ensued, the report commented, "Forget for a moment the conventional wisdom: No pundit, professor or political pro believes Ventura can win" (p. 1A). On the night of election results, the news media continued to believe Ventura could not win. Of the three network affiliate television stations, only one sent a lead reporter to cover the event at the Ventura campaign party; the other two stations had reporters present, but not those who traditionally covered politics. In his book *Electing Jesse Ventura, A Third-Party Success Story*, Jacob Lentz reports that Ventura rarely received scrutiny by the media covering his campaign. The media typically cover the horse race among candidates but also try to uncover skeletons and conduct some truth-testing on candidates' statements, but compared to the coverage Minnesota Attorney General Skip Humphrey and St. Paul Mayor Norm Coleman received, there was an absence of scrutiny of Jesse Ventura.

With regard to media framing, Ventura was framed primarily as the popular outsider whose campaign was based more on stunts (what he wore to political events, for example) and publicity than real politics. Minnesota certainly witnessed an explosion of national attention on the election outcome, but there was little national media attention to Ventura's bid for governor before he won the election. Ventura adman Bill Hillsman describes in his book *Run the Other Way: Fixing the Two-Party System, One Campaign at a Time*, that once news reports had called the race in Minnesota to Jesse Ventura,

> Terry's [Jesse Ventura's wife] cell phone rang. It was Maria Shriver, calling from NBC. Her husband, Arnold Schwarzenegger, was one of Jesse's Hollywood buddies, and the two couples were close friends. But right now she was calling not just with congratulations, but to make sure NBC's Tom Brokaw got the first national interview with Jesse, at midnight Central time. (p. 140)

One unique media-related factor in Jesse Ventura's campaign was his employment as a talk radio host on sports-oriented KFAN Radio prior to his campaign for governor. The same day he filed to run, July 21, 1998, KFAN took his 10:00 P.M. to 1:00 A.M. show off the air. Although Ventura had hoped he could stay on the air, his contract included a clause that he could be suspended if he ran for office (he had previously been the mayor of Twin Cities' suburb Brooklyn Park). Equal time rules as established by the Federal Communications Commission (FCC) were apparently not part of the decision, according to KFAN general manager Mick Anselmo, who stated, "I don't think I would want to allow any political candidate a platform that some would interpret as an unfair advantage."[15] The FCC's equal time rule requires broadcasters to make available equal time to political candidates for the same office; if a broadcaster accepts the political advertising for one candidate, it must accept advertising for opposing candidates, for example. Jesse was disappointed by KFAN's decision, but others in his campaign were pleased that he would no longer have to be in the Twin Cities every weeknight to do his radio show, and competing radio stations were now more willing to have him on the air.[16] Most candidates do not resign

---

[15]Conrad deFiebre, "Ventura loses KFAN job in his race for another: Governor," *Minneapolis Star Tribune*, July 23, 1998.

[16]Dane Smith and Dean Barkley. "Diary of an Upset," *Minneapolis Star Tribune*, November 8, 1998.

positions to run for political office, but the potential conflict between Ventura as a media personality and as a gubernatorial candidate led to him becoming unemployed, at least temporarily.

Once the national spectacle of Jesse Ventura's victory died down, how did the local media respond in their coverage? Coffman (1999) found in the first 7 months of Ventura becoming governor of Minnesota that Twin Cities' media continued to pay plenty of attention to their new state leader.[17] The analysis found 168 front page stories in the *St. Paul Pioneer Press*, and 132 page one stories in the *Minneapolis Star Tribune*, and although substantive news pieces regularly appeared, so did celebrity or fluff stories, with such headings as "Crowd rolls with Stones; Gov. Ventura proclaimed it Rolling Stone Day and then danced at show." The celebrity and spectacle that preceded his running for governor, and continued into his campaign, did not disappear when he was sworn in to lead the state of Minnesota.

Political Advertisements and Campaign Finance

Ventura's creative political advertisements are noteworthy on their own, but understanding the financial restraints of his campaign makes them memorable for additional reasons. Although money can influence political campaign at local, state, and national levels, the lack of financial resources in the Ventura campaign made his victory even more noteworthy, because he won while spending so little.

As long as Ventura received 5 percent of the vote for governor, he would qualify to receive $310,000 from the state for his campaign expenditures. However, his campaign would not receive those funds until the votes were tallied in the election and not until December. His campaign struggled to secure a $300,000 loan to fund his advertising campaign, even taking out insurance to repay the loan in case they didn't reach the 5 percent vote result; their loan came through less than 2 weeks before Election Day.[18] The Reform Party contributed very little to Ventura's campaign, and Ventura would not accept individual donations of more than $50. He sold more than $100,000 in $22 campaign t-shirts.

The loan came through just in time for the campaign to produce and air a handful of advertisements. Bill Hillsman, creator of the award-winning and inventive ads for Paul Wellstone's 1990 victory for the U.S. Senate in Minnesota, joined the Ventura campaign 5 days after the DFL primary of September 15 (he had been working with DFL nominee Doug Johnson in the five-way race in the primary).

Negative advertisements have been found to be effective in close races and in other particular circumstances, but Hillsman's approach is to use humor and keep it clean; when he criticizes opponents in advertisements, he still uses humor to thwart any potential backlash effects from voters. Hillsman describes the work they do at North Woods Advertising as the following: "Instead of doing ads that drive people

---

[17]Jack B. Coffman, "Ventura Highway," *American Journalism Review* 21 (September 1999): 54.

[18]Dane Smith and Dean Barkley. "Diary of an Upset," *Minneapolis Star Tribune*, November 8, 1998.

from the room, we put together ads that get people to call out, 'Hey, get in here! That ad is on again.'"[19]

Instead of buying advertising time during local news broadcasts, as is common in local elections and was done heavily by Ventura's opponents Coleman and Humphrey, the Ventura campaign instead frequently aired their advertisements on the local Fox channel, in an appeal to younger viewers and potential voters. Additionally, media in the Twin Cities can reach 80 percent of the state, so advertising time did not need to be purchased in multiple markets, which is often the case in many state-level races in states of greater size or with more metropolitan areas and media markets.

Bill Hillsman describes his pitch to Ventura of the "Action Figure" ad (described in the introduction to this case), with the Jesse Ventura action figure taking on special interests and lobbyists:

> . . . he took about two seconds, said "We're doing that. What else have you got?" It was the fastest decision I've ever seen a politician make. No 17 layers of handlers telling him, "It's too risky, let's test it." Just boom. Go do it.[20]

When the Ventura campaign launched a 72-hour "Road to Victory" tour of the state of Minnesota by RV, a miniature RV made it into a new version of the "Action Figure" advertisement. The popular "Action Figure" ad was followed by "The Thinker," airing during the last days of the campaign. Here is a description of that ad:

> If anyone harbored the assumption Jesse was your run-of-the-mill candidate, that belief was undoubtedly put to rest in Hillsman's "The Thinker" spot. In that commercial, a body double for Jesse clothed in briefs posed as the Rodin sculpture, while strains of "La Casta Diva" played in the background. A voice-over details Jesse's achievements and family background, and bestowed the candidate with a new moniker: Jesse is no longer The Body, but The Mind. In case the audience suspects Ventura is taking himself too seriously, the spot closed with a sly smile and wink from the candidate.[21]

Campaigning on the Internet

The Ventura campaign of 1998 was also novel for its use of the Internet. It successfully received campaign contributions from supporters through the campaign website and sold t-shirts and other items to raise money for the race. Such political marketing is commonplace in elections today, but it was rare in the late 1990s, as was online campaigning in general.

E-mail was successfully used to reach and mobilize volunteers cheaply and quickly. The campaign had compiled a "Jessenet" database of 26,000 supporters,

---

[19]Alexandra Starr, "The Man behind Ventura," *Washington Monthly* 31.6 (1999): 25.

[20]Patricia Lopez Baden, "This candidate knew how to market himself," *Minneapolis Star Tribune*, November 5, 1998.

[21]Starr.

3,000 of whom volunteered to help Ventura's campaign. For example, during Ventura's final 72-hour "Road to Victory" tour of the state, e-mail would be sent to supporters in particular areas of the state and 600 or more people would show up at the last-minute rallies.

Contacting volunteers through e-mail also aided in diffusing a potential controversy in Ventura's campaign. Before running for governor, Ventura spoke on his radio show about drug and prostitution legalization. At a campaign luncheon he was asked to state his position publicly, to which Ventura first stated, "I have never stated that I want to legalize prostitution or drugs"[22] but then continued with a rambling response. The opposition attacked Ventura, and many media reports showed excerpts of his comments but not his initial statement. The campaign immediately created a press release and sent it to the 3,000 volunteers, who then handed the press release about what Ventura had really said that day to people in communities throughout the state. They were able to diffuse attention and concern regarding Ventura's comments by quickly sharing information that the mass media were not reporting.

Regarding Ventura's success and the use of online resources, Steve Clift, who coordinated the Red White and Blue election website for the Markle Foundation, concludes the following, "Here's my line: Ventura did not win the election because of the Internet. But he could not have won without it."[23] The Ventura campaign's use of online technology relied most heavily on e-mail to supporters to mobilize, to organize, and even to finance the campaign. Although campaigns of the twenty-first century see extensive use of sophisticated online resources, such as elaborate websites, streaming video, and involvement in online social networks, Ventura's run for governor demonstrates the power of the Internet in reaching supporters simply through e-mail. Research by Bimber in 1996 on the use of the Internet in political mobilization confirms the success that could be obtained by e-mail over other approaches to contacting potential voters.[24]

Conclusion

Ventura's campaign for governor of Minnesota demonstrates the potential for victory against numerous challenges that defeat candidates regularly. Most mainstream media did not take Jesse Ventura seriously, and his own campaign faced serious financial challenges to promote his candidacy through advertising. However, Ventura's past in sports and entertainment certainly aided his name recognition, as well as garnered him more media attention than most other third-party candidates would receive. His campaign's creative use of the few advertisements they could run and innovative use of the Internet to reach supporters are also noteworthy in this surprise victory.

---

[22]Kevin Featherly, "Body-Slamming the Election and the Media," *Editor and Publisher* (February 13, 1999): 32.

[23]Featherly.

[24]Bruce Bimber, "The Internet and Political Mobilization," *Social Science Computer Review* 16 (1998): 391–401.

CONCLUSION

All three approaches discuss Ventura as the outsider, the nontraditional candidate; in this election, that worked in his favor. Political expectations were low, so the opposition in the race (Norm Coleman and Skip Humphrey) did not take his candidacy seriously or respond to his campaign in any meaningful way. Ventura's rhetoric appealed to voters otherwise turned off by politics, and the political system in Minnesota allowed these otherwise disinterested voters to same-day register to vote on Election Day. His ability to relate to the "regular guy" and to keep his political discourse simple in communicating with them contributed to his success. The news media focused on Ventura's spectacle as well and did not participate in the critical "kingmaking" tests of scrutiny that they do of candidates deemed as "serious contenders" in an election. Although there was not much else to deem as "serious" about Ventura's campaign, given the offbeat political ads, the carnivalesque approach against his opponents, and the questions about politics versus publicity stunts that surround many celebrity candidates, Ventura effectively directed his message to a meaningful 37 percent of Minnesota voters.

Each perspective does offer potentially competing explanations for Ventura's victory in the 1998 governor's race. Ventura may have capitalized on the electoral system in Minnesota and avoided partisan politics in the election. The Ventura campaign may have been savvy in assessing the pulse of voters in Minnesota and delivering successful messages to them through nontraditional avenues. Or perhaps the news media's lack of scrutiny of Ventura as a candidate aided his success in reaching voters without having gotten involved in mudslinging himself.

What may have taken place is the coincidence of these various aspects of the campaign and political climate—that they all fell into place at the same time, to result in Ventura's arrival at the governor's mansion in Minnesota from 1999 to 2003. His being "a little different from the other candidates" led to novel messages and innovative strategies to succeed in a state that is "a little different" from other states in its political history and process.

■ ■ ■ ■ ■ ▬▬▬▬▬▬▬▬▬▬▬▬▬▬▬▬▬▬▬▬▬▬▬▬▬▬▬▬▬▬▬

ADDITIONAL CASES

On third-party candidates:

- **Angus King, Independent, governor of Maine (elected in 1994, reelected in 1998)**
  Resource: Howard J. Gold, Third-Party Voting in Gubernatorial Elections: A Study of Angus King of Maine and Jesse Ventura of Minnesota, *Polity* 35 (Winter 2002): 265–82.

(continued)

■ ■ ■ ■ ■ ▬▬▬▬▬▬▬▬▬▬▬▬▬▬▬▬▬▬▬▬▬▬▬▬▬▬▬▬▬▬▬

ADDITIONAL CASES   CONTINUED

- **Ralph Nader, Green Party candidate for president in 2000**
  Resources: Ralph Nader, My Untold Story: What If We Threw a Presidential Campaign and Nobody Came? *Brill's Content* 4 (February 2001): 100–103, 153; Barry C. Burden, Ralph Nader's campaign strategy in the 2000 U.S. presidential election. *American Politics Research* 35 (September 2005): 672–99.

  On Athletes/Celebrities as candidates:

- **Arnold Schwarzenegger's 2003 election to Governor of California (and the Recall of Gray Davis)**
  Resources: William Babcock and Virginia Whitehouse, Celebrity as a Postmodern Phenomenon, Ethical Crisis for Democracy, and Media Nightmare. *Journal of Mass Media Ethics* 20 (2005): 176–91; Matt A. Barreto, Matthew J. Streb, Mara Marks, and Fernando Guerra, Do Absentee Voters Differ from Polling Place Voters? New Evidence from California. *Public Opinion Quarterly* 70 (2006): 224–34.

- **Jack Kemp (former Buffalo Bills quarterback), member of U.S. House of Representatives from 1971 to 1989, Vice Presidential running mate of Bob Dole in 1996**
  Resource: Gage Chapel, Rhetorical Synthesis and the Discourse of Jack Kemp. *Southern Communication Journal* 61 (1996): 342–61.

- **Lynn Swann (former Pittsburgh Steeler and ABC sports broadcaster), who faced incumbent Ed Rendell in the 2006 gubernatorial election in Pennsylvania**
  Resource: Mark Leibovich, 88 Goes Long: In the Game for Pennsylvania Governor, NFL Hall of Famer Lynn Swann Is Running Like a Pro. *Washington Post* (April 3, 2006): C01

CHAPTER 7

CASE THREE: THE 2000 PRESIDENTIAL ELECTION

THE CASE

In 2000, then-Vice President Al Gore asked voters to endorse him as their choice for president and, in so doing, express their satisfaction with the direction the country was heading after 8 years of Democratic presidential control under President Bill Clinton. Gore's challenger, Republican George W. Bush, then the governor of Texas, asked voters to think of Gore as inexorably linked to the scandals of the Clinton White House and to see Bush as the "outsider" alternative, even though he was the son of former President George H. W. Bush.

In the end, voters seemed to have a difficult time making a choice. As the polls closed in state after state on election night, it became clear that in Florida, the race was too close to call. Without knowing which of the candidates won in Florida, it was impossible to determine who had been elected president, since the race was so close that each candidate needed Florida's Electoral College votes to win. For more than a month, the country was focused on recounts, hanging chads, and multiple decisions of both the Florida and U.S. Supreme courts. When all was said and done, Al Gore narrowly won the popular vote (as aggregated nationally), but George W. Bush won in more and larger states, including Florida, giving him a larger share of the Electoral College vote—the one that actually determines who is elected.

As the dust settled and pollsters and pundits tried to make sense of the outcome, the consensus seemed to be that the Gore campaign had botched a number of key campaign events. One of the most important was the first presidential debate, which Gore had been expected to win easily. Instead, Gore came across as an impatient know-it-all with a tendency to stretch the truth. An excerpt of the first debate between Gore and Bush follows.

> **Bush:** . . . We need to reform Medicare. This administration has failed to do it. . . . You've had your chance, Vice President, you've been there for eight years and nothing has been done. My point is, is that my plan not only trusts seniors with options, my plan sets aside $3.4 trillion for Medicare over the next ten years. My plan also says it requires a new approach in Washington, D.C. It's going to require somebody who can work across the partisan divide.

Republican presidential candidate Texas Governor George W. Bush and Democratic presidential candidate Vice President Al Gore square off in their first debate in 2000.

Gore: If I could respond to that. Under my plan I will put Medicare in an ironclad lockbox and prevent the money from being used for anything other than Medicare. . . . Let me give you one quick example. There is a man here tonight named George McKinney from Milwaukee. He's 70 years old, has high blood pressure, his wife has heart trouble. They have an income of $25,000 a year. They can't pay for their prescription drugs. They're some of the ones that go to Canada regularly in order to get their prescription drugs . . . .

Bush: I cannot let this go by, the old-style Washington politics, if we're going to scare you in the voting booth. Under my plan the man gets immediate help with prescription drugs. It's called Immediate Helping Hand. Instead of squabbling and finger pointing, he gets immediate help. Let me say something.

Gore: They get $25,000 a year income, that makes them ineligible.

Bush: Look, this is a man who has great numbers. He talks about numbers. I'm beginning to think not only did he invent the Internet, but he invented the calculator. It's fuzzy math. It's a scaring—he's trying to scare people in the voting booth. Under my tax plan that he continues to criticize, I set one-third. The federal government should take no more than a third of anybody's check. But I also dropped the bottom rate from 15% to 10%. Because by far the vast majority of the help goes to people at the bottom end of the economic ladder. . . .

Moderator: . . . On the Supreme Court question. Should a voter assume— you're pro-life.

Bush: I am pro-life.

Moderator: Should a voter assume that all judicial appointments you make to the supreme court or any other court, federal court, will also be pro-life?

Bush: The voters should assume I have no litmus test on that issue or any other issue. Voters will know I'll put competent judges on the bench. People who will strictly interpret the Constitution and not use the bench for writing social policy. That is going to be a big difference between my opponent and me. I believe that the judges ought not to take the place of the legislative branch of government. That they're appointed for life and that they ought to look at the Constitution as sacred. They shouldn't misuse their bench. I don't believe in liberal activist judges. I believe in strict constructionists. Those are the kind of judges I will appoint . . . .

Gore: We both use similar language to reach an exactly opposite outcome. I don't favor a litmus test, but I know that there are ways to assess how a potential justice interprets the Constitution. And in my view, the Constitution ought to be interpreted as a document that grows with our country and our history. And I believe, for example, that there is a right of privacy in the Fourth Amendment. And when the phrase "a strict constructionist" is used and when the names of Scalia and Thomas are used as the benchmarks for who would be appointed, those are code words, and nobody should mistake this, for saying the governor would appoint people who would overturn *Roe v. Wade*. It's very clear to me. I would appoint people that have a philosophy that I think will be quite likely would uphold *Roe v. Wade*.

Moderator: Is the vice president right?

Bush: It sounds like he's not very right tonight. I just told you the criteria on which I'll appoint judges. I have a record of appointing judges in the State of Texas. That's what a governor gets to do. A governor gets to name supreme court judges. . . .

Moderator: Reverse the question. What code phrases should we read by what you said about what kind of people you would appoint?

Gore: It would be likely that they would uphold *Roe v. Wade*. I do believe it's wrong to use a litmus test. If you look at the history of a lower court judge's rulings, you can get a pretty good idea of how they'll interpret questions. . . .

Bush: I'll tell you what kind of judges he'll put on. He'll put liberal activist justices who will use their bench to subvert the legislature, that's what he'll do. . . .

Moderator: . . . On that wonderful note of disagreement, we have to stop here and we want to go now to your closing statements. Governor Bush is first. You have two minutes.

Bush: Thank you, Jim. Thank the University of Massachusetts and Mr. Vice President, thank you. It has been a good, lively exchange. There is a huge difference of opinion. Mine is I want to empower people in their own lives. I also want to go to Washington to get some positive things done. It is going to require a new spirit. A spirit of cooperation. It will require the ability of a Republican president to reach out across the partisan divide and to say to Democrats, let's come together to do what is right for America. It's been my record as Governor of Texas, it will be how I conduct myself if I'm fortunate enough to earn your vote as President of the United States. I want to finally get something done on Medicare. I want to make sure prescription drugs are available for all seniors. And I want seniors to have additional choices when it comes to choosing their health care plans. I want to finally get something done on Social Security. I want to make sure the seniors have the promise made will be a promise kept, but I want younger workers to be able to manage some of their own money, some of their own payroll taxes in the private sector under certain guidelines to get a better rate of return on your own money. I want to rebuild our military to keep the peace. I want to have a strong hand when it comes to the United States in world affairs. I don't want to try to put our troops in all places at all times. I don't want to be the world's policeman, I want to be the world's peacemaker by having a military of high morale and a military that is well-equipped. I want anti-ballistic missile systems to protect ourselves and our allies from a rogue nation that may try to hold us hostage or blackmail our allies and friends. I want to make sure the education system fulfills its hope and promise. I've had a strong record of working with Democrats and Republicans in Texas to make sure no child is left behind. I understand the limited role of the federal government, but it could be a constructive role when it comes to reform, by insisting that there be a strong accountability systems. My intentions are to earn your vote and earn your confidence. I'm asking for your vote. I want you to be on my team. And for those of you working, thanks from the bottom of my heart. For those of you making up your mind, I would be honored to have your support.

Moderator: Vice President Gore, two minutes.

Gore: I want to thank everybody who watched and listened tonight because this is indeed a crucial time in American history. We're at a fork in the road. We have this incredible prosperity, but a lot of people have been left behind. And we have a very important decision to make. Will we use the prosperity to enrich all of our families and not just a few? One important way of looking at this is to ask who are you going to fight for? Throughout my career in public service, I have fought for the working men and women of this country, middle-class families. Why? Because you are the ones who have the hardest time paying taxes, the hardest time making ends meet. You are the ones who are making car payments and mortgage payments and doing right by your kids. And a lot of times there are powerful forces that are against you. Make no mistake about it, they do have undue influence in Washington, D.C. and it makes a difference if you have a president who will fight for you. I know one thing about the position of president, it's the only position in our Constitution that is filled by an individual who is given the responsibility to fight not just for one state or one district or the well-connected or wealthy, but to fight for all of the people, including especially those who most need somebody who will stand up and take on whatever powerful forces might stand in the way. There is a woman named Winifred Skinner here tonight from Iowa. I mentioned her earlier. She's 79 years old. She has Social Security. I'm not going to cut her benefits or support any proposal that would. She gets a small pension, but in order to pay for her prescription drug benefits, she has to go out seven days a week several hours a day picking up cans. She came all the way from Iowa in a Winnebago with her poodle in order attend here tonight. I want to tell her, I'll fight for a prescription drug benefit for all seniors and fight for the people of this country for a prosperity that benefits all.

THE POLITICAL SCIENCE PERSPECTIVE

A strange thing happened in November 2000 while the nation waited to learn who would be the forty-third president of the United States. Amid the news coverage of the recounts taking place in Florida, the outrage over misinterpreted exit poll data, and the allegations of improprieties at the voting booth, the American people actually engaged in a conversation about the Electoral College, presidential succession, and the importance of elections. The U.S. Constitution was, for a few short weeks, in the forefront of the public's consciousness—and for a few short weeks, there was actually political discourse, and not only within the halls of government, but also among rank-and-file citizens who sought to recall the nuances of elector selection from their high school civics classes.

In many respects, the heightened levels of substantive political discourse that followed the 2000 presidential election were anomalous, at least by comparison with the lack of interest that many people showed in the months and weeks leading up to Election Day. Political pundits and citizens were more apt to discuss whether adding "Earth tones" to Al Gore's wardrobe was a good campaign strategy than they were to talk about the effects on the Earth of the U.S. failure to ratify the proposed Kyoto Protocol, a multilateral treaty whose provisions were designed to help reduce environmental degradation. A *Mother Jones* editorial in the November/December 2000 issue described the 2000 presidential election:

> It was dubbed by some as "The Thrilla in Vanilla," and it struggled vainly for much of the year to win the attention of a public whose taste in elections ran instead to a fake-reality

soap opera set on a faraway tropical island. As Curtis Gans, director of the Committee for the Study of the American Electorate, noted, twice as many Americans watched a single episode of *Survivor* on one network this past summer than watched any night of the national political conventions on all the networks combined.[1]

What accounted for the public's lack of interest in the election? It was likely the combination of three factors. First, both of the major party candidates were weak. Although Al Gore was not a part of the vast majority of scandals that plagued the Clinton Administration (the investigation into whether he accepted campaign contributions from foreign nationals is an exception), Gore was, after all, Bill Clinton's vice president. Thus, from the outset, his campaign had to demonstrate that Gore was a man of literally unimpeachable integrity. Unfortunately, Gore's penchant for hyperbole—such as the over-the-top examples he used of "average" citizens in his first debate with George W. Bush—left many voters convinced that he, like Clinton, was willing to stretch the truth to his own advantage. Another factor that weakened Gore (although the alternative decision likely would have had the same effect) was that he made the decision to campaign without significant support from President Bill Clinton. As presidency scholar Mark Wattier notes in a 2004 assessment of the Gore campaign:

> Several signs indicated that Gore campaigned as a non-incumbent. Gore distanced himself from the administration's policy toward Elian Gonzalez. He moved the campaign headquarters from Washington, D.C., to Nashville, Tennessee, making him a Washington outsider. . . . His acceptance speech contained a politically significant line: "This election is not a reward for past performance." Two of his resume advertisements omitted his eight years as Vice President."[2]

For his part, George W. Bush had been pretty badly beaten up during the primary election season by war hero and U.S. Senator John McCain, and he was widely perceived as an intellectual lightweight who lacked either the substantive expertise or the innate intelligence to govern effectively.

A second factor that likely affected the public's interest (or lack thereof) in the election was the fact that—as the excerpt from the first debate demonstrated—both candidates had difficultly presenting their proposals to the public in concrete terms. Although both candidates focused their campaigns heavily on economic issues—taxes, Medicare, and social security, for example—neither seemed to be able to articulate either what the problems were that they wanted to fix or why their solution would be the best one. Gore tended to get bogged down in minute policy details, while Bush tended to speak in sweeping generalizations. The result was that neither

[1] Paul Taylor, *The New Political Theatre. Mother Jones*. November/December 2000 issue. Available online at: http://www.motherjones.com/commentary/power_plays/2000/11/powerplays.html. Accessed June 28, 2006.

[2] Mark J. Wattier, "The Clinton Factor: The Effects of Clinton's Personal Image in 2000 Presidential Primaries and in the General Election," *White House Studies* 4(4) (2004): 17.

candidate seemed to be offering realistic, commonsense policy proposals to steer the course of the country's next 4 years.

The third factor that likely contributed to public apathy about the 2000 election was that times were good in 2000. Economically, unemployment rates were low, the stock market was high, and the federal government was projecting enormous budget surpluses for years into the future. Politically, the country was at peace. No overriding issue confronted the country, making it difficult for either candidate to stir a groundswell of support for his candidacy.[3]

Given the lack of overriding issues, the candidates' inability to articulate clear programs and policies, and the fact that neither candidate was particularly strong, it is hardly surprising that voters had difficultly deciding whether they wanted to elect Bush or Gore. The result, of course, was that in several states one candidate or the other only narrowly won the popular vote; of course, since nearly all states (the exceptions are Maine and Nebraska) have winner-take-all systems of allocating Electoral College votes, even narrow popular vote victories were sufficient to add a state's electors to the winner's tally. Unfortunately, as state after state declared a winner on election night, it became clear that in Florida, the race was too close to call. Indeed, it was not until the U.S. Supreme Court interceded, more than a month after Election Day, that George W. Bush was finally certified as the winner in Florida, and the election of 2000 was over.

Postelection Mythmaking

With the increased discussion about the presidential election process in 2000 came the propagation of several myths in the public discourse that circulated in the weeks and months that followed the election. One such myth was that to have an election and not know the outcome for several weeks was "unprecedented." In fact, it was not until 1845 that Congress chose a uniform date for the selection of electors from all states, and not until 1860 did South Carolina switch from state legislative selection of electors to direct popular election like all other states.[4] The lack of a uniform date for selecting electors meant that states that chose their electors (and thus settled on a choice for president and/or vice president) did not know the result of the election until after all electors were selected and had cast their votes, which might not happen until several weeks later. In addition, in several early elections, the House of Representatives was forced to decide the outcome of the presidential election since no candidate received a majority in the Electoral College. In one case—the election of 1800—it took the House of Representatives thirty-six ballots to determine that Thomas Jefferson had defeated Aaron Burr for the presidency. Although the monthlong delay in 2000 and the dramatic media coverage of the Florida recount and subsequent judicial decisions kept the public guessing about who would succeed President Bill Clinton, the delay was hardly unprecedented.

---

[3]For more on this point, see Arthur H. Mille and Thomas F. Klobucar. "The Role of Issues in the 2000 U.S. Presidential Election." *Presidential Studies Quarterly*, 33 (1) (2003).

[4]Kimberling, William. Undated. "The Electoral College." Federal Election Commission report. Available online at: http://www.fec.gov/pdf/eleccoll.pdf. Accessed June 28, 2006.

TABLE 7.1   FEC-Compiled Voter Turnout Rates, 1964-2000

YEAR	PERCENT OF CITIZENS CLAIMING TO HAVE VOTED
1964	62%
1968	61%
1972	55%
1976	53.5%
1980	52.5%
1984	53%
1988	50%
1992	55%
1996	49%
2000	51%

Source: Compiled by authors from data gathered by the Federal Election Commission.

Nor was voter turnout unprecedented, another myth that was prevalent after the polls closed on Election Day 2000. As the media recounted stories of lines of voters waiting outside polling places and of polling places having to be kept open past the normal closing time to accommodate the huge number of people in line, rumors swirled that turnout levels would be higher than they had been in recent memory. Unfortunately, by whatever measure one consults, turnout in 2000 was roughly the same as in the two previous elections (1996 and 1992) and was substantially lower than elections held in the 1960s. Official tallies of voter turnout from the Federal Election Commission (FEC) demonstrate that turnout in 2000 was hardly unusually high. Table 7.1 presents data compiled from the FEC.

Clearly, voter turnout was not especially impressive in 2000; the turnout figure for that year suggests that, in contrast to media reports of long lines and lengthy waits to vote, voters did not feel particularly inspired to go to the polls.

A final myth that was propagated following the election of 2000 was that it was unheard of for a person to gain a majority of the popular vote but to lose the election to another candidate because of a failure to achieve a majority in the Electoral College. In fact, this was also untrue. The best example of another instance in which this occurred was 1888, when incumbent President Grover Cleveland won an over-whelming number of popular votes in eighteen states, but his opponent, Benjamin Harrison, won narrow majorities in twenty states; the twenty states collectively controlled a greater share of the Electoral College vote, however, and Harrison was elected president, despite Cleveland's popular vote victory.[5]

---

[5]William Kimberling "The Electoral College," Federal Election Commission report (n.d.). Available online at: http://www.fec.gov/pdf/eleccoll.pdf. Accessed June 28, 2006.

To some extent, public confusion over the relationship between the popular vote and the Electoral College vote got bogged down by the extensive concern about the exit poll data reported by the major broadcast and cable networks that had led the media to call the election in Al Gore's favor. To understand how the networks' pollsters could have gotten the story so wrong on the basis of exit polls, a few words about the science of exit polling are necessary.[6] Exit polling, like any other kind of polling, capitalizes on statistical principles to allow a sample—a small subset—of the population of interest to be used to draw conclusions about the way the entire population would behave. It is calculated using the formula $[\sqrt{(var/N)}]^*2$, where N = the size of the sample and var is the amount of variation in the survey results. The result of that equation is multiplied by 2, because it is standard to report sampling error at two standard deviations away from the mean. In layman's terms, by multiplying by 2 we are able to report a sampling error that gives us 95 percent confidence that the actual population values for the item of interest on our survey would be within the plus or minus range of the result we reported based on our sample.

The problem in 2000 was that being 95 percent confident wasn't enough. When only a few votes of many hundreds of thousands ultimately separate two candidates, there is no way that standard polling techniques can be precise enough.

Conclusion

The 2000 presidential election was an important one from the political science perspective, because it got people talking about important questions of civic responsibility and election design that too often go undiscussed in American civic discourse. Although issues of ballot design, Electoral College reform, and winner-take-all elections are beyond the scope of this brief response to the 2000 presidential election, they joined issues of voter turnout, vote counting, and presidential succession as among the important political subjects that enjoyed a renewed and vigorous public discourse following the 2000 presidential election. Although the candidates might themselves have been nothing terribly exciting, the 2000 election will long be remembered for its dramatic finish and for the renewed civic engagement it engendered.

THE RHETORICAL PERSPECTIVE

Political communication scholars like to talk about elections, and based on what's in print, they evidently like to talk especially about two election topics: the advertising the candidates use and the debates they engage in. Much of this talk makes its way into print, and thanks to this literature, we can offer a number of fairly safe generalizations

---

[6]Portions of the discussion that follows appeared as an invited guest column in *Virginia Capital Connections*, a publication of David Bailey and Associates, cited as: Lauren C. Bell, "Lies, Damned Lies, and Statistics: A Cautionary Tale About the Use of Exit Poll Data," *Virginia Capital Connections* (Winter 2004).

about both of these major aspects of contemporary presidential campaigns. About the debates, let me offer four such generalizations.[7]

Assumptions about the Debates

First, no one seems entirely happy with the way the presidential debates are conducted. The early debates (1960, 1976, 1980, 1984, 1988) seemed more like joint press conferences than debates. There was little opportunity for the candidates to engage in a discussion. If there had been, that discussion would have necessarily featured underdeveloped arguments because of the time limits that had been placed on the candidates so that many topics could be covered in the allotted airtime. Limiting direct confrontation and keeping answers brief (and, therefore, superficial) also kept the candidates on relatively "safe" footing. So, since 1992, although the format has been revised to promote a public discussion that might provide voters with more insight, there has been a counterbalancing desire on the candidates' part to remain on safe ground. Given this desire, one might ask if the debates accomplish anything in the election drama. Despite the absence of the full discussion of issues, the debates do seem to have effects.

Second, the debates seem primarily to reinforce the voting preference the audience members bring to the debates. This effect should not be dismissed as unimportant. Candidates need to sustain their support, and they need to get those who so support them to the polls. Also, in close elections, the relatively few undecided voters who might be swayed one way or the other by the debates are important.

Third, to the extent the debates influence the undecided or maybe even change voters' minds, they do so because of how the candidates come across and not their position on the issues.[8] Relevant to the current discussion is *ethos* (see Chapter 3). On the dimensions of competence, character, and dynamism, the candidates can perform in such a way that viewers' assessments of the candidates change.

Fourth, although candidates guard against saying or doing anything that might lead to dramatic changes in how they are perceived, they can make mistakes. These mistakes can affect how they are viewed in the areas of competence, character, and dynamism as shown in the following examples.

---

[7]For good reviews of the research on the presidential debates, see The Racine Group, "White Paper on Televised Political Campaign Debates," *Argumentation & Advocacy* 39 (2002): 199–218; and Mitchell S. McKinney and Diana B. Carlin, "Political Campaign Debates," in Lynda Lee Kaid, ed., *Handbook of Political Communication Research* (Mahwah, NJ: Lawrence Erlbaum Associates, 2004), 203–34.

[8]With the 2000 election as subject and using different approaches, this conclusion was reached both by Mitchell S. McKinney, Elizabeth Dudash, and Georgine Hodgkinson, "Viewer Reactions to the 2000 Presidential Debates: Learning Issue and Image Information, " in Lynda Lee Kaid et al., eds., *The Millennium Election: Communication in the 2000 Campaign* (Lanham, MD: Rowman & Littlefield, 2003), 43–58; and Theodore F. Sheckels and Lauren Cohen Bell, "Character versus Competence: Evidence from the 2000 Presidential Debates and Election," in Lynda Lee Kaid et al., eds., *The Millennium Election: Communication in the 2000 Campaign* (Lanham, MD: Rowman & Littlefield, 2003), 59–71.

In 1960, Richard Nixon's aggressiveness and appearance may have strongly reinforced the view that he was an unsavory character, a political "hit man," whereas John F. Kennedy's eloquence and appearance may have caused some to believe he had a higher level of competence than they had previously thought.

In 1976, what the press would term Gerald Ford's misstatement about Soviet domination in Eastern Europe may have reinforced the view that he was not especially bright and, therefore, not competent.

In 1980, sitting President Jimmy Carter may have undermined his character by being unduly aggressive as well as bit condescending toward challenger Ronald Reagan.

In 1984, sitting and aging President Reagan may have undermined his competence with a shaky performance in one debate, only to restore it with a strong performance in the next.

In 1988, Michael Dukakis may have confirmed the voters' view of his character as lacking in compassion by answering without emotion a hypothetical question involving his wife's rape and murder.

In 1992, George H. W. Bush may have confirmed voters' view of his character as distanced by responding with defensiveness to a citizen's question about economic hardship and repeatedly checking the time on his wristwatch.

These are all famous "moments" in the history of the presidential debates. Every four years, commentators and scholars alike wait and watch for another to join the list.

The questions then to be asked of the 2000 presidential debates are the following:

1. How did Bush and Gore use the resources of rhetoric to reinforce the candidate preferences of their supporters?
2. How did Bush and Gore use these resources to improve their ethos and, thereby, perhaps gain new support?
3. Did either candidate say or do anything that might hurt their candidacy?

Reinforcing One's Support

A candidate's supporters listen as much for key words and phrases as for fully developed arguments. These words and phrases suggest to supporters that the candidate sees "things" pretty much as the partisans do. Both Bush and Gore used such words and phrases to reinforce their supporters' allegiance. On the Medicare question, Bush says he "trusts seniors with options"; on tax relief, he says that "[t]he federal government should take no more than a third." His phrasing suggests he does not want to see the federal government either dictating to people or taking too much of their money. On the Supreme Court question, Bush's language is even more overtly in line with a particular political ideology. He will appoint "[p]eople who will strictly interpret the Constitution," not write "social policy"—"strict constructionists," not "liberal activist[s]."

Gore's language positions him as defender of the less affluent. He wants to serve the "people who have been left behind." He believes the nation is prosperous, but he says the prosperity has yet to enrich "all of our families and not just the few." He will fight, he says, "for the working men and women of this country," for "middle-class families," for "those who most need somebody who will stand up" for them. Gore's supporters then heard the kind of language they were hoping to hear, just as Bush's supporters did. Both candidates were using what Burke calls "terministic screens." Although the language contains few instances of "God terms" or "devil terms," it nonetheless implies ways of seeing the relationship between the governing and the governed (as well as the Supreme Court and the Constitution). Gore, for example, presupposes that government's role is to be an advocate, whereas Bush envisions a less overt role.

Improving One's Ethos

Going into the debates, Bush was thought to be a nice guy but, perhaps, not presidential timber. He was also thought to be one who stumbles over his words (i.e., not an especially dynamic candidate). Bush, by all reports, exceeded expectations insofar as he did not mispronounce words or get tangled in his sentences. So, he thereby improved his ethos on the dynamism dimension. To boost his ethos on the competence dimension, he cited specifics of his various plans, and he referred to his experience as governor of Texas. His style also may have helped him communicate a higher level of competence than some thought he possessed. As is especially noticeable in his closing statement, he heavily uses parallel structure. He tells the audience a succession of things he "wants" or "wants to" do. This anaphora—to use the formal term for the rhetorical scheme—conveys an orderly mind, a quality one might associate with competence. Bush's reliance on this rather formal style will be especially striking when we consider how Gore structured his remarks.

Gore's ethos situation was different. As sitting vice president, he was presumed competent. His having a reputation as something of a policy wonk helped with the perception of competence as well. He had also spoken enough in various venues to establish that he was articulate, but he was thought to be somewhat stiff. Nonetheless, he was expected to be a good debater. However, his being a policy wonk and being stiff together resulted in his being thought not especially warm. This lack of warmth gave Gore a problem when it came to character. He also had a character problem because of his reputation for stretching the truth somewhat.

Gore's rather aggressive style during the debates was probably a reflection of his attempt to put some warmth into his persona. But, whereas his long, passionate kiss with wife Tipper at the Democratic National Convention worked in overcoming the cold, robotic persona, the aggressive style in the debate may have backfired. His

Democratic presidential candidate Al Gore seems to be invading the space of George W. Bush during the third debate in 2000.

audible sighing at Bush's comments (in the first debate) and his invading Bush's personal space on stage (in the third) suggested that he, at best, was enacting a role that was not naturally his.[9]

Gore's rhetorical style worked a bit better. He borrowed it from Bill Clinton, who had borrowed it from Ronald Reagan. Rather than string together policy pronouncements using parallel structure, Gore established his position and then offered an anecdote to show the human side of the problem—and to show he was attuned to the human side. Thus, in talking about Medicare, Gore quickly shifts to the story of George McKinney from Milwaukee; and, in talking about those who are struggling economically, Gore shifts eventually to the story of Winifred Skinner from Iowa. The rhetorical style did convey a warm Gore; unfortunately, the overaggressiveness may have muted the style, resulting in no significant gain in how the audience evaluated his character.

The character dimension of ethos, however, arguably did take a hit when Gore confirmed for viewers that he had a tendency to overclaim. Two examples from the first debate illustrate Gore's "problem." When talking about education, Gore told the story of Kaylee Ellis from Sarasota, Florida, a supposed victim of overcrowding in

[9]Criticism of Gore's style emerged days after the debates, not immediately. See Diana B. Carlin, Eric Morris, and Shawna Smith, "The Influence of Format and Questions on Candidates' Strategic Argument Choices in the 2000 Presidential Debates," *American Behavioral Scientist* 44 (2001): 2196–2218.

that city's public schools. After the debate, the press quickly discovered that the story was full of errors: this disadvantaged 15-year-old was actually in an excellent high school that might have encountered problems in the first couple of days of the school year before $150,000 of new science equipment was set up in the laboratory poor Kaylee was supposedly standing in because there were not even enough desks. This example reveals, perhaps, poor research by Gore's staff. The second reveals more about Gore.

In the same debate, Bush had spoken of fires that had swept Texas in 1996 while he was governor. Gore acknowledged the governor's actions in response, and then he claimed that he had accompanied Federal Emergency Management Agency (FEMA) head James Lee Witt on his tour of the disaster. Again, the press quickly discovered that Gore had not done so. Perhaps Gore had his fires confused: in 1998 he had visited after other fires. Perhaps Gore had somehow confused an airport briefing on the latter occasion with an actual visit to the disaster site. But, even giving Gore every benefit of the doubt, one has to conclude that he claimed to have done more than he had really done.[10]

People who watch the quadrennial presidential debates may come away with some information about how the candidates stand on the issues; however, they seem to come away with more of a sense of who the candidates are as people—in other words, their ethos. Weeks later, this information seems to linger.

Ultimately, if anything is going to sway voters, it is probably this kind of competence, character, and dynamism information. In 2000, Bush seems to have helped himself and perhaps persuaded some by sustaining the audience's sense of his nice-guy character while improving its sense of his competence and dynamism. Gore, on the other hand, seems to have hurt himself. He may have sustained the audience's sense of his competence, but he raised questions about his dynamism, and—more seriously—he confirmed negative views of his character.

Gore's "Gaffe"

Gore's overclaiming during the debates may well rank right up there with the gaffes that have been made by other presidential candidates during debates. History remembers Gerald Ford for what seemed to be outlandish statements about the political situation in Poland, and history may remember Al Gore for taking credit for things he had very little to do with. Although Gore never claimed to have invented the Internet, that supposed claim has become connected in the public's mind with Gore. Thus, any instances of credit-taking, especially if they did not seem to be borne out by the facts, added to Gore's unfortunate public image.

---

[10]For a review of Gore's claims (as well as other details about the three debates), see Robert V. Friedenberg, "The 2000 Presidential Debates," in Robert E. Denton, Jr., ed., *The 2000 Presidential Campaign: A Communication Perspective* (Westport: CT: Praeger, 2002), 135–65.

Gore entered the general election period after Labor Day in strong shape. The debates hurt his candidacy. Very late revelations in the press that Bush had years before been arrested for driving while intoxicated may have helped Gore get back into the game by Election Day. Absent that news story and its possible effects on voters (i.e., keeping religious conservatives away from the polls), Gore's debate performance would probably have resulted in sufficiently decisive election results to keep "hanging chads" out of the news and the issue of a Florida recount out of the U.S. Supreme Court.

Conclusion

As those that took place in 2000 reveal, presidential debates can have effects. Both Bush and Gore reinforced the support they had through the key words and phrases they used. Bush sustained his relatively high ethos on the character dimension, while boosting it on both the competence and dynamism ones. Gore, perhaps, sustained his relatively high ethos on the competence dimension. However, behavior that some saw as emotionally out of control and several claims he made that quickly proved inaccurate hurt his ethos on the dynamism and character dimensions. The inaccurate claims represented a major gaffe in his campaign.

THE MASS COMMUNICATION PERSPECTIVE

"I'm always reminded of those west Texas saloons, where they had a sign that says, 'Please don't shoot the piano player; he's doing the best he can. . . ' That's pretty much the case here tonight over this election."
—Quote from Dan Rather, November 8, 2000, approximately 3:45 A.M.[11]

As CBS News anchor during the 2000 presidential elections, Dan Rather summed up many sentiments regarding the confusion over the election night calls for who would be the next president. The confusion continued until the U.S. Supreme Court decision on December 12, 2000, ended Florida's recount, which led the state to certify its vote and resulted in George W. Bush's victory for president. Beyond the chaos that plagued the news media and the electoral process in 2000, this section will also discuss the media attention to and impact of the 2000 presidential debates between George W. Bush and Al Gore.

---

[11]This quote originally came from Seth Mnookin, "It Happened One Night." *Brills' Content*, February 2001: 98, 152. The quote also appeared in Stephen K. Medvic and David A. Dulio's chapter on "The Media and Public Opinion" (under the section "Election Night 2000: What went wrong?") in Mark J. Rozell, ed., *Media Power, Media Politics* 207–33. (Lanham, MD: Rowman & Littlefield, 2003).

News Media and Election Night "Predictions"

Let's start with a short time line of the confusion surrounding the news media on election night, November 7, 2000.

7:48 P.M., EST: NBC News projects a Gore win in Florida.

7:50 P.M.: CNN and CBS News project Gore to win Florida.[12]

7:52 P.M.: Voter News Service (VNS) calls Florida for Gore.

8:02 P.M.: All major news networks and the Associated Press (AP) have projected Gore to win Florida.

9:50 P.M.: Associated Press retracts their call for Gore in Florida.

9:54 P.M.: CNN and CBS retract their call for Gore in Florida.

10:16 P.M.: VNS retracts their call for Florida.

10:18 P.M.: All news networks have retracted the call.

1:45 A.M.: CNN reports the count in Florida is still "too close to call."

2:15 A.M.: Fox News calls Florida for Bush.

2:16 A.M.: NBC News calls Florida for Bush.

2:17 A.M.: CNN and CBS News call Florida for Bush.

2:20 A.M.: ABC News calls Florida for Bush; AP and VNS did not call Florida for Bush that night.

3:00 A.M.: CNN reports that Gore has called Bush to concede.

3:40 A.M.: CNN reports that Gore has re-called Bush to retract his concession.

3:57 A.M.: CNN and CBS retract the call for Bush in Florida, with the other news networks following.

One can understand Dan Rather's 3:45 A.M. comment when considering the mass confusion in network news on the night of the 2000 presidential election. Not only did we wake up the next morning not knowing who would be our next president, we also did not learn that information for another 5 weeks. The drama continued with Florida Secretary of State Katherine Harris (who in 2002 was elected to the House of Representatives for Florida's 13th District) certifying Bush as the winner of Florida's 25 electoral votes on November 26, and battles that reached the Supreme Court in the case, Al Gore conceded to George Bush on December 13, 2000.

---

[12]CBS News and CNN jointly relied on a "Decision Team" from Voter News Service for additional advice on announcing the state projections, although individual decisions were still made within both news operations. The time line summary is based on Joan Konner, James Risser, and Ben Wattenberg, "Television's Performance on Election Night 2000: A Report for CNN," January 29, 2001. http://archives.cnn.com/2001/ALLPOLITICS/stories/02/02/cnn.report/cnn.pdf.

Why did this confusion occur on election night? Looking at the news media, the pressure to beat other networks in calling states, to not get scooped by the competition, is a strong motivator to take chances on election night. And if a news organization isn't "leading the pack" by announcing results first, they're quick to follow the pack in confirming results when possible and making announcements of their own. The time line above displays how quickly the "scooped" news organizations' announcements are made. What is most at risk in such a competitive environment is accuracy; even though networks had added "decision teams" to aid them in making their moves on election night, the lack of accuracy that night, as well as the on-air chaos that ensued, hurt the news media's credibility with their audience. Looking at Voter News Service (VNS), which conducted the exit polls reported by the news organizations, errors in their predictions may have arisen from a number of factors. Voters may have voted early or by absentee ballot and were therefore not included in the exit polling process. VNS initially estimated that about 7 percent of Florida voters would return absentee ballots, but they ended up casting 12 percent of the vote. Surveys in general can be subject to errors in many forms; in close elections those errors may lead to incorrect projections.

We should note that this is not the first controversy involving exit polls and presidential elections. Many of the news organization policies on using and reporting exit polls date back to the 1980 presidential election. For instance, news organizations agree not to announce any national exit poll results until the polls in California had closed. In 1980, NBC News reported exit poll results predicting a victory for Ronald Reagan at 8:15 eastern standard time (EST), and by 10:00 P.M. EST (before California polls had closed) Jimmy Carter had already conceded the race. Although Reagan did enjoy a landslide victory in 1980, many raised concerns that the early exit poll announcements, as well as Carter conceding so early, hurt the turnout in West Coast states, which had substantial implications for state-level elections.

Given the fiasco in the news media predicting the 2000 election results, newsrooms will continue to revise their policies regarding exit polls and reporting results in future election cycles. Shortly after President Bush was sworn into office in January 2001, CNN had already received a commission report of recommendations regarding changes they should make in their policy regarding future exit poll results (from Konner, Risser, and Wattenberg, 2001).

The Media's Role in the 2000 Presidential Debates

In addition to an analysis of Gore's and Bush's performance during the 2000 debate provided earlier in this case study, we should consider the other candidates in the race for president in 2000, including most prominently Green Party candidate Ralph Nader, as well as Reform Party candidate Patrick Buchanan. They were not allowed to participate in any of the three 2000 presidential debates.

The media do not decide who gets to participate in the debate, and although the candidates might like to have that control, they do not get to decide either. The Commission on Presidential Debates (CPD) decides who will and will not participate in the presidential debates. The CPD was organized in 1987 to sponsor and produce presidential and vice presidential debates and to be involved in research on debates. The CPD is a bipartisan group and is directed by former chairs of both the Republican National Committee and the Democratic National Committee. Before the CPD's involvement in organizing debates, other groups such as the League of Women Voters sponsored and organized presidential debates.

Regarding the CPD's determination of who will and will not be allowed to participate in presidential debates, we, the public, have input on that decision of which some may not be aware. Candidates allowed to participate in the presidential debates must be "serious" contenders, in that they must have received at least 15 percent support of the electorate as measured in public opinion surveys. The CPD takes the average of five national news polls to determine whether a candidate has achieved 15 percent support from the public. This type of system reflects a chicken-and-egg dilemma. To participate in the debates, one must be identified as a contender garnering 15 percent support in public opinion polls. However, to be seen as a contender and gain support, candidates need media access and attention, of which political debates are part. If an individual is not perceived as a serious contender, his or her campaign may get little media coverage in general, which might affect the public's awareness of him or her as a candidate. This may also limit knowledge about the campaign and the candidate's policy positions, which could have otherwise evolved into potential support for the candidate.

To get media attention by participating in presidential debates, a candidate needs to have public support as measured in news media polls. But to have public support, one relies to some degree on media attention to create awareness and knowledge in potential voters, as well as favorable attitudes. Not all candidates are as wealthy as Ross Perot when he ran for president in 1992; he was able to bypass "free" media coverage by the news organizations and buy an infinite amount of advertising time.

Other factors or decisions regarding the 2000 debates involved the format of the debates. Al Gore supported the CPD proposal of three presidential debates that differed in format and one vice presidential debate. George Bush wanted a debate in the format of a face-to-face joint appearance, like those on programs such as NBC's *Meet the Press*. Although Bush's preference did not win out, the second debate was most similar to that style, with both candidates seated at a table with moderator Jim Lehrer from the Public Broadcasting System (PBS). The calendar for the debate schedule was created by the CPD to be sensitive to competition from fall sporting events.[13] The debates took place after the 2000 Olympics concluded, but before the World Series began. Networks that still faced programming conflicts, such as NBC and Fox Broadcasting, had the luxury of keeping their prime time programming intact and airing the presidential debates on their sister cable stations, MSNBC and Fox News. Representatives of the presidential candidates are involved in debate negotiations on issues ranging from which reporters will be invited to ask questions

[13]Robert V. Friedenberg, "The 2000 Presidential Debates." In Robert E. Denton, Jr., ed., *The 2000 Presidential Campaign: A Communication Perspective* (Westport, CT: Praeger, 2002), 135–65.

of the candidates, to podium height, to format style. However, the 2000 debates demonstrated the influence of other media variables, beyond the control of campaign representatives, in shaping the schedule of the debate. As news organizations were reducing their coverage of campaign events, such as presidential nominating conventions, to ensure that commercial network television would focus on the presidential debates the schedule was arranged to accommodate competing programming.

The spin doctors' assessment of the presidential debates worked in Bush's favor in 2000, by creating low expectations for his performance, which he could easily meet. In *The Media in American Politics: Contents and Consequences*, David L. Paletz concludes the following regarding the 2000 debates between Bush and Gore:

> In 2000, expectations were so low for Governor Bush that for many observers he exceeded them by showing up and not torturing the English language. His misstatements and errors were little noticed. In contrast, Vice President Gore was accused of displaying arrogance and condescension in the first debate and of pseudo self-deprecation and passivity in the second.[14]

The media postdebate analysis following the first presidential debate of 2000 focused on three issues, according to Robert Friedenberg's (2002) analysis of the debates. First, while Bush met the low expectations for his performance, Gore failed to live up to expectations of his performance, based on his past political experience and involvement in political debates, as well as his stated willingness to debate Bush "anywhere, anytime." Second, media coverage raised questions regarding Gore's exaggerations during the debate. While some information was made available through Internet sources such as the Drudge Report, the mainstream media repeated claims and information made on the Drudge Report that questioned the accuracy of many of Gore's assertions. A CNN-Time poll 3 days after the first debate found that although 54 percent of respondents said Gore was trustworthy, 60 percent agreed that he would say anything to get elected. This differed considerably from the assessment on Bush; more than 66 percent said Bush was trustworthy, and 40 percent agreed that he would say anything to get elected. The third main news story that followed the first debate had little to do with candidates' experience in debating or with the statements made, but rather how they were made, specifically with regard to Al Gore's conduct. Gore could be heard sighing while Bush spoke, his facial expressions were distracting, and his interruptions of Bush as well as the moderator also annoyed viewers.

Postdebate media coverage traditionally involves news media analysis of performance; postdebate entertainment media have also focused on aspects of debate performance in the context of parody. Presidential debates in 2000 become fodder on comedies such as *Saturday Night Live*, with parodies of George W. Bush's mispronunciation of

---

[14]Quote from David L. Paletz, *The Media in American Politics: Contents and Consequences*. 2nd ed. (New York: Longman, 2002), p. 228. Paletz reports the change in Gore from the first to the second debate was due to seeing the *Saturday Night Live* parody of his first debate performance, which his campaign staff showed him.

words (Will Ferrell who portrayed Bush coined the term "strategery") or catchwords used by Al Gore ("lockbox"). Such parodies can become even more memorable than the original debate events.

Impact of the Debates

In terms of possible media effects from the 2000 debates, one study that examined the impact on learning after the debate asked focus group participants (after viewing each 2000 debate), "Did you learn anything about the candidates or the issues that you didn't know before watching tonight's debate?"[15] This research specifically examined learning about the issues and image of the candidates and found that voters reported learning more about the candidates' image than their issues by a two to one margin (67 percent of comments dealt with image, and 33 percent of comments were about issues). The researchers rated comments as positive, negative, or neutral toward Gore or Bush or both candidates together and found that the evaluations of Bush's image became more positive with each debate, while the assessments of Gore's image declined with each debate. Although the study did not measure vote likelihood, this snapshot of knowledge and evaluations reflects a similar tenor found in media coverage of the 2000 presidential debates.

Conclusion

As we have seen in the aftermath of past elections, the problems in one election cycle led to changes in future campaigns. The election night chaos of the news media to predict and report the outcome of the 2000 presidential election led to changes in how news organizations use exit polls and report voting results. In 2000 we saw the news media continuing to cover the process of political debates (e.g., formats, negotiations over details), as well as obsess over the debate outcomes, which may have been as influential on voters as the debates themselves.

CONCLUSION

As this chapter has demonstrated, the 2000 presidential election offered political scientists, rhetoricians, and mass communication scholars a wealth of material to analyze. For many political scientists, the campaign itself offered little of interest; the candidates were weak, there were no overwhelming issues, and the public seemed relatively disinterested. Other than the usual speculation about who would win, many political scientists became interested in the election only after Election Day, when it

[15]Mitchell S. McKinney, Elizabeth Dudash, and Georgine Hodgkinson, "Viewer Reactions to the 2000 Presidential Debates: Learning Issue and Image Information." In Lynda Lee Kaid, John C. Tedesco, Dianne G. Bystrom, and Mitchell S. McKinney, eds., *The Millennium Election: Communication in the 2000 Campaign*, (Lanham, MD: Rowman and Littlefield, 2003), 43–58.

became clear that the election results would be determined on the basis of the recount in Florida. In contrast, rhetoricians and media scholars found much to analyze throughout the campaign, including the debate performances, speaking styles, and media coverage of Al Gore and George W. Bush. Of course, all of these things affected the behavior of the electorate on Election Day and thus are at least implicit in all three perspectives on the 2000 presidential election.

One area of consensus seems clear, however: no matter what perspective is used, Vice President Al Gore failed to capitalize on all the things that should have helped him to win the presidency—including incumbency and rhetorical skill—whereas George W. Bush exceeded the public's expectations and in so doing gained favorable media coverage that, in the end, resulted in an election that was too close to call.

ADDITIONAL CASES

Students interested in learning more about elections similar to that of 2000, including those in which the candidate debates were important, may wish to consider the following additional cases:

- **The 1960 Presidential Election**
  See, for example, *The Great Debates: Kennedy vs. Nixon 1960.* Sidney Kraus, ed. (Bloomington, IN: Indiana University Press, 1977). Another good starting point is Theodore H. White, *The Making of the President, 1960* (New York: Atheneum Publishers, 1961).

- **The 1992 Presidential Election**
  See, for example, Gerald M. Pomper, ed., *The Election of 1992: Reports and Interpretations* (Chatham, NJ: Chatham House Publishers, 1993). See also Jack W. Germond and Jules Witcover, *Mad As Hell: Revolt at the Ballot Box, 1992* (New York: Warner Books., 1993).

- **The 1994 Ann Richards–George W. Bush Texas Gubernatorial Race**
  See: James Fallows, "When George meets John: A viewer's guide to this fall's version of 'asymmetric warfare,'" *Atlantic Monthly* 294.1 (July-August 2004), 67–80. For coverage of the 1994 gubernatorial election itself, see David Elliot, "Sparks, No Fires," *Austin American Statesman* (October 21, 1994); and Dave McNeely. "Richards Can Claim Victory in Debate," *Austin American Statesman* (October 25, 1994), A11.

CHAPTER 8

CASE FOUR: THE 2004 PRESIDENTIAL ELECTION

THE CASE

The 2004 election results were not nearly as drama-filled as those of 2000. George W. Bush was reelected to a second term against Democrat John Kerry, winning 286 electoral votes to Kerry's 252. Bush garnered 51 percent of the popular vote to Kerry's 48 percent (a margin of 3.3 million votes between Bush and Kerry), and 1 percent for Independent Ralph Nader.

Noteworthy items in the 2004 presidential campaign that may have impact on future campaigns and distinguish it from past campaigns are three factors: the use of the Internet in the campaign, the role of 527 groups in the election, and the attention given to mistakes made by presidential candidates.

Internet Use in the 2004 Presidential Campaigns

The campaigns of both George Bush and John Kerry used online resources to reach voters in a variety of ways in 2004. For example, campaign websites were successfully used to recruit volunteers. The Bush campaign website reported having 6 million e-citizens or supporters who spread the campaign's messages and communicated with others online. E-mail was also used by the campaigns, as John Kerry announced his choice of John Edwards as his running mate by e-mail to his supporters. Anticipating the announcement of the vice presidential candidate by the Kerry campaign, 150,000 people signed up for a campaign e-mail listserv.

We may associate the greatest developments in the use of the Internet in presidential campaigns not with Bush or Kerry, but rather with Howard Dean. His campaign's use of weblogs, online grassroots support, and fund-raising success are all indicators of the potential online resources had in the 2004 election. Blog for America, associated with the Howard Dean campaign, allowed users to post comments to threads on issues of all sorts, including policy positions, campaign strategy, and the candidate's personality. This online discourse developed an online community of "Deaniacs." Another online resource used successfully by the Dean campaign was pairing with Meetup.com, an online resource that facilitates real-world meetings of people interested in common issues and topics. The Dean campaign promoted Meetup sessions on the first Wednesday of each month of the campaign, to engage in letter-writing campaigns or coordinate volunteer activities. By the end of 2003, 160,000 individuals had signed up to participate in Howard Dean Meetup groups. Dean's ability to collect campaign contributions online was most enviable; in total the Dean campaign raised more than $40 million, $20 million of that via the Internet, including a record $7.4 million online in the third quarter of 2003 alone.

527 Groups in the 2004 Elections

One change seen in the 2004 election compared to previous years was the rise of the 527 groups. The label of "527 group" refers to the section of the Internal Revenue Code involving political organizations that are "organized and operated primarily for the purpose of directly or indirectly accepting contributions or making expenditures, or both, for" the purpose of "influencing or attempting to influence the selection, nomination, election, or appointment of any individual to any Federal, State, or local public office" (26 U.S.C. 527(e)(1)-(2)).

Where did the 527 groups originate in their political influence? The Bipartisan Campaign Reform Act of 2002, also known as the BCRA, became effective on November 6, 2002, immediately after the 2002 midterm elections. The BCRA was established to ban the national political parties and congressional campaigns from raising and spending soft money. It placed a limit on individual contributions of $2,000 per candidate per election, as well as limits on individual contributions to local, state, and national party organizations. Although 527 groups had minimal reporting requirements regarding their financial information, the BCRA did not restrict their fund-raising or their spending, and 527 groups were not subject to the disclosure requirements of candidates, as long as they did not advocate the election or defeat of a particular candidate. The 2004 election saw the organization of the pro-Democratic group Americans Coming Together (ACT), which raised $125 million, as well as the pro-Bush 527 group Progress for America, which raised approximately $50 million. Perhaps the most noteworthy 527 group of the 2004 election was the Swift Boat Veterans for Truth, a group that sponsored advertisements questioning John Kerry's military record; they report raising $26 million in the 2004 election.

The first ad sponsored by the Swift Boat Veterans for Truth, "Any questions?" aired on August 5, 2004, in Wisconsin, Ohio, and West Virginia. Although the organization had hoped to air the ad the night of John Kerry's "Reporting for Duty" speech to the Democratic National Convention, the ad was delayed for 1 week to wait for a check to clear to pay to air it. The visuals of this ad included "talking heads" of the veterans speaking, with the background comprising images from photographs of the veterans and John Kerry from the Vietnam War. The veterans' names, military rank, and honors of bronze stars and purple hearts are included as text at the bottom of the screen. The following is the transcript of the first Swift Boat Veterans for Truth advertisement.

Roy Hoffmann
Rear Admiral
Distinguished Service Medal, Silver Star
www.swiftvets.com

The Swift Boat Veterans for Truth attacked John Kerry's record in Vietnam in a series of advertisements in 2004.

"Any questions?"

John Edwards: "If you have any questions about what John Kerry is made of, just spend 3 minutes with the men who served with him."

(On screen: Here's what those men think of John Kerry.)

Al French: I served with John Kerry.

Bob Elder: I served with John Kerry.

George Elliott: John Kerry has not been honest about what happened in Vietnam.

Al French: He is lying about his record.

Louis Letson: I know John Kerry is lying about his first Purple Heart because I treated him for that injury.

Van O'Dell: John Kerry lied to get his bronze star . . . I know, I was there, I saw what happened.

Jack Chenoweth: His account of what happened and what actually happened are the difference between night and day.

Admiral Hoffman: John Kerry has not been honest.

Adrian Lonsdale: And he lacks the capacity to lead.

Larry Thurlow: When he chips were down, you could not count on John Kerry.

Bob Elder: John Kerry is no war hero.

Grant Hibbard: He betrayed all his shipmates . . . he lied before the Senate.

Shelton White: John Kerry betrayed the men and women he served with in Vietnam.

Joe Ponder: He dishonored his country . . . he most certainly did.

Bob Hildreth: I served with John Kerry . . .

Bob Hildreth (*off camera*):   John Kerry cannot be trusted.

Announcer: Swift Boat Veterans for Truth is responsible for the content of this ad.

(On screen: Paid for by Swift Boat Veterans for Truth and not authorized by any candidate or candidate's committee. www.swiftvets.com. Swift Boat Veterans for Truth is responsible for the content of this ad.)

Media and public attention quickly turned to focus on Swift Boat Veterans for Truth, who followed with additional ads attacking Kerry's military service and his campaign positioning of him as a war hero. An August 2004 National Annenberg Election Survey reported that one third of respondents had seen the first television advertisement.

Political Gaffes

The 2004 presidential election is certainly not the first to highlight errors made by candidates—for example, Bob Dole falling off the front of a campaign stage in 1996, and Gerald Ford's erroneous response in a 1976 presidential debate that Eastern Europeans did not live under Soviet domination. The 2004 presidential campaign saw two particular candidate errors that were prominent, memorable, and potentially damaging to the candidates involved.

Howard Dean was the leading Democratic candidate for the nomination heading into the 2004 primaries. His campaign had raised record contributions online, and he had strong momentum particularly with young voters. Although there were problems within the Dean campaign before the Iowa caucus, his bid for the Democratic nomination quickly unraveled after Iowa. The event receiving the greatest attention for the Howard Dean campaign overall was his concession speech following the Iowa caucus and his surprising third place finish (following John Kerry and John Edwards) on January 19, 2004. Some have jokingly called it his "I have a scream" speech.

More than 3,000 people reportedly attended Dean's rally that night in a Des Moines ballroom, and many say they were not aware of his yell as the media have portrayed it. However, Dean was using a noise-canceling microphone that was being recorded by the media, so the crowd noise he was shouting over was not as apparent on the news recording. Howard Dean wanted to give his supporters the same passion they gave him, but his speech—out of context and as recorded and rebroadcast by news media—hurt his image. The following is an excerpt from that Iowa caucus concession speech.

Howard Dean enthusiastically rallies his supporters following his poor showing in the Iowa Caucus in 2004.

"If you had told us one year ago that we were going to come in third in Iowa, we would have given anything for that. Not only are we going to New Hampshire. We're going to South Carolina and Arizona and North Dakota and New Mexico, and we're going to California and Texas and New York. And we're going to South Dakota and Oregon and Washington and Michigan. And then we're going to Washington, DC to take back the White House! YAAARRRHH!

"We will not give up! We will not give up in New Hampshire! We will not give up in South Carolina! We will not give up in Arizona or New Mexico, Oklahoma, North Dakota, Delaware, Pennsylvania, Ohio, Michigan! We will not quit now or ever! We'll earn our country back for ordinary Americans! And we're going to win in Massachusetts! And North Carolina! And Missouri! And Arkansas! And Connecticut! And New York! And Ohio!" (These last states were the home states of the other Democratic challengers for the nomination.)

The Bush campaign had already labeled John Kerry as a flip-flopper, but Kerry's own words helped reinforce that portrayal, as did Bush's subsequent advertising. The following is one news account of Kerry's remarks in response to a question about his vote against an $87 billion war expenditure, at a campaign visit to Marshall University in West Virginia, on March 16, 2004:

"Ladies and gentlemen, the president made the decision as to when to send our troops to war, no one else—he decided the date," he began. "And on the date they went into Iraq, they didn't have the armament on the Humvees, the armored doors, they didn't have the equipment they needed in some regards, and they didn't have the state-of-the-art body armor at that moment when they went in.

"Secondly, this is very important, I actually did vote for the $87 billion—before I voted against it. Joe Biden and I thought this: we thought since a lot of mainstream, regular folks in America were sharing a big burden of this war, we thought since those families are sacrificing, that just maybe the wealthiest people in America would be willing to also contribute, and so Joe and I brought an amendment to the $87 billion, and we said, 'This should be paid for now, not adding to the deficit,' and the way we should pay for it is say to the wealthiest 1 or 2 percent of Americans, instead of accepting $690 billion of tax cuts over the next 10 years, wouldn't you just be willing, in the spirit of patriotism and sacrifice, to just take $600 billion?

"And you know what? The president said no; the Republicans voted no."[1]

The following is a summary from W. Lance Bennett (2005) of John Kerry's campaign visit and the subsequent Bush advertising:

> The state had been blitzed with Bush campaign ads sent electronically to local TV stations just ahead of Kerry's arrival. The ads accused Kerry of flip-flopping in his votes, first for the Iraq War and then against the US$87 billion to fund it. A questioner in the audience asked Kerry about those votes, and the candidate launched into his scripted response about the president's poor planning for the war. Then he went off script and made a meandering statement on the vote against the funding, beginning with the now infamous line, "Secondly, this is very important, I actually did vote for the $87 billion—before I voted against it" . . . . That sound bite was inserted into the Bush campaign flip-flopper ads and run nationally within 2 days—often in the same newscasts containing stories about Kerry's remark. The news often featured the Bush ads rather than the dull elaborations of Kerry's reasoning following the remark (p. 366).[2]

THE POLITICAL SCIENCE PERSPECTIVE

With apologies to Charles Dickens, the 2004 presidential election was the best of times and it was the worst of times. After the 2000 presidential election, the U.S. Congress and state legislatures had promised better election administration in 2004. In many respects, they delivered. Polling places featured improved voting technology and state and local election officials, with the cooperation of the media, provided more information about the location of polling places and the procedural aspects of registration and voting. Voter News Service, the public opinion and exit poll clearing-house that had been unable to assist the media with determining the winner of the 2000 election, was disbanded, and the media promised not to use exit poll data to

---

[1]Jodi Wilgoren, "Kerry's Words, and Bush's Use of Them, Offer Valuable Lesson in '04 Campaigning," *New York Times*, May 8, 2004, A14.

[2]The summary of the Kerry event and Bush advertising came from W.L. Bennett, "Beyond Pseudoevents: Election News as Reality TV," *American Behavioral Scientist 4* (3) (2005), 364–78. The Wilgoren piece cited in Bennett's summary is the article by Jodi Wilgoren cited in note 1.

declare a winner in an election within a state before all polls had closed statewide. In these respects, the election of 2004 was a great improvement over the 2000 election.

At the same time, the 2004 presidential election was all too similar to its 2000 counterpart. Incumbent President George W. Bush was again the Republicans' nominee, while the Democrats again nominated a wonkish member of the Washington establishment, this time U.S. Senator John Kerry. Just as in 2000, the election outcome hinged on the popular vote total in one state—this time, Ohio. Just as in 2000, allegations of voter fraud circulated after the election. And just as in 2000, the exit polls got it wrong, with even well-respected pollsters reporting that John Kerry was winning overwhelming majorities of the popular vote.

What Went Right

The biggest thing that went right in 2004, from the perspective of political scientists who study elections, is that people voted. Voter turnout is the keystone of representative democracy and is a necessary condition of free and fair elections. In that respect, the 2004 election was a dramatic improvement over 2000. According to the *Washington Post*, voter turnout in the 2004 presidential election neared 61 percent, the highest turnout level since 1968, and the largest jump in turnout from one presidential election to the next since 1952.[3] The Federal Election Commission's report on voter turnout claims a more modest turnout level—56.7 percent[4]—but it is clear that in 2004 greater numbers of voters than in other recent elections went to the polls to express their opinions through voting.

Several factors contributed to the higher turnout rates. The electoral context was certainly important, because the election pitted a controversial incumbent against a well-known Washington insider during a time of war and economic uncertainty. Moreover, it was the first opportunity for voters to directly express their opinions of President Bush in a tangible way since his controversial election victory in 2000. Political scientists Alan Abramowitz and Walter Stone note that incumbent President George W. Bush was one of the most polarizing presidential candidates in history. People had an opinion about Bush—either positive or negative—and they were motivated to go the polls to express it.[5] In addition, a number of significant issues were of interest to the public in 2004.

Voter turnout also was likely enhanced by the creative use of new campaign technologies, such as the Internet, to reach younger voters. According to the

---

[3]Brian Faler, "Election Turnout in 2004 Was Highest Since 1968," *The Washington Post*, (January 15, 2005), A5.

[4]See: Federal Election Commission, "Federal Elections 2004: Election Results for the U.S. President, the U.S. Senate, and the U.S. House of Representatives." Available online at http://www.fec.gov/pubrec/fe2004/federalelections2004.shtml. Accessed June 30, 2006.

[5]Alan I. Abramowitz and Walter J. Stone, "The Bush Effect: Polarization, Turnout, and Activism in the 2004 Presidential Election," *Presidential Studies Quarterly* 36.2 (2006), Pp. 141–154.

Center for Information and Research on Civic Learning and Engagement (CIRCLE), youth voting was up more than 9 percent overall and increased at even greater rates in battleground states.[6] The marked increase in younger voters going to the polls illustrates a broader phenomenon in 2004: individuals who might otherwise not have been interested in politics or willing to make the effort to vote did so in 2004. These members of the "inattentive public," which R. Douglas Arnold noted in his 1990 study *The Logic of Congressional Action* generally do not follow politics, can be mobilized quickly by an interest group or other catalyst because they lack sufficient prior information to determine the veracity of the messages they hear.[7] It is likely that both the war in Iraq and the advertisements run by the group Swift Boat Veterans for Truth mobilized some people to vote who might otherwise have stayed home. Younger voters may have been moved to the polls by appeals coming to them via e-mail. According to Arnold, these individuals likely would have voted based on whatever information they had received in the near term just before the election; according to CIRCLE, younger voters were the only age group to prefer Democrats, as a group voting 54–44 percent for the Kerry-Edwards ticket.[8]

Something else that went right in 2004 was that the media did not use exit poll data to make projections about which presidential candidate won in each state. After the 2000 presidential elections, news organizations across the country learned an important lesson: don't call elections before the polls close, because exit polls don't always reveal the whole story. During their coverage of the November 2004 election, these media outlets did somewhat better; some, like CNN, were overcautious in their election night coverage. The discussion of the science of exit polling in Chapter 7 makes clear the networks' wisdom when they decided not to project winners on the basis of exit polls.

To put this in practical terms, when the exit polls reported on Election Day that John Kerry would win with 54 percent of the vote (± 3 percent), that meant that if every voter in the precincts from which the sample was drawn had been surveyed, we could be 95 percent certain that Kerry would win the election, with his actual share of the vote being between 51 and 57 percent. Continuing to capitalize on statistical principles, at a 99 percent level of confidence (or three standard deviations away from the mean), the election would be too close to call; in that case, the actual population value for Kerry's share of the vote would have fallen between 49.5 percent and 58.5 percent. Even then, we're only 99 percent confident in our results, so the actual population values could be outside even these extremes. In other words, in a close election, even the best exit poll can get it wrong.

---

[6]See: "Youth Voting Up Sharply in 2004." Center for Information and Research on Civic Learning and Engagement. Available online at: http://www.civicyouth.org/PopUps/Release_Turnout2004.pdf. Accessed July 3, 2006.

[7]Arnold, R. Douglas, *The Logic of Congressional Action* (New Haven, CT: Yale University Press, 1990).

[8]See: "Youth Voting Up Sharply in 2004."

What Went Wrong

Even though the news networks did not use exit poll data to project the winner of the election in each state, incongruous exit poll and official results led to conspiracy theories about the election being rigged in Bush's favor and were even cited in a lawsuit challenging Ohio's election results. Of course, as the earlier discussion makes clear, the exit polls were not wrong, they were simply too blunt an instrument to measure the minute differences in vote totals that each of the major party candidates received. Moreover, a variety of other factors could have contributed to the disparate poll data and election results. Perhaps Kerry voters were more willing than Bush voters to talk with pollsters, for example. The election results were simply too close to draw meaningful conclusions from the surveys taken by pollsters on Election Day. Unfortunately, in 2004, just as in 2000, too few people fully understood what the data meant.

The impressive increase in voter awareness and participation, as well as the media's new caution in interpreting results data in 2004, did not fully overcome the problems encountered in the 2004 presidential election. In some states, voters continued to vote using outdated lever or punch-card machines. New touch-screen computerized voting machines in many localities made the voting process easier for some voters, but other voters found themselves confused by the technology, and in a few cases, technological glitches created difficulties for voters and precinct workers. Anecdotal evidence suggests that for some older voters, the touch-screen systems were not an improvement; for a generation that may never have used an automated teller machine (ATM) or e-mail, the notion that their vote was stored in a computer rather than recorded on paper did not sit well.

Conclusion

In many respects, the 2004 presidential election was an improvement over the previous one. Voters were more attentive to the processes and procedures of voting, and the media were more professional in the ways in which they covered the election. The marked increase in voter turnout demonstrates that the 2004 presidential election was more of a high-stimulus election than the one in 2000 had been. Angus Campbell's seminal work on elections notes that "'core' voters are joined in a high stimulus election by additional 'peripheral' voters whose levels of interest is lower but whose motivation to vote has been sufficiently increased by the stimulation of the election situation to carry them to the polls."[9] Clearly, this is what occurred in 2004. As the director of electionline.org, a group dedicated to monitoring election reform, noted in his introduction to the group's 2004 election preview report:

> At the heart of it all, American voters return to the polls a changed breed—better informed, wiser to the strengths and weaknesses of the electoral process and more willing to ask questions and/or complain when things fail to go right. This change in

[9]Campbell, pp. 42–3.

voter awareness could have tremendous impact on the perceived success or failure of election reform since 2000.[10]

Nevertheless, the election of 2004 was not perfect. A disparity between exit poll and official voting results led to continuing skepticism among some segments of the public that fair elections are possible. New voting machines in some areas stymied voters, and decrepit technology in other areas reminded voters and election watchers that much work remains to be done to modernize and standardize the national election process.

THE RHETORICAL PERSPECTIVE

The Internet has been around for almost two decades, and politicians seeking public support in their campaigns for public office have used it. During this period, rhetoricians—because they are primarily concerned with effects that messages have on audiences—have waited for those Internet effects to become evident. How has the Internet changed voters' minds? Or, short of that, how has the Internet increased enthusiasm for a candidate and, as a result, voter turnout among his or her adherents?

The Dean Campaign and the Internet

The Dean campaign's use of the Internet highlighted much of what a candidate website can do. And, although providing information about the candidate is important and raising funds for the candidate is crucial, the Howard Dean site demonstrated other purposes. These purposes have less to do with winning votes and more to do with creating a community that cares about the campaign. Yes, one would hope that such a community would vote in large numbers for the candidate; however, the primary effect of the website's communication is simply the creation of that community. Oddly, rhetor and audience merge: the rhetor is the website's interacting user; the audience is the website's interacting user; and the website becomes not so much a source for information as the site where communication occurs and community is built. The candidate—or, more accurately, the candidate's campaign—facilitates this process but is not as involved in the communication as the traditional rhetorical model, when superimposed on a website, would suggest. The Dean website, then, was less about Dean speaking and achieving effects and more about the "Deaniacs" speaking among themselves and creating a shared identity.

For a while, this identity was quite strong. The rhetorician, accustomed to asking how messages affect audiences, needs to alter the question slightly. How does the communication facilitated by the campaign website, as illustrated by Howard Dean's,

[10]"Election Preview 2004: What's Changed, What Hasn't, and Why." A Report of Electionline.org, available online at http://www.electionline.org/Portals/1/Publications/Election.preview.2004.report.final. update.pdf. Accessed July 1, 2006.

affect those who are engaged in the communication as both creators of and receivers of that communication? Even though the question represents a twist on traditional rhetorical thinking, traditional rhetorical thought does provide a basis for an answer. That answer is found in three very different theoretical places: the ideas of Kenneth Burke, the rhetorical thoughts of many about social movements, and the ideas of Michel Foucault.

Burke first. The cornerstone of Burke's approach to rhetoric is identification. A rhetorical act is successful if it achieves identification or—to use Burke's other term—consubstantiality. The process is usually conceived of as something the rhetor orchestrates through his or her choices. In the case of the Dean website, the rhetors (i.e., those who blog and so forth) orchestrate identification not so much through what they say but through the very fact that they are both saying it and, then, acting as a receptive audience to responses and other rhetors' ideas. As stated earlier, rhetor and audience become blurred. That blurring in and of itself suggests how the one is becoming identified—consubstantial—with the other by choosing to communicate. A community comes to exist online; through Meetup.com that community takes the next step and meets offline, in person. The community created through website-facilitated communication expresses its identification and identity by accepting the name "Deaniacs." To the extent the website buzzes with communication, there is consubstantiality and there has been—and continues to be—successful rhetoric, as Burke conceives of rhetoric.

What occurred as the Dean website developed its following has some of the energy one associates with a social movement. Some who study such movements have insisted that they be directed against something, and the accounts they offer of the strategies movements use (e.g., vilification) or the phases movements proceed through (e.g., arguing that those opposed to change are not united) suggest as much. However, others have argued that this definition is restricting—that, in other words, a movement can exist without there being a clear target.[11] Several accounts of the rhetorical functions of social movements map well onto what we see the "Deaniacs" doing. To use one, Charles J. Stewart's, the "Deaniacs" are trying to transform how politics are perceived, prescribing courses of action, mobilizing for action (the Meetup groups), and sustaining the movement through their high level of "conversation" on the site.[12]

Social movements, nonetheless, seem more fired up when they are opposed to something—war, racism, sexism, or environmental degradation, for example. But the "Deaniacs" were pretty fired up. What gave them their peculiar energy? The answer may be found in the writings of Michel Foucault. He talks about epistemes, eras in

[11]See, for example, arguing for the necessity of an opposition stance, Robert S. Cathcart, "Movements: Confrontations as Rhetorical Form," *Southern Speech Communication Journal* 43 (1978): 233–47; and, arguing against, Malcolm O. Sillars, "Defining Social Movements Rhetorically: Casting the Widest Net," *Southern Speech Communication Journal* 46 (1980): 17–32.

[12]For Stewart's schemas, as well as others, see Charles J. Stewart, "A Functional Approach to the Rhetoric of Social Movements," *Central States Speech Journal* 31 (1980): 298–305.

which certain assumptions, almost unquestioned, reigned true; and he also talks about rhetoric that is "counter-discursive" (i.e., runs contrary to the dominant episteme). The dominant episteme in politics, one might argue, has been elitist: candidates and other insiders deliver messages; the prospective voters cheer and, ultimately, vote. Communication has been top-down, premised on the assumption that the elites know and the voters need to be informed and swayed. Yes, the voters have power—the power to vote—but even this power is regulated in a way by the elites who poll and predict and analyze, so much so that some voters wonder why they should bother to vote when the elites have already told them what the results of the voting will be. The "Deaniacs" acted contrary to this episteme: they acted as if they knew and were, perhaps with former elites, determining what the substance of politics would be. The result not only results in what Bruce E. Gronbeck and Danielle R. Wiese have termed "the repersonalization" of politics but, perhaps, something more radical.[13] The result of the "Deaniacs'" counterdiscursive rhetoric could have been a new political episteme, one in which people set the agenda. No wonder the "Deaniacs" had energy! And, although the Dean campaign ultimately imploded, the website communication set a powerful precedent for future campaign communication.

Dean's Declining Moment

The implosion requires a comment. Whether Howard Dean's rallying speech on January 19 wrecked the campaign or not is certainly a matter of debate. From a rhetorical perspective, that speech raises two interesting problems. The first concerns the difference between a hotel ballroom and America's television screens as media for a public speech. What Dean did may well have been perfectly acceptable in the first medium, but not in the second, which, because it is in McLuhan's terms a "cooler" medium, presupposes minimal audience involvement. Candidates must, therefore, be aware of the different media in which their remarks might be heard and, if there is a conflict among the media, make a rhetorical decision about the communication based on which medium is ultimately the most important. Dean, evidently, did not think along these lines that evening in Des Moines. The second concerns the genre he used. When rallying the masses, one speaks in a particular genre, but is that the genre that is typically used by the candidate on a primary election night? Those who have attended such nights might observe that speakers other than the candidate typically give the rallying addresses (when the television cameras are off); then, the candidate uses a different genre to thank and encourage supporters, without the shrillness of a rallying cry. Candidates must also understand that there are different genres, and they must choose carefully among them—another rhetorical choice. Dean arguably did not.

---

[13]Bruce E. Gronbeck and Danielle R. Wiese, "The Repersonalization of Presidential Campaigning in 2004," *American Behavioral Scientist* 49 (2005): 520–34.

The Candidates' Narratives

Dean's campaign was a "big" story in 2004, but ultimately one must shift from the candidacy that almost was to the Kerry candidacy and ask what went wrong with it. At the same time, of course, one is asking what went right with the Bush campaign.

The ability of the Bush campaign to get out the vote in carefully selected areas of the country (e.g., southern Ohio) may have been the deciding factor in the election.[14] However, long before Election Day, campaign advertising was tilting things Bush's way.

Fisher tells rhetoricians how powerful narratives can be in persuasion. Voters recall issue positions vaguely, but they recall the candidates' "stories" well. And I don't mean the stories they tell; I mean the stories they embody. In 2004, Kerry chose to embody a particular story. Advertising by the 527 group Swift Boat Veterans for Truth managed to undercut that story.

Increasingly over the years, the party conventions have become staged events. Because the primaries began selecting most of the delegates and because the primary season became heavily front-end loaded, the identity of the nominees is now known long before the summer gatherings. (Once upon a time, these gatherings selected the nominees, sometimes proceeding through many, many rounds of balloting.) The nominees then have the opportunity to craft the convention so that it presents a coherent story. Obviously, any candidate might choose among several stories. That choice is a rhetorical one: the candidate ought to be choosing the story that will prove the most persuasive.

Kerry chose "Reporting for Duty" as his story line. He would highlight his service during the Vietnam War; he would suggest that he was ready to provide comparable leadership now, in another time of war. In retrospect, his choice is questionable, but he probably made it for two reasons: first, the United States was in the midst of an armed conflict; second, Democrats are traditionally viewed as less capable of dealing with military matters than Republicans.

The period between the party conventions and Labor Day (traditional general election kickoff) is traditionally a "dead" period. The enthusiastic campaigning of Clinton and Gore in 1992 during this period has led some to question whether this pre–Labor Day period ought to be "dead," but, still, candidates seem to be holding their fire—and their funds—until September. So, into this void came the Swift Boat Veterans for Truth, running a succession of ads that call the Kerry narrative into question. They offered the testimony of some of those who served with Kerry in Vietnam. They essentially called the Democratic presidential candidate a liar. The

---

[14]See Robert E. Denton, Jr., "Religions, Evangelicals, and Moral Issues in the 2004 Presidential Campaign," in Robert E. Denton, Jr., ed., *The 2004 Presidential Campaign: A Communication Perspective* (Lanham, MD: Rowman & Littlefield, 2005), 255–81; Henry C. Kenski and Kate M. Kenski, "Explaining the Vote in a Divided Country: The Presidential Election of 2004," in Robert E. Denton, Jr., ed., *The 2004 Presidential Campaign: A Communication Perspective* (Lanham, MD: Rowman & Littlefield, 2005), 301–42.

ads, which were not initially shown widely, received a great deal of media attention. The Kerry campaign, perhaps lulled into thinking that they did not need to respond quickly because the campaigns were in this "dead" period, responded slowly and poorly. The Kerry narrative was certainly weakened.

Meanwhile, in a succession of ads, the Bush campaign was creating and sustaining a narrative for him. In July, the campaign ran four ads entitled "Safer/Stronger," "Tested," "Lead," and "Time," the last of which actually used 9/11 footage. Bush's response to the terrorist attack was clearly the story his campaign was going to push. But the story was, in various ways, going to suggest that Bush was a compassionate leader.[15] Later in the campaign, the ad entitled "Wolves" reminded voters of the threats from which the nation needed Bush's leadership to be safe. Keeping the full Bush story very much alive was a late ad sponsored by the 527 group Progress for America. This ad, entitled "Ashley," evoked 9/11 but stressed the president's compassionate response to a teenage girl who lost her mother in the attack. The ad powerfully kept the Bush story before the voters. As Kerry's advertising man Bob Shrum noted, "'Ashley' probably cost us Ohio and cost us the presidency!"[16]

From a rhetorical point of view, single ads are powerful, but even more powerful is their ability to affect the narratives the candidates are offering the voters about themselves. In 2004, the 527 ads muted Kerry's narrative, and a combination of Bush ads and 527 ads sustained Bush's, very much to the president's advantage.

Using a Candidate's Words against the Candidate

Kerry's remark in West Virginia was also used to the president's advantage. Individuals running for president (or any elected office, for that matter) must watch what they do and what they say. Kerry's windsurfing off Nantucket proved unfortunate: it was used as a visual image in two ads to suggests that Kerry's views on issues shifted with the wind. But the West Virginia remark was more unfortunate. If one were to look at all that Kerry said, one would understand that Kerry, after voting for the measure, voted against funding the war effort out of general federal revenue and thereby increasing the deficit, because Kerry preferred an alternative funding mechanism: asking the wealthiest to forgo $90 billion out of a $690 billion tax cut. He voted against after voting for to make an editorial comment on both war spending and tax cuts for the rich. But only Kerry's initial words, words almost defining "flip-flop," were all the Bush campaign strategist needed to hear—and all they wanted the public to hear. At the time he offered the comment, the Bush campaign was preparing an ad entitled "Troops." The campaign immediately reedited the ad, naming the new version "Troops/Fog," to include the Kerry comment and used it heavily in battleground states.

---

[15]For an excellent account of the advertising used by both campaigns as well as by 527 groups, see L. Patrick Devlin, "Contrasts in Presidential Campaign Commercials of 2004," *American Behavioral Scientist* 49 (2005), 279–313.

[16]The comment was made in an interview conducted by Devlin.

Television ads are quick hitting. In a relatively short period of time (15, 30, or 60 seconds), visual images, spoken words, written words—what radio journalists call "actualities"—and ambient sound are paraded before a semiattentive viewer. Their rhetoric (i.e., what makes them persuasive) is not easy to discern, given both the brevity of the message and how much "stuff" is included. A rhetorician can best generalize from what has worked in arriving at such a rhetoric. The defunct *George* magazine ran a feature article in 2000 on the "Top 10" ads ever. These ads provide us with clues as to what works in ads.

Number 10 was a 1996 ad directed against Bob Dole by the Clinton campaign. It visually paired Dole with the then-unpopular Speaker of the House of Representatives, Newt Gingrich of Georgia. So, one effective rhetorical technique would be associating one's opponent with someone or something negative. Number 9 was a 1960 ad in which Jackie Kennedy spoke to Latino voters in Spanish. It worked because the use of Spanish was a surprise, a welcome surprise where the ad was shown. Number 8 was a 1968 Nixon ad that evoked voters' fear of crime. So, another technique would be to evoke fear. Number 7 was the 1988 Bush ad depicting Michael Dukakis's M1 tank ride, a ride during which the grinning Democrat looked silly. So, use negative pictures of your opponent if you have them. The 2004 "Surfer" ad also uses that strategy. In the Number 6 position, we find the 1984 Reagan ad that reminded voters that there was probably "a bear in the woods." It again evoked fear too—fear of the Soviet Union.

Number 5 is a 1968 Hubert Humphrey ad that laughs hysterically and at length at the idea of Spiro T. Agnew as vice president. Mockery can work. Number 4 is the 1952 "Eisenhower Answers America" ad series, effective because they brought the president personally into American homes, sincerely answering citizens' questions. So, being genuine works too. Number 3 is a 1984 Reagan ad, a very positive one, telling voters that "It's Morning Again in America." Positive messages work if you can associate yourself with the positive and your opponent with the negative. The Reagan campaign succeeded in suggesting that the Mondale campaign was unduly pessimistic. Number 2 is the 1988 PAC ad entitled "Willie Horton" (oddly, created by the same man who designed "Ashley") that associated Massachusetts Governor Dukakis with the very negative image of a dangerous furloughed criminal. And Number 1 is the 1964 "Daisy Girl" ad used by Lyndon Johnson to associate his opponent, Senator Barry Goldwater, with nuclear annihilation, a holocaust that would presumably take the life of the innocent young girl trying to count the petals on a daisy. Besides making a negative association, this "classic" ad evokes fear.

We need to add to this list—this rhetoric—the tactic of using an opponent's words against him or her. Clinton used the strategy effectively against George H. W. Bush in 1992, recalling the Republican's "Read my lips: No new taxes" pledge. George W. Bush used it effectively against Kerry. It should therefore come as no surprise that an opponents' "people" are always trailing a candidate, with recorders—as well as cameras—trying to capture words such as those that Kerry uttered in West Virginia that would give credence to the claim that he was a "flip-flopper."

Conclusion

During the 2004 primary season, the interesting story was that of former Vermont Governor Howard Dean. His website showed the potential such a communication medium has to foster identification and inspire high levels of energy among supporters. It signaled the possibility of a new kind of politics, a kind that emerges from the ground up, not from political elites down. The Dean campaign, however, fizzled after a single communication event that revealed how important it is for speakers to make intelligent rhetorical choices among media and genres. During the 2004 general election period, the interesting story was the stories—the narratives—the two candidates offered voters. The Bush campaign sustained his narrative as a strong, but compassionate leader through its televised advertising. Advertising by a 527 group helped call Kerry's chosen narrative as military leader into question. In addition, the Bush campaign strategically used Kerry's words and images of Kerry against him.

THE MASS COMMUNICATION PERSPECTIVE

Although much media attention and mass communication research regarding elections typically focuses on the final "showdown" between the party nominees for president, 2004 is atypical when compared to previous presidential elections. The 2004 campaign was perhaps more noteworthy for developments and events within the Democratic primary, as well as the early stages of the race between John Kerry and George Bush, than for the outcome in November 2004. This section will address the rise of campaign blogs, the influence in advertising of the 527 group Swift Boat Veterans for Truth, and media attention and framing of presidential candidate gaffes.

Blogging and Political Campaigns

In addition to the record-breaking success of the Howard Dean campaign in online fund-raising, his presidential campaign was also in the forefront of the use of other Internet technologies within a political campaign. Weblogs, or blogs, have proliferated the Internet, but Howard Dean's presidential campaign was one of the first to consistently use the campaign blog as a tool for communicating with and mobilizing supporters. Blog for America began as the Dean Call for Action Blog, on March 13, 2003, with this message from campaign manager Joe Trippi:

> This is the place where we at the campaign can let people know when, where, and how you can help. We are going to need as much support from the netroots and grassroots as we can possibly get. Please check back here regularly.

One analysis[17] of Blog for America reports that 82 percent of blog posts were essays written by the campaign Internet staff, 9 percent were press releases, and 2 percent were messages from Howard Dean or Joe Trippi. Another 5 percent were reprints of political news stories, and 2 percent were blogs pasted from other sites. "Deaniacs" were very involved in responding to the blog postings in building an online community, as well as taking action when requested, such as spreading messages to others or contributing to the campaign. One unique method of fund-raising via Blog for America arose spontaneously from supporters; when an individual posted a negative comment to Blog for America, supporters responded by promising if more inflammatory comments were posted, they would donate $10 or $20 to Howard Dean's campaign, and dozens if not hundreds of others agreed to do so as well. As promised, when flaming comments were posted next, the campaign received over ten thousand dollars in these very small donations.

Beyond the role of campaign blogs, the news media has faced challenges from bloggers outside of political campaigns. Blogs have increased scrutiny on news stories (as with Dan Rather's report for CBS News regarding George Bush's National Guard service), as well as provided audiences with another source of information to use. Fred Brown, journalist and former president of the Society for Professional Journalists, makes the distinction between "citizen" journalists (bloggers) and "professional" journalists.[18] He says that although professional journalists' first goal is to be accurate, the main goal of citizen journalists is to be interesting. He does, however, praise blogs for providing additional scrutiny of the accuracy of the media.

Former journalist Joe Pollack takes the side that bloggers are not journalists. In his critique of blogs, he says, "More than anything, I resent that bloggers hide behind the well known cloak of anonymity. They can say what they please, without regard for truth, accuracy or even common decency, and let the Devil take the hindmost, defending their actions by saying that they are free to speak the truth (as they see it)."[19] To demonstrate exactly what some bloggers do, especially those tracking mass media, his essay was critiqued on the blog The Commonspace in late March 2005. The critique points out that not all blogs are anonymous (many do identify authors of blogs) and that Pollack erroneously lumps all blogs together as lacking quality. Regardless of how Brown or Pollack perceive them, the proliferation, increasing prominence, and potential impact of blogs on mainstream media since the 2004 elections cannot be denied.

The successful use of blogs by the Howard Dean campaign is considered a milestone in the developments in Internet campaigning for its ability to mobilize supporters quickly and to maintain contact with supporters and also invite the public's response to campaign announcements and activities. Past milestones of note in the Internet and political campaigns include the first major candidate website

---

[17]Matthew R. Kerbel and Joel. D. Bloom, "Blog for America and Civic Involvement," *Harvard International Journal of Press/Politics* 10.4 (2005): 8–27.

[18]Fred Brown, "'Citizen' Journalism is Not Professional Journalism," *Quill Magazine* 93.6 (2005): 42.

[19]Joe Pollack, "Blogs Are Not Journalism," *St. Louis Journalism Review* 35 (2005), 25.

(in 1994 for Dianne Feinstein's U.S. Senate campaign), the first presidential candidate to announce his candidacy online (in 1999 with Steve Forbes' announcement that he was running for the Republican nomination, and the first publication of a candidate's campaign contributors online (in 2000 with George W. Bush's presidential campaign).[20] These three particular milestones demonstrate increasing access to information provided for voters; the Howard Dean campaign's use of blogs, as well as other technological developments such as Meetup.com groups, took the next step in using such technologies not only to inform voters but also to motivate and mobilize them.

Swift Boat Veterans for Truth

Another new development witnessed in the 2004 elections was the potential influence and power of 527 groups, interest groups outside of political parties and campaigns that could fund-raise without the limits set for others by the BCRA and could sponsor their own advertisements amid political campaigns.

The Swift Boat Veterans for Truth[21] began their involvement in the 2004 presidential elements not with their anti-Kerry advertising, but with a press conference they held in May 2004, three months before their anti-Kerry advertising began. The press conference was held at the National Press Club and was aired on C-SPAN, but only one broadcast news program mentioned the group on the evening news. The competing news of the day was breaking news of the Iraqi prisoner abuse in Abu Ghraib, which grabbed the majority of media attention. Albert May's analysis of media attention found that the group disappeared from the news until August 2004, with U.S. newspapers mentioning them 58 times between May and July 2004. In August 2004, the month Swift Boat Veterans for Truth began their advertising campaign, U.S. newspapers mentioned the group in more than 1,200 stories. Some of the increased media attention did turn scrutiny toward the Swift Boat veterans themselves, when a couple of the veterans featured in the ad recanted their criticisms of Kerry and questions about the accusations the Swift Boat vets made against John Kerry arose.

Beyond the advertisements themselves, the Swift Boat campaign received considerable media attention. The first ad was aired in only three states, yet it was the focus of news reports, cable television discussions, talk radio, and the Internet. *American Journalism Review* editor Rim Rieder likens the news media's decision to cover the Swift Boat Veterans for Truth to Gennifer Flowers' announcement in 1992 that she had had a 12-year affair with Bill Clinton.[22] That story broke in the tabloid

---

[20]Dennis W. Johnson, "Campaigning on the Internet." In *The Electoral Challenge: Theory Meets Practice.* Ed. Stephen C. Craig. (Washington, DC: CQ Press, 2006), 121–42.

[21]For a detailed review of the Swift Boat Veterans for Truth advertising in 2004, as well as campaign finance law changes, see. Albert L. May, "Swift Boat Vets in 2004: Press Coverage of an Independent Campaign," *First Amendment Law Review* 4 (2005): 66–106.

[22]Rem Rieder, "The Swift Boat Conundrum," *American Journalism Review* 26 (October/November 2005): 6.

Star Magazine but was eventually picked up by mainstream news organizations. Rieder credits not the "elite" news media but cable news, talk radio, and the Internet for bringing attention to the Swift Boat group. The role of the gatekeeper in determining what is newsworthy and what facts can be verified is leaving the control of mainstream news organizations and shifting to cable news and the Internet. This shift also includes bloggers who investigate and bring attention to many accusations before they might be covered by traditional news organizations.

Were the Swift Boat Veterans for Truth ads effective? They were highly negative, but since they were not sponsored by the Bush campaign there was no backlash effect against Bush. They certainly raised doubts in voters' minds about John Kerry, perhaps the minds of the Independent voters more than clear Democrats or Republicans, but, in a close race, that doubt could result in the difference between winning and losing. The potential effects of the Swift Boat ads were primarily on voters' attitudes regarding John Kerry, and for some voters' the advertisements may have had an effect on their behavior in terms of their vote choice.

Dean's and Kerry's Gaffes

Voters have often criticized the news media for their pack-journalism mentality and focus in campaigns on the strategy over issues. The 2004 presidential campaign demonstrated how unexpected and spontaneous events of political campaigns can become the obsession of news coverage and the focus of political advertising.

According to the *National Journal*'s Hotline, broadcast news and cable prime time programs aired Howard Dean's yell 633 times in the 4 days following the Iowa caucus. One report, from Diane Sawyer at ABC News, was rare in that it included a comparison of the broadcast version of Dean's scream as well as recordings from members of the audience at the speech itself, in which the scream could not be heard. Sawyer's report included comments from news executives at CBS, ABC, Fox News, and CNN that the media had overplayed the clip of Howard Dean's "scream."[23]

The distinction in how the media portrayed the event and how it appeared in person are confirmed by Howard Dean himself. Jane Hall interviewed Howard Dean for an article in *Columbia Journalism Review* , which included this exchange:

Hall: Let's talk about the infamous scream speech after your loss in the Iowa caucus. You say the incident didn't happen, at least not the way it was reported.

Dean: That's right, I was in front of 1,200 screaming kids who couldn't hear the speech, and the cable networks ran it as a speech with a directional

---

[23]Rachel Smolkin, "Not Too Shabby," *American Journalism Review* 26 (April/May 2004): 40–45.

mic[rophone]–no crowd noise and no pictures of the crowd. So it didn't happen at all the way it was on television.

Hall: I heard that reporters in the room didn't think it was that big a deal, and then their editors said, "Did you see that?" And that's how it started.

Dean: The editors said, "How come you didn't say anything about this?" The reporters were there; they didn't think it was a big deal.[24]

The distinction between the media coverage and the reports from those who were at the speech regarding Howard Dean's "scream" is similar to a historical example of the potential change in accuracy with the media process of a news event. Kurt Lang and Gladys Engel Lang studied the television coverage versus real viewing of General Douglas MacArthur's parade in 1952 when he returned from the Korean War.[25] They found that, in person, the parade was described as being boring and the crowds were not very enthusiastic, whereas from the television footage, the parade was assessed as being exciting and noisy and crowds appeared to be enthusiastic. The Langs concluded that the media did not reflect reality, but rather they constituted their own realty of the event, which was then presented to the audience. This example suggests that the media portrayal of the event, as compared to what the reality of the event actually was, may have the potential for media effects, perhaps affecting attitudes more than knowledge or behavior in this case.

Regarding John Kerry's confirmation through his own words of Bush's accusation of flip-flopping, Lance Bennett refers to the media attention over these factors as the "candidate challenge" news frame, in which "the challenge often begins with journalists' raising unsourced 'concerns' about a candidate or campaign. The ensuing pundit-journalist buzz then leads journalists to become the sources of reported rumors as real and important campaign elements."[26] In this instance the public did not see only the media attention toward John Kerry's statements. Those statements were reinforced in Bush's campaign advertising, which may have further enhanced this frame of Kerry in the news media.

The conventions of news reporting encourage the use of news frames as narrative devices in coverage, and the Bush campaign advertising enhanced the news frame of Kerry through a media genre other than reporting. The 24/7 news cycle, competition from the proliferation of cable news outlets and Internet news sources, and the business model of news operations in the twenty-first century offer additional pressure on newsrooms to reinforce existing frames in coverage rather than spend the time creating different approaches in news coverage. Although Martin Linksy's work examined case studies from 1969 through 1984, his findings about the relationship between the mass

[24]Jane Hall, "Burned by the Spotlight," Columbia Journalism Review 43 (September/October 2004): 14–15.

[25]Kurt Lang and Gladys Engel Lang, "The Unique Perspective of Television and Its Effects: A Pilot Study," *American Sociological Review* 18.1 (1953): 3–12.

[26]Quote from W. Lance Bennett, "Beyond Pseudoevents: Election News as Reality TV," *American Behavioral Scientist* 49.3 (2005): 365.

media and political officials remain accurate today.[27] Policy making coincides with public relations for many officials and candidates, because the power of the media to dramatize events, sway emotions, and affect citizens and voters can be considerable.

Conclusion

We continued to see the evolution of the use of the Internet in political campaigns with the popularity of blogs arising in the 2004 campaign and their relationship with mainstream news organizations. We also saw the success of Howard Dean's campaign in mobilizing supporters and donors and also communicating with voters via the Internet in the 2004 Democratic primary. The 2004 election also presented initial developments regarding interest groups' involvement in political advertising following the Bipartisan Campaign Reform Act with the Swift Boat Veterans for Truth advertising campaign against John Kerry, which received considerable news media attention, as have political advertisements of controversy in the past. Of the two political gaffes of the 2004 campaign spotlighted here, we saw one that the news media unduly obsessed over and one that the media all but ignored except when reminded of it by the Bush campaign advertisement that quickly capitalized on Kerry's own words.

CONCLUSION

The 2004 presidential election, like its precursor in 2000, offers rich material for analysis. Whether the focus is on the Democratic primary election, the advertising produced by the major-party candidates, or the use of the Internet to mobilize groups of typically underrepresented voters, it is clear that political scientists, rhetoricians, and mass communication scholars all see technological advances in campaign communication techniques as important in 2004.

Technology can be used to the benefit or to the detriment of candidates for public office. The Internet allows candidates to contact potential voters who might not be as easily reached using traditional methods of communication; it is likely that at least some of the increase in voter turnout in 2004 resulted from the innovative use of campaign communication technology. As Howard Dean learned during the Democratic primary, however, microphones that filter out crowd noise can ensure that the media are able to broadcast a campaign speech, but they can also have the effect of removing the context from a speaker's remarks.

Election 2004 was notable for the use of third-party ads, the Internet, and efforts to reform media coverage of everything from the debates to the exit polls. It remains to be seen whether the changes of 2004 continue in future elections. One thing seems clear, however—subsequent elections are likely to continue to see the use of emerging technologies in their efforts to bring voters to the polls.

[27]Martin Linsky, *Impact: How the Press Affects Federal Policymaking* (New York: W. W. Norton, 1986).

ADDITIONAL CASES

Students wishing to learn more about the media and the use of technology in elections or about situations in which gaffes damaged a candidate may wish to consult the following additional cases/sources:

- **2004 Illinois Senate race: Jack Ryan sex scandal**
  See: Maura Kelly Lannon, "Ryan Pulls Name off Illinois U.S. Senate Ballot," Associated Press State and Local Wire, July 29, 2004. See also: Peter Savodnik, "Republicans Rebuke LaHood for Asking Ryan to Step Down," *The Hill: The Newspaper for and about the U.S. Congress*, June 23, 2004.

- **Moveon.org**
  Access the website of this collection of progressive organizations at http://www.moveon.org. During the 2004 presidential election, moveon.org was active in trying to identify progressive-minded voters. The hope was that if enough progressive voters went to the polls, incumbent President George W. Bush would be defeated. Their website contains a brief history of the organization, a list of their success stories, and a discussion of their plans, strategies, current projects, and techniques.

- **Bob Dole's fall from a stage during the 1996 presidential election**
  See: Robert Moran, "Falling Down: Not All Spills Are Equal at the Washington Post," available online at National Review Online: http://www.nationalreview.com/comment/moran200403200946.asp. In addition, see: Donna Hale and Janet Church, "Helping Hands: News Photographer's Save of Dole in Continuing Tradition," *News Photographer* 51(12) (December 1996). For a good overview of concerns about Dole's age, see: Herbert L. Abrams and Richard Brody, "Bob Dole's Age and Health in the 1996 Election: Did the Media Let Us Down?" *Political Science Quarterly* 113(3) (Fall 1998).

- **1994 Health care debate**
  Issue ads produced by the Health Insurance Association of America (HIAA) featuring a fictional husband-and-wife couple ("Harry and Louise") were among the first issue-based ads to appear outside the context of an election. See, for example: Darrell M. West, Diane Heith, and Chris Goodwin, "Harry and Louise Go to Washington: Political Advertising and Health Care Reform," *Journal of Health, Politics, Policy and Law*, 21(1) (Spring 1996).

- **1988 Democratic primary/Gary Hart sex scandal**
  See: John B. Judis, "The Gary Hart Affair: The Media's Role," *Current* (297) (November 1987). See also: "Gary Hart's Dare: Media Stake Out Rendezvous with Model; Sex Lives of Politicians Become Popular News Subjects," *Columbia Journalism Review* 40 (November-December 2001), 4.

CHAPTER 9

CASE FIVE: THE 2006 MIDTERM ELECTIONS

THE CASE

The media try to turn any election into a big story, but, with regard to the 2006 congressional midterm election, the media may have been right about how big the story was. Because of the election's results, control of the U.S. House of Representatives shifted from control by the Republican Party to Democratic control. That was an accomplishment, but one that many political pundits thought attainable. The election, however, also shifted control of the U.S. Senate. That task was thought to be quite difficult to accomplish.

In the language of billiards, the Democrats would have to "run the table" on election night in order to regain the Senate. They would have to retain two highly contested seats in Maryland and New Jersey, and then they would have to capture six of seven seats held by the GOP: Missouri, Montana, Ohio, Pennsylvania, Rhode Island, Tennessee, and Virginia; Democrats won all but one of these races as well as held onto the Maryland and New Jersey seats.

This chapter focuses on the Senate races in these nine states. In the remainder of the chapter, we highlight the major issues involved in each state's Senate race and then offer an analysis of the 2006 midterm election.

Maryland

The retirement of senior Senator Paul Sarbanes (D) made the Maryland Senate race an open-seat election. Such elections are often hotly contested, and this was especially true within the Democratic Party. The Democratic primary featured long-term Congressman Ben Cardin against former NAACP official (and former Maryland Congressman) Kweisi Mfume. Cardin won, leaving some African American Democrats displeased. The Republicans quickly settled on incumbent Lieutenant Governor Michael Steele, an African American, as their candidate.

Maryland is a fairly reliable "blue" state; therefore, one would expect Cardin to be the favorite. He was, but Steele made the race close. Using highly stylized campaign advertisements, Steele positioned himself as a reformer. He did not identify himself as a Republican, and he publicly criticized both parties. He also did not specify where he stood on major issues. Nonetheless, the ads captured voters' attention. The fact that Steele was African American also captured attention. Maryland Democratic Party officials worried that Steele would make significant inroads into the traditionally heavy Democratic vote among the state's African American voters.

The Cardin camp responded, first by associating Steele with President George W. Bush and second by identifying Steele's conservative positions on several policy matters. During their debates, including one televised nationally on NBC's *Meet the Press*, Cardin stressed the Steele-Bush link and pressed Steele for his positions on policy issues.

The text of a late Cardin ad ("Straight") illustrates well the Cardin strategy:

Narrator: The truth about Michael Steele? Check the facts:

Recruited by Bush and Cheney. Taken six million in special interest money. Supports Bush's plan to privatize social security and Bush's war in Iraq. Now Steele wants you to believe he'll follow his own convictions. The truth?

Steele: (clip from RNC convention speech) The standard bearer of these convictions is George W. Bush.

Narrator: Michael Steele: Right for Bush. Wrong for Maryland.

Cardin: I'm Ben Cardin, and I approve this message.

Very late in the campaign, the Steele campaign issued controversial fliers and sample ballots. The fliers implied that three prominent African American Democrats supported Steele and Republican Governor Robert Ehrlich. In truth, only one of the pictured Democrats had endorsed Steele, and none had endorsed Ehrlich. The sample ballots were labeled "Democratic" ballots, but had Steele and Ehrlich listed, not Cardin and Baltimore Mayor Martin O'Malley, the Democratic candidate for governor. These fliers and ballots were targeted at African American precincts in Prince George's County and distributed by homeless people the Steele campaign had bused in from Philadelphia. Despite these efforts, however, on Election Day Cardin, the Democrat, was victorious.

Missouri

Missouri is frequently a "battleground" state that pits the more urban areas of the state (Democratic) against the more rural segments (Republican). A blue-and-red map of the state would in many ways mirror that of the nation as a whole. This urban-rural split showed up in the race between incumbent Republican Senator Jim Talent and his Democratic challenger, Attorney General Claire McCaskill. In fact, while McCaskill won, it was late returns from the St. Louis metropolitan area that sealed her victory.

One issue that played a major role in the campaign was stem cell research. Talent had taken a very conservative position on the issue. McCaskill's view was quite opposite. Thus, her campaign attracted the attention of those at the national level who were concerned about this issue. Actor Michael J. Fox, who has Parkinson's disease, was featured in one of her campaign ads that focused on this issue. In this ad, versions of which Fox prepared for other candidates such as Maryland's Cardin and Jim Doyle in Wisconsin's gubernatorial race, Fox's Parkinson's symptoms are quite pronounced—so pronounced that conservative commentator Rush Limbaugh accused Fox of faking extreme symptoms for political effect.[1] The following is the text of Fox's ad:

> As you might know, I care deeply about stem cell research. In Missouri you can elect Claire McCaskill, who shares my hope for cures. Unfortunately, Senator Jim Talent opposes expanding stem cell research. Senator Talent even wanted to criminalize the science that gives us a chance for hope. They say all politics is local, but that's not always the case. What you do in Missouri matters to millions of Americans. Americans like me.

Montana

Montana has lately been very, very red, as has the rest of the West. Thus, incumbent Republican Senator Conrad Burns was the presumed the favorite for reelection. Burns, unfortunately, became entangled in the scandal involving Jack Abramoff. Abramoff was a lobbyist who pled guilty to defrauding American Indian tribes and corruption of public officials in January 2006. Allegations of his influence peddling connected him to Conrad Burns, who oversaw the budget for the Bureau of Indian Affairs. Questions arose when Burns pushed for a $3 million grant to go to one of the richest tribes in the United States (who had hired Abramoff for representation in Washington, DC), when the program was designed to help support poor Indian tribal schools.[2] Burns received $150,000 in campaign contributions from Abramoff and his clients, and then gave it away when the allegations against Abramoff arose.[3]

Burns' connections to Abramoff weakened Burns' chances for reelection and prompted a challenge by Jon Tester, a former farmer and popular president of the Montana Senate. Tester's popularity is at least partially the result of an outgoing personality that makes him a dynamic campaigner on the stump. Burns, by contrast, is not especially dynamic.

In other parts of the country, Republicans were running away from President George W. Bush. Presidential coattails are often desirable for state-level officials, but declining public support for the president resulted in less desirability for that association in 2006. The decline in public support for George W. Bush was a result of growing public sentiment against the continued involvement of U.S. military in Iraq and President Bush's plan to continue a military presence in the region. Many candidates, therefore, did not want Bush campaigning on their behalf and distanced themselves even further from the president. Burns, however, invited George W. Bush to Montana

[1]Limbaugh's comments regarding Fox were aired on his syndicated radio program on October 23, 2006.

[2]Susan Schmidt, "Tribal Grant Is Being Questioned," *Washington Post*, March 1, 2005, A3.

[3]Karen Tumulty, "The Man Who Bought Washington," *Time Magazine* (January 16, 2006): 30–1.

and had the embattled president speak on his behalf at selected campaign stops, sites in Montana thought to be very "red."

Bush's words on Burns' behalf (quoted below from his rally in Billings) prompted some pro-Republican votes. However, they were not enough. Tester won in a very close race.

> **The President:**   On all these vital measures—measures necessary to fight and win the war on terror —the Democrats in Washington have followed a simple philosophy: Just say no. When it comes to listening on to the terrorist —listening to the terrorists, what's the Democrats' answer? Just say no. When it comes to detaining terrorists, what's the Democrats' answer?
>
> **Audience:**   Just say no.
>
> **The President:**   When it came time to renew the Patriot Act, what was the Democrats' answer?
>
> **Audience:**   Just say no.
>
> **The President:**   When it comes time to questioning the terrorists, what's the Democrats' answer?
>
> **Audience:**   Just say no.
>
> **The President:**   So, when the Democrats ask for your vote on November the 7th, what's your answer?
>
> **Audience:**   No! (*Applause.*)
>
> **The President:**   We are on the offense against the enemy wherever we can find them. One of the important lessons of September the 11th, in this new kind of war, America must take threats seriously before they come to the homeland. It's important for the people of this state to understand that lesson. In other words, when we see a threat we just can no longer hope that oceans will protect us. We can no longer hope for the best, that in order to protect you, we must be on the offense.

New Jersey

Senator Robert Menendez had been appointed to his seat by Democratic Governor Jon Corzine when Corzine moved from the Senate to the governor's mansion. Thought by his party to be highly competent, Menendez was known to be an uninspiring campaigner. His opponent was Tom Kean, Jr., the son of popular former Republican Governor Thomas H. Kean, and a more dynamic candidate.

Menendez added some style to his campaign by bringing in several Democratic Party "stars" to speak on behalf of his campaign. Here are some snippets from what they said on Menendez's behalf:

> **Massachusetts Senator John Kerry:**   "It is clear that Bob Menendez has been right about the war. He has been courageous about this war. And he

understands the connection of this war to all the other priorities of the State of New Jersey."

Reverend Jesse Jackson: "We've lost too much, we've bled too profusely. Don't miss the moment—Tuesday is your time. It's 'hope' time. It's Bob Menendez time."

Massachusetts Senator Edward Kennedy: "On November 7, the people of New Jersey will send Bob Menendez back to the Senate so that he can continue to stand up to George Bush and fight for a new direction in this country."

On Election Day, Menendez held onto his Senate seat, beating Kean handily, especially in traditional Democratic areas.

Ohio

Incumbent Republican Senator Mike DeWine was certainly not the darling of conservatives within his party after he joined with other Republicans and some Democrats to defuse a potentially explosive confrontation over nominations to the federal judiciary in 2005. Lukewarm GOP support may have hurt DeWine, but the poor state of Ohio's economy under Bush as well as repeated scandals within the Ohio Republican Party probably hurt him more.

The Democrat challenger, Cleveland area Congressman Sherrod Brown, was aided by a populist style that played well with prospective voters. He talked about numerous issues, but he focused a great deal of attention on the economy. When the DeWine-Brown race continued to be close in the final days of the campaign, negative advertising attacks by DeWine were closely followed by a response ad from Brown. The following is the text from both final advertisements:

DEWINE'S AD

Ad text: (*The spot opens with Vicki Almay, a former narcotics agent with the Ohio Bureau of Criminal Identification and Investigation.*)

"You've been hearing about drug allegations in Sherrod Brown's office when he was Ohio's secretary of state. I thought it was important to come forward and to tell you the truth. I was a narcotics officer sent undercover to Brown's office and I made a drug buy from one of Brown's employees.

"Instead of firing her, Sherrod Brown promoted her. And he even gave her a raise. That's the kind of person he is.

"I don't trust Sherrod Brown, and I don't think you should either."

Mike DeWine: "I'm Mike DeWine and I approved this message."

BROWN'S AD

Ad text: (*The spot uses images of Vicki Almay from Sen. Mike DeWine's commercial.*)

Male announcer: "Mike DeWine has reached a new low. Attacking Sherrod Brown about an employee in the secretary of state's office 20 years ago.

"But DeWine's charges are lies. The *Dayton Daily News* said these allegations have been investigated and rejected. They called the attack 'junk.'

"The *Plain Dealer* called it 'pathetic' and said DeWine's attack 'smacked of desperation.' After 12 years in the Senate, doesn't DeWine owe Ohio more than this? Isn't it time for a change?"

Brown: "I'm Sherrod Brown and I approve this message."

Pennsylvania

Incumbent Republican Senator Rick Santorum was a target that Democrats had long had in their sights. He seemed vulnerable in a state that was increasingly voting "blue." And his incendiary conservative rhetoric and his leadership position in the Republican-controlled Senate had made him someone Democrats wanted to "take out." The Democrat chosen to take on Santorum was State Treasurer Robert Casey, Jr., the son of former Democratic Governor Robert Casey.

Casey was not the liberals' darling. He had fairly conservative positions on issues such as reproductive rights. His "moderation," however, made him attractive to a larger number of voters than a liberal Democrat would have been. He was acceptable to the Democratic Party because he could help it accomplish the ultimate goal: retaking the Senate. Although he was not known for being especially dynamic, he was very likeable. In addition, his laid-back style contrasted with Santorum's intensity. Casey's victory over Santorum was the largest margin of victory for a Democrat running for U.S. Senate in Pennsylvania, with 58.7 percent of the vote to Santorum's 41.3 percent.

One week before Election Day, the *Pittsburgh Post-Gazette* published columns by Casey and Santorum, both of whom had accepted the paper's invitation to set out their top three priorities if they were elected. In his statement, Santorum does not acknowledge his opponent whatsoever; in Casey's statement, he offers three priorities if elected but also three attacks against Santorum. The following are excerpts from the beginning of both candidates' columns:

Rick Santorum: Nothing is more important to the people of Pennsylvania than their security, whether that be security from violent threats, both foreign and domestic, security from financial troubles or security from volatile energy markets that impact both. And so nothing will receive more of my attention, in the first 100 days next year and beyond, than the physical security, the economic security and the energy security of the people of Pennsylvania.

Bob Casey: There are many important issues facing Pennsylvania and the United States. Three of the top issues include the following: Moving the focus away from the special interests and the wealthiest Americans and toward Pennsylvania and working families. Making our country more secure. And reducing the partisanship and corruption in Washington. Over the course of this campaign I have outlined the many differences between myself and Rick Santorum. And I have put specific plans on the table to combat global warming, bolster homeland security and slash corporate welfare.[4]

---

[4]Both columns were published by the *Pittsburgh Post-Gazette* (October 29, 2006), p. H-1.

Rhode Island

Rhode Island's incumbent Republican Senator Lincoln Chafee was even less popular with the GOP than Ohio's DeWine. Chafee had disagreed so often with President Bush that his voting record was arguably more Democratic than that of many Democrats. Many political pundits even speculated that after his election to the Senate in 2000, Chafee would announce he was switching parties and become a Democrat. Chafee's narrow victory in the Republican primary was the first sign that his reelection would be a struggle.

Chafee's challenger, state Attorney General Sheldon Whitehouse, focused his campaign on the need to send a Democrat to the Senate, not on any faults that Chafee might have had. The following text from Whitehouse's "Real Solutions" ad is typical of the appeals his campaign made to Democratic voters in the state:

> **Announcer:** "In Washington, we have a president and a Republican Congress that have failed our families and our nation. This year, we can change that. Sheldon Whitehouse will be a senator who will work with Jack Reed [Rhode Island's senior senator] for real solutions to the toughest problems facing our families, our seniors and our kids. For our seniors, fixing the new Medicare prescription drug plan so it helps people, not the big drug companies. For our families, a full-scale investigation into price gouging at the pump and a commitment to making America energy independent of foreign oil. For our kids, a doubling of Pell Grants for college. For our future, repealing the Bush tax cuts for the rich and putting Medicare and Social Security back on solid ground. For our national interest, our troops out of Iraq this year. Real solutions to real problems. Sheldon Whitehouse. Finally, a Whitehouse in Washington you can trust."

Tennessee

Tennessee had a rare open seat for the Senate when Republican Senator and Senate Majority Leader Bill Frist retired after two terms. The race to replace him saw two highly capable campaigners, Republican Chattanooga Mayor Bob Corker and Democratic Congressman Harold Ford, Jr., run spirited campaigns. For the most part, both campaigns stuck to the issues but media commentators noted that there were not striking differences between the candidates on the issues. Thus, the candidates needed to find other ways to distinguish themselves, and each did so at least once. One departure that benefited Corker was a campaign ad; Ford departed from issues-based campaigning when he crashed a Corker public appearance.

The controversial ad, sponsored by the Republican National Committee and not by Corker himself, was quickly removed from the air after it was criticized by the NAACP for sexual innuendo "that plays to pre-existing prejudices about African American men and white women"[5] Corker attempted to distance himself from the

---

[5]Beth Rucker, "Critics Say Republican Ad Uses Racial Code to Criticize Ford," *Associated Press*, October 25, 2006.

WAL-MART'S CHINA POLICY BOTOX CONFESSIONS

Newsweek

NOT YOUR DADDY'S DEMOCRATS

CAMPAIGN 2006

HUNGRY TO TAKE BACK
CONGRESS, MODERATES LIKE
HAROLD FORD JR. HAVE
THE GOP RUNNING SCARED.
WOULD A DEMOCRATIC
MAJORITY GO WILD, OR
GOVERN FROM THE MIDDLE?

By Jonathan Darman

Ford, the Democratic nominee for the Senate from Tennessee.

Harold Ford, Jr. appears on a Newsweek cover profiling Senate races of 2006.

RNC ad, saying it was "tacky, over the top and is not reflective of the kind of campaign we are running." The following is the description of the ad from an editorial in the *Chattanooga Times Free Press*:

> The ad features a bare-shouldered blonde woman who coyly says she met "Harold at the Playboy party last year." Other actors in the ad pose for man-on-the-street style interviews that sarcastically trade on distortions and lies about Rep. Ford's voting record on hot-button issues. Then the blonde returns to close the ad with a suggestive wink and a 'Harold, call me' come-on. The reference to a Playboy party refers to Mr. Ford's invitation to a 2005 Super Bowl party sponsored by Playboy magazine.[6]

The confrontation between Corker and Ford occurred in a parking lot as Bob Corker was about to head inside for a press conference on lobbying reform and ethics. Harold Ford and his campaign bus arrived at the location, with news cameras rolling, and shouted, "It's good to see you" as Corker approached, followed by, "I'd love to debate you on this Iraq thing." Corker responded, "I came to talk about ethics and I have a press conference. And I think it's a true sign of desperation that you

---

[6]"Republicans Still Run Dirty Ad," *Chattanooga Times Free Press* (October 28, 2006): B6.

would pull your bus up when I'm having a press conference," to which Ford replied, "I can never find you."[7]

Up until the end, the race seemed too close to call. In the end, Corker won by a surprisingly comfortable margin. It was the only election of the nine chronicled in this chapter that the candidate from the Republican Party won.

Virginia

Early public opinion polls in Virginia had incumbent Republican Senator George Allen easily defeating his Democratic challenger, former Secretary of the Navy (under Ronald Reagan) James Webb. Webb had been a Republican, but, propelled by his opposition to the war in Iraq, he became a Democrat, although his positions on some social issues seemed more attuned to the GOP than the Democrats. Like Casey in Pennsylvania, he was a moderate or conservative Democrat and, thus, more likely to be elected in Virginia than a liberal would be.

Webb campaigned using a mixture of positive and negative messages. The negative ones stressed the extent to which Allen had stood by George W. Bush: voters were repeatedly told that Allen voted with Bush 96 percent of the time. As the gap between the candidates narrowed, the Allen campaign turned unremittingly negative. Statements that Webb had made decades earlier on women in the military were held against him, as were allegedly steamy sex scenes and explicit language in his novels.

The Allen campaign looked into Webb's past. Allen's past also came into play. News stories reminded voters that Allen had once displayed the Confederate flag in his law office and told voters that, while a student at the University of Virginia, Allen had used the "n-word" and had once stuffed a severed deer head in an African American family's mailbox.

The event that arguably hurt Allen the most was not in the past. It occurred at a mid-August rally in rural southwestern Virginia. From the stage, he singled out a Webb supporter of Indian descent who had been following the Allen entourage and filming the appearances for the Webb campaign. S. R. Sidarth recorded Allen saying the following to him at a late summer rally:

> "This fellow over here with the yellow shirt—Macaca or whatever his name is—he's with my opponent. He's following us around everywhere. . . . Let's give a welcome to Macaca here. Welcome to America and the real world of Virginia."

The national media attention to this gaffe, as well as Allen's delay in an apology for his remarks, hurt Allen not only in his reelection bid in 2006. Pundits suggested this error may have also removed him from being a contender for the Republican nomination for president in 2008, which before his 2006 reelection attempt, Allen had indicated he would seek.

---

[7]Bartholomew Sullivan, "Ford Crashes Corker News Conference," *The Commercial Appeal* (October 21, 2006): A1.

Jim Webb greets his supporters at a victory celebration after his 2006 victory over Senator George Allen in Virginia.

THE POLITICAL SCIENCE PERSPECTIVE

If, as political scientists Robert Erikson and Gerald Wright have noted,[8] "House elections provide a regular biennial measure of the electoral pulse of the nation," then the electorate's pulse was racing in 2006. Not only did the Democratic Party pick up nearly 30 seats and take control of the U.S. House of Representatives, but the party picked up six seats in the United States Senate—enough to recapture that chamber from the Republican Party as well. And, within the states, Democrats picked up six governorships. As the November 7, 2006, election results demonstrated, the Republican Party did not take a single seat in any statewide or congressional election away from a Democrat in 2006.

Almost as soon as the polls closed and Democratic control of the House and Senate seemed assured, political pundits and politicians were calling election 2006 a "repudiation" of President George W. Bush's policies, especially with regard to the war in Iraq. To be sure, there is likely some truth to that statement, as in numerous races—most notably, perhaps, in the race for Virginia's Senate seat—the Iraq war was

[8]Robert S. Erikson and Gerald C. Wright "Voters, Candidates, and Issues in Congressional Elections." In Lawrence C. Dodd and Bruce I. Oppenheimer, eds., *Congress Reconsidered*, 7th edition (Washington, DC: Congressional Quarterly, 2001), 67.

a major issue during the campaign. But, understanding what happened in the 2006 congressional midterm election requires as much understanding of midterm elections generally as it requires knowledge of the specific issues confronting candidates in 2006. The remainder of this section addresses both the general and specific issues affecting congressional elections, to offer some context for the 2006 election results.

Congressional Midterm Elections

People who are unfamiliar with the literature on congressional elections might wonder how Larry J. Sabato and David Wasserman of the University of Virginia's Center for Politics were able to predict on November 2, 2006—*five days before* the 2006 congressional midterm election—that the Democrats would pick up six seats in the U.S. Senate and twenty-seven seats in the U.S. House of Representatives, giving the party control of both houses of Congress for the first time in 12 years. Although Sabato and Wasserman were off by two seats in the House, their predictions were uncannily accurate.

The ability of political scientists to predict the outcome of congressional elections with a good degree of accuracy results from the careful analysis of decades of midterm election results in combination with detailed information about electoral conditions at the time of an election. Pundits and prognosticators rely on the surfeit of public opinion polls taken on a near-daily basis in the weeks leading up to the election to make predictions about the outcome. As the science of polling has increasingly become better able to predict outcomes within a small margin of error (usually ±3 percent), polls have become an important component of the analysis undergirding experts' predictive models.

One thing that helps political scientists with making predictions, however, is the small number of congressional races that are actually competitive. Taking all factors into consideration, the number of competitive races for the House of Representatives is now roughly 5 percent of the total number of House seats, or about 22, in an average election.[9] The proportion is frequently greater in Senate elections, although the number remains small because of the small number of senators who are up for reelection in any given election (at most, 34). These small numbers of seats include those that are open (whether or not they are contested) and those in which an incumbent is vulnerable due to scandal; examples of the latter include Mark Foley in 2006, who was forced to resign from Congress when it was revealed that he had engaged in inappropriate e-mail and Instant Messenger exchanges with congressional pages, and Gary Condit, who lost his bid for reelection in 2002 in the wake of the investigation of the disappearance of Chandra Levy, during which it was revealed that Condit was having a relationship with the young woman.

When a seat is contested, the extensive literature on congressional elections has led scholars to conclude that congressional election results generally are a function of several factors: the number of incumbents running for reelection/the number of open seats, the partisan balance between the White House and Congress, campaign

---

[9]See David W. Brady and Jeremy C. Pope, "Congress: Still in the Balance? How Congress May Look after the Election," *Hoover Digest* (Stanford, CA: Hoover Institution Press, 2004).

finance laws and practices, and the strength and cohesion of the national political parties. Midterm elections also often channel public disaffection with the sitting president. With the exceptions of 1934 and 1998, the party in control of the White House has lost seats in every single congressional midterm election since 1900. Generally speaking, the extent to which the party in the White House loses seats in any given midterm election depends not only on the public's animosity toward the incumbent president, but also on the way that the other factors listed above converge. As political commentator Jay Cost has noted on the Real Clear Politics blog: "Our House elections are not referenda [on the President] strictly speaking. They are qualified referenda—the qualifications are (a) good recruitment, (b) good fundraising and (c) good campaigns."[10]

Candidate Recruitment. Finding candidates willing to stand for election is the most important factor in congressional elections. Nationwide in 2006, roughly 30 percent of elections (some 6,100 candidates) for state legislatures and the U.S. Congress featured candidates running unopposed.[11] There are a variety of reasons why elections at all levels in the United States feature candidates running unopposed, but one of the biggest—especially with regard to congressional elections—is that running against an incumbent is virtually always a losing proposition.

As Table 9.1 demonstrates, congressional incumbents win the vast majority of contests in which they compete. This is because they almost always are better funded than their challengers and because they already have a connection with the constituency whose votes they are seeking. Moreover, the perquisites of office to which they already have access—regular contact with constituents, staff to assist with constituency service, the ability to send mail to the district free of charge, contacts with interest group and political action committee (PAC) leaders, among others—serve as often insurmountable hurdles for challengers. It is for these reasons that political scientist David Canon has noted that only certain types of challengers—"actors, athletes, and astronauts"—with extensive name recognition and the ability to raise significant amounts of money are able to compete in most contested elections in which an incumbent is in the race.[12]

Candidate Fund-Raising. The ability to raise money is crucial to waging a competitive campaign for Congress. It is not unusual for candidates for the House of Representatives to spend a million dollars or more on their campaigns,

---

[10]See: Jay Cost, "Why I Jumped The Shark," posted on Real Clear Politics (November 8, 2006). Available online at http://time-blog.com/real_clear_politics/2006/11/index.html. The Real Clear Politics blog searches the web for online content from media sources and makes it available, along with staff commentary, to the public. It is a clearinghouse of political commentary and is read by or contributed to by a large number of respected print and electronic journalists.

[11]See Associated Press, "Incumbency Level Running High: While There Are Some Races to Watch in the National Picture, There are More Incumbents Than in Past Years" (October 28, 2006).

[12]See David T. Canon, *Actors, Athletes, and Astronauts: Political Amateurs in the United States Congress* (Chicago: University of Chicago Press, 1990.).

TABLE 9.1 Incumbency Rates, U.S. Congress 1984-2004

YEAR	HOUSE OF REPRESENTATIVES	UNITED STATES SENATE
2004	98%	96%
2002	96%	86%
2000	98%	79%
1998	98%	90%
1996	94%	91%
1994	90%	92%
1992	88%	83%
1990	96%	96%
1988	98%	85%
1986	98%	75%
1984	95%	90%

Source: The Center for Responsive Politics. See http://www.opensecrets.org/bigpicture/ reelect.asp?Cycle=2004&chamb=S and http://www.opensecrets.org/bigpicture/reelect.asp? Cycle=2004&chamb=H. Last accessed January 5, 2007.

and U.S. Senate candidates will often spend ten or more times that amount to seek election or reelection. Given these large sums of money, candidates who are independently wealthy or who are able to raise large sums of money from private donations or contributions from PACs or the political parties will have a significant advantage over those who are unable to do so. As noted earlier, incumbents frequently are able to raise money because of the greater number of connections they are likely to have with constituents, PACs, and party leaders who can assist them.

What does all of this money buy? Much of the money goes into paying the high cost of television advertising, especially in Senate races with multiple media markets. Other significant costs of campaigning include paying campaign staff members' salaries, paying for nontelevision ads (e.g., placards, yard signs, buttons, stickers, banners), and covering the costs of campaign-related travel across a district or state. Of course, the larger the geographic size of a state or district, the greater the costs of campaigning.

As electronic media have dominated campaigns in recent decades, the cost of campaigning has increased. A 2005 report in the *Washington Post* indicates that there has also been a concomitant increase in the proportion of individuals who claim that money now has too much influence in politics, with sizable majorities of Americans polled expressing concern about both political parties' fund-raising efforts.[13]

[13]See Jeffrey H. Birnbaum, "A Growing Wariness about Money in Politics," *Washington Post* (November 29, 2005), A1.

Common Cause, a public interest group that has been active for more than three decades in the push for public financing of elections, sums up these concerns this way:

> The dominating influence of wealthy special interests in the funding of campaigns has eroded public trust in our political system and discouraged political participation. In a system that gives undue access to lawmakers and influence on legislation to those who contribute large amounts to campaigns, most citizens believe their voice is not being heard.[14]

However, efforts to limit the influence of money in politics have generally stalled or been rather narrowly tailored, largely because of the U.S. Supreme Court's decision in *Buckley v. Valeo* (1976), in which the Court restricted the ability of Congress to put limits on campaign expenditures, reasoning that when it comes to supporting a candidate, restricting money spent is equivalent to restricting the ability of individuals (or candidates themselves) to advocate for a particular candidate. This gave fairly broad First Amendment protection to campaign expenditures.

Good Campaigns. It is somewhat difficult to distinguish a "good" campaign from a "bad" campaign, but in general a good campaign is one in which a candidate runs the campaign free from gaffes or scandal, the candidate (or his or her staff) does not mischaracterize the candidate's qualifications or record, and the candidate takes advantage of broader political forces to shore up local support and conserve resources.

An example of this latter characteristic of a good campaign was the "nationalized" congressional midterm election of 1994. As political scientist Thomas Little has explained, in 1994 the Republican Party for the first time nationalized not only the congressional midterm election but also the coincident state and local elections by encouraging candidates at all levels to sign on to modified versions of the party's national "Contract With America." This "Contract" was a list of specific legislative proposals and philosophical principles that signatory congressional incumbents and challengers agreed to promote if elected. Little explains:

> In 1994, the Republican National Committee (RNC) encouraged and coordinated the adoption of a basic set of issues by Republican candidates at all levels of government. They put in place an organization dedicated to encouraging the development of state specific electoral contracts that would reflect the conservative themes of opportunity, responsibility, and accountability.[15]

The result of this nationalized strategy in 1994 was that the Republican party not only recaptured majority status in the U.S. House of Representatives for the first

---

[14]See http://www.commoncause.org/site/pp.asp?c=dkLNK1MQIwG&b=191979 (accessed January 5, 2007).

[15]See Thomas H. Little, "On the Coattails of a Contract: RNC Activities and Republican Gains in the 1994 State Legislative Elections," *Political Research Quarterly* (Salt Lake City, UT: University of Utah Press, 1998), 178.

time in more than 40 years, but that it also was able to take control of several state legislatures and governorships. By virtually any account, the 1994 congressional midterm elections were an example of a good campaign.

The 2006 Midterm Election

Taking all of this into consideration, what lessons can be drawn about the 2006 elections? First, as the previous section has explained, the fact that the Republican Party lost seats in 2006 is hardly a surprise. In fact, Erikson and Wright note that since 1946, "each party has enjoyed an increase of about thirty-five more House seats when it did *not* control the presidency."[16] With that in mind, the twenty-nine House seats picked up by the Democrats in 2006 is actually slightly below the average gain for the party out of power at the time of the midterm election. Although Senate elections are more volatile, the Senate switched from Republican to Democratic control after the 1986 midterm election, during Republican Ronald Reagan's presidency, and then switched from Democratic control to Republican control in 1995, following the 1994 midterm election, when Democrat Bill Clinton occupied the White House.

Next, 2006 highlights the consequences of a lack of electoral competitiveness within and across congressional elections. That is, because many House and Senate incumbents were running unopposed, or were opposed by challengers who were underfunded or were just plain underqualified, the outcomes of many of the races were foregone conclusions not only before the polls closed, but even before they *opened*. As Jay Cost noted on the Real Clear Politics blog:

> If [midterm elections] were true referenda, the GOP would have lost many more seats than they actually did [in 2006]. Fortunately for them, most voters did not get a true choice [on election day] because their Democratic challengers were under-funded and under-qualified relative to their incumbents. The incumbents who lost were the incumbents who either faced strong challenges or who themselves ran very weak campaigns. Indeed, by my count—there were only 3 Republican incumbents who ran essentially flawless campaigns and nevertheless lost: Nancy Johnson, Mike Sodrel, and Clay Shaw. Mike Fitzpatrick and Rob Simmons both appear headed for losses, so I would add them to the list. The rest of the Democratic pickups, 83.33% in all, were pickups in either (a) open seats, (b) seats held by scandal-ridden incumbents or (c) seats held by ineffective campaigners. Thus, Republican mistakes, specifically campaign-related mistakes, very clearly were a major factor in the loss of the House.[17]

Relatedly, 2006—and especially the Senate races highlighted in the case that introduces this chapter—reveals the phenomenal sums of money that are now

[16]Robert S. Erikson and Gerald C. Wright, "Voters, Candidates, and Issues in Congressional Elections." In Lawrence C. Dodd and Bruce I. Oppenheimer, eds. *Congress Reconsidered*, 7th ed.. (Washington, DC: Congressional Quarterly, 2001), 72.

[17]Jay Cost, "Why I Jumped the Shark." Posted on Real Clear Politics (November 8, 2006). Available online at http://time-blog.com/real_clear_politics/2006/11/index. html.

involved in running for Congress. According to Federal Election Committee data posted on the Center for Responsive Politics' website (www.opensecrets.org), the Pennsylvania, Connecticut, Missouri, Tennessee, Ohio, and Virginia Senate races were among the ten most expensive races of 2006. In those six races alone, more than *$2 billion* was spent by the candidates; that sum would be much greater if it included the independent expenditures made on behalf of the candidates by PACs and other interested parties.[18] The average expenditure by a candidate for Senate in 2006 was $3.2 million, and the average House candidate spent $629,000 and change. Other data available from the Center for Responsive Politics makes it clear that the incumbency advantage in fund-raising is roughly 11 to 1 in the Senate and nearly 5 to 1 in the House.[19]

Conclusion

Given all of this information, what should be made of the media claims—cited frequently throughout the immediate coverage of the election's aftermath—that the election was a referendum on the Bush presidency, on the Iraq war, and on economic issues such as high gasoline prices? There is likely some truth to these assessments; after all, the Democrats were "on message" nationally about these issues, and polls taken across the country demonstrated that Americans were generally concerned about the lingering conflict in Iraq and the state of the national economy. Certainly, as the example of the Republican "Contract With America" demonstrates, when the party that is out of power nationalizes a congressional midterm and when its candidates emphasize common themes throughout their campaigns, there does seem to be some positive impact on Election Day.

Nevertheless, although Real Clear Politics' Jay Cost's comments were specific to the 2006 congressional midterm election, his point can be applied to virtually any contemporary congressional midterm: midterm elections cannot be assumed to be full referenda on presidential performance. Indeed, as the case study at the outset of this chapter demonstrates, although some candidates (most notably Michael Steele in Maryland and Conrad Burns in Montana) lost in large part because of voters' frustration with President Bush and the policies of his administration, Bush was not the singular factor in determining the outcome of the 2006 midterm elections. Harold Ford lost in Tennessee because of a provocative television ad, Lincoln Chafee lost because Democratic voters who had previously voted for him recognized that control of the Senate hung in the balance, and George Allen lost because his verbal gaffes and missteps were too frequent—and too disturbing—for voters to overlook. The bottom line is that no matter how much a party seeks to nationalize (for good or for ill) current political conditions, the idiosyncrasies of the 435 congressional districts and 33 states

---

[18]A list of the most expensive races of 2006 can be found on the Center for Responsive Politics' website at: http://www.opensecrets.org/overview/topraces.asp?cycle=2006 (Accessed January 5, 2007).

[19]See http://www.opensecrets.org/overview/incumbs.asp?cycle=2006 (Accessed January 5, 2007).

with candidates seeking election are too great to credit to any one factor—even one as important as the president—with full responsibility for the election results.

THE RHETORICAL PERSPECTIVE

Candidates for public office of course make arguments. The media they use largely determine how full the arguments are. But whether the medium is the stump speech, the pamphlet, or the 30-second television spot, the arguments will of necessity be abbreviated.

Enthymemes

In Classical terms, the candidates will be offering enthymemes, which by definition require audience participation. Enthymemes, as explained in Chapter 3, are abbreviated arguments. The audience is invited to complete them. If the audience accepts the invitation, the audience becomes a co-creator of the arguments, making them—arguably—more compelling.[20] If the audience does not accept the invitation, the audience may, unwittingly, end up accepting an ill-formed argument as embodying some kind of truth about the candidates. As Kathleen Hall Jamieson has noted in *Dirty Politics*, negative ads heavily use just such ill-formed enthymemes.[21]

The spot that actor Michael J. Fox filmed for candidates who favored stem cell research offers a rather complete enthymeme. He argues that stem cell research can be beneficial and that listeners should support a given candidate (Claire McCaskill in Missouri, Ben Cardin in Maryland) because she or he supports this beneficial research. The candidate is associated with a positively viewed idea; a cause-effect prediction is implied: if you elect McCaskill or Cardin, then she or he will vote for such research. The ad's appeal was considerably enhanced by the emotional appeal Fox made through both his words and the visual picture he, a sufferer of Parkinson's disease, offered by exhibiting many of that malady's symptoms. The ad had what Perelman has termed "presence." That the Michael J. Fox ad worked better in Missouri than in Maryland is perhaps explained by the Classical concept of *kairos*. It was a timely issue in Missouri because the issue was on the ballot there, and, as a result, considerable media attention had been devoted to it.

Other ads used in 2006 were less complete. The negative ad aired against McCaskill associated her with her husband's nursing home enterprise. One property had been the subject of an investigation, and the business had also evidently been quite lucrative. Of course, McCaskill's husband had long since sold the business;

---

[20]See Karlyn Kohrs Campbell and Susan Schultz Huxman, *The Rhetorical Act: Thinking, Speaking, and Writing Critically*, 3rd ed. (Belmont, CA: Thomson Wadsworth, 2003), 100, for a brief discussion of audience participation in enthymemes.

[21]Kathleen Hall Jamieson, *Dirty Politics: Deception, Distraction, and Democracy* (New York: Oxford University Press, 1992), 60–63.

furthermore, the couple were not married at the time he had owned it. So what argument was the ad making? Her husband had been unethical; therefore, she will be? The ad seems to simply associate McCaskill with something "bad" that is tenuously linked to her in hope that the aura of "badness" will envelop her. The ad then seems to assume a less than critical viewer.

The controversial ad that was directed against Tennessee Democrat Harold Ford seems to have assumed a racist viewer. The ad implies that Ford is quite the partygoer. The implication may have been an attempt to reduce his ethos on the character dimension or to suggest that he would be socializing, not legislating, if elected to the Senate. The ad also associates Ford with *Playboy*, since the party in question was hosted by *Playboy* at the 2005 Super Bowl. That association might further reduce Ford's ethos in some eyes. The ad, however, goes farther: it implies past and future sexual liaisons between African American Ford and a sexy white woman. In the American South, the idea of sex between African American men and white women evokes a long, ugly history. African American men who crossed the line established (largely) by white men invited lynching, not election to the U.S. Senate. The ad then may have invited viewers to construct a racist enthymeme which suggested that Ford, given how he was behaving, did not know "his place." The ad was, of course, quickly withdrawn, but, like the famous "Daisy Girl" ad in the 1964 presidential campaign, it received a great deal of coverage in the news.

The ads used in Ohio against Sherrod Brown and in Virginia against Jim Webb are similar to the negative ad against McCaskill discussed earlier: Brown is being linked to something that supposedly happened in his office years earlier; Webb is being linked to both remarks he made about women in the military years earlier and supposedly "steamy" sex scenes in novels he wrote years earlier. The link in these ads, however, is stronger than that in the anti-McCaskill ad because the accusations do involve Brown and Webb. The ads impugn the candidates' ethos on the character dimension. Brown supposedly tolerated—even rewarded—drug activity in the Ohio secretary of state's office; Webb saw women in a sexist light. Audience members were being asked to complete an enthymeme that posited a present-day generalization about the opposed candidates based on events or statements that were in the past. Were the examples sufficient to warrant the jump to the generalization? Does the fact that the examples were dated affect the validity of the jump? Ad makers hope that those in the audience don't ask such simple critical questions.

The ads used against McCaskill, Brown, and Webb all tried to establish a link between something in the past and the opposed candidate. Ads used in Maryland, Virginia, and Rhode Island on behalf of Democratic candidates tried to establish a different kind of link, one between the opposed candidate and an unpopular president. Maryland voters were told that Michael Steele "loves George W. Bush"; Virginia voters were told that George Allen voted with Bush 96 percent of the time. The enthymeme then used a comparison *topos*: the Republican candidate is like Bush; Bush is objectionable; therefore, the Republican candidate is objectionable.

Rhode Island voters had to construct a more complex enthymeme. They had to assume that Republican control of the Senate was the crucial issue and, then, grant that Lincoln Chaffee, although unobjectionable based on his voting record, stood in the way of Democrats wrestling control away. Since the voters held a negative view of Bush, and not necessarily the Republican-controlled Senate, they had to grant that rejecting Republicans in the Senate was, in some way, rejecting Bush. Were they trying to stop pro-Bush Senate votes? Were they trying to send the president a message? In all likelihood, the enthymeme they constructed did not spell out exactly why it was important that Rhode Island replace a liked Republican with Democrat Sheldon Whitehouse.

Associations are created by campaign communication events, not just by advertising. In New Jersey, the numerous Democrats who visited the state and campaigned on Menendez' behalf established an association between themselves and Menendez. Voters again were invited to complete the enthymeme: Menendez is comparable to well-known Democrats; these well-known Democrats are—for whatever reason—good; therefore, Menendez is good. Since voters are being invited to link the favored candidate with the visiting Democrats, campaign advisers need to exercise care in selecting the visiting Democrats. In the 2000 presidential campaign, for example, outgoing President Bill Clinton was an asset in some areas but a liability in others. Democratic candidate Al Gore wanted the association where it might help, but did not want the association where it would hurt his chances. In 2006, most Republicans were therefore choosing not to invite President Bush to campaign on their behalf: he was viewed more often than not as a liability. In Montana, however, Conrad Burns did invite Bush to visit. The Burns campaign assumed that Bush was more of an asset than a liability in typically "red" Montana and wanted voters to associate him with the president and the president's strong responses to global terrorism. Burns' strategy was not necessarily wrong. He lost, but he may have lost more because of the ethos his opponent had and sustained during the campaign.

Ethos

Ethos can be part of the enthymeme an audience is invited to create or partially create. In Montana, Democrat Jon Tester was perceived by voters to be a much more engaging person than Republican Burns. Plus, Burns' ethos was tainted a bit by his involvement with lobbyist Jack Abramoff. Voters—by a narrow margin—may have selected the man they perceived as being more dynamic and having the better character. The dynamism dimension of ethos may also have been a factor in Ohio. Brown was a lively campaigner who communicated the stereotypical populist's energy; DeWine was not as lively. Ethos may also have been the deciding factor in Pennsylvania. Incumbent Republican Rick Santorum was an aggressive advocate of a national conservative agenda; challenging Democrat Robert Casey was a friendly moderate who seemed attuned to the people of Pennsylvania. Voters may have simply liked Casey more, having found his character to consist of qualities such as humility and empathy that they sought in a leader.

In Maryland, ethos could well have gone against the Democratic candidate. Ben Cardin came across as likable but dull, whereas Republican Michael Steele came across as both likable and exciting. Steele's stylish ads played a major role in assist-ing voters in constructing this ethos for him. Another part of that ethos that the ads pushed on voters was his supposed anti-Washington and bipartisan attitudes. He crit-icized the way the people's business was being done in the national capital, and he argued that Democrats *and* Republicans were at fault.

Steele's ethos might well have carried the election if it were not for the campaign's other communication events. First, ads on behalf of Cardin undermined Steele's claims by noting the conservative insiders who were funding his campaign and by connecting Steele with Bush. In a reliably "blue" state, these ads, although not as attention catching as Steele's, were probably enough to neutralize Steele's persona. Second, the Election Day tactics used by Steele's supporters may have produced a backlash against the Republican with the very voters he was targeting. On that day, a flier and a sample ballot were distributed in a heavily African American jurisdic-tion. The one implied endorsements by prominent Democrats that Steele did not have; the other listed Steele (and Republican gubernatorial candidate Robert Ehrlich) as if they were Democrats. If these materials were designed to dupe voters presumed to be uninformed enough to be so misled, then they may have called Steele's charac-ter—and thus his ethos—into question.

Actions That Speak

It is not clear who was responsible for these Election Day materials that may have hurt—not helped—the Steele campaign. It is clear, however, who was responsible for campaign events that seem to have hurt the chances of Harold Ford in Tennessee and George Allen in Virginia. Ford and Allen communicated through their actions messages they did not intend to communicate.

Ford aggressively confronted his opponent in a parking lot, challenging the opponent to debate the campaign's issues with him. His opponent was on his way to a news conference; he, therefore, declined, expressing his indignation at being assaulted en route by Ford. What message did Ford intend his actions to send to vot-ers? He probably wanted them to see him as interested in talking about the issues, especially the war in Iraq, and he probably had no problem with voters seeing him as aggressive. What message did his actions send? They perhaps sent the message that he was *over*aggressive because he was either rude or desperate. The staged confrontation seems to have hurt, not helped, Ford.

Allen singled out a Webb supporter who had been following the Allen entourage and capturing its campaign activities on videotape. The Webb campaign worker, a University of Virginia undergraduate of Indian descent, was performing a common function in political campaigns. Allen pointed to him, referred to him by an arguably derisive and racist name, "Macaca," and welcomed him to the real America of southwestern Virginia as if he were an immigrant and not someone who had been born in the country. The Allen campaign's explanations for the confrontation were unconvincing, and its extensive coverage in the media invited others to come forward with stories from the past that painted Allen as racist. It is difficult to discern what message Allen was attempting to send to voters. Arguably, he was trying to highlight his "true American values," as opposed to those of people such as the young man. Even if such an argument might have been effective in the specific area Allen was speaking in that day, he ought to have been savvy enough to realize that the remark would not be heard just in that area. (And, Allen did not win the jurisdiction in which he made the remark on Election Day.)

Conclusion

Candidates in 2006 offered arguments, usually abbreviated, to convince voters to elect them, as do candidates in general. They offered these arguments in ads, through personal appearances staged on their behalf, through the ethos they projected by the ways they campaigned, and by actions that spoke louder than words. One might step back from the 2000 and 2004 presidential elections and conclude that character matters. And character mattered again in 2006. Voters elected candidates they liked and did not elect candidates they felt were aloof or overaggressive or nasty. But trumping character in 2006 was the anti-Bush sentiment that many Democrats could tap. Not all of the decisive 2006 Senate races were referenda on the Bush presidency, but many of them were. The strong anti-Bush sentiment gave Democrats an enthymeme that was both very easy to use and very evocative.

THE MASS COMMUNICATION PERSPECTIVE

The 2006 Senate races described in this chapter were noteworthy for a number of reasons related to mass media issues. Political advertising spending broke past records, campaign coverage was considerable, and new communication technologies played a new role in how candidates reached voters and in how voters received information regarding the 2006 elections.

Political Advertising Spending

The races profiled here reflect not only elections that contributed toward the change in control of the Senate, but also some of the most expensive races in the country regarding political advertising. A *Media Week* report estimated that $2.1 billion was spent on television advertising in the 2006 midterm elections, compared with $1 billion in 2002.[22] The final two months of the election were the primary source of advertising spending with 76 percent spent in the final 60 days of the campaign. Of that $2.1 billion, $365 million was spent on advertising in U.S. Senate races, compared with $652 million in gubernatorial races, $391 million in U.S. House races, and $302 million for ballot measures.

---

[22]"Political Spending on TV Hits $2.1 Billion," *Media Week* (November 20, 2006): 18.

Early estimates[23] forecasted many of the Senate races profiled here to be the costliest in 2006 in terms of advertising spending: Tennessee, Ohio, Pennsylvania, Maryland, Virginia, and Rhode Island. Many of these were very close races that resulted in an incumbent losing his seat or, in Tennessee, an open seat. New Jersey should be added to that list, as candidates there must advertise on television stations in New York City as well as Philadelphia, two of the most expensive markets in the country.

One factor that boosted the advertising spending of most of these Senate campaigns was support from their respective party campaign committees. For example, in the final weeks of the 2006 Senate race, the Democratic Senatorial Campaign Committee ran $4 million worth of adverting attacking Tom Kean in New Jersey and gave Jim Webb's campaign in Virginia $3.5 million for last-minute advertising.[24] The National Republican Senatorial Committee spent $3.5 million for last-minute ads attacking Bob Menendez in New Jersey and $1.5 million for George Allen's campaign in Virginia. The exception to extensive party financial support was Montana's Senate race; Republicans criticized the National Republican Senatorial Committee after Burns' narrow loss to Tester that the NRSC had aired no advertisements in Montana in September and October of the campaign.[25]

Campaign Coverage

Not only had advertising spending increased in Senate 2006 races, but so had national news coverage, especially of the close races. One study, by the Center for Media and Public Affairs (CMPA), of network news coverage in September 2006 found that coverage had increased substantially over past elections.[26] Broadcast networks aired eighty-three campaign stories in September 2006, compared to twenty during the midterm elections of 2002. CMPA also compared coverage to that in 1994, the "Republican Revolution" midterm election when Republicans took over control of the House and Senate, which resulted in sixty stories in September 1994.

Although this study explores more than just Senate race coverage, what might be some explanations for the growing increase in network news attention toward midterm elections? The closeness of many of these races, as well as the controversial

---

[23]"2006 Candidate Ad Spending up 150 Percent from Last Mid-Terms; Spending Could Surpass Record 2004 Levels." *TNS Media Intelligence* (August 22, 2006).

[24]See Jeffrey Gold, "Sprint to Finish for N.J. Senate Candidates Includes More Ads." *Associated Press* (October 31, 2006); and Annie Gowen, "Political Ad Nauseam: Candidates Blanket the Airwaves Because Such Tactics May Work in Close Races," *Washington Post* (November 4, 2006): B1.

[25]David Epso, "In Wake of Senate Loss, GOP Turns Anger on Campaign Committee," *Associated Press* (December 23, 2006).

[26]Center for Media and Public Affairs (2006, October 18). *Networks Triple Their Mid-Term Coverage.* Report available online at http://www.cmpa.com/documents/06.10.18.Mid-Term.Coverage.pdf

advertising described earlier from some of the campaigns, may explain greater media attention in 2006. The news media's temptation to follow the horse race, who is ahead and who is trailing, feeds many news stories, as does the scrutiny over the contenders in the race, as part of "kingmaking."

Once primary elections for state-level races have concluded, and the field has been narrowed down to the "real" contenders, media attention increases. In close primaries involving incumbents, such as Lincoln Chafee's in Rhode Island, that media attention and scrutiny begin even earlier, questioning a candidate's "electability." The lack of an incumbent candidate, as in Tennessee's open seat race with Bob Corker and Harold Ford, Jr., makes a campaign more intriguing to follow because it lacks the predictability of an incumbent being reelected. The serious challenges (and eventual defeats) that incumbents Conrad Burns in Montana, Jim Talent in Missouri, Mike DeWine in Ohio, Rick Santorum in Pennsylvania, Lincoln Chafee in Rhode Island, and George Allen in Virginia all faced made these races more newsworthy than races in which candidates consistently led challengers by 20 points in the polls.

Because these were midterm elections, there was no presidential election to consume news organizations' attention and resources. But the president is still considered in coverage of such midterm races, in terms of who the president is campaigning on behalf of and what the outcome of the congressional elections might say about public sentiment toward the president. The growing unpopularity of the war in Iraq and declining public opinion about President Bush were both issues in Senate campaign coverage in 2006. Although Bush did campaign on behalf of many candidates and received media coverage for such visits, such as campaigning for Conrad Burns in Montana, news reports also focused on Republican candidates' desire to distance themselves from Bush, given his declining approval ratings and the growing concern over Iraq.

Much campaign coverage, at a national as well as a local level, focuses on campaign strategy and performance. Political debates, as well as political advertising, often merit considerable attention in local news coverage of campaigns. The political advertising examples described earlier in these Senate races also received considerable news attention and analysis. Michael J. Fox's stem cell advertisements, and Rush Limbaugh's comments about them, increased the news attention on the advertisements themselves as well as on the controversy they stirred. Candidate response ads to negative attacks, such as the exchange between DeWine and Brown's ads in Ohio, also merit news attention to the response and therefore the earlier attack.

Many news organizations also conduct "ad watches" or advertising analyses of political ads. In newspapers, they may feature a frame of video from an ad, as well as a summary of the content of the ad, in addition to an analysis of the advertisement's claims. This "truth-testing" seen in the print news coverage also occurs in television news coverage, although it usually provides a short video clip from the ad itself. Early ad watches (from the 1988 "Willie Horton" ad and 1990 campaigns) often provided a free replay of the ad in full followed by an analysis, which even with critique by the news media was still desirable for a campaign, to have their advertisement replayed at no cost during a local news program. Later ad watches, including those in 2006, were more likely to provide only short clips from ads rather than provide a full 30-second replay.

Scandal and controversy explain greater media coverage as well, with more news stories covering George Allen in Virginia after video of his "Macaca" comment and its distribution through the Internet, as well as the scandal involving e-mail messages sent by Congressman Mark Foley to congressional pages. The Mark Foley scandal that arose and led to his resignation in September 2006 was the focus of many of the news stories in the fall of 2006. However, when those are removed from the count, The Center for Media and Public Affairs study reported there were still sixty news stories about the midterm elections on ABC, CBS, and NBC in 1 month fairly early in the election cycle. Most coverage, national or local, does not intensify until after the summer primaries for political office, and Labor Day often marks an unofficial start to news attention toward political campaigns. Although the shift in control of the House and Senate was likely not a serious consideration so early in the 2006 campaign, the coverage was as intense as it had been during the last change of control in Congress back in 1994.

The change of control of Congress, at least in the House, was a primary focus of news coverage on November 8, 2006. An analysis was conducted by the by the Project for Excellence in Journalism of 230 newspaper front pages the day after the 2006 midterm elections.[27] They found that more than half of U.S. newspaper front pages focused on their own local elections, and approximately 25 percent reported some version of the national election headline "Democrats Take House." Although predictions regarding control of the Senate could not be concluded due to close-call races in Montana and Virginia, the possibility of a shift of control in the Senate arose in next-day coverage.

Another study of election coverage suggests the influence new technologies have in the role of news in campaigns and where we as news consumers might go to get information. The Project for Excellence in Journalism assessed the election night coverage of thirty-two news outlets, including websites, blogs, broadcast networks, cable TV, and public radio and concluded that television news websites may have out-performed the others.[28] Their analysis suggests television websites may have been the most successful in election night coverage, in their ability to provide rapid coverage and greater depth of information than television channels could provide. The Project for Excellence in Journalism concludes about television websites, "It may be that they have finally found a platform through which they can deliver the heavy volume of information they had always collected but had never felt they could offer viewers on television" (p. 3). In contrast, blogs about politics were more opinion than

---

[27]Project for Excellence in Journalism, "Post Election Headlines Play It Safe." http://www.journalism.org/node/2861. Accessed Jan. 3, 2007.

[28]Project for Excellence in Journalism, "Election Night 2006: An Evening in the Life of the American Media," http://www.journalism.org/node/3015. Accessed Jan. 3, 2007.

information on election night, and newspaper websites offered some real-time news coverage online that was similar to that of television coverage. Broadcast network TV has reduced its coverage and staff—most election night reporting came directly from the news anchors—but cable news had plenty of hours to fill with live coverage, often with talking head "spin doctors" between election result reports.

A Pew Internet and American Life Project study confirms the growing popularity of online resources as sources of information for potential voters.[29] It reported that the number of Americans who relied on the Internet as a source for political news in 2006 was 15 percent, double the amount who reported relying on the Internet in the last midterm election, in 2002. Not only have online news sources increased in number and improved in quality of original news, they are also growing in audience popularity as reliable sources of information.

Campaigns and Technology

While online news resources grew in popularity during the 2006 elections, political campaigns continued to use online technologies in a variety of ways in their elections in 2006. Given what had recently been considered revolutionary tactics in online campaigns (in particular with Howard Dean in 2004), online fund-raising and campaign blogs, the Senate candidates profiled from 2006 races were technologically attuned.

Campaign e-mail had become conventional for candidates by the 2006 races, offering visitors to their websites an opportunity to sign up to receive candidate e-mails or newsletters. Although some candidates and campaigns communicated with potential voters minimally through such online resources (e.g., Conrad Burns, Tom Kean, Sheldon Whitehouse), others offered regular communication with citizens. The most prolific campaign e-mailers of these 2006 Senate races included Missouri's Jim Talent and Claire McCaskill, Ohio's Mike DeWine, and Maryland's Michael Steele and Ben Cardin. For example, Mike DeWine's campaign regularly sent out to prospective voters (who had signed up to receive e-mail messages via his campaign website) "The Truth Held Hostage" messages attacking Sherrod Brown, "In case you missed it" news events such as endorsements for DeWine, as well as a reminder "countdown" to Election Day. Messages provided through such campaign e-mails may reinforce information posted on campaign websites or through "message of the day" campaign events garnering other media attention, but prospective voters do not need to go out and seek out these messages, because they arrive in e-mail boxes throughout the campaign cycle.

All Senate candidates discussed in the beginning of this chapter had a campaign website, and a number of them featured a blog. Some candidate blogs were little more than online photo albums of events, such as Maryland's Michael Steele

---

[29]Lee Rannie and John Horrigan, "Election 2006 Online." Pew Internet and American Life Project, http://www. pewinternet.org/PPF/r/199/report_display.asp. Accessed Jan. 4, 2007.

or Pennsylvania's Bob Casey. Most campaign blogs are maintained and authored by a campaign staff member, but in some campaigns candidates themselves occasionally post their own comments, as did Missouri's Claire McCaskill, New Jersey's Bob Menendez, Rhode Island's Sheldon Whitehouse, and Virginia's Jim Webb. Three Senate candidate blogs that stand out from the rest in terms of offerings are those of Montana's Jon Tester and Pennsylvania's Rick Santorum and Bob Casey. Tester posted attacks against Burns in his blog, as well as links to campaign-related news stories and even video clips posted on YouTube. Rick Santorum's website featured the "Running with Rick" blog, with many postings authored by Santorum himself, and "Karen's Corner," a blog by his wife that offered photos from many campaign events. Casey's blog featured a "From the Road" photo album from campaign events in addition to "Manager's Memo" (where attacks could be made but not directly by Casey), plus "Santorum Watch," where the opponent's own words and actions were the subject of critique. Campaign websites and campaign blogs are used to attack one's opponent in a less direct way than through a political ad. For example, Virginia's Jim Webb's blog "Born Fighting" was filled more with attacks against George Allen than any other category of information, such as issue explanations by Webb or campaign event announcements or updates after the event.

In addition to the popularity of blogs by campaigns and candidates, contemporary elections are also the fodder for many blogs about campaigns and candidates. In 2006 the Pew Internet and American Life Project estimated that 12 million American adults operate blogs on a variety of subjects on the Internet, and 57 million American adults are blog readers (or 39 percent of the online population).[30] When categorizing blog content, more than one third of bloggers write about their own lives and experiences, followed next by 11 percent of blogs writing primarily about politics. Blogs have become so popular as a source of information and commentary by Internet users that many mainstream media (MSM) organizations have their own bloggers and include them in some broadcast segments of television news as well. Even traditional newspapers have gravitated toward covering blogs that discuss politics, with stories such as "The Blog House: A Worried GOP Attacks the Ailing, Minorities" in the Minneapolis *Star Tribune* on October 28, 2006.

The use of blogs by candidates and campaigns, as well as news organizations, has changed the role of this relatively recent addition to sources of campaign information. Project for Excellence in Journalism director Tom Rosenstiel said the role of blogs has changed, and "Campaigns have taken over the blogs as part of the political operation and that's undermined the notion that blogs are citizen media."[31] Senate campaign websites in 2006 not only provided their own blogs often, but also linked to blogs that discussed their campaigns. For example, the campaign website of Montana's Jon Tester linked to seventeen blogs. Tester spokesman Matt McKenna

[30]Amanda Lenhart and Susannah Fox, "Bloggers: A Portrait of the Internet's New Storytellers," Pew Internet and American Life Project. http://www.pewinternet.org/PPF/r/186/report_display.asp. Accessed Jan. 4, 2007.

[31]Erica Iacono, "Analysis: New Media Tactics Alter Face of Election," *PR Week* (November 6, 2006): 14.

offered their rationale for this as "The Tester campaign understands that blogging is a conversational medium, and so we provide links to other blogs that are talking about the 2006 race in Montana. But we don't monitor what other blogs say. It's simply a resource to point our visitors to other blogs that may be of interest to voters."[32]

We have heard of blogs outside of politics leading to people being fired for posting negative or proprietary information about employers, and the same has occurred in political campaigns. New Jersey's Bob Menendez accused Tom Kean's campaign manager of anonymously posting negative comments about Menendez to a Democratic blog, and Maryland's Ben Cardin fired a staff member for comments she posted on her blog that were racist in nature about the Senate candidates.[33] An example of candidate supporters trying to influence content online to enhance or harm a candidate's reputation took place with the online encyclopedia Wikipedia in 2006. New Jersey's Bob Menendez and Tom Kean, Jr. both had their Wikipedia profiles "vandalized" throughout their campaign that included distorted records, racial slurs, and name-calling. The changes were quickly undone, as Wikipedia is open to editing by any users.[34]

Social networking sites, such as Facebook and MySpace, also evolved as a possible tool in political campaigns in 2006 Senate races. For example, Pennsylvania's Rick Santorum had a Facebook profile, with more than 6,000 users tagging him as the candidate they support and posting supportive messages to him; more than 9,000 users tagged his opponent Bob Casey as their choice.[35] New Jersey's Bob Menendez and Tom Kean, Jr. had Facebook profiles during the 2006 Senate race, as did Missouri's Jim Talent and Claire McCaskill (set up by her supporters). As we saw in the earlier examples of the "dark side" of blogs, social network sites have also faced issues in politics. Fourteen governors reportedly had profiles in MySpace in 2005, but questions arose over the authenticity and accuracy of many of them.[36]

Why are candidates going to MySpace or Facebook? Besides providing information in a format that is appealing to many voters, and in particular to young tech-savvy voters, online networks are used to drive offline activity. For example, a report by the Institute of Politics, Democracy and the Internet (IPDI) suggests that such an online presence works to drive volunteers to events, to radio call-in shows, to blogs about the campaign.[37] They may also encourage citizens to communicate with

---

[32]Melissa Drosjack, "Blogs Offer Arena for Political Attacks," Fox News. http://foxnews.com/story/0.2933.207874.00.html.

[33]Aaron Blake. "Candidates' Staffers Increasingly Caught (Red-Handed) on the Web." *The Hill*, October 5, 2006. http://www.thehill.com/thehill/export/TheHill/News/Campaigns/100506_caught.html.

[34]J. Scott Orr. "Bring Your Own Filter to the Political 'Wild West.'" *Newark Star Ledger*, October 30, 2006.

[35]"Candidates Reach Internet Generation on MySpace, YouTube." November 3, 2006. http://www.playfuls.com/news05005_Candidates_Reach_Internet_Generation_On_MySpace_YouTube.html.

[36]Brady Averil, "Fake MySpace Profiles Pose a Dilemma for Politicians," *Minneapolis Star Tribune* (August 14, 2005): 1B.

[37]Institute of Politics, Democracy, and the Internet, "Person-To-Person-To-Person: Harnessing the Political Power of Online Social Networks and User-Generated Content." http://ipdi.org/uploadedfiles/PtPtP%20ExecSum.pdf. Accessed Jan. 3, 2007.

others online, publish their own blogs, or post videos. The IPDI reports a number of approaches in which online networking leads to offline communities of voters and involvement on behalf of candidates.

The online video website YouTube also grew in popularity in 2006, and it grew in connections to political campaign as well. YouTube had more than 19 million visitors just in the month of August 2006, and although not all were seeing political video clips, plenty of users were. Both Bob Casey and Rick Santorum in Pennsylvania's Senate race posted video and advertisements to YouTube for potential supporters to see. The more noteworthy postings in 2006 politics, however, reflect that "dark side" of the Internet once again. In the "be careful of what you say" category, Montana's Conrad Burns and Virginia's George Allen offer two examples of less than flattering video that became wildly popular online. One was a clip of Conrad Burns nodding off during a meeting on farm policy, with the piece posted and the music "Happy Trails" playing in the background. George Allen's "Macaca" comment, recorded by the college student whom Allen was poking fun at with his statement, was likely the most widely seen "gaffe" of the 2006 Senate races, watched by millions online through YouTube and replayed in news broadcasts accessing the digital video, Allen's off-the-cuff remark would have been quickly ignored had it not been recorded and distributed as it was. John deTar, cofounder of networking and discussion site www.hotsoup.com, said about such news events going online: "Used to be, it'd be on the nightly news one night and it would just be over with after that. Today, it's a viral effect. It's around the world overnight."[38] A report by the Pew Internet and American Life Project puts these technological innovations of 2006 in perspective regarding political utility:

> YouTube now takes its place in the procession of internet-driven innovations in politics: candidate web sites in 1996, email in 1998 (the Jesse Ventura campaign), online fundraising in 2000 (John McCain), blogs in 2003 (Howard Dean), net-organized house parties in 2004 (Bush-Cheney). (p. 4).[39]

Conclusion

The 2006 Senate races were "big" in many ways: big changes in terms of control of Congress, big money being spent on political ads, big news being made, and big technological developments that both helped and hindered campaigns. Several factors may explain the heightened news attention on these Senate races, including the serious challenges incumbents faced, the focus on the ads being run by and on behalf of candidates, the declining support for President Bush and how public opinion

---

[38] Adam Sichko, "The New World of E-lections: Social Networking Web Sites" *St. Louis Post-Dispatch* (October 2, 2006).

[39] Michael Cornfield and Lee Rainie, "The Impact of the Internet on Politics," Pew Internet and American Life Project (November 5, 2006). http://www.pewinternet.org/ppt/PIP_Internet_and_Politics.pdf. Accessed Jan. 3, 2007.

might be reflected in the 2006 vote, and controversy within many races. The evolving online environment provides avenues for further news and discussion of these campaigns through candidate e-mail, blogs by campaigns and about campaigns, and social networking websites. We as voters can watch the political ads online (for candidates in our own state races and also throughout the country), we can see satires produced to mimic the candidates and replay clips of unflattering political moments ourselves (and watch them via mainstream media as well), and we can communicate with others about what we saw, what we thought, and what our vote will be.

CONCLUSION

Given that U.S. elections have few truly competitive races, the Senate races profiled here were some of the most competitive in 2006, and the most costly as well. One theme across the three perspectives presented in this chapter is the importance of money in running a serious bid for elected office. Fund-raising is crucial to cover campaign costs, particularly the growing amount dedicated to political advertising that offers many arguments, as well as critiques of character, within an election.

Some of these Senate campaigns would not qualify as having been "good" campaigns, as scandals and gaffes plagued candidates, as did tactics in political advertising that raised questions of character. These controversies within campaigns were not just highlighted in campaign coverage as was done in the past, but now are also widely disseminated and discussed through the Internet.

■ ■ ■ ■ ■ ▬▬▬▬▬▬▬▬▬▬▬▬▬▬▬▬▬▬▬▬▬▬▬▬

ADDITIONAL CASES

Each of the nine Senate races briefly described in this chapter could be explored further as an individual case study regarding the political, rhetorical, and mass communication factors within those elections. Many other interesting races of the 2006 elections may offer the basis for additional case studies:

- **Connecticut Senate race: Joseph Lieberman and Ned Lamont**
  Resources: David Lightman, "Joe & Ned Seek Support Inside the Beltway," *Hartford Courant* (September 7, 2006); Elizabeth Mehren, "Lieberman Bounces Back from Primary Loss: Now an Independent, the Senator's Leading His Democratic Opponent," *Los Angeles Times* (November 4, 2006): A11.

- **Florida's 16th District race, House of Representatives, Mark Foley resigned seat in September 2006**
  Resources: Warren Richey, "GOP slips at Foley Scandal's Epicenter" *Christian Science Monitor* (October 27, 2006): 2; Carol J. Williams, "GOP's Sure Bets in Florida Now Appear in Question" *Los Angeles Times* (October 14, 2006): A1.

(continued)

ADDITIONAL CASES   CONTINUED

■ **New York's 26th District race, House of Representatives, Tom Reynolds**
Resources: Ben Smith, "GOP Aides Took Early Foley 'Damage Control' Call," *New York Daily News* (November 3, 2006): 6; Dan Majors, "'The Foley Thing' Roils N.Y. Congressional Race," *Pittsburgh Post-Gazette* (November 3, 2006): A1.

■ **Louisiana's 2nd District race, House of Representatives, William Jefferson**
Resources: Frank Donze, "William Jefferson Undeterred by Allegations: Incumbent Stresses Years of Effectiveness," *Times-Picayune* (October 18, 2006): 1; Frank Donze and Michelle Krupa, "Carter, Jefferson Gear Up for Runoff: They Must Scramble to Plug Vote Gaps," *Times-Picayune* (November 9, 2006): 1.

■ **Texas Governor's Race, 2006, Independent candidate Kinky Friedman**
Resources: My-Thuan Tran, "Friedman Clicks with Online Social Web Sites the Best," *Houston Chronicle* (November 3, 2006): B3; Carlos Guerra, "Democratic Nominee for Governor Sees Big Post-Debate Changes," *San Antonio Express-News* (October 17, 2006): 1B.

■ ■ ■ ■ ■

CHAPTER 10

CASE SIX: RONALD REAGAN'S 1981 INAUGURAL ADDRESS

THE CASE

Presidential inaugurals enact the important ritual of passing executive power on, peacefully, from one president to the next. They typically have a solemnity befitting such an occasion. In addition, they often forecast what the incoming president will attempt to do in the 4 years that follow. Mixing ritualistic solemnity and practical politics, inaugurals invite study from multiple perspectives.

Many inaugurals have proved to be quite memorable. Ronald Reagan's 1981 address was one. Reagan had challenged incumbent Democrat Jimmy Carter in the 1980 election and had won a clear victory. The Carter administration had seen a major diplomatic triumph in the accords it brokered between Israel and Egypt, but the administration had also seen economic difficulties, including a continuing energy "crisis," and, late in the Carter presidency, the holding hostage of fifty-two Americans by Iranian militant students at the U.S. embassy in Tehran. Carter had also spoken to the nation in July 1979 about a "crisis of confidence" he saw affecting the nation. He never used the word *malaise*, but press coverage stressed that "malaise" was what the president felt had settled over the nation. In contrast, Reagan, in the campaign and in the inaugural, offered an optimistic view.

Presidential inaugurals are traditionally delivered on the U.S. Capitol's east side, a flat area with the Supreme Court and the Library of Congress somewhat in view. Because of construction on the east side, Reagan's 1981 inaugural was delivered on the west side. This site put the president in a high position, looking down and out onto the Mall with the Washington Monument and Lincoln Memorial in view. Reagan will refer to this view as well as the political context in his memorable speech. Kenneth Khachigian drafted the speech for Reagan; Reagan revised it, adding the concluding story of World War I soldier Martin Treptow and its penultimate sentence.

> To a few of us here today this is a solemn and most momentous occasion, and yet in the history of our nation it is a commonplace occurrence. The orderly transfer of authority as called for in the Constitution routinely takes place, as it has for almost two centuries, and few of us stop to think how unique we really are. In the eyes of many in the world, this every-4-year ceremony we accept as normal is nothing less than a miracle.

Mr. President, I want our fellow citizens to know how much you did to carry on this tradition. By your gracious cooperation in the transition process, you have shown a watching world that we are a united people pledged to maintaining a political system which guarantees individual liberty to a greater degree than any other, and I thank you and your people for all your help in maintaining the continuity which is the bulwark of our Republic.

The business of our nation goes forward. These United States are confronted with an economic affliction of great proportions. We suffer from the longest and one of the worst sustained inflations in our national history. It distorts our economic decisions, penalizes thrift, and crushes the struggling young and the fixed-income elderly alike. It threatens to shatter the lives of millions of our people.

Idle industries have cast workers into unemployment, human misery, and personal indignity. Those who do work are denied a fair return for their labor by a tax system which penalizes successful achievement and keeps us from maintaining full productivity.

But great as our tax burden is, it has not kept pace with public spending. For decades, we have piled deficit upon deficit, mortgaging our future and our children's future for the temporary convenience of the present. To continue this long trend is to guarantee tremendous social, cultural, political, and economic upheavals.

You and I, as individuals, can, by borrowing, live beyond our means, but for only a limited period of time. Why, then, should we think that collectively, as a nation, we're not bound by that same limitation? We must act today in order to preserve tomorrow. And let there be no misunderstanding: We are going to begin to act, beginning today.

The economic ills we suffer have come upon us over several decades. They will not go away in days, weeks, or months, but they will go away. They will go away because we as Americans have the capacity now, as we've had in the past, to do whatever needs to be done to preserve this last and greatest bastion of freedom.

In this present crisis, government is not the solution to our problem; government is the problem. From time to time, we've been tempted to believe that society has become too complex to be managed by self-rule, that government by an elite group is superior to government for, by, and of the people. Well, if no one among us is capable of governing himself, then who among us has the capacity to govern someone else? All of us together, in and out of government, must bear the burden. The solutions we seek must be equitable, with no one group singled out to pay a higher price.

We hear much of special interest groups. Well, our concern must be for a special interest group that has been too long neglected. It knows no sectional boundaries or ethnic and racial divisions, and it crosses political party lines. It is made up of men and women who raise our food, patrol our streets, man our mines and our factories, teach our children, keep our homes, and heal us when we're sick—professionals, industrialists, shopkeepers, clerks, cabbies, and truck-drivers. They are, in short, "We the people," this breed called Americans.

Well, this administration's objective will be a healthy, vigorous, growing economy that provides equal opportunities for all Americans, with no barriers born of bigotry or discrimination. Putting America back to work means putting all Americans back to work. Ending inflation means freeing all Americans from the terror of runaway living costs. All must share in the productive work of this "new beginning," and all must share in the bounty of a revived economy. With the idealism and fair play which are the core of our system and our strength, we can have a strong and prosperous America, at peace with itself and the world.

Ronald Reagan takes the oath of office as president.

So, as we begin, let us take inventory. We are a nation that has a government—not the other way around. And this makes us special among the nations of the Earth. Our government has no power except that granted it by the people. It is time to check and reverse the growth of government, which shows signs of having grown beyond the consent of the governed.

It is my intention to curb the size and influence of the Federal establishment and to demand recognition of the distinction between the powers granted to the Federal Government and those reserved to the States or to the people. All of us need to be reminded that the Federal Government did not create the States; the States created the Federal Government.

Now, so there will be no misunderstanding, it's not my intention to do away with government. It is rather to make it work—work with us, not over us; to stand by our side, not ride on our back. Government can and must provide opportunity, not smother it; foster productivity, not stifle it.

If we look to the answer as to why for so many years we achieved so much, prospered as no other people on Earth, it was because here in this land we unleashed the energy and individual genius of man to a greater extent than has ever been done before. Freedom and the dignity of the individual have been more available and assured here than in any other place on Earth. The price for this freedom at times has been high, but we have never been unwilling to pay that price.

It is no coincidence that our present troubles parallel and are proportionate to the intervention and intrusion on our lives that result from unnecessary and excessive growth of government. It is time for us to realize that we're too great a nation to limit ourselves to small dreams. We're not, as some would have us believe, doomed to an inevitable decline. I do not believe in a fate that will fall on us no matter what we do. I do believe in a fate that will fall on us if we do nothing. So, with all the creative energy at our command, let us begin an era of national renewal. Let us renew our determination, our courage, and our strength. And let us renew our faith and our hope.

We have every right to dream heroic dreams. Those who say that we're in a time when there are not heroes, they just don't know where to look. You can see heroes every day going in and out of factory gates. Others, a handful in number, produce enough food to feed all of us and then the world beyond. You meet heroes across a counter, and they're on both sides of that counter. There are entrepreneurs with faith in themselves and faith in an idea who create new jobs, new wealth and opportunity. They're individuals and families whose taxes support the government and whose voluntary gifts support church, charity, culture, art, and education. Their patriotism is quiet, but deep. Their values sustain our national life.

Now, I have used the words "they" and "their" in speaking of these heroes. I could say "you" and "your," because I'm addressing the heroes of whom I speak— you, the citizens of this blessed land. Your dreams, your hopes, your goals are going to be the dreams, the hopes, and the goals of this administration, so help me God.

We shall reflect the compassion that is so much a part of your makeup. How can we love our country and not love our countrymen; and loving them, reach out a hand when they fall, heal them when they're sick, and provide opportunity to make them self-sufficient so they will be equal in fact and not just in theory?

Can we solve the problems confronting us? Well, the answer is an unequivocal and emphatic "yes." To paraphrase Winston Churchill, I did not take the oath I've just taken with the intention of presiding over the dissolution of the world's strongest economy.

In the days ahead I will propose removing the roadblocks that have slowed our economy and reduced productivity. Steps will be taken aimed at restoring the balance between the various levels of government. Progress may be slow, measured in inches and feet, not miles, but we will progress. It is time to reawaken this industrial giant, to get government back within its means, and to lighten our punitive tax burden. And these will be our first priorities, and on these principles there will be no compromise.

On the eve of our struggle for independence a man who might have been one of the greatest among the Founding Fathers, Dr. Joseph Warren, president of the Massachusetts Congress, said to his fellow Americans, "Our country is in danger, but not to be despaired of. . . . On you depend the fortunes of America. You are to decide the important questions upon which rests the happiness and the liberty of millions yet unborn. Act worthy of yourselves."

Well, I believe we, the Americans of today, are ready to act worthy of ourselves, ready to do what must be done to ensure happiness and liberty for ourselves, our children, and our children's children. And as we renew ourselves here in our own land, we will be seen as having greater strength throughout the world. We will again be the exemplar of freedom and a beacon of hope for those who do not now have freedom.

To those neighbors and allies who share our freedom, we will strengthen our historic ties and assure them of our support and firm commitment. We will match loyalty with loyalty. We will strive for mutually beneficial relations. We will not use our friendship to impose on their sovereignty, for our own sovereignty is not for sale.

As for the enemies of freedom, those who are potential adversaries, they will be reminded that peace is the highest aspiration of the American people. We will negotiate for it, sacrifice for it; we will not surrender for it, now or ever.

Our forbearance should never be misunderstood. Our reluctance for conflict should not be misjudged as a failure of will. When action is required to preserve our national security, we will act. We will maintain sufficient strength to prevail if need be, knowing that if we do so we have the best chance of never having to use that strength.

Above all, we must realize that no arsenal or no weapons in the arsenals of the world is so formidable as the will and moral courage of free men and women. It is a weapon our adversaries in today's world do not have. It is a weapon that we Americans do have. Let that be understood by those who practice terrorism and prey upon their neighbors.

I'm told that tens of thousands of prayer meetings are being held on this day, and for that I'm deeply grateful. We are a nation under God, and I believe God intended for us to be free. It would be fitting and good, I think, if on each Inaugural Day in future years it should be declared a day of prayer.

This is the first time in our history that this ceremony has been held, as you've been told, on this West Front of the Capitol. Standing here, one faces a magnificent vista, opening up on this city's special beauty and history. At the end of this open mall are those shrines to the giants on whose shoulders we stand.

Directly in front of me, the monument to a monumental man, George Washington, father of our country. A man of humility who came to greatness reluctantly. He led

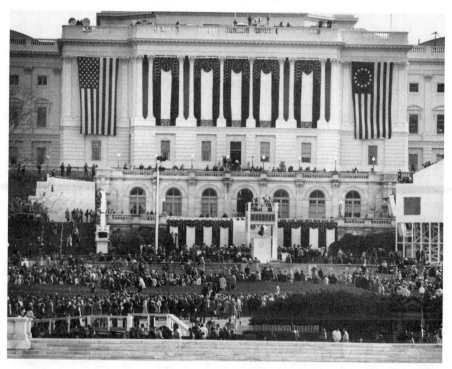

The 1981 Reagan inaugural takes place on the U.S. Capitol's west side, giving Reagan a view of Washington's numerous memorials.

America out of revolutionary violence into infant nationhood. Off to one side, the stately memorial to Thomas Jefferson. The Declaration of Independence flames with his eloquence. And then, beyond the Reflecting Pool, the dignified columns of the Lincoln Memorial. Whoever would understand in his heart the meaning of America will find it in the life of Abraham Lincoln.

Beyond those monuments to heroism is the Potomac River, and on the far shore the sloping hills of Arlington National Cemetery, with its row upon row of simple white markers bearing crosses or Stars of David. They add up to only a tiny fraction of the price that has been paid for our freedom.

Each one of those markers is a monument to the kind of hero I spoke of earlier. Their lives ended in places called Belleau Wood, The Argonne, Omaha Beach, Salerno, and halfway around the world on Guadalcanal, Tarawa, Pork Chop Hill, the Chosin Reservoir, and in a hundred rice paddies and jungles of a place called Vietnam.

Under one such marker lies a young man, Martin Treptow, who left his job in a small town barbershop in 1917 to go to France with the famed Rainbow Division. There, on the western front, he was killed trying to carry a message between battalions under heavy artillery fire.

We're told that on his body was found a diary. On the flyleaf under the heading, "My Pledge," he had written these words: "America must win this war. Therefore, I will work, I will save, I will sacrifice, I will endure, I will fight cheerfully and do my utmost, as if the issue of the whole struggle depended on me alone."

The crisis we are facing today does not require of us the kinds of sacrifice that Martin Treptow and so many thousands of others were called upon to make. It does require, however, our best effort and our willingness to believe in ourselves and to believe in our capacity to perform great deeds, to believe that together with God's help we can and will resolve the problems which now confront us.

And after all, why shouldn't we believe that? We are Americans.

God bless you, and thank you.[1]

THE POLITICAL SCIENCE PERSPECTIVE

There is nothing in the Constitution of the United States that requires presidents to give a speech upon their inauguration. Nevertheless, since President George Washington took the oath of office in 1789, presidents have used their inauguration ceremonies to create impressions—in both subtle and overt ways—about the ways in which they intend to lead. In his 2004 article in *Congress & the Presidency*, Michael Korzi identifies three types of presidential images that are conveyed through presidential inaugural addresses: constitutional, party, and plebiscitary.[2] Each of these differs from the others with respect to the ways in which presidents locate themselves

[1]The text is derived from that in *The Public Papers of the President: Ronald Reagan, 1981–89*, http://www.reagan.utexas.edu/archives/speeches/publicpapers.html.

[2]Michael J. Korzi, "The President and the Public: Inaugural Addresses in American History," *Congress & the Presidency* 31.1 (Spring 2004): p21(32).

in the constitutional system of checks and balances as well as whether or not the president claims a mandate for partisan goals.

In his first inaugural address, President Ronald Reagan took a plebiscitary approach. The word *plebiscite* refers to a direct vote of the people on a specific proposal, and presidents who take plebiscitary approaches, either to governing or to presenting themselves in their inaugural addresses, convey the message that they will do only what the people specifically endorse. President Reagan and his advisers knew very well that Reagan would define himself to the world through his first inaugural address, and he used the occasion to characterize himself as a steward of the will of the people. This is apparent when he says, midway through his address: "Your dreams, your hopes, your goals are going to be the dreams, the hopes, and the goals of this administration, so help me God." Reagan repeatedly used these sorts of rhetorical appeals to collective interests throughout his two terms in office.

Political scientist John Pitney, Jr. reminds us that "an inaugural address is a contrived effort at image-building, not a spontaneous exercise in soul-baring."[3] In his first inaugural address, President Reagan returned repeatedly to two separate themes. The first was the failure of government; the second was the triumph of the individual. Each of these is discussed below in greater detail. Although in an editorial a few days after the inauguration, *New York Times* columnist and analyst William Safire argued that the two themes were unrelated,[4] Reagan used concern about the failures of government to segue into his emotional appeal to the American spirit of renewal.

One thing that Reagan's inaugural address did not do was offer an extensive list of specific policy proposals. Unlike his predecessor, President James E. Carter, or his successors, Presidents George H. W. Bush and William Jefferson Clinton, Reagan made reference to very few specific public policies or goals. Whereas the other presidents referenced poverty, AIDS, health care, deficit reduction, and several other specific policy goals, Reagan's speech focused on broad themes that together promoted a vision of American society with which few could disagree.

The Failure of Government

It is not unusual for politicians to run for office by running against the institution in which they wish to serve. For example, candidates for Congress have long railed against the national legislature during their campaigns. The strategy is effective because people have a tendency to support their own member of Congress while expressing the attitude that the rest of the institution is corrupt. Presidential candidates also frequently campaign as Washington outsiders seeking to reform government.[5]

[3]John J. Pitney Jr., "President Clinton's 1993 Inaugural Address," *Presidential Studies Quarterly* 27(1) (1987).

[4]See William Safire, "The Land Is Bright," *The New York Times* (January 22, 1981), A27.

[5]See Fenno, Richard. See also Thomas E. Cronin and Michael A. Genovese, *The Paradoxes of the American Presidency*, 2nd ed. (New York: Oxford University Press, 2004).

Reagan, in his first inaugural, made it clear that in his view the U.S. federal government had grown too large and was a hindrance to American progress.

Nowhere does Reagan state this concern about the role of the federal government more clearly than when he says "government is not the solution to our problem; government is the problem." But Reagan's critique of government begins much earlier in the address. He references "a tax system which penalizes successful achievement and keeps us from maintaining full productivity" in the fourth paragraph and complains in the very next paragraph that government has "piled deficit upon deficit, mortgaging our future and our children's future for the temporary convenience of the present." Later in the speech, Reagan states: "It is time to check and reverse the growth of government, which shows signs of having grown beyond the consent of the governed."

Despite the clearly negative tone these comments conveyed about the role of the federal government in public life, Reagan offered little substantive support for these assertions. Moreover, with the exception of his reference to the tax system, the president did not criticize any particular aspect of the federal government, focusing instead on the vague assertion that government, in general, was the problem. This was likely a smart strategy on his part, since politicians who are hypercritical of the very government to which they have just been elected to serve do little to inspire confidence in their own leadership abilities.[6]

Likewise, Reagan did not provide significant amounts of detail about the ways in which he intended to shrink the scope and size of government, but he did indicate that one part of the solution would be a return to the principle of federalism—the idea that the federal, state, and local governments each have autonomous powers that cannot be encroached on by the other levels of government. Reagan explains: "It is my intention to curb the size and influence of the Federal establishment and to demand recognition of the distinction between the powers granted to the Federal Government and those reserved to the States or to the people." This is a statement with which it is difficult to disagree, because it is firmly grounded in the Tenth Amendment to the U.S. Constitution. With his reference to returning power to the people, Reagan was able to tie in his critique of the government with the second major theme of his speech, the triumph of American individualism.

The Triumph of American Individualism

President Reagan's messages about the endurance of Americans, both individually and collectively, are equally as impassioned as his critique of the U.S. federal government. Reagan notes that "we as Americans have the capacity now, as we've had in the past, to do whatever needs to be done to preserve this last and greatest bastion of freedom," and that

> . . . our concern must be for a special interest group that has been too long neglected. It knows no sectional boundaries or ethnic and racial divisions, and it crosses political

---

[6]Thomas E. Cronin and Michael A. Genovese, *The Paradoxes of the American Presidency*, 2nd ed. (New York: Oxford University Press, 2004).

party lines. It is made up of men and women who raise our food, patrol our streets, man our mines and our factories, teach our children, keep our homes, and heal us when we're sick—professionals, industrialists, shopkeepers, clerks, cabbies, and truck-drivers. They are, in short, "We the people," this breed called Americans.

By making reference to Americans from all walks of life, Reagan sought to personalize his message of individual responsibility and liberty.

Without reading it verbatim, the second half of Reagan's inaugural address invoked the principles of the "American Creed," a statement written by William Tyler Page in 1917, and approved by the U.S. House of Representatives a year later. That statement reads, in part:

> I believe in the United States of America as a government of the people, by the people, for the people; whose just powers are derived from the consent of the governed, a democracy in a republic, a sovereign Nation of many sovereign States; a perfect union, one and inseparable; established upon those principles of freedom, equality, justice, and humanity for which American patriots sacrificed their lives and fortunes.[7]

Reagan, in his inaugural address attempts to emphasize the important role of the individual in promoting his or her own success, and in the success more generally of the country. As other political observers have noted, this is consistent with the messages conveyed by other presidents, including John F. Kennedy and Franklin D. Roosevelt, in their inaugural addresses.

Tying It Together

Although, as noted above, William Safire asserted that Reagan did not tie together his two themes—reducing the size of government and the triumph of the individual—it is clear that Reagan believed he could not accomplish the former unless he could convince the public, and its elected representatives in Congress, that individuals would be better able to maximize their own human potential through hard work and self-sacrifice rather than with the assistance of government. As Thomas Cronin and Michael Genovese explain, presidents frequently find it difficult to enact the changes they desire in the absence of a spirit of cooperation from the public and the Congress. They write in *The Paradoxes of the American Presidency*: "In order to promote change, presidents must simultaneously affirm and create order. They begin by affirming the past, and use that past to undo the present and recreate it on the basis of past values."[8] (2004, 25). Reagan does exactly this in the historical examples he uses toward the end of his address when he references American heroes such as Thomas Jefferson, Dr. Joseph Warren, and

---

[7]The American Creed is available online at http://www.ushistory.org/documents/creed.htm.

[8]Thomas E. Cronin and Michael A. Genovese, *The Paradoxes of the American Presidency*, 2nd ed. (New York: Oxford University Press, 2004).

Martin Treptow. By using historical examples of men whose individual contributions to history were separate from a specific act of government, Reagan appealed to the American spirit of individual responsibility and collective American pride. In so doing, he created the impression that people can succeed without government to guide them.

Conclusion

Inaugural addresses do not have the force of law, nor do they typically offer specific policy proposals for the country to consider. In large part, these presidential speeches are symbolic events that give the president the opportunity to share his vision of government with the public. With its references to limited government and restoring the balance of power between the national government and its counterparts within the states, President Ronald Reagan's first inaugural address appealed to the American spirit of self-reliance as it built an image of Reagan as a champion of limited government. By telling the national and international audience for the address that "our present troubles parallel and are proportionate to the intervention and intrusion on our lives that result from unnecessary and excessive growth of government" and then articulating a vision of a smaller government that exists to promote human potential, Reagan created an impression of himself in his first inaugural address as a president who understood and acted in the best interests of the people. This impression carried through his first term as president, and likely contributed to his policy successes with a Congress controlled by the Democratic party.[9]

Following on events such as the oil crisis of the late 1970s and the Iran hostage crisis that was the backdrop to the 1980 presidential campaign, Reagan's first inaugural address made an appeal to every American to work to his or her full potential, and it made a promise that the government would not impede individual progress.

THE RHETORICAL PERSPECTIVE

These days, presidents speak and speak and speak. Some of the occasions and some of the messages are trivial, but many are important.[10] Arguably the most important—and certainly the most solemn—is the inaugural address offered every 4 years. This speech is important because it offers the incoming president's view of the nation—its problems and its potentialities—and suggests the directions the new government will take. It is more important because it reestablishes by its words and by its very being what we are as a constitutional democracy.

[9]Thomas E. Cronin and Michael A. Genovese, *The Paradoxes of the American Presidency*, 2nd ed. (New York: Oxford University Press, 2004).

[10]For a historical account of how often, see Roderick P. Hart, *The Sound of Leadership: Presidential Communication in the Modern Age* (Chicago: University of Chicago Press, 1987).

Inaugural as Speech Act

An inaugural, thus, should be considered as a speech act. Those who study speech acts often make a distinction between the locutionary and illocutionary. The former deals with the actual arguments that a text makes; the latter with what that text *does*. Speech act theorists, such as Habermas and Ehninger, have found the latter category far more interesting than the first, perhaps because rhetoricians have long looked at a speech's message but have not adequately attended to its performative dimension.

So what does an inaugural address perform? It performs the peaceful transfer of executive power from president to president, that transfer being based on the outcome of a democratic election. We take this action for granted, but in both the eighteenth-century context and in the present-day global context, this action is astonishing. No monarch must die; no coup must occur: the people's vote effects a change in power. The inaugural enacts this change, and, furthermore, it celebrates both the change itself and the fact that, under our Constitution, we make the change both in peace and with dignity.

To be such a speech act, an inaugural simply needs to be. Although some inaugural addresses have seemed inappropriately partisan (Grant's) or inappropriately casual (Carter's), they have only created dissonance. They have not prevented the power-transferring ritual from taking place. So, one might conclude that an inaugural's words and ideas matter little. Not so. They contribute to the ritual, and they say things that the incoming president believes are important. When the president's judgment is shared by others and when the president does a particularly good job of expressing these ideas, an inaugural can become not just an important speech act but a truly great instance of oratory.

Inaugural as Genre

An incoming president, however, is not free to do whatever he or she feels like when crafting this speech. Every new inaugural is part of a tradition of inaugural addresses. These speeches, taken together, establish a genre. Presidents use many genres when they speak: the State of the Union address is a genre, as are apologies and farewells. Some genres are loosely defined, permitting a president a fair amount of freedom in using them. The inaugural address, however, is probably the most tightly defined presidential address.

Karlyn Kohrs Campbell and Kathleen Hall Jamieson defined several presidential genres in their influential 1990 study *Deeds Done in Words*. We can acquire a good understanding of Ronald Reagan's 1981 inaugural if we consider it in the terms Campbell and Jamieson establish in their book.[11] They establish, more or less, eight characteristics for the genre.

First, the inaugural unifies its audience as "the people." When the speech follows a particularly divisive election, this reunification may be vital—even more so if the

---

[11]Karlyn Kohrs Campbell and Kathleen Hall Jamieson, *Deeds Done in Words: Presidential Rhetoric and the Genres of Governance* (Chicago: University of Chicago Press, 1990), 14–36.

party or president in power loses to a challenger as in 1980. The need to reunify the audience as "the people" is also a tremendous rhetorical opportunity, for the president has the opportunity to tell "the people" who they are. Franklin Delano Roosevelt, for example, redefined a people battered by economic hardship into a people who could overcome both fear and adversity; John F. Kennedy redefined a self-absorbed people who were enjoying the "happy days" of the 1950s into citizens of the world.

Reagan's reunification of "the people" begins in his rejection of those who "would have us believe" that we are "doomed to an inevitable decline." Veiled in that reference is the pessimistic rhetoric that sometimes emerged from the Carter administration. Jimmy Carter's infamous speech in which he declared the nation was suffering from "a crisis of confidence" had been delivered in July 1979.[12] During the 1980 campaign, Reagan had frequently accused Carter of having a pessimistic view of the nation's future. To overcome this "malaise," Reagan calls for "an era of national renewal." He says, "Let us renew our determination, our courage, and our strength. And let us renew or faith and our hope." If we do so, then "We have every right to dream heroic dreams." There are, according to Reagan, heroes all around us. In fact, he says, "I'm addressing the heroes of whom I speak—you, the citizens of this blessed land." He redefines "the people," then, as everyday heroes and declares, "Your dreams, your hopes, your goals are going to be the dreams, the hopes, and the goals of this administration, so help me God." His redefinition offers a powerful counterpoint to the lack of power many Americans may have felt in the declining months of the Carter administration.[13]

Reagan also rejects another Carter idea in the way he redefines and reunifies "the people." In Carter's farewell address, in keeping with that genre, he warned the American people about the increasing power of special interest groups. In Reagan's inaugural, he seems to have Carter's warning in mind:

> We hear much of special interest groups. Well, our concern must be for a special interest group that has been too long neglected. It knows no sectional boundaries or ethnic and racial divisions, and it crosses political party lines. It is made up of men and women who raise our food, patrol our streets, man our mines and our factories, teach our children, keep our homes, and heal us when we're sick—professionals, industrialists, shopkeepers, clerks, cabbies, and truck-drivers. They are, in short, "We the people," the breed called Americans.

Second, the inaugural rehearses common values. In doing so, the speech is very epideictic—to use the Classical term for oratory that blames or praises. Here, American values are being praised.

---

[12]This Carter speech is often referred to as his "malaise" speech, although he never uses that word in it. The word was picked up by the press from a prespeech briefing they received.

[13]The fact that Americans were being held hostage by radical students in the U.S. embassy in Tehran during this period and the fact that an attempt by the Carter administration to rescue them failed added to the public's feeling of impotence.

An orator in 1980 is facing an audience that wants both the ideal and the real. Reagan offers the audience just such a mixture by stressing the values of freedom (the ideal) and prosperity (the real). Reagan calls for measures—such as a tax cut— to ensure the latter. The former, he repeatedly salutes. He refers to America as "this last and greatest bastion of freedom," and he declares that, once we act as heroes, "[w]e will again be the exemplar of freedom and beacon of hope for those who do not now have freedom."

Third, the inaugural sets forth the governing principles of the incoming administration. Here, the speech drifts in a deliberative direction, but it usually drifts only so far. The principles remain vague; very rarely are specific policy initiatives mentioned.

Reagan wastes little time in his speech naming the problems that beset the nation: inflation, stifling taxes, idle industries, and excessive public spending. The last is symptomatic of a larger problem he will address, "the growth of government, which shows signs of having grown beyond the consent of the governed." He says he will "get government back within its means" and, being a bit specific, "lighten our punitive tax burden." He says that, "on these principles there will be no compromise," thereby establishing for the incoming administration a strong conservative ideology.

Fourth, the inaugural demonstrates the incoming president's recognition of the limits on his or her power. That power might be limited by a Congress populated by many with different ideas; that power is certainly limited by the various checks and balances set in place by the U.S. Constitution.

Reagan does not mention the Democratic Congress, and he only alludes to the Constitution. He makes it clear that "[o]ur government has no power except that granted it by the people." He reminds his audience that, "the Federal government did not create the States; the States created the Federal government," thus embracing federalism as another governing principle for the incoming administration. The states have power; the people have power. The federal government that he will lead must, he declares, "work with us, not over us."

Reagan also cites how time limits what a president can do. He says that the problems "will not go away in days, weeks, or months. . . ." (He also seems to echo a similar disclaimer made by Kennedy in his famous 1961 inaugural.)

Fifth, the inaugural is contemplative. It is like a prayer, frequently punctuated with Biblical allusions. Like many public addresses, the inaugural tends to follow the Classical organizational pattern (proem-statement-argument-epilogue). Religious language frequently dominates the proem and the epilogue.

Reagan does not sound a prayerlike note in the proem. But, toward the speech's end, he devotes a paragraph to the topic of prayer:

> I'm told that tens of thousands of prayer meetings are being held on this day; and for that I'm deeply grateful. We are a nation under God, and I believe God intended for us to be free. It would be fitting and good, I think, if on each Inaugural Day in future years it should be declared a day of prayer.

Furthermore, Reagan ends the address asking for "God's help" in solving the nation's problems. And he prays, ending with "God bless you."

Sixth, since, after all, in America we embrace a civil religion as well as a religion per se, the inaugural typically reviews history so as to contextualize the new administration's vision within that history. As we all know, history can be told in many different ways. Thus, the president on inaugural day has the power in his or her speech to interpret the nation's history as he or she wants. Many presidents, for example, have chosen to speak about this nation's almost-divine mission, following in the footsteps of George Washington who sounds that note in the very first inaugural.

Reagan takes advantage of the fact that this inaugural will be delivered from the Capitol's west side for the first time ever. He invites viewers to gaze out on the mall and, on or near it, "those shrines to the giants on whose shoulders we stand." He proceeds chronologically and geographically westward and talks about Washington (the Washington Monument), Jefferson (the Jefferson Memorial), Lincoln (the Lincoln Memorial), and all the soldiers who lost their lives in World War I and II (Arlington National Cemetery). He thus moved from "giants" to average Americans, and he concludes his review of history by telling the story of a World War I soldier named Martin Treptow. Throughout Reagan's gaze westward, he stresses American heroism, the quality that unites "giants" such as Washington with men such as Treptow.[14]

Seventh, the inaugural, as an epideictic speech, praises American "institutions." Foremost among them would be the U. S. Constitution and the governing principles and processes it established.

Reagan begins his inaugural by paying tribute to "[t]he orderly transfer of authority as called for in the Constitution." He notes how, "In the eyes of many in the world, this every-four-year ceremony we accept as normal is nothing less than a miracle." He tells exiting President Carter that, in his "gracious cooperation in the transition process," he has "shown a watching world that we are a united people pledged to maintaining a political system. . . ."

Finally, eighth, the inaugural is typically written in a high style (as befitting epideictic oratory). Rhetorical schemes abound; tropes such as extended metaphors and allusions are numerous. There are lines worth savoring and quoting, lines that endure as have ones from Lincoln's inaugurals and Franklin Roosevelt's first and Kennedy's only.

Reagan quotes Winston Churchill and Founding Father Joseph Warren. He uses an extended metaphor of mortgaging to explain the nation's economic plight. He also, curiously, seems to "stylize" (i.e., use words and phrases and sentence rhythms the audience will associate with famous others) John F. Kennedy, for there are places

---

[14]How Reagan incorporated the vista offered by the Capitol's west side has been noted by several. For example, see Kurt Ritter and David Henry's reading of the address in *Ronald Reagan: The Great Communicator* (Westport, CT: Greenwood, 1992).

in the inaugural where Kennedy's words in his 1961 inaugural seem to shine through—for example, when Reagan addresses comments to "those neighbors and allies who share our freedom." Reagan, a former Democrat, was not averse to using Kennedy's words or Roosevelt's words to support his presidential vision. Here and throughout Reagan's speeches he offers what Bakhtin terms "polyphony." Many of these other voices contribute to a fairly high style.

Reagan's style, in general, was not as high as Kennedy's or Roosevelt's. What characterizes Reagan's style is his use of rhetorical schemes but with words that have a commonality. The effect is an everyday eloquence. A few examples will illustrate this style:

> All of us need to be reminded that the Federal Government did not create the States; the States created the Federal government.—*antimetabole*

> Now, so there will be no misunderstanding, it's not my intention to do away with government. It is rather to make it work—work with us, not over us; to stand by our side, not ride on our back. Government can and must provide opportunity, not smother it; foster productivity, not stifle it.—*antithesis*

> Let us renew our determination, our courage, and our strength. And let us renew our faith and our hope.—*anaphora*

> Your dreams, your hopes, your goals are going to be the dreams, the hopes, and the goals of this administration, so help me God.—*anaphora/parallelism*

> . . . peace is the highest aspiration of the American people. We will negotiate for it, sacrifice for it; we will not surrender for it, now or ever.—*antithesis/epistrophe*

> It [freedom] is a weapon our adversaries in today's world do not have. It is a weapon that we as Americans do have.—*antithesis*

The archaic names given to various rhetorical schemes can be assigned to these lines, but note how the vocabulary's register remains within the easy reach of the common man or woman. This everyday eloquence will be imitated by others in the years following the Reagan presidency.

The Reagan Style

Kathleen Hall Jamieson in *Eloquence in an Electronic Age* identifies several characteristics of a political style that she argues has gradually emerged in the television era.[15] Two of these characteristics are storytelling and offering a memorable picture; both of these are striking in the Reagan inaugural. At the speech's conclusion,

---

[15]Kathleen Hall Jamieson, *Eloquence in an Electronic Age: The Transformation of Political Speechmaking* (New York: Oxford University Press, 1988).

Reagan tells the story of Martin Treptow. Such stories will pop up in many Reagan speeches—as well as in those of his successors. In telling stories, Reagan recognizes the persuasive quality narrative has always had, in addition to shifting to a presentational mode especially suited to electronic media. Toward the end of the speech, Reagan offers his audience the picture of Washington's many monuments.

Reagan also, at a few points, speaks more personally than many of his predecessors on their inaugural days. He personally thanks outgoing President Jimmy Carter; and he personally thanks those who are praying for him for their prayers. This tendency toward self-revelation in a style that seems, at moments, more conversational than oratorical is another characteristic Jamieson cites. It is not surprising then that Reagan is Jamieson's exemplar for this new style.

Interestingly, Jamieson raises questions about this new style. She sees it as a television style, although, as Michael Weiler and W. Barnett Pearce have argued, there is a fair amount of traditional populism in it as well.[16] Jamieson worries that it may promote a separation of speech and thought. The result would be speeches that move or persuade but not by presenting reasoned discourse. Since Reagan's style, as exemplified well by the 1981 inaugural, has influenced others, it may be well worth considering if Jamieson's fears in her 1988 book have proved well-founded or not.

Conclusion

An inaugural address, no matter what its content, is an important act. It signals the peaceful transition from one national leader to another. Reagan's 1981 inaugural performs this act, but it does much more. It conforms to the tradition of the genre, but it also redefines both who the American people are and what the American federal government is. The speech refutes the pessimism associated with outgoing President Jimmy Carter by highlighting American heroism, a heroism exhibited by ordinary men and women as well as by revered national leaders. Reagan uses the view from the site of his speech to underscore the grander heroism and the story of GI Martin Treptow to underscore the more common. Reagan uses the high style typical of inaugurals, but uses it in a manner that minimizes its elevated tone so as to keep his remarks accessible to average Americans. He adds visual and narrative elements, creating a highly effective television style.

THE MASS COMMUNICATION PERSPECTIVE

Ronald Reagan, fortieth president of the United States, came to the White House in 1981 as a media-savvy politician. His time in front of the camera as an actor and his 8 years as governor of California had prepared him for his encounters with the

---

[16]Weiler and Pearce, "Ceremonial Discourse: The Rhetorical Ecology of the Reagan Administration." In Michael Weiler and W. Barnett Perace, eds., *Reagan and Public Discourse in America* (Tuscaloosa, AL: University of Alabama Press, 1992), 11–42.

press as well as his political opposition. Former Chief of Staff Ken Duberstein recounted the following of Reagan becoming president: "People used to say, 'How can an actor be president?' And Reagan's answer was, 'How can somebody be president without being an actor?'" In considering media issues of his inauguration, we see the news media dealing with the predictable as well as the unpredictable in their coverage. After the news media obsession with the presidential campaign process, from the primaries through Election Day, the attention continues through to the inauguration.

Media Coverage of Reagan's Inauguration

Although news coverage is not as sustained as in the final days of the election, the week of the presidential inauguration we do see daily reports of the upcoming events, early inaugural celebrations, the weather predictions for the parade and swearing in outside the Capitol, and the excitement that fills Washington, DC, during the week of the inauguration.

Let's consider the news environment at the time of Reagan's inauguration, in 1981. If you wanted to watch the inaugural address on television, you would have tuned in to CBS, ABC, or NBC for live coverage; estimates were that 75 million would do so. Some viewers might have been able to see coverage on CNN, because it was founded in 1980, but cable concentration was then low—16 million households subscribed to cable television in 1980, compared with 65.5 million in 2006.[17] In his column highlighting the media coverage of Reagan's inauguration in the *Washington Post*, TV critic Tom Shales discussed CNN's potential advantage that day, as he reported the following:

> CNN anchor Chris Curle insists the fledgling cable network will have the best or at least most coverage. CNN will stay with the story all day. "The networks can't bear to cut away from their money-making soaps," she says. "We don't have any money-making soaps. The big news is the inaugural and we'll stay with it as long as we can for all it's worth."[18]

Inaugurations are important in political history because they mark the transition from one president to another, but they are not the most interesting news stories to cover, since they tend to lack spontaneity. From the perspective of newsworthiness, prominence is the motivation for covering otherwise highly predictable events. The presidential transition is an event in U.S. history that news media are reluctant to ignore. News routines and rituals require that media cover such milestone events, but they are highly scripted, predictable, and controlled by those who organize them.

---

[17]Statistics come from the National Cable & Telecommunications Association (www.ncta.com), "History of Cable Television" and "Industry Statistics."

[18]Tom Shales, "The Inauguration: Watching the Watchers: How the Networks Are Covering All the Angles for 75 Million Viewers," *Washington Post*, January 18, 1981.

Washington Post TV critic Shales summarizes the television network's approach to presidential inaugurations as the following:

> In network TV, inaugural coverage isn't considered a plum beat because it's not easy to keep it from coming across exactly the way its organizers intended it. This makes the networks feel they aren't doing their jobs. "I don't do parades" is the way one veteran TV news executive rejected the thrill of supervising the inaugural one year. (p. H1)

One analysis comparing news coverage of presidential inaugural addresses and State of the Union addresses points out some unique factors in covering inaugurations. McDevitt (1986) examined the news coverage of State of the Union addresses and inaugural addresses from 1973 to 1985 from five U.S. newspapers.[19] His analysis found Ronald Reagan's most frequently used ideographs[20] included the following: freedom, peace, progress, opportunity, prosperity, democracy, and liberty. Although McDevitt's analysis does not pinpoint specific characteristics of Reagan's 1981 address, he found that news coverage of inaugural addresses includes about 60 percent of the ideological references (phrases including language such as *freedom, justice, peace,* and so on). He suggests that this implies reporters "actively scrutinize presidential messages as opposed to passively reporting what is presented to them." (p. 21). We are more likely to see a "watchdog" role of the media rather than a "reporter as stenographer" even for key presidential addresses.

An alternative explanation for the limited use of references in news reports from the original address might be the limits of the "news hole." Newspapers contain a certain a number of column inches, and to include more pages to add more coverage, we will also see more advertising on the pages to cover those additional costs. Traditional news broadcasts run in 30-minute increments (usually 19 to 20 minutes being the actual newscast); only for breaking news do we see those limits expanded. The confines of the news hole explain why presidential address coverage is limited to the degree that McDevitt's analysis found. We need to consider the other events that occur in the world on the day of presidential addresses that merit news attention, in particular those that coincided with Reagan's 1981 inaugural address.

Competing Political News: Reagan's Inauguration versus the End of the Hostage Crisis

What makes Reagan's inauguration memorable and important from a news media perspective has little to do with his inaugural address itself. Rather, the news media simultaneously covering the quadrennial event that was staged and produced for the

---

[19]Mike McDevitt, "Ideological Language and the Press: Coverage of Inaugural, State of the Union Addresses," *Mass Communication Review* 13.1 (1986): 18–24. The five newspapers examined were the *New York Times, Washington Post, Los Angeles Times, Chicago Tribune,* and *Atlanta Journal-Constitution.*

[20]McDevitt's quantitative analysis of ideology uses the qualitative unit of an ideograph, which he defines as "a concept developed in speech communication defined as 'a high-order abstraction representing collective commitment to a particular but equivocal and ill-defined normative goal'". His definition comes from Michael Calvin McGee's work on rhetoric and ideology.

news cameras and the breaking news of the release of the 52 American hostages from Iran after they had been held captive for 444 days created a day of excitement as well as of chaos and confusion. One news account of January 20, 1981, described the inauguration as "overshadowed, or perhaps more aptly, upstaged by the hostages' story."[21]

Newsrooms had predicted the potential timing of these two events to compete for their attention in the days before Reagan's inauguration. *Washington Post* TV critic Tom Shales notes this in his preview of media coverage of the inauguration, saying, "On Friday, the networks also began gearing up for the possibility that inaugural coverage may have to be interrupted for coverage of the end of the Iranian hostage crisis. That could make this, from a TV point of view, the most unforgettable inaugural in history" (p. H1).

The first U.S. report of the release of the hostages came from the NBC radio network, as recounted by NBC radio anchor Don Blair in his article "The News Scoop to End All News Scoops."[22] Blair explains the conflict they faced when their London bureau chief had learned that an agreement had been reached to release the hostages on January 18, but they lacked a second source to confirm the story before airing it, which had been their news routine for past stories. In this instance, their "two-source" rule was bypassed and NBC was the first to break the news with the following report as Blair recounts:

> **Blair:** This is an NBC News Hotline Report. This is Don Blair, NBC News. We take you now to NBC's Fred Kennedy in London.
>
> **Kennedy:** This is exclusive! It's an answer [pause] to all our prayers. The prayers of a nation have been answered! The captivity of the 52 American hostages is ending, and freedom, freedom is absolutely just around the corner! We have been told in an exclusive interview with Pars News Agency, the official Iranian news agency, that has just spoken with the Prime Minister's advisor and the head of Iran's hostage negotiation team, Mr. Nabavi. He said the final reply from the U.S. government had been received a few minutes ago, and they have reached an agreement. Nabavi says there are some small disagreements, but they are not important. They are not important at all. He says that an agreement has been reached. (p. 64)

It took another 5 hours for an interview with negotiator Behzad Nebavi to be released by Tehran radio and for other news organizations to report the story. We can sense from Blair's account, as well as Fred Kennedy's excitement in his report, the emotional roller-coaster the hostage crisis produced and the newsroom decisions on coverage.

---

[21]Lee Lescaze, "Hostage Release Opens Presidency on a Dramatic High Note," *Washington Post*, January 21, 1981.

[22]Blair, Don, "The News Scoop to End All News Scoops," *Television Quarterly* 35.3 and 4 (2005): 63–66.

A survey of nearly 400 newspaper editors[23] the week following the inauguration and hostage release in 1981 found that most papers published two separate
stories on the events, rather than condense both into one news story. Newspapers ran
more photographs of the inauguration than of the hostage release, likely because of
the availability of photographs of the two events. The analysis examined the influence
of publication time (morning versus afternoon newspapers), ownership, and circulation size on the editorial decision in covering these two news stories. Ostman and
Babcock provide the following conclusion for differences in coverage of these two
important events:

> The inauguration story generally was superior in solid facts and lent itself to greater
> access by the American press corps. The hostages' release story, played out mostly in a
> country with which the U.S. had no formal diplomatic relations, which was relatively
> ill-understood by the American public, and which was hostile to the U.S., meant that
> wire coverage of both stories and photographs was less dependable, less plentiful and,
> when available, often of a poorer quality. (p. 33)

Many newspapers, however, did make connections in coverage between the
two events, whether in a combined story on both events (about one sixth of newspapers did so) or in other approaches to the coverage. For example, in Bormann's
(1982) analysis of fantasy themes of the coverage of Reagan's inaugural and the
hostage release,[24] one example of the theme of "renewal" for both events was a page
one image from the *Minneapolis Tribune* from January 21, 1981. The top story was
headlined "Day 1 of a new life" above a photograph of the only two female released
hostages, Kathryn Koob and Elizabeth Ann Swift. Immediately below appeared the
headline "Day 1 for a new leader" with a photograph below of Ronald and Nancy
Reagan waving toward the camera from the inaugural parade route.

Inauguration and Presidential Honeymoon

Beyond the presidential campaign and the inauguration, what then occurs with news
coverage of the president? There are a couple different conceptualizations of what a
"presidential honeymoon" is. From a political science perspective, it is the period at
the beginning of a president's term in office when Congress, as well as the opposing
political party, is most cooperative with the president. From a mass communication
perspective, it is the period at the beginning of a president's term in office when
media coverage of the president is not as negative or critical as it will likely become
the longer the president is in office.

---

[23]Ronald E. Ostman and William. A. Babcock, "Reagan Inauguration, Hostage Release, or Both?: Publication Time, Ownership and Circulation Size in Daily Newspaper Editorial Decisions," *Newspaper Research
Journal* 3.4 (1982): 24–35.

[24]Ernest G. Bormann, "A Fantasy Theme Analysis of the Television Coverage of the Hostage Release and
the Reagan Inaugural," *Quarterly Journal of Speech* 68 (1982): 133–45.

We may hear references to the honeymoon as the first 100 days the president is in office; mass communication research has examined these first 100 days, as well as perhaps what we might consider the "pre-honeymoon" period from the day after Election Day to the day of the inauguration. In research on the media coverage in the pre-honeymoon period for the presidencies of Reagan, Carter, and Nixon, the presidential honeymoon was portrayed as a time for healing, a time for political opponents to make up and work together.[25] Although the analysis of Reagan, Carter, and Nixon found that at least half of news coverage before the president took office was neutral, Reagan and Carter faced more negative than positive coverage in the 2 months between the election and taking office. The challenges and criticism both Reagan and Carter faced in cabinet selections may explain much of the early negativity. In contrast to the celebratory coverage of Inauguration Day as well as the release of the American hostages in Iran, the press had started scrutinizing Reagan as president well before he took the oath of office in January 1981.

Conclusion

Even while covering such a highly scripted and predictable event as a presidential inauguration, we still find variation in media coverage. The advent of CNN coverage of politics just before Reagan's presidency changed how news media could cover political events. News routines and limitations in how much can be covered do explain differences in media coverage versus the event of Reagan's inauguration itself. The challenges and emotions involved in covering Reagan's inauguration as well as the release of the American hostages in Iran resulted in perhaps the most unique inaugural coverage American has listened to, watched, and read about to date.

CONCLUSION

An inauguration is an important event. It signals continuity in American government; it also signals what the incoming administration will be like. The political scientist is drawn to that message. Reagan signaled that his administration would push for a limited government, one that would allow the individual American to thrive and thus that American would realize his or her full potential. This picture was a counterpoint to the more pessimistic message that had become associated with outgoing President Jimmy Carter. The rhetorician is drawn to this same message, but more to how Reagan, working within the confines of the inaugural genre, conveyed it. The rhetorician notes how Reagan redefines Americans—all Americans—as heroes and uses visual and narrative elements to convey this redefinition.

To the media covering the inaugural, the crucial constraint is not the one genre imposes on the incoming president but, rather, the one the incoming administration

[25]Karen S. Johnson, "The Honeymoon Period: Fact or Fiction?" *Journalism Quarterly*, 62.4 (1985): 869–76.

imposes on the media, virtually compelling newspeople to tell the new president's "story." The mass communication scholar is drawn to how the media resists this control by interpreting as well as reporting events. In general, the inauguration would be the day's biggest story, although not necessarily the "juiciest." In 1981, however, the release of the American hostages in Iran competed with the Reagan inaugural for the headlines. The media had to determine whether to report the two events as separate or connected. Thus, media coverage of the 1981 inaugural was far from typical.

ADDITIONAL CASES

Many other presidential inaugurals could be considered from these three perspectives. Among the more interesting ones would be:

- **George Washington's April 1789 Inaugural**
- **Abraham Lincoln's 1865 Inaugural**
- **Franklin Delano Roosevelt's 1933 Inaugural**
- **John F. Kennedy's 1961 Inaugural**
- **Bill Clinton's 1993 Inaugural**

The text of the first four can be found in Michael Waldman, *My Fellow Americans: The Most Important Speeches of America's Presidents* (Naperville, IL: Sourcebooks, 2003). A useful initial discussion of them is Karlyn Kohrs Campbell and Kathleen Hall Jamieson's *Deeds Done in Words*. The Clinton inaugural is available in *Vital Speeches* 59.9 (February 15, 1993): 258–59.

CHAPTER 11

CASE SEVEN: CLINTON RESPONDS TO THE LEWINSKY SCANDAL

THE CASE

Political leaders, especially when faced with the conclusion of their term in office, consider what legacy they will leave with the public. For William Jefferson Clinton, memories of his presidency may be based more on the events of 1998 than on any other, when he became only the second president in history to be impeached by the House of Representatives. The first was not Richard M. Nixon, as he resigned when faced with an impeachment trial; the first president to be impeached was Andrew Johnson in 1868. Clinton was impeached on grounds of perjury to a grand jury and obstruction of justice. Clinton remained in office and continued to maintain impressive public approval ratings through the rest of his presidency.

Time Line of Events of the Clinton-Lewinsky Scandal:[1]

November 1992	William Jefferson Clinton elected president of the United States
May 1994	Paula Jones files lawsuit against President Clinton
July 1995	Monica S. Lewinsky begins White House internship
November 15, 1995	President begins sexual relationship with Lewinsky
April 5, 1996	Lewinsky transferred from White House to Pentagon
November 1996	President Clinton reelected
March 29, 1997	Last intimate contact between president and Monica Lewinsky
December 5, 1997	Lewinsky appears on Jones Witness List
December 19, 1997	Lewinsky served with subpoena to appear at deposition and produce gifts from President Clinton
December 24, 1997	Lewinsky's last day of work at the Pentagon

[1]The majority of this time line originates from the Starr Report, with additional dates from the *Washington Post* at http://www.washingtonpost.com/wp-srv/politics/special/clinton/how/how.htm.

December 28, 1997	Lewinsky meets with the president and receives gifts; later gives box of gifts from the president to Bettie Currie
January 7, 1998	Lewinsky signs affidavit intended for filing in Jones case
January 13, 1998	Lewinsky accepts job offer at Revlon in New York
January 16, 1998	Special Division appoints Independent Counsel Kenneth W. Starr to investigate the Lewinsky matter
January 17, 1998	President deposed in Jones case
January 18, 1998	President meets with Betty Currie to discuss president's deposition
January 21, 1998	Lewinsky matter reported in press; president denies allegations of a sexual relationship and of suborning perjury
January 26, 1998	President publicly denies sexual relationship with Lewinsky
April 1, 1998	Judge Wright grants summary judgment for President Clinton in the Jones litigation
July 17, 1998	President served with grand jury subpoena, which was later withdrawn in return for testimony
July 28, 1998	Immunity/Cooperation Agreement reached between Lewinsky and Office of Independent Counsel (OIC)
August 17, 1998	President testifies before the grand jury for more than 4 hours; later he publicly acknowledges improper relationship
September 9, 1998	Kenneth Starr submits his 453-page report to the House, report released in full on the Internet on September 11, 1998
December 11, 1998	After 7 days of hearings, a House Judiciary Committee votes to recommend impeachment of President Clinton
December 19, 1998	House of Representatives impeaches President Clinton for lying under oath and obstructing justice by attempting to cover up his affair with Lewinsky

Clinton's Denial

The first allegations of a relationship between Monica Lewinsky and President Clinton were reported on January 21, 1998. Clinton first publicly denied the allegations 5 days later. At the conclusion of a White House news conference on education the morning of January 26, 1998 (the day before his State of the Union address) in the Roosevelt Room of the White House, Clinton ended with this statement:

Now I have to go back to work on my State of the Union speech, and I worked on it till pretty late last night. But I want to say one thing to the American people. I want you to listen to me. I'm going to say this again: I did not have sexual relations with that woman, Miss Lewinsky. I never told anybody to lie, not a single time. Never. These allegations are false. And I need to go back to work for the American people.

Clinton's Apology

On August 17, 1998, the day of his testimony before Kenneth Starr's grand jury, President Clinton addressed the nation with a 4-minute live statement. Nielsen ratings estimated that more than 67 million viewers tuned in to their televisions to watch the following statement from Clinton:

> Good evening. This afternoon in this room, from this chair, I testified before the Office of Independent Counsel and the grand jury. I answered their questions truthfully, including questions about my private life, questions no American citizen would ever want to answer.
>
> Still, I must take complete responsibility for all my actions, both public and private. And that is why I am speaking to you tonight.
>
> As you know, in a deposition in January, I was asked questions about my relationship with Monica Lewinsky. While my answers were legally accurate, I did not volunteer information. Indeed, I did have a relationship with Miss Lewinsky that was not appropriate. In fact, it was wrong. It constituted a critical lapse in judgment and a personal failure on my part for which I am solely and completely responsible.

Bill Clinton publicly denies his relationship with Monica Lewinsky in January 1998, as Hillary Rodham Clinton looks on.

But I told the grand jury today and I say to you now that at no time did I ask anyone to lie, to hide or destroy evidence or to take any other unlawful action.

I know that my public comments and my silence about this matter gave a false impression. I misled people, including even my wife. I deeply regret that.

I can only tell you I was motivated by many factors. First, by a desire to protect myself from the embarrassment of my own conduct. I was also very concerned about protecting my family. The fact that these questions were being asked in a politically inspired lawsuit, which has since been dismissed, was a consideration, too.

In addition, I had real and serious concerns about an independent counsel investigation that began with private business dealings 20 years ago, dealings, I might add, about which an independent federal agency found no evidence of any wrongdoing by me or my wife over two years ago.

The independent counsel investigation moved on to my staff and friends, then into my private life. And now the investigation itself is under investigation.

This has gone on too long, cost too much and hurt too many innocent people. Now, this matter is between me, the two people I love most—my wife and our daughter—and our God. I must put it right, and I am prepared to do whatever it takes to do so. Nothing is more important to me personally. But it is private, and I intend to reclaim my family life for my family. It's nobody's business but ours. Even presidents have private lives.

It is time to stop the pursuit of personal destruction and the prying into private lives and get on with our national life.

Our country has been distracted by this matter for too long, and I take my responsibility for my part in all of this. That is all I can do. Now it is time—in fact, it is past time—to move on.

We have important work to do—real opportunities to seize, real problems to solve, real security matters to face.

And so tonight, I ask you to turn away from the spectacle of the past seven months, to repair the fabric of our national discourse, and to return our attention to all the challenges and all the promise of the next American century.

Thank you for watching. And good night.

THE POLITICAL SCIENCE PERSPECTIVE

For much of U.S. history, the power of the presidential office conferred substantial persuasive authority on presidents, and presidents used their authority with relatively little oversight from the other branches of government. With the ability to command instantaneous media attention, the authority that comes with being one of only two individuals elected from a national constituency (the vice president is the second), and with significant power conferred by the Constitution of the United States, American presidents have often been thought of as the centers of governmental power.

At the same time, the president's constitutional powers are unquestionably weaker than those granted to the U.S. Congress. Moreover, as public distrust in the nation's presidents waned in the wake of the Vietnam War and the Watergate scandal, presidential action became more highly scrutinized by all quarters. Whereas the media during the 1930s and 1940s were largely complicit in helping President Franklin Roosevelt to conceal his physical disabilities, by the 1970s the media seized on every potentially questionable act of the president. Today, there is literally no aspect of the president's personal or professional life that goes unscrutinized. President Bill Clinton should have realized this long before he ascended to the office; that he did not, and that he ultimately was impeached for lying about an illicit relationship with a former White House intern, demonstrates the extent to which in the modern era, presidential power is tenuous and contingent on the support of others.

Presidential Power

In his classic work *Presidential Power and the Modern Presidents*, Richard Neustadt notes that because the Constitution of the United States grants few formal powers to the president, the most important power of the U.S. president is the power to persuade others to do what he wants them to do. For example, since presidents can not introduce legislation in Congress or single-handedly create new laws, they must persuade the public and the Congress that what they want is the correct course of action to effect positive change. Neustadt rightly points out that presidential persuasion is a two-way street, because the public, the Congress, and even other government actors with whom the president interacts all enjoy powers and advantages the president does not.[2] For this reason, presidents must cultivate the powers they can control while neutralizing the advantages held by other political actors if they want to accomplish their goals.

In the case of former President Bill Clinton, repeated lapses in personal judgment undermined his ability to fully exploit the persuasive authority of the office of president of the United States and undermined his ability to achieve his policy and political objectives over the course of his two terms as president. Clinton would have likely enjoyed far more policy success had he not been in the position of defending himself publicly from multiple sex scandals. Moreover, Clinton's miscalculation about how best to handle the situation compounded the outrage related to his affair with Monica Lewinsky. Clinton's mishandling of the fallout from the Monica Lewinsky scandal likely further undermined his own legacy and had implications for future presidents.

The Badly Handled Cover-Up

As problematic as the sex scandals themselves were for the president, he did not help himself by the way he handled them. President Clinton's public denial of any sexual relationship with Monica Lewinsky only compounded the fallout from the scandal. Although he later apologized both for the pain the relationship caused his family and

[2]Richard Neustadt, *Presidential Power and the Modern Presidents: The Politics of Leadership from Roosevelt to Reagan* (New York: The Free Press, 1991).

for lying about it to the public and to a grand jury, the House of Representatives' decision to impeach Clinton suggested that the apology was too little, too late. As a 2001 editorial in the *New Jersey Law Journal* notes:

> The public apology is in vogue. During his term of office, President Clinton apologized for our history of slavery, for America's past support of foreign dictators and its indifference to various atrocities in the world and, of course, for lying about his relationship with that White House intern. . . . Pope John Paul II apologized for the sins and injustices committed by the Roman Catholic Church over its 2,000 years. The Japanese government has apologized for Japan's role in World War II. Ford and Firestone have apologized for selling dangerous tires. Boxer Mike Tyson has apologized for biting off Evander Holyfield's ear, and Atlanta Braves pitcher John Rocker has apologized to New Yorkers for giving them an earful of abuse. . . . [But] we tend to look askance upon apologies. They can strike us as staged and insincere, something said for effect without any true feeling of remorse. We are especially cynical about apologies uttered by public officials, suspecting that they have been made for crass political advantage.[3]

Clinton would likely have helped himself and reduced the long-term effects of the scandal had he simply taken responsibility for his behavior at the time the media first reported the news of his relationship with Monica Lewinsky. In the past, public officials that have taken responsibility for misconduct have fared better than those that have denied or refused to address such allegations. For example, when it was revealed in 1989 that Massachusetts Congressman Barney Frank's driver, a former male escort, was running a prostitution ring out of Frank's Capitol Hill home, Frank "admitted what he'd done, denied what he hadn't, and took his case to the House ethics committee, which recommended a reprimand by the full House, a lesser penalty than the censure that had been requested in a motion by a notorious back-bench bomb thrower named Newt Gingrich."[4] Despite the damage that was done to Frank's reputation and standing in the House, Frank survived the scandal and continues to represent Massachusetts' fourth congressional district.

Former California congressman Gary Condit's handling of his own public scandal offers additional evidence that Clinton mishandled the Lewinsky scandal. When Condit was implicated in both a relationship with and the disappearance of one of his staff members, Chandra Levy, Condit refused to cooperate with police investigators. *Media Relations Handbook* author Brad Fitch notes that Condit's strategy was similar to Clinton's and the opposite of Frank's—likely the reason that congressional Democrats abandoned Condit, who lost in the 2002 Democratic primary election as he sought to retain his seat in Congress.[5] As the New York *Daily News* noted: "Though every political counselor under the sun has said the Democratic congressman's one

---

[3]Unsigned editorial. 2001. "The Role of Apology." *New Jersey Law Journal* 163.3 (Jan 15, 2001): 26.

[4]See: Charles P. Pierce, "To Be Frank," *Boston Globe Magazine*, October 2, 2005.

[5]Brad Fitch, *Media Relations Handbook* (Washington, DC: Congressional Management Foundation, 2005).

chance to save his career was to display remorse and candor, Condit repeatedly refused to admit he had an affair with Levy."[6] The lesson of the Clinton, Condit, and Frank scandals, according to Fitch's *Media Relations Handbook*, is that defusing a scandal by accepting responsibility will reduce the long-term implications for a politician's career and legacy.

The Effects of the Scandal on the Clinton Presidency

In Clinton's case, he suffered both short-term and longer-term effects of his behavior and the cover-up. One possible measure of presidential *policy* success is the extent to which Congress supports the president. This measure, although it too has its flaws, at least offers scholars and students some mechanism by which to understand how often the Congress is willing to assist the president with achieving his policy goals. Over the 8 years of his presidency, Clinton's success rate with Congress averaged roughly 58 percent. In 1999, the year in which the House of Representatives impeached Clinton and the Senate adjudicated the charges, Clinton's success rate in Congress dropped to 37.8 percent; this was the second lowest level of presidential success in Congress of any president from Eisenhower through the second year of the George W. Bush presidency.[7]

The Effects of the Scandal on the Presidency More Generally

During both the 1992 and 1996 presidential campaigns, rumors of relationships with women during his tenure as governor of Arkansas dogged Clinton's candidacy. One allegation—that of sexual harassment made by Paula Jones—led to a Supreme Court case (*Clinton v. Jones* [1997]) in which the justices determined that a sitting president can be sued in a civil court for conduct not relating to his official responsibilities as president of the United States. The consequences of this decision refined the evolving legal consequences for the personal conduct of elected officials and undoubtedly will have long-term effects on future presidents. This is because Clinton had invoked a defense of executive privilege in claiming that he did not have to answer questions about his personal conduct—either at all or truthfully. He claimed that his position as president of the United States entitled him to immunity from investigation and prosecution because of the interference with his responsibilities as president that such

---

[6]See: Helen Kennedy, "California Pol Talks, Says Little on TV: Condit Provides Few Details and No Remorse," *New York Daily News* August 24, 2001.

[7]In fact, Clinton also holds the record for the lowest level of presidential success in Congress. In 1995, Clinton achieved only a 36.2 percent success rate with Congress; 1995 was the first time in 40 years that the Republican Party controlled both houses of Congress, and the Republicans were focused on promoting their own agenda rather than working closely with a Democratic president. See Cronin, Thomas E. and Michael A. Genovese. *The Paradoxes of the American Presidency*, 2nd ed. New York: Oxford University Press, 2004).

legal proceedings would cause. As Mark Rozell explains, "Clinton's White House counsel tried to make the argument that by harming "the president's ability to 'influence' the public," the investigation undermined his ability to lead foreign policy."[8] The Supreme Court disagreed, noting:

> [W]e have never suggested that the President, or any other official, has an immunity that extends beyond the scope of any action taken in an official capacity. . . . Moreover, when defining the scope of an immunity for acts clearly taken *within* an official capacity, we have applied a functional approach. . . . Hence, for example, a judge's absolute immunity does not extend to actions performed in a purely administrative capacity. As our opinions have made clear, immunities are grounded in 'the nature of the function performed, not the identity of the actor who performed it.' [Clinton's] effort to construct an immunity from suit for unofficial acts grounded purely in the identity of his office is unsupported by precedent.[9]

Although the Supreme Court rejected the notion that its decision in *Clinton v. Jones* would lead to a flood of frivolous civil litigation against sitting presidents, many legal scholars raised precisely this concern in the wake of the decision in the case. Regardless of whether the Court's decision would have led to a torrent of litigation against Clinton, or any future president, the decision did indicate the extent to which presidents—and the presidency—are not above the law and are subject to regulation by the other branches of government and by the public.

Conclusion

Former President Bill Clinton, by virtually every account, was a gifted politician with the uncanny ability to empathize with others and to use his intellect, political skill, and ability to connect with others to hone his persuasive skills. Had he exercised more control over his personal life, or at least kept it secret from the press and the public, there is no telling how well he might be remembered by history. As Temple University scholar Russell Weigley noted, Clinton's "personal failings compromised any accomplishments he managed, [for] he always had trouble in keeping to a consistent policy course."[10] It is likely that both the romantic dalliances themselves and the time and effort it took to manage the fallout had enormous effects on Clinton's legacy.

Clinton's lies to the public and to the grand jury did not merely damage his own credibility and affect his ability to accomplish his policy objectives, they also damaged the credibility of the office of the president and may ultimately have longer-term

---

[8]Mark J. Rozell, "Executive Privilege in the Lewinsky Scandal: Giving a Good Doctrine a Bad Name (Monica Lewinsky)," *Presidential Studies Quarterly* 28.4 (Fall 1998): 816(1).

[9]See: *Clinton v. Jones* (95–1853), 520 U.S. 681 (1997).

[10]"Scholars Rank Clinton Both High and Low," *USA Today Magazine*, August 14, 2001.

legal implications for future sitting presidents. Richard Neustadt notes that successful presidents recognize that their persuasive power includes the power to bargain, and they use the special status and authority of their office to provide bargaining advantages. In this way, presidents' own choices can determine the extent to which they are able to be persuasive and the extent to which he will be able to bargain with others. Presidents who seek out and exploit opportunities to gain bargaining advantages typically enjoy success, whereas presidents who squander the advantages of their office frequently find themselves stymied by the other branches of government. Unfortunately for Clinton, he opted for the latter course, faced an uphill battle with the Congress for much of his second term as president, and squandered the opportunity to secure a long-term positive legacy for himself.

THE RHETORICAL PERSPECTIVE

The genre of the *apologia* has a long, venerable history. For those well versed in English literature, the classic example is John Henry Newman's nineteenth-century *Apologia pro Vita Sua*, which is but one of many examples in the Western literary tradition. The term *apologia*, as used in such treatises, has little to do with saying "I'm sorry"; rather, the term denotes a text in which a person offers an explanation. Thus, John Henry Newman offers an explanation for his life—for the choices he has made and the course that his life took. The explanation is usually prompted by some need to explain, such as the accusation that one has made the wrong choice or committed some kind of error. Of course, when the accusation is well-founded, "I'm sorry" could be a part of what the rhetor offers.

Political *Apologia*

The most famous *apologia* in American politics is undoubtedly U.S. Senator Richard M. Nixon's "Checkers" speech. Nixon was the Republican candidate for vice president at the time (1952), and he had been accused of having a "secret fund." Nixon bought 30 minutes of television time and delivered a masterful address. He explained what the "secret fund" really was, and he went further and laid bare before viewers his entire financial history. He presented himself as a man of humble origins and limited means. He furthermore used the situation to attack his political opponents for financial shenanigans and to salute his running mate, retired General Dwight D. Eisenhower, as America's only hope to combat communism and clean up "the mess" in Washington. Eisenhower had been seriously considering replacing Nixon on the ticket. The "Checkers" speech effectively painted Eisenhower into a corner: he had no choice but to stick with Nixon.[11]

---

[11]This is called the "Checkers speech" because that is the name Nixon's young daughters gave a cocker spaniel puppy he and they had received as a gift. Nixon, in a rather maudlin moment in the speech, made it clear that this was a gift they were not going to return, no matter what his opponents might say.

Nixon's "Checkers speech" was an *apologia* in the strictest sense: a rather full accounting of his political life thus far. Most political examples of the genre are different from Nixon's insofar as there really is something to apologize for. As Karlyn Kohrs Campbell and Kathleen Hall Jamieson describe the genre in their *Deeds Done in Words*, the essence is twofold: one must admit some error, while in some way minimizing it; and one must rehabilitate his or her ethos.[12] The ways of accomplishing the latter goal are numerous. They range from demonstrating humility to brazenly attacking opponents and thereby demonstrating them to be "bad" and you to be "not so bad" or even "good." More usual would be either demonstrating that an admirable quality of character led to the error or noting that subordinates were the ones who were really responsible.

Other rhetorical scholars have listed the available strategies differently.[13] In the 1970s, Ware and Linkugel suggested that denial, bolstering, differentiation, and transcendence are the chief strategies one would use in an apology.[14] More recently, Benoit has suggested that denial, evading responsibility, reducing offensiveness, corrective action, and mortification represent a more exhaustive list.[15] In Nixon's case, denial—on either list—would be a major strategy, as would bolstering and differentiation on Ware and Linkugel's. Nixon does indeed promote himself as well as skillfully attack his political opponents by differentiating his conduct from theirs.

Senator Edward M. Kennedy delivered another famous apology to the people of Massachusetts on June 25, 1969. Late one night, he had driven a car off a narrow bridge on Martha's Vineyard and into a deep pond. His passenger, Mary Jo Kopechne, drowned. In his speech, Kennedy denied any improper relationship between the two, and he denied that he was driving under the influence of alcohol. He noted the efforts he made to save the girl's life. But he also admitted that he irresponsibly left the scene of the accident and did not call the authorities until the following morning. He offered a mix of denial and mortification. Kennedy also tried to evade responsibility by claiming that he "was overcome . . . by a jumble of emotions, grief, fear, doubt, exhaustion, panic, confusion, and shock" and citing the darkness. Writing in the *Central States Speech Journal*, David A. Ling argues that, in Kenneth Burke's terms, Kennedy creates a drama in which the scene is the dominant element, overwhelming him, the actor. Well, people perhaps don't want a president who is so easily overwhelmed, and, therefore, the accident and Kennedy's apology for it may

---

[12]Karlyn Kohrs Campbell and Kathleen Hall Jamieson, *Deeds Done in Words: Presidential Rhetoric and the Genres of Governance* (Chicago: University of Chicago Press, 1990), 127–43.

[13]There is also a considerable body of social science research on strategies for apologizing, ably summarized by William L. Benoit, *Accounts, Excuses, and Apologies: A Theory of Image Restoration Strategies* (Albany, NY: State University of New York Press, 1995).

[14]See "They Spoke in Defense of Themselves: On the Generic Criticism of the Apologia," *Quarterly Journal of Speech* 59 (1973): 273–83. For an example of their approach applied, see Jackson Harrell, B. L. Ware, and W. A. Linkugel, "Failure of Apology in American Politics: Nixon on Watergate," *Speech Monographs* 42 (1975): 245–60.

[15]See Benoit, *Accounts*, 74–80.

have cost the senator the presidency.[16] People understood why Kennedy reacted as he did—it was, after all, a very human reaction; but they did not want someone that human in the White House.

Richard M. Nixon, now president, delivered several speeches in 1974 that we might consider examples of the genre. On April 29, he addressed the nation on television. He denied the accusations being made against him about both the Watergate break-in and a supposed plot to cover it up. He was at that time releasing transcripts of tapes he had made of Oval Office conversations. Knowing that his opponents would use the words on those tapes against him, he offered his interpretation. Up to that point, only one witness had accused Nixon—his former aide John Dean. Nixon used the April 29 speech to evade responsibility by shifting as much blame as he could to Dean. On August 8, Nixon spoke again, this time to resign the presidency. He still did not admit to the charges against him. However, he did say that "if some of my judgments were wrong—and some were wrong—they were made in what I believed at the time to be the best interest of the Nation." Ware and Linkugel would refer to this as an attempt (failed) at transcending—that is, shifting the audience's focus to something more important; Benoit would point to it as an attempt to reduce offensiveness. In a way, Nixon admitted fault, but he quickly tried to rebound from the offense by noting, vaguely, the positive goals that had motivated him.

Perhaps the best example of the more literally apologizing version of the genre would be a speech President Ronald Reagan delivered on March 4, 1987. The speech dealt with a double "scandal": Reagan's administration had secretly sold weapons to Iran (in violation of stated neutrality in the war between Iran and neighboring Iraq) and then diverted the revenue to anticommunist revolutionaries in Nicaragua (in violation of a law passed by the Congress). Reagan took "full responsibility for my own actions and for those of my administration." He argued that he had no recollection of having approved the sale and no personal knowledge of what aides then did with the money but, "as President, I cannot escape responsibility."[17] Reagan managed to engage simultaneously in mortification and evasion of responsibility. Besides blaming subordinates, he blamed his management style, which was to appoint the best staff and to give them the freedom to do their work. He also noted that he was taking action—what had been recommended by an independent commission and then some—to prevent further problems. His speech seemed designed to evoke admiration for (and thereby bolster) the president on at least three counts: he was nobly taking responsibility for what had gone wrong on his watch; he had a management style many Americans liked; and he was acting to modify this style so that no future "scandals" would occur.

---

[16]David A. Ling, "A Pentadic Analysis of Senator Edward Kennedy's Address to the People of Massachusetts, July 25, 1969," *Central States Speech Journal* 21 (1970): 81–86.

[17]The speech is quoted from Theodore Windt, *Presidential Rhetoric (1961 to the Present)* (Dubuque, IA: Kendall-Hunt, 1994).

Clinton's January Remarks

President Bill Clinton's remarks in 1998 should be viewed in the context established by these previous political apologies. The January 21 denial might be contrasted with those offered by Nixon. In the "Checkers speech" and again on April 29, 1974, Nixon spoke at length on the accusations against him. Clinton, on the other hand, spoke very briefly. Each denied the accusations, and each attempted to present positive pictures of himself. Nixon presented himself as humble, honest, and—like most in his audience—middle class in "Checkers"; he presented himself as responding with all the right questions when he first found out about a Watergate cover-up on April 29. Clinton presented himself as hard at "work for the American people." The night before, he had "worked on [the State of the Union address] till pretty late," and he had to get back to that important task now. In Benoit's terms, Clinton relies heavily on the strategy of denial, but he does attempt to reduce the offensiveness of the denied action by bolstering his image as working hard for America and encouraging the viewers to rise above (i.e., transcend) a supposed sex scandal and focus on the nation's business.[18]

Nixon, in both speeches, presented a drama in which he was the victim of attacks. In "Checkers," he attacks his attackers. On April 29, 1974, he does so only implicitly, although he does take a few shots at John Dean. Clinton presented a different drama: rather than depicting himself as being a victim of attacks, he depicted himself as being distracted. He was trying to do the business of the country; others, he implies, are doing something else. But he keeps that "something else" vague. Were they inappropriately prying into his personal life? Were they playing politics? Were they engaging still in the kinds of personal attacks that had been plaguing Clinton and his wife for years? Clinton does not specify, just as he keeps his remarks brief. He is hoping that, by not giving the accusation of an improper relationship with Monica Lewinsky much attention, it will go away. The January comments are dismissive, even though they do try, in their very few words, to portray the president positively as a hard-working victim.

Clinton's August Address

The later Clinton speech is better compared to Kennedy's address after the Chappaquiddick accident and Reagan's after the Iran/Contra affair had been uncovered. Like Kennedy and Reagan, Clinton does admit wrongdoing.

Clinton, early in the speech, says, "I must take complete responsibility for all my actions, both public and private." He thereby implies that he is taking responsibility for the particular events he is talking about in the speech, but he never directly

---

[18]See Joseph R. Blaney and William L. Benoit, *The Clinton Scandals and the Politics of Image Restoration* (Westport, CT: Praeger, 2001) for a full discussion of Clinton's image repair strategies. In Benoit, *Accounts*, he outlines six ways of reducing the offensiveness of a transgression: bolstering, minimization, differentiation, transcendence, attacking one's accuser, and compensation.

says so. In fact, no sooner does Clinton utter the word "responsibility" than he begins chipping away at what he might be held responsible for. He denies lying to a grand jury—"my answers were legally accurate"; he denies obstruction of justice—"at no time did I ask anyone to lie, to hide or destroy evidence or to take any other unlawful action." So, what is he taking responsibility for—for giving "a false impression," for misleading "people, including even my wife" and for "a relationship with Miss Lewinsky" that was "not appropriate," that was "wrong," and that represented "a critical lapse in judgment and a personal failure on my part." Since the relationship did not involve vaginal intercourse, Clinton holds that his statement to the grand jury was accurate but misleading. He is implicitly saying the same about his January remark: he did indeed not have sex with her if sex is, by definition, vaginal intercourse.[19]

Clinton then admits wrongdoing on his part in language that lacks Nixon's tentativeness, but like Reagan and Kennedy, he admits wrongdoing while almost simultaneously backing away from the admission. Reagan took responsibility but shifted much (if not all) of the blame to aides and to his management style; Kennedy took responsibility but shifted much (if not all) of the blame to the "scene" and his understandably human emotional response to the scene. Clinton tries less to shift than to narrow down what he's responsible for so that it is no longer important or it is solely between himself and his wife and daughter.

Kennedy, it has been argued, hurt himself politically by admitting that he, in essence, panicked. Did Clinton hurt himself politically? Being slick with one's words so as to avoid personal and political problems—is that a behavior that disqualifies one from high office? Engaging in sexual activities with someone other than his wife? Someone quite a bit younger? Someone in a subordinate position?—are these behaviors that disqualify one? Or are they behaviors one would simply rather not see in the nation's chief executive?

After admitting guilt—albeit for limited offenses—Clinton attempts to rebuild his character. In doing so, he, of course, is doing what is common in this kind of speech. He uses four strategies to do so.

First, like Kennedy, he cites his humanity. Clinton says he did what he did (i.e., misled people) prompted "by a desire to protect myself from the embarrassment of my own conduct." Those in the audience would certainly understand this motive. How many in that audience would "go public" with an embarrassing admission if it were possible to avoid doing so?

Second, like Reagan, he cites an admirable quality that motivated his behavior. For Reagan, it was his admirable management style. For Clinton, it is his admirable desire to protect his family from embarrassment. One might respond to Clinton's

[19]Clinton's claim that "he did not have sexual relations with that woman" may have more validity than may at first seem to be the case. See Walter Kirn, "When Sex Is Not Really Having Sex," *Time* (February 2, 1998): 34, for a discussion of the legal and popular basis of Clinton's claim that oral sex is not sex. Also, for evidence that youth do not think oral sex "counts" as sex, see "Teens Break No-Sex Vows, Study Suggests; Some Say Oral Sex Not Sex," *Christian Century* (December 27, 2003): 14.

claim with disbelieving cynicism; however, if one believes the claim, then one affirms that Clinton acted nobly in trying to cover up his indiscrete behavior, saving Hillary and Chelsea pain.

Third, like Nixon, he attacks those who are attacking him. He mentions the "politically inspired lawsuit" launched by Paula Jones; he notes that it was dismissed to prove it to be also an unfounded lawsuit. He mentions the independent counsel's investigation that is looking into 20-year-old allegations, of which an independent federal agency had cleared him, and he mentions how the counsel is now investigating "my staff and friends" and "my private life." That investigation is "now ... itself ... under investigation," a fact that Clinton offers to discredit it. Later, he refers to "the pursuit of personal destruction." Obviously, those suing him and investigating him so doggedly are the ones he wants his audience to see as engaged in that pursuit. He is their victim.

Fourth, he tries to establish a dividing line in people's minds between what's public and what's private. The grand jury is asking "questions about my private life, questions no American would ever want to answer." Clinton is implicitly asking: Should they be?. Later, he argues that "this matter is between me, the two people I love most—my wife and our daughter—and our God." He says, like Reagan, that he will "put it right," but he insists that the matter "is private." It should not be before the public, and he "intend[s] to reclaim my family life for my family. It's nobody's business but ours. Even presidents have private lives." Those who will not let private be private are "prying into private lives" and doing damage to "the fabric of our national discourse" and distracting attention from "all the challenges and all the promises of the next American century." Clinton wants his audience to accept the public–private division and see him—and not his opponents—as trying to focus the nation on those important public matters. Clinton wants his audience to rise above (i.e., transcend) and forget his private affairs.

Nixon's "Checkers speech" was a masterful success, but his Watergate speeches probably were not. Reagan's "apology" for Iran/Contra probably succeeded; Kennedy's for Chappaquiddick helped him get reelected to the U.S. Senate but probably kept him from the White House. The verdict on Clinton's "apology" is less clear than those for the other addresses. What one thinks of the speech may ultimately depend on what one thinks of Bill Clinton, and that may depend largely on one's politics. Many Republicans thought in 2000 that he was a disgrace to the presidency, but many Democrats thought he would have won reelection if a third term had been Constitutionally permitted.

All that a rhetorician can ultimately do is point to the strategies the rhetor (Clinton) chose to use. He took responsibly but shrunk as much as he could what he was responsible for. He admitted that his personal (not presidential) conduct was wrong. He tried to rebuild his lowered character by citing his humanity, his nobility, and his victim status. He also tried to clear the field for further presidential successes by arguing that that field should grow public policy, not personal matters. Viewed objectively, these strategies could well have succeeded. But strategies are not always viewed so. Strategies are displayed before audiences, and audiences have strongly held attitudes as well as a sense of who the speaker is. Rhetoric is then not just about strategic choices among possible messages to deliver and possible ways to deliver them. Rhetoric is about the process of persuading audiences. And different audiences, as this case shows, might well have very different reactions to the same speech. Some might say, leave the man's private life alone; others might say, impeach and convict.

Critics Joseph R. Blaney and William L. Benoit offer an analysis that is highly critical of the speech. They see the address as both insufficiently contrite and too aggressive in its attacks on others. Rather than try to reduce the offensiveness of his actions, they would have preferred that Clinton engage in mortification. Thus, they find the president's September 11, 1998, speech at the White House Prayer Breakfast to be a more successful *apologia*. They do admit, however, that polling showed that the viewing public largely granted Clinton's arguments on August 17. They note, to the contrary, that many columnists and writers of letters to the editor felt differently. Clearly, audiences were not considering Clinton's arguments neutrally: the audience's politics were affecting how successful they found the *apologia* to be.

Conclusion

Clinton's speeches on the subject of his relationship with intern Monica Lewinsky are best seen in the context of the genre of *apologia*. His brief January statement is somewhat like Nixon's famous "Checkers speech," although far briefer. His August address is more like later apologies. In it, like others who have used the genre, he takes responsibility but immediately backpedals from the act. Then, like the others, he tries to rebuild his image. The extent to which Clinton rhetorically succeeded may have as much to do with the audience's attitudes as with the president's strategies.

THE MASS COMMUNICATION PERSPECTIVE

Watergate and the Clinton–Lewinsky scandal may quickly come to mind when we think back to presidential scandals of the twentieth century. When considering media aspects of these two scandals, however, the connection between them quickly ends. The 1998 feeding frenzy over Monica Lewinsky's relationship with President Bill Clinton differed dramatically from the investigative reporting of Watergate. In the Clinton case we see how technology, competition, and newsroom decisions influenced how the news media covered this scandal, how the coverage was evaluated (by the public as well as those in the news media), and the potential impact of the coverage mass communication research found.

News, Gossip, and Scoops

Besides the scandal in 1998 making household names of Linda Tripp, Monica Lewinsky, and Kenneth Starr, there are two other key names to address when considering mass media issues of this presidential crisis: Michael Isikoff and Matt Drudge.

Michael Isikoff was the *Newsweek* investigative reporter who first learned of the relationship between Clinton and Lewinsky. Although the scandal broke publicly in January 1998, Isikoff had heard back in March 1997 that Clinton was having an affair with a former White House intern. He had covered the case involving Paula Jones's sexual harassment lawsuit against President Clinton since 1994. Even with Isikoff's background and thorough reporting in the past, *Newsweek* was divided on how to handle the developing stories about whether Lewinsky had lied about having an affair with the president when she testified in the Paula Jones case, and whether Clinton or others had coached her to do so.[20]

Matt Drudge was the first to name Monica Lewinsky as the intern who had had an affair with President Clinton by posting a report online, while *Newsweek* was holding the story to complete additional reporting (although Drudge claimed they had killed the story, not just held it). Drudge, who is often referred to as an Internet gossip and not a journalist, sent out and posted his story early the morning of Sunday, January 18, 1998.

Some news organizations discredited Drudge as a credible source of information and dismissed Drudge's claims. But hearing that *Newsweek* was about to break some story prior to Drudge's e-mail, many news organizations quickly developed their own stories on the case. As a weekly news magazine, *Newsweek* postponed the story from their January 19 edition and ended up posting their version of the story online on January 21 (only the second time they published a story online before it appeared in the print version of the magazine), to avoid being scooped further by their competition. By then, however, most mainstream news organizations, daily newspapers and television news, had already begun their own reporting on the story.

According to Alicia Shepard's account of the Lewinsky coverage in *American Journalism Review*, the news obsession continued to grow.

> There are 19 minutes of news on each of the three major network nightly newscasts—a possible total of 57 minutes combined. On Wednesday, January 21, 28.5 minutes were devoted to Clinton, 22 minutes to Cuba. By Friday, the ratio was 46 minutes for Clinton, five for Cuba. "Any time you get over 30 minutes a day combined on the nightly newscast on one story, it's a great story," says [Andrew] Tyndall [of the *Tyndall Report*], who closely monitors network coverage. "In the last 10 years, only one inside Washington story got more coverage than this did during the first week: Clarence Thomas."[21]

A later analysis of network news confirmed the media obsession with this story. The three news networks, ABC, CBS, and NBC, devoted more airtime to covering the Clinton scandal than the next seven most-aired stories combined in 1998. However, broadcast news alone is not to blame in this apparent frenzy. The Associated Press wire service had twenty-five reporters working regularly on the Lewinsky story, and the *New York Times* had twelve reporters in Washington, DC, covering it as well as reporters in other cities.[22]

---

[20]For further details on the early developments in the reporting on Monica Lewinsky, see Alicia C. Shepard, "A Scandal Unfolds," *American Journalism Review* 20.2 (March 1998): 20–28.

[21]Shepard, "A Scandal Unfolds," p. 28.

[22]Michael Gartner, "How the Monica Story Played in Mid-America," *Columbia Journalism Review* 38.1 (May/June, 1999): 34–36.

Although the media coverage in 1998 indicates a fascination with this scandal story, news consumers report not being as interested in it as the media were. Just 10 days after the story broke on January 21, 1998, a *Washington Post* poll found that 74 percent of respondents said the news media were giving the story "too much attention." In that same poll, 56 percent agreed that the news media were treating Clinton unfairly.[23] A survey by the Pew Research Center for People and Press at the end of 1998 confirms the lack of public interest in the Clinton scandal story. Only 36 percent reported following the Clinton–Lewinsky scandal story closely in 1998, with only 34 percent saying they watched the coverage of the House impeachment of Clinton closely.[24] Stories meriting more public attention in 1998 than the scandal and impeachment included school shootings in Jonesboro, Arkansas, and Oregon; the U.S. Capitol shooting; military strikes against Iraq, Sudan, and Afghanistan; election results for 1998; and that summer's heat wave.

"Darts and Laurels" for News Coverage[25]

Some have praised the media for its willingness to pursue this story, to explain why a private matter may have public importance. Defenders of media coverage of this scandal would defend the public's right to know as well as the press's right to scrutinize those in elected office. Others have criticized the news media for its invasion into the privacy of Bill Clinton, Monica Lewinsky, and others involved in this case. Although we may support in general the "watchdog role" of the press, the news media were criticized for operating like an angry pack of dogs in covering this story and for substituting a healthy dose of skepticism with antagonism.[26] In a *Columbia Journalism Review* column, former NBC News president Michael Gartner defended the reporting by news media, in light of considerable speculation and gossip being conveyed on the Internet and some cable channels.[27] Gartner's comment on the coverage reflects two divergent opinions on the coverage as well as the event itself:

> Was all of this coverage—as some charge—a "feeding frenzy" by an overeager press pushed by Washington bureau chiefs who delight in seeing big politicians tumble? In my view it's outrageous to make such a charge. This was the greatest human, moral, political, and constitutional drama in our country since the end of the Civil War. (p. 35)

[23]Poll summarized in Jules Witcover, "Where We Went Wrong," *Columbia Journalism Review* 36.6 (March/April 1998): 19–26.

[24]Pew Research Center for the People and the Press, "Turned off: Public Tuned Out Impeachment," December 21, 1998. http://people-press.org/reports/display.php3?ReportID=73.

[25]"Darts and Laurels" are the critiques and praise offered for news media practices by *Columbia Journalism Review* in each issue.

[26]Rem Rieder, "Clinton's Legacy to Journalism," *American Journalism Review* 20.8 (October 1998): 6.

[27]Michael Gartner, "How the Monica Story Played in Mid-America," *Columbia Journalism Review* 38.1 (May/June, 1999): 34–36.

As we saw Clinton's approval ratings continue to remain strong throughout this crisis, public opinion criticizing the media's coverage of the scandal persisted as well. A February poll by the Pew Center found that 36 percent of those surveyed thought the media were doing either an excellent or a good job in maintaining their objectivity in covering the scandal.[28] That skepticism of the media was also reflected in a finding that 69 percent of the public thought the news media presumed Clinton guilty of perjury. In August 1998, another Pew Center poll found only 40 percent of respondents thought the media were doing an excellent or good job in maintaining their objectivity in covering the scandal.[29]

Journalists graded themselves poorly for the news coverage of the Clinton–Lewinsky scandal. In a small poll of senior journalists conducted by *Columbia Journalism Review*, 61 percent said they would give the news media a grade of A or B in the overall press coverage of the Monica Lewinsky scandal,[30] with 23 percent grading the coverage a C, 14% giving it a D, and 2% giving the news media an F. The *Columbia Journalism Review* survey of senior journalists also found that only 11 percent planned to change the way they covered the private lives of political officials and candidates, whereas 89 percent did not plan on changing their coverage. Beyond the assessments of coverage of this particular scandal, it has also been the subject of considerable speculation and research regarding its potential impact on the public.

Media Theory and the Clinton-Lewinsky Scandal

Media scholars have studied the Clinton–Lewinsky scandal with the "trifecta" of media theories: agenda setting, framing, and priming. If we think of traditional agenda-setting research in the context of the scandal, we might assume that the concentration of media coverage noted earlier would produce a heightened concern about the scandal as an issue for Americans. However, such a relationship was not found, perhaps because a scandal is not an issue affecting most Americans, not in the way that issues such as crime or the economy affect individuals.

Public opinion polls found a heightened awareness of the scandal, and perhaps concern for how it might affect the presidency, or speculation about details of the affair, but not in establishing it as an issue of importance to the American public. Yioutas and Segvic note this inconsistency, stating that "observing this contradiction between media and public priorities, some have described the Clinton/Lewinsky scandal as a classic case of the media failing to set the public agenda"[31] (p. 571).

---

[28]Pew Research Center for the People and the Press, "Popular Policies and Unpopular Press Lift Clinton Ratings," February 6, 1998. http://people-press.org/reports/display.php3?ReportID=96.

[29]Pew Research Center for People and the Press, "It's still the economy, they say," August 27, 1998. http://people-press.org/reports/display.php3?ReportID=82.

[30]Neil Hickey, "After Monica, What Next?" *Columbia Journalism Review* 37 (November/December 1998): 30–33.

[31]Julie Yioutas and Ivana Segvic, "Revisiting the Clinton/Lewinsky Scandal: The Convergence of Agenda-Setting and Framing," *Journalism and Mass Communication Quarterly* 80.3 (2003): 567–82.

They suggest rather that "if the attribute agenda of the media emphasized the sexual nature of the scandal rather than the implications for the presidency" (p. 572), the public would not see the scandal as relevant to Clinton's presidency or governance. Their analysis found 55 percent of *New York Times* and *Washington Post* news articles on the scandal included attention toward the affair itself, while only 21 percent referred to the impact on the presidency.

The news coverage surrounding this scandal demonstrates a unique factor in agenda-setting research. Given the poll results cited earlier regarding the public's lack of interest in this scandal, their critique of media coverage, and their continuing support for President Clinton, along with the noted concentration of media coverage on this scandal, we see that it may not always be a direct effect of media attention to public attention. Rather, the public's opinion of the event, and of the media coverage itself, may insulate potential agenda-setting effects by the media. If the public concludes, as they did in this case, that there was too much coverage of the story, perhaps agenda-setting effects will not occur. Yioutas and Segvic also suggest that how the event was covered, or framed, as a sex scandal versus one having political implications, may have affected the public's evaluation of its importance as well.

Framing research on the Clinton scandal examines how the news media covered the scandal, to explore to what extent the media focused on the events of the affair itself or the political implications of the scandal overall. An analysis of coverage by Shah, Watts, Domke, and Fan identified three frames in news coverage of the Lewinsky scandal: a Clinton behavior frame (the nature of the affair, Clinton avoiding discussing his relationship, the scandal's process toward impeachment), a conservative attack frame (actions by Republicans in critiquing Clinton and discussing means to remove him from office), and a liberal response frame (defending Clinton, claiming attacks on Clinton served to embarrass and discredit him for others' political gain).[32] Furthermore, they found the two competing frames, the conservative attack and liberal response, both contributed to public support for Clinton. While media audiences saw stories including attacks on Clinton for his conduct, they also saw stories criticizing those attacks.

The concept of priming in this case would examine to what extent news coverage of the sex scandal primed particular attitudes or opinions about President Clinton. Kiousis studied priming effects by tracking media coverage (from the *New York Times* and ABC News) with public opinion evaluations of President Clinton throughout 1998.[33] Kiousis found that media attention to the Lewinsky scandal did prime people's evaluations of President Clinton. Kiousis found a stronger correlation between news coverage and perceived favorability of Clinton than with news coverage

[32]Dhavan V. Shah, Mark D. Watts, David Domke, and David P. Fan, "News Framing and Cueing of Issue Regimes: Explaining Clinton's Public Approval in Spite of Scandal," *Public Opinion Quarterly* 66 (2002): 339–70.

[33]Spiro Kiousis, "Job Approval and Favorability: The Impact of Media Attention to the Monica Lewinsky Scandal on Public Opinion of President Bill Clinton," *Mass Communication and Society* 6.4 (2003): 435–51.

and job approval, identifying distinctions in evaluating Clinton personally and professionally. The concentration of media coverage on this scandal clearly had agenda-setting, framing, and priming effects, although those effects varied among citizens in their attention to the coverage and their assessment of President Clinton.

Conclusion

Although we might hope, or expect, the news media to proceed with caution in dealing with similar news events in the future, the feeding frenzy and the news environment in 1998 might once again impact coverage and the newsroom decisions on reporting. The immediacy of information available online and the heightened competition from online news, traditional network news, cable news, and various sources of print news contributed to the frenzy we saw in 1998 in covering President Clinton's relationship with Monica Lewinsky. The news coverage in this case demonstrates when agenda setting may *not* occur, that is, when the news attention on a particular topic does not lead to public evaluations of importance of that topic. Consistent frames were identified in analysis of news coverage of this scandal, and connections were also found between news coverage and the potential priming of opinions, although the connections differed in favorability and job approval ratings of Clinton.

CONCLUSION

A number of themes are consistent among the perspectives presented in this chapter. The rhetorical and political science perspectives address Clinton's initial denial of his relationship with Monica Lewinsky, and his later apology, and the potential damage that not taking responsibility earlier may have caused in his presidency. The distinction Clinton made in his apology speech between public and private matters is at the center of most media debates regarding the coverage of the Clinton–Lewinsky scandal. In the "court" of public opinion, Clinton's speech was successful, because his approval ratings remained strong throughout his impeachment process. Finally, a number of effects of this scandal were identified, politically for Clinton's presidency in the short term and long term, as well as effects of the media coverage on the public's attention to the scandal and their interpretation of it.

Although many common issues are raised, these perspectives do diverge in this case study. Clinton's speeches are compared to past apologies, and in what ways his remarks were successful with the public. A focus in mass communication was not Clinton's remarks themselves, but how the mass media covered the scandal in general, from the transformation of gossip into news to the feeding frenzy that persisted. Although public opinion polls reported in the news media found support for Clinton strong, politically the scandal had repercussions for Clinton in terms of less success in Congress and the potential of the scandal undermining his legacy as president.

ADDITIONAL CASES

Students interested in exploring other instances of political "scandal," which required a deft response, might consider the following:

- **Iran/Contra Hearings, 1986**
  Resource: David Bogen and Michael Lynch, "Taking Account of the Hostile Narrative: Plausible Deniability and the Production of Convention History in the Iran-Contra hearings." *Social Problems, 36* (June 1989): 197–224.

- **U.S. Attorney General Janet Reno's comments regarding the 1993 standoff between the FBI and David Koresh at the Branch Davidian compound in Waco, Texas**
  Resource: Attorney General Janet Reno's Opening Statement before the Crime Subcommittee of the House Judiciary Committee and the National Security International Affairs and Criminal Justice Subcommittee of the House Government Reform and Oversight Committee, August 1, 1995; available online at http://www.pbs.org/wgbh/pages/frontline/waco/renoopeningst.html

- **Nixon's resignation speech amid the Watergate scandal**
  Resource: President Nixon's Resignation Speech, August 8, 1974, available online at http://www.americanrhetoric.com/speeches/richardnixonresignationspeech.html

- **New Jersey Governor James McGreevey's resignation after confessing to having a homosexual affair**
  Resource: Michael Isikoff and Evan Thomas, "He Wanted to Clean up Politics in the Jersey Capital. It Didn't Work out That Way. A Series of Scandals, and a Gay Secret Life, Cut James McGreevey's Career Short." *Newsweek* (August 23, 2004): 24.

- **Congressman Bob Livingston's resignation from Congress during the Clinton impeachment**
  Resource: Brian Duffy, Kenneth T. Walsh, Michael J. Gerson, Major Garrett, Franklin Foer, Joseph P. Shapiro, Michael Barone, Mike Tharp, James Morrow, and Brian Kelly, "End Games." *U.S. News & World Report, 125* (December 28, 1998): 16.

CHAPTER 12

CASE EIGHT: GEORGE W. BUSH RESPONDS TO TERRORISM

THE CASE

On September 11, 2001, terrorists trained and financed by al Qaeda flew commercial airplanes into the World Trade Center towers in New York City and the Pentagon just outside Washington, DC. Another airplane crashed in western Pennsylvania before reaching its intended target. That evening, President George W. Bush addressed the American people.

> Good evening. Today, our fellow citizens, our way of life, our very freedom came under attack in a series of deliberate and deadly terrorist attacks. The victims were in airplanes, or in their offices; secretaries, businessmen and women, military and federal workers; moms and dads, friends and neighbors. Thousands of lives were suddenly ended by evil, despicable acts of terror. The pictures of airplanes flying into buildings, fires burning, huge structures collapsing, have filled us with disbelief, terrible sadness, and a quiet, unyielding anger. These acts of mass murder were intended to frighten our nation into chaos and retreat. But they have failed; our country is strong.
>
> A great people has been moved to defend a great nation. Terrorist attacks can shake the foundations of our biggest buildings, but they cannot touch the foundation of America. These acts shattered steel, but they cannot dent the steel of American resolve. America was targeted for attack because we're the brightest beacon for freedom and opportunity in the world. And no one will keep that light from shining.
>
> Today, our nation saw evil, the very worst of human nature. And we responded with the best of America—with the daring of our rescue workers, with the caring for strangers and neighbors who came to give blood and help in any way they could.
>
> Immediately following the first attack, I implemented our government's emergency response plans. Our military is powerful, and it's prepared. Our emergency teams are working in New York City and Washington, D.C. to help with local rescue efforts.
>
> *****
>
> The search is underway for those who are behind these evil acts. I've directed the full resources of our intelligence and law enforcement communities to find those responsible and to bring them to justice. We will make no distinction between the terrorists who committed these acts and those who harbor them.
>
> *****
>
> America and our friends and allies join with all those who want peace and security in the world, and we stand together to win the war against terrorism. Tonight, I ask for your

prayers for all those who grieve, for the children whose worlds have been shattered, for all whose sense of safety and security has been threatened. And I pray they will be comforted by a power greater than any of us, spoken through the ages in Psalm 23: "Even though I walk through the valley of the shadow of death, I fear no evil, for You are with me."

This is a day when all Americans from every walk of life unite in our resolve for justice and peace. America has stood down enemies before, and we will do so this time. None of us will ever forget this day. Yet, we go forward to defend freedom and all that is good and just in our world. Thank you. Good night, and God bless America.[1]

Several days later, on September 20, Bush addressed Congress in an emergency State of the Union speech, outlining the nation's response to the terrorist attacks. Michael Gerson was its primary author, with input from Bush aide Karen Hughes and advice from others.

In the normal course of events, Presidents come to this chamber to report on the state of the Union. Tonight, no such report is needed. It has already been delivered by the American people.

We have seen it in the courage of passengers, who rushed terrorists to save others on the ground—passengers like an exceptional man named Todd Beamer. And would you please help me welcome his wife, Lisa Beamer, here tonight.

We have seen the state of our Union in the endurance of rescuers, working past exhaustion. We have seen the unfurling of flags, the lighting of candles, the giving of blood, the saying of prayers—in English, Hebrew, and Arabic. We have seen the decency of a loving and giving people who have made the grief of strangers their own.

My fellow citizens, for the last nine days, the entire world has seen for itself the state of our Union—and it is strong.

Tonight we are a country awakened to danger and called to defend freedom. Our grief has turned to anger, and anger to resolution. Whether we bring our enemies to justice, or bring justice to our enemies, justice will be done.

*****

... On September the 11th, enemies of freedom committed an act of war against our country. Americans have known wars—but for the past 136 years, they have been wars on foreign soil, except for one Sunday in 1941. Americans have known the casualties of war—but not at the center of a great city on a peaceful morning. Americans have known surprise attacks—but never before on thousands of civilians. All of this was brought upon us in a single day—and night fell on a different world, a world where freedom itself is under attack.

Americans have many questions tonight. Americans are asking: Who attacked our country? The evidence we have gathered all points to a collection of loosely affiliated terrorist organizations known as al Qaeda. They are the same murderers indicted for bombing American embassies in Tanzania and Kenya, and responsible for bombing the USS *Cole*. Al Qaeda is to terror what the mafia is to crime. But its goal is not making money; its goal is remaking the world—and imposing its radical beliefs on people everywhere.

The terrorists practice a fringe form of Islamic extremism that has been rejected by Muslim scholars and the vast majority of Muslim clerics—a fringe movement that perverts the peaceful teachings of Islam. The terrorists' directive demands them to kill

[1]The text is derived from that available at http://www.whitehouse.gov/news/releases.

Christians and Jews, to kill all Americans, and make no distinction among military and civilians, including women and children.

This group and its leader—a person named Osama bin Laden—are linked to many other organizations in different countries, including the Egyptian Islamic Jihad and the Islamic Movement of Uzbekistan. There are thousands of these terrorists in more than 60 countries. They are recruited from their own nations and neighborhoods and brought to camps in places like Afghanistan, where they are trained in the tactics of terror. They are sent back to their homes or sent to hide in countries around the world to plot evil and destruction.

The leadership of al Qaeda has great influence in Afghanistan and supports the Taliban regime in controlling most of that country. In Afghanistan, we see al Qaeda's vision for the world.

Afghanistan's people have been brutalized—many are starving and many have fled. Women are not allowed to attend school. You can be jailed for owning a television. Religion can be practiced only as their leaders dictate. A man can be jailed in Afghanistan if his beard is not long enough.

The United States respects the people of Afghanistan—after all, we are currently its largest source of humanitarian aid—but we condemn the Taliban regime. It is not only repressing its own people, it is threatening people everywhere by sponsoring and sheltering and supplying terrorists. By aiding and abetting murder, the Taliban regime is committing murder.

*****

. . . I also want to speak tonight directly to Muslims throughout the world. We respect your faith. It's practiced freely by many millions of Americans, and by millions more in countries that America counts as friends. Its teachings are good and peaceful, and those who commit evil in the name of Allah blaspheme the name of Allah. The terrorists are traitors to their own faith, trying, in effect, to hijack Islam itself. The enemy of America is not our many Muslim friends; it is not our many Arab friends. Our enemy is a radical network of terrorists and every government that supports them.

Our war on terror begins with al Qaeda, but it does not end there. It will not end until every terrorist group of global reach has been found, stopped and defeated.

Americans are asking, why do they hate us? They hate what we see right here in this chamber—a democratically elected government. Their leaders are self-appointed. They hate our freedoms—our freedom of religion, our freedom of speech, our freedom to vote and assemble and disagree with each other.

*****

These terrorists kill not merely to end lives, but to disrupt and end a way of life. With every atrocity, they hope that America grows fearful, retreating from the world and forsaking our friends. They stand against us, because we stand in their way.

We are not deceived by their pretenses to piety. We have seen their kind before. They are the heirs of all the murderous ideologies of the 20th century. By sacrificing human life to serve their radical visions—by abandoning every value except the will to power—they follow in the path of fascism and Nazism, and totalitarianism. And they will follow that path all the way, to where it ends: in history's unmarked grave of discarded lies.

*****

Our response involves far more than instant retaliation and isolated strikes. Americans should not expect one battle, but a lengthy campaign, unlike any other we have ever seen. It may include dramatic strikes, visible on TV, and covert operations, secret even in success. We will starve terrorists of funding, turn them against one another, drive them from place to place, until there is no refuge or no rest. And we will pursue nations that provide aid or safe haven to terrorism. Every nation, in every region, now has a decision to make. Either you are with us, or you are with the terrorists. From this day forward, any nation that continues to harbor or support terrorism will be regarded by the United States as a hostile regime.

*****

It is my hope that in the months and years ahead, life will return almost to normal. We'll go back to our lives and routines, and that is good. Even grief recedes with time and grace. But our resolve must not pass. Each of us will remember what happened that day, and to whom it happened. We'll remember the moment the news came—where we were and what we were doing. Some will remember an image of a fire, or a story of a rescue. Some will carry memories of a face and a voice gone forever.

And I will carry this: It is the police shield of a man named George Howard, who died at the World Trade Center trying to save others. It was given to me by his mom, Arlene, as a proud memorial to her son. This is my reminder of lives that ended, and a task that does not end.

I will not forget this wound to our country or those who inflicted it. I will not yield; I will not rest; I will not relent in waging this struggle for freedom and security for the American people.

The course of this conflict is not known, yet its outcome is certain. Freedom and fear, justice and cruelty, have always been at war, and we know that God is not neutral between them.

Fellow citizens, we'll meet violence with patient justice—assured of the rightness of our cause, and confident of the victories to come. In all that lies before us, may God grant us wisdom, and may He watch over the United States of America.[2]

Several months later, on January 29, 2002, Bush gave his "regularly scheduled" State of the Union address. Michael Gerson was, again, its primary author.

We last met in an hour of shock and suffering. In four short months, our nation has comforted the victims, begun to rebuild New York and the Pentagon, rallied a great coalition, captured, arrested, and rid the world of thousands of terrorists, destroyed Afghanistan's terrorist training camps, saved a people from starvation, and freed a country from brutal oppression.

*****

Our cause is just, and it continues. Our discoveries in Afghanistan confirmed our worst fears, and showed us the true scope of the task ahead. We have seen the depth of our enemies' hatred in videos, where they laugh about the loss of innocent life. And the depth of their hatred is equaled by the madness of the destruction they design. We have found diagrams of American nuclear power plants and public water facilities, detailed instructions for making chemical weapons, surveillance maps of American cities, and thorough descriptions of landmarks in America and throughout the world.

*****

Our nation will continue to be steadfast and patient and persistent in the pursuit of two great objectives. First, we will shut down terrorist camps, disrupt terrorist plans, and bring terrorists to justice. And, second, we must prevent the terrorists and regimes

---

[2]The text is derived from that available at http://www.whitehouse.gov/news/releases.

who seek chemical, biological or nuclear weapons from threatening the United States and the world.

Our military has put the terror training camps of Afghanistan out of business, yet camps still exist in at least a dozen countries. A terrorist underworld—including groups like Hamas, Hezbollah, Islamic Jihad, Jaish-i-Mohammed—operates in remote jungles and deserts, and hides in the centers of large cities.

*****

Our second goal is to prevent regimes that sponsor terror from threatening America or our friends and allies with weapons of mass destruction. Some of these regimes have been pretty quiet since September the 11th. But we know their true nature. North Korea is a regime arming with missiles and weapons of mass destruction, while starving its citizens.

Iran aggressively pursues these weapons and exports terror, while an unelected few repress the Iranian people's hope for freedom.

Iraq continues to flaunt its hostility toward America and to support terror. The Iraqi regime has plotted to develop anthrax and nerve gas and nuclear weapons for over a decade. This is a regime that has already used poison gas to murder thousands of its own citizens—leaving the bodies of mothers huddled over their dead children. This is a regime that agreed to international inspections—then kicked out the inspectors. This is a regime that has something to hide from the civilized world.

States like these, and their terrorist allies, constitute an axis of evil, arming to threaten the peace of the world. By seeking weapons of mass destruction, these regimes pose a grave and growing danger. They could provide these arms to terrorists, giving them the means to match their hatred. They could attack our allies or attempt to blackmail the United States. In any of these cases, the price of indifference would be catastrophic.

We will work closely with our coalition to deny terrorists and their state sponsors the materials, technology, and expertise to make and deliver weapons of mass destruction. We will develop and deploy effective missile defenses to protect America and our allies from sudden attack. And all nations should know: America will do what is necessary to ensure our nation's security.

We'll be deliberate, yet time is not on our side. I will not wait on events while dangers gather. I will not stand by, as peril draws closer and closer. The United States of America will not permit the world's most dangerous regimes to threaten us with the world's most destructive weapons.

Our war on terror is well begun, but it is only begun. This campaign may not be finished on our watch—yet it must be and it will be waged on our watch.

We can't stop short. If we stop now—leaving terror camps intact and terror states unchecked—our sense of security would be false and temporary. History has called America and our allies into action, and it is both our responsibility and our privilege to fight freedom's fight.[3]

On March 17, 2003, Bush took this fight into Iraq. Here are some excerpts from his televised address:

The danger is clear: using chemical, biological, or, one day, nuclear weapons, obtained with the help of Iraq, the terrorists could fulfill their stated ambitions and kill thousands or hundred of thousands of innocent people in our country, or any other.

*****

[3]The text is derived from that available at http://www.whitehouse.gov/news/releases.

Before the day of horror can come, before it is too late to act, this danger will be removed.

*****

Many Iraqis can hear me tonight in a translated radio broadcast, and I have a message for them. If we must begin a military campaign, it will be directed against the lawless men who rule your country and not against you. As our coalition takes away their power, we will deliver the food and medicine you need. We will tear down the apparatus of terror and we will help you to build a new Iraq that is prosperous and free. In a free Iraq, there will be no more wars of aggression against your neighbors, no more poison factories, no more executions of dissidents, no more torture chambers and rape rooms.

The tyrant will soon be gone. The day of your liberation is near.

*****

Should enemies strike our country, they would be attempting to shift our attention with panic and weaken our morale with fear. In this, they would fail. No act of theirs can alter the course or shake the resolve of this country. We are a peaceful people—yet we're not a fragile people, and we will not be intimidated by thugs and killers.

*****

The cause of peace requires all free nations to recognize new and undeniable realities. In the 20th century, some chose to appease murderous dictators, whose threats were allowed to grow into genocide and global war. In this century, when evil men plot chemical, biological, and nuclear terror, a policy of appeasement could bring destruction of a kind never before seen on this earth.[4]

Then, on May 1, Bush landed on the deck of the USS *Abraham Lincoln* and, with a banner proclaiming "Mission Accomplished," declared Operation Iraqi Freedom a success and saluted the troops, comparing them to those who fought in World War II. Bush also looked to the future in the following two excerpts:

Our war against terror is proceeding according to principles that I have made clear to all: Any person involved in committing or planning terrorist attacks against the American people becomes an enemy of this country, and a target of American justice. Any person, organization, or government that supports, protects, or harbors terrorists is complicit in the murder of the innocent, and equally guilty of terrorist crimes. Any outlaw regime that has ties to terrorist groups or seeks or possesses weapons of mass destruction is a grave danger to the civilized world—and will be confronted.

Our mission continues. Al Qaeda is wounded, not destroyed. The scattered cells of the terrorist network still operate in many nations, and we know from daily intelligence that they continue to plot against free people. The proliferation of deadly weapons remains a serious danger. The enemies of freedom are not idle, and neither are we. Our government has taken unprecedented measures to defend the homeland. And we will continue to hunt down the enemy before he can strike. The war on terror is not over; yet it is not endless. We do not know the day of final victory, but we have seen the turning of the tide. No act of the terrorists will change our purpose, or weaken our resolve, or alter their fate. Their cause is lost. Free nations will press on to victory.[5]

[4]The text is derived from that available at http://www.whitehouse.gov/news/releases.

[5]The text is derived from that available at http://www.whitehouse.gov/news/releases.

President George W. Bush declares that our mission has been accomplished in Iraq in a speech aboard the aircraft carrier USS Abraham Lincoln *on May 1, 2003.*

THE POLITICAL SCIENCE PERSPECTIVE

Whatever else will ultimately be said about the presidency of George W. Bush, an inescapable part of his legacy will be his administration's response to the horrific attacks of September 11, 2001. However, any analysis of President Bush's response to the attacks must begin with the attacks themselves. Political violence—what most people think of as terrorism—is a form of political communication, although it is thankfully not a common one. As San Francisco State University communication professor Joseph Tuman, quoted in a 2002 *Chronicle of Higher Education* article, has pointed out: "'When a terrorist hurts someone or destroys property, it's not only violence, it's communicating a message.' . . . Terrorism is not just about blowing something up. What's important is the message being sent.'"[6]

---

[6]Author unknown. "Examining the Symbols of Terrorism to Understand Its Message." *The Chronicle of Higher Education* 49.15 (December 6, 2002).

Those who engage in political violence frequently do so because they believe (correctly or not) that traditional avenues of influencing their political environment have been closed to them. Politically motivated violence alters the traditional relationships between those in power and those who feel powerless, because governments must shift their priorities in response to an attack. Certainly this is what occurred as a result of September 11. Before the attacks, the nation was engaged in a debate over the appropriateness of stem cell research using human embryos; after the attacks, the nation's priorities shifted to homeland security, counterterrorism and prosecuting a multifront war on terror. As presidency scholars Thomas Cronin and Michael Genovese explain: "The attack changed the political circumstances under which Bush governed, and created a 'crisis presidency.'"[7]

The Crisis Presidency

Of course, terrorism is only one form—and an extreme one at that—of political communication. The responses of political leaders to terrorist incidents likewise constitute political communication. As Cronin and Genovese note, during times of crisis, a "crisis presidency" typically emerges. This term refers to the tendency of the other branches of the federal government to defer to the president during national emergencies. Because the president oversees a vast national security and diplomatic staff, Congress and the federal courts frequently are reluctant to limit his power during a time of crisis. Moreover, the president's constitutionally assigned role of commander-in-chief makes him the focal point for leadership during times of emergency. As presidency scholar Jon Roper has noted, "[T]he president's heroic talent is latent. It is to be called upon in times of crisis."[8] It should be noted that the president-as-focal-point model of American national government is contrary to the Constitution's delegation of greater institutional power to the U.S. Congress in Article I than to the president, which is not discussed until Article II. Nevertheless, because the Constitution makes the president the commander-in-chief of the nation's armed forces, he is able to act decisively in times of crisis.

In addition to the constitutional roles assigned to the president, he has a number of extraconstitutional powers that permit him to govern effectively when a national emergency takes place. Always an important agenda setter, when a crisis hits the president is able to act almost unilaterally. This is largely because the public rallies around the president; regardless of how popular the president was before a crisis incident, his popularity will rise as he appears to take charge of the situation.

The president's job during these times is to help people cope with whatever traumatic event has occurred. Part of what the president must do during times of crisis is to reassure the public both that he has a plan and is in control of the situation and that the course of action he intends to follow is justified by American values. This is certainly what happened after September 11, 2001. For example, in his address to the nation a week after the 2001 attacks, Bush stated:

---

[7]Thomas E. Cronin and Michael A. Genovese, *The Paradoxes of the American Presidency*, 2nd ed. (New York: Oxford University Press, 2004), 137.

[8]Jon Roper, "The Contemporary Presidency: George W. Bush and the Myth of Heroic Presidential Leadership," *Presidential Studies Quarterly* 34.1 (March 2004): 132(11).

> Freedom and fear, justice and cruelty, have always been at war, and we kn
> is not neutral between them. . . . Fellow citizens, we'll meet violence
> justice—assured of the rightness of our cause, and confident of the victories ...... in
> all that lies before us, may God grant us wisdom, and may He watch over the United
> States of America.[9]

With these words, Bush sought to reassure the public that those who attacked the country were wrong, not just politically, or because of their methods, but wrong because the course of action they selected was an offense against natural, or God-given, law. In so doing, the president attempted to justify the course of action the country would pursue in response. Bush, like crisis presidents before him, offered a dichotomy that pitted the wrongheaded terrorists against the righteousness of the United States.

Often, however, to demonstrate the rightness of his own course of action, a president must demonize enemies, both domestic and foreign. Presidents do this to clarify the roots of the conflict and to make clear the official position of the U.S. national government. Thus, rather than helping the public to understand the nuances and complexities of what has occurred, presidents rally support and assuage public fears through appeals to patriotism and by casting enemies in the worst possible light. For example, writing about the vilification of Saddam Hussein that the George H. W. Bush administration engaged in during the first Gulf War, one observer noted: "That the leader of a modern nation such as the United States, filled with people allegedly educated and civilized, had to resort to name calling attests to two things: that leaders still must maintain a visceral rather than a rational connection to their people, and that words are vital in war and the preparation for war."[10] George W. Bush's repeated references to war in the excerpts of the speeches above also illustrate presidential crisis rhetoric. As Bruce Ackerman noted, in a 2004 commentary in *The American Prospect*: "Almost two centuries ago, Andrew Jackson was making war on the Bank of the United States. More recently, presidents have waged wars on drugs, crime, and poverty. Even at its most metaphorical, martial rhetoric gives presidents a chance to invoke their mystique as Commander-in-Chief."[11]

It is the president's role as commander-in-chief, cultivated through patriotic words and tough talk to the nation's enemies, which was strengthened by the speeches made by George W. Bush in reaction to the September 11 attacks. His speeches were filled with explanations for the attacks that were designed both to demonstrate his resolve as president and to comfort people about the place of our public values. His explanation—"They hate what we see right here in this chamber— a democratically elected government. . . . They hate our freedoms—our freedom of religion, our freedom of speech, our freedom to vote and assemble and disagree with

---

[9]Source: President's Address to a Joint Session of Congress and the American People. Washington, DC. September 20, 2001. Available online at: http://www.whitehouse.gov/news/releases/2001/09/20010920-8. html.

[10]Richard O'Mara, "A Terrorist Is a Guerrilla Is a Freedom Fighter: 'Reality' Is a Long and Slippery Slope," *The Quill* 78.8 (October 1990): 22(3).

[11]Bruce Ackerman, "States of Emergency," *The American Prospect* 15.9 (September 2004): 40(1).

each other"—was patriotic and in keeping with the Bush's role as a crisis president. Yet, it was an oversimplified view of the reasons underlying the September 11 attacks. That fact illustrates the principle, articulated by Cronin and Genovese, that the public frequently cares less about the substance of a president's message than it does about the appearance of strength and resolve. They write:

> Although Americans like to view themselves as hardheaded pragmatists, they, like humans everywhere cannot stand too much reality. People do not live by reason alone. Myths and dreams are an age-old form of escape. People will continue to believe what they want to believe. And people turn to national leaders just as indigenous people turn to shamans—yearning for meaning, healing, empowerment, legitimacy, assurance, and a sense of purpose.[12]

During times of crisis, a president's words offer reassurance that the nation will rebound from whatever tragedy has occurred. Clearly, Bush's role as national healer was in evidence throughout the speeches he made during 2001 and 2002, both in response to the September 11 attacks and, later, to explain his rationale for the war in Iraq. According to Communication professor Denise Bottsdorff: "Bush's rhetorical response to the terrorist attacks [of September 11, 2001] constituted citizens as part of a special, sacred community involved in the same monumental battle against evil that the greatest generation fought during World War II."[13]

Just as presidential rhetoric during a time of crisis can be used to rally the public to the president's proposed response, the rhetoric can later come back to haunt a president if he cannot meet the public's expectations. For example, as the years since the September 11 attacks have passed, the Bush administration has increasingly been criticized for the lengthy conflict in Iraq that ensued, and for the rhetoric that he used in the speeches he made in response to September 11, specifically his reference to an "axis of evil" consisting of Iran, Iraq, and North Korea. Indeed, the president's "axis of evil" designation came back to haunt him when the Democratic People's Republic of Korea (DPRK)—North Korea—test fired several nuclear missiles in early July 2006. When the United Nations' Security Council unanimously condemned the DPRK, the North Korean ambassador to the United Nations unequivocally rejected the Security Council's resolution, claiming that President Bush had previously designated North Korea as a part of an axis of evil, and then had attacked Iraq preemptively (in their view).[14] Even at home, public concerns began to surface about the wisdom of the Bush Administration's decision to engage in a war in Iraq,

---

[12]Thomas E. Cronin and Michael A. Genovese, *The Paradoxes of the American Presidency*, 2nd ed. (New York: Oxford University Press, 2004), 147.

[13]Denise M. Bostdorff, "George W. Bush's Post-September 11 Rhetoric of Covenant Renewal: Upholding the Faith of the Greatest Generation," *Quarterly Journal of Speech* 89 (2003): 293–319.

[14]United Nations Security Council. "Security Council Condemns Democratic People's Republic of Korea's Missile Launches, Unanimously Adopting Resolution 1695" (New York: United Nations, 2006).

especially because both Iran and North Korea announced that they were continuing to pursue the development of nuclear weapons.

Conclusion

Although the Constitution does not give the president unilateral power to act during times of domestic tranquility, when a crisis hits a number of factors converge that give him extensive power. This was certainly in evidence after the attacks of September 11, when President George W. Bush was put in the position of articulating a U.S. response to the terrorist incidents. Bush's response, delivered through a series of speeches, sought to distill the issues underlying the attacks to a simple dichotomy between good and evil. This strategy is consistent with what presidents have done throughout history during times of crisis, but it is not without its pitfalls. Although tough rhetoric directed at the nation's enemies may help to ease the country through a difficult time, as President Bush learned in 2005 and 2006, it may also raise the public's expectations for presidential leadership more generally.

THE RHETORICAL PERSPECTIVE

Aristotle loved to classify things: three kinds of this; four types of that. Some sense that the scientist in Aristotle is coming through. But his classifications are rarely just for the sake of neatening things up, nor are they based on differences one might call trivial.

Thus, Aristotle divided oratory into three types: forensic, epideictic, and deliberative. It might seem that this classification is based on where the communication occurs: forensic in the courtroom, epideictic in the town square, deliberative in the legislative assembly. However, Aristotle seemed to discern that more differentiated these types of oratory from each other than just location. He seemed to discern that rhetors were constructing very different kinds of arguments.

If we map Toulmin onto Aristotle, we can perhaps see what Aristotle did. Forensic discourse is characterized by designative claims, with the rules of evidence determining which of these claims should be attended to.[15] Some definitive claims (e.g., the definition of "hate crime") and some evaluative claims (e.g., crime was heinous) may enter into forensic discourse, but most of the claims are designative. Epideictic discourse is characterized by evaluative claims: people or events or actions are being praised or condemned. Some definitive claims may also appear since the warrants for the evaluative claims tend to be definitions of what is "good" or what is "bad." Deliberative discourse is characterized by advocative claims, but buried in

---

[15]For a full discussion of how argumentation would proceed in a forensic context, see Stephen Toulmin, Richard Rieke, and Allan Janik, *Introduction to Reasoning* (New York: Macmillan, 1979): 203–27.

those are the three other types. To justify action by the state, one needs to know what the facts are (designative), what key terms mean (definitive), and what's advisable and what's not (evaluative). The key is that the different types of discourse necessitate different combinations of claims. One does not proceed rhetorically in the legislative assembly, where public policy is being discussed, in the same way as in the town square, where praising and blaming are occurring and the public is being rallied.

Bush's Immediate Response as Epideictic

The terrorist attack on the United States on September 11, 2001, called initially for the president to come into the electronic town square. He needed to praise those who had come to the aid of victims as well as the victims themselves; he needed to blame—vaguely, if necessary—those responsible for the attack. He also needed to suggest to those in his audience that the crisis was being managed well. This last task required that he offer some designative claims—facts about rescue and recovery efforts at the disaster sites. But, for the most part, he would be offering the evaluative claims characteristic of epideictic discourse.

Bush evaluates the work of rescue personnel as "daring," and the volunteering to help on the part of average citizens as "caring." He provides a litany of those who died and asks for "prayers for all those who grieve," especially the children. In a paragraph of the speech not reprinted, he talks about how the government, the nation's financial institutions, and the economy in general are "open for business," per usual. And in a crucial paragraph that is reprinted, he talks about how "the full resources" of the government are being devoted to rooting out all responsible for the attack. Bush's language in this September 11 speech is strong—more about that later, but he generally does what needs to be done rhetorically in a crisis.

Bush's Call for Attack on Afghanistan

President Bush's rhetorical situation quickly changes, however. Several days later, he is beginning a war effort that will start with attacks on Afghanistan and later extend to Iraq. He is presenting foreign policy decisions to the legislature and the public and asking for (at least implicitly) their assent. His situation calls for deliberative discourse and the offering of advocative claims underpinned by designative, definitive, and evaluative ones. Does Bush offer this kind of discourse, or does he continue in an epideictic vein? In the present day, rarely does oratory fall neatly into one of Aristotle's categories. So, we should not expect to find Bush offering nothing but evaluative claims if he is offering epideictic discourse, not the requisite deliberative. The question then becomes does he do so sufficiently to overwhelm the kind of reasoning deliberative discourse requires.[16]

---

[16]A fuller version of some of the analysis offered is found in John M. Murphy, "'Our Mission and Our Moment': George W. Bush and September 11th," *Rhetoric & Public Affairs* 6 (2003): 607–32.

The September 11 speech is, as one would expect, dominated by evaluative claims. The acts of the terrorists are called "evil, despicable" and termed "mass murder"; the United States, on the other hand, is evaluated as "strong" and the actions taken in response to the attack are evaluated as demonstrating "the best of America." Even the quoting of Psalm 23 toward the speech's conclusion evaluates the terrorist acts as "evil." In contrast, the U.S. effort is evaluated as being in service of "freedom and all that is good and just."

The address to Congress 9 days later is more of a policy address, for, in it, Bush is announcing what U.S. policy toward the Taliban regime in Afghanistan will be. However, the claims are overwhelmingly evaluative. The passengers on United Flight 93 are praised; so are those "loving and giving" Americans who came to people's aid on September 11. On the contrary, the Taliban is condemned for both brutalizing its own people (especially its women) and "aiding and abetting murder" abroad. The U.S. cause is evaluated as serving freedom and justice; the Taliban's as serving fear and cruelty. And, in conclusion, to confirm absolutely his evaluation of the U.S. cause, Bush tells us that "God is not neutral."

Epideictic discourse is, by its very nature, emotional. The September 11 speech evokes anger; the September 20 address is longer and more complex, as the president tries to move his audience from grief and anger toward the resolution necessary for a lengthy war on terror. Bush evokes these emotions through strong language but also by having Lisa Beamer, the widow of a courageous United Flight 93 passenger, present in the gallery and by telling the audience that he will carry the police shield of George Howard, who died during rescue operations on September 11 in New York City, with him as a reminder of the day. These are very Reaganesque moves, bringing visually before the audience compelling stories featuring average Americans.

The January 29, 2002, State of the Union address, like the two speeches before it, seems very epideictic. The president praises all that the United States has accomplished thus far on both the domestic and the foreign fronts. And he evaluates our cause as "just" and in service of freedom. He also evaluates Iraq, Iran, and North Korea as "an axis of evil" that poses a "grave and growing danger." The designative claims that might have been offered to prove that these nations are a danger are largely lacking. There are few facts in the address about what these three nations have done or are doing. Evaluations, laden with emotion, dominate.

Bush's Call for Action against Iraq

The March 17, 2003, address that extends the war on terror into Iraq is a bit more balanced between epideictic and deliberative. Some attempt is made by the president to prove—through designative claims—that Iraq has not cooperated with the international community and that Iraq has weapons of mass destruction. However, Bush very quickly jumps to judgment, declaring Iraq's leadership "not ... peaceful men" and "lawless men" and Saddam Hussein "the tyrant" and associating the Iraqi regime with "reckless aggression," "a deep hatred of America," "horror," "deceit and cruelty," and "terror."

These two addresses take the nation into war. They present a policy. One would hope that they would offer the mix of claims that characterize deliberative discourse. Instead, they rely very heavily on the evaluations characteristic of the epideictic. The result of sticking with the epideictic may well have been to undermine the policy-making process that requires claims other than evaluative ones to ensure sound decisions.

Bush's "Victory" Address

The May 1, 2003, speech aboard the USS *Abraham Lincoln* is different: it is not a policy-making speech; rather, it is a celebratory one. Its purpose is to praise the troops and to celebrate the American cause. It is appropriately epideictic. In being so, however, it does offer at least one evaluative claim—that Iraq is now free—that time will call into question. However, in a speech designed to celebrate it would have been out of keeping for the kind of reasoning and evidence appropriate to policy deliberation to have been offered. The "Mission Accomplished" speech, then, is rhetorically what it ought to be. The problem is that the epideictic mode, appropriately turned to here, was inappropriately turned to in the preceding three policy-making speeches. Bush is, as it were, "stuck" in an epideictic way of speechmaking.

Bush and Genre Confusion

There are other rhetorical problems evidenced in those speeches. Karlyn Kohrs Campbell and Kathleen Hall Jamieson in *Deeds Done in Words* define several genres of speeches that presidents, through many years, have delivered. Two of these genres are relevant to the speeches Bush delivered between the September 11 address and the "Mission Accomplished" one: State of the Union addresses and war declaration speeches.[17] Bush conflates the two genres, thus arguably setting up in the minds of audience members a confusing set of expectations. He also allows his emphasis on praising and blaming to lead him away from conforming to the norms for either genre.

The speech in February 2002 is a State of the Union address; the previous speech, although not delivered at what has come to be the normal time for a State of the Union speech, is foregrounded as such by Bush in its initial paragraphs. As defined by Campbell and Jamieson, such a speech serves both epideictic and deliberative needs. It offers a public meditation on the values that define the nation, and it sustains or creates a national identity. In doing so, it usually takes listeners back into the nation's history. These are epideictic functions and, not surprisingly, the style can be rather high when the speech is serving these functions. Furthermore, the speech usually has a nonpartisan quality at these times. On the other hand, a State of the Union address presents and assesses information about the nation and offers policy

---

[17]Karlyn Kohrs Campbell and Kathleen Hall Jamieson, *Deeds Done in Words: Presidential Rhetoric and Genres of Governance* (Chicago: University of Chicago Press, 1990): 52–75; 101–26.

recommendations based on it. The style tends to be lower when the speech is serving these deliberative functions, and partisanship sometimes rears its ugly head.

Bush's two addresses arguably become hijacked by the war on terror. The values that are promoted and the national identity that is presented are tied to the war. Thus, we stand for freedom, and we *are* that nation in the world that will act to defend freedom. The posture we are asked to assume is an at-war one. Furthermore, the information presented as preparation for policy recommendations is skewed toward this war. In the September speech, the war excludes all else; in the February one, the war squeezes other issues into a relatively small section of the address. And, in that section, the war keeps intruding. Arguably, this deliberative discourse dealing with matters such as unemployment, education, energy, trade, taxation, retirement security, health care, and volunteerism becomes lost in a speech dominated by the war. Neither this speech nor the September one fully functions as a State of the Union address. The emphasis on the epideictic as well as the way the epideictic is used to push certain values and a particular national identity prevent the speech from achieving the aims of the State of the Union address as—at least partially—deliberative discourse.

These two speeches, as well as the March 2003 one, are also flawed examples of the presidential address declaring war. Whereas the inaugural address is a fairly stable genre, the war declaration speech has proved quite unstable. This instability is linked to two connected political "facts": the war power has evolved; and "war" has become increasingly difficult to define. When Woodrow Wilson addresses Congress on April 2, 1917, he asked that the Congress declare war; when Franklin Delano Roosevelt addressed Congress after the Japanese attack on Pearl Harbor, he asked that the Congress declare that a state of war already exists—a subtle shift. But then there were police actions, and then there were volatile situations requiring an immediate military response. As a result, presidents after John F. Kennedy began asking Congress to support a military operation already under way. Legislation was enacted defining exactly when and how presidents had to consult and report. Still, through all of the presidencies until George W. Bush's, there was an expectation that, when the president reported, he would refer to the careful consultation that had taken place and he would call explicitly for national unity and ask for Congressional commitment to the operation, be it called a "war" or not.

Bush's speeches that led America's armed forces into Afghanistan and Iraq largely lack both of these characteristics. In September 2001, he thanks Congress and he invites other nations to join us in the war on terror, but Bush does not mention consulting with either. He assumes that others are with him, but he does not explicitly ask for support. His remark, "I will not yield; I will not rest; I will not relent in waging this struggle for freedom and security for the American people," perhaps suggests how much Bush sees waging the war as something he the president does, with others, perhaps, following his personal lead.

In February 2002, he refers to "the coalition" pursuing the war, but he does not talk about consulting with them, let alone other leaders in Washington, DC. He does, however, call for support—for the budget necessary to fight the war and to provide for homeland security.

In March 2003, he mentions that other nations that might join us in acting against Iraq. However, he makes it clear that the United States is acting because of the failure of others in the international community to do so. And, in talking about using military force, Bush says, "That duty falls to me as Commander-in-chief, by the oath I have sworn, by the oath that I will keep." He refers to the congressional support he has previously received for the idea of using force against Iraq; however, he suggests that the decision to do so is his alone to make. And he certainly does not in this speech ask Congress to second his decision.

Bush, then, has taken the declaration of war speech further away from its historical norm. What the speeches lack are references to deliberation—either that with others preceding the use of arms or that afterward. Lacking these references, the president perhaps no longer needs to offer much by way of a rationale for such deliberations. War declaration speeches have typically offered a narrative justifying the use of force. Although it was often dramatized, simplified, and sometimes even characterized by misrepresentations of the facts, the narrative was there—so that others could nod assent or support. In Bush's three speeches, the narrative is so severely truncated as to be barely present. Bush declares rather than narrates with some supporting detail. And, from these declarations, he moves quickly to good/bad evaluative claims and, then, military threats. One might argue once again that a tendency to engage in epideictic discourse when some level of deliberative is expected caused Bush's war declaration speeches to be quite far removed from what Wilson or Roosevelt delivered in the twentieth century's first half or even what Lyndon B. Johnson (Vietnam) or George H. W. Bush (the first Gulf War) delivered in its second half.

Bush's Language

Epideictic discourse tends to be high style. This style can exhibit itself in rhetorical flourishes or, more simply, in highly evocative language. The Bush speeches exhibit the latter. The following are the phrases used in association with the terrorists and those who support them:

> "evil, despicable acts of terror" (9/11/01)
> "acts of mass murder" (9/11/01)
> "evil" (9/11/01)
> "evil acts" (9/11/01)
> "evil" [in quotation from Psalm 23] (9/11/01)
> "enemies of freedom" (9/20/01)
> "Islamic extremists" (9/20/01)
> "a fringe movement that perverts the peaceful teachings" (9/20/01)
> "to kill Christians and Jews, to kill all Americans" (9/20/01)
> "to plot evil and destruction" (9/20/01)
> "Afghanistan's people have been brutalized" (9/20/01)
> "aiding and abetting murder . . . committing murder" (9/20/01)
> "those who commit evil in the name of Allah" (9/20/01)

"traitors to their own faith, trying . . . to hijack Islam" (9/20/01)
"brutal oppression" (1/29/02)
"hatred. . . . madness" (1/29/02)
"leaving the bodies of mothers huddled over their dead children" (1/29/02)
"axis of evil" (1/29/02)
"tyranny and death" (1/29/02)
"reckless aggression" (3/17/03)
"deep hatred of America" (3/17/03)
"the day of horror" (3/17/03)
"the lawless men" (3/17/03)
"thugs and killers" (3/17/03)
"oppressors" (5/15/03)
"enslavement" (5/15/03)

Several rhetoricians have written about the emotive power of language. Richard Weaver, in particular, has talked about "god" terms and their opposite. Here is a catalogue of terms that would fall into that devilish second category. Given the repetition of such terms throughout Bush's speeches, it is clear that he is seeing the war on terrorism through what Kenneth Burke would call a "terministic screen," a rather simple one that shades those opposed to the United States as "evil."

Bush and Identification

All that has been said thus far might lead one to think that the rhetoric of these Bush speeches on terrorism is a failure. If it is, it is because they short-circuit policy making: they replace well-reasoned policy making with emotionally laden evaluations. These evaluations, however, can be very successful in persuading an audience of the president's position. As humans, we respond powerfully to pathos, and there is plenty of pathos in these speeches. The speeches can also be seen as effective, persuasive ones insofar as they offer very powerful negative depictions of "the enemy." Kenneth Burke talks about the rhetorical power of positive identification that brings about what he terms "consubstantiality." Also powerful is the negative insofar as it can unite those on the other side against "the enemy": the audience becomes consubstantial—one body—against this enemy.

In depicting this enemy, who, then, does Bush identify the enemy with in order to solidify himself and the audience against this enemy? On September 20, 2001, Bush identified the terrorists with the Japanese attacking Pearl Harbor in 1941, with the mafia, and with "all the murderous ideologies of the 20th century" including "fascism, and Nazism, and totalitarianism." On March 17, 2003, Bush identified Hussein with the "aggressive dictators" whose actions necessitated the establishment of the United Nations and the "murderous dictators, whose threats were allowed to grow into genocide and global war." On May 15, 2003, Bush identified the defeated Iraqi military with the Nazis we fought on D-Day and the Japanese we fought on Iwo Jima. These negative identifications, of course, demean the enemy. They also put those fighting against terrorism in the ennobled shoes of "the greatest generation" that fought in World War II. That positive identification, besides unifying those in his audience, also gave the American efforts against terror a much clearer sense that they, in fighting terror, were, of course, the good combating the starkly evil.

Conclusion

The rhetorical lens, with its close focus on texts, gives us much to ponder when considering George W. Bush's oratorical responses to terrorism. The president conflates epideictic and deliberative, perhaps resulting in policy making that is too tied to emotional responses. The president also conflates genres, causing further problems with the fullness of the arguments he offers. Bush's language, however, has power to persuade, as does the way he identifies America's enemies with evil and the nation's defenders with good.

THE MASS COMMUNICATION PERSPECTIVE

In considering the events outlined in the introduction to this chapter, one could write multiple books just on the media and September 11 and the media and the war in Iraq.[18] To fit the confines of this case study, however, the mass communication section of this chapter will focus on a few key issues: news decisions and coverage issues in covering the war in Iraq, reporters' relationship with President Bush, and how the embedded reporting affected journalists' relationships with the military, as well as coverage of the war.

News Media Coverage of the War in Iraq

The war in Iraq was a dominant focus in American news for much of 2003. A content analysis of network news broke the year into three segments: January to March 18, before the war started; March 19 to May 1, the start of the war until Bush declared an end to major hostilities; and then the rest of the year as the third segment.[19] These are not equal length segments of that year, but they do reflect key time periods of the conflict, by which we can examine the focus of the television news agenda in attending to the Iraq war. In the 10 weeks of 2003 before the start of the war, network news aired 810 stories about the conflict. In the approximately 6 weeks of key conflict, network news aired 1,052 stories about Iraq. And in the remaining 8 months of 2003, there

---

[18]A few titles to consult for in-depth discussions on these issues include: Ralph D. Berenger, ed., *Global Media Go to War: Role of News and Entertainment Media during the 2004 Iraqi War* (Spokane, WA: Marquette Books, 2004); Stuart Allan and Barbie Zelizer, eds., *Reporting War: Journalism in Wartime* (London: Routledge, 2004); Barbie Zelizer and Stuart Allan, eds., *Journalism after September 11* (London: Routledge, 2002).

[19]S. J. Farnsworth and S. R. Lichter, *The Mediated Presidency: Television News and Presidential Governance* (Lanham, MD: Rowman and Littlefield, 2006).

were 1,571 stories about Iraq aired on U.S. television. As we saw the political transitions take place in Iraq, as well as continuing violence by insurgents, news attention did not decline dramatically.

Cable television appeared to be the biggest "winner" of growing audiences during the war in Iraq. Sharkey cites a *Los Angeles Times* poll from early April 2003 which found that almost 70 percent of Americans reported getting most of their news about the war from cable TV.[20] The number of average daily viewers for MSNBC, CNN, and Fox News skyrocketed during the first 2 weeks of the Iraqi war. Whereas *NBC Nightly News* had 11.3 million viewers nightly according to Nielsen ratings, another 3.3 million were watching Fox News each day, and not necessarily for a 30-minute evening newscast.

Given the length of time of escalation before the war started in March 2003, news organizations had considerable time to plan their news strategies and prepare for extended reporting abroad. Before going to the Middle East to cover the pending war in Iraq, many reporters trained physically for the rigors of war coverage, especially when embedded with U.S. military troops. Some news organizations hired personal trainers to work with their staff going to Iraq, and others took advantage of Pentagon-sponsored "basic training" for reporters.[21] Ricchiardi offers the following description of such training in "Preparing for War":

> To prepare, reporters and photographers climbed ropes, crawled on their bellies, lifted weights and trekked for miles during rugged training offered by the Pentagon at places like Georgia's Fort Benning and Virginia's Quantico Marine Corps Base. NPR's [John] Burnett reported: 'Our escorts for the week were mostly Army drill sergeants. They compared supervising correspondents to herding cats.' (p. 30)

In addition to preparing news staff for reporting on the war, news organizations were also busy establishing news bureaus in the Middle East to facilitate their coverage. Although we may think of embedded reporters and the restrictions placed on journalists by U.S. military, reporters were also restricted by Iraqi officials in their coverage and access. NBC News reporter Richard Engel recounts his experiences in Iraq just before the war's onset in 2003:

> When you arrived, the Ministry of Information gave you a minder, and his job was to follow you and write reports. And to make sure that you didn't point your cameras at any presidential sites, which were everywhere. There were certain areas where you could film one way but you couldn't move your camera four inches to the left.[22]

Engel also suggests that although Iraq's Ministry of Information worked to control outside news reporters' access to information, they were more concerned with what Iraqis said to reporters than with what reporters said or did.

---

[20]Jacqueline Sharkey, "The Television War." *American Journalism Review* 25.4 (May 2003): 18–27.

[21]Sherry Ricchiardi, "Preparing for War," *American Journalism Review* 25.2 (March 2003): 29–33.

[22]Mark Lasswell, "Life During Wartime," *Broadcasting and Cable* (February 7, 2005): 8.

One area of discussion and possible concern regarding the news coverage of the war in Iraq was the effect television coverage in particular might have had in distancing viewers from the emotional power of the war. Such accusations occurred even with the embedded coverage, which we might think would provide a more realistic picture of war. A quote from Anthony Swofford, author of *Jarhead: A Marine's Chronicle of the Gulf War and Other Battles* (the basis for the 2005 film by the same name) suggests one perspective on this issue: "Television reports soften war and allow it to penetrate even deeper into the living rooms and minds of America. War can't be that bad if they let us watch it."[23] Paul McMasters of the Freedom Forum First Amendment Center says the reporting on Iraq worked "to grind the grit of war into a fine powder that makes the war more palatable."[24]

The media attention toward casualties may reinforce the "sanitizing" of the war even further. An analysis of news broadcasts from ABC, NBC, CBS, CNN, and Fox News by the Project for Excellence in Journalism found that half the reports from embedded journalists depicted combat action, but never people hit by weapons.[25] Although weapons were shown being fired, their impact was not shown; moving and military maneuvers were the most common images of action shown from the war. A contrasting analysis by Farnsworth and Lichter compared network coverage of the Iraq war in 2003 to the coverage of the Persian Gulf War in 1991. They found that 35 percent of news stories in 2003 on Iraq contained some image of combat, whereas only 20 percent of news stories in 1991 did so.[26] They attribute this shift to journalists embedded with troops, as well as new technology that allowed for such coverage. When it came to coverage of casualties, they found that images of military casualties had declined from 1991 to 2003, but that images of civilian casualties had actually increased: appearing in 3 percent of news reports in 1991 but appearing in 18 percent of news reports in 2003. When comparing coverage of the Persian Gulf War to that of the 2003 war in Iraq, the human consequences of war appear to be a more common image. This could also be explained by additional access to the areas of combat, as well as the length of the conflict in Iraq in 2003 compared with the very short Persian Gulf War in 1991.[27] What to show and how much to show continue to be debated in newsrooms when covering such conflicts.

---

[23]Sharkey, p. 21.

[24]Sharkey, p. 23.

[25]Project for Excellence in Journalism, "Embedded Reporters: What Are Americans Getting?" April 3, 2003. http://www.journalism.org/resources/research/reports/war/embed/default.asp.

[26]Farnsworth and Lichter.

[27]For further research and discussion on the news images of the Iraqi war, see Cynthia King and Paul Martin Lester, "Photographic Coverage during the Persian Gulf and Iraqi Wars in Three U.S. Newspapers," *Journalism and Mass Communication Quarterly* 82.3 (2005): 623–37; and Lori Robertson, "Images of War," *American Journalism Review* 26.5 (2004): 44–51.

Reporters' Relationships

Looking specifically at media coverage of Bush's "Mission Accomplished" speech included in the introduction of this chapter, we can sense aspects of the news media's relationship with President Bush during this international conflict. A report in the *San Francisco Chronicle* on May 2, 2003, is consistent with most coverage of Bush's speech:

> Speaking from the deck of one of America's most potent weapons of war, President Bush announced Thursday that "major combat operations in Iraq have ended" while warning that "our coalition will stay until the work is done." . . .
>
> The day's carefully choreographed events allowed the president a picturesque— and powerful—opportunity to express the nation's gratitude to the troops in the glow of sunset while the *Lincoln* plowed toward San Diego after more than nine months at sea.[28]

The report also detailed specifications of the S-3B Viking that Bush flew as "the first-ever jet arrival by a commander in chief on an aircraft carrier," as well as his landing carrier, the USS *Abraham Lincoln*. Many other reports similarly focused on the contents of Bush's remarks as well as his dramatic entrance and the environment from where they were given. Although reports may have included quotes by Democrats criticizing Bush for his comments or the venue for the speech, most press was neutral and potentially even positive toward Bush.

However, some news organizations continued to explore the circumstances of Bush's landing the jet before his speech, which resulted in less favorable coverage of the president. For example, a May 7, 2003, *Washington Post* report raises issues regarding Bush's choice to land on the carrier by jet rather than by helicopter, with this lead into the story: "President Bush chose to make a jet landing on an aircraft carrier last week even after he was told he could easily reach the ship by helicopter, the White House said yesterday, changing the explanation it gave for Bush's 'Top Gun' style event."[29] When looking at this type of coverage, some may conclude media bias, that the *Washington Post* is one of many papers that is "out to get" the president in its coverage. Although they did publish such a story, it was not "page 1" news, as Bush's speech initially was in the papers throughout the United States; this piece was published on page 20 of the first section of the *Post*. Although the reporting raised questions about such coverage, it was not given much prominence by the paper itself.

If we consider the tone of coverage toward President Bush overall during the war in Iraq, and not just surrounding this single event, we see that it declined in favorability as the conflict continued after Bush's "Mission Accomplished" speech. In *The Mediated Presidency: Television News and Presidential Governance*, Farnsworth and Lichter evaluated the tone of network coverage of President Bush during the crisis of September 11, 2001, as well as during the war in Iraq in 2003.[30] They found that in

[28]Carla Marinucci, "Bush Thanks Troops; 'The Tyrant Has Fallen,'" *San Francisco Chronicle*, May 2, 2003.

[29]Dana Milbank, "Explanation for Bush's Carrier Landing Altered," *Washington Post*, May 7, 2003.

[30]Farnsworth and Lichter.

the 2 months following the September 11 terrorist attacks, 64 percent of network news coverage of President Bush was positive; in 2003 in the combat phase of the war in Iraq, 49 percent of news coverage of Bush was positive. In the "early occupation" phase in Iraq, from May 1 through October 31, 2003, only 32 percent of network news was favorable toward President Bush. Farnsworth and Lichter note that once a war ends, or in this case once a president declares it has ended, coverage of the president typically increases in negativity.

A debate regarding the role of the news media in the war in Iraq has developed, with one side accusing the news media of patriotic coverage that did not seriously investigate the administration's justification for the war, while the other side suggests the news media doubted and questioned every move President Bush or Secretary of Defense Donald Rumsfeld made. The "news as lapdog" accusations suggested the news media wagged the flag for the United States in the war in Iraq and did not maintain their objectivity. Both Fox News and MSNBC terms their coverage "Operation Iraqi Freedom," the government's name for the conflict, while other news organizations selected more general terms ("Showdown in Iraq," for example).[31] The Pentagon reportedly twice convinced CBS News to delay the broadcast of a *60 Minutes II* report airing photographs from Abu Ghraib prison that showed American military forcing Iraqi prisoners into humiliating poses.[32] The *New York Times* published an apology on May 26, 2003, to readers for not being "more aggressive" in investigating the White House decision to invade Iraq. The "news as watchdog" accusations suggested reporters were not objective in their coverage of the war in Iraq, perhaps because of their own opposition of military involvement in the conflict. The focus on the events surrounding Bush's landing on the USS *Abraham Lincoln* before his May 1, 2003, speech might be an example raised for "undue scrutiny" by the press.

Beyond the news media's relationship with President Bush, the war in Iraq also offers the opportunity to explore the relationship between news media and the U.S. military in a time of war. More than 500 reporters were embedded with American troops during the war in Iraq. The embedded journalist program evolved over dissatisfaction with the "pool coverage" model used in the Persian Gulf War in 1991, in which a small number of reporters were allowed to travel with troops on a given day, but their access was severely limited and they were required to provide their information back to the pool of other reporters who were not permitted to travel with the troops on that given day. Such a news structure leads to homogeneous coverage, as all reporters are basing their news stories on the same information, and when much of the news process is competitive, this required information-sharing approach was counterintuitive to news routines.

Reporters embedded with troops agreed to Pentagon ground rules that outlined what was "releasable" information and what they could not report on from the war.[33]

---

[31]Sharkey.

[32]Stephen J. Berry, "CBS Lets the Pentagon Taint Its News Process," *Nieman Reports* 58.3 (Fall 2004): 76–78.

[33]A complete list of Pentagon guidelines for embedded reporters in the war in Iraq can be found online at http://www.defenselink.mil/news/Feb2003/d20030228pag.pdf.

If reporters revealed prohibited information, such as troop locations, they would no longer be allowed to accompany troops and they were, in some cases, removed from Iraq and returned home.

In general, the conclusion is that the embedded reporting process worked. Journalists reported feeling free to report as long as they were not risking security, although there were instances of reporters not being given access to particular locations. There was in-depth reporting on particular troop operations by embedded journalists, but what was lacking was a broad overview of the war.[34] One evaluation of the embedded reporting was quite favorable, saying the following:

> And despite initial skepticism about how well the system would work, and some dead-on criticism of overly enthusiastic reporting in the war's early stages, the net result was a far more complete mosaic of the fighting—replete with heroism, tragedy, and human error—than would have been possible without it.[35] (p. 30)

Concerns regarding this "enthusiasm" of coverage tie to questions regarding the objectivity of reporting on the war. Would embedded reporters be even more likely to provide patriotic coverage? The conclusion may be that the coverage was different from what it would have been without embedded reporters, but not necessarily more biased. Ricchiardi notes that embedded TV reporters often referred to the troops' activities using the term "we," associating themselves with soldiers in Iraq. Fox and Park examined what they call the "I of embedded reporting" of CNN coverage in March 2003, during the "Shock and Awe" campaign. Their analysis found a higher use of personal pronouns in embedded reporting than news stories written by journalists not embedded with troops, although in some ways embedded reporters may have attempted to show greater objectivity in their coverage of the troops. Fox and Park conclude, "embedded reporters may have been more mindful of seeming biased in favor of the Bush administration's Shock and Awe campaign."[36]

Another analysis examined the framing of newspaper stories by embedded reporters compared to those not embedded with the troops.[37] The findings of Pfau and colleagues are consistent with the critique of embedded war coverage: it lacked a broad perspective on the war. They found embedded coverage was more episodic than nonembedded coverage, to use Shanto Iyengar's distinction between episodic and thematic framing. Episodic news frames were narrow in focus, which provided in-depth attention on a particular issue, and also personalized the issues. But because

[34]Jennifer LaFleur, "Embed Program Worked, Broader War Coverage Lagged," *News Media and the Law* 27.2 (2003): 4–6.

[35]Sherry Ricchiardi, "Close to the Action," *American Journalism Review* 25.4 (May 2003): 28–35.

[36]Julia R. Fox and B. Park, "The 'I' of Embedded Reporting: An Analysis of CNN Coverage of the 'Shock and Awe' Campaign," *Journal of Broadcasting and Electronic Media* 50.1 (2006): 36–51. (Quote from Discussion, para. 2).

[37]Michael Pfau et al., "Embedding Journalists in Military Combat Units: Impact on Newspaper Story Frames and Tone," *Journalism and Mass Communication Quarterly* 81.1 (2004): 74–88.

embedded journalists were so strongly connected to particular units of the military during their coverage, they were isolated from the larger issues of the war and also the context to understand their unit's events in a broader picture. News organizations that had embedded reporters providing episodic yet in-depth frames and non-embedded reporters covering the thematic frames for a broader overview of the war in Iraq may have been able to provide coverage that gave audiences depth as well as breadth to understanding the war in Iraq.

Conclusion

The war in Iraq received considerable media attention in news coverage, as well as substantial audiences for the news, with cable news having considerable growth in audiences compared to past conflicts. The notion of a "TV war" continues to be a concern; although embedded reporting brought more detail of the war to audiences (perhaps in exchange for a broad understanding of the war), debates continue in newsrooms over showing casualties, and balancing coverage to maintain objectivity while supporting troops being covered. Coverage of President Bush was consistent with news attention toward presidents of past conflicts; coverage is quite favorable during the conflict, but as soon as there is a sign of an "end" to the conflict negative coverage increases. The most significant change in the news media's involvement in covering the war in Iraq compared to past conflicts is the development of embedded reporting with the military. Such coverage presented its own set of challenges in terms of access to information, objectivity, and reporter safety, but we do see differences in the type of coverage audiences received.

CONCLUSION

Whether so intended by the Founding Fathers or not, presidents have long taken the helm of our national government. This fact is striking in times of war, and this chapter has looked closely at President George W. Bush's actions during what he termed the "war on terrorism."

The political scientist, not surprisingly, goes first to the U.S. Constitution and the "war-making" powers outlined within it. In this case, as in many others in recent times, the president has responded to a crisis in ways that seemed to him and his advisers as appropriate and necessary, even if technically not in line with the Constitution. Others in government have acceded, as in the past, to the president because a crisis required a strong commander-in-chief. This particular commander-in-chief exhibited this strength very much through the words he spoke: he offered comfort, but he also clearly outlined who in the world was "evil" and who was "good." Although flamboyant, Bush's words were consistent with the behavior of other presidents in times of crisis. This crisis communication, however, has risks, including increased expectations of the president.

Bush's words also draw the rhetorician's attention. Their emotionally evocative power, in addition to how they identify terrorists with evil entities and America with good ones, marks the speeches the words make up as epideictic. Bush, however, uses epideictic oratory at times when deliberative oratory would be more appropriate—and more useful. In addition to this rhetorical confusion, Bush confuses genres and thereby offers incomplete examples of common presidential discourse.

These speeches were covered by the media much as presidential addresses long have been. What was covered differently, as the mass communication perspective highlights, was the warfare itself. The combat was even more a "TV war" because of the use of embedded reporters. They were able to offer coverage that was new to American viewers. Also striking in this case was the full emergence of a pattern seen in previous instances of combat: positive media coverage during the combat phase, shifting to more negative coverage after that phase supposedly ends.

■ ■ ■ ■ ■ ▬▬▬▬▬▬▬▬▬▬▬▬▬▬▬▬▬▬▬▬▬▬▬▬▬▬▬▬▬▬

ADDITIONAL CASES

Students might want to consider the following instances when presidents spoke about the use of American forces abroad.

- **President Franklin Delano Roosevelt's address to Congress after the Japanese attack on Pearl Harbor**
  A text of this widely available speech can be found in Michael Waldman's *My Fellow Americans: The Most Important Speeches of America's Presidents.*

- **President Harry S Truman's use of the atomic bomb in Japan**
  For the documents surrounding this controversial event, see Robert H. Ferrell, ed., *Harry S Truman and the Atomic Bomb: A Documentary History* (Worland, WY: High Plains Publishing, 1996).

- **President Lyndon B. Johnson's and President Richard M. Nixon's addresses expanding American involvement in Vietnam**
  See Jules Davids, ed., *Documents in American Foreign Relations 1964* (New York: Harper and Row, 1965): 212–13, for Johnson's August 4, 1964, address to the people (as well as his next-day message to Congress); see *Vital Speeches of the Day* 36.15 (1970): 450–52 for Nixon's April 30, 1970, address.

- **President George H. W. Bush's address initiating U.S. military action in defense of Kuwait**
  See *Weekly Compilation of Presidential Documents* 26 (1990): 1358–63 for Bush's September 11, 1990, address.

- **President Bill Clinton's address on the use of American troops in Bosnia**
  See *Weekly Compilation of Presidential Documents* 30 (1994): 329–31 for Clinton's comments on Bosnia.

CHAPTER 13

CASE NINE: CLARENCE THOMAS'S CONFIRMATION HEARING

THE CASE

On July 8, 1991, President George H. W. Bush, nominated Clarence Thomas to replace the retiring Thurgood Marshall as an associate justice on the United States Supreme Court. Thomas was a 43-year-old federal judge whom President Bush had appointed to the District of Columbia Court of Appeals just the year before.

For most of the several weeks of hearings, Thomas's confirmation seemed reasonably certain. Although he had received only tepid support from the American Bar Association and had not been on the federal bench for very long, many senators believed that, barring a major scandal, the Senate ought to give President Bush his selection. Nevertheless, the Senate Judiciary Committee deadlocked on a recommendation, voting 7–7 in its executive business meeting to send Thomas's name to the floor of the Senate. Ordinarily a tie vote in committee would result in a failure to forward the name to the Senate for confirmation; in this case the Committee agreed to send the name forward with no recommendation, in light of the importance of a Supreme Court nomination.

Just a few days before the full Senate was to vote on Thomas's confirmation, the results of a Federal Bureau of Investigation (FBI) investigation into allegations that Thomas had sexually harassed a former co-worker, Anita Hill, were leaked to the press. The result was that the vote to confirm was postponed, and the Senate Judiciary Committee held additional hearings into the allegations. Following these hearings, Thomas was ultimately confirmed by the full Senate, but by an extraordinarily narrow margin of 52–48. Excerpts of both Hill's and Thomas's testimony, as well as some of the questioning by members of the Senate Judiciary Committee, follow.

*****

Ms. Hill: . . . After approximately 3 months of working [at the U.S. Department of Education], [Clarence Thomas] asked me to go out socially with him. . . . I declined the invitation to go out socially with him, and explained to him that I thought it would jeopardize what at the time I considered to be a very good working relationship. . . . [Later] Judge Thomas began to use work situations to discuss sex. On these occasions, he would call me into his office for reports on education issues and projects or he might suggest that because of the time pressures of his schedule, we go to lunch to a government cafeteria. After a brief discussion of work, he would turn the conversation to a discussion of sexual matters. His conversations were very vivid. He spoke about acts that he had seen in pornographic films involving such matters as women having sex with animals, and films showing group sex or rape scenes. He talked about pornographic materials depicting individuals with large penises, or large breasts involved in various sex acts. On several occasions Thomas told me graphically of his own sexual prowess. . . .

During the latter part of my time at the Department of Education, the social pressures and any conversation of his offensive behavior ended. I began both to believe and hope that our working relationship could be a proper, cordial, and professional one. When Judge Thomas was made chair of the EEOC, I needed to face the question of whether to go with him. I was asked to do so and I did. The work, itself, was interesting, and at that time, it appeared that the sexual overtures, which had so troubled me, had ended. . . .

For my first months at the EEOC, where I continued to be an assistant to Judge Thomas, there were no sexual conversations or overtures. However, during the fall and winter of 1982, these began again. . . . One of the oddest episodes I remember was an occasion in which Thomas was drinking a Coke in his office, he got up from the table, at which we were working, went over to his desk to get the Coke, looked at the can and asked, "Who has put pubic hair on my Coke?" On other occasions he referred to the size of his own penis as being larger than normal and he also spoke on some occasions of the pleasures he had given to women with oral sex. At this point, late 1982, I began to feel severe stress on the job. I began to be concerned that Clarence Thomas might take out his anger with me by degrading me or not giving me important assignments. I also thought that he might find an excuse for dismissing me. . . .

*****

Judge Thomas: . . . Let me describe my relationship with Anita Hill. In 1981, after I went to the Department of Education as an Assistant Secretary in the Office of Civil Rights, one of my closest friends, from both college and law school, Gil Hardy, brought Anita Hill to my attention. As I remember, he indicated that she was dissatisfied with her law firm and wanted to work in Government. Based primarily, if not solely, on Gil's recommendation, I hired Anita Hill. During my tenure at the Department of Education, Anita Hill was an attorney-adviser who worked directly with me. . . . Upon my nomination to become Chairman of the Equal Employment Opportunity Commission, Anita Hill, to the best of my recollection, assisted me in the nomination and confirmation process. After my confirmation, she and Diane Holt, then my secretary, joined me at EEOC. . . . Throughout the time that Anita Hill worked with me I treated her as I treated my other special assistants. I tried to treat them all cordially, professionally, and respectfully. And I tried to support them in their endeavors, and be interested in and supportive of their success. . . .

This is a person I have helped at every turn in the road, since we met. She seemed to appreciate the continued cordial relationship we had since day one. She sought my advice and counsel, as did virtually all of the members of my personal staff. During my tenure in the executive branch as a manager, as a policymaker, and as a person, I have adamantly condemned sex harassment. There is no member of this committee or this Senate who feels stronger about sex harassment than I do. As a manager, I made every effort to take swift and decisive action when sex harassment raised or reared its ugly head. The fact that I feel so very strongly about sex harassment and spoke loudly about it at EEOC has made these allegations doubly hard on me. I cannot imagine anything that I said or did to Anita Hill that could have been mistaken for sexual harassment. . . . Mr. Chairman, I am a victim of this process and my name has been harmed, my integrity has been harmed, my character has been harmed, my family has been harmed, my friends have been harmed. There is nothing this committee, this body or this country can do to give me my good name back, nothing. I will not provide the rope for my own lynching or for further humiliation. I am not going to engage in discussions, nor will I submit to roving questions of what goes on in the most intimate parts of my private life or the sanctity of my bedroom. These are the most intimate parts of my privacy, and they will remain just that, private.

*****

Senator Leahy: . . . Professor Hill said the two of you went out to dinner as she was leaving. Professor Hill, of course, further alleges—and this would be a major and explosive matter—that you said something to her to the effect, "If you ever tell about this, it will damage or destroy my career." Now, that was her statement. I want you to have a chance to give yours. Am I correct in understanding your testimony now that you have no recollection of ever having such a conversation at any time? Is that correct?

Judge Thomas: No, I have no recollection of having dinner with her as she left, although I do not think that it would be unusual for me to have gone either to lunch or to particularly an early dinner with a member of my staff who was leaving. I would categorically deny that, under any circumstances, whether it is breakfast, lunch or dinner, that I made those statements.

Senator Leahy: Then, would it be safe to say your testimony is: At any time, whether in a social, business or any other setting, you never made the statement, "If this comes out, it would ruin my career," or anything even relating to that kind of a statement. Is that correct?

Judge Thomas: That's right. . . .

Senator Leahy: Going back to the charges that Professor Hill made yesterday, one was of your discussing pornographic films with her. She stated this happened on a number of occasions and that she had found it uncomfortable and asked you not to. Let me ask you—she has been asked whether this happened—let me ask you: Did you ever have a discussion of pornographic films with Professor Hill?

Judge Thomas: Absolutely not.

Senator Leahy: Have you ever had such discussions with any other women?

Judge Thomas: Senator, I will not get into any discussions that I might have about my personal life or my sex life with any person outside of the workplace.

Senator Leahy: I'm not asking

Judge Thomas: I will categorically say I have not had any such discussions with Professor Hill. . . .

*****

Senator Hatch: Thank you, Chairman Biden. Judge there are a lot of things in Anita Hill's testimony that just don't make sense to me. I liked her personally. . . . But, Judge, it bothers me because it just doesn't square with what I think is—some of it doesn't square with what I think is common experience, and just basic sense, common sense. . . .

Judge Thomas: Senator, my reaction to this has been, over the last 2 weeks, has been one of horror. I can't tell you what I have lived through. I can't tell you what my wife has lived through or my family. I can't tell you what my son has lived through. I don't know what to tell him about this. If I were going to date someone outside of the workplace, I would certainly not approach anyone I was attempting to date, as a person, with this kind of grotesque language.

Senator Hatch: I have to interrupt you here, Judge, but there was an implication that you not only repetitively asked her for dates—I don't know, I guess that can be construed as sexual harassment, repetitively asking a woman for dates—but the implication was, and the clear implication which she spoke about was that you wanted more than dates, if her allegations were true.

Judge Thomas: Senator, I did not ask her out, and I did not use that language. One of the things that has tormented me over the last 2 weeks has been how do I defend myself against this kind of language and these kind of charges? How do I defend myself? That's what I asked the FBI agent, I believe, for the first time. That's what I have asked myself, how do I defend myself? If I used that kind of grotesque language with one person, it would seem to me that there would be traces of it throughout the employees who worked closely with me; there would be other individuals who heard it, or bits and pieces of it, or various levels of it.

Senator Hatch: Don't worry, Judge, probably before the weekend's out they will find somebody who will say that.

Judge Thomas: Well, the difficulty also was that, from my standpoint, is that in this country when it comes to sexual conduct we still have underlying racial attitudes about black men and their views of sex. And once you pin that on me, I can't get it off. That is why I am so adamant in this committee about what has been done to me. I made it a point at EEOC and at Education not to play into those stereotypes, at all. I made it a point to have the people at those agencies, the black men, the black women to conduct themselves in a way that is not consistent with those stereotypes, and I did the same thing myself. . . .

Senator Hatch: Before we get to that, Judge, I am going to get to that, that's an interesting concept that you have just raised, and I promise I will get back to it. You are a very intelligent man, there is no question about it. Anybody who watches you knows that. You could not have risen to these high positions in Government, been confirmed four times by the august U.S. Senate, three times by the Labor Committee—upon which a number of us, here on this committee serve, and whose staff members were used in this investigation—and I might add, once now before the Judiciary Committee, august committees. She is an extremely intelligent woman and from all appearances a lovely human being. Do you think an intelligent African American male, like you, or any other intelligent male, regardless of race, would use this kind of language to try and start a relationship with an intelligent, attractive woman?

Judge Thomas: Senator, I don't know anyone who would try to establish a relationship with that kind of language.

Senator Hatch: Unless they were sick.

Judge Thomas: I don't know of anyone.

Senator Hatch: I don't even know of people who might have emotional disturbances who would try this. Now, I want to ask you about this intriguing thing you just said. You said some of this language is stereotype language? What does that mean, I don't understand.

Judge Thomas: Senator, the language throughout the history of this country, and certainly throughout my life, language about the sexual prowess of black men, language about the sex organs of black men, and the sizes, et cetera, that kind of language has been used about black men as long as I have been on the face of this Earth. These are charges that play into racist, bigoted stereotypes and these are the kind of charges that are impossible to wash off. . . .

Senator Hatch: Well, I saw—I didn't understand the television program, there were two black men—I may have it wrong, but as I recall—there were two black men talking about this matter and one of them said, she is trying to demonize us. I didn't understand it at the time. Do you understand that?

Judge Thomas: Well, I understand it and any black man in this country— Senator, in the 1970s I became very interested in the issue of lynching. And if you want to track through this country, in the 19th and 20th centuries, the lynchings of black men, you will see that there is invariably or in many instances a relationship with sex—an accusation that that person cannot shake off. That is the point that I am trying to make. And that is the point that I was making last night that this is high-tech lynching. I cannot shake off these accusations because they play to the worst stereotypes we have about black men in this country.

Senator Hatch: Well, this bothers me.

Judge Thomas: It bothers me.

Senator Hatch: I can see why. Let me, I hate to do this, but let me ask you some tough questions. You have talked about stereotypes used against black males in this society. In the first statement of Anita Hill she alleges that he told her about his experiences and preferences and would ask her what she liked or if she had ever done the same thing. Is that a black stereotype?

Judge Thomas: No.

Senator Hatch: OK. Anita Hill said that he discussed oral sex between men and women. Is that a black stereotype?

Judge Thomas: No.

Senator Hatch: Thomas also discussed viewing films of people having sex with each other and with animals. What about that?

Judge Thomas: That's not a stereotype about blacks.

Senator Hatch: OK. He told her that he enjoyed watching the films and told her that she should see them. Watching X-rated films or pornographic films, is that a stereotype?

Judge Thomas: No.

Senator Hatch: . . . He liked to discuss specific sex acts and frequency of sex.

Judge Clarence Thomas testifies before the Senate Judiciary Committee in 1991, flatly denying the sexual harassment charges levied against him by Anita Hill.

Judge Thomas: No, I don't think so. I think that could—the last, frequency— could have to do with black men supposedly being very promiscuous or something like that.

Senator Hatch: So it could be partially stereotypical?

Judge Thomas: Yes.

Senator Hatch: In the next statement she said, "His conversations were very vivid. He spoke about acts that he had seen in pornographic films involving such things as women having sex with animals and films involving group sex or rape scenes. He talked about pornographic materials depicting individuals with large penises or breasts involved in various sex acts." What about those things?

Judge Thomas: I think certainly the size of sexual organs would be something.

Senator Hatch: Well, I am concerned. "Thomas told me graphically of his own sexual prowess," the third statement.

Judge Thomas: That is clearly

Senator Hatch: Clearly a black stereotype.

Judge Thomas [continuing]: Stereotypical, clearly. . . .

Senator Hatch: Let me just give you one more. . . . She testified: "One of the oddest episodes I remember was an occasion in which Thomas was drinking a Coke in his office, he got up from the table, at which we were working, went over to his desk to get the Coke, looked at the can and asked, 'Who has put pubic hair on my Coke?'" That's what she said. Did you ever say that?

Judge Thomas: No, absolutely not.

Senator Hatch: Did you ever think of saying something like that?

Judge Thomas: No.

Senator Hatch: That's a gross thing to say, isn't it? Whether it is said by you or by somebody else, it is a gross thing to say, isn't it?

Judge Thomas: As far as I am concerned, Senator, it is and it is something I did not nor would I say.

Senator Hatch: . . . She would have us believe that you were saying these things, because you wanted to date her? What do you think about that, Judge?

Judge Thomas: Senator, I think this whole affair is sick.

Senator Hatch: I think it's sick, too.

Judge Thomas: I don't think I should be here today. I don't think that this inquisition should be going on. I don't think that the FBI file should have been leaked. I don't think that my name should have been destroyed, and

I don't think that my family and I should have been put through this ordeal, and I don't think that our country should be brought low by this kind of garbage.

*****

Senator Specter: Professor Hill, you testified that you drew an inference that Judge Thomas might want you to look at pornographic films, but you told the FBI specifically that he never asked you to watch the films. Is that correct?

Ms. Hill: He never said, "Let's go to my apartment and watch films," or "go to my house and watch films." He did say, "You ought to see this material."

Senator Specter: . . . [T]he fact is, flatly, he never asked you to look at pornographic movies with him.

Ms. Hill: With him? No, he did not. . . .

Senator Specter: Professor Hill, now that you have read the FBI report, you can see that it contains no reference to any mention of Judge Thomas's private parts or sexual prowess or size, et cetera. . . .

Ms. Hill: Senator, in paragraph 2 on page 2 of the report it says that he liked to discuss specific sex acts and frequency of sex. And I am not sure what all that summarizes, but his sexual prowess, his sexual preferences, could have . . .

Senator Specter: Which line are you referring to, Professor?

Ms. Hill: The very last line in paragraph 2 of page 2.

Senator Specter: Well, that says—and this is not too bad, I can read it— "Thomas liked to discuss specific sex acts and frequency of sex." Now are you saying, in response to my question as to why you didn't tell the FBI about the size of his private parts and his sexual prowess and "Long John Silver." That information was comprehended within the statement, "Thomas liked to discuss specific sex acts and frequency of sex"?

Ms. Hill: I am not saying that that information was included in that. I don't know that it was. I don't believe that I even mentioned the latter information to the FBI agent, and I could only respond again that at the time of the investigation I tried to cooperate as fully as I could, to recall information to answer the questions that they asked. . . .

Senator Specter: Professor Hill, the next subject I want to take up with you involves the kind of strong language which you say Judge Thomas used in a very unique setting, where there you have the Chairman of the EEOC, the Nation's chief law enforcement officer on sexual harassment, and here you have a lawyer who is an expert in this field, later goes on to teach civil rights and has a dedication to making sure that women are not discriminated against. . . . [M]y question is: . . . [G]iven your own expert standing and the fact that here you have the chief law enforcement officer of the country on this subject and the whole purpose of the civil right law is being perverted right in the office of the Chairman with one of his own female subordinates, what went through your mind, if anything, on whether you ought to come forward at that stage? If you had, you would have stopped this man from being head of the EEOC perhaps for another decade. What went on through your mind? I know you decided not to make a complaint, but did you give that any consideration, and, if so, how could you allow this kind of reprehensible conduct to go on right in the headquarters, without doing something about it?

Ms. Hill: Well, it was a very trying and difficult decision for me not to say anything further. I can only say that when I made the decision to just withdraw from the situation and not press a claim or charge against him, that I may have shirked a duty, a responsibility that I had, and to that extent I confess that I am very sorry that I did not do something or say something, but at the time that was my best judgment. Maybe it was a poor judgment, but it wasn't dishonest and it wasn't a completely unreasonable choice that I made, given the circumstances.

THE POLITICAL SCIENCE PERSPECTIVE

In an April 2006 online column, Paul Jenks wrote of the Clarence Thomas confirmation hearings:

> Many years ago I was watching a playoff hockey game on television and just as the first intermission began, the network switched to live coverage of the Clarence Thomas confirmation hearing for the Supreme Court before the Senate Judiciary Committee. I was struck by the odd similarity of watching a hockey game and a Senate committee hearing breaking out.[1]

Jenks's comment was a reference to an old joke about going to watch a fight and a hockey game breaking out, but the point he was making was that Clarence Thomas's confirmation hearing was fraught with conflict. More important, however, the Thomas confirmation hearing was a watershed moment in American politics because of the messages that it conveyed—both overt and subtle—about the status of men and women in society and about the proper subjects of inquiry for public debate.

The hearings didn't begin that way, however. In fact, the first several days of hearings were typical of hearings for most Supreme Court nominees—they were downright dull. Thomas refused to answer questions about political issues, such as abortion, citing the possibility that cases about such questions might one day be posed to him as a sitting justice. Thomas's practice of avoiding controversial issues

[1]Paul Jenks, "Congressional Hearings," 2006. Available online at: http://www.llrx.com/congress/hearings.htm.

kept the initial set of hearings from getting too contentious. *Newsweek* described the Thomas hearings on September 23, 1991, as follows:

> [M]ost senators were a study in docility. Except for the prosecutorial Arlen Specter, the Republican members of the Judiciary Committee saw themselves as speechifying cheerleaders for the nominee. Orrin Hatch asked Thomas this mind twister: "When you become a justice on the U.S. Supreme Court, do you intend to uphold the Constitution of the United States?" At times, Alan Simpson didn't bother with questions; on Wednesday he went on for 15 minutes seemingly without even indicating where one sentence stopped and the next one began. The Democrats promised better. . . . The result? Some senators certainly have pressed Thomas. Joe Biden of Delaware scolded him, calling one answer "the most unartful dodge I have heard." No one, though, would confuse any of the interrogators with Perry Mason.[2]

To be sure, there were concerns about Clarence Thomas among both the Republican and Democrat members of the Senate Judiciary Committee, despite the Committee's apparent unwillingness to engage, at least initially, in confrontation with President George H. W. Bush's nominee to the U.S. Supreme Court. The American Bar Association had given him only a "Qualified" rating—essentially signaling that Thomas was an average nominee. Thomas had been on the federal appellate bench only about 18 months, which meant that he lacked much substantive experience in handling difficult cases. His answers to many of the questions asked by the Senate Judiciary Committee revealed little about his attitudes toward legal issues or future cases that might be heard by the Supreme Court. Thus, many senators on both sides of the aisle were frustrated by Thomas's refusal to offer any insights into his personal attitudes about such controversial topics as abortion. On September 27, 1991, the Senate Judiciary Committee deadlocked 7–7 on whether to send the Thomas nomination to the Senate floor with a positive recommendation.

Ordinarily, measures or nominations that receive a tie vote in committee are failed under the Senate's rules of procedure. However, committees have the option to refer items of business to the floor without a recommendation when ties occur on matters of important national business. That is what the Senate Judiciary Committee decided to do with Clarence Thomas's nomination. During the full chamber's deliberations over the Thomas nomination, allegations of sexual harassment were leaked to the press. University of Oklahoma law professor Anita Hill, who formerly had worked for Thomas when he was the head of the Equal Employment Opportunity Commission under President Ronald Reagan, had previously informed Committee investigators and the FBI of her claims of sexual harassment. She had not, however, wanted to make those claims public. However, during the full Senate's deliberations on the Thomas nomination, Hill's allegations were leaked, prompting the nomination to be sent back to the Senate Judiciary Committee for additional hearings. The excerpt that appears earlier in this chapter is taken from those additional hearings.

[2]David A. Kaplan (with Bob Cohn), "Court Charade," *Newsweek* (September 23, 1991): 18.

Unfortunately for Clarence Thomas, who eventually was confirmed by a vote of 52–48 in the full Senate, few people recall much else from his hearings besides the supplemental hearings that were held to determine whether he did or did not sexually harass Anita Hill.

The Hill–Thomas Spectacle

There were no women on the U.S. Senate Committee on the Judiciary in 1991. There were no African American members of the United States Senate at all. So, when the public watched the gavel-to-gavel coverage of the Thomas confirmation hearings on television, courtesy of the Public Broadcasting System (PBS) and C-SPAN, what people saw was a panel of middle-aged to quite elderly white men awkwardly asking the African American nominee and his African American accuser very graphic questions about their sexual proclivities.

If her allegations were truthful, then Hill was describing a classic example of a hostile work environment, in which a powerful supervisor used sexual innuendo to demean a subordinate. But most senators on the Judiciary Committee panel seemed to believe that the comments Thomas was alleged to have made could only have been made in the context of seeking to ask her out on a date, and they used that assumption to discount her allegations. While praising Hill for being articulate and poised, senators wondered out loud—and on camera—why any man would say the sorts of things that she alleged Thomas had said if he had wanted to date her. Many senators' comments demonstrated that they did not understand what sexual harassment was and implied that Hill had misheard or misunderstood or was simply a woman with an unrequited crush. Senators on the hearing panel were accused of talking down to Professor Hill, and politicians and pundits alike lamented the lack of women on the Senate Judiciary Committee.[3]

Representative Barbara Boxer, a Democratic member of Congress who in November 1992 won a seat in the U.S. Senate from California, ran a campaign commercial shortly after the Thomas hearings concluded and shortly before Election Day that declared: "If there had been only one woman on the Judiciary Committee, things would have been different."[4] Political scientists Michael Delli Carpini and Ester Fuchs, in their analysis of the 1992 presidential and congressional elections, offer a scholarly reaffirmation of this view, writing:

> [T]hat men and women exercise their franchise with equal regularity is not to suggest that gender equality has been achieved in electoral politics. . . Equally important [as voting] is for women to be directly involved in the day-to-day process of making public policy. This requires that women be adequately represented in the ranks of local, state,

---

[3]David Finkel, "Women on the Verge of a Power Breakthrough," *Washington Post Magazine* (May 10, 1992): W15.

[4]"Judiciary Committee Needs Woman On It," Editorial in the *Chicago Sun-Times* December 1, 1992), A27.

and national elected officials—a point dramatically illustrated during the televised Senate confirmation hearings for Clarence Thomas's appointment to the Supreme Court.[5]

Although Thomas's confirmation hearings were not the first to be televised (Sandra Day O'Connor's confirmation hearings in 1981 hold that honor), something about the images that people saw when they tuned in gave many Americans pause. Senators debating with a Supreme Court nominee whether he had or had not ever mentioned a character in an X-rated film by the name of "Long Dong Silver," for example, was far afield from anything most citizens ever expected to hear their elected officials discuss. Moreover, with alleged womanizers like Ted Kennedy on the Judiciary Committee, the images of senators of supposed questionable moral virtue holding a nominee to account for allegations of sexual misconduct struck many observers as hypocritical. Even Orrin Hatch, whose Mormon faith and strong family values should have made him above reproach, was singled out for particularly harsh treatment by late night talk show hosts and other comedians for his naive and banal questions to Thomas about African American men, race and sex stereotypes, and what Thomas allegedly did or did not say to Anita Hill.

In the end, the Thomas hearings ended up being about far more than the nominee's fitness to hold one of the highest judicial offices in the country. A December 1, 1992, editorial in the *Chicago Sun-Times* noted:

> Those hearings gave many women and minorities the impetus, the final push, to seek elective office. And some of the new senators made the race and gender of the panel and the tenor of the hearings an issue in their campaigns. Carol Moseley Braun of Illinois, the first black woman elected to the Senate, owes her success in significant measure to the outrage over Hill's treatment by the all-male panel.[6]

Although the *Sun-Times* editorial may overstate the impact of the Hill–Thomas hearings on the November 1992 election (many of the women and minorities who ran for office in 1992 had made up their minds to do so long before the Thomas hearings began), the analysis is generally correct. The female and minority candidates who were successful in 1992 were so largely as a result of voters deciding it was time for a change. Women and minorities have long been perceived as political outsiders, in large part because they have held a very small proportion of positions in government through U.S. history. When voters weighed their options in November 1992, they did so with two events in mind—the House banking scandal and the Clarence Thomas confirmation hearings. The House banking scandal led to the ouster of several incumbent members of both parties in the House of Representatives; in the Senate, four women senators—Moseley Braun, Boxer, Patty Murray (D-WA), and Dianne

---

[5]Delli Scarpini, Michael X. Fuchs, and Ester R. Fuchs. "The Year of the Woman? Candidates, Voters, and the 1992 Elections," *Political Science Quarterly* (1993): 108(1).

[6]"Judiciary Committee Needs Woman On It," Editorial in the *Chicago Sun-Times* (December 1, 1992), A27.

Feinstein (D-CA)—joined Senators Nancy Kassebaum (R-KS) and Barbara Mikulski (D-MD) to bring the total number of women in the Senate to six at the start of the 103rd Congress (1993–1994). These six women were joined a few months later by Kay Bailey Hutchison (R-TX), who was elected in a special election.[7]

Conclusion

The late communication scholar and theorist Marshall McLuhan is credited with the oft-cited phrase "the medium is the message." He meant that when the form of communication is a visual one—such as television—viewers will remember what they see, not what they hear. If the medium is an aural one—such as radio—listeners will receive no message other than what they have heard. In the context of the Thomas confirmation hearings, televised nationwide on both public and cable airwaves, the message that most viewers took away was the image of the all-white, all-male Senate Judiciary Committee seated high on the dais literally looking down on the African American nominee and his accuser. By many accounts, the tremendous success of women in seeking and attaining public office in 1992 and early 1993 can be attributed, at least in part, to these stark images of the all-male Senate Judiciary Committee that were broadcast nationally in the fall of 1991. Those who listened to the hearings heard suspicion in the tone of the senators interrogating Anita Hill—suspicion that is revealed even from reading the excerpt of the transcript that appears earlier in this chapter.

Because the timing of the Thomas confirmation hearings coincided with the run-up to both the presidential and congressional elections in 1992, the hearings became a powerful catalyst to encourage women, minorities, and those who were dissatisfied with the status quo to vote. The Thomas hearings thus provide an excellent illustration of the point that the ways in which political messages are communicated—both through image and through the spoken word—can have tremendous implications for public governance and policy.

THE RHETORICAL PERSPECTIVE

Postmodern critics of written or spoken texts have called into question the "stability" of those texts. In years past, a rhetorician would have assumed that there was a single text that he or she might analyze. Now, a rhetorician needs to be aware that what looks like a single text might, in fact, be several.

How can this be, you might ask. The different texts exist because readers and listeners construct their sense of the text as they read and listen. Yes, there are words, phrases, and sentences; and, yes, they are strung together in a discernible order. Based on that order, we ought to be able to identify what a given rhetor is arguing,

---

[7]For more information on each of these senators, as well as the other women who have served in the U.S. Senate throughout history, see the United States Senate's website: http://www.senate.gov/artandhistory/history/common/briefing/women_senators.htm.

and based on the words and phrases, we ought to be able to posit that there is a particular tone or style to the text under examination. However, when readers and listeners go through this process—and even when supposedly objective critics do so—they bring who they are into it. Their political experiences and their political views, as well as other elements of their "subjectivity," color their interpretation. There is usually enough in common among the different readings that have been constructed for a conversation to occur among the different readers and listeners. However, this conversation will sometimes suggest that they read or heard different communication events. "You must have heard a different speech," one conversant might be tempted to say to another.

Individuals more often than not construct their sense of a text socially. This statement means two things. First, they tend to form their construction through interaction with those they might talk about the text with, be they family members, fellow students, or coworkers. Second, individuals tend to form their construction based on group characteristics such as gender, race, ethnicity, and class—especially when the communication event in view relates to any of these variables. The hearings held by the Senate Judiciary Committee on Clarence Thomas's nomination to the Supreme Court rather obviously touched on the first two of these variables.

Political scientists Dan Thomas, Craig McCoy, and Allan McBride played off these ideas of "social construction" current in literary and rhetoric circles and identified five different constructions of the Clarence Thomas–Anita Hill controversy.[8] Perhaps the most interesting differences they found are tied to the variable of gender.

Males tended to side with Thomas; females with Hill. In fact, Hill's testimony—and the way the interrogating U.S. senators responded to it—provoked a great deal of solidarity among females. One can say, "Well, of course, males will agree with Thomas and females with Hill," but a rhetorician, who is interested in how texts persuade or fail to persuade, would not stop there. A rhetorician would ask why did males construct a "reading" that credited Thomas and why did females construct a "reading" that credited Hill.

Males and Clarence Thomas

William L. Benoit and Dawn M. Nill, writing in *Communication Studies*, analyzed Thomas's statement to the Judiciary Committee. They found that Thomas used three defensive strategies: denial, bolstering, and attacking.[9] He denied that any of the conversations or behavior Hill had cited occurred; he bolstered both his argument and his ethos by offering positive information about his relationship with Hill. As he told the story, he was a good mentor, who expressed concern for her professional

[8]Dan Thomas, Craig McCoy, and Allan McBride, "Deconstructing the Political Spectacle: Sex, Race, and Subjectivity in Public Response to the Clarence Thomas/Anita Hill 'Sexual Harassment' Hearings," *American Journal of Political Science* 37 (1993): 699–721.

[9]William L. Benoit and Dawn M. Nill, "A Critical Analysis of Judge Clarence Thomas' Statement Before the Senate Judiciary Committee," *Communication Studies* 49, no. 3 (1998): 179–96.

development. "This is a person," he said, "I have helped at every turn in the road, since we met." The denying and the bolstering are, however, less interesting than the attacking. Thomas quite shrewdly did not attack Hill. If he had done so, he would have reinforced the view of some in the public that she was a victim. Rather, he attacked those who were attacking his character. These counterattacks are rhetorically fascinating insofar as he accuses those who are trying to defeat him of vicious racism while focusing that accusation more on the process than on particular opponents.

Thomas initially positions himself as a victim: "Mr. Chairman, I am a victim of this process and my name has been harmed, my integrity has been harmed, my character has been harmed, my family has been harmed, my friends have been harmed." His use of the rhetorical scheme of epistrophe emphasizes how victimized he felt. "There is nothing this committee, this body or this country can do to give me my good name back, nothing."

Race is not relevant to the victim position Thomas has thus far assigned himself. However, Thomas adds race in when he, first, refers to what has occurred as a "lynching" and, second, talks about how the accusations play off stereotypes of the African American male. Lynchings, as Thomas tells the committee, in the nineteenth and twentieth centuries were a fate experienced by black men, and sex frequently played a role in the accusations that prompted the lynchings. He is being subjected to a "high-tech lynching" because of an alleged sex-based offense. And in being charged with that offense, those lynching him are evoking in the minds of listeners "the worst stereotypes we have about black men in this country" as dangerously oversexed and overendowed.

But note how Thomas refers to his accusers. As Alison Regan notes in an essay in *Political Communication*, Thomas does not point the finger of blame at Hill. Neither does he blame particular Senators or even particular special-interest groups. He blames "the process." Regan suggests that he thereby constructs a drama that is not a woman accusing him of harassment but, rather, a politicized process bringing him down.[10] And it was far easier for those supporting him to reject a politicized process than someone Senator Orrin Hatch refers to as "a lovely human being," "an intelligent, attractive woman."

Thomas's counterattacking—and how he executed it—was effective in convincing male audience members, but other rhetorical dimensions of the hearings also helped his cause. First, he had power on his side; second, he benefited from the "adversarial discourse" directed at Anita Hill; and, third, he benefited from the tendency of some of his supporters to "silence" Hill by removing her personally from the discussion. Each of these elements that gave his defense rhetorical strength needs to be explained briefly.

Power: Thomas had power behind him—because he was highly educated and held a high position in the judiciary; because he was nominated by a president and

---

[10]Alison Regan, "Rhetoric and Political Process in the Hill-Thomas Hearings," *Political Communication* 11, no. 3 (1994): 277–86.

supported by that president's political party; because he was male.[11] In contrast, Hill, although highly educated, had held only supporting positions, came out of nowhere to accuse Thomas, and was female in an arguably patriarchal society.

Hill told a detailed story; Thomas just said no. Hill had not only failed to act on the matter but had, arguably, acted contrary to it by continuing her working relationship with Thomas; Thomas's behavior, carefully scrutinized by the Judiciary Committee staff, seemed beyond serious reproach. So, in a "she said/he said" situation, what and who, if you wanted to get at the truth, would you interrogate? The honest desire to find a route around the "she said/he said" situation seemed to have led committee members to focus their scrutiny on Hill. This focus—that is, that her story and she were targets of "adversarial discourse"—implied that Thomas's version of events was presumed to be true.[12]

Paige K. Turner and Patricia Ryden suggest in an essay in *Argumentation & Advocacy* that George H. W. Bush silenced Anita Hill in his discussion of the controversy by foregrounding Thomas and the accusations against Thomas and drawing a contrast between the noble man and words and actions that seemed so beneath him. With the man and his supposed deeds foregrounded, Anita Hill the person as well as Anita Hill the victim largely vanish from the discussion.[13] Some Senate supporters framed the matter in much the same way, thereby removing Hill from the picture and effectively "silencing" her. One can understand why Bush and some senators proceeded in this manner. Besides being an effective rhetorical strategy to set up a tense contrast between Thomas the person and deeds unlikely to be his and, then, resolve the tension in his favor, the framing of the matter allowed Bush and others to avoid facing Hill, a sympathetic witness whose story was difficult to impeach. They thus avoided discomfort in addition to enacting a shrewd rhetorical move.

A gloss on this "silencing" strategy is useful. Years later, the Senate is debating a proposed ban on a medical procedure that has become known as "partial birth abortion." Senator Bob Smith of New Hampshire is leading the call for a ban. He talks about the medical procedure and what it does to "the baby," and he uses charts showing a cutaway of a woman's lower anatomy diagrammatically and "the baby." Missing from his framing is the mother as a person. So, in response, Senator Barbara Boxer of California shows pictures of women—not diagrammatic segments—who have been helped by the procedure. She dramatically brings women, "silenced" in Smith's framing, into focus. It is easy, Boxer implies, to enact laws against the interests of women

---

[11]For a discussion of how power trumped the right to justice in the hearings' text, see Vanessa Bowles Beasley, "The Logic of Power in the Hill-Thomas Hearings: A Rhetorical Evaluation," *Political Communication* 11, no. 3 (1994): 287–98.

[12]For a discussion of "adversarial discourse," especially that engaged in by Senator Arlen Specter of Pennsylvania, see S. Ashley Armstrong, "Arlen Specter and the Construction of Adversarial Discourse: Selective Representation in the Clarence Thomas–Anita Hill Hearings," *Argumentation & Advocacy* 32, no. 2 (1995): 75–90.

[13]Paige K. Turner and Patricia Ryden, "How George Bush Silenced Anita Hill: A Derridean View of the Third Persona in Public Argument," *Argumentation & Advocacy*, 37, no. 2 (2000): 86–98.

when you can't see their faces.[14] Similarly, it was easy to reject Anita Hill's story when you could neither see her face nor hear her voice.

Females and Anita Hill

The "adversarial discourse" that benefited Thomas's case with males benefited Hill's case with females. It did so because it intensified how females perceived her as victim. Although Senators such as Arlen Specter were interrogating the only narrative they had before them in their attempt to figure out who to believe, that interrogation and, at times, its persistence conveyed a spectacle of further victimization—further sexual harassment—to those inclined to socially construct the scene in that manner. Visual dimensions of this scene reinforced this construction, for Hill came across as almost meek; Specter and others as aggressive.

Anita Hill's story does indeed contain information that is difficult to believe. It is difficult to believe that a man of Clarence Thomas's stature and seeming refinement would talk to a female coworker in a manner Senator Hatch refers to as "sick." And, as Hatch tries to point out in his questioning of Thomas, it is difficult to believe that any man trying to get a date or initiate a relationship with a woman would proceed so crudely. The substance of Hill's story, then, may have been a barrier to its acceptance. However, it was not that much of a barrier for females. This was so not primarily because they might have experienced crude sexual harassment themselves and therefore knew such behavior was indeed possible, but because they were, arguably, paying less attention to the specifics of Hill's narrative than to her speech act itself.

At that time, it was very difficult for a woman to come forward and make an accusation of sexual harassment. The term was beginning to make its way into employment and everyday vocabulary, so Hill, unlike previous generations of women, was at least talking about behavior that had a name and, therefore, a reality. However, it was still difficult for a woman to make the charge. The charge was usually made against a more powerful male, who had behind him the presumption that power gives. The charge involved speaking publicly about matters that, traditionally at least, made many women uncomfortable. And, in this case, that public speaking would be before an overwhelmingly male audience in a "regal" capitol environment that would be somewhat intimidating even without the lights and cameras.

Despite all of these difficulties, Anita Hill did speak—clearly and with vivid detail. The very fact that she spoke was what was crucial in the female social construction of the event. Furthermore, given the difficulties any woman who chose to go public would encounter, a woman had to make sure her testimony was accurate. To do otherwise was to invite rhetorical disaster. Understanding this dynamic, females presumed that Hill's story, as bizarre as it was at points, must be true.

Women also had a better understanding of sexual harassment than did many of the men watching the confirmation hearings. They knew that sexual harassment was

---

[14]For a full account of the rhetoric of this debate, see Theodore F. Sheckels, *When Congress Debates: A Bakhtinian Paradigm* (Westport, CT: Praeger, 2000): 67–85.

often not about initiating a relationship but, rather, exerting power. That exertion might mean a demand for sexual favors, or it might just be part of the creation of a hostile work environment. Either way, the harassing male was playing a power game, not trying to win favor. If understood in this context, the bizarre details of Hill's story are less of an interpretive problem, for what would be highly unlikely to lead to a romantic relationship could indeed create intimidating discomfort. Women understood this dynamic.

The Nature of Congressional Hearings

This hearing had more than its share of theater. The accusation was sensational, and the two characters involved, for various reasons, were compelling. One might think, however, that congressional hearings are usually not this way. Rarely are they quite as theatrical as this one. Furthermore, they are also fairly rarely events featuring disinterested communication.

One might presume that the purpose of a hearing is to gather information that will inform what a committee recommends and what the full Senate or the full House of Representatives will decide. This is the ostensible purpose, and sometimes it is served. However, hearings are far more political than they may seem.

Whichever party holds the majority in either the Senate or the House controls the committee structure, through which the legislature does much of its business. The majority party will appoint the committee chair; that chair will set the committee's agenda. As Lisa Gring-Pemble points out in an article in the *Quarterly Journal of Speech*, this latter power is far from benign: committee chairs can use it make sure their party's side of an issue gets more time and gets more media coverage. As a result, communication on an issue at a hearing is often not balanced between opposing viewpoints.[15] On the floor of the Senate or the House, procedures governing communication ensure equal time, but the same is not true in committee. So, who testifies is controlled. So is who questions. Questioning proceeds hierarchically, with the majority party taking the lead. A committee chair—with perhaps the assistance of another senior colleague—could so dominate the questioning as to silence opponents with less seniority. A newly elected senator might well have much to say—through her or his questions—on a matter but not get much of a chance to do so.

Hearings on matters such as Supreme Court nominations do not typically see as much partisan manipulation of information as less prominent issues such as welfare reform, research on AIDS, or military appropriations. Anti-Thomas speakers and pro-Thomas speakers probably did receive their due: Democrat Joseph Biden of Delaware, the Committee's chair, did not skew testimony in an anti-Thomas direction. But, in other cases, the communication may well have a bias. Hearings are rarely as theatrical as the one that saw Anita Hill accuse and Clarence Thomas defend, but hearings are almost always political—sometimes distressingly so.

[15]Lisa M. Gring-Pemble, "Are We Going to Govern by Anecdote," *Quarterly Journal of Speech*, 87 (2001): 341–65.

Hearings also showcase legislators' style. Whereas legislators have long had an understanding that it is important to "sound good" when debating on the floor of the Senate or the House—even if few people are actually watching—they may not have quite as firm a grasp over how they are coming across when questioning witnesses. Pennsylvania Senator Arlen Specter's style has already been mentioned. It was so aggressive that it became an issue the next time he stood for reelection—against a woman.

Utah Senator Orrin Hatch's style, in the excerpt above, is also worth noting. It is difficult to discern what Hatch was trying to project, but he projects a naïveté that is astounding. If we accept Hatch's questioning at face value, he is clueless about sexual stereotypes concerning African American males. He therefore has to lead Thomas through a sequence of questions in which he presents an instance of sexual behavior and asks Thomas if it's a black stereotype or not. Besides coming across as naive, Hatch also may have been inadvertently undermining Thomas's defense. Thomas had relied on counterattacking: his opponents were trying to stereotype him as an African American male. Hatch asks Thomas about sharing sexual histories and preferences and asking a prospective partner about hers, about oral sex, about bestiality, about viewing pornography, about sexual frequency and prowess, about large penises, about large breasts, and about pubic hair on Coke cans. In only two instances—about the level of sexual activity and about large penises—did Thomas link the details in Hill's story to the stereotype of an African American male. Hatch's questioning then may have inadvertently revealed the disjunction between the story being told about Thomas and the stereotype and undermined Thomas's attempt to portray himself as a victim of racism. If Hatch was trying to help Thomas's defense, the Senator may have inadvertently undermined it by using a naive style.

Conclusion

The Senate Judiciary Committee hearings that saw Anita Hill accuse Clarence Thomas of sexual harassment and, then, Clarence Thomas defend himself offer an excellent example of how political discourse is socially constructed by its audience. Males saw the hearings one way, and they believed Thomas to be "not guilty." Thomas's counterattacking—and how he did that—played a major role in swaying the male audience. Thomas also benefited from power, others' "adversarial interrogation" of Hill and her story, and a tendency males had to construct the story in a way that removed Hill the person from the picture. Females saw the hearings very differently. They attended to Hill's speech act and, knowing how difficult it was, believed her narrative. The way she was treated by Senators made her even more the victim, reinforcing the female construction that had her playing that role.

These hearings also demonstrate that such proceedings can be dramatic. In general, it is important to note that hearings, which are an important kind of Congressional communication, are not as neutral as one might think. Because the communication is controlled by the majority party, hearings are often politically biased. They also showcase individual Senators' styles, sometimes positively and sometimes not.

THE MASS COMMUNICATION PERSPECTIVE

Supreme Court hearings are important because they will lead to an appointment to the highest court in the nation. These hearings tend to be predictable: they typically contain a review of the judge's record, questions on particular issues of controversy that may come before the Court, and political posturing by the members of the Senate Judiciary Committee. They also tend to be predictable in the news media coverage of the nomination process and Senate hearings, with a focus on the conflict or the emotions to heighten the drama of the event. The Clarence Thomas hearing in 1991 needed no further dramatization, once Anita Hill came forward with her allegations of sexual harassment against Thomas.

Focus on Clarence Thomas Hearing Coverage

Richard Davis acknowledges the potential for drama in news coverage of the Supreme Court nominee hearings, given the structure of contemporary hearings he describes as the following:

> The nominee's appearance before the Judiciary Committee resembles the famous gunfight at the OK Corral with the protagonists in place. At least a significant minority, if not a majority, of the Judiciary Committee members may oppose the nominee. Moreover, although confirmations are not unique, they are infrequent enough to retain their newsworthiness. The significance of the outcome, given the policy role of the Court and the salience of any single member on narrowly decided cases, guarantees press coverage.[16]

Three phases of news coverage of the confirmation hearing of Clarence Thomas reflected in news headlines, as well as broader coverage in print and broadcast, can be identified. First, we see attempts at "prehearing drama" in the news stories that appeared in the days just before the start of the hearings before the Senate Judiciary Committee. Although others had speculated that Thomas should proceed through the hearings uneventfully, the news media were still looking for the possible drama, as reflected in the following news headlines:

Days of reckoning finally arrive for Thomas (*USA Today*, September 9, 1991)

Thomas opposition grows louder as confirmation hearings approach (*Washington Post*, September 7, 1991)

Thomas image diverts scrutiny; Bootstraps story outshines record (*Boston Globe*, September 8, 1991)

When the Thomas hearings began, the first 2 weeks were predictable in news coverage. In addition to traditional stories reflecting the questions asked and the

[16]Richard Davis, "Supreme Court Nominations and the News Media," *Albany Law Review* 57 (Fall 1994): 1061–79. Quote from section D, para. 8.

responses given, and challenges made toward the nominee, we see examples of the second phase, "attempts at dramatizing the hearing" in the following headlines:

Thomas rules in Redskins vs. Cowboys (*USA Today*, September 12, 1991)

The Thomas hearings: Witness list notable for its absences (*Washington Post*, September 27, 1991)

Thomas may face tie vote today: New opposition could give high court bid a rougher ride (*Houston Chronicle*, September 27, 1991)

Although most political nomination hearings might conclude quietly and be reported simply, the 7–7 tie vote to send Thomas's name to the full Senate provided some drama on its own. But then we arrive in the Thomas hearings case to phase three of news coverage, "Finally, drama arrives!" Looking at the following headlines, the nomination hearing became material for the tabloids, and was reported in extensive detail by traditional news media as well:

Law professor accuses Thomas of sexual harassment in 1980s (*New York Times*, October 7, 1991)

Senate hearing was mesmerizing viewing (*Minneapolis Star Tribune*, October 12, 1991)

Thomas denies everything, decries 'high-tech lynching' (*St. Petersburg Times*, October 12, 1991)

The Thomas Nomination: Accuser of accuser is accused (*New York Times*, October 14, 1991)

Larry Sabato suggested this later stage of the Thomas hearing and Hill testimony is an instance of a "feeding frenzy," of the news media blowing an event out of proportion with endless coverage and speculation. We may think of such feeding frenzies surrounding political campaigns, but the Thomas hearing was an example of the frenzy going beyond the election arena. In the midst of Hill's accusations coming to public attention and the confirmation hearings continuing after a 1-week postponement, Sabato commented on the frenzy in this case with the following:

> It's lunacy. It is just another sad spectacle of soap opera made for television. It's absurd that a nomination to the Supreme Court is hanging on one 10-year-old allegation of sexual harassment raised at the last minute rather than what this man will do for the next 30 or 40 years on the court. Unfortunately, the character issue has taken deep roots in our politics. Now everybody gets sidetracked about a matter we're not likely to see resolved.[17]

---

[17]As quoted in John Aloysius Farrell, "Debate gives way to a morality play: The Thomas hearings news analysis," *Boston Globe* (October 11, 1991), 1.

From an analysis of newsworthiness, the Clarence Thomas hearings met many criteria. The prominence of the Supreme Court as a political institution, and of such hearings as part of the political rituals, was a primary factor in the newsworthiness of these events. The impact of a new justice, while difficult to predict, has the potential to shift and shape policy through Court decisions. Conflict certainly heightened media's interest in covering the hearing, as Anita Hill's testimony brought unexpected conflict to what are otherwise predictable events in the judicial-appointment process. That conflict fed the dramatic news frame applied in much of the news coverage of the hearings.

The Thomas confirmation hearings and Anita Hill's testimony also brought drama to the news media themselves, not just in their coverage of events. The news media also became part of the news story, as National Public Radio legal affairs reporter Nina Totenberg and *Newsday* reporter Timothy Phelps both faced subpoenas from a special independent counsel appointed by the Senate to surrender confidential information they had gathered in reporting Anita Hill's accusations against Clarence Thomas.[18] Both reporters resisted the efforts to discover the source of their information about the confidential Senate investigation, but these examples reflected a rise in subpoenas issued against reporters and news organizations to turn over notes and video footage at both the national level and in local news markets in other news stories. *Washington Times* reporter Dawn Ceol resigned after editors rewrote her front-page story with the headline "Thomas accuser lauded, assailed" to a story with the headline "Miss Hill painted as 'fantasizer'," based on testimony that suggested Hill fantasized about relationships with men with whom she worked.[19]

As seen in campaign coverage, the reporting of public opinion polls may add to the drama and frenzy of an event, as was the case with the Thomas hearing and Anita Hill's testimony. One example was an ABC News poll taken after the first two days of testimony regarding Hill's allegations, which found that 46 percent of the public believed Thomas to be more credible than Hill, and 24 percent reported that Hill was more credible than Thomas. Additionally, 34 percent believed Hill's charges to be true, and 55 percent said they were false. Such polls were not only reported by the sponsoring organization, but were repeated in other news media as well.[20] Ruckinski[21] summarized polls regarding Hill and Thomas testimony as the following:

> The initial portrayal of public opinion by elites and in media discourse was one of consensus: that a majority of the American people, both men and women, believed Thomas' denials of Hill's charges, that African-Americans overwhelmingly rallied behind Thomas after the charges were leveled, and that a majority of the public supported

---

[18]Rich Brown, "Press fears subpoena chill: First Amendment advocates decry rise in requests for confidential information from reporters," *Broadcasting* 122.7 (1992): 34–5.

[19]Howard Kurtz, "Reporter quits over rewrite of Thomas story," *Washington Post* (October 16, 1991).

[20]Walter V. Robinson, "Hill's friends bolster her account; Thomas ex-aids defend character," *Boston Globe* (October 14, 1991).

[21]Dianne Ruckinski, "Rush to judgment? Fast reaction polls in the Anita Hill–Clarence Thomas controversy," *Public Opinion Quarterly* 57 (1993): 575–92.

his confirmation. Thomas' support in the polls was cited by those favoring his confirmation as evidence of his veracity and fitness for the Supreme Court.

Although Ruckinski describes the tenor of public opinion polls as above, her research explores a number of questions and possible problems with such "fast-reaction" polls on breaking news, as one year later polls indicated opinion had shifted in favor of Anita Hill.

Which "Soap Opera" to Air?

No soap opera fan can complain that the Senate Judiciary Committee hearings that usurped the network tales of sex and power could not deliver their daily emotional fix. It was an astounding day for television viewers, right up there with Watergate.[22]

One conflict in the Thomas hearing that media organizations faced, specifically television broadcasters, was programming issues. Network television chose to air the hearing live and preempt their daytime programs, primarily comprising soap operas and talk shows. Given the drama of the hearings and the numbers of viewers compelled to watch (more than 30 million viewers or network television the first night of the hearing), media organizations that provided news and entertainment programming could not resist. NBC aired 30.5 hours of the Thomas hearings involving Anita Hill's testimony, ABC aired 23 hours, and CBS followed with 13 hours. CBS coverage trailed the other two networks considerably because of contractual obligations to broadcast the Major League Baseball play-offs that October. The three commercial networks were estimated to have lost a combined $15 to 20 million in advertising revenue by preempting daytime television with live coverage of the nomination hearing.[23]

C-SPAN increased its public attention by providing "gavel-to-gavel" coverage of the hearings, and attracted new viewers; they reported 700 calls in to discuss the hearings, and more than 400 callers had not called C-SPAN previously. PBS aired 44 hours of coverage of the week of hearing and in some cases provided coverage when the networks no longer did. The fourth network in the 1990s, Fox, found its ratings increased Saturday morning when they provided children's programming against the other network's coverage of the Thomas hearing. We are quickly reminded by these numbers that beyond news issues of coverage and content, the media are still businesses.

Cameras in the Supreme Court

One news story that garnered little attention from the early days of the Clarence Thomas hearing, before Anita Hill's accusations were made public, is still relevant to consider today. Wisconsin Senator Herbert Kohl asked Thomas during the hearing if

---

[22]Walter Goodman, "In Dramatic Hearings on Thomas, No Soap Opera Fan Need Feel Cheated," *New York Times* (October 12, 1991), 10.

[23]Rich Brown, "Thomas Takes TV's Center Stage," *Broadcasting* (October 21, 1991): 23–25.

cameras should be allowed in the Supreme Court to televise oral arguments, and Thomas stated the oral arguments should be televised.[24] That 1991 news story continued, "Most believe it may be another five years—and perhaps a decade—before purely ceremonial coverage begins. It may be five to 10 years more before oral arguments are covered." Yet more than 15 years later, we can watch the nomination hearings for Supreme Court justice, but we still have no televised oral arguments from the Court.

Recent comments from Supreme Court justices suggest we will not be seeing cameras in their court anytime soon. In 2005, Justices Stephen Breyer, Sandra Day O'Connor, and Antonin Scalia spoke out against television coverage of oral arguments made before the Supreme Court. They expressed concerns that the short segments of court arguments that television would broadcast might portray cases out of context.[25] The concerns for news media's brevity in coverage, reliance on visuals, and the potential for sensationalism, as witnessed in coverage of the Thomas hearing, are likely key factors for the justices' concerns.

Conclusion

The testimony in the final week of Clarence Thomas's nomination hearing involving Anita Hill's allegations of sexual harassment was dramatic on its own for such a hearing. However, the news coverage of the testimony, and responses to it, heightened the drama even further. News coverage surrounding Hill's testimony had implications for the news media as well, for one reporter who saw her story changed by editors to be more sensationalistic, and for two other reporters who faced subpoenas to reveal how they had learned of Hill's allegations. Television networks willingly substituted the drama of daytime soap operas with the drama of the testimony at the hearing and also faced the economic implications of doing so. Whether the public will ever be able to watch more than the Supreme Court nomination hearings on television, and see the oral arguments of cases as they are given before the Court, is yet to be determined.

CONCLUSION

The three perspectives presented here focus on the drama created surrounding Anita Hill's testimony and subsequent responses to it during Clarence Thomas's Supreme Court nomination hearing before the Senate Judiciary Committee. We see in the hearing the drama involving the senators themselves, the spectacle created surrounding Hill's allegations, and the deadlocked 7–7 committee tie before Hill's testimony, and the emotions reinforced through news coverage. Differences were also acknowledged

---

[24]Patrick J. Sheridan, "Cameras in the Supreme Court a Distinct, if Distant, Possibility," *Broadcasting* (September 23, 1991): 48–49.

[25]Andrew Brenner, "Courtrooms Shuttered to Cameras in Three Trials." *News Media & the Law*, 29.2 (2005): 33.

by each perspective in how men versus women reacted to the testimony, the contrast of white senators overseeing a hearing involving an African American accuser and an African American nominee, and the public opinion disagreement identified regarding who believed Clarence Thomas and who believed Anita Hill during the hearings.

The perspectives also diverged in additional issues raised regarding these hearings, with a focus on the social construction of the hearings by male and female viewers, the political implications of the hearing on the 1992 elections, and the economic decisions made in network television to air dozens of hours of testimony live into American households.

ADDITIONAL CASES

- **Nomination of Thurgood Marshall to the Supreme Court, the first African American justice**
  Resource: L. Martin Overby, Beth M. Henschen, Julie Strauss, and Michael H. Walsh, African-American constituents and Supreme Court nominees: An examination of the Senate confirmation of Thurgood Marshall. *Political Research Quarterly, 47* (December 1994): 839–855.

- **The Watergate hearings**
  Resource: Harvey L. Molotch and Deidre Boden, Talking social structure: Discourse, domination and the Watergate hearings. *American Sociological Review, 50* (June 1985): 57–68.

- **McCarthy hearings, 1954**
  Resources: Lewis A. Kaplan, The House Un-American Activities Committee and its opponents: A study in congressional dissonance. *Journal of Politics, 30* (August 1968): 647–671; G. D. Wiebe, The Army-McCarthy hearings and the public conscience. *Public Opinion Quarterly, 22* (Winter 1958): 490–502.

- **House hearings on Bill Clinton's impeachment**
  Resource: Virginia Anderson, "The perfect enemy": Clinton, the contradictions of capitalism, and slaying the sin within. *Rhetoric Review, 21* (2002): 384–400.

- **Nomination hearings of John Ashcroft for U.S. Attorney General, 2001**
  Resource: Benjamin R. Bates, Ashcroft among the Senators: Justification, Strategy, and Tactics in the 2001 Attorney General confirmation hearing. *Argumentation & Advocacy, 39* (Spring 2003): 254–273.

CHAPTER 14

CASE TEN: THE GOP'S "REVERSE FILIBUSTER" OVER GEORGE W. BUSH'S JUDICIAL NOMINEES

THE CASE

When President George W. Bush made his first judicial nominations in the spring of 2001, the Republican party controlled the Senate. Within a matter of weeks, however, Vermont Republican Senator James Jeffords announced that irreconcilable differences between him and the Republican leadership and the president would lead him to leave the Republican Party over the summer. When Jeffords' defection occurred, it gave control of the Senate to the Democrats, who maintained majority party status through the November 2002 elections. Unfortunately for judicial nominees who had been selected early in 2001, the Democrats were not amenable to the conservative choices the president made initially. Before the 107th Congress ended in 2002, the Democrats had rejected several of President Bush's nominees.

However, the 2002 congressional midterm elections restored Republicans to majority party status in the chamber, and early in 2003 President Bush opted to renominate several of the individuals who had been rejected by the Democratically controlled Senate only months before. With their options for recourse constrained, the Democrats began employing filibusters to keep the most objectionable nominees from being brought to a vote. Filibusters require a vote of sixty members of the chamber in order to end, in the event that the filibusterer(s) refuse to relinquish control of the floor voluntarily. Because the Republican leadership was never able to secure sixty votes, it began to pursue other options to bring about the end of these filibusters. Senate Majority Leader Bill Frist proposed a change to the rule requiring sixty votes to cut off debate on a judicial nominee. Dubbed the "nuclear option," Frist's proposal involved having the presiding officer of the Senate rule—in violation of the Senate's Standing Rules—that only 51 votes were necessary to cut off debate. Because this proposal was so controversial, the Republicans decided it could be attempted only after all other mechanisms for negotiating an end to the filibusters had been exhausted.

One of the alternatives that the Republican leadership decided to pursue was the so-called reverse filibuster. The brainchild of Republican Whip Rick Santorum (R-PA), the plan was that Republicans would take control of the Senate floor and force the Democrats to engage in a marathon session to debate the merits of confirming President Bush's nominees. Convinced that they would be able to prevail in winning public support for their view that the nominees deserved confirmation, and hopeful that the Democrats would be unequal to the challenge presented by the 30 hours of constant debate, the Republicans decided that from 6:00 P.M. on November 12, until midnight on November 13, 2003, they would force the Democrats to consume 30 minutes of every hour in debate. If, at any point, there was no Democrat on the floor to object, they would simply move the confirmation of each of the filibustered nominees by unanimous consent.

Excerpt from the Debate

Mr. Frist: [T]onight we embark upon an extraordinary session for the next 30 hours. Republicans and Democrats will debate the merits of three judicial nominees. We will be considering the meaning of our constitutional responsibility to advise and consent on nominations. We will discuss whether there is a need to enact filibuster reform so that nominations taken to the floor can get a vote. . . .

We hold this extraordinary session for truly extraordinary reasons. In the history of this Senate, through 107 Congresses, the filibuster was never used to block confirmation of judicial nominees enjoying majority support. When the Senate has refused to confirm a nominee brought to the floor, it has done so on an up or down vote. Permitting a vote was fair to the nominees and fair to the President who sent them to us. In theory, the filibuster has always been available as a tool to derail a nomination, but until this Congress it has not been successfully used. . . .

Filibustering judicial nominations breaks dangerous new ground. It is unprecedented. These filibusters are not business as usual. . . . Under the Constitution, the Senate has a confirmation veto; a majority can vote a nominee down but obstruction by filibuster is veto by a minority. Never did the framers envision that anti-democratic outcome.

*****

Mr. Specter: I thank the Chair. Tonight the Senate is engaging in a proceeding to call the attention of the American people to a very serious matter which exists on the confirmation of Federal judges. It is not a matter which occurs just when there has been a Republican President, but it has occurred also when there has been a President of the Democratic party, when the Republicans controlled the Senate. It has gone back at least to 1987, during the second 2 years of President Reagan's administration. . . .

The last time there was a [traditional] filibuster in the Senate was 1987 when the subject was campaign finance reform. Senator Byrd was the leader of the Democrats. Senator Dole, the leader of the Republicans, called all of us into the cloakroom behind us in the Senate Chamber at about 2 o'clock one morning and said: I would like all Republican Senators to stay off the floor. The reason Senator Dole asked everyone to stay off the floor was to compel the party in power, the Democrats, to maintain a quorum of 51 Senators because if there are not 51 Senators present, then any Senator may suggest the absence of a quorum, and the Senate conducts no further business.

When Republican Senators, including Arlen Specter, absented ourselves from the floor at Senator Dole's request, Senator Byrd, the leader of the Democrats, countered with a motion to arrest absent Senators. Sergeant at Arms Henry Giugni was then armed with warrants of arrest and started to patrol the halls, and the first Senator he found was Senator Lowell Weicker. Sergeant at Arms Henry Giugni was a little fellow, about 5 foot 6 inches, 150 pounds. Senator Weicker was a big guy—still is—about 6 foot 4 inches, 240 pounds. This was at about 3:30 in the morning. Sergeant at Arms Giugni decided not to arrest Senator Weicker. I think he made a good judgment. Then he started to go around and knock on Senators' doors. Senator

Iowa Senator Tom Harkin signals his opinion to the press before the start of the 30-hour session in protest of the Democrat's blocking of GOP judicial nominees in November 2003.

Packwood foolishly answered his door. Senator Packwood was then carried feet first into the Senate Chamber. This is a true story. You don't get many out of Washington, but this is a true story. That incident attracted a great deal of attention. C-SPAN became the channel of choice instead of Jay Leno.

In having this proceeding, it is more accurately called a marathon than a filibuster because it is not a filibuster. Republicans are doing most of the talking. We seek to attract the attention of the American people to what is going on in the judicial system. We have at the present time judicial emergencies in four of the circuit courts of appeals in the United States: the Fourth Circuit, the Fifth Circuit, the Sixth Circuit, and the Ninth Circuit. When these judicial emergencies occur, people are denied their day in court, cases languish, the matters are not decided, and the fact of life is that justice delayed is justice denied. . . .

*****

Mr. Durbin: . . . My people living back home in Springfield, IL, and Chicago, IL, I am sure, turned off C-SPAN a long, long time ago, if this is the best we can offer them. Sadly, that is all we are offering them. We left the Veterans Administration appropriations bill—we could have finished it— for veterans hospitals and the millions of veterans across America because we did not have time; we had to start this never-ending 30-hour debate. We cannot entertain a motion made by the Senator from Indiana, a motion I made, as well, to try to do something about the 9 million unemployed Americans whose benefits are running out. We do not have time for that. We have time for this political debate. That is unfortunate. It is distressing.

I have given 21 years of my adult life to public service. I have never regretted a moment of it. I walked away from a law practice and never looked back. This is the most exciting and interesting thing I can think of to do with your life, to be involved in public service. I encourage everyone, regardless of your political stripe, to get involved. You will love the opportunity it gives you to help people. But, frankly, we are not seizing that opportunity or we would not be here tonight. We would not be here discussing a question about whether 168 or 172 judges is the right number.

. . . Let me try to synthesize this into what it is about. It is not about the four judges or two more who might be added on Friday. It is about the next appointment to the Supreme Court across the street. That is the real story. There are a lot of good reasons we are here tonight but the real reason is the next Supreme Court vacancy and the belief on the Republican side of the aisle that if we can hold fast with our approach in stopping people unqualified, unfit, to serve on a Federal court, they will have a difficult time passing through a controversial nominee to the U.S. Supreme Court. I think, in my heart of hearts, that is why we are here this evening. They are trying to smooth the road, prepare the way for that Supreme Court nominee from this President. Now, let me give advice to my friends—and they are not likely to take it—on the Republican side. There is a way to avoid all that. Pick a man or a woman who is of such impeccable legal background, great credentials, the kind of person with the integrity that they will be above this kind of political debate. It can happen and it has happened.

. . . [W]e have to move away from those who are ideological extremes. We have to move away from those who are lightning rods. We have to move to a center path, which most Americans expect of us. Sadly, tonight, we are being told this Senate should not even ask questions of these nominees. That is wrong. We have a constitutional responsibility, a responsibility that must be met.

Some have said, incidentally, that ours are the first to ever filibuster nominees. In fact, the Senator from Pennsylvania said it is the first time in the history of the United States anyone has ever filibustered a judicial nominee. Well, this chart shows that is not correct. Abe Fortas of the Supreme Court, subject to cloture motion, filibuster; Stephen Breyer, First Circuit—I am going through the list—Rosemary Barkett, Eleventh Circuit; Lee Sarokin, Third Circuit; Marsha Berzon, Ninth Circuit; and Richard Paez, Ninth Circuit.

The fact is, there have been judges brought to the Senate floor who have been filibustered in the past. The fact is, most of those filibusters failed. The motion for cloture prevailed but the filibuster was on. On the four who are under contention this evening, the filibuster has succeeded. The motion for cloture has not been filed successfully. That is the difference. To say it has never happened before in our history is to defy the obvious. It certainly has happened before. The point we are trying to make is it is not unreasonable to have 4 nominees out of 172 questioned, to be found lacking. Let me close by saying, again I commend my colleague from Indiana because I think he put it in perspective. We all know it is true. We could be spending our time doing a lot more important things for America and a lot more important things for the people we represent than squabbling over four judges.

THE POLITICAL SCIENCE PERSPECTIVE

The November 2003 reverse filibuster is an interesting case of political communication aimed at both the attentive and inattentive publics. The fact that only cable and satellite subscribers whose packages include C-SPAN2, the public affairs channel that covers the Senate, would be able to tune in, coupled with the fact that only those viewers who stayed awake for 30 straight hours would be able to watch the debate in real time suggests that senators' comments were directed at political elites. However, the nature of the rhetoric employed by the senators who participated in the marathon debate, especially the ways in which facts were distorted or omitted from the discussion, suggests that senators also expected their messages to be filtered to less attentive publics who would be less likely to know the history of the confirmation process and the filibuster and who, therefore, could potentially be more easily swayed to the positions being advanced during the debate.

To understand the reverse filibuster debate, it is essential to understand some basic facts about both the confirmation process and the ways in which the Senate has employed the filibuster over the course of its history. The Senate is required by Article II, Section 2 of the Constitution to advise and consent to presidents' selections to fill vacancies in the federal courts and other federal offices. The Constitution does not offer any guidance about what constitutes presidential advice-seeking from the Senate, nor does it offer any guidance about what the rules of approving a presidential nomination might be. Moreover, Article I, Section 5 permits each chamber of the Congress to determine its own rules of procedure. This section is important both to understanding the evolution of the Senate's confirmation process and for understanding the origins and usage of the Senate filibuster, the right of any member of the Senate to have the privilege of the floor—in other words, to debate—until such time as he or she decides to relinquish it voluntarily or is simply no longer capable of continuing the debate.

Because Article I, Section 5 makes each chamber responsible for setting its own rules, the Senate has been able to create its own procedures for processing presidential nominations. Presidents nominate individuals to fill vacancies in the federal judiciary by transmitting the name of their selections to the Senate clerk. Upon receipt of a nomination, the Senate would consider the candidate and would offer its assessment of the nominee's fitness for office. George Washington's nominees to the federal courts were typically approved (or, rarely, rejected) within a day of receipt of their nominations in the Senate. In the first several decades of its existence, in the rare event that the Senate rejected a nominee, it generally was because the home state senators who represented the state in which there was a vacancy found the nominee "personally obnoxious." The process of rejecting presidential nominees who lack the support of home state senators is known as senatorial courtesy; the practice continues today.

Although today the names of all nominees to the federal courts are sent to the Senate Judiciary Committee for preliminary consideration, during the first several decades of its existence the Senate did not make use of smaller jurisdiction-specific committees to process nominations, but simply considered presidential nominees in the committee of the whole. Following the Judiciary Committee's creation as one of the chamber's original standing committees in 1816, the Judiciary Committee took an active role in screening presidential nominees, although its current practices did not fully develop until the early 1980s.

Once the Committee determines that the full Senate should act on a nomination to the federal courts, the nomination is scheduled for a vote of the full Senate. Consent to an appointment has, from the very first Senate, required a majority vote of the members of the full chamber. Initially, this vote took place in secrecy. As necessary, the Senate would go into a true executive session in which all outside observers would be cleared from the galleries and it would debate the merits of presidential nominees and then vote on each individual. In 1929, the Senate abandoned its use of the true executive session for discussing presidential nominations, but it still uses its executive calendar to organize debate on pending nominations. The only other item of pending business that is in order on the Executive Calendar is treaties pending Senate ratification. To discuss a nomination or a treaty, the Senate must suspend its work on pending legislation, which is scheduled on the chamber's legislative calendar.

Moving from a closed executive session to an open one had a profound effect on the Senate's work in general, and in the judicial confirmation process specifically. Rather than being able to debate freely the merits and liabilities of nominees to the federal judiciary, the fact that senators' remarks were now part of the official record of proceedings and were available for public scrutiny changed senators' incentive structures. Moreover, because of ratification of the Seventeenth Amendment to the Constitution in 1913, senators faced direct election by statewide constituencies, which likewise gave them incentives to promote their constituents' policy preferences in the confirmation process. External political actors, such as interest groups, also took advantage of the openness in the process. Because senators' votes on nominees are cast in public, the groups can offer inducements for senators to vote in the direction that the groups prefer. In the 1960s and 1970s, as the number of interest groups in the United States exploded, the confirmation process gradually began to change. What had once taken President George Washington only a day began to take weeks or even months. When C-SPAN began broadcasting Senate debates in 1986, senators' incentives again changed, as they could use the increased visibility among political elites to curry favor with powerful national and home state interests.

Deconstructing the Reverse Filibuster

As noted in the introduction to this chapter, Senate Republicans hoped that their reverse filibuster would succeed in both drawing attention to Democratic filibusters of President George W. Bush's judicial nominees and in persuading the public that the Democrats were wrong to delay the confirmation of these nominees. By most accounts, however, the Republicans were not successful in achieving their objectives. The public generally has little sympathy for pending judicial nominees. Such nominees tend to be sitting judges or prominent attorneys in their home states and communities, and most Americans will never be litigants in federal court. In addition, the vast majority of the public do not know anything about the appointment process for federal judges. In fact, a June 2003 survey of 800 Hispanic voters determined that at least a third of them had confused federal appeals court nominee Miguel Estrada, one of the targets of the Democrats' filibustering efforts, with the actor Erik Estrada, who played "Ponch" on the 1980s motorcycle cop drama *CHiPS*.[1]

Because the confirmation of federal judges is not a highly salient issue to most Americans, with many other pressing items of pending business, including Medicare reform, the War in Iraq, and the federal budget resolutions, many people wondered why the Senate was conducting a marathon session that most observers agreed was

---

[1]Steven Dinan, "Hispanics Tune Out Estrada Filibuster; Nominee Mistaken for Actor, Poll Finds." *Washington Times*, June 19, 2003, A6.

little more than a publicity stunt. A closer look at the specific arguments that were advanced by senators on both sides of the aisle reveals that the reverse filibuster is an excellent example of a political spectacle orchestrated to promote image rather than substance and characterized by hyperbole and distortions designed to support the speakers' versions of the confirmation process conflict.

Majority Leader Bill Frist began the 30-hour debate by presenting his version of the circumstances that led to the event. Only moments into his remarks, he presents the first bit of misleading information, when he states: "Up until now, no judicial nominee has ever failed on a filibuster. For the past 200 years, no judicial nominee has ever failed on a filibuster" (*Congressional Record*, November 12, 2003; S.14528). Moments later, he continued: "Filibustering judicial nominations breaks dangerous new ground. It is unprecedented. These filibusters are not business as usual" (*Congressional Record*, November 12, 2003; S. 14528). When it is Senate Judiciary Chairman Orrin Hatch's turn to speak following the conclusion of Frist's remarks, he too repeats the statement that the Democrat-led filibusters are unprecedented. But, in fact, President Lyndon Johnson's 1968 nomination of Abe Fortas to be Chief Justice of the United States Supreme Court failed as a result of a bipartisan filibuster against his nomination. And, throughout the history of the Senate, several additional judicial nominees were subject to filibusters that were eventually overcome by cloture votes. These notable filibusters were highlighted by subsequent Democratic speakers, who sought to minimize the magnitude of their actions.

In addition, Democrats emphasized the fact that beginning in 1995, when Republicans regained control of the Senate for the first time in nearly a decade, conservative interest groups began to pursue a more aggressive strategy designed to keep President Bill Clinton's nominees off of the federal bench. A key part of this strategy was encouraging their allies in the Senate to use holds to keep nominees from being brought to a vote. Holds are requests made to the majority leader, who is responsible for deciding which measures to bring up for debate. In the context of judicial nominations, they are most often made by a senator or senators who wish to derail a nomination. They are secret, so the senator who has requested the hold is not known to anyone but the majority leader. Some scholars who study holds consider them to be equivalent to threatened filibusters. Dozens of Clinton's nominees to the federal judiciary and to other federal positions were delayed or denied confirmation as a result of senatorial holds during the period 1995–2000. However, the Republicans who spoke during the 30 hours of debate did not acknowledge their own efforts during the Clinton Administration to deny "up or down" votes to the president's nominees.

A few minutes further into his opening remarks, Majority Leader Frist continues to be less than fully accurate in his depiction of the way in which the Senate's confirmation process operates. Claiming that "[u]nder the Constitution, the Senate has a confirmation veto; a majority can vote a nominee down but obstruction by filibuster is veto by a minority. Never did the framers envision that anti-democratic outcome." Frist capitalizes on the public's lack of knowledge about the constitutional language that describes the process as well as the lack of public information about the debates that occurred during the Constitutional Convention. In actuality, Article II does not indicate what "by and with the advice and consent of the Senate" means in terms of confirming presidents' nominees. Consent has always been construed to mean a simple majority, but there is nothing in the document that mandates that be the case. Moreover, because of the language in Article I, Section 5 that allows each chamber to set its own rules of procedure, there is no constitutional prohibition against the use of filibusters in the confirmation process.

The Political Spectacle of the Reverse Filibuster

The reverse filibuster is an excellent example of Edelman's "political spectacle." Both the words and visual images used throughout the marathon debate were carefully constructed to communicate the respective positions of the Republican and Democratic parties. Predictably, however, as it was the Republican party who organized the talkathon, the Republican party was more "on message," than was the Democratic party. The Republicans' message was that President George W. Bush's judicial nominees deserved "up or down" votes, rather than being subject to filibusters by Senate Democrats. In fact, Republican Senators repeated this line more than 200 times during the 30 hours of debate—that's an average of almost four mentions per senator, and between six and seven mentions per hour.

It is not surprising that the Republicans were so united in the language that they used during the debate. They had been specifically encouraged to use the "up or down" votes line by their strategists. A memorandum written in the spring of 2003 by former Republican Frank Luntz detailed how Republican strategists tested several ways of talking about judicial nominations. The memo noted (emphasis original):

> We tested seven individual themes and more than a dozen articulations. Unfortunately, only a few are strong enough to cut through the political clutter. We also saw firsthand how a single word or phrase can often mean the difference between effective speech and ineffective rhetoric. With a Supreme Court vacancy approaching, you need to get it right . . . NOW. Here's what we recommend: **Your Best Argument: "As a matter of principle, judicial nominees deserve a simple up or down vote."** Americans expect and want the Senate confirmation process to be thoughtful and thorough, but they certainly don't think it should drag on month after month (The Language of Judicial Nominations 2003).

Media accounts of the reverse filibuster noted that the Republicans had copies of Luntz's memo and were consulting them throughout the lengthy debate.[2]

It wasn't just what was said in the debate that mattered, it was the use of visual images and props to communicate the messages each side wanted the public to remember. The Senate's rules for displays in its buildings constrain the use of props on the chamber floor, limiting them to signs of no greater than three by four feet, to be displayed only at the senator's desk or at the back of the Senate chamber and only when the senator is engaged in debate.

---

[2]Ed Henry, "How about the Language of Truth Telling." *Roll Call* (November 19, 2003).

The debate transcripts indicate that the Republicans employed several posters to communicate the content of their message visually. When New York Senator Charles Schumer, one of the leaders of the Democrats' filibuster efforts, took to the Senate floor, he appeared with a large sign that read "168 to 4" to indicate the number of George W. Bush's nominees that the Senate had confirmed—168—compared with the number that had been blocked by the Democrats—4 (*Congressional Record*, November 12, 2003; S 14533). Schumer's Democratic colleague, Minority Whip Richard Durbin (D-IL) used a poster to highlight past judicial nominees whose nominations were stalled or derailed by a filibuster. Iowa's senior senator Democrat Tom Harkin's poster read: "I'll be home watching the Bachelor" which prompted a fairly scathing response from Pennsylvania Republican Senator and reverse filibuster architect Rick Santorum, who accused the Democrats of trying to divert attention from the Republicans' message.

On the Republican side, Senator Orrin Hatch used two posters to highlight the credentials of several beleaguered nominees (*Congressional Record*, November 12, 2003; S 14535). Republican John Cornyn used a poster to depict the amount of business accomplished by the Senate throughout various presidential administrations (*Congressional Record*, November 12, 2003; S 14542). Rick Santorum (R-PA) had his own chart made to counter Senator Schumer's chart; Santorum's chart read: "2,372 to 0," to represent the number of nominees—2,372—who have been confirmed since the cloture rule was adopted in 1925, as compared with the number of nominees—0—who had actually been subject to a filibuster; however, Santorum's chart, like the claims of his colleagues, was not technically correct. As noted above, several nominees were filibustered between 1968 and 2005.

Conclusion

As much as Republicans had hoped that the reverse filibuster would both highlight their quest to confirm several of President George W. Bush's nominees (and that perhaps a Democratic lapse would give them the opportunity to do so during the course of the period set aside for the debate), they did not accomplish this goal. As noted earlier, the vast majority of the public paid little attention to the speech making occurring in the Senate while it happened. Moreover, the media coverage of the event was limited to C-SPAN2 during the debate and brief articles in national news sources afterward, and many of the articles written about the debate focused on the humorous aspects, such as Senator Harkin's "Bachelor" sign.

In the short term, although the Republicans did a better job getting their message across, the Democrats successfully were able to argue that the Republicans could have better spent the time debating issues of substantive importance to a sizable segment of the American population—issues such as unemployment, health care, and funding veterans' benefits. In addition, the Democrats met the Republicans' challenge and successfully held the floor throughout the 30-hour period, preventing the Republicans from moving any of the beleaguered judicial nominees to a vote.

In the longer term, the Democrats successfully thwarted Majority Leader Bill Frist's proposed Senate rules change that would have reduced the number of votes needed to invoke cloture and thus cut off debate on judicial nominations. A spring 2005 compromise between seven moderate Democrats and seven moderate Republicans ensured that the majority leader would not have sufficient votes to abolish the filibuster. Although Democrats were forced to accept the nominations of four of President Bush's more controversial judicial nominees, the net effect of the compromise was to preserve the filibuster, which is a larger victory. Moreover, the compromise, which led seven Republicans to break with the majority leader, was an embarrassment to Majority Leader Frist, because it called into question his ability to lead his own party. The result was that the Democrats successfully weakened the Republican Party in the Senate and strengthened their own position.

THE RHETORICAL PERSPECTIVE

Congress is a busy place, featuring communication of all sorts. Certainly the most visible kind of communication is that which occurs in either the Senate or the House chamber. There—at least in popular lore—great debates decide what policies the nation will adopt.

How Congressional Debates Have Been Viewed

One would think that debates on the floor of either the Senate or the House of Representatives would attract a great deal of attention from rhetorical critics: after all, such critics are interested in arguments, and members of Congress certainly make many of them as they discuss various policies. However, these debates have drawn relatively little attention. Why? Because they, despite the many words uttered, have been thought to be of little consequence. Why? Matters of public policy are typically decided in committee meetings and in private conversation, and, as a result, as a debate proceeds through its hours or days, everybody knows what the ultimate vote will be.

There, of course, have been debates that have indeed swayed votes one way or the other and, therefore, had consequence. However, most debates are indeed *seemingly* beside the point, and the members of Congress *seem* to be engaging in exercises in rhetorical bluster.

Note that the previous sentence said "seemingly" and "seem." These words were used because—as will be explained shortly—beneath the surface, much that is of importance may be going on during a typical Congressional debate. However, the surface debate can be interesting too when the speaking has consequence—such as preventing the ultimate vote. That is, simply speaking, what a filibuster is. Members of the Senate do not filibuster casually. Rather, they do so when they believe the issue before the Senate is of importance. This so-called reverse filibuster is not really a filibuster; rather, it is a nonstop 30-hour period of extended debate. It nonetheless has the feel of a filibuster—because it is nonstop 30-hour period of extended debate, in this case orchestrated by the Republican majority. They plan to keep talking, and, if the Democrats don't follow suit by always having someone there to take the Democrats' turn talking, the Republicans plan to take advantage of this failure to move the immediate approval of controversial judicial nominees. Therefore, both the surface and the subsurface are well worth examining rhetorically in this marathon debate.

The Debate's Surface

Toulmin's classification of claims into the categories of designative, definitive, evaluative, and advocative provides a useful framework for examining what the debating Senators are arguing.

The Designative Claims   A designative claim deals with questions of fact. The crucial questions in this debate are (1) how often have Democrats blocked President George W. Bush's judicial nominations and (2) how often did Republicans block President Bill Clinton's? One would think that the relevant numbers would be a matter of public record and, therefore, determined by citing that record, but the issue is not that simple. On the first argument, the Democrats claimed that they had supported 168 Bush nominees and blocked only 4. The Republicans responded that the 4 would shortly increase and that the better numbers to cite would be for just the circuit court positions, where the Democrats had approved 40 but rejected 4 and may reject 8 more.

On the second argument, the Democrats claimed that Republicans had failed to approve 63 of Clinton's 311 nominees. The Republicans responded that they had never successfully filibustered a Clinton nominee who had been reported out of the Judiciary Committee. They argued that what may have happened within the Committee was beside the point.

The audience for this debate, as is almost always the case since the advent of C-SPAN2, was neither on the floor of the Senate chamber nor in the gallery but beyond the Capitol—those either watching C-SPAN2 or excerpts conveyed by television news media. This audience—to the extent it could be swayed from a preconceived opinion—might have found the simplicity of the Democrats' 168–4 and 248–63 easier to grasp than what might have come across as the Republicans' massaging of this data. The Democrats seemed to be counting on this audience reaction: thus, they repeated the numbers frequently and used visuals to drive the numbers into the audience's consciousness even more. They displayed the 186–4 visually with a poster, and they showcased the numerous blocked Clinton nominees visually with their pictures.

The Definitive Claims   A definitive claim deals with questions of meaning—in other words, with definitions. The crucial term requiring a definition in this debate is "filibuster." The Republicans preferred a narrow definition. Not only must it be extended debate but extended debate that also succeeds in preventing a majority vote.

Based on this narrow definition, they could claim that the Democrats were doing something unprecedented in filibustering Bush's judicial nominees. The Democrats, on the other hand, preferred a broader definition. Their definition would include not only examples of extended debate that did not succeed (thus including GOP filibusters against Clinton nominees Berzon and Paez), but also any procedural moves that prevented nominees from getting a vote on the Senate floor, including the moves used in the Judiciary Committee to prevent Clinton nominees from either receiving a hearing or being sent to the Senate floor after a hearing.

The Democrats were stretching the term a bit. However, the Republicans were arguably playing with words so that what the Democrats had done by way of extended debate against Bush nominees was a filibuster because it had succeeded in preventing a vote, whereas what the Republicans had done by way of extended debate against Clinton nominees was not because it had not succeeded. Most in the audience beyond the Capitol probably tuned this argument out rather quickly. Whatever was being done, no matter by which party, they wanted to know whether it was good or bad.

The Evaluative Claims Which brings us to the evaluative claims being made. The Republicans claimed that what the Democrats were doing was (1) an unprecedented violation of the U.S. Constitution and (2) unfair to both Bush and his nominees.

The first claim has two parts. The "unprecedented" part—that the Democrats were filibustering a judicial nominee for the first time ever and, therefore, thwarting majority rule—takes us back to the definitive claim. What the Republicans were arguing can be valid only if you accept their narrow definition of *filibuster*. The "violation" part depends on whether you believe that the Constitution specifies the *only* circumstances under which a super-majority is required or whether you believe that, since the Constitution gives the Senate the power to set its own rules, its rules of cloture (which have developed over the years) can be used, in essence, to require super-majority votes on other matters. Most in the audience, however, were unlikely to get inside these constitutional arguments. Rather, they would likely process the Republican claim as a highly emotional attack akin to saying the Democrats were desecrating the flag and either agree or disagree with it based on their predisposition.

The second claim evoked two Democratic responses. First, they claimed that, rather than being unfair to Bush, they were simply doing their job under the "advise and consent" clause in the Constitution. They argued that the Senate was never envisioned as a "rubber stamp" but, rather, as an equal participant in the process of appointing men and women to lifetime judicial posts. They further argued that, if there were problems, they existed because Bush was refusing to seek and take the advice of the Senate. Several Democratic senators noted states (e.g., Florida, Washington) in which there was "true" "advice and consent" and, thus, no problem with confirmations. Second, the Democrats claimed that, in blocking Bush nominees, they were simply doing to Bush what the GOP had done to Clinton. Although this second argument was perhaps unavoidable in a political arena, it did undermine the more principled first argument. The Democrats may have then made a strategic error in comparing their responses to Bush nominees to Republican responses to Clinton's. They tried to make the Republican behavior seem worse; they even tried to suggest that both parties correctly used the Senate's power to pare extremists from the lists. The public, however, is likely to process the comparison as proof that *both* parties had played politics.

Whereas the Democrats made a careful distinction between cabinet appointments, where the president should be entitled to have "his people," and judicial appointments, where the lifetime nature of the appointment requires closer scrutiny, the Republicans combined the two sets. They seemed to be hoping that the audience would embrace the simple "The President is entitled to his choices" and apply it equally to cabinet officers and federal judges. They may have been correct. Further helping the Republicans make their case was that they could freely quote Democrats saying, back during the Clinton administration, that blocking the President's choices was unfair. In response, the Democrats did note that Republicans back then were absolutely silent about such blocking being either unconstitutional or unfair. Words, however, trump silence. Thus, the Democrats may seem to the debate's audience to be more hypocritical than the Republicans.

Stepping back from the debate, however, a critic would probably suggest that its audience—except for those predisposed to side, almost blindly, with the one side or the other—would dismiss as too complex the constitutional argument, just as they had dismissed the definitive claims about what a filibuster is or is not and would conclude that both parties were being far too political. This audience would probably grant that the numbers suggest that the Republicans were worse during the Clinton years than the Democrats were being now under Bush. But the difference would not prevent that audience from negatively evaluating *both* parties and asking that they proceed onward in a less purely political manner.

The Democrats clearly wanted the Republicans to be viewed in such a manner. Thus, the Democrats noted throughout the debate all of the matters important to the American people—most of them economic—that the Republicans were ignoring in order to have this 30-hour reverse filibuster: creating jobs, increasing the minimum wage, extending unemployment benefits, increasing veterans' benefits, and so on. The Democrats repeatedly offered unanimous consent requests to debate or vote on such matters, making the Republicans look bad when they objected. This maneuver on the Democrats' part would be dismissed with a bit of laughter by anyone savvy about Senate procedure. The Democrats, however, seemed to be counting on there being some in the audience who were not that savvy and would think the Republicans wanted to waste 30 hours talking about a small number of Bush's judicial nominees rather than act on important economic matters or even hear a briefing on the conduct of postwar operations in Iraq.

It is then very much a matter of opinion who came out ahead once the debate ended. In the final analysis, it may be more important that neither side did, prompting the audience to ask both parties to do better in the future.

The evaluative claims were, in this debate, its *stasis*—that is, the point on which the overall argument hinged. The designative and definitive claims became, to some extent, mixed in with the evaluative, but they mattered less than the fundamental question: were the Democrats doing something wrong? My reading of the debate would suggest that the audience would conclude that, although the Democrats were not doing something horribly wrong, they were playing partisan political games just as the Republicans had when Clinton was in the White House. Thus, both sides were guilty—not of violating the Constitution but of politicking, not governing.

The Advocative Claims   Some advocative claims were advanced about how nominees might be better processed by revising cloture procedures. However, these claims seemed almost beside the point—the point being to make the other party look bad.

Beneath the Surface of the Debate

This particular debate was an interesting one on its surface. Ultimately, however, it may be what was beneath the surface that truly mattered. As Bakhtin has suggested, discourse is frequently multileveled. In Congress, even when votes are not in doubt, much can be "happening" at levels beneath the debate's surface. For example, debating senators might be trying to set the stage for a future issue.

Beneath the surface of this reverse filibuster was rather clearly the next nomination(s) to serve on the U.S. Supreme Court. The Republicans seemed to be anticipating strongly conservative choice(s) by Bush. Should the Democrats filibuster and, in essence, insist on a super-majority of 60 to confirm these future nominee(s), the Republicans wanted the public to see such action as both unconstitutional and unfair. The Democrats, on the other hand, wanted the public to see them as principled— insisting that the president consult and, within reason, heed the Senate's advice and, if necessary, blocking someone so ideologically extreme that he or she would be unable to work within the confines of existing law.

The way in which the Republicans conducted the reverse filibuster debate suggests another way in which they hoped the public would interpret present and future Democratic objections. Frequently, Republicans noted that these objections to nominees were primarily because of their presumed position on abortion. Republicans wanted Democratic objections to Bush Supreme Court nominees to be processed as tied to one issue. So-called pro-life voters would then reject the Democratic position, but so would other voters who don't like important political decisions to be unduly influenced by a single issue or by lobbying groups focused on that single issue.

So, who "won" this subtextual debate? Which party set itself up better for the battles ahead? As already suggested, both parties came across as being too political when it came to judicial nominees. Thus, the public was positioned by the reverse filibuster debate to want neither party to "play politics" and block nominees. Neither the blocking techniques used by Republicans during the Clinton presidency nor those used by Democrats during the Bush presidency should be turned to. Of course, this advice offered to both parties had to be heeded first by the Democrats. Therefore, although the reverse filibuster did not succeed in painting the Democrats as "evil," it did put Democrats in a difficult position should they go too far in blocking Bush's Supreme Court nominee(s).

The "Carnivalesque"

Just as Bakhtin suggests that critics look beneath the surface "voice" of a text at the other things it says or suggests, he suggests that critics be alert to the possibility of the "carnivalesque." By definition, the "carnivalesque" is an eruption of irreverent energy directed against those "power-up" by those "power-down." Although in public affairs the "carnivalesque" usually lacks the crudeness it exhibited in medieval times or in renaissance and neoclassical satire, it has something of a "circus" quality—at times, outlandish; at times, going too far; at times, parodic; and, almost always, high-energy as those "down," in solidarity, "act up."

This particular debate was doubly carnivalesque. Although numerically the majority, the Republicans were in a "power-down" position because they could not muster 60 votes for cloture against a well-orchestrated Democratic filibuster. So, the Republicans, during this 30-hour period, acted up against the Democrats. However, the Democrats, "power-down" because of fewer total votes, responded by acting up against the Republicans.

Both sides had signs. Both sides thought nothing of calling the other "hypocrites" (arguably in violation of Senate rules). Both sides delighted in quoting each other, saying, "Well, once you said just the opposite." They thereby satirized each other. They praised their compatriots; they attacked their foes. And, although there clearly were angry voices on both sides, there were others who seem to be enjoying the debate—having a good time. They called it "theater"; they called it a "circus"; they called it a "charade"—even a "partisan food fight." It was clearly in the irreverent spirit of "carnival."

So what, you might ask. The carnivalesque is an attempt to showcase the abuse of power. In this debate, because it was doubly carnivalesque, both sides were trying to showcase how the other was abusing power. The Democrats wanted the audience to see that the Republicans were abusing power by insisting that Bush get his way 100 percent of the time; the Republicans wanted the audience to see that the Democrats were abusing power by using a procedural tactic to prevent majority rule. The audience, however, probably saw both as playing politics with whatever tools were available. Thus, the carnivalesque, as a rhetorical move, ultimately failed both parties.

Conclusion

Reading this 30-hour debate or watching it on C-SPAN2 would be exhausting—something you wouldn't want to undertake unless you become a political junkie, with a particular fondness for the legislature. But you should not let the length and the tedious moments lull you into thinking that the communication was no more than political "hot air." Arguments were being made—important ones. Attempts were being made not only to win the day but also to win the future days. And attempts were being made to paint the opposite party as abusers of power. An analysis of the arguments not only helps one to make sense of 30 hours of political talking but to assess what goes right and wrong for the rhetors as they and their arguments interact. An analysis helps one say, with some confidence, what ultimately transpired. Rhetorical analysis is such that several critics might see the debate somewhat differently. Usually, those differences can be worked out as they discuss their interpretations. That discussion, however, is informed not by knee-jerk impressions but, rather, by a disciplined examination of the text before them.

The speakers offered designative, definitive, and evaluative arguments. The evaluative ones ultimately proved to be the ones the debate turned on in the eyes of the audience. Who were the "bad guys," the Democrats or the Republicans? Many in the audience, those watching C-SPAN2 or seeing clips on television news programs, perhaps concluded that both were "bad" insofar as they were playing politics, not governing. Beneath the surface, the two parties were getting ready for Bush's anticipated nominees to the Supreme Court. Both wanted to make the other's anticipated behavior presumptively "bad" in the public's eyes. Both parties also engaged in carnivalesque behavior to highlight how they were victims of other party's abuses of power. Both the subsurface arguments and the carnivalesque displays probably rallied partisans on both sides but also probably further convinced more neutral viewers that politics was triumphing over governing.

THE MASS COMMUNICATION PERSPECTIVE

The mass communication perspective of this case study will discuss the following five issues: media attention to this event in the Senate, news values used in decision making regarding covering such events, attracting media attention, the role of C-SPAN in coverage of Congress, and the potential impact this coverage and event had on audience members.

Media Attention

"Senate Slumber Party" (ABC's *Good Morning America*, November 13, 2003)

"Republicans Stage 39 Hour Talk-a-thon" (NBC *Nightly News*, November 13, 2003)

"A Manufactured Crisis on Judges" (*New York Times*, November 10, 2003)

These are just a few of the headlines given to the "reverse filibuster" by news media in their coverage of the November 12 and 13, 2003, nonstop "debate." No, none of these are very flattering or complimentary to the events of the Senate. Yet news media covered the events of the Senate more during that single week in November than most weeks in 2003. Reviewing broadcast news transcripts and archives of major U.S.

newspapers, every news organization searched gave some degree of attention to the debate.[3] Reasons why this story was considered newsworthy are addressed below, but it is also important to note that U.S. senators facilitated the coverage of this event in a number of ways. Press conferences were held before the 6:00 P.M. start on November 12 and were held throughout the 39 hours of debate. In addition to being interviewed for stories days leading up to the debate, senators also made the rounds of live interview TV news programs on November 12 and 13, 2003, during the hours of the reverse filibuster.

Many news reports provided a brief historical perspective regarding filibusters, and some reports included a list of "modern-day" marathon Senate sessions (as in, "For 30 Hours, Senate Will Be Talk of Nation," *Star Tribune*, November 12, 2003). Many news stories put this event in context by describing previous challenges of presidents in getting judicial nominees through Congress (for example, "Senate to Talk the Night away over Judges," *St. Petersburg Times*, November 12, 2003). Many reports stated that cots were being set up in a room named for the late senator Strom Thurmond (R-SC), as well as his still-standing 24-hour, 18-minute record for holding the Senate floor in opposition to a civil rights bill in 1957. These types of details were much more common in newspaper reports than in broadcast news stories, as print media continue to enjoy the luxury of longer stories that can provide more context, background, and detail of the event.

Overall, news reports did provide a clear explanation of what the reverse filibuster was and why it was occurring. Many news stories addressed the serious issues under way and the rationale behind this marathon in the Senate, whereas others took a lighter approach to covering the subject. For example, NPR's (National Public Radio) "All Things Considered" aired a report on November 12 offering Senators tips from "experienced all-nighters," including a new mom and college students, on how to stay awake and alert. Fox News aired a "person-on-the-street" report on November 13, which involved asking people on the streets of Washington, DC, what the Senate had been doing for 30 hours. The most common response was that people didn't "have a clue." Another example of "soft news" on the reverse filibuster was a report by ABC's *Good Morning America's* Jake Tapper's on Rick Santorum (R-PA), during which he reported that coffee was not on Santorum's menu for staying awake.

Tapper: Have you had coffee yet tonight?

Santorum: I don't drink coffee.

Tapper: You don't drink coffee at all?

Santorum: No. No caffeine. It, it gives me the shakes.

---

[3]This analysis included a review of news transcripts of the following broadcast organizations: ABC, CBS, NBC, CNN, FOX News, and MSNBC. Newspapers analyzed included the *New York Times, Washington Post, USA Today, Los Angeles Times*, and *Chicago Tribune*, among others.

Not surprising, the late night comedy shows also attended to the nearly 40-hour Senate filibuster. In addition to their late-night audiences, jokes regarding the filibuster were also replayed on other news-oriented programs, which sustained further the attention to the humor in the event. CNBC's *Capital Report* and ABC's *This Week with George Stephanopoulos* rebroadcast these late-night jokes (according to their program transcripts):

> From Conan O'Brien's *Late Night*: Just about a half hour ago, the U.S. Senate finished a marathon session on judicial nominees that lasted 30 straight hours . . . in fact, around 5:00 A.M., Ted Kennedy was so tired he put his head down on several desks.

> From Jon Stewart's *The Daily Show*: Aired a clip of Rick Santorum, "We're trying to change the rules? We're not being good temporary stewards? Methinks thou doth protest too much" Followed by Stewart "Is he quoting Hamlet? I'll tell you, for a guy who once equaled gayness with bestiality, he's awfully familiar with 'the theater'."

Although traditionally not considered "real news," discussions of current events in late-night comedy venues are now being considered part of the information landscape for audiences. For example, the Center on Media and Public Affairs has been tracking politicians as the source of late-night comedy since 1989. A study conducted by the Pew Research Center for the People and the Press found in 2004 that one in five people, age 18 to 29, were turning to late-night comedy shows for political news.[4]

Adding further legitimacy to this television genre as an important information source, presidential candidates have made guest appearances on late-night television programs, such as the noteworthy visit in the 1992 presidential campaign by Bill Clinton to the *Arsenio Hall Show*, saxophone in tow. He was not the first to do so, however,; earlier examples include John F. Kennedy's visit to the *Tonight Show* as well as Richard M. Nixon's cameo on *Laugh-In*.

Newsworthiness

Why would the news media choose to cover an event such as this Senate debate? When we consider the news values of timeliness, proximity, conflict, impact, prominence, currency, and uniqueness, and look at the November 2003 Senate filibuster through these criteria, we can find a number of newsworthy factors in this story. Timeliness was a key factor, as most media attention concentrated on the day or two leading up to the filibuster and also covered events during the debate, but once it was over, news media directed their attention to other "news of the day" very quickly.

Proximity may have been the case for Washington, DC,–affiliated media, but the story had potential for newsworthiness on proximity depending on news markets and elected representatives from those areas. For senators who were quite publicly

---

[4]Pew Research Center for the People and the Press, "Cable and Internet Loom Large in Fragmented Political News Universe." January 2004. http://people-press.org/reports/display.php3?ReportID=200.

involved in stages of the filibuster, proximity was likely a factor in the amount of coverage dedicated to the story from news media in their home state. Given that most news organizations have Washington bureaus for such coverage, or use those available through syndication services from other news outlets, the convenience of locale for coverage is not such an issue for news from Washington, DC.

Why the mainstream news media covered this event to the extent it did (versus most other days in the Senate) was due primarily to conflict and the potential drama that might develop in this political standoff. Values of impact, prominence, and currency likely did not shape the decision making in newsrooms covering this event versus other news values.

One could argue there was an element of uniqueness in this story that merited the news attention it received; although filibusters are not unique to politics, the process and procedure in this debate (media attention on cots being set up in Senate office hallways, for example), and potential length (nearly 40 hours) were unique. The types of "stunts" we saw reported in some coverage would also play into this criterion as events surrounding this marathon were attention-getting.

Playing to the Camera? Attracting Media Attention

As discussed in Chapter 4, news media and elected officials have what may be a challenging relationship with respect to balancing the interests of both parties. While news media are trying to get access to elected officials for interviews and leads for stories, media are expected to cover elected officials fairly, without bias, and be willing to ask the tough questions when necessary. In the instances of this Senate debate, even though some elected officials were not taking this debate seriously themselves, what approach should media coverage take?

Looking at this relationship from the perspective of elected officials, they want to control the media reports about them in order to put forth the most favorable image possible. In periods before reelection, they are seeking as much media attention as possible to reach potential voters and donors. We see a number of instances in the reverse filibuster that demonstrate Senators' attempts to make sure they were part of the news story. They garnered their own media attention in approaches such as the following:

- Tom Harkin (D-IA) held up a handwritten sign at the start of the 6:00 P.M. debate, as Republicans entered the Senate floor, that read "I'll be home watching 'The Bachelor'." Harkin's sign may have appeared to be promotional for ABC's reality show, but his sound bite about the sign was less complimentary. NPR's *Morning Edition* on November 13 quoted Harkin as saying "Why join in the circus? I'll go home and watch something that's about as stupid as what they're doing here." For those who only saw the visual of the sign and did not hear his sound bite, they likely interpreted this "stunt" differently.
- Interest groups provided "care packages" to Republican senators that included coffee and breath mints. A *Pittsburgh Post-Gazette* report on November 13

identified civil rights and abortion rights groups who had opposed the judicial nominees provided such support.

- In protest of the November 12 intended "talk-fest," Harry Reid (D-NV) responded with a lengthy soliloquy of his own, for 9 hours, 37 minutes on November 10 to protest the pending Republican tactic. Such an event might have been quickly ignored by news media without the context of the 39-hour debate that took place the same week.
- T-shirt wars between staffers broke out; according to the *Washington Post* (November 14), Democrats were wearing shirts that read, "We confirmed 98% of Bush's Judges and All We Got Was this Lousy T-Shirt," and Republican staffers appeared wearing "Justice for Judges Marathon" shirts.
- President Bush also chimed in for his own claim to airtime on television (and column inches in newspapers), hosting a photo opportunity with three of the judicial nominees who were being blocked by the Democratic filibusters to the White House.

These examples raise the question of what these political events would be like without the media attention we see today. Between cable news organizations having 24 hours to fill and live cameras recording the events in the House and Senate chambers, we must ask to what extent political events are being manipulated for those cameras. Without the cameras and reporters present, many of the above examples may not have occurred. And because the media were attending to and covering these events, other portions of the debate that may have been substantively important were ignored. Many of these media-garnering events could be considered pseudoevents, because they may contained no real or original news but were events structured to attract media coverage. The parallel of the real events in Congress during this reverse filibuster and these staged and scripted events demonstrates the ambiguity that exists in such pseudoevents.

C-SPAN: Gavel-to-Gavel Coverage

Although we've seen examples above of mainstream or national media attention on the Senate filibuster, the one source we would expect to see cover this event is C-SPAN. Created by the cable industry in 1979, C-SPAN (Cable-Satellite Public Affairs Network) started by providing coverage of the U.S. House of Representatives, included "gavel-to-gavel" coverage of House hearings in 1981, and expanded to 24-hour programming in 1982. In 1986, the Senate began televising its proceedings, and C-SPAN2 was created to air Senate debates. C-SPAN reports that in 2001, 13 percent of their programming was composed of U.S. House debates.[5] C-SPAN's main purpose may be the coverage of Congress, but a small proportion of that time is

---

[5]"C-Span by the Numbers." http://www.cspan.org.

dedicated to live coverage of debates in the House. Press conferences, political speeches, author lectures, and other public affairs events are covered as well during the 24-hour broadcast cycle of C-SPAN and C-SPAN2.

Although the "talking head" format of much of C-SPAN coverage is not visually compelling compared with other television content, plenty of viewers are tuning in to see "politics in action." A study by Peter D. Hart Research Associates found that 20 percent of the cable and satellite audiences watched C-SPAN at least once or twice a week.[6] They estimated that this percentage equates to an audience of 34.5 million people watching C-SPAN weekly.

C-SPAN would argue that it is objective in its coverage of the House and Senate, because they provide an unedited record of House and Senate hearings and debates, but other programming on the cable channel may affect the public's perceptions of the network. According to a Pew Research Center for the People and the Press study, Democrat viewers rate C-SPAN's believability as higher than Republicans do (36 percent to 23 percent)[7]. However, compared to other broadcast sources such as CNN or Fox News, C-SPAN is typically exempt from any "media bias" debates. When comparing Republican, Democrat, and Independent respondents, C-SPAN was one of three sources on each groups' list of most trusted sources for information (in addition to CNN and CBS' *60 Minutes*).

In terms of potential effects of C-SPAN coverage of the House and Senate, a 2004 study of congressional scholars of the American Political Science Association reported by C-SPAN found mixed results.[8] For example, 37 percent of scholars say television has had a negative effect on public perception of the House, while 36 percent said television has had a positive effect. C-SPAN is praised for allowing people to see their government at work and its potential for civic engagement, but it is criticized for producing longer congressional sessions and questionable motivation of speakers. When considering House members' motivation for speaking on the floor, 42 percent of respondents said it was to raise their personal visibility, versus communicating with their constituents (26 percent), informing the general public about policy (11 percent), or influencing other members (7 percent).

Even though C-SPAN as well as mainstream media covered the reverse filibuster, it did not make for "good TV." Mark Dayton (D-MN) noted in one news report that the event would discourage people's interest in government, saying, "I would not recommend it to anybody who has any interest in the public process."[9]

[6]Peter D. Hart Research, "C-Span and the American People: 25 Years Later," March 18, 2004. http://www.cspan.org/about/research/index.asp?code=HART.

[7]Pew Research Center for the People and the Press, "News Audiences Increasingly Politicized," June 2004. http://people-press.org/reports/display.php3?PageID=833.

[8]"New C-SPAN Study: Congressional Scholars Examine House Television after Twenty-Five Years," April 2004. http://www.cspan.org/C-SPAN25/survey_release.asp.

[9]Rob Hotakainen, "For 30 Hours, Senate Will Be Talk of Nation," *Star Tribune* (November 12, 2003), 1.

Impact of Filibuster Coverage on Audience

In considering issues of media effects in this case, the media coverage of this marathon debate was most likely just a small "blip" on the radar screens of most audience members. It may have been amusing for some and frustrating for others, but likely it was quickly forgotten in the consumption of more news, entertainment, and information in the days that followed the debate. One news report addressed the "effects" issue as well.[10] The report quoted three political scientists who argued that the event took place unnoticed by most ordinary people, although Brookings fellow Stephen Hess was quoted as saying, "It was for political junkies, but it can have a ripple effect." (p. 6) However, the report did not explain what that ripple effect would be, and it may be a positive or negative outcome.

Perhaps the American public, whose attention is directed to such events by the mass media, will pay more attention to the decision making of Congress. They could be more informed on the judicial nomination process following some media attention to this debate. And if intrigued by this event, citizens may become more engaged in other aspects of government. On the other hand, the media's focus on the gimmicks within this marathon debate may instead have degraded public opinion of Congress as an institution.

Conclusion

The reverse filibuster highlighted a number of factors of media coverage, such as managing press conferences that could be held any hour of the day, and considering the newsworthiness of the events during the filibuster to determine news coverage. However, C-SPAN's coverage offers a visual transcript of the official speeches made in Congress and does not consider the news values of one event over another. Although important speeches were given during this reverse filibuster, and key issues regarding judicial nominees were newsworthy to cover, we saw news media attending to less serious aspects of this debate and politicians offering plenty such diversions for reporters to cover.

CONCLUSION

The so-called reverse filibuster offered those who were interested and brave enough to watch an opportunity to see a dress rehearsal of the arguments that each Senate party would later use in challenging President Bush's nominees to the U.S. Supreme Court in late 2005 and early 2006. Each party sought to position itself as the most reasonable side, with Republicans arguing that the president's nominees to the federal bench merited a presumption of fitness for office and swift confirmation, and the Democrats arguing that the pending nominees should not be confirmed.

---

[10]Helen Dewar, "Bush, Daschle Trade Charges: Senate's Talkathon on Judicial Nominees Exceeds 30 Hours," *Washington Post* (November 14, 2003).

The three perspectives offered in this chapter on the reverse filibuster reach remarkably consistent conclusions. All three note that the talkathon was more show than substance and that what substantive issues were addressed were subject to factual and political distortion. Relatedly, all three perspectives focus on the extent to which the substantive arguments that the participating senators made were subsumed beneath the more humorous or entertaining aspects of the 30-hour spectacle.

ADDITIONAL CASES

- **Nomination of Miguel Estrada**
  President George W. Bush nominated Estrada to the United States Court of Appeals for the Federal Circuit in 2001, but he was denied confirmation as a result of a Democratic filibuster and withdrew his name from consideration in 2003. A good overview of the events related to his nomination can be found in the following *Baltimore Sun* article: Julie Hirschfield Davis, "Estrada withdraws as nominee for bench; Democrats are successful in blocking Bush's pick for federal appeals court." *Baltimore Sun*, September 5, 2003. A1.

- **The Medicare Prescription Drug Bill**
  On December 8, 2003, President Bush signed into a law a major overhaul of the nation's Medicare prescription drugs program, which provides low-cost medications for senior citizens. The bill was among the most contentious of the 108th Congress, and was an issue in the 2004 presidential and congressional elections. For an overview of the issues and the debate surrounding passage of the bill, see: Jackie Koszczuk and Gebe Martinez, "Parties Agree Medicare Has Political Legs," *Congressional Quarterly Weekly* (November 22, 2003).

- **Filibuster of the Helms Amendment to the 1993 Community Service Bill by former Senator Carol Moseley-Braun**
  An interesting perspective on Moseley-Braun's filibuster of a proposed amendment to extend the patent for the insignia of the United Daughters of the Confederacy comes from former U.S. Senator Howell Heflin (D-AL). See: Howell Heflin, "Congressional Remarks on USCCR Reauthorization—Reflections on Progress in Civil Rights." Tuesday, October 1, 1996; 104th Congress 2nd Session: *142 Cong Rec S 12080*.

- **Anti–Flag Desecration Amendment**
  Anti–flag burning amendment proposals have been introduced in every recent Congress. The text of the 109th Congress's debate in the Senate on the proposal on June 27, 2006, is a good representation of the issues in the debate. The *Congressional Record* from June 27, 2006, is available at the Congress's official website, http://thomas.loc.gov.

CHAPTER 15

CASE ELEVEN:
TEXAS V. JOHNSON,
491 U.S. 397 (1989)

THE CASE

In 1984, the Republican Party held its national nominating convention in Dallas, Texas. During the convention, protestors of Reagan administration and Dallas-area corporation policies took to the streets. The protestors demonstrated under the banner "The Republican War Chest Tour," and engaged in marches and demonstrations that were focused especially on the protestors' opposition to nuclear weapons and their concerns about the consequences of nuclear war. At the end of the protest, the group assembled on the steps of the Dallas City Hall, where Gregory Lee Johnson, one of the protestors, held aloft an American flag, doused it with kerosene, and then set it on fire.

Johnson was arrested under the Texas law that prohibited "desecration of a venerated object" and was convicted and sentenced to one year in prison and a fine of $2,000. After a series of appeals, the Texas Court of Criminal Appeals reversed Johnson's conviction, stating that the state could not punish Johnson for burning the flag, since he did so as a form of political protest that was protected by the First Amendment. The state of Texas appealed the decision of its high court to the Supreme Court.

Writing on behalf of a very narrow majority, Justice William Brennan explained that the Texas law used to convict Johnson could not, in fact, be used to convict a person for burning a flag in protest under the First Amendment. Justice John Paul Stevens, one of the dissenters in the case, offered an alternative view of the First Amendment and flag burning. An excerpt of Brennan's opinion and of Stevens' dissent follows.

We must first determine whether Johnson's burning of the flag constituted expressive conduct, permitting him to invoke the First Amendment in challenging his conviction. If his conduct was expressive, we next decide whether the State's regulation is related to the suppression of free expression.

The First Amendment literally forbids the abridgment only of "speech," but we have long recognized that its protection does not end at the spoken or written word. While we have rejected "the view that an apparently limitless variety of conduct can be labeled 'speech' whenever the person engaging in the conduct intends thereby to express an idea," (*United States v. O'Brien*), we have acknowledged that conduct may

Gregory Johnson is arrested after his flag-burning demonstration to express anger against Reagan policies during the Republican National Convention in 1984.

be "sufficiently imbued with elements of communication to fall within the scope of the First and Fourteenth Amendments," (*U.S. v. Spence*).

Especially pertinent to this case are our decisions recognizing the communicative nature of conduct relating to flags. Attaching a peace sign to the flag, refusing to salute the flag, and displaying a red flag, we have held, all may find shelter under the First Amendment. That we have had little difficulty identifying an expressive element in conduct relating to flags should not be surprising. The very purpose of a national flag is to serve as a symbol of our country; it is, one might say, the one visible manifestation of two hundred years of nationhood. Thus, we have observed:

> "[T]he flag salute is a form of utterance. Symbolism is a primitive but effective way of communicating ideas. The use of an emblem or flag to symbolize some system, idea, institution, or personality, is a short cut from mind to mind. Causes and nations, political parties, lodges and ecclesiastical groups seek to knit the loyalty of their followings to a flag or banner, a color or design." (*U.S. v. Barnette*).

We have not automatically concluded, however, that any action taken with respect to our flag is expressive. Instead, in characterizing such action for First Amendment purposes, we have considered the context in which it occurred. The State of Texas conceded for purposes of its oral argument in this case that Johnson's conduct was expressive conduct . . . Johnson burned an American flag as part—indeed, as the culmination—of a political demonstration that coincided with the convening of the Republican Party and its renomination of Ronald Reagan for President. The expressive, overtly political nature of this conduct was both intentional and overwhelmingly apparent.

The government generally has a freer hand in restricting expressive conduct than it has in restricting the written or spoken word. It may not, however, proscribe particular conduct because it has expressive elements. It is, in short, not simply the verbal or non-verbal nature of the expression, but the governmental interest at stake, that helps to determine whether a restriction on that expression is valid. . . . [T]herefore, we must decide whether Texas has asserted an interest in support of Johnson's conviction that is unrelated to the suppression of expression. . . . The State offers two separate interests to justify this conviction: preventing breaches of the peace and preserving the flag as a symbol of nationhood and national unity. We hold that the first interest is not implicated on this record and that the second is related to the suppression of expression. . . .

Texas claims that its interest in preventing breaches of the peace justifies Johnson's conviction for flag desecration.[4] However, no disturbance of the peace actually occurred or threatened to occur because of Johnson's burning of the flag. Although the State stresses the disruptive behavior of the protestors during their march toward City Hall, it admits that no actual breach of the peace occurred at the time of the flag burning or in response to the flag burning. . . . No reasonable onlooker would have regarded Johnson's generalized expression of dissatisfaction with the policies of the Federal Government as a direct personal insult or an invitation to exchange fisticuffs. We thus conclude that the State's interest in maintaining order is not implicated on these facts. The State need not worry that our holding will disable it from preserving the peace. We do not suggest that the First Amendment forbids a State to prevent "imminent lawless action." (*Brandenburg v. Ohio*). And, in fact, Texas already has a statute specifically prohibiting breaches of the peace, Tex. Penal Code Ann. 42.01 (1989), which tends to confirm that Texas need not punish this flag desecration in order to keep the peace.

---

[4]Relying on our decision in *Boos v. Barry*, 485 U.S. 312 (1988), Johnson argues that this state interest is related to the suppression of free expression within the meaning of *United States v. O'Brien*, 391 U.S. 367 (1968). He reasons that the violent reaction to flag burnings feared by Texas would be the result of the message conveyed by them, and that this fact connects the State's interest to the suppression of expression. This view has found some favor in the lower courts. Johnson's theory may overread Boos insofar as it suggests that a desire to prevent a violent audience reaction is "related to expression" in the same way that a desire to prevent an audience from being offended is "related to expression." Because we find that the State's interest in preventing breaches of the peace is not implicated on these facts, however, we need not venture further into this area.

The State also asserts an interest in preserving the flag as a symbol of nationhood and national unity. The State, apparently, is concerned that [Johnson's] conduct will lead people to believe either that the flag does not stand for nationhood and national unity, but instead reflects other, less positive concepts, or that the concepts reflected in the flag do not in fact exist, that is, that we do not enjoy unity as a Nation.

It remains to consider whether the State's interest in preserving the flag as a symbol of nationhood and national unity justifies Johnson's conviction. Johnson was not prosecuted for the expression of just any idea; he was prosecuted for his expression of dissatisfaction with the policies of this country, expression situated at the core of our First Amendment values. Moreover, Johnson was prosecuted because he knew that his politically charged expression would cause "serious offense." If he had burned the flag as a means of disposing of it because it was dirty or torn, he would not have been convicted of flag desecration under this Texas law: federal law designates burning as the preferred means of disposing of a flag "when it is in such condition that it is no longer a fitting emblem for display," [36 U.S.C. 176(k)], and Texas has no quarrel with this means of disposal. The Texas law is thus not aimed at protecting the physical integrity of the flag in all circumstances, but is designed instead to protect it only against impairments that would cause serious offense to others. Whether Johnson's treatment of the flag violated Texas law thus depended on the likely communicative impact of his expressive conduct.[7]

---

[7]Texas suggests that Johnson's conviction did not depend on the onlookers' reaction to the flag burning because 42.09 is violated only when a person physically mistreats the flag in a way that he "knows will seriously offend one or more persons likely to observe or discover his action." Tex. Penal Code Ann. 42.09(b) (1989). "The 'serious offense' language of the statute," Texas argues, "refers to an individual's intent and to the manner in which the conduct is effectuated, not to the reaction of the crowd." If the statute were aimed only at the actor's intent and not at the communicative impact of his actions, however, there would be little reason for the law to be triggered only when an audience is "likely" to be present. At Johnson's trial, indeed, the State itself seems not to have seen the distinction between knowledge and actual communicative impact that it now stresses; it proved the element of knowledge by offering the testimony of persons who had in fact been seriously offended by Johnson's conduct. In any event, we find the distinction between Texas' statute and one dependent on actual audience reaction too precious to be of constitutional significance. Both kinds of statutes clearly are aimed at protecting onlookers from being offended by the ideas expressed by the prohibited activity.

If there is a bedrock principle underlying the First Amendment, it is that the government may not prohibit the expression of an idea simply because society finds the idea itself offensive or disagreeable. We have not recognized an exception to this principle even where our flag has been involved. Nor may the government, we have held, compel conduct that would evince respect for the flag. . . .

In short, nothing in our precedents suggests that a State may foster its own view of the flag by prohibiting expressive conduct relating to it. Texas' focus on the precise nature of Johnson's expression, moreover, misses the point of our prior decisions: their enduring lesson, that the government may not prohibit expression simply because it disagrees with its message, is not dependent on the particular mode in which one chooses to express an idea. If we were to hold that a State may forbid flag burning wherever it is likely to endanger the flag's symbolic role, but allow it wherever burning a flag promotes that role—as where, for example, a person ceremoniously burns a dirty flag—we would be saying that when it comes to impairing the flag's physical integrity, the flag itself may be used as a symbol—as a substitute for the written or spoken word or a "short cut from mind to mind"—only in one direction. We would be permitting a State to "prescribe what shall be orthodox" by saying that one may burn the flag to convey one's attitude toward it and its referents only if one does not endanger the flag's representation of nationhood and national unity.

We never before have held that the Government may ensure that a symbol be used to express only one view of that symbol or its referents. To conclude that the government may permit designated symbols to be used to communicate only a limited set of messages would be to enter territory having no discernible or defensible boundaries.

Could the government, on this theory, prohibit the burning of state flags? Of copies of the Presidential seal? Of the Constitution? In evaluating these choices under the First Amendment, how would we decide which symbols were sufficiently special to warrant this unique status? To do so, we would be forced to consult our own political preferences, and impose them on the citizenry, in the very way that the First Amendment forbids us to do. The First Amendment does not guarantee that other concepts virtually sacred to our Nation as a whole—such as the principle that discrimination on the basis of race is odious and destructive—will go unquestioned in the marketplace of ideas. We decline, therefore, to create for the flag an exception to the joust of principles protected by the First Amendment.

It is not the State's ends, but its means, to which we object. It cannot be gainsaid that there is a special place reserved for the flag in this Nation, and thus we do not doubt that the government has a legitimate interest in making efforts to preserve the national flag as an unalloyed symbol of our country. To say that the government has an interest in encouraging proper treatment of the flag, however, is not to say that it may criminally punish a person for burning a flag as a means of political protest. We are fortified in today's conclusion by our conviction that forbidding criminal punishment for conduct such as Johnson's will not endanger the special role played by our flag or the feelings it inspires. To paraphrase Justice Holmes, we submit that nobody can suppose that this one gesture of an unknown man will change our Nation's attitude towards its flag. Indeed, Texas' argument that the burning of an American flag "'is an act having a high likelihood to cause a breach of the peace,'" and its statute's implicit assumption that physical mistreatment of the flag will lead to "serious offense," tend to confirm that the flag's special role is not in danger; if it were, no one would riot or take offense because a flag had been burned.

We are tempted to say, in fact, that the flag's deservedly cherished place in our community will be strengthened, not weakened, by our holding today. Our decision is a reaffirmation of the principles of freedom and inclusiveness that the flag best reflects, and of the conviction that our toleration of criticism such as Johnson's is a sign and source of our strength. The way to preserve the flag's special role is not to punish those who feel differently about these matters. It is to persuade them that they are wrong. And, precisely because it is our flag that is involved, one's response to the flag burner may exploit the uniquely persuasive power of the flag itself. We can imagine no more appropriate response to burning a flag than waving one's own, no better way to counter a flag burner's message than by saluting the flag that burns, no surer means of preserving the dignity even of the flag that burned than by—as one witness here did—according its remains a respectful burial. We do not consecrate the flag by punishing its desecration, for in doing so we dilute the freedom that this cherished emblem represents.

Johnson was convicted for engaging in expressive conduct. The State's interest in preventing breaches of the peace does not support his conviction because Johnson's conduct did not threaten to disturb the peace. Nor does the State's interest in preserving the flag as a symbol of nationhood and national unity justify his criminal conviction for engaging in political expression. The judgment of the Texas Court of Criminal Appeals is therefore affirmed.

JUSTICE STEVENS, dissenting.

A country's flag is a symbol of more than "nationhood and national unity." It also signifies the ideas that characterize the society that has chosen that emblem as well as the special history that has animated the growth and power of those ideas. The fleurs-de-lis and the tricolor both symbolized "nationhood and national unity," but they had vastly different meanings. The message conveyed by some flags—the swastika, for example—may survive long after it has outlived its usefulness as a symbol of regimented unity in a particular nation.

So it is with the American flag. It is more than a proud symbol of the courage, the determination, and the gifts of nature that transformed 13 fledgling Colonies into a world power. It is a symbol of freedom, of equal opportunity, of religious tolerance, and of good will for other peoples who share our aspirations. The symbol carries its message to dissidents both at home and abroad who may have no interest at all in our national unity or survival.

The value of the flag as a symbol cannot be measured. Even so, I have no doubt that the interest in preserving that value for the future is both significant and legitimate. Conceivably that value will be enhanced by the Court's conclusion that our national commitment to free expression is so strong that even the United States as ultimate guarantor of that freedom is without power to prohibit the desecration of its unique symbol. But I am unpersuaded. The creation of a federal right to post bulletin boards and graffiti on the Washington Monument might enlarge the market for free expression, but at a cost I would not pay. Similarly, in my considered judgment, sanctioning the public desecration of the flag will tarnish its value—both for those who cherish the ideas for which it waves and for those who desire to don the robes of martyrdom by burning it. That tarnish is not justified by the trivial burden on free expression occasioned by requiring that an available, alternative mode of expression—including uttering words critical of the flag—be employed.

The Court is therefore quite wrong in blandly asserting that respondent "was prosecuted for his expression of dissatisfaction with the policies of this country, expression situated at the core of our First Amendment values." Respondent was prosecuted because of the method he chose to express his dissatisfaction with those policies. Had he chosen to spray-paint—or perhaps convey with a motion picture projector—his message of dissatisfaction on the facade of the Lincoln Memorial, there would be no question about the power of the Government to prohibit his means of expression. The prohibition would be supported by the legitimate interest in preserving the quality of an important national asset. Though the asset at stake in this case is intangible, given its unique value, the same interest supports a prohibition on the desecration of the American flag. I respectfully dissent.

THE POLITICAL SCIENCE PERSPECTIVE

Few political images convey as much meaning to as many people as does the American flag. United States Senator Dianne Feinstein (D-CA), one of the sponsors of the anti–flag desecration constitutional amendment in the 109th Congress summed up what the flag means to hundreds of thousands of people when she said:

> In a sense, our flag is the physical fabric of our society, knitting together disparate peoples from distant lands, uniting us in a common bond, not just of individual liberty but also of responsibility to one another. Supreme Court Justice Felix Frankfurter called the flag "The symbol of our national life." I, too, have always looked at the flag as the

symbol of our democracy, our shared values, our commitment to justice, our remembrance to those who have sacrificed to defend these principles. For our veterans, the flag represents the democracy and freedom they fought so hard to protect. Today there are almost 300,000 troops serving overseas, putting their lives on the line every day to fight for the fundamental principles that our flag symbolizes.[1]

On June 27, 2006, the United States Senate rejected the proposed amendment to the United States Constitution that Feinstein cosponsored. That amendment would have given Congress the power to prevent the physical desecration of the U.S. flag, but ultimately it was a single vote short of achieving the two thirds vote necessary to send the amendment to the states for ratification (the U.S. House of Representatives had already passed the proposal by the required two thirds vote in 2005). Had the proposed amendment passed the Senate and then been ratified by three fourths of the states, it would not directly have banned flag burning and other forms of flag desecration, but Congress would almost certainly have acted almost immediately thereafter to do so.

Proposals to outlaw flag burning are not new. Indeed, until the Supreme Court invalidated the Texas antidesecration law in *Texas v. Johnson* in 1989, virtually every state (forty-eight of the fifty) prohibited a range of activities as they related to the U.S. flag. And, since the Court's decision, every Congress has attempted to ban flag burning by constitutional amendment—the only way to overturn the Court's decision in *Texas v. Johnson*, because the Court held that the First Amendment to the U.S. Constitution prohibits using laws passed by the state or federal legislatures in order to outlaw flag desecration.

The Court's decision was controversial, to say the least. As the excerpt of the decision shows, the Court struck down the Texas antidesecration law because it determined that what was objected to by the state of Texas was not the action of burning the flag itself, but the message the burning flag was intended to convey. As the majority of the Court noted in its opinion, burning a flag is the legally prescribed method of disposing of a flag that is no longer in suitable condition to be flown. That law declares: "The flag, when it is in such condition that it is no longer a fitting emblem for display, should be destroyed in a dignified way, preferably by burning."[2] Thus, had Johnson carried a well-worn flag to the courthouse steps in Dallas, joined a solemn gathering of veterans, and ceremoniously burned it as a means of disposal, he would not have been arrested, because he would have conformed to federal law. A majority of the Court therefore reasoned that the act of burning a flag is not in and of itself objectionable. What was objectionable was the message that Johnson wished to convey at the time he burned it.

Proponents of protecting the flag disagreed, of course. For them, burning the flag in the manner that Johnson did was itself objectionable. This is because when a flag is burned after flying in service to the point it can no longer be used, it is burned

---

[1]Remarks of Senator Dianne Feinstein. *Congressional Record*, June 27, 2006, p. S6501.
[2]36 U.S.C. 176(k).

in a solemn ceremony using "strict rules of etiquette."[3] A person who burns the flag in protest abides by none of these rules, and therefore, the act of burning a flag in that circumstance—according to supporters of the constitutional amendment—is fundamentally different and can be punished without offending the First Amendment. However, until such time as the U.S. Supreme Court either reverses its decision in *Texas v. Johnson* or an amendment to the Constitution is passed and ratified, flag burning remains legal.

Flag Protection as Symbolic Politics

Following the Court's decision in *Texas v. Johnson*, the U.S. Congress began efforts to try to protect the flag from desecration. Before the decision, the vast majority of states protected the flag, making a federal law or constitutional amendment unnecessary. However, with all state laws invalidated by the high court's decision, Congress felt it had to react. To be sure, some of this reaction was based on the principles of separation of powers and federalism; there is a long history of Congress reacting to Supreme Court decisions that overturn acts of Congress or the state legislatures. The objection that Congress typically raises is that the laws that were overturned by the Court were passed by elected representatives of the people, and that representative democracy should triumph over judicial invalidation of such laws. However, Congress has rarely been so persistent when attempting to overturn a Supreme Court decision as it has been in its efforts to overturn *Texas v. Johnson* with an amendment to the U.S. Constitution.

Why is protecting the flag so important to elected members of Congress? There are, of course, members of Congress who feel very deeply about protecting the flag and who believe that it is absolutely the right thing to do. These members take very principled stands—some are veterans, others lost family members in military conflicts—and believe that protecting the U.S. flag from harm sends an important message about national unity. In this sense, protecting the flag is psychologically comforting. However, a second, more cynical explanation for why some members of Congress are anxious to protect the flag is that it is politically expedient. Each of these explanations is addressed briefly.

Psychological Explanation. Murray Edelman's work on the role of symbols in political life offers important insights into the psychological dimensions of symbolic actions like flag protection. According to Edelman, the vast majority of the public is underinformed about, or even disinterested in, politics and governance. At the same time, people recognize the importance of what governments do but feel powerless to participate in a meaningful way. These feelings of powerlessness lead individuals to latch on to symbolic efforts, because the symbolism provides a form of stability and comfort. In *The Symbolic Uses of Politics* (1964) Edelman explains: "Alienation, anomie, despair of being able to chart one's own course in a complex, cold and bewildering world have

---

[3]Remarks of Senator John Cornyn (R-TX). *Congressional Record*, June 27, 2006, p. S6509.

become characteristic of a large part of the population of advanced countries. As the world can be neither understood nor influenced, attachment to reassuring abstract symbols rather than to one's own efforts becomes chronic."[4]

Extrapolating from Edelman's argument, it is clear that both members of Congress and the mass public are comforted by the idea of protecting the flag. For members of Congress who confront difficult, if not impossible, policy decisions on a daily basis, flag protection is easy. Regardless of the position one takes—pro or con—the issue is straightforward. By comparison, other items on Congress's agenda—military conflict, the economy, the development of nuclear weapons by foreign governments—are difficult and may have life-or-death consequences. Members of Congress frequently feel powerless to solve these problems or to improve the quality of life for their constituents. Thus, as Edelman suggests, members of Congress naturally gravitate to the easy, symbolic decisions that let them feel good and that offer psychological comfort in tumultuous times. The public does this as well; for the average citizen, gaining sufficient political knowledge to allow him or her to make rational, informed decisions about issues of national or international significance is time-consuming and difficult. Instead of investing the time and effort, people gravitate to the quick, easy cognitive heuristics (shortcuts) that help them to order the political world. If the flag, as a symbol of the United States, is safe from harm, that may provide comfort to an anxious citizen in a time of national security threats. At least that is what Edelman would suggest.

Political Expediency Explanation.   However, some members of Congress have other reasons for attempting to protect the flag from desecration. As David Mayhew has said, members of Congress (and other elected officials) are "single-minded seekers of reelection."[5] Because they recognize that their constituents expect them to do something, and because they know that positive, even symbolic, legislation will win them favor with their constituents, members of Congress frequently champion legislation that does little, but makes constituents happy. Senator Jim Jeffords (I-VT) articulated this perspective during the June 27, 2006, Senate debate on the anti–flag burning amendment when he said:

> I am very troubled by priorities put forth by the Senate majority. Our domestic programs are facing serious budget cuts. Millions of Americans are without health insurance. Gas prices are out of control while our Nation's reliance on foreign oil shows no sign of easing. And we still have no strategy for the war in Iraq. However, the Senate leadership has chosen to spend a portion of our limited days in session to bring up a constitutional amendment to ban flag burning. Once again, we seem to be searching for a solution in need of a problem, and I am afraid the reason we are spending time on this topic is only for political gain.[6]

---

[4]Murray Edelman, *The Symbolic Uses of Politics* (Chicago: University of Chicago Press, 1964), 76.

[5]David R. Mayhew, *Congress: The Electoral Connection*, 1975.

[6]Remarks by Senator James Jeffords (I-VT). *Congressional Record*, June 27, 2006, p. S6501.

Opponents of the anti–flag burning amendment, like Jeffords, have long objected to the use of congressional time to debate flag burning. Flag burning, they argue, is a rare event. By one measure, it occurs an average of one time per year.[7] Opponents of the amendment also object precisely because they believe that prohibiting flag burning is a symbolic action, especially when compared with other proposals of national importance that would actually offer a tangible benefit to the public.

Conclusion

When the U.S. Supreme Court overturned the Texas antidesecration law, as well as the laws of forty-seven other states, in *Texas v. Johnson* in 1989, the Court created the impetus for Congress to try to protect the flag through constitutional amendment. These efforts are an excellent example of what Murray Edelman called the "symbolic uses of politics" in his 1964 book by that title. Although there are politicians and citizens on both sides of the issue, the momentum for a constitutional amendment for flag protection is increased by the psychological and electoral benefits that are offered.

THE RHETORICAL PERSPECTIVE

Upon reading a U.S. Supreme Court decision such as *Texas v. Johnson*, a rhetorician would go straight to the arguments. The widely held impression that the decisions, the concurring opinions, and the dissents are tightly reasoned texts would invite this scrutiny. How are these legal arguments made, the rhetorician would ask.

Describing the Legal Arguments

Classical theorists such as Aristotle and Cicero would provide the rhetorician with a lens through which to consider these arguments. And, at first glance, the way the arguments are presented in *Texas v. Johnson* fits well within a Classical framework. Classical orators are, for example, encouraged to divide a question into its parts. Brennan, in the excerpt from the majority opinion earlier, does that twice. In its very first paragraph, he presents what he sees as the two crucial legal questions: "We must first determine whether Johnson's burning of the flag constituted expressive conduct. . . . If his conduct was expressive, we next decide whether the State's regulation is related to the suppression of free expression." Later, Brennan divides the State's justification for conviction into an "A" part and a "B" part before rejecting both.

Also Classical is Brennan's and Stevens' use of topoi in constructing the logical part (logos) of their arguments. As noted in Chapter 3, there are a variety of ways

---

[7]See: Senate Report 108-334—Constitutional Amendment to Prohibit Physical Desecration of U.S. Flag. Filed under authority of the order of the Senate, July 22, 2004.

these topoi have been listed (and revised) by recent rhetoricians who are trying to make the Classical idea useful. Weaver, for example, lists definition, cause/effect, similarity/dissimilarity, circumstances, and testimony as five basic topoi. Brennan uses definition—defining expressive conduct as a communicative extension of "speech." Later, he contrasts expressive conduct with "the written or spoken word," establishing that the government is freer to regulate the former. Still later, he relies on the topos of effects by suggesting where government regulation of this particular expressive act—flag burning—may lead. Stevens in his dissent also uses the topos of definition, defining what the flag is. He then relies heavily on similarities, connecting burning the flag to desecrating the façades of the Washington Monument and the Lincoln Memorial with graffiti or a message. Just as those actions would be prohibited, so should the burning of the American flag, he argues. And he also cites the effects of permitting flag burning: how it will tarnish the flag's value as symbol.

Ethos and pathos are not lacking from the arguments either. Both men, through their citations of law and their learned language, play off the high ethos they enjoy as Supreme Court justices. And pathos is certainly not lacking in Stevens' dissent. He seems indignant—even angry—that the majority of the court has decided to extend constitutional protection to flag burning.

Some of the arguments offered are rather clearly enthymemes that can easily be expanded into full syllogisms. Thus, the majority argument might be rendered as follows:

The First Amendment to the U.S. Constitution prohibits a ban on expressive conduct based on its expression;

Texas law banned an expressive conduct (i.e., flag-burning) based on what it expressed;

Therefore, the First Amendment to the U.S. Constitution prohibits the Texas law.

Classical rhetoric, however, would not illuminate all aspects of the justices' arguments. Stephen Toulmin's twentieth-century work on the structure of arguments would provide a valuable additional lens. Both the majority opinion and the Stevens dissent offer arguments that one might understand better by being put in Toulmin's terms. For example, Brennan claims that expressive conduct is constitutionally protected. Why? The grounds for his claim are the Supreme Court cases of *Spence v. Washington* and *United States v. O'Brien* (with *West Virginia Board of Education v. Barnette* linking the topic of expressive conduct directly to the flag). Unstated in the argument is the warrant that precedent should be honored; stated is the rebuttal that admits that the conduct might be prohibited if the state had a compelling interest in doing so other than to thwart the demonstrator's expression.

Toulmin, however, recognized that this basic model, despite its general utility, did not fully describe argumentation in specialized fields such as ethics, management, the arts, science, and law. He discussed these specialized argument fields in philosophical terms in *The Uses of Argument*; he (and two colleagues) outlined their particular claims, grounds, and warrants in *An Introduction to Reasoning*.[8] When discussing argumentation in the law, Toulmin, Rieke, and Janik note that there is a difference between the appellate level and the courts of original jurisdiction. The grounds typically used are different, as are the warrants cited or implied. For example, the grounds we saw above, a preceding Supreme Court decision, would not be used at the lower level, where the grounds are usually evidence of several sorts. At that lower level, warrants are typically the standards for admitting evidence, such as relevancy, materiality, and competency. At the appellate level, however, the grounds are such items as the records of the original trial, the texts of pertinent laws, the contents of lower appellate decisions, the contents of past decisions by appellate courts (especially the U.S. Supreme Court), and the testimony of legal authorities. A common warrant is *stare decisis*, the principle that precedent prevails.

In applying what Toulmin, Rieke, and Janik have to say to the majority opinion in *Texas v. Johnson* and Stevens' dissent, it is apparent that the former proceeds as a typical legal argument but the latter really does not: there are citations of precedents, but they are extraneous to the main thrust of Stevens' dissent . It is tempting to theorize that majority opinions and dissents are different genres, with the latter being free from some of the constraints of legal reasoning. But, in looking at the other dissent written by Rehnquist and joined by White and O'Connor, it is more like the majority opinion than Stevens' dissent. It premises its argument that flag burning is so provocative an act that it can be prohibited based on *Chaplinsky v. New Hampshire*. Its reasoning is similar to Brennan's, but it begins with different grounds (i.e., a different and a conflicting precedent).

From the nature of the Stevens dissent, one may conclude that whereas court decisions are part of a specialized argument field, they sometimes depart from that field's characteristic reasoning and read more like an "op-ed" piece. Toulmin, Rieke, and Janik explain why dissents are more likely to go in this popular direction:

> Because the majority opinion reflects a compromise between the personal viewpoints of several justices, and has to stand as an expression of the law, it is typically written in careful style, showing close reasoning and severe restraint. Dissents, on the other hand, often reflect the personal opinion of a single justice, and it is not their function to express the law. Instead it is their business to impute faults to the majority reasoning. As a result, dissents tend to be worded more strongly, written in more flamboyant style, and aimed not merely at expressing concern over the present case but also at swaying future courts in the hope that one day the dissent may become the *majority*—and therefore *operative*—opinion.

The argument field is not impermeably fenced. Those using legal argument may proceed legally or offer argumentation that is more "popular."

---

[8]See Stephen Toulmin, *The Use of Argument* (Cambridge: Cambridge University Press, 1968); and Stephen Toulmin, Richard Rieke, and Allan Janik, *An Introduction to Reasoning* (New York: Macmillan, 1979).

Justices also do not write the same way. They are, after all, different jurists with different takes on how their statements should read. An examination of the opinions written by a handful of famous Supreme Court justices would uncover a wide variation in style. Some are a pleasure to read; others are written in a style that seems almost "scientific." Across history, the gradual ascendancy of this more "scientific" style is apparent.

Critiquing the Legal Arguments

The tendency to write in that "scientific" style has increased as law has become more professionalized in this nation. That style, however, has dangers: it suggests an objectivity and certainty that may be more of a judicial illusion than a reality. At least this is the conclusion reached by several who have critiqued the Supreme Court as being more political and more ideological than its justices may think. The Critical Legal Studies movement has used the insights of postmodern literary and rhetorical theorists to point not just to the justices' inadvertent prejudices one way or another on an issue but also to systemic class, gender, and race biases in the way legal reasoning works.

Two critiques offered by communication scholars are especially useful to consider because they allow us to see the opposed rhetoric in a case such as *Texas v. Johnson* as more than just a choice between cases such as *Spence v. Washington*, *United States v. O'Brien*, and West *Virginia Board of Education v. Barnette* as opposed to *Chaplinsky v. New Hampshire* as precedent in determining when a state may prohibit expressive conduct.

One critique, offered by William Lewis in the *Southern Communication Journal*, invites us to consider the mythic dimension of Supreme Court argumentation.[9] The other, offered by Marouf Hasian, Jr., Celeste Michelle Condit, and John Louis Lucaites in the *Quarterly Journal of Speech*, invites us to consider the extent to which law is a rhetorical construction.[10]

Lewis begins by noting, "Judicial discourse is predominantly conceived as the application of pre-existing principles to determinate cases," a formulation that makes such discourse sound rather neutral. However, Lewis argues, judicial discourse does more than apply principles; it offers narratives. To understand these narratives, Lewis goes to the literary theory of Northrop Frye, who, in the *Anatomy of Criticism*, posits that there are four master narratives or myths. Frye names them comedy, romance, tragedy, and irony. Legal discourse, as Lewis sees it, has offered romantic narratives. *Texas v. Johnson* offers two. In the majority decision, "The Law" as hero defends dissident Johnson against the suppressive inclinations of government. In the

---

[9]William Lewis, "Of Innocence, Exclusion, and the Burning of Flags: The Romantic Realism of the Law," *Southern Communication Journal*, 60, no. 1 (1994): 4–21.

[10]Marouf Hasian, Jr., Celeste Michelle Condit, and John Louis Lucaites, "The Rhetorical Boundaries of 'the Law:' A Consideration of the Rhetorical Culture of Legal Practice and the Case of the 'Separate But Equal' Doctrine," *Quarterly Journal of Speech* 82 (1996): 323–42.

dissents, "The Law" as hero defends the victimized flag against those who represent disorder, indecorum, immorality—in short, a kind of barbarism. Either romance, however, reduces the matter at hand to an "agon of good and evil," when in reality there are positive and negative things to be said about dissent and positive and negative things to be said about the flag and the nation it represents. The matter at hand is not as simple as either romance narrative suggests. Worse, to the extent that either narrative labels one party "evil" and the other "good," it can oppress those the law rules against or enshrine as innocent those victims for whom the law rules.

Lewis rejects comic (too soothing) and ironic (too cynical) alternatives and calls for a tragic mythos. Such a mythos would admit the ambiguity and the pain experienced when the law tilts one way or the other. Dissent can be violent; the flag "has stood as a symbol of bondage as well as a symbol of freedom." A tragic mythos would have The Law work its way through this ambiguity and arrive at a resolution that might restore community. It would be less interested in "good" and "evil" than in purging the difficulties inherent in the case by bringing them into the open and then trying to move beyond them. Those involved in legal reasoning, first, must grant that they are offering mythic narratives and, once they have done so, shift to ones that serve society well.

Hasian, Condit, and Lucaites reject both the illusion that legal reasoning is "rationally constructed discourse" and the vehement Critical Legal Studies movement's assault on legal reasoning. To them, law is "an active and protean component of a hegemonically crafted rhetorical culture," and legal reasoning should reflect this. Now, you might well ask, what does that quoted phrase mean? Put simply, law does not exist "up there" to be revered from below. No, rather law reflects the culture it is part of, and because that culture is not of one mind or one voice, law has, simultaneously, many sides. Attempting to contain the law within a supposedly objective, technical language runs contrary to what law is. Nonetheless, there will be a push, if not in this "scientific" direction, then in the direction dictated by "prevailing social alignments." That push exists because those who "do" law are products of those "alignments" and they are concerned about avoiding controversy. Nonetheless, as a product of the culture, the law can and does change. Demographics, economic changes, and technology (defined very broadly) are among the forces that prompt change.

So, how should legal reasoning reflect what law as a "rhetorical construct" is? Reasoning should give up on legal jargon for such language separates the law from the culture; reasoning should give up on the warrant of *stare decisis* for that "rule" prevents—actually, just slows—adaptation; reasoning should give up on the illusion that law is "above politics" for it is just an illusion. In sum, "the judiciary should promote itself as an institution that attempts to generate reasonable decisions, often entailing reasonable compromises, about important political issues."

Perhaps the matter of burning the American flag doesn't make the essence of this critique clear. So, let's try another issue: "the right to bear arms" as stated in the Second Amendment to the U.S. Constitution. The "traditional" take on legal reasoning would hold that there is a universal position toward an understanding of which a sequence of Supreme Court cases, each subsequent one building on what preceded it, should take us. But isn't this right to bear arms—this constitutionally established law—more of a cultural construction? In the late eighteenth century, there was no standing army. The fledgling United States needed militia to protect itself, and those citizens who would make up these militia would need their own arms. In the nine-teenth century, as the nation expanded westward, the purpose of the arms one might own and bear changed: they became a tool of self-protection on the frontier. More recently, they have become recreational equipment as well as a tool of self-protection against crime . In some subcultures, but not in others, learning how to use a weapon has become an important rite of passage. It is difficult to sustain the premise that the right is universally true in this nation when its basis has shifted from era to era. It is also difficult to sustain the premise when so many other nations, including ones with strong democratic traditions, fail to extend the "right" to their citizens. The critique offered by Hasian, Condit, and Lucaites calls for legal reasoning to reflect the cultural, rhetorical, political nature of the law by abandoning deduction based on precedents and replacing it with a full and thoughtful discussion of matters that are inherently far more complex than deduction, no matter how painstakingly meticulous it might be.

These two critiques, if heeded, would push the text of *Texas v. Johnson* away from warring deductions. Rather than offering the universal statement that expressive conduct cannot be suppressed based on what is expressed or its opposite and reason-ing from it, the jurists would use reasoning to create a middle ground that acknow-ledges the difficulties of crafting such a space.

In the recent discussions of George W. Bush's nominees to the U.S. Supreme Court, many observed that the 5–4 votes that were going one way would soon be 5–4 votes going the other. Basically, those who offered this observation were acknowledg-ing that the current jurists were tending to engage in the kind of legal reasoning Lewis and Hasian, Condit, and Lucaites critique. They were fighting for their view of the law and then were ready to witness the law triumphing over evil, as opposed to recognizing that it is a culturally created rhetorical construct full of tensions and using reasoning to reflect and work past this reality. The vote in *Texas v. Johnson* was 5–4: four joined Brennan in the majority opinion; the others dissented, three together and Stevens alone. Given how the composition of the court has changed since this decision, a reconsideration of the matter would likely go in the opposite direction now, perhaps 4–5. In the firmness of the positions taken in the decision and the dissents, one can see how such a flip might have occurred: just delete the firm voices on the one side and add equally firm voices to the other. The critique of legal reasoning summarized here would suggest that the reasoning, on both sides, should not be so distanced from the culture, so intent on denying ambiguities, and so tied to finding a precedent and following it closely that no middle ground on the issue at hand seems to exist.

Conclusion

The rhetorician, then, looks at the arguments that are offered in an appellate court case such as *Texas v. Johnson*. The rhetorician would try to account for how they work, paying close attention to logos—both the topoi the justices use and the ways they structure their arguments. Classical insights would assist the rhetorician, as would those offered by Stephen Toulmin and his colleagues. But the rhetorician would not stop at describing what's there in the text. The rhetorician would also critique what's there, premised on the assumption that a mythic structure may be present or that legal reasoning used implies a misleading view of what the law is.

THE MASS COMMUNICATION PERSPECTIVE

The timing of the decision by the Supreme Court in *Texas v. Johnson* heightened media attention to the case, as well as related events. The attention may have also been greater because of events that took place before the court case. The case demonstrates an intersection of newsworthiness, Supreme Court attention to a particular issue, and related current events. Prior events may have shaped news attention to this court decision; the controversy over the Pledge of Allegiance in the 1988 presidential campaign is believed to have led to increased interest in the decision in *Texas v. Johnson*.

A number of events in March 1989 also intersected to heighten attention in this case. Oral arguments in *Texas v. Johnson* were made on March 21, 1989. Just days earlier, on March 16, 1989, the Senate had passed (97–0) and sent to the House of Representatives a bill making it a crime to "knowingly display" the flag on the floor or ground. The proposed law was a response to an exhibit at the School of the Art Institute of Chicago titled "What Is the Proper Way to Display the U.S. Flag?" that invited visitors to comment on the question. However, to write their comments in the book of the display, one would have to stand on an American flag placed on the floor. One story covering the controversy ran a news headline stating "Emotional disputes flare over flag desecration; Supreme Court to hear arguments Tuesday."[11]

Media Coverage of *Texas v. Johnson*

The original flag-burning incident was almost completely ignored in the news coverage of the 1984 Republican Convention. The oral arguments in the case on March 21 also received little attention in the news media. Although the oral arguments in the case got little attention in the news media, the reporting on the decision itself usually provides background on the case. Not all Supreme Court cases are covered by news media; one analysis of Supreme Court decisions from 1981 to 1988, just before the *Texas v. Johnson* decision in 1989, found that 10 percent of decisions were covered in U.S. news magazines (*Time, Newsweek, U.S. News & World Report*).[12]

What made *Texas v. Johnson* a case meriting media attention? In addition to the timing factors discussed above, Richard Davis discusses issues of newsworthiness

[11]Al Kamen, "Emotional Disputes Flare Over Flag Desecration; Supreme Court to Hear Arguments Tuesday," *Washington Post* (March 19, 1989), A9.

[12]Dorothy A. Bowles and Rebekah V. Bromley, "Newsmagazine Coverage of the Supreme Court During the Reagan Administration," *Journalism Quarterly* 69.4 (2002): 948–59.

of court cases in *Decisions and Images: The Supreme Court and the Press*. If an issue has already been defined as newsworthy, it is likely to be covered when involved in Supreme Court cases as well. Davis recounts comments from *Baltimore Sun* reporter Lyle Denniston specifically about the newsworthiness of the flag-burning case:

> Flag burning for a year and a half was an exciting and inciteful issue. I couldn't give my editors enough on that. It was wonderful because it was kind of a residual carryover from the campaign in '88. It was such a wonderful mix of personality and patriotism. I thought it was the best case of the lot.[13]

When considering traditional criteria of newsworthiness, a number of factors apply to this case. Conflict is likely the most predominant news value of coverage of this Supreme Court case and the events leading up to it. Opinions on flag burning are quite polarized in public opinion, laying the ideal groundwork for a conflict story in the news media. Flag burning often occurs as part of protest events laden with conflict without the involvement of the flag. The currency of the issue, as flag-related issues were the focus of other news reports and public discussion, also contributed to the newsworthiness of this case, as did its prominence in that the case was one of few late-twentieth-century First Amendment cases that reached the level of the Supreme Court.

What information traditionally appears in Supreme Court decision reporting? The analysis by Bowles and Bromley found that the following factors appeared in at least 75 percent of news stories on Supreme Court cases in their analysis from 1981 to 1988:[14] name of the case or identification of parties involved in the case; litigative history; vote count of the Court; mention or discussion of majority reasoning; discussion of probable or expected impact of the decision; and reactions to the court decisions. Less likely to appear (but still in more than half of the stories) was a mention or discussion of dissenting opinion; and rules, statutes, or precedents that apply to the case.

The decision in *Texas v. Johnson* received extensive coverage by both print and broadcast news organizations in 1989. Some news coverage was traditional and included many of the elements outlined earlier found in Supreme Court decision coverage. The coverage in *USA Today* on June 22, 1989, was particularly unique; the paper included excerpts of opinions in the case, but they were not included simply as part of other news stories on the case. Rather, the paper published the opinions of Justices Brennan and Rehnquist under the headline: "Face-off: The Supreme Court on Old Glory." The subheadline that preceded Brennan's comments was "Don't jail flag-burners; wave yours," and for Rehnquist's comments the subheadline read "Don't waive jail for flag-burners." The bylines that accompanied both pieces listed the justice as a "Guest columnist," which suggests they crafted an original piece to be published. However, that was not the case. Both pieces began with a statement clarifying that the views of the justices were condensed or excerpted from their written opinions on the case.

---

[13]Richard Davis, *Decisions and Images: The Supreme Court and the Press* (Englewood Cliffs, NJ: Prentice Hall, 1994), 72–73.

[14]Dorothy A. Bowles and Rebekah V. Bromley.

Another unique factor of this case that received media attention from a *USA Today* report as well as other news was the rare fact that Justice Stevens read his dissenting opinion from the bench. For example, a *USA Today* article stated:

> The ruling roused strong emotions. Justice John Paul Stevens—a Bronze Star recipient in World War II—took the unusual step of reading his dissent from the bench. His voice cracking, Stevens recalled "the soldiers who scaled the bluff at Omaha Beach" and said, "The American flag is more than a proud symbol." Permitting burning will "tarnish its value."[15]

A number of organizations and interests were represented in news coverage regarding reaction to the decision in *Texas v. Johnson*. Those who reacted to the decision and merited media coverage (or were contacted by the media to get a response) and were satisfied with the Court's decision included the following: People for the American Way, Center for Constitutional Rights, and Gregory Johnson, the defendant in the original case. Among organizations covered in news reports that were dissatisfied with the decision were the National Commander of the American Legion, Washington Legal Foundation (who argued for veterans groups), Veterans of Foreign Wars, National Flag Foundation, and the Free Congress Center for Law and Democracy. To have balance and fairness in reporting, journalists strive to get opinions from both sides. In a review of decision reporting in this case from the *New York Times, USA Today*, the *Washington Post*, and the *Boston Globe* (which cited the sources identified above in their coverage), all decision news stories included responses from both sides, from groups who either supported or opposed the decision on flag burning.

President George H. W. Bush also commented on the decision, which is rare for a president to do in most Supreme Court cases. Given the potential connections of issues of patriotism surrounding flag burning and the 1988 presidential campaign, it may have been more likely that Bush would comment on the case than if it was later in his presidency. Since much of what a president says or does makes news, so did his response to *Texas v. Johnson*. At a luncheon on June 22 to promote volunteerism in New York, Bush opened with comments regarding the Supreme Court decision that was covered in a number of news stories:

> I understand the legal basis for the decision and I respect the Supreme Court, and as president of the United States, I will see that the law of the land is fully supported. But I have to give you my personal, emotional response. Flag burning is wrong; dead wrong. And the flag of the United States is very, very special.

His reaction was quoted in many news stories covering the decision of the case. On June 27, Bush began a White House press conference with comments on the case and the issue of flag burning. Although just days earlier he had commented that he would see the law is "fully supported," he announced that he was reviewing proposed language for a constitutional amendment. Only one reporter at the press conference followed up with

[15]Tony Mauro, "Vets See Flag Ruling as 'Slap,'" *USA Today*, June 22, 1989.

questions about his comments—not about the case, but about the politicization of the American flag as an instrument in party politics. On June 30, in front of the World War II Iwo Jima Memorial, Bush received media coverage of his comments on a constitutional amendment banning flag desecration.

A separate event received news coverage the same week of the Supreme Court decision, one that otherwise likely would have been ignored. But because of the timing of the decision in the case and the ongoing discussions of patriotism since the 1988 presidential campaign, it was deemed more newsworthy. Any other week, this story would not have been covered by any news organization. But with the headline "A Patriotic Sideshow to Flag-Burning Flap," the reporter connected a separate event that week with the Court decision:

> The verbal explosion surprised almost everyone. "Look, look, two members of the press not standing!" Rep. Gerald B. H. Solomon (R-N.Y.) shouted from the House floor up to the Press Gallery.
>
> Rep. William E. Dannemeyer (R-Calif.) picked up the chorus. "Get out! Get out!" he shouted at two young reporters who had been buried in reading material, apparently unaware that the House had turned its attention from the confusion and hubbub of an opening vote to the Pledge of Allegiance.
>
> The House seemed confused a moment, a little shocked at the scene, then went about its business as if nothing had happened.
>
> The incident last week might have been passed off as just another of the odd things that occasionally afflict "the people's house," but Solomon decided not to let it lie. He wrote House Speaker Thomas S. Foley (D-Wash.) to ask that gallery Superintendent Thayer V. Illsley be informed "in writing, that reporters in the gallery are expected to stand during renderings of the pledge."
>
> So, while most politicians yesterday spent their patriotic fervor on the Supreme Court decision decriminalizing the burning of the flag, a patriotic sideshow appeared to be playing itself out behind the scenes.[16]

This example demonstrates how the newsworthiness of a story, and its correlated likelihood of being reported, relies on the currency of the related issues and public discussion of them. Any other week of the year, this story likely would have been ignored by all news organizations. That particular week in the summer of 1989, however, this event's tie to other current issues, and its ability to fuel the conflict and controversy over patriotism further, resulted in news attention and coverage.

The Supreme Court and Agenda Building

Although media effect research often examines agenda setting, in how the media may influence (or reflect) public opinion, agenda building is often a consideration in media research as well. Such research examines how individuals, organizations, and

---

[16]Don Phillips, "A Patriotic Sideshow to Flag-Burning Flap; Failure to Stand During Pledge Jars the House," *Washington Post* (June 23, 1989), A21.

institutions influence media attention and possibly shape coverage through their prominence and strategy, beyond the newsworthiness of a potential story on its own.

We associate the Supreme Court with deciding key cases such as *Texas v. Johnson* that influence American life, but the Court may also influence and shape media coverage of the issue. In his book *Decisions and Images: The Supreme Court and the Press*, Richard Davis suggests the Supreme Court may utilize the media, as well as influence media attention, to a greater extent than we might expect. He states that although the Supreme Court agrees to take cases to settle constitutional issues, it may also do so to give a constitutional issue more media coverage. For example, Associated Press reporter Richard Carelli suggested such agenda building occurred in the *Texas v. Johnson* case:

> Why did they take it? The court could have denied cert. with the same effect. The court embraced the case, agreed to hear it, then agreed with the Texas court and struck it down. I'd like to know if those who wrote dissents knew it would spark passion (from outside the court). The court does perceive, with great precision, what the press' role is.[17]

When we consider issues of agenda setting, they traditionally involve the influence of the media to set the agenda for issues of concern for the public, the audience of news media. Agenda building, however, involves the influence on the media agenda, by way of what they might choose to cover or not. Davis suggests the Supreme Court has that agenda-building power, whether it is conscious of it or not. In deciding which cases it will hear, it is influencing what issues the media might be covering, what stories will emerge. Finally, this case is an example of the potential influence of news factors in the timing of the announcement of decisions in *Texas v. Johnson*; in the height of pending legislation and heightened attention to flag desecration, the Supreme Court decision was announced within one week of Flag Day 1989.

Conclusion

The media coverage surrounding *Texas v. Johnson* demonstrates the intersection of court cases and timing with other events that have the potential to influence news attention, as well as public attention, in such decisions. Although there may be some conventional patterns in covering Supreme Court decisions, the coverage of this decision and the related issues of flag desecration reflected some uniqueness, including President Bush's involvement in the issue and his media-related events that followed the Court's decision. The Supreme Court itself has the potential to influence the newsworthiness of its own decisions, as well as to shape media coverage in a variety of ways, as seen in the reporting on the *Texas v. Johnson* decision.

[17]Richard Davis, p. 115.

CONCLUSION

As the rhetorical section of this chapter has discussed, something of a mythology surrounds Supreme Court decisions. The justices hear cases at law perched high above the litigants in what has been called a marble temple. The mythology of the Court insulates it from the political whims of Congress, the president, and the public, but it cannot protect the Court completely when it issues an unpopular decision, even (or sometimes especially) when—as is the case with flag burning—the decision is largely symbolic. The Court is further insulated because it communicates only through its written opinions; in this case, however, the mass communication perspective illustrates the ways in which the reporting on *Texas v. Johnson* contributed to the public outrage that surrounded the Court's decision. Taken together, however, this chapter has demonstrated the importance of symbolism to political communication.

ADDITIONAL CASES

Students interested in the symbolic nature of political communication may wish to consider the following additional cases:

■ *Regents of the University of California v. Bakke* **(1978)**:
This decision was the first landmark Supreme Court case to grapple with the question of affirmative action. The opinion declared that race could be a factor in college and graduate school admissions decisions, but that it could not be the only factor. The full text of the case is available online at: **http://laws.findlaw.com/us/438/265.html**.

■ *Buckley v. Valeo* **(1976)**:
This Supreme Court decision about campaign financing has defined what is acceptable for political campaigning for three decades. From this decision the notion of campaign contributions as a form of political speech was canonized. The full text of the decision can be viewed at Findlaw.com: **http://laws.findlaw.com/us/424/1.html**.

■ **The Congress's March 11, 2003, decision to rename "French fries" and "French toast," in all of the U.S. House of Representatives' eateries, to protest France's stance against the United States concerning the War in Iraq**.
See: "Debate Real Issues and Leave the Jokes to Comedians" (Floor statement by Representative McGovern). *Congressional Record*, March 12, 2003. P. H1753. See also: Stolberg, Sheryl Gay, "An Order of Fries, Please, But Do Hold the French," *The New York Times* (March 12, 2003), A1.

■ ■ ■ ■ ■

CHAPTER 16

CASE TWELVE: THE GAY-LESBIAN RIGHTS MOVEMENT

THE CASE

A social movement is best described by telling its story, and a handy way to do so is to offer a time line, especially if the movement extends over many years. Otherwise, one imposes an interpretation on it. Along the time line below, actions and events that one might "read" as if texts are emphasized:

- 1948—Kinsey's *Sexual Behavior in the Human Male* is published.
- 1951—The Mattachine Society is founded, with chapters in several U.S. cities.
- 1951—Edward Sagarin, using the pseudonym Donald Webster Cory, publishes *The Homosexual in America*.
- 1953—Mattachine Society members begin publishing the gay magazine *One*.
- 1954—U.S. Post Office bans the mailing of *One*.
- 1955—The Daughters of Bilitis (DOB) is founded, with chapters in several cities.
- 1957—Frank Kameny is fired from U.S. Army Map Service because of his sexual orientation.
- 1958—U.S. Supreme Court rules against the Post Office and *One* is allowed in the mails.
- 1958—Barbara Gittings becomes editor of the DOB's magazine, *The Ladder*, and steers it in more militant direction.
- 1961—U.S. Supreme Court refuses to hear Frank Kameny's case, letting lower court's ruling, which validated his firing, stand.
- 1961—Kameny founds Washington, DC, Mattachine chapter and takes a more militant tack, arguing against the idea that homosexuality is a disease. Later, Kameny, indebted to the "Black Power" movement, argues that "Gay is Good."
- 1965—In San Francisco, Council on Religion and the Homosexual holds New Year's Day costume ball; attendees are harassed by police.
- 1965—Gittings is removed as *The Ladder*'s editor by DOB members fearful of her militancy.
- 1965—Demonstrations are held in Washington at the White House, the Pentagon, and the Civil Service Commission and in Philadelphia at Independence Hall; demonstrations receive considerable mass media coverage.

- 1967—Homophile Action League is founded in Philadelphia, with chapters in other cities soon to follow.
- 1968—The North American Conference of Homophile Organizations adopts a Homosexual Bill of Rights focusing on the decriminalization of homosexuality and an end to discrimination in matters such as employment, military service, security clearances, and citizenship.
- 1969—Police raid on Greenwich Village (New York City) gay bar the Stonewall erupts into antipolice riot.
- 1969—Gay Liberation Front (GLF) and Gay Activist Alliance (GAA) are founded in New York City, largely in response to the Stonewall Riot. Both groups begin staging "zaps" and instances of civil disobedience.
- 1970—GAA lobbies successfully for gay rights ordinance in New York City and then stages march on state capital.
- 1970—Large demonstrations are held in several cities to commemorate Stonewall Riot.
- 1970—"Zaps" are staged against media offices, including an on-the-air "zap" during the *CBS Evening News with Walter Cronkite*.
- 1971—First Gay Pride Day is celebrated.
- 1972—*The New Republic* publishes an article, "The Gay Vote," testifying to the group's increasing political power.
- 1972—ABC airs made-for-TV movie "That Certain Summer," which positively portrays a gay couple.
- 1973—National Gay Task Force and the Lambda Legal Defense and Education Fund are incorporated to raise funds for gay cause.
- 1973—Several Protestant denominations launch National Task Force on Gay People in the Church.
- 1973—American Psychiatric Association removes homosexuality from its list of mental disorders.
- 1973—American Bar Association calls for repeal of all sodomy laws.
- 1973–77—Antidiscrimination legislation is adopted in many cities.
- 1973+—Lesbian separatism divides gay and lesbian movements over former's "allegiance to men."
- 1974—National Teachers Association adds sexual orientation to its antidiscrimination policy.
- 1975—U.S. Civil Service Commission revokes ban on hiring gays for civilian federal government jobs.
- 1976—Attempt to stage protest outside Democratic National Convention draws 600, not the 10,000 called for.
- 1977–78—Singer Anita Bryant leads "Save Our Children" campaign to reverse gay civil rights legislation, leading to several repeals.
- 1978—California State Senator John Briggs introduces "initiative" to expel all gay and lesbian teachers from the state's public schools; "initiative" is on California ballot in November.

- 1978—250,000 turn out for Gay Pride Day in San Francisco to protest Briggs Initiative; efforts are mobilized throughout state, with organized labor support, to defeat it.
- 1978—Briggs Initiative defeated 58 percent to 42 percent; Seattle retains its gay rights ordinance, 63 percent to 37 percent.
- 1978—Gay activist San Francisco Mayor Harvey Milk is assassinated.
- 1979—Riots occur when Milk's assassin is convicted of only manslaughter; the next day, 10,000 demonstrators celebrate Milk's birthday.
- 1979—First national gay rights march on Washington, DC, draws 100,000.
- 1983—Larry Kramer's "1,112 and Counting" is published in *The New York Native*.
- 1985—Actor Rock Hudson dies of AIDS, drawing mass media attention to disease ravaging gay population.
- 1986—U.S. Supreme Court upholds Georgia ban on just homosexual sodomy in *Bowers v. Hardwick*.
- 1987—Randy Shilts publishes *And The Band Played On*.
- 1989—Larry Kramer publishes *Reports from the Holocaust*.
- Late 1980s—Religious Right launches backlash; Jerry Falwell terms AIDS "God's punishment upon homosexuals."

Protesters march through a New York City street during a demonstration in favor of more AIDS funding.

- Late 1980s—National Gay and Lesbian Task Force and Human Rights Campaign Fund begin documenting antigay hate crimes.
- Late 1980s—AIDS Coalition to Unleash Power protests national indifference toward disease.
- 1987—500,000 march on U.S. Capitol; 600 stage civil disobedience actions at Supreme Court.
- 1990—The Americans with Disabilities Act includes HIV/AIDS in its antidiscrimination provisions.
- 1990—Hate Crimes Statistics Act becomes law.
- Early 1990s—More states pass antidiscrimination laws.
- 1992—Backlash amendment prohibiting antidiscrimination laws passes in Colorado.
- 1994—Colorado Supreme Court declares Colorado amendment unconstitutional.
- 1996—U.S. Supreme Court upholds ruling of Colorado Supreme Court.
- 1996—Congress enacts Defense of Marriage Act.
- 1998—University of Wyoming student Matthew Shepard is tortured and murdered because he was gay.
- 2000—President Bill Clinton addresses, via videotape, Millennium March on Washington for Equality.
- 2000—Vermont passes Act Relating to Civil Unions.
- 2000—"Big 3" U.S. automakers, with union backing, extend benefits to partners of gay and lesbian workers.
- 2000—Coca-Cola extends healthcare benefit to same-sex partners of its workers.
- 2000—U.S. Supreme Court in *Boy Scouts of America v. Dale* says Boy Scouts can exclude gays from organization.
- 2003–04—Supreme Judicial Court of Massachusetts offers rulings interpreted as favorable toward gay marriages; legislature, however, ultimately bans them.
- 2004—President Bush in his State of Union Address calls for protection of sanctity of marriage; a month later, he calls for a Constitutional amendment defining marriage as between a man and a woman.
- 2004—San Francisco sues the state of California, challenging its ban on gay marriage.
- 2004—New Platz, New York, mayor arrested for performing nineteen gay marriages.
- Late 2004—Anti–"gay marriage" initiatives appear on many state ballots.

In *Doing Democracy*, Bill Moyer offers his Movement Action Plan (MAP) as a framework within which to understand the dynamics of social movements. The MAP model traces movements through eight stages: (1) normal times; (2) prove the failure of official institutions; (3) ripening conditions; (4) take off; (5) perception of failure; (6) majority public opinion; (7) success; (8) continuing the struggle. This model

Gays and lesbians protest the 2004 California Supreme Court decision voiding gay marriages.

provides a lens through which one can look at a time line and extract from it the actions and events that may be the richest in what they communicate.[1]

Early groups such as the Mattachine societies and the DOB chapters provided gays and lesbians with support, but activists Kameny and Gittings gave the movement leadership. The 1965 New Year's masquerade ball in San Francisco inspired solidarity and anger—at police harassment. The 1965 demonstrations in Washington, DC, brought these feelings to a national audience. But the true "trigger event"—which allowed the movement to truly "take off"—was probably the Stonewall Riot in New York City in 1969. In its wake, activism increased, culminating in the first Gay Pride Day in 1971. Then, in rapid succession, establishment bodies for psychiatrists, lawyers, and teachers, and then the U.S. Civil Service Commission embraced the gay-lesbian civil rights claims.

The "Save Our Children" campaign, which demonized gays and lesbians in the late 1970s, was a setback for the gay-lesbian cause. But the Briggs Initiative in California and the assassination of Harvey Milk in San Francisco "retriggered" the cause. Political action against the initiative and demonstrations at the light sentence given Milk's assassin led to the highly visible gay rights march on Washington in 1979.

---

[1]Bill Moyer, *Doing Democracy: The MAP Model for Organizing Social Movements* (Gabriola Island, BC, Canada: New Society Publishers, 2001).

The movement was on the verge of achieving considerable success—at least on the basic civil rights front.

The gay-lesbian movement, extending as it does over six decades, seems to repeat stages four through eight. In the 1980s, the focus shifted from civil rights to AIDS. Increased public awareness of AIDS and the *Bowers v. Harwick* decision provided fuel for another backlash against the gay-lesbian movement, but these events also retriggered the movement, which rallied, staging large demonstrations in 1987 and achieving some success when HIV/AIDS was cited in the Americans with Disabilities Act as an illegal basis for discrimination.

The movement then refocused one again on the rights of gay and lesbian couples. The Defense of Marriage Act in 1996 (as well as the murder of Matthew Shepard in 1998) were setbacks. However, they were followed by a legislative victory in Vermont as well as nonlegislative ones as large corporations such as General Motors and Coca-Cola granted some of what the movement was asking for. Since then, there have been losses as well as victories in a very up-and-down battle, with the presence in 2004 of anti–gay marriage initiatives on many state ballots being a rather negative omen. The matter remains very volatile.

THE POLITICAL SCIENCE PERSPECTIVE

On July 18, 2006, as the United States House of Representatives debated a national constitutional amendment to prevent gay marriage, openly gay Member of Congress, Barney Frank (D-MA) made a speech on the House floor, in which he stated, in part:

> People will remember the commercial for V8 juice years ago in which a cartoon character who was feeling poorly drank various juices to see if he or she could be energized. None of them worked. Tomato juice didn't work. Apple juice didn't work. Pineapple juice didn't work, and then someone gives him a V8. The cartoon character gets pumped up, literally, and steam comes out of his ears. He is literally now raring to go, because he had a V8. He says to himself, wow, I could have had a V8. Note for the record, I just smacked myself in the forehead to represent what happened in the commercial. Now, that is apparently the logical structure of same-sex marriages. Apparently there were these 37-, 38-, 42-year-long marriages all over the place. There are happily married men all over America, and they are content with their wives. They are heterosexual, and they feel this physical and emotional attraction to each other. Then they read in the paper that in the State of Massachusetts it is now possible for there to be a same-sex marriage. How is a marriage endangered? Apparently, people happily married in Indiana, Nebraska, Kansas, and Mississippi read that we have had same-sex marriage quite successfully in Massachusetts, and they look in the mirror and they say, wow, I could have married a guy. So, apparently, same-sex marriage is the V8 juice of America. And apparently there are people who fear that knowing that two men who love each other, want to be committed to each other, somehow will dissolve the bonds of matrimony between two heterosexuals, it is, of course, nonsense. I will do

my friends the credit of acknowledging that they don't believe it. There is a political motive here.[2]

Frank's comment was directed at other members of Congress who had made the claim that if gay people were allowed to marry, it would threaten the sanctity of marriage.

As the introduction of this chapter points out, issues relating to equality for homosexuals are numerous, and the rhetoric and action surrounding them are at times volatile. Although representations of homosexual relationships are common today and the movement for gay marriage and equal rights is more organized than it was a decade or two ago, the movement has not fully accomplished the objective of achieving equality for all citizens regardless of sexual orientation.

The Marriage Issue

The issue of gay marriage provides an excellent lens through which to understand the movement for equal rights for homosexuals more generally. As Katherine Franke notes in the *Columbia Journal of Gender and Law*: "In a very short period of time, this issue has moved to the center of the gay and lesbian rights movement as well as larger mainstream political and legal debates."[3] To understand the issue fully, it is necessary to cover some important political and legal facts. First, because of the principle of federalism, articulated primarily in the Tenth Amendment to the Constitution, the federal government has certain powers but other powers are reserved explicitly for the states. Because of federalism, it is up to the states to set policies about who may marry. States regulate a variety of aspects of marriage, from the age at which people may marry to whether or not they must have blood tests to prove they do not have sexually transmitted diseases. Without an overarching set of federal regulations to constrain them, every state is different with regard to what is regulated.

However, despite the differences in how they regulate marriage, each state is obligated to recognize the validity of a marriage endorsed by any other state. This is because of the Full Faith and Credit clause of Article IV of the U.S. Constitution, which provides that each state must recognize the legal acts of every other state as being valid and binding. In other words, if two people marry, divorce, or adopt a child in Delaware, Virginia must acknowledge the legality of those acts and treat the individuals accordingly. Without states affording full faith and credit to each other's legal actions, every time a person crossed a state line, he or she would have to get a new driver's license or remarry their spouse. So, the full faith and credit provision makes good sense.

---

[2]Debate on the Marriage Protection Amendment. United States House of Representatives. *Congressional Record*, July 18, 2006, p. H5295.

[3]Katherine M. Franke, "The Politics of Same-Sex Marriage Politics," *Columbia Journal of Gender and Law* 15.1 (Winter 2006).

However, the Full Faith and Credit clause of the Constitution is at the core of the gay marriage issue. If Massachusetts permits gay marriage, and gay or lesbian couples marry there, the Constitution requires that all other states—even states that have adopted bans on gay marriage—recognize the legitimacy of the marriage. In fact, opponents of gay marriage frequently use states' rights rhetoric to declare that what liberal states decide is appropriate should not be forced onto more conservative states simply by virtue of the Full Faith and Credit clause.

The full faith and credit provision is not the only constitutional principle at issue when considering gay marriage. The Fourteenth Amendment to the Constitution provides that all citizens of the United States are entitled to "equal protection of the laws." This suggests (although the courts have not yet reached a definitive conclusion) that if a state permits heterosexuals to marry, then that state must also permit homosexuals to marry because the Constitution speaks to issues of citizenship, not to issues of sexual orientation.

For both opponents and proponents of gay marriage, the issue masks more deeply held beliefs. Opponents of gay marriage frequently view marriage as a covenant not only between two people but also with a higher authority. For those who believe that homosexuality is a sin, the notion of gays being permitted to marry undermines their deeply held belief in covenantal marriage. On the other hand, proponents of gay marriage make the argument that gay marriage is less about the marriage bond itself and more about ensuring the equal protection of the laws, many of which preference married couples over unmarried ones. As Timothy Stewart-Winter writes in the Winter 2006 issue of *The Gay and Lesbian Review Worldwide*,

> the current marriage debate is profoundly structured by a series of changes, dating at least to the New Deal but expanding in the World War II era, by which marriage became a primary mechanism for distributing state and private benefits. In postwar America, gay marriage dreams correspond rather precisely to the shifting menu of rights enjoyed by heterosexual couples only.[4]

For example, a married couple may choose to hold assets jointly with survivorship, meaning that in the event that one spouse dies, the other automatically retains ownership of any property or assets held jointly prior to the death. However, unmarried people generally cannot establish jointly held property or assets in this way. To be sure, two unmarried people can hold property jointly, but if one dies, the other either pays an inheritance tax if the property was willed to him or her, or he or she must buy out the other person's share of the asset. Thus, someone who is a legal co-owner of a piece of property with another person to whom they are not married does not automatically retain ownership of the property in the event that the co-owner dies. This is true whether the co-owner is a parent, sibling, friend, or lifelong partner.

[4]Timothy Stewart-Winter, " What Was Same-Sex Marriage?" *The Gay & Lesbian Review Worldwide* 13.1 (January-February 2006): 33(3).

Gay Rights in Context

To some extent the movement for gay marriage and for gay rights more generally parallels previous social movements that have been grounded in constitutional protections. Further, the movements both in favor and against rights for homosexual couples, like other social movements before them, is a multifront movement, with individuals on both sides of the question attempting to influence both legislative and judicial action. For example, the pro– and anti–gay rights sides of the movement are much like the two sides of the African American rights movement of the mid-twentieth century. In that case, proponents of civil rights were bringing litigation into the state and federal courts, while opponents of race-neutral policies were attempting to use the legislative authority of the state and national legislatures to thwart rapid social change. This is much the same situation that exists today; it is the judicial branch primarily that has been leading the charge to confer equal rights on gay Americans, while state and federal legislation to ban same-sex marriages has found support in the legislative branch. According to Elon University professor of women's history and African American history Mary Jo Festle, writing in an essay in *The Gay and Lesbian Review Worldwide*,

> we are in a historic period somewhat comparable to the African-American struggle for justice in the mid-1950s. At that crucial turning point, African Americans were enjoying some important gains but still endured blatantly discriminatory laws and practices, notably in the South. . . . Although racism and homophobia are different animals, and the context now surely differs from the 1960s, the black Civil Rights Movement has many lessons for us, whether we are GLBT movement strategists or just average people who care about equality.[5]

Brandeis professor E. J. Graff disagrees to some extent that the movement for gay rights parallels the movement for civil rights for African Americans. He notes that whereas gay men and lesbians frequently mirror their heterosexual counterparts with regard to economic and social status, African Americans have not enjoyed the same kind of parity with those of European descent in the United States.[6]

Nevertheless, there are parallels between the two movements. Both movements rely on the language of the Fourteenth Amendment's Due Process and Equal Protection clauses to support their equality claims. Those provisions of the Fourteenth Amendment prohibit any state from denying to citizens the rights and protections enjoyed by any other citizens. Although the Fourteenth Amendment was written to protect former slaves from racially inspired discrimination, its protections have been expanded over time to protect other political minorities from discrimination.

---

[5]Mary Jo Festle, "Listening to the Civil Rights Movement," *The Gay & Lesbian Review Worldwide* 12.6 (November-December 2005): 10(5).

[6]E. J. Graff, "How the Culture War Was Won: Lesbians and Gay Men Defeated the Right in the 1990s, But Tougher Battles Lie Ahead, " *The American Prospect* 13.19 (October 21, 2002): 33(4).

Another important similarity between the racial equality and gay rights move-ments is the extent to which courts in the states and at the federal level paved the way for rights for both groups. For example, it was the Supreme Court's decisions in 1954 and 1955 in *Brown v. Board of Education I* and *II* that ultimately led desegregation efforts in the states. The *Brown* decisions came nearly six decades after an earlier decision by the Supreme Court in *Plessy v. Ferguson* (1896) that allowed that black and white citizens could legally be kept from one another in public places; because the rulings in *Brown* overturned *Plessy*, they were heralded as truly landmark deci-sions. However, the Court's decisions did not in and of themselves lead to increased civil rights for African Americans; instead, it took legislative action both within the states and ultimately at the federal level to ensure equality. And this legislative action did not come without protracted battles over the issue of granting full equality to all citizens regardless of the color of their skin.

Similar to its decision in *Plessy*, the Supreme Court issued a decision ninety years later in *Bowers v. Hardwick* (1986), which declared that the U.S. Constitution does not provide equal protection for homosexuals. Likely because homosexuals in America are more similar to their heterosexual counterparts in terms of socioeco-nomic status and, ultimately, political power than were African Americans in the early twentieth century, it took far less time for the Court to overturn its decision in *Bowers*. In 2004, the Supreme Court revisited its *Bowers* decision in the case of *Lawrence v. Texas*. In this case, two homosexual men contested the state of Texas's criminalization of private, consensual homosexual conduct. In striking down the law, and overturning the *Bowers* decision, Associate Justice Anthony Kennedy wrote for the majority:

> *Bowers* was not correct when it was decided, and it is not correct today. It ought not to remain binding precedent. *Bowers v. Hardwick* should be and now is overruled. . . . The petitioners are entitled to respect for their private lives. The State cannot demean their existence or control their destiny by making their private sexual conduct a crime. Their right to liberty under the Due Process Clause gives them the full right to engage in their conduct without intervention of the government.

Because of the broad language Justice Kennedy used in his opinion, some political observers have speculated that the precedent established in *Lawrence* might one day be used to justify a Supreme Court decision legalizing gay marriage.

Conclusion

The movement for equality for homosexuals has made substantial progress in the last two decades. In that time period, there have been significant changes to state and fed-eral laws that previously had been invoked to prevent gays and lesbians from sharing the rights enjoyed by heterosexuals. This is a relatively short time frame when com-pared with the movement for civil rights that was fought more than seventy years by African Americans and other racial minorities. The relatively rapid success to date for the gay rights movement may be the result of the similarity of homosexual couples to heterosexual couples in terms of their demographic and socioeconomic characteristics. Moreover, because the movement for gay rights has been character-ized not only as a social issue but also in terms of economic parity, proponents of equality for homosexuals have been able to debate changes in social policy on grounds that are more comfortable for opponents. This has likely contributed to the gains made by gay men and lesbians since the mid-1980s.

Nevertheless, the movement for rights for gay men and lesbians has to some extent mirrored the struggle that has confronted other groups that have sought civil and political equality over U.S. history. Gains made in the judicial branch have been counteracted by anti–gay rights legislation at both the federal and state levels, and several states have amended their constitutions to ban gay marriage. Although the U.S. Congress has thus far been unable to pass a constitutional amendment to ban gay marriage nationally, proposals are introduced annually in Congress to do so. Thus, the movement for gay and lesbian rights, while progressing rapidly when compared with previous social movements, still faces substantial opposition.

THE RHETORICAL PERSPECTIVE

Social movements are "messy." They involve many people who communicate using various media as well as their symbolic actions. These movements can extend over decades. Within such movements, there are obviously instances of discourse that a rhetorician might study. The goal, however, of understanding the rhetoric of social movements is not to be met by simply studying selected texts. The goal requires understanding how, over the many years, those involved in the movement (the rhetors) get their message(s) out to various audiences with the goal of persuading them to embrace the movement's ideas. Once a given movement's rhetorical story is known, then, to meet the goal fully, rhetoricians would have to set that story next to the stories of other movements. The task is a daunting one—and one rhetorical scholars have not yet completed.

Here, in brief, is what a rhetorician might do. Stepping back from the gay-les-bian movement and keeping other well-known American social movements in mind, rhetoricians might posit the following eight generalizations about the rhetoric of social movements.

Traditional Texts

First, a social movement will have its crucial traditional texts. A traditional text might be a speech, but it might also be a book, an article, or even a pamphlet. The Civil Rights movement had speeches by Martin Luther King, Jr., Malcolm X, and Stokely Carmichael. The women's movement had the classic texts by Simone De Beauvoir and Kate Millett. The antiwar movement had mainstream speeches by the likes of

Senator Wayne Morse of Oregon and Senator Eugene McCarthy of Minnesota as well as many pamphlets authored and distributed by the radical Students for a Democratic Society (SDS) and other antiwar groups that popped up. Vilification and legitimization, two strategies Arthur Smith finds in Civil Rights rhetoric, are common throughout these texts.[7] We learn who the enemy is, and we learn "who's got it right." In the terms used by Bowers, Ochs, and Jensen, these texts enact three phases in the rhetoric of agitation: they promulgate the movement's principles, they solidify its members, and set it against the "enemy" and thereby polarize matters.[8]

Early in the gay-lesbian movement, Kinsey's *Sexual Behavior in the Human Male* (1948) and Cory's *The Homosexual in America* (1951) played a major role in depathologizing homosexuality in the eyes of homosexuals. That legitimizing role was also played by the periodicals *One* and *The Ladder*, although the second retreated from radicalism in the mid-1960s. The Homosexual Bill of Rights, written and adopted in 1968, was an important manifesto, but perhaps more influential—because externally addressed—were the mainstream "texts" "The Gay Vote" (in *The New Republic* in 1972) and "That Certain Summer" (on ABC that same year). At this point, the gay-lesbian movement needed to be legitimized both in the eyes of its participants and in the eyes of the society at large.

The AIDS crisis prompted its own crucial texts. Larry Kramer's "1,112 and Counting," which first appeared in 1983 in *The New York Native* and was reprinted in many gay publications, used shocking rhetoric to wake up the gay community to the AIDS crisis.[9] More mainstream were the 1987 *And The Band Played On* by Randy Shilts and the 1979 *Reports from the Holocaust* by Larry Kramer.

Crucial Moments

Second, a social movement will have its crucial moments of communication. These will be moments of triumph as well as ones reflecting struggle. The Civil Rights movement had the 1963 March on Washington as well as bus boycotts in Montgomery, Alabama, and luncheonette sit-ins in Greensboro, North Carolina. The women's movement had the Seneca Falls Convention back in 1848 and the election of several women to the U.S. Senate in 1992, the "Year of the Woman."[10] The antiwar movement had numerous demonstrations, none as riveting as those that occurred in Chicago during the 1968 Democratic National Convention. The antiwar movement also had the tragic shootings of student demonstrators at Kent State University in May 1970. All of these moments sent a message.

---

[7]Arthur Smith, *Rhetoric of Black Revolution* (Boston: Allyn and Bacon, 1969).

[8]John W. Bowers, Donovan J. Ochs, and Richard J. Jensen, *The Rhetoric of Agitation and Control*, 2nd ed. (Prospect Heights, IL: Waveland, 1993).

[9]For a close reading on Kramer's article, see Bonnie J. Dow, "AIDS, Perspective by Incongruity, and Gay Identity in Larry Kramer's '1,112 and Counting," *Communication Studies* 45 (1994): 225–40.

[10]See Barbara Mikulski et al., *Nine and Counting: The Women of the Senate* (New York: Perennial, 2001).

Observers may well disagree on what the crucial moments have been in the gay and lesbian rights movement. Bill Moyer terms such moments "triggers"; James Darsey calls them "catalysts."[11] So, they obviously both speak and do. Frank Kameny's story, although it extended over many years, might be one. He was fired, and he sued. When the U.S. Supreme Court refused to hear his final appeal in 1961, he took the movement in a more militant direction. A San Francisco costume ball in 1965 might be one, as might demonstrations held in Washington, DC, that same year. Most certainly, the Stonewall Riot in 1969 was a crucial moment as was the first Gay Pride Day celebrated in 1971. After 1971, the movement experienced a number of successes as the American Psychiatric Association, the American Bar Association, the National Teachers Association, and the U.S. Civil Service Commission altered their prejudicial or discriminatory stances. And the movement became—arguably—complacent. Anita Bryant's "Save Our Children" campaign in Florida and the Briggs Initiative in California certainly triggered renewed activism, culminating in a turnout of 250,000 for the Gay Pride Day rally in San Francisco in 1978. The next year, the first national gay rights march on Washington, which drew 100,000, might be a crucial moment; but, certainly, the 1987 march, which drew 500,000, was. Post-1987, there have been lows—the passage by Congress in 1996 of the Defense of Marriage Act and the murder of gay student Matthew Shepard in 1998. There have also been highs—the passage by Congress in 1990 of the Hate Crimes Statistics Act and the passage by Vermont in 2000 of its Acts Relating to Civil Unions, which was followed by pro-gay/lesbian actions by the "Big 3" automakers and Coca-Cola to extend benefits to same-sex partners of their employees.

All of these moments both conveyed a message and had an effect on the movement: they spoke and *did*. Darsey suggests that truly crucial moments also constrain discourse, focusing it on a particular matter, and become part of the movement's rhetoric for years to come. Those criteria would certainly push the Stonewall Riot, the defeat of the Briggs Initiative, and the 1987 march on Washington to the top of the list—along with an event not listed in the previous paragraph: the death of actor Rock Hudson in 1985. That death not only alerted the gay community and the larger community to the reality of AIDS—something the very radical "1,112 and Counting" had not accomplished, but it also gave the movement a focus it sustained for a decade.

Rhetorical Leaders

Third, a social movement will have its rhetorical leaders.[12] The Civil Rights movement had Martin Luther King, Malcolm X, Stokely Carmichael, and others. The women's movement had, early on, Elizabeth Cady Stanton, and, in more recent times, Gloria Steinem, Betty Friedan, and Ti-Grace Atkinson. The antiwar movement had

[11]Bill Moyer, *Doing Democracy: The MAP Model for Organizing Social Movements* (Gabriola Island, BC, Canada: New Society Publishers, 2001); James Darsey, "From 'Gay is Good' to the Scourge of AIDS: The Evolution of Gay Liberation Rhetoric," *Communication Studies* 42 (1991): 43–66.

[12]Bill Moyer in *Doing Democracy: The MAP Model for Organizing Social Movements* lists and describes four different roles, all of which have a rhetorical component: citizen, rebel, reformer, and change agent.

mainstream politicians, but also radicals such as The Chicago Seven and Veterans Against the War, with its spokesman John Kerry.

The gay and lesbian movement had early leaders in Frank Kameny and Barbara Gittings. Both represented radical voices that were, perhaps, too much so for the movement. Kameny's "Gay is Good" just did not catch on as well as "Black is Beautiful," and Gittings lost her position as editor of *The Ladder* in 1965. Later, Larry Kramer and Randy Shilts took a leading role in alerting the gay community to AIDS and crusading against both the community's and the government's inaction. However, in general, the gay and lesbian movement has not had strong individual leaders. Certainly, early on, there was a stigma associated with "coming out." Perhaps that stigma still exists and constrains individuals from assuming rhetorical leadership. The few mainstream political figures who have been openly gay or lesbian have typically not positioned themselves as movement leaders, the exception being San Francisco Mayor Harvey Milk, who was assassinated.

Confrontational Strategies

Fourth, a social movement will employ some confrontational strategies. It must do so to both provoke conversation (and, then, action) and gain media attention. The Civil Rights movement had its bus boycotts, sit-ins, and marches. The women's movement had its "Take Back the Night" marches. The antiwar movement staged guerilla theatre. As described by Bowers, Ochs, and Jensen, movements tend to progress from nonviolent to more overtly confrontational strategies.

Like other social movements, the gay-lesbian rights movement has relied on marches and rallies. They also staged what one might term their own variation on guerilla theatre—"zaps." These were quick, somewhat comical hits at establishment venues, such as media offices. The *CBS Evening News with Walter Cronkite* was even "zapped." The atmosphere surrounding these events exhibited a carnivalesque irreverence. Back in the early 1970s, Saul D. Alinsky wrote *Rules for Radicals: A Practical Primer for Realistic Radicals*. He recommended that, in choosing confrontational strategies, radical groups take the establishment outside its comfort zone and that groups use tactics its members enjoy. The "zaps" would seem to fulfill Alinksy's prescription.[13] More recently, the movement has staged mass marriages of same-sex couples. They have thereby taken advantage of the few opportunities they have had to wed, but they've also visually confronted those who have seen these events with the reality of gay and lesbian couples.

Paths in Time

Fifth, social movements follow similar but not identical paths, with times of triumph, complacency, backlash, despair, and reenergizing or redirecting characteristic of most if not all long-term movements. The Civil Rights movement, for example,

---

[13]See Saul D. Alinsky, *Rules for Radicals: A Practical Primer for Realistic Radicals* (New York: Random House, 1971). See especially the chapter entitled "Tactics," pp. 126–64.

experienced triumphs as Congress passed several pieces of landmark legislation in the mid-1960s. The movement may have become complacent and, then, experienced a backlash after American cities erupted into flaming riots after Dr. King's assassination in 1968 and Americans became concerned about the violence. The women's movement, after overcoming many sexist barriers in the 1970s, may have become complacent. In this country, a focus on gendered violence and lingering workplace discrimination has reenergized the movement somewhat; however, it has also experienced backlashes from both some women, who reject the term "feminist," and some men, who label feminists "femi-Nazis." The antiwar movement scared many voters into supporting Nixon-Agnew in 1968 and 1972. Then, the movement faded, only to be reenergized by George W. Bush's military adventures in Afghanistan and Iraq.

The gay-lesbian movement slowly gained energy in the 1950s. In the 1960s, it became more radical. Police action against a New York City gay bar, The Stonewall, led to a fiery riot that galvanized the movement. So steeled, the movement was triumphant on the first Gay Pride Day in 1971 and upon the end to discrimination by mainstream groups such as the American Psychiatric Association. Then, there was complacency as well as a something of a split between gay and lesbian groups; then, there was the backlash of Anita Bryant's "Save Our Children" movement and the Briggs Initiative directed against California's gay-lesbian teachers. This assault brought the splintering movement back together, and its triumph over the backlash reenergized the movement, but then it quickly fell back into complacency. It took AIDS to rally it again. Then, after the 1987 march on Washington, further complacency—even some despair as AIDS took its toll and the "establishment" did little. Recently, the related issues of benefits for same-sex partners, civil unions, and gay marriage have reenergized—and redirected—the movement. This movement's numerous ups and downs may make it an extreme case of what we see in social movements in general, or the roller-coaster rhythm may just be a reflection of how long the movement has existed.

Inward Direction

Sixth, social movements feature as much (if not more) discourse that is inwardly directed as is outwardly directed. Much material from all of the noteworthy American social movements received little attention from outside—because it was not directed outside. For example, within the women's movement, a large body of poetry and song circulated in cheaply published collections. And even some communication that we all read when studying the Civil Rights movement—Malcolm X's call to arms and Stokely Carmichael's call to black pride—had as its primary audience those in the movement, not those outside. A primary function of this inwardly directed writing was, of course, the ongoing solidification of the movement.

The gay-lesbian movement had—and has—its own journalism. Cities have gay and lesbian newspapers, and there were—and are—transmunicipal papers as well. To understand the discourse of the movement one must follow the lead of Darsey and look closely at the pages of these periodicals. Doing so is important because, often, social movements achieve their greatest successes internally. The rhetoric persuades those who are part of the movement that they are not "sick," that "gay is good," and that AIDS is not, as the religious right claimed in the 1980s, the wrath of God. These are not inconsequential rhetorical successes either, for although changes in laws would affect a group's public life, changes in self-assessment affect each member's very person.

Different Values at Different Times

Seventh, a social movement's discourse, especially that inwardly directed, will stress different values at different points in the movement's history. One might conjecture that, in the rhetoric of the Civil Rights movement, the Southern Christian Leadership Conference's emphasis on justice led to the Student Non-violent Coordinating Committee's emphasis on pride; then, after the 1968 riots and the law-and-order atmosphere of the Nixon-Agnew years, pride led to an emphasis on determination and work.

We need work comparable to that by Darsey on the gay-lesbian movement for the other American social movements. Darsey uses content analytical techniques to discern what the dominant values or themes were at different points in the movement. So, early on in the gay-lesbian rights movement, he finds an emphasis on truthfulness—this at a point when gays and lesbians, as well as the larger audience, needed to know the truth that homosexuality was not a sickness. After the "Save Our Children" backlash, he finds unity dominant followed by the cluster of work, determination, and strength. At that point, the movement needed to hold together and keep at it. Responding to the Reagan administration, the rhetoric deemphasized unity: evidently, responding to "Save Our Children" and the Briggs Initiative had unified the movement again. The dominant values became work, determination, and strength followed by achievement. At this point, the movement needed to be sustained; thus, the discourse pushed while reminding those reading or listening of what had been accomplished. Post-AIDS, work, determination, and strength remained dominant, but they were joined by justice, truthfulness, safety and security, and tolerance. The movement's focus had shifted from rights in general to rights in the context of an AIDS epidemic. Hard work was necessary, but so were justice and tolerance on the parts of those in power and truthfulness and safety on the parts of those who could be exposed to AIDS. Darsey's overall point is that the rhetorical exigence causes the themes of social movement discourse to shift. Sometimes a movement needs to work; sometimes, it needs to be reborn.

Dependent on Those with Power

Eighth, a social movement, no matter how enthusiastic, is dependent for its success on cultural and governmental institutions that, although not always hostile, do not always share the movement's agenda. Fortunately for the Civil Rights movement, the relatively new medium of television needed the kinds of highly dramatic, highly visual stories the movement produced to help stake its claim to journalistic legitimacy. The antiwar movement and the women's movement, unfortunately, had to rely on the sensationalistic to get attention. In the latter case, the most sensationalistic event covered, massive bra burnings, never actually took place. In that case, the media distorted the movement.

The political climate eventually turned warm for the Civil Rights movement, as President Lyndon B. Johnson pushed landmark legislation through the Congress. Then, the climate turned chilly—with statewide candidates running against equal housing and national and statewide candidates running against school busing to achieve integration and with a new emphasis on law and order, an emphasis often racially tinged. The women's movement found periodic support in government circles, but it was far from constant. The antiwar movement has needed a war and, then, time to generate opposition to that war. It has not sustained that political support during times of peace when wars are usually embarked upon.

The gay-lesbian movement has received media coverage for its marches and rallies. Its "zaps" helped it gain more. Rock Hudson's death attracted the media, and the cause of AIDS sufferers was helped. Matthew Shepard's murder attracted the media, and the cause of stopping hate crimes was aided. But the media has needed "a good story," and it has not always been there. In addition, some good stories—gay men parading in "S and M" leather or attending costume balls in drag—have received coverage, prompting "concern" among the straight community and internal bickering about "image" among the gay community.

The political battles that have dominated the gay-lesbian movement have been more local. Through the years, they have seen victories and defeats when it comes to local antidiscriminatory ordinances. Only recently have gays turned their attention to the federal level. In 1990 the Hate Crimes Statistics Act was a positive, but six years later the Defense of Marriage Act was a negative. In 2000, President Bill Clinton addressed (safely, via videotape) the Millennium March on Washington for Equality, and that was a positive. In 2004 President George W. Bush called for the protection of marriage as a union between a man and a woman through a constitutional amendment, and that was a negative. The gay-lesbian movement has also had positive and negative experiences in its dealings with the U.S. Supreme Court as the preceding political science perspective noted.

Conclusion

The rhetorical study of social movements has not yet reached the point at which scholars can say what is common and, then, look at the extent a given movement conforms to or departs from this norm. One can, nonetheless, conjecture as to what those common threads might be and examine the gay-lesbian liberation movement in those terms.

The movement then has its traditional texts and its important moments. It has had rhetorical leaders, but not to the extent other American social movements have. It has confronted audiences with its messages using conventional (e.g., marches) and unconventional (e.g., "zaps") methods. Its path through time has seen many ups and downs—perhaps more so than other movements. The values stressed in its communication have changed through time, based on a given time's rhetorical exigence. Like other movements, its message has frequently been inwardly directed, and that message has succeeded in changing the self-assessment of gays and lesbians. And, like other movements, it has ultimately been dependent on those with power—media and government—for visibility and success.

THE MASS COMMUNICATION PERSPECTIVE

The time line in the introduction to this chapter highlights a number of events that garnered considerable news media attention. Some issues and concerns may be common in the coverage of any social movement, when a group seeks public recognition, and perhaps media attention, for its cause. Looking at the coverage of the AIDS crisis since the 1980s, as well as the contemporary issues of covering gay marriage, newsrooms have faced a number of issues and decisions regarding news coverage of gays, lesbians, bisexuals, and transgender individuals.

Media Coverage of Social Movements

Media coverage of protests or demonstrations may be a double-edged sword. A group may desire media attention and coverage, but it may not in the end be satisfied by how the group was portrayed by that coverage. Many of the activities garnering media attention from the time line in the chapter introduction involved violence in terms of protestors clashing with police or arrests being made, which provide compelling visuals for news coverage. William Gamson (1989) suggests that to gain media attention, social movements may construct events or responses that provide action footage to appeal particularly to television news coverage.[14] He says that "to keep media attention, challengers are tempted to ever more extravagant and dramatic actions— regardless of their contribution to the challenger's goals" (p. 465).

In their analysis of 40 years of news coverage of protests, Boyle, McCluskey, McLeod, and Stein (2005) identify a number of motivations for social movements working to gain media attention:[15]

> Often, social movement groups use events such as marches, rallies, or demonstrations to attract media coverage to reach both the public and elected officials. Coverage can allow groups to disseminate information, frame movements, and shape official and public perceptions. (p. 638)

[14]William A. Gamson, "Reflections on the Strategy of Social Protest," *Sociological Forum* 4 (1989): 455–67.

[15]Michael P. Boyle, Michael R. McCluskey, Douglas M. McLeod, and Sue E. Stein, "Newspapers and Protest: An Examination of Protest Coverage from 1960 to 1999," *Journalism and Mass Communication Quarterly* 82.3 (2005): 638–53.

However, Boyle and colleagues also identify that many social movements struggle to receive any media attention for their events or issues, and when the news media does cover them, that coverage may often be negative toward the organization. Specifically they suggest that the more "protest groups threaten the status quo, the more harshly they will be treated by the media" (p. 639).

The framing of participants in protests or marches as deviant is a consistent pattern in news coverage of social movements. Todd Gitlin's analysis[16] of news coverage of the antiwar movement in the 1960s found a number of ways protestors were portrayed as deviant in coverage of the antiwar movement. McLeod and Hertog also found media coverage of social movements involved framing protestors as violating mainstream norms and laws and portraying protestors in contrast to bystanders, who witnessed events and often commented negatively on them in news reports.[17]

Another way a particular segment of the population may feel marginalized from society is not by negative coverage in the media, or being treated as deviant, but by being ignored as a population with its own voice. Whereas racial groups such as Latinos or Asian Americans would offer the same complaint, historically gays and lesbians have been excluded from mainstream news reports except for those dealing with particular issues such as AIDS or gay marriage legislation. An analysis of 50 years of *Time* and *Newsweek* magazines from 1947 to 1997 found little coverage of gays and lesbians before the movements of the 1970s.[18] Since then, mainstream news coverage has steadily increased, although the majority of stories continue to focus on controversies such as employment discrimination and gays in the military.

This past research, although not on social movements involving gay and lesbian issues specifically, offers us a framework to understand coverage of gay pride parades in many communities, as well as the coverage of the AIDS crisis and gay marriage initiatives debated in many states.

Media Coverage of AIDS

The AIDS story has been driven by a series of big, attention-grabbing events. In the early years, it was the effect on the blood supply and debate over San Francisco bathhouses being shut down. Next came the public infections of Rock Hudson and Magic Johnson, followed by a pair of very large events, the discovery of the drugs that have staved off death for so many people, and finally, by the AIDS devastation in Africa.[19]

---

[16]Todd Gitlin, *The Whole World is Watching: Mass Media in the Making and Unmaking of the New Left* (Berkeley: University of California Press, 1980).

[17]Doug M. McLeod, and James K. Hertog, "The Manufacture of Public Opinion by Reporters: Informal Cues for Public Perceptions of Protest Groups," *Discourse and Society* 3 (1992): 259–75.

[18]Lisa Bennett, "Fifty Years of Prejudice in the Media," *Gay and Lesbian Review Worldwide* 7.2 (2000): 30.

[19]Kai Wright, "AIDS: Hiding in Plain Sight," *Columbia Journalism Review* 42.6 (March/April 2004): 5.

The above description from a *Columbia Journalism Review* analysis omits some key events and factors of coverage, but it does encapsulate primary patterns of coverage of AIDS we have seen in the United States. Although heterosexual men and women have also contracted HIV and developed AIDS, the syndrome was first identified in gay men, and has continued to be framed by the media as a "gay disease." We have seen reports of the treatments for AIDS, often referring to the dozens of pills an individual needs to take each day as a "cocktail," which softens the notion of an aggressive treatment that produces its own side effects.

In true agenda-setting patterns of media and public opinion, declining media attention on AIDS has occurred at the same time that public opinion concern over AIDS has also dropped. The Kaiser Family Foundation has conducted one of the most extensive analyses of media coverage of AIDS, as well as public opinion on the subject.[20] They found in examining public opinion that the percentage of people who believe HIV/AIDS is the "most urgent health problem facing the nation/world" has declined from 68 percent in 1987 to 17 percent in 2002. Replacing HIV/AIDS in public concern has been cancer, health care costs, health insurance, and access to health care.

Kaiser's study also found a consistent decline in media coverage of AIDS since 1987. Although there have been slight "peaks" in the coverage since 1987, such as the FDA approval of protease inhibitors for the treatment of AIDS in 1996, media attention has continued to decline. The study suggests that the pattern of declining coverage confirms a media "fatigue" in covering the AIDS story. When the nature of the syndrome shifted from an epidemic to a disease people can manage with treatment, and when attention shifted from the United States to a global focus on AIDS as seen predominantly in the 1990s, the AIDS story became more routine and not as newsworthy. Lehrman suggests that coverage of AIDS has continued to decline since the *New York Times Magazine* published "The End of AIDS: The Twilight of an Epidemic" in 1996.[21] Lehrman also identifies one consequence of the declining and sometimes inaccurate coverage: waning public concern over AIDS. Such disinterest may be the cause of declining fund-raising as well as ignorance among people who might be at risk of contracting HIV.

Early in the AIDS crisis, media coverage sparked a new focus of some within the gay and lesbian movement. Media coverage of the gay and lesbian community launched a new form of media activism, focusing on the stereotypes contained in media reports, as well as the lack of representation of gays and lesbians in mass media. In response to media coverage, GLAAD, the Gay and Lesbian Alliance Against Defamation, was formed in 1985. The activist group began amid protests

---

[20]Mollyann Brodie, Elizabeth Hamel, Lee Ann Brady, Jennifer Kates, and Drew E. Altman, "AIDS at 21: Media Coverage of the HIV Epidemic 1981–2002." Supplement to *Columbia Journalism Review* 42.6 (March/April 2004): 1–8.

[21]Sally Lehrman, "AIDS Coverage Has Been Lost in Recent Years," *Quill Magazine* 92.2 (March 2004): 24–25.

against the *New York Post* for its negative coverage of people with AIDS. GLAAD and others accused the *Post* of homophobic coverage of HIV, which referred to gay bars as "AIDS dens" in one instance. GLAAD continues to work today to criticize as well as celebrate accuracy and representation of gays and lesbians in news media as well as entertainment content.

Media Coverage of Gay Marriage

Following the June 2006 failed Senate vote for the Marriage Protection Amendment, which would have defined marriage as exclusively between one man and one woman (49 were in favor, 48 opposed, but it needed a two thirds majority), CNN.com published a commentary criticizing the news organizations' role in the vote failure. James Dobson, founder of Focus on the Family, authored a commentary titled "Media provides cover for assault on traditional marriage" and blamed the media for the vote result:

> Rarely has there been a greater disconnect between members of the Senate and the American people who put them in power. With the help of the media, which laid down "cover" by claiming voters didn't care about marriage, 40 Democrats, one Independent and seven Republicans turned their backs on this most basic social institution.[22]

Although there have not been any guidelines from the Associated Press (the most common source of newsroom style rules) for covering gay marriage, GLAAD recommends the use of "marriage rights for same-sex couples" in news coverage rather than to contrast gay marriage to traditional marriage. A LexisNexis search of the *New York Times* and *Washington Post* for 2005 found that more often the phrase "gay marriage" is used than "civil union." In articles that included these phrases in either the headline or lead paragraph, the *New York Times* used "gay marriage" in seventy articles in 2005, whereas the *Washington Post* included the phrase in forty-five articles. The use of "civil union" by the *New York Times* appeared in twenty-six articles, although this included some announcements, and the *Washington Post* had fifteen articles that used the phrase "civil union." Similar patterns were found in an analysis of news stories in the two months before the 2000 elections, in which "homosexual marriage" was used in news stories considerably more often than was "gay civil union," although some news stories included both terms.[23]

In a study of the effects of framing of this issue, Price, Nir, and Cappella examined how two frames often used in the news media shape how citizens think about

---

[22]James C. Dobson, "Media Provides Cover for Assault on Traditional Marriage," June 28, 2006. http://www.cnn.com/2006/US/06/28/dobson.gaymarriage/index.html, para. 3.

[23]Vincent Price, Lilach Nir, and Joseph. N. Cappella, "Framing Public Discussion of Gay Civil Unions," *Public Opinion Quarterly* 69.2 (2005): 179–212.

and talk about the issue. They found political ideology influenced reactions to these two frames ("homosexual marriage/special rights," and "civil union/equal rights"), with the "homosexual marriage" frame in particular leading to ideological polarization.

Newsroom Decisions

One specific aspect of the gay marriage controversy that has led to decisions in many newsrooms is the coverage of gay marriage in wedding announcements. A growing number of newspapers have accepted same-sex ceremony announcements for publication, with more than 500 U.S. newspapers doing so in 2004, according to GLAAD. The policy in many newsrooms has been that if same-sex marriages are legally recognized in the state, the newspaper will publish the announcement. Two of the United States' most prestigious and high-profile newspapers, the *New York Times* and the *Washington Post*, both began publishing same-sex union announcements in 2002 and 2003, respectively.

Identifying someone as gay or lesbian in an obituary has also been the focus of many newsroom debates, with many questions of "outing" an individual in an obituary. Most newsroom policies are to follow the wishes of the individual if stated before death, or of the family after an individual has died. This issue arose in many newsrooms, as well as journalism trade publications, following the death of essayist and novelist Susan Sontag, as many obituaries made no mention of her bisexuality, including a relationship with photographer Annie Leibovitz. The *New York Times* responded to critiques that they could not find a source to confirm details of the relationship and therefore omitted it. In a panel discussion on the issue at the convention of the National Lesbian and Gay Journalists Association (NLGJA), *Washington Post* Style writer Hank Stuever changed the focus of the issue, stating, "Instead of all the blogging about how badly newspapers do in covering gay people in obits—we should focus on how badly newspapers do in covering gay people who are alive."[24]

Finally, newsrooms have made progress toward policies regarding identifying sexual orientation within news stories outside of the above types of announcements. Similar to criticism against news media for identifying the race of individuals in news stories, in particular in crime stories, newsrooms have had to make decisions about reporting an individual's sexual orientation as well. Most newsrooms identify a person's race if it is pertinent to the story, and this same policy is often used for identifying a person's sexual orientation. If the story is on gay marriage or another issue with direct impact on gays or lesbians, a news report would likely identify those news sources who are gay, lesbian, bisexual, or transgender, but would not do so in other news stories.

---

[24]Mark Fitzgerald, "Bring 'Out' Your Dead," *Editor and Publisher* (September 26, 2005), para 15.

Conclusion

As in other social movements, gay and lesbian issues have been either ignored by news media or covered as being deviant in some way as a group "out of the mainstream" of society. The AIDS crisis is one example of considerable news coverage that followed such patterns, and it also had agenda-setting effects on declining public concern over the disease. Finally, news coverage of gay marriage, as well as gay and lesbians in other stories, has required newsrooms to discuss and determine policy on a number of coverage issues in wedding announcements, obituaries, and general daily news.

CONCLUSION

Social movements are important insofar as they can effect change in American society. The political scientist looks for the change in the law. The ongoing debate over homosexual marriage is a good example of how such change can occur. Initially, advocates treated the matter as a social issue and evoked opponents' ire, but once they shifted the focus to equal protection and economic parity, they found an ally in the courts. This progress was similar to that characteristic of the Civil Rights movement but more rapid, suggesting that despite deeply held attitudes about sexual orientation heterosexuals have been quicker to find common ground with homosexuals than whites with blacks.

The rhetorician also both examines the particular movement and compares it to others. The rhetorician's focus is less on the law and more on how the movement "works." In the case of the gay-lesbian rights movement, it works much as others insofar as it has its important texts, dramatic moments, rhetorical leaders, ups and downs, changes in expressed values, occasional inward focus, and dependence on those with greater power for its ultimate success.

The media have this very power. Unfortunately, there is a tendency for the media to either ignore or treat as out-of-the-mainstream those whom many social movements crusade on behalf of. The media's treatment of AIDS exemplifies this process. However, as in the case of AIDS, the very fact of media coverage can have an agenda-setting function, prompting changes in public policy. At present, the issue of homosexual marriage is prompting not only news coverage but also discussions within media organizations about seemingly trivial matters, such as obituaries and marriage announcements.

All then who look at social movements are concerned with both their effects and how these effects are achieved. Whether the focus is on court decisions, internal organizational activity, or media coverage, the overriding question is how and to what extent did the movements effect social and political change.

ADDITIONAL CASES

Students who wish to consider additional social movements might want to look at the following:

- **The U.S. Civil Rights Movement**
- **The Anti–Nuclear Energy Movement**
- **The Breast Cancer Social Movement**
- **The Anti-Global Economy Movement**
- **The Women's Movement**

A good initial resource for the first four cases is Bill Moyer's *Doing Democracy: The MAP Model for Organizing Social Movements* (Gabriola Island, BC, Canada: New Society Publishers, 2001). Good initial resources for the last case are numerous. An overview of the movement can be found in Chapter 3 of Julia T. Wood's *Gendered Lives: Communication, Gender, and Culture*, 5th ed. (Belmont, CA: Wadsworth/Thompson, 2003). A particularly insightful discussion of the role of media in the movement is Bonnie J. Dow's *Prime-Time Feminism: Television, Media Culture, and the Women's Movement Since 1970* (Philadelphia: University of Pennsylvania Press, 1996).

■ ■ ■ ■ ■ ▬▬▬▬▬▬▬▬▬▬▬▬▬▬▬▬▬▬▬▬▬▬▬▬▬▬▬▬

CHAPTER 17

CASE THIRTEEN: POLITICS IN POPULAR CULTURE

THE CASE

Some might consider the following examples to be political fads, but the presence of popular culture in politics is not a new development. The current popular culture of music, film, television, and other forms of entertainment may have the potential to be influential in the political arena, which might be disturbing to many in politics. And there are likely pop culture connections with every event or person featured in the other case studies in this book. This chapter highlights and discusses a few particular examples of the relationship between popular culture and politics.

Comedy and Politics

Shortly after the Iowa caucus and Howard Dean's "scream" that was heard around the political world, thanks to broadcast television and the Internet, he recorded a Top Ten list for David Letterman's CBS *Late Show* in 2004, on "Ways I, Howard Dean, Can Turn Things Around." Number 10 on the list was "Switch to decaf" and Number 1 was "Oh, I don't know, maybe fewer crazy, red-faced rants?" Late-night comedy has enjoyed vast amounts of material from politics to use for jokes and skits.

It is safe to conclude that every presidency, or presidential campaign, has been parodied on NBC's *Saturday Night Live* since its inception in 1974. To name a few, Chevy Chase has played an uncoordinated Gerald Ford, Dan Akroyd portrayed Richard Nixon and Jimmy Carter, Randy Quaid featured Ronald Reagan, Dana Carvey played both George H. W. Bush and presidential candidate Ross Perot, Phil Hartman played Bill Clinton, and Will Ferrell and then Will Forte portrayed George W. Bush.

Presidential candidates have also appeared on SNL. Both Al Gore and George Bush taped a segment to open *Saturday Night Live*'s Presidential Bash 2000, which aired two days before Election Day. Gore returned (while not a candidate) to highlight his film *An Inconvenient Truth* in 2006. In 1996, candidates for the Republican nomination Steve Forbes, Lamar Alexander, and Bill Bradley all made appearances on the NBC comedy.

George W. Bush kids around with Dana Carvey, well known for his impersonation of George H. W. Bush, before the 2000 Saturday Night Live election special.

Jon Stewart took over *The Daily Show* on Comedy Central from Craig Kilbourn in 1999, and although we might associate this late-night comedy with its own "spin" on news, wacky correspondent reporters, and prominent guests for interviews, two elements related to the show came to prominence during the 2004 elections. In September 2004 Warner Books published *America (The Book): A Citizen's Guide to Democracy Inaction*, the creation of Stewart and *Daily Show* writers. The book provides *The Daily Show*'s interpretation of the history of democracy, mass media in America, and the 2004 elections. When published, the book immediately topped the *New York Times* best seller list and remained at number one for 18 consecutive weeks.

Jon Stewart received more media attention for an event not on his own show, but instead from his appearance on CNN's *Crossfire* (hosted by Democrat Paul Begala and Republican Tucker Carlson) in October 2004, in which Stewart transformed from a comic to a critic. Although the banter back and forth between Stewart, Begala, and Tucker is missing, the following are excerpts of Stewart's critique of *Crosstalk* while on the show[1]:

---

[1]The interchange among Stewart, Begala, and Tucker has been available online at websites such as www.ifilm.com and others. The excerpts of Stewart's comments come from CNN's transcript of the October 15, 2004, *Crossfire* program.

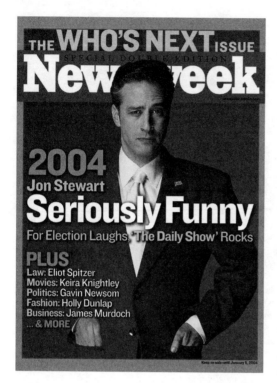

Newsweek suggests that Jon Stewart's The Daily Show has become a major source of political information for television viewers.

I think, oftentimes, the person that knows they can't win is allowed to speak the most freely, because, otherwise, shows with titles, such as CROSSFIRE or "HARDBALL" or "I'm Going to Kick Your Ass" or. . .

In many ways, it's funny. And I made a special effort to come on the show today, because I have privately, amongst my friends and also in occasional newspapers and television shows, mentioned this show as being bad. And I wanted to—I felt that that wasn't fair and I should come here and tell you that I don't—it's not so much that it's bad, as it's hurting America.

Here's just what I wanted to tell you guys. Stop, stop, stop, stop hurting America. See, the thing is, we need your help. Right now, you're helping the politicians and the corporations. And we're left out there to mow our lawns.

I didn't realize that—and maybe this explains quite a bit. . . . is that the news organizations look to Comedy Central for their cues on integrity.

But the thing is that this—you're doing theater, when you should be doing debate, which would be great. It's not honest. What you do is not honest. What you do is partisan hackery. And I will tell you why I know it. You know, the interesting thing I have is, you have a responsibility to the public discourse, and you fail miserably. You know, because we need what you do. This is such a great opportunity you have here to actually get politicians off of their marketing and strategy.

Stewart gave a similar critique of the media and lack of political discourse in an interview for the CBS news program *60 Minutes*, which was conducted before his *Crosstalk* appearance but aired after it.

Fiction and Politics

One example of the blurring of reality and fiction in politics involves a book published by Random House in January 1996. *Primary Colors: A Novel* was a fictional account of a presidential primary campaign, a *roman à clef*, believed to be based on Bill Clinton's campaign in 1992. With the main character described as a "womanizing, doughnut-eating Southerner seeking the presidency," some critics alleged a campaign staff member must be its author, given the similarities to the story and Clinton. In July 1996, after months of public denials, *Newsweek* columnist Joe Klein admitted being the author. In 1998, the book was turned into a film starring John Travolta (as Governor Jack Stanton) and Emma Thompson (as his wife and potential first lady).

We also have a number of contemporary portrayals of the presidency in feature films. In the 1993 film *Dave*, the president falls into a coma and rather than officials acknowledging that publicly, Kevin Kline's character becomes a substitute for the president whom he closely resembles. In 1995, Michael Douglas played a widowed president who falls in love with a lobbyist in *The American President*. Harrison Ford portrays the president in the 1997 film *Air Force One*, who deals with hijackers taking over the presidential aircraft. One example of politicians in film that suggests a connection between fiction and reality is Warren Beatty. The 1998 film *Bulworth* was written and directed by Warren Beatty, who also played the starring role of Senator Jay Bulworth. After he takes out a substantial life insurance policy and hires a hit man to kill him, Bulworth transforms into a politician who is not afraid to "tell it like it is" and critique elected officials, both the Democrats and Republicans, as well as the political campaign process. In 1999, Warren Beatty was contemplating a run for the presidency, according to Bill Hillsman,[2] who worked on the political advertising for Minnesota Senator Paul Wellstone, Minnesota Governor Jesse Ventura, and presidential candidate Ralph Nader, among others.

In stark contrast to the humorous portrayals of presidents we associate with *Saturday Night Live, The West Wing* was a drama that featured the fictional presidency of Democrat Jed Bartlet, played by Martin Sheen. *The West Wing*[3] premiered on September 22, 1999, the year Bill Clinton was impeached for lying under oath

---

[2]An account of Hillsman's meeting with Warren Beatty and discussion of a presidential campaign can be found in Bill Hillsman, *Run the Other Way: Fixing the Two-Party System, One Campaign at a Time* (New York: Free Press, 2004).

[3]The detailed Oval Office set used in *The West Wing* was originally constructed for the film *Dave* and also was used in *The American President*. It is reportedly such an accurate set that tour groups at Warner Brothers studios were not permitted through the set, out of White House security concerns.

about his affair with Monica Lewinsky. Originally, President Bartlet was to appear in only a handful of episodes per season, and the main focus of the program would be on the president's staff. After the pilot was filmed, the creators decided to feature Sheen as a regular cast member. *The West Wing* was a top-10 show from 1999 to 2002 and lasted for seven seasons until its conclusion on May 14, 2006. It received eighteen Emmy Awards during its run, including four consecutive wins for best television drama. When asked in the first season if creator Aaron Sorkin envisioned *The West Wing* to be teaching civics lessons to the audience, he responded:

> No! It's not my goal to get you to eat your vegetables. *The West Wing* isn't meant to be good for you. We're not doing an after-school special. I think government is, by definition, dramatic and very theatrical. I find an argument over the Census makes interesting dialogue that connects with the audience because the characters really are passionate about what they do. These are people going about work they love with great energy and wit.[4]

The short-lived drama *Commander in Chief* featured Geena Davis as the first female president. The drama premiered on September 27, 2005, and quickly ended on June 14, 2006. Davis's character, Mackenzie Allen, begins as the Vice President, an Independent, selected by a Republican president, who dies while in office. Although she is asked by the president to resign, she refuses and ascends to the presidency. The drama was created by Rod Lurie, director of the 2000 film *The Contender*, which featured Joan Allen as a female presidential candidate; Lurie reportedly planned the television drama as a sequel to the film.

Whether it is comedy, fiction, music, or other forms of entertainment fostered by new technology, we find popular culture and politics intertwined in many ways. Should we be concerned? One argument is that such connections degrade the images of political institutions they reflect, and another argument suggests that people who might otherwise be disinterested in politics may find some connection through popular culture and become more involved. Another argument by Michael Parenti in *Make-Believe Media: The Politics of Entertainment* raises still other issues:

> What the media actually give us is something that is neither purely entertainment nor purely political. It is a hybrid that might be called "political entertainment." The entertainment format makes political propagation all the more insidious. Beliefs are less likely to be preached than assumed. Woven into the story line and into the characterizations, they are perceived as entertainment rather than as political judgments about the world.[5]

---

[4]C.L. Grossman, Lessons in Entertainment: 'West Wing' Manages to Teach Civics without Going by the Textbook. *USA Today* (1999, Dec. 15), 9D.

[5]M. Parenti, *Make-Believe Media: The Politics of Entertainment* (New York: St. Martin's Press, 1992), 3.

THE POLITICAL SCIENCE PERSPECTIVE

Three months before the 2000 presidential election, in August 2000, the *Washington Post* ran a column on the front page of the Sunday editorial section, written by the newspaper's movie critic. Under the headline "You Don't Just Want a Leader, You Want a Leading Man," the column made this point:

> Life in America has been a movie for years. We've become so conditioned by the movies, we've fuzzed up the borders between dramatic truth and reality. . . . And that's why the electorate isn't going to vote for the candidate who will lead this country to a better health plan or eight more years of economic growth. We're voting Best Actor in a Movie of His Own Devising.[6]

The line between politics and entertainment has long been blurred. As we noted previously in Chapter 6 on Jesse Ventura, celebrity candidates are among the most successful amateur politicians. This is because the same characteristics that create celebrity buzz—gaining name recognition, being good looking, commanding media attention—are also important in seeking and winning public office. But politics and entertainment are intertwined in more ways than just elections. In particular, government and politics intersect with popular culture by affecting the ways in which people are socialized to think about politics and by influencing the regulatory processes that the government uses to monitor popular culture. Each of these will be discussed in more detail. However, it is worth noting that the regulatory and socialization processes are related to one another. Figure 17.1 offers a model of the relationships that exist between citizens, government, and popular culture. As the model indicates, citizens are both affected by popular culture and, through their elected and appointed officials, involved with the regulation of the messages they receive. The result of the network of relationships between citizens, government, and popular culture can be the reinforcement of particular ideas about politics—both positive and negative.

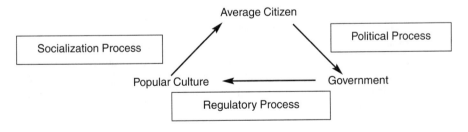

FIGURE 17.1

Source: Created by the authors.

[6]Desson Howe, "You Don't Just Want a Leader, You Want a Leading Man," *Washington Post* (August 6, 2000), B1.

Political Socialization

The term *political socialization* refers to the ways in which individuals gain knowledge about the political world and learn to orient themselves to politics. Political socialization is a lifetime learning process that for most individuals begins in their childhood and starts with their parents. Children learn whether politics is important to their family, which political party their parents support, and the extent to which they should participate in politics simply by absorbing messages their parents give them through their words and actions. These messages may be altered or reinforced as children enter elementary school. One consistent message that children receive through their primary school educations is that government is legitimate. For example, reciting the Pledge of Allegiance, learning about Betsy Ross or Francis Scott Key, or being taught about the "father of our country," George Washington, reinforces the existing political order.

As children mature and are exposed to political messages from outside the home or their schools, they begin to develop their own sense of political efficacy (the feeling that they can—or cannot—make a difference to the political environment). Many of the messages that adolescents and adults receive about the political world come from the media. Although this has long been the case, in recent decades the types of media and the types of messages have evolved to include parodies and satirical explorations concerning politics. According to data compiled from a January 2000 Pew Research Center for the People and the Press survey, 28 percent of Americans "regularly" or "sometimes" get their news about political campaigns from "comedy shows such as *Saturday Night Live* and *Politically Incorrect.*" Among voters aged 18 to 24, 45.4 percent "regularly" or "sometimes" get their news about political campaigns from such shows.[7]

The fact that large numbers of people get their news about political campaigns, or politics generally, from comedy shows has changed the ways in which people orient themselves to politics. According to recent studies, people who watch programs like *The Daily Show* and *Saturday Night Live* tend to have more negative perceptions of politicians and government and tend to believe less in the principle that their participation in politics matters than people who do not view such programs.[8] In addition, as the results of the Pew study cited previously indicate, younger viewers rely more heavily on late-night and comedic news sources for their information about politics. As Hollander (2005) notes, younger viewers are able to recognize that they have heard political information from these shows, although their recall of specific facts is less apparent from their survey responses. Hollander concludes:

[7]Pew Research Center for the People and the Press, "The Tough Job of Communicating with Voters," January 2000.

[8]See Jody Baumgartner and Jonathan S. Morris, "*The Daily Show* Effect: Candidate Evaluations, Efficacy, and American Youth," *American Politics Research* 34.3 (May 2006): 341(27).

As the political content of comedy and late-night television programs continues to rise, as does an audience turned off by mainstream news sources, then the significance of this exposure increases to the point where, for many, they become the lone source of news. . . . There is some good news here, that young people are capable of gleaning at least modest amounts of campaign information from such content, but how competent it leaves them to participate in a meaningful manner remains an open question.[9]

The Regulatory Context

On February 1, 2004, during the Super Bowl halftime show, singer Justin Timberlake tore off part of singer Janet Jackson's wardrobe and revealed her bare breast. The episode lasted only a second or two, but the Federal Communications Commission (FCC), which is charged by federal statute to uphold standards for content broadcast over public airwaves, fined the CBS broadcasting company $550,000 after more than 500,000 viewers of the halftime show contacted the FCC to complain.[10] CBS appealed the fine, but the episode demonstrates the role that government regulators play in determining what elements of popular culture the public can watch, hear, or experience.[11]

The regulatory process is an especially important part of understanding popular culture. A variety of federal government actors regulate popular culture in one way or another. For example, the U.S. Congress passes statutes and appropriates funds for monitoring agencies to ensure that the messages the public receives through the media and other popular culture outlets are free from illegal or indecent content. Federal executive branch agencies including the FCC and the National Endowment for the Arts (NEA) are also involved in regulating popular culture. These agencies create rules and standards, as well as grant licenses (in the case of the FCC) or allocate grant monies (in the case of the NEA) to promote the expression of ideas.

The federal courts have played a tremendously important role in regulating the media and popular culture; several of the U.S. Supreme Court's landmark decisions in these areas are worth mentioning. In *Hustler v. Falwell (1983)*, the Supreme Court ruled that parodious speech—that is, speech that is satirical or a parody—is protected by the First Amendment. It is this ruling that allows television shows like *Saturday Night Live* or *The Daily Show* to mock elected and appointed officials so mercilessly. Because no one watching *Saturday Night Live* or *The Daily Show* assumes that the sketches are truthful representations of the politicians' characteristics or behaviors, shows like this are able to broadcast their satirical reflections on political life without fear of repercussions.

[9]Barry A. Hollander, "Late-Night Learning: Do Entertainment Programs Increase Political Campaign Knowledge for Young Viewers?" *Journal of Broadcasting & Electronic Media* 49.4 (December 2005): 402(14).

[10]"CBS Dealt Record Fine Over Janet," 2004. http://www.cbsnews.com/stories/2004/07/01/entertainment/main626925.shtml. Accessed August 1, 2006.

[11]John Dunbar, "CBS Appeals 'Wardrobe Malfunction' Fine." *Chicago Tribune*, July 28, 2006. Available online at: http://www.chicagotribune.com/technology/sns-ap-cbs-janet-jackson,1,1991749.story?coll=chi-news-hed. Accessed August 1, 2006.

This is not to say that the courts permit any or all messages to enjoy the protection of the First Amendment. For example, in *Jacobellis v. Ohio (1964)*, the Court allowed that material that is "utterly without redeeming social value" could be banned. In *Miller v. California (1973)*, the Court clarified that materials can be banned as obscene if they meet a three-part test:

1. The average person, applying contemporary community standards, would find that the work, taken as a whole, appeals to the prurient interest;
2. The work depicts, in a patently offensive way, sexual conduct specifically defined by the applicable state law;
3. The work, taken as a whole, lacks serious literary, artistic, political or scientific value.

In *New York v. Ferber (1982)*, the Court unanimously outlawed child pornography, even if the pictures would not be considered obscene under the *Miller* test.

The regulation of the media and popular culture remains a controversial area of the law. Because the First Amendment prohibits the Congress from legislating against a free press, the courts are forced to step in and determine when Congress has overstepped its bounds as legislators attempt to be responsive to citizens who complain about the types of messages they or their children are exposed to by broadcasters.

Conclusion

Although democratic theory suggests that an informed citizenry is the cornerstone of popular control of government, it is clear that the source of information matters. Political subjects have become an important component of late-night and comedic programs such as *Saturday Night Live* and *The Daily Show*. On the positive side, an increasing number of younger viewers are now being exposed to political information. On the negative side, however, recent studies demonstrate that this increased exposure may be creating generations of citizens who are disenfranchised from politics with low levels of political efficacy and a general suspicion of the competence of public officials.

At the same time, the government is an important part of determining the content of public broadcasts, although it is constrained by the First Amendment to the Constitution. In that context, it cannot prevent satire and parody from dominating the late-night airwaves and ultimately affecting public opinion about politics and government.

THE RHETORICAL PERSPECTIVE

Rhetoricians typically look at serious, purposeful communication—speeches and the like that rhetors craft to persuade audiences. Popular culture flies in the face of this traditional rhetorical transaction. Those who write late-night comedy monologues or sketch comedy or television and motion picture drama are trying to entertain, not persuade. Yet, their less-than-serious purpose aside, what they craft may well persuade. And it may persuade large numbers, including many in demographic categories that politicians find difficult to move with all of their more "normal" appeals. Recognizing that popular culture does indeed reach a large, difficult-to-reach audience, politicians are increasingly choosing to use popular culture as a medium whereby they might send messages. These messages are not the reasoned ones of those antiquated political "stump" speeches; rather, these messages are ones that the candidates deliver more by being present than by anything specific they might say.

Rhetoricians, then, see two very interesting facets in popular culture: the messages it inadvertently communicates and the messages political figures send by turning onto popular culture avenues.

The Messages Popular Culture Sends

Motion pictures and television programs have long been important parts of American popular culture. During the Great Depression and again during World War II, motion pictures offered an entertaining escape to troubled Americans. They could enter the darkened theater and, for an hour or two, simply allow what was on the screen to affect them, as they somewhat mindlessly absorbed an entertaining story. At times, a director or a screenwriter would go beyond merely entertaining and try to offer a message. In more recent times, perhaps more filmmakers are trying to deliver a message than in the 1930s and 1940s. Still, the bulk of the "Hollywood" fare has as its primary goal to entertain. Messages nonetheless are sent—some intended, some not.

Many American films have dealt with political subjects. Needing heroes, some have focused on legislators, but far more have focused on American presidents.[12] These films may well send messages about a political issue crucial at the time the film hits the theaters, but far more important may be the message sent about the president. Judith S. Trent has studied what qualities voters seek in a president.[13] Do voters simply know what these qualities are? Or have they been persuaded to want certain characteristics in a chief executive because of what they have seen on the movie screen? Harrison Ford's portrayal of the president in *Air Force One* (1997) may have subtly persuaded voters that they wanted a family-loving action hero as their next president. It may have corrected ever so slightly the message sent by Michael Douglas's president in *The American President* (1995) that a president could be both very human and very enamored with an attractive younger woman. The Michael Douglas–Harrison Ford double whammy may have been a subtle corrective to

[12]An excellent overview of political films is offered in Terry Christensen and Peter J. Haas, *Projecting Politics: Political Messages in American Films* (Armonk, NY: M. E. Sharpe, 2005). In their filmography, they list over 400 American films with political themes.

[13]For example, see Judith S. Trent, et al., "The Idealized Presidential Candidate: A Vision Over Time," *American Behavioral Scientist* 49 (2005): 130–56.

William Jefferson Clinton. That corrective may have created a predisposition for a compassionate man who can be tough when it comes to "evil-doers." Trent's succession of studies shows little variation in the qualities voters sought across five presidential elections. However, these studies do not address either how voters arrive at their preferences or what role popular culture might have in both prompting these preferences and providing correcting visions when the actual president deviates from what is desired.

Aaron Sorkin claims his highly acclaimed television show *The West Wing* was intended to entertain, not offer civics lessons. Nonetheless, after Jed Bartlett begins to dominate the ensemble show, Sorkin offers a president American liberals loved—to the point of affixing "Jed Bartlet is My President" bumper stickers on their cars. He was intelligent, enlightened, and eloquent. And, as the 2000 and 2004 elections unfolded in real time, Bartlet made Al Gore, George W. Bush, and John Kerry look wooden, simple, and wishy-washy. The political left's delight in Bartlet may have, however, caused them to overlook how he presented "presidentiality." In, first, a controversial article in the *Quarterly Journal of Speech* and then the book *The Prime-Time Presidency: The West Wing and U.S. Nationalism* (2006), Trevor and Shawn J. Parry-Giles have argued that the "presidentiality" *The West Wing* sold viewers was premised on sexism, racism, and an almost macho militancy.[14] "Pornography for liberals"—John Podhoretz's quip in *The Weekly Standard* in March 2000—*The West Wing* was not.[15] Although these rhetorical critics backed off from their initial thesis in the book, probably because the book was based on more seasons of the program, they nonetheless suggest that the weekly drama may have been selling an image of both the presidency and "presidentiality" (i.e., how one, officially and ceremonially, executes the office) that would have surprised the show's fans.[16]

Commander in Chief, although it barely lived for a single season, also conveyed more than mere entertainment; however, it was more overt in delivering a message about who or what our president should be. It offered a woman in the White House at the very time New York Senator Hillary Clinton was moving toward a presidential campaign. Who could help but read the show as answering the "woman in the White House" question? The program, however, failed to deliver a clear answer. President Mackenzie Allen was clearly up to the job; however, she also struggled to play the roles of spouse and mother while serving as commander-in-chief. The program's take on a female president—and on the Hillary Clinton candidacy—was ambiguous.

---

[14]Trevor Parry-Giles and Shawn J. Parry-Giles, "*The West Wing*'s Prime-Time Presidentiality: Mimesis and Catharsis in a Postmodern Romance," *Quarterly Journal of Speech* 88 (2002), 209–27; Trevor Parry-Giles and Shawn J. Parry Giles, *The Prime-Time Presidency: The West Wing and U.S. Nationalism* (Urbana, IL: University of Illinois Press, 2006).

[15]Reprinted as John Podhoretz, "The Liberal Imagination," in Peter C. Rollins and John E. O'Connor, eds., *The West Wing: The American Presidency as Television Drama* (Syracuse, NY: Syracuse University Press, 2003), 222–31.

[16]The implicit racism and sexism in the initial two seasons were muted by the inclusion of more and more empowered African American and female characters in the later seasons.

Whereas motion picture and television drama may well tell us what we want our political leaders to be, comedy tends to tell us what, unfortunately, they often are.[17] They become the butt of stand-up comedy on late-night programs such as NBC's *The Tonight Show* and CBS's *Late Night with David Letterman* and sketch comedy on NBC's *Saturday Night Live* (SNL). The latter has proved especially effective in calling into comic question the ethos of presidents and presidential candidates. Dana Carvey's portrayal of President George H. W. Bush may well have convinced voters in 1992 that he did not have much to say to them about matters of public policy. More devastatingly, Chevy Chase's portrayal of President Gerald R. Ford may well have convinced voters in 1976 that he lacked intelligence as he, in one sketch, spoke to a stuffed dog as if it were alive and tried to putt with a tennis racquet. Bush's character took a hit; Ford's competence. Other politicians have suffered as well.

SNL's rhetoric demands a full study by someone. But, in advance of that, I would conjecture that two interesting principles are operating in determining which skits have an effect and whether the effect is negative or *really* negative. First, the skit's portrayal has to be reasonably consonant with the ethos the public already has of the man. SNL's portrayal of Massachusetts Governor Michael Dukakis as cold and unfeeling would not have worked if voters had not already viewed the Democratic presidential candidate in that manner. SNL's portrayal of businessman H. Ross Perot, third-party presidential candidate in 1992, as quirky and eccentric would not have worked if voters thought he was a more usual candidate. Second, the skit has to zero in on a quality thought to be crucial to do maximum damage. Thus, skits that show George W. Bush as lacking intelligence—as reflected in his inability to use the English language correctly—may be more devastating than ones that show Bill Clinton "chasing the ladies." Intelligence is a crucial quality for a president; marital fidelity only a desirable one. Skits that show Richard M. Nixon as brooding and paranoid may be more devastating than ones that depict Al Gore being "in love" with the word "lockbox." Psychological stability is crucial; a varied vocabulary only nice.

Some of SNL's most interesting quick hits have been through the show's ever-evolving Weekend Update segment. Taking this segment several steps further is Jon Stewart's *The Daily Show* on Comedy Central. Although Stewart does fairly accurately present the news, he presents it in such a manner as to highlight its absurdities. His coverage of the 2004 Democratic and Republican conventions is a case in point. All conventions have their absurdities: all one has to do is look at some of the costumes and funny hats the delegates are wearing to discern that. Stewart exaggerates each and every one. Thus, former Georgia Governor Zell Miller's rage at John Kerry, which was so overdone as to border on the absurd, is pushed beyond that border through *The Daily Show's* coverage. The emphasis on 9/11 during that GOP convention was comically emphasized by being framed within a "Drink every time someone says '9-11'"

[17]For a discussion of how candidates are predominantly presented negatively on late-night comedy programs, see Michael Nitz et al., "Candidates as Comedy: Political Presidential Humor on Late-Night Television Shows," in Lynda Lee Kaid et al., eds., *The Millennium Election: Communication in the 2000 Campaign* (Lanham, MD: Rowman and Littlefield, 2003): 165–75.

message. And, on the Democratic side, *The Daily Show* offered the "real" John Kerry campaign film, which parodied both the actual Kerry film and the genre. Exaggerating absurdities for laughs entertains, but it also may inadvertently send the message that politics and politicians are absurd. If viewers, many of whom are rather young, absorb this message, how likely are they to participate in the election by voting?

Politicians' Use of Popular Culture

Saturday Night Live and *The Daily Show* do indeed reach a demographic group both parties want to get more involved, a group that has tuned out more traditional political appeals. Aware that popular culture can reach groups that otherwise might not be reached, political figures have, for more than a decade, used popular culture. At the same time as it may be inadvertently sending negative messages about politics (messages of which it may not be fully cognizant), popular culture can be used to send the messages candidates and elected officials desire.

Bill Clinton, in both 1992 and 1996, used popular culture vehicles. The very fact that he appeared on the likes of the Arsenio Hall talk show and MTV sent a message: Clinton was not being aloof, like many political figures, holding himself at a distance from which average Americans must revere him; rather, he was more "one of us." That's an important message for a populist candidate to send. He also played the saxophone when visiting Arsenio Hall and answered questions when visiting MTV on whether he'd still just inhale (if he could relive his Oxford days) and whether he wore boxers or briefs. At the time, some pundits wondered if Clinton was lowering the presidency by using pop culture vehicles. The ultimate verdict is that, the presidency aside, he helped his candidacy—by communicating that he's "one of us" and that he's "cool."[18] So, after Clinton, everybody began appearing on a variety of previously "undignified" television programs.

Although we do remember a few of the things these candidates have said, their appearances are probably best thought of as "speech acts." They communicate positive messages about themselves simply by "doing" the show. They show that they are not full of themselves; they show that they want to connect with the kinds of people watching the particular shows; they exhibit a sense of humor. This sense of humor extends to jokes about themselves since, in many cases, they are walking onto a stage that has been the site of quip after quip directed against them. So, just by showing up and talking, they communicate humility, accessibility, and a sense of humor—all of which would seem to be positive qualities.

Just appearing, however, doesn't necessarily ensure rhetorical success. There needs to be some consonance between the image the political figure has and the image he or she is trying to walk away from popular culture venues with. If not, the

---

[18]In 1996, Republican presidential candidate Bob Dole tried to use some of Clinton's comments on MTV against him in late ads attacking the president's character. That these ads failed may be attributed partially to the positive effects Clinton's speech act (i.e., just appearing) had.

political figure suffers from political dissonance—for instance, President Richard Nixon appearing on NBC's *Laugh-In* and saying "Sock it to me"—or comes across as pandering. These pitfalls might well be kept in mind by candidates and their advisers in deciding which shows to appear on and which shows to skip.

Conclusion

Politics and popular culture is a big topic, and rhetoricians have only looked at pieces of it. That examination is sufficient, however, to conclude that popular culture can send powerful messages. Feature films and television programs may well send messages about the presidency as an institution as well as the kind of people we collectively wish to see in the White House. Comedy may inadvertently convince some pop culture consumers that politics is absurd. At the same time, it may undermine our leaders and our candidates for leadership. These political figures can, however, use the venues of popular culture themselves to communicate messages. These messages may get to citizens who are not very fully engaged in the political process.

THE MASS COMMUNICATION PERSPECTIVE

The introduction to this chapter identifies some particular examples of popular culture with connections to politics, but what do we mean by popular culture? In her review of *Hop on Pop: The Politics and Pleasure of Popular Culture*, Denise Bielby offers a list of qualities of what she calls "well established understandings of popular culture" (p. 261):

> . . . that it is marked by the immediacy of experience; that it can emanate from outsider groups; that it should strive to be jargon-free and accessible to those beyond the academy; that empirical evidence that challenges theoretical pre-conceptualizations should be acknowledged; that historical, political, and cultural context is essential for understanding the particulars of otherwise isolated case studies; and that time and space frame the very questions that inform inquiry, analysis, and interpretation.[19]

So we may be talking about reality television, computer games, or Internet fandom, all considered to be "pure entertainment," but they are part of our contemporary popular culture and the focus of considerable analysis and research.

---

[19]Denise D. Bielby, Review: *Hop on Pop: The Politics and Pleasures of Popular Culture. Popular Communication* 2.4 (2004): 261–62.

Blurring of News and Entertainment

Many of the examples in the time line suggest that any clear lines that once existed between news and entertainment in the past are now gone. Weekend Update on NBC's *Saturday Night Live* and *The Daily Show* with Jon Stewart are both examples of programs that appear to be like a newscast, but are entertainment and comedy. If we consider a typical television network today, there will be a substantial news operation that is costly to run but also quite profitable for a network; there will also be an entertainment division that selects and possibly produces daytime and evening programming; there may also be a sports division separate from entertainment that deals with the sports broadcast contracts as well as staffing the coverage of games; there will also be an advertising department that sells airtime to companies and organizations promoting various products or services. And while these entities may still exist as different units at the network level, we are seeing more cases of content that merges what had been clearly distinguishable units in mass media. For example:

- Julie Chen hosts *Big Brother* on CBS and also co-hosts the CBS News' *The Early Show*.
- *60 Minutes* correspondent Steve Croft played a TV news broadcaster in Woody Allen's *Small Time Crooks*.
- PBS *Newshour* anchor Jim Lehrer is also author of the novel *The Last Debate* about a presidential campaign.
- Leonardo DiCaprio, rather than one of ABC News' own correspondents, interviewed former President Bill Clinton on Earth Day 2000 for ABC News.
- Local television anchors make guest appearances and serve as hosts for events and fund-raisers in their communities.[20]

Why does this blurring of the distinction between news and entertainment occur? We can look at media ownership for one possible answer. Although "who owns whom" continues to change, here are a few examples of entertainment businesses also playing a role in the news today: Disney owns ESPN as well as ABC; CNN is owned by Time-Warner, which also owns America Online, New Line Cinemas, Turner Broadcasting, *Time* magazine, and Warner Broadcasting. MSNBC, owned by General Electric as is the NBC network, included a variety of clips from Jay Leno and *Saturday Night Live* skits (both NBC productions) in their "news" coverage of the 2000 election results in Florida. Eric Effron noted how the mix of news and entertainment in the 2000 election coverage played into the spectacle of the election:

> So more than ever before, the news we consumed was filtered through a comedic lens. Whether we actually tuned in to the comedy shows or left our televisions tuned to the news, there were the funny-men, wisecracking, making light of Bush's

---

[20]Many of these examples come from Lawrence K. Grossman, "Shilling for Prime Time: Can CBS News Survive *Survivor*," *Columbia Journalism Review* 39.3 (September/October 2000): 70–71.

intellect and of Gore's demeanor and of the morass of confounding legal strategies and relentless partisanship and—naturally—of the media's handling of the entire spectacle. (p. 72)[21]

Stewart's appearance on CNN's *Crossfire* reinforces the blurring even further. The talk show that regularly hosted political elites as guests invited Jon Stewart for the October 2004 episode. Carlson and Begala wanted Stewart to be his funny *Daily Show* self, but not only was he more serious than expected, he also critiqued the very show he was a guest on for its lack of serious political discourse. The event went beyond the talk show itself, and clips of Stewart's critique were played on news as well as entertainment programs.

Programs such as *The Daily Show* and *Saturday Night Live*'s Weekend Update may contribute to this blurring between news and entertainment, and it appears that audiences are accepting these "alternative" sources of information as well. According to a 2004 study[22] by the Pew Research Center for People and the Press, such programs are becoming as common a source of information on political campaigns as traditional news sources:

> One-in-five young people say they regularly get campaign news from the Internet, and about as many (21%) say the same about comedy shows such as *Saturday Night Live* and the *Daily Show*. For Americans under 30, these comedy shows are now mentioned almost as frequently as newspapers and evening network news programs as regular sources for election news. (p. 2)

A subsequent Pew Research Center study of Deaniacs, voters who enthusiastically supported Howard Dean's candidacy for president in 2004 and were involved online in promoting his campaign, found Deaniacs' viewing of *The Daily Show* was considerably higher than the general public's.[23] While 3 percent of the general public reported regularly watching *The Daily Show* in 2004, 29 percent of Dean activists were regular viewers. Its appeal was most notable with younger viewers: 8 percent of all 18- to 29-year-olds reported watching *The Daily Show* regularly, compared to 44 percent of Deaniacs ages 18 to 29.

Beyond the blurring between news and entertainment, there have also been examples of entertainment media impacting political discourse. One recent example is the discussion following the 2002 film *John Q* starring Denzel Washington as a father who navigates a complex health care system while pursing a heart transplant for his son. The Kaiser Family Foundation, a nonprofit organization that studies health care issues, followed with a conference on "John Q. Goes to Washington:

[21]Eric Effron, "Laughing Matters," *Brill's Content* (February 2001): 72–73.

[22]Pew Research Center for the People and the Press, "Cable and Internet Loom Large in Fragmented Political News Universe," January 11, 2004. http://people-press.org/reports/display.php3?ReportID=200.

[23]Pew Research Center for the People and The Press, "The Dean Activists: Their Profile and Prospects," April 6, 2005. http://people-press.org/reports/display.php3?ReportID=240.

Health Policy Issues in Popular Culture," which included speakers from both the entertainment and the health care industries.

The West Wing: Fiction and Images of the Presidency

The West Wing presents a different blurring in the media, between idealistic portrayals of the president in fiction, and the realistic expectations of a president in society. In addition to the numerous Emmy Awards *The West Wing* received over its seven-year run, it also received praise from media critics for its portrayal of politics, such as the following:

> ". . . the fictional *West Wing* conveys more truth about the humanness of those who run our government and sometimes even the complexities of the issues they face than most of the reports we get from Sam Donaldson and other TV marionettes who stand in front of the White House each night talking about who won and who lost that day."[24]

Perhaps such comments further blur the distinction between reality and fiction, as a prime-time drama is being compared to traditional broadcast news coverage of the presidency. Beyond the praise from the media itself, it was also highly regarded by scholars who studied the political-based drama, such as research by Lance Holbert and colleagues:[25]

> This fictional show offers something to the American public that it cannot get from any other source, an insider's view of what it is like to be president on a daily basis. In short, *The West Wing* represents the fly on the wall that the press wishes it could be. (p. 505)

This quote sets the basis for research conducted on *The West Wing* on the effects of framing and priming, which suggests that the fictional portrayal of the presidency may have real-world effects on citizens' perspectives of the presidency. In a content analysis of the *West Wing*, Holbert and colleagues examined the 2000–2001 season for depictions of President Jed Bartlet as chief executive, a political candidate, and a private citizen. They suggest each role offers an opportunity for viewers to create a relationship with the presidency, and in the season of *The West Wing* analyzed, more than one quarter of the scenes including President Bartlet portrayed him as a private citizen. The analysis also assessed the portrayal of Bartlet as principled (honest, hard-working, determined) as compared to Bartlet as engaged (loving, warm, compassionate) and found the principled qualities most often were associated with the president in his role as chief executive, whereas the engaged qualities were more often associated with Bartlet as a private citizen. The analysis confirms that audiences see a different

---

[24]Steven Brill, "Truth or Fiction: Pick One: Fictional *West Wing* Bests Many Reporters in Depicting a Nuanced Washington," *Brill's Content* 3.2 (March 2000): 25.

[25]R. Lance Holbert et al., "The West Wing and Depictions of the American Presidency: Expanding the Domains of Framing in Political Communication," *Communication Quarterly*, 53.4 (2005): 505–522.

"type" of president with different qualities in these the role as chief executive, political candidate, and private citizen. The distinction made between chief executive and private citizen may be important to consider in the context of Bill Clinton's presidency after his impeachment, when people thought he was doing a good job as chief executive, even as they were disappointed with him personally.

In addition to the analysis of the framing of President Bartlet from *West Wing*, another study by Holbert and colleagues considered to what extent the images of Bartlet primed particular attitudes or expectations in our real-world president.[26] They found that *West Wing*'s President Bartlet was evaluated more favorably than either President George W. Bush or President Bill Clinton (the study was conducted in early 2002). Their study also found that viewers' evaluations, just after viewing *The West Wing*, of both Bush and Clinton were higher, in that viewers saw both in a more positive light after seeing the favorable Bartlet image of the presidency than they did before watching a particular episode of *West Wing*. In this study, watching *The West Wing* primed viewers to have more positive evaluations of contemporary real-world presidents.

It is not clear how long such priming may last, or what further impact it might have on a person's actions, but it does indicate that media audiences may have attitudes primed by entertainment content rather than news content. The study by Holbert and colleagues may provide evidence to support what one analysis early in *The West Wing* series suggested: that *The West Wing* is "what a number of journalists, former White House aides, and media analysts say may be a promising antidote for today's widespread disenchantment with politics. Can a smart TV show renew interest in public life in ways that real politics brought to us by the real press corps can't?"[27] (p. 90). Holbert's research suggests there could be such an intersection between viewing fictional portrayals of politics and real-world political opinions.

Conclusion

The comedy versions of news from programs such as *Saturday Night Live* and *The Daily Show* are just one factor contributing to the blurring of news and entertainment in contemporary mass media. Other examples of such blurring stem more directly from the news side of the media industry, as well as the business organization and pressure within current media ownership patterns. The consequences are unclear, however; do media consumers find potential "truth" in these entertainment venues, or do they not take traditional news as seriously as they once did? Both results may occur. The focus on *The West Wing* not only as entertainment, but also a possible source of change in attitudes toward real-world political institutions, blurs the distinction made between fiction and reality of media content. The research suggests, however,

[26]R. Lance Holbert, et al., "The West Wing as Endorsement of the U.S. Presidency: Expanding the Bounds of Priming in Political Communication," *Journal of Communication* 53.3 (2003): 427–43.

[27]Matthew Miller, "Real White House: Can a Smart TV Show Inspire Interest in Public Life in Ways that Real Politics—Brought to Us by the Real Press Corps—Can't? Absolutely," *Brill's Content* 3.2 (March 2000): 88–113.

that we may need to consider the potential influence of a variety of entertainment media on current political attitudes and behavior.

CONCLUSION

The three perspectives presented in this case all addressed the potential power of popular culture, in the types of messages audiences received and the possible effects of those messages. It is clear that those effects may vary, some of which may be positive for citizens, elected officials, and political institutions, and others that may be damaging to those individuals or institutions.

The three perspectives also raised unique issues in the context of politics and popular culture, including the legal protection political satire receives, the influence of media ownership on the blurring of traditional news with entertainment, and the extent to which politicians and candidates themselves have capitalized on popular culture to reach audiences and potential voters.

■ ■ ■ ■ ■ ▬▬▬▬▬▬▬▬▬▬▬▬▬▬▬▬▬▬▬▬▬▬▬▬▬▬▬▬▬

ADDITIONAL CASES

- **MTV's "Choose or Lose 20 Million Loud" campaign, 2004**
  Resource: Allison Romano, Stand and Deliver: MTV News Challenges Young Viewers to Vote, *Broadcasting & Cable*, 134 (2004, June 21), 10.

- **Editorial cartoons, such as Gary Trudeau's *Doonesbury*.**
  In 2000, Doonesbury character Ambassador Duke ran for President and was featured in animated form on CNN's *Larry King Live*. Resource: Ken Kerschbaumer, Duke on the Campaign Trail, *Broadcasting & Cable*, 130 (2000, March 20), 76.

- **Musicals with political themes: historic examples include "The Cradle Will Rock," "Pins and Needles," and "Hooray for What"; one contemporary political musical is "Rent."**
  Resource: Charles Isherwood, Rent control: Political issues of the Broadway musical 'Rent,' *The Advocate*, #734 (1997, May 27), 75–77.

- **National Endowment for the Art's funding of controversial art**
  Resource: John J. Miller, Up from Mapplethorpe, *National Review* 56 (2004, March 8), 24.

- **Political Fiction, including authors such as Tom Clancy, David Baldacci, and Margaret Truman**
  Resource: Walker L. Hixson, "Red Storm Rising": Tom Clancy Novels and the Cult of National Security. *Diplomatic History* 17 (1993 Fall), 599–613.

CHAPTER 18

CONCLUSION

As we conclude this text, we pose three questions to consider in reflecting on the case studies presented, as well as the political science, rhetorical, and mass communication perspectives discussed.

- What are the basics of political communication?
- What do the three disciplinary perspectives offer?
- What insights do those perspectives give the reader?

The answers to these questions that follow provide a summary of topics and issues this book has raised in the previous chapters.

WHAT ARE THE BASICS OF POLITICAL COMMUNICATION?

This book's cases deal with six topics that are common in political communication courses: (1) elections; (2) the presidency; (3) the legislature; (4) the judiciary; (5) social movements; and (6) popular culture. There are more cases on the earlier topics than the latter ones because most political communication courses concentrate the majority of their attention on the first few. They tend to treat elections at length and topics such as social movements and popular culture only briefly and if time allows. Yet some of the later topics are key components of political communication and for many of us are the most frequent interaction we have with the subject.

Our approach has been to let the basics emerge as we discuss real political communication situations. In the paragraphs that follow, we offer a summary of the basics of each of the six topics on which this book is focused.

Elections

As the case studies have demonstrated, U.S. elections follow a time line, one that begins long before the now-condensed caucuses and primaries of February and March. Once the major parties have determined who their nominees will be, the time line moves through the late summer nominating conventions and into the general election period, during which there will be personal appearances and advertising and probably debates. There is also a great deal of Internet activity—visits to websites, e-mails, blogs. These are all communication activities that can be studied. One can look at how each activity has evolved and can gain an understanding of what communication behavior is expected. Scholars of electoral political communication look at the communication behavior itself, at the texts (both visual and written) that are created during the election, at the media the candidates choose to communicate their messages, and at how the media establishment (e.g., newspapers, television networks) chooses to cover these communication events. Citizens learn and make decisions about the candidates through all of these means. Those who study elections point to the predictable, highlight any departures from the norm, and become really interested when there is a dramatic departure, such as when a third-party candidate wins.

As the case studies have demonstrated, many elements of election campaign communication are predictable. Candidates almost always appeal to party loyalists during primaries, offering messages that might seem starkly liberal or conservative, only to move to the center during the general-election phase. The candidates and their advisers try to manage the nominating conventions in order to deliver as strong a message about their leadership abilities as possible. During the elections, the candidates offer both positive image and issue advertising to highlight their own credentials, and then they frequently shift to comparative or negative ads to raise questions about their opponents. In the weeks preceding a debate, many candidates attempt to lower voters' expectation of them as debaters and then try to exceed those expectations while avoiding anything that might be considered a mistake. Certainly, this was the case for George W. Bush during the 2000 presidential election.

Throughout the process, there is above all else a concern with winning and losing. A variety of factors can affect both a candidate's likelihood of winning election and his or her communication strategy for victory: Is there an incumbent? What issues are most salient to voters? What do public opinion polls suggest? Which campaign is making the better strategic decisions? Have sufficient funds been raised to carry out these decisions? These and many other questions are considered in the practice as well as the study of political elections in the United States.

The Presidency

Presidents communicate a great deal and they, more than any other single political official in the United States, command an audience when they do. What they say is often important insofar as it affects both the policies the Congress may choose to consider and the actions of our diplomats and our troops abroad. Presidents also seek to communicate directly with citizens to rally support for their proposed courses of action.

As the introductions to the presidency case studies point out (Chapters 10, 11, and 12), the president has not always been the focal point of the American system of government in the way he or she is today. For this reason, it is important to understand the presidency from both a constitutional and a historical point of view to contextualize the contemporary state of presidential communication.

Although presidents communicate in ways other than giving speeches, scholars focus on speeches because they are public and recorded. All of these speeches are not the same; they are of different genres and therefore do different things and follow different conventions. They are also covered differently by the media depending on variables such as at what time during the day or at what point in his or her 4-year term the president speaks, as well as what else is newsworthy. The media have not always covered the presidency in the same way, however, and as the case studies suggest, they have arguably become more aggressive over the years. Similarly, presidents have not always spoken the same way, and changes in media—for example, the shift from radio to television and the shift from speaking to Congress to speaking to Congress and the general public—have important roles in altering how presidents have communicated.

The Legislature

Members of Congress—and state legislatures as well—also communicate a lot, both internally between and among their own members, and externally with their constituents. But much of this communication is either invisible (such as chats in the cloak rooms off the floor of House and Senate chambers) or is rarely or only superficially covered by the media, which is the case for most committee hearings and floor debates. In fact, except when the pending legislative proposal is either extremely important or extremely controversial, most congressional communication escapes the public's attention because it's not on the media's agenda. With 535 individual House and Senate members at the federal level, and literally thousands of state legislators, no member of a legislative body can command the kind of media attention that the president of the United States enjoys. Legislative communication thus is relegated to a few periodic sound bites rather than being a central focus of reporting.

Nonetheless, communication in Congress and state legislatures is vital and often compelling. Legislators don't just talk. What they do is governed by rules, rules that more often than not reflect power relationships. As the case studies of the reverse filibuster and Clarence Thomas hearing demonstrate, scholars are interested in how legislators work within the confines of the rules to send messages that either affect specific legislation or affect public policy more broadly. Of special interest to scholars and observers are those times when legislators seem to thwart the norms and the rules, for these are undoubtedly moments when lawmakers believe that they are saying something crucial.

As the case studies we've included in the text have demonstrated, congressional communication does garner media attention. But the moments the media choose to cover, as well as the ways in which these moments are framed, have important consequences for the impact of this particular form of political communication. There are implications when the media take matters that are complicated enough to entail hours and days of talking and reduce them to 15 seconds for the evening news. The case studies in this text have explored these issues as well as others such as the impact of the change from network television to cable television and to public affairs television such as C-SPAN and C-SPAN2.

The Judiciary

As we noted in the discussion of *Texas v. Johnson*, much of the communication that takes place in the judicial branch of government is private. Unless we are lucky enough to be among a select few attendees at oral arguments, we can hear—but not see—the arguments presented before the U.S. Supreme Court; we can read decisions as well as concurring and dissenting opinions. But a great deal that matters is not available to scholars. For example, we know little about the conversations that take place between and among the justices as they cast their votes in cases or as they negotiate about the language to include in their written opinions. Still, the writings of the justices provide us important communication to consider. How the majority is reasoning is well worth noting. Scholars typically look at the way in which the justices are interpreting the Constitution—whether they are strictly interpreting the document or adapting it to situations that the Framers never could have envisioned. Perhaps even more interesting is how dissents are cast, since freed from the constraints that govern the decisions per se, authors of dissents can challenge prevailing views, perhaps weakening the impact of the current decision and even perhaps initiating shifts in the law that will not come to fruition for years.

Social Movements

Social movements may also take years to bring about meaningful change. They occur within time frames that make election cycles look brief, and often adapt and change as time passes. These attributes can make them difficult to study, but there are certain regularities that characterize most social movements. As the case study on the contemporary movement for political, economic, and social equality for gays and lesbians (Chapter 16) demonstrated, social movements have leaders, overarching goals and interests, and messages that are communicated to the public and to policy makers. Social movements are organized to deliver messages, whether through marches or rallies or "zaps" or even violent confrontations. Although the public and public opinion are frequently the focus of social movements, leaders of these movements also often communicate among themselves in ways that are important.

Social movements, as noisy as they can be, have limited power if the media and policy makers are not receptive to their messages. Thus, any social movement's influence waxes and wanes depending on how much those in power embrace its messages and how much—and in what manner—the media establishment chooses to cover its activities.

Popular Culture

As Chapter 17 on popular culture demonstrates, pop culture is—and has always been—all around us, but historically there seemed to be a boundary between popular culture and politics that was not crossed. Although popular culture has always been concerned with, and offered commentary on, politics, those in politics tended to ignore the comments. Serious politicians certainly did not participate in popular culture programming. Today, the boundary has shifted. In 2000, Vice President Al Gore and Texas Governor George W. Bush appeared on *Saturday Night Live*'s Presidential Bash 2000, and today, it is not unusual to find candidates and officeholders appearing on television talk shows or entertainment programs. The result is that popular culture seems to have more power today because its messages are being heard (or being seen) more than messages from political elites, especially among younger voters. Thus, scholars and students then need to know about the history of *Saturday Night Live* and about what *The Daily Show* and Jib-Jab.com are up to. They need to understand how motion picture and television portrayals of government and politics are offering, rightly or wrongly, a lesson in civics to many who make political decisions when they cast votes for candidates and referenda.

WHAT DO THE THREE DISCIPLINARY PERSPECTIVES OFFER?

As is undoubtedly evident by now, the three perspectives offered throughout this textbook ask different questions about political communication because they have different primary concerns. What each perspective has to say may overlap with the others because they are, after all, considering the same political events. But each perspective comes at those events from different directions, producing opportunities for comparison as well as contrast.

Political scientists are interested in power and the governmental structures that parcel it out. Thus, any specialist in American government is likely to be obsessed to some extent with the U.S. Constitution, for it is *the* document in this country that parcels out power. Certainly, the Constitution is the point of departure for most analyses of power in American politics. But the parceling out is not static; it changes as the nation changes. Moreover, within government, smaller power shifts are occurring all the time. For example, the power to wage war gradually became more and more a presidential prerogative, but who has more power in a congressional committee or in a presidential-legislative showdown or in an ongoing election is constantly changing. Communication is both what causes and what marks these shifts, whether they are grand ones or smaller ones.

The rhetorician is interested in the texts, broadly defined, that make up political communication. More particularly, he or she is interested in how these texts—and their authors—use various resources to persuade diverse audiences. In times past, the rhetorical perspective might have been limited to examining specific speeches or specific debates. Nowadays, the perspective is broader; an entire presidential campaign can be and is thought of as a text, as is a decades-long social movement. Also, as time has passed, rhetoricians have acquired more theoretical lenses to use when examining texts. They still might cite Aristotle and Cicero, but the insights of others, ranging from Kenneth Burke and Chaim Perelman and Stephen Toulmin to Bakhtin and Foucault, just as often will inform the commentary.

Mass communication scholars focus on how and through what media the messages are delivered. The political scientist and the rhetorician are not only aware that media have changed, they are also alert to how these changes affect power and alter how messages come across. The mass communication scholar, however, delves into these questions more fully. These scholars are just as much—if not more—interested in how the media industries have played a role in these dynamics. After all, although a communicator may think of his or her message as being televised and as being covered by the news media in a certain manner, if it televised, how it is televised, if it is covered, and how it is covered may be largely up to the people in the media. Media keep evolving; the media industries keep changing. These developments, very much in the eye of the mass communication scholar, necessarily affect how political communication proceeds. Therefore, the mass communication scholar is quick to point out how power dynamics may be changing and what texts now must be scrutinized.

WHAT INSIGHTS DID THOSE PERSPECTIVES GIVE THE READER?

In this text, we have offered many instances in which the three perspectives led us to highlight different aspects of the case in question. These differences, however, usually coalesced into coherent readings, which exhibit a richness because the three perspectives have been brought to bear on political communication event.

The three perspectives offered strikingly similar conclusions about the elections covered in this book, even though each approached the subject from a different direction. For example, the three perspectives, in combination, noted that in the 1988 presidential election, the "Willie Horton" and "Revolving Door" ads coalesced with Jesse Jackson's role at the Democratic National Convention to hurt Dukakis with white ethnics and white Southerners. Moreover, the two ads seem to have coalesced in people's minds—so much so that viewers of the latter saw African American men moving through the revolving door when, on close examination, only one of the actors portraying the inmates might have been an African American. Combined, the ads evoked fear of African American males (portrayed as more likely to commit violent crimes) on the parts of white viewers. When all three perspectives on the 1988 presidential election are read together, it becomes apparent that the ads, combined with the manner in which the Democratic National Convention showcased Jesse Jackson, established a climate in which two white constituencies, ethnic voters and Southerners, were already inclined to abandon the Dukakis-Bentsen ticket because they perceived it as too pro-black.

Another point of convergence can be found by examining what the three perspectives had to say about Jesse Ventura's surprising gubernatorial victory. Jesse surprised people on Election Day, especially because he was not considered—by opponents or the media—much of a threat. His campaign's astute use of the Internet rallied a surprising number of voters, many of whom felt disconnected from one or the other of the two major parties, to his candidacy at the very last minute; the structural feature of Minnesota's same-day voter registration law allowed many of these individuals to cast ballots. Taken together, the three perspectives invite readers to consider Ventura's victory in the context of specific electoral constraints and to think about whether he would have won had Minnesota required all voters to be registered a month ahead of the election.

Our other election case studies likewise converged around a few important themes. For example, as was demonstrated in the case study of the 2000 presidential election, voters received important information about the candidates' image or *ethos* from presidential election debates. This information, in the absence of strong issue positions or externally important issue debates, may be crucial to citizens' voting decisions. This conclusion about candidate image is reinforced by the election of 2004, when Howard Dean's speech after the Iowa caucuses—as it was covered by the media—led to the end of his campaign. The ballroom was so noisy that neither Dean nor audience members (media representatives included) heard his infamous scream as television audiences later did. If one was covering what took place in that ballroom, the scream was not news, but news people made the scream the news nonetheless.

Likewise, our chapters on the presidency reached important points of convergence as well. The Reagan inaugural is considered by public address scholars to be one of the more effective presidential inaugural addresses. Viewed in isolation from its context, it was effective, but viewing it in context—that is, with what was happening simultaneously in Iran—makes its messages all the more powerful and alters how one sees the inaugural. The coexistence of the two stories also presented the media with coverage problems. Which one do they stress? Do they draw a connection between the two events or not? Far more than a speech was occurring that January day.

Similarly, Bill Clinton's words on his relationship with intern Monica Lewinsky followed in the strategic footsteps of predecessors Richard Nixon and Ronald Reagan, each of whom addressed the public during his presidency to offer an apology for misconduct. Clinton's words left many dissatisfied, but they may have been more carefully planned out than at first seems to be the case. Each perspective on Clinton's speech notes that he drew on lessons learned from previous presidential apologies to craft a speech that would allow him to maintain some credibility as president. Finally, all three of the perspectives in this text pointed out the way that George W. Bush, in his speeches following September 11, and his decision to send troops into Iraq, used the emotional language characteristic of one kind of discourse in a situation that required more logic and evidence. His rhetoric may well have been appropriate to condemn the September 11 terrorists and to celebrate our alleged victory in Iraq but not appropriate for speeches leading the nation into military action.

Other important areas of convergence among the three perspectives can be found by looking at how all three highlighted the ways in which male and female viewers socially constructed very different versions of the conflicting testimony offered by Clarence Thomas and Anita Hill and how Republicans and Democrats alike tried many different gimmicks during the daylong "reverse filibuster" in their efforts to attract media attention and then to get the media to highlight a particular take on the event. The perspectives converged in the chapter on the judicial branch as well. Regarding flag burning, all three perspectives noted that flag burning is more of a symbolic issue than a real one, and that its power as an issue is tied to what the flag and flag burning symbolize and how action on this front might be psychologically comforting to some voters.

There are differences as well in the ways in which the three perspectives view the case studies presented in this book and these differences sometimes end up offering complementary, not coalescing, viewpoints. For example, the political science approach to gay marriage highlighted the ways in which the U. S. Constitution doubly enters into the gay marriage debate by compelling (in Article IV) all states to recognize certain legal proceedings in any state and by enshrining "equal protection" under the Fourteenth Amendment. This constitutional approach is different from that taken by the rhetorical perspective, which considered the text of the current movement, and different from the mass communication approach, which charted the coverage of the movement as well as the way in which the issue was made salient to the public. Certainly the three approaches complement each other even though they do not reach a specific point of agreement about the gay rights movement.

CONCLUSION

None of the insights offered or conclusions reached by any of the three perspectives presented in this text are totally outside the realms in which political scientist, rhetorician, and mass communication scholars operate. As the examples above illustrate, all might have arrived at the same points. But the political scientist and the mass communication scholar do not usually think in terms of "epideictic discourse" or "social construction of meaning"; the political scientist and the rhetorician do not usually ask what were the headlines on a given day or what was an event really like from a reporter's (and thus the immediate audience's) vantage point; and the rhetorician and the mass communication scholar do not usually think about same-day registration laws and the precise terms of the U.S. Constitution. Because the three perspectives tend to come at political communication from different angles, they attend to and discuss different aspects.

A goal of this textbook is to lead the student to a discovery of the important basics of political communication through the close examination of case studies. Another goal is to equip the student with three separate but related points of view from which to analyze political communication events. Some students may find that they are drawn to the discussion of power dynamics and how communication affects them in a way characteristic of the political scientist. Others may find that they are drawn to the close analyses of texts in a way characteristic of the rhetorician. And still others might be drawn to a discussion of how the mediation of political messages affects how they come across and what they do. Regardless of the perspective taken, all who have been exposed to this textbook's multidisciplinary approach will be attuned to the other ways of looking at political communication. We hope they will, as a result, be better students of the subject and better citizens in this democratic society where political communication abounds.

SELECTED BIBLIOGRAPHY

Abramowitz, Alan I., and Walter J. Stone. "The Bush Effect: Polarization, Turnout, and Activism in the 2004 Presidential Election." *Presidential Studies Quarterly* 36.2 (2006): 141–54.

Ackerman, Bruce. "States of Emergency." *The American Prospect* 15.9 (September 2004): 40–41.

Alinsky, Saul D. *Rules for Radicals: A Practical Primer for Realistic Radicals*. New York: Random House, 1971.

Allan, Stuart, and Barbie Zelizer, eds. *Reporting War: Journalism in Wartime*. London: Routledge, 2004.

Ansolabehere, Stephen, and Shanto Iyengar. *Going Negative: How Political Advertisements Shrink & Polarize the Electorate*. New York: Free Press, 1995.

Armstrong, S. Ashley. "Arlen Specter and the Construction of Adversarial Discourse: Selective Representation in the Clarence Thomas–Anita Hill Hearings." *Argumentation and Advocacy* 32.2 (1995): 75–90.

Arnold, R. Douglas. *The Logic of Congressional Action*. New Haven, CT: Yale University Press, 1990.

Asher, Herbert. *Polling and the Public: What Every Citizen Should Know*. Washington, DC: Congressional Quarterly Press, 2004.

Bagdikian, Ben. *The New Media Monopoly*. Boston: Beacon Press, 2004.

Bakhtin, Mikhail. *Problems of Dostoevsky's Poetics*. Ed. and trans. Caryl Emerson. Minneapolis: University of Minnesota Press, 1984.

Bakhtin, Mikhail. *Rabelais and His World*. Ed. and trans. Helene Iswolsky. Bloomington: Indiana University Press, 1984.

Baumgartner, Jody, and Jonathan S. Morris. "The Daily Show Effect: Candidate Evaluations, Efficacy, and American Youth." *American Politics Research* 34.3 (May 2006): 341–68.

Beasley, Vanessa Bowles. "The Logic of Power in the Hill-Thomas Hearings: A Rhetorical Evaluation." *Political Communication* 11.3 (1994): 287–98.

Beiler, David. "The Body Politic Registers a Protest: Jesse Ventura's Stunning Victory in Minnesota as More Than a Fluke." *Campaigns and Elections* 20.1 (1999): 34–42.

Bennett, L. "Fifty Years of Prejudice in the Media." *Gay and Lesbian Review Worldwide* 7.2 (2000): 30.

Bennett, W. Lance. "Beyond Pseudoevents: Election News as Reality TV." *American Behavioral Scientist* 49.3 (2005): 364–78.

Bennett, W. Lance. *News: The Politics of Illusion*, 6th ed. New York: Pearson/Longman, 2004.

Benoit, William L. *Seeing Spots: A Functional Analysis of Presidential Television Advertising, 1952–1996*. Westport, CT: Praeger, 1999.

Benoit, William L., *Accounts, Excuses, and Apologies: A Theory of Image Restoration Strategies*. Albany: State University of New York Press, 1995.

Benoit, William L., and Dawn M. Nill. "A Critical Analysis of Judge Clarence Thomas' Statement before the Senate Judiciary Committee." *Communication Studies* 49.3 (1998): 179–96.

Berenger, Ralph D., ed. *Global Media Go to War: Role of News and Entertainment Media During the 2004 Iraqi War*. Spokane, WA: Marquette Books, 2004.

Berry, Stephen J. "CBS Lets the Pentagon Taint Its News Process." *Nieman Reports* 58.3 (Fall 2004): 76–78.

Bielby, Denise D. Review: *Hop on Pop: The Politics and Pleasures of Popular Culture. Popular Communication* 2.4 (2004): 261–62.

Bimber, Bruce. "The Internet and Political Mobilization." *Social Science Computer Review* 16 (1998): 391–401.

Blair, Carole, and Neil Michel. "Commemorating in the Theme Park Zone: Reading the Astronauts' Memorial." In *At the Intersection: Cultural Studies and Rhetorical Studies*, edited by Thomas Rostack, pp. 29–83. New York: Guilford, 1999.

Blaney, Joseph R., and William L. Benoit. *The Clinton Scandals and the Politics of Image Restoration*. Westport, CT: Praeger, 2001.

Boorstin, Dan. *The Image: A Guide to Pseudo-Events in America*, reissue ed. New York: Vintage, 1994.

Bormann, Ernest G. "A Fantasy Theme Analysis of the Television Coverage of the Hostage Release and the Reagan Inaugural." *Quarterly Journal of Speech* 68 (1982): 133–45.

Bostdorff, Denise. "George W. Bush's Post-September 11 Rhetoric of Covenant Renewal: Upholding the Faith of the Greatest Generation." *Quarterly Journal of Speech* 89 (2003): 293–319.

Bowers, John W., Donovan Ochs, and Richard J. Jensen. *The Rhetoric of Agitation and Control.* 2nd ed. Prospect Heights, IL: Waveland, 1993.

Bowles, Dorothy A., and Rebekah V. Bromley. "Newsmagazine Coverage of the Supreme Court During the Reagan Administration." *Journalism Quarterly* 69.4 (1002): 948–59.

Boyle, Michael P., Michael R. McCluskey, Douglas M. McLeod, and Sue E. Stein. "Newspapers and Protest: An Examination of Protest Coverage from 1960 to 1999." *Journalism and Mass Communication Quarterly* 82.3 (2005): 638–53.

Brady, David W., and Jeremy C. Pope. "Congress: Still in the Balance? How Congress May Look after the Election." *Hoover Digest*, Winter, 2004.

Brenner, Andrew. "Courtrooms Shuttered to Cameras in Three Trials." *News Media and the Law* 29.2 (Spring 2005): 33.

Brill, Steven. "Truth or Fiction: Pick One: Fictional *West Wing* Bests Many Reporters in Depicting a Nuanced Washington." *Brill's Content* 3.2 (March 2000): 25.

Brodie, Mollyann, Elizabeth Hamel, Lee Ann Kates, and Drew E. Altman. "AIDS at 21: Media Coverage of the HIV Epidemic 1981–2002." Supplement to *Columbia Journalism Review* 42.6 (March/April 2004): 1–8.

Brown, Rich. "Press Fears Subpoena Chill: First Amendment Advocates Decry Rise in Requests for Confidential Information from Reporters." *Broadcasting*, February 10, 1992: 34–35.

Brown, Rich. "Thomas Takes TV's Center Stage." *Broadcasting*, October 21, 1991: 23–25.

Buchanan, Bruce. "Presidential Campaign Quality: What the Variance Implies." *Presidential Studies Quarterly* 29.4 (1999): 798–820.

Campbell, Karlyn Kohrs, and Kathleen Hall Jamieson. *Deeds Done in Words: Presidential Rhetoric and the Genres of Governance.* Chicago: University of Chicago Press, 1990.

"Candidates Reach Internet Generation on MySpace, YouTube." November 3, 2006. http://www .playfuls.com/news-05005_Candidates_Reach_Internet_Generation_On_MySpace_YouTube. html.

Canon, David T. *Actors, Athletes, and Astronauts: Political Amateurs in the United States Congress.* Chicago: University of Chicago Press, 1990.

Carlin, Diana B., Eric Morris, and Shawna Smith. "The Influence of Format and Questions on Candidates' Strategic Argument Choices in the 2000 Presidential Debates." *American Behavioral Scientist* 44 (2001): 2196–218.

Cathcart, Robert S. "Movements: Confrontations as Rhetorical Form." *Southern Speech Communication Journal* 43 (1978): 233–47.

Center for Information and Research on Civic Learning and Engagement. "Youth Voting Up Sharply in 2004." http:/ /www. civicyouth. org/ PopUps/ Release_Turnout2004. pdf.

Center for Media and Public Affairs. "Networks Triple Their Mid-Term Coverage." http:/ /www. cmpa. com/ documents/ 06. 10. 18. Mid-Term. Coverage. pdf.

Christensen, Terry, and Haas, Peter J. *Projecting Politics: Political Messages in American Films.* Armonk, NY: M. E. Sharpe, 2005.

Clinton v. Jones (95–1853), 520 U.S. 681 (1997).

Conover, Pamela Johnston, and Stanley Feldman. "How People Organize the Political World." *American Journal of Political Science* 28.1 (1984): 95–126.

Constitutional Amendment to Prohibit Physical Desecration of U.S. Flag. Senate Report 108–334. Washington, DC: Government Printing Office, 2004.

Corbett, Edward P. J., and Robert Connors. *Classical Rhetoric for the Modern Student*, 4th ed. New York: Oxford University Press, 1999.

Cornfield, Michael, and Lee Rainie. "The Impact of the Internet on Politics." Pew Internet and American Life Project. November 5, 2006. http:/ /www. pewinternet. org/ ppt/ PIP_Internet _and_Politics. pdf.

Cronin, Thomas E., and Michael A. Genovese. *The Paradoxes of the American Presidency*, 2nd ed. New York: Oxford University Press, 2004.

Crouse, Tim. *The Boys on the Bus.* New York: Ballantine Books, 1973.

Darsey, James. "From 'Gay is Good' to the Scourge of AIDS: The Evolution of Gay Liberation Rhetoric." *Communication Studies* 42 (1991): 43–66.

Davis, R. "Supreme Court Nominations and the News Media." *Albany Law Review* 57 (Fall 1994): 1061–79.

Davis, R. *Decisions and Images: The Supreme Court and the Press.* Englewood Cliffs, NJ: Prentice Hall, 1994.

Debate on the Marriage Protection Amendment. United States House of Representatives. *Congressional Record*, July 18, 2006.

Delli Carpini, Michael X., and Ester R. Fuchs. "The Year of the Woman? Candidates, Voters, and the 1992 Elections." *Political Science Quarterly* 108.1 (1993): 29–36.

Denton, Robert E., Jr. "Religions, Evangelicals, and Moral Issues in the 2004 Presidential Campaign." In *The 2004 Presidential Campaign: A Communication Perspective*, edited by Robert E. Denton, Jr., 255–81. Lanham, MD: Rowman and Littlefield, 2005.

Denton, Robert E., Jr., ed. *The 2000 Presidential Campaign: A Communication Perspective*. Westport, CT: Praeger, 2002.

Devlin, L. Patrick. "Contrasts in Presidential Campaign Commercials of 2004." *American Behavioral Scientist* 49 (2005): 279–313.

Dinan, Steven. "Hispanics Tune Out Estrada Filibuster; Nominee Mistaken for Actor, Poll Finds." *The Washington Times*, June 19, 2003, A6.

Dobson, James C. "Media Provides Cover for Assault on Traditional Marriage." June 28, 2006. http://www.cnn.com/2006/US/06/28/dobson.gaymarriage/index.html.

Dow, Bonnie J. "AIDS, Perspective by Incongruity, and Gay Identity in Larry Kramer's '1,112 and Counting.'" *Communication Studies* 45 (1994): 225–40.

Edelman, Murray. *The Symbolic Uses of Politics*. Urbana, IL: University of Illinois Press, 1964.

Effron, Eric. "Laughing Matters." *Brill's Content*, February 2001: 72–73.

Emerson, Thomas I. *The System of Freedom of Expression*. New York: Random House, 1970.

Entman, Robert M. "Framing: Toward Clarification of a Fractured Paradigm." *Journal of Communication* 43.4 (1993): 51–58.

Erickson, Robert S., and Gerald C. Wright. "Voters, Candidates, and Issues in Congressional Elections." In *Congress Reconsidered*, 7th ed., edited by Lawrence C. Dodd and Bruce I. Oppenheimer, 67–96. Washington, DC: Congressional Quarterly Press.

Farnsworth, S. J., and S. R. Lichter. *The Mediated Presidency: Television News and Presidential Governance*. Lanham, MD: Rowman and Littlefield, 2006.

Featherly, Kevin. "Body-Slamming the Election and the Media." *Editor and Publisher*, February 13, 1999: 32.

Federal Election Commission. "Federal Elections 2004: Election Results for U.S. President, the U.S. Senate, and the U.S. House of Representatives." http://www.fec.gov/pubrec/fe2004/federalelections2004.shtml.

Fenno, Richard. "U.S. House Members in Their Districts: An Exploration." *American Political Science Review* 71 (1977): 883–917.

Festle, Mary Jo. "Listening to the Civil Rights Movement." *The Gay and Lesbian Review Worldwide* 12.6 (November-December 2005): 10–15.

Fisher, Walter. *Human Communication as Narration: Toward a Philosophy of Reason, Value, and Action*. Columbia: University of South Carolina Press, 1987.

Fitch, Brad. *Media Relations Handbook*. Washington, DC: Congressional Management Foundation, 2004.

Fitzgerald, M. "Bring 'Out' Your Dead." *Editor and Publisher*, September 26, 2005.

Foss, Karen A., Sonja K. Foss, and Cindy L. Griffin. *Feminist Rhetorical Tradition*. Thousand Oaks, CA: Sage, 1999.

Fox, J. R., and B. Park. "The 'I' of Embedded Reporting: An Analysis of CNN Coverage of the 'Shock and Awe' Campaign." *Journal of Broadcasting and Electronic Media* 50.1 (2006): 36–51.

Franke, Katherine M. "The Politics of Same-Sex Marriage Politics." *Columbia Journal of Gender and Law* 15.1 (2006): 236–48.

Frantzich, Steven, and Sullivan, John. *The C-SPAN Revolution*. Norman, OK: University of Oklahoma Press, 1996.

Friedenberg, Robert V. "The 2000 Presidential Debates." In *The 2000 Presidential Campaign: A Communication Perspective*, edited by Robert E. Denton, Jr., 135–65. Westport, CT: Praeger, 2002.

Gamson, W. A. "Reflections on the Strategy of Social Protest." *Sociological Forum* 4 (1989): 455–67.

Gartner, Michael. "How the Monica Story Played in Mid-America." *Columbia Journalism Review* 38.1 (May/June, 1999): 34–36.

Gitlin, T. *The Whole World is Watching: Mass Media in the Making and Unmaking of the New Left*. Berkeley: University of California Press, 1980.

Glowacki, C., T. Johnson, and K. E. Kranenberg. "Use of Newspaper Political Adwatches from 1988–2000." *Newspaper Research Journal* 25.4 (2004): 40–54.

Gold, Howard J. "Third-Party Voting in Gubernatorial Elections: A Study of Angus King of Maine and Jesse Ventura of Minnesota." *Polity* 35.2 (2002): 270–71.

Golden, James L., et al. *The Rhetoric of Western Thought: From the Mediterranean World to the Global Setting*, 8th ed. Dubuque, IA: Kendall/Hunt, 2004.

Graber, Doris. *Mass Media and American Politics*, 7th ed. Washington, DC: Congressional Quarterly Press, 2006.

Graff, E. J. "How the Culture War Was Won: Lesbian and Gay Men Defeated the Right in the 1990s, but Tougher Battles Lie Ahead." *The American Prospect* October 21, 2002: 33–37.

Gray, Virginia, and Wyman Spano. "The Irresistible Force Meets the Immovable Object: Minnesota's Moralistic Culture Confronts Jesse Ventura." *Daedalus* 129.3 (2000): 221–26.

Gring-Pemble, Lisa M. "Are We Going to Govern by Anecdote." *Quarterly Journal of Speech*, 87 (2001): 341–65.

Gronbeck, Bruce E., and Danielle R. Wiese. "The Repersonalization of Presidential Campaigning in 2004." *American Behavioral Scientist* 49 (2005): 520–34.

Grossman, C. L. "Lessons in Entertainment: 'West Wing' Manages to Teach Civics Without Going by the Textbook." *USA Today*, December 15, 1999.

Grossman, Lawrence K. "Shilling for Prime Time: Can CBS News Survive Survivor." *Columbia Journalism Review* 39.3 (September/October 2000): 70–71.

Harrell, Jackson, B. L. Ware, and Wil A. Linkugel. "Failure of Apology in American Politics: Nixon on Watergate." *Speech Monographs* 42 (1975): 245–60.

Hart, Roderick P. *Campaign Talk: Why Elections Are Good for Us*. Princeton, NJ: Princeton University Press, 2000.

Hart, Roderick P. *The Sound of Leadership: Presidential Communication in the Modern Age*. Chicago: University of Chicago Press, 1987.

Hart, Roderick P. *Verbal Style and the Presidency: A Computer-Based Analysis*. Orlando, FL: Academic Press, 1984.

Hasian, Marouf, Jr., Celeste Michaelle Condit, and John Louis Lucaites. "The Rhetorical Boundaries of 'the Law': A Consideration of the Rhetorical Culture of Legal Practice and the Case of the 'Separate But Equal' Doctrine." *Quarterly Journal of Speech* 82 (1996): 323–42.

Hertsgaard, Mark. *On Bended Knee: The Press and the Reagan Presidency*. New York: Farrar, Strauss, and Giroux, 1988.

Hillsman, W. G. *Run the Other Way: Fixing the Two-Party System, One Campaign at a Time*. New York: Free Press, 2004.

Holbert, R. Lance, et al. "*The West Wing* as Endorsement of the U.S. Presidency: Expanding the Bounds of Priming in Political Communication." *Communication Quarterly* 53.4 (2005): 505–22.

Hollander, Barry A. "Late-night Learning: Do Entertainment Programs Increase Political Campaign Knowledge for Young Viewers?" *Journal of Broadcasting and Electronic Media* 49.4 (December 2005): 402–16.

"Incumbency Level Running High: While There Are Some Races to Watch in the National Picture, There Are More Incumbents Than in Past Years." *Associated Press*, October 28, 2006.

Institute of Politics, Democracy, and the Internet. "Person-to-Person-to-Person: Harnessing the Political Power of Online Social Networks and User-Generated Content." http://ipdi.org/uploadedfiles/PtPtP%20ExecSum.pdf.

Iyengar, Shanto, and Kinder, D. *News That Matters*. Chicago: University of Chicago Press, 1987.

Iyengar, Shanto. *Is Anyone Responsible? How Television Frames Political Issues*. Chicago: University of Chicago Press, 1991.

Jamieson, Kathleen Hall, ed. *Electing the President 2004: The Insiders' View*. Philadelphia: University of Pennsylvania Press, 2006.

Jamieson, Kathleen Hall. *Dirty Politics: Deception, Distraction, and Democracy*. New York: Oxford University Press, 1992.

Jamieson, Kathleen Hall. *Eloquence in an Electronic Age: The Transformation of Political Speechmaking*. New York: Oxford University Press, 1988.

Jamieson, Kathleen Hall. *Packaging the Presidency: A History and Criticism of Presidential Campaign Advertising*, 3rd ed. New York: Oxford University Press, 1996.

Johnson, K. S. "The Honeymoon Period: Fact or Fiction?" *Journalism Quarterly* 62.4 (1985): 869–76.

Johnson-Cartee, Karen S., and Gary A. Copeland. *Manipulation of the American Voter: Political Campaign Commercials*. Westport, CT: Praeger, 1997.

Kaid, L. L., Chris M. Leland, and Susan Whitney. "The Impact of Televised Political Ads: Evoking Viewer Responses in the 1988 Presidential Campaign." *Southern Communication Journal* 57 (1992): 285–95.

Kaid, Lynda Lee, and Anne Johnston. *Videostyle in Presidential Elections: Style and Content of Televised Political Advertising*. Westport, CT: Praeger, 2001.

Kaid, Lynda Lee, John C. Tedesco, Dianne G. Bystrom, and Mitchell S. McKinney, eds. *The Millennium Election: Communication in the 2000 Campaign*. Lanham, MD: Rowman and Littlefield, 2003.

Kaid, Lynda Lee. "Political Advertising." In *Handbook of Political Communication Research*, edited by Lynda Lee Kaid, 155–202. Mahwah, NJ: Lawrence Erlbaum Associates, 2004.

Kan, K., and C. C. Yang. "On Expressive Voting: Evidence from the 1988 U.S. Presidential Election." *Public Choice* 108.3 (2001): 295–313.

Kenski, Henry C., and Kate M. Kenski. "Explaining the Vote in a Divided Country: The Presidential Election of 2004." In *The 2004 Presidential Campaign: A Communication Perspective*, edited by Robert E. Denton, Jr., 301–42. Lanham, MD: Rowman and Littlefield, 2005.

Kerbel, Matthew R., and Joel D. Bloom. "Blog for America and Civic Involvement." *Harvard International Journal of Press/Politics* 10.4 (2005): 8–27.

Kimberling, William. "The Electoral College." Federal Election Commission Report. http://www.fec.gov/pdf/eleccoll.pdf.

King, Cynthia, and Paul Martin Lester. "Photographic Coverage During the Persian Gulf and Iraqi Wars in Three U.S. Newspapers." *Journalism and Mass Communication Quarterly* 82.3 (2005): 623–37.

Kiousis, S. "Job Approval and Favorability: The Impact of Media Attention to the Monica Lewinsky Scandal on Public Opinion of President Bill Clinton." *Mass Communication and Society* 6.4 (2003): 435–51.

Konner, Joan, James Risser, and Ben Wattenberg. "Television's Performance on Election Night 2000: A Report for CNN." January 29, 2001. http://archives.cnn.com/2001/ ALLPOLITICS/stories/02/02/cnn.report/cnn.pdf.

Korzi, Michael J. "The President and the Public: Inaugural Addresses in American History." *Congress and the Presidency* 31.1 (2004): 21–53.

Kraus, Sidney. *Televised Presidential Debates and Public Policy*, 2nd ed. Mahwah, NJ: Lawrence Erlbaum Associates, 2000.

LaFleur, J. "Embed Program Worked, Broader War Coverage Lagged." *News Media and the Law* 27.2 (2003): 4–6.

Lang, Kurt, and Gladys Engel Lang. "The Unique Perspective of Television and Its Effects: A Pilot Study." *American Sociological Review* 18.1 (1953): 3–12.

Lehrman, S. "AIDS Coverage Has Been Lost in Recent Years." *Quill Magazine* 92.2 (March 2004): 24–25.

Lenhart, Amanda, and Susannah Fox. "Bloggers: A Portrait of the Internet's New Storytellers." Pew Internet and American Life Project. http://www.pewinternet.org/PPF/r/186/ report _display. asp.

Lentz, Jacob. *Electing Jesse Ventura: A Third-Party Success Story*. Boulder, CO: Lynne Rienner, 2002.

Lescaze, Lee. "Hostage Release Opens Presidency on a Dramatic High Note." *Washington Post*, January 21, 1981, A31.

Lewis, William. "Of Innocence, Exclusion, and the Burning of Flags: The Romantic Realism of the Law." *Southern Communication Journal* 60 (1994): 4–21.

Lieske, Joel. "Cultural Issues and Images in the 1988 Presidential Campaign: Why the Democrats Lost Again!" *PS: Political Science and Politics* 24 (1991): 2.

Ling, David A. "A Pentadic Analysis of Senator Edward Kennedy's Address to the People of Massachusetts, July 15, 1969." *Central States Speech Journal* 21 (1970): 81–86.

Lippman, Walter. *Public Opinion*. New York: Harcourt, Brace, and Company, 1922.

Little, Thomas H. "On the Coattails of a Contract: RNC Activities and Republican Gains in the 1994 State Legislative Elections." *Political Research Quarterly* 51 (1998): 173–90.

Lorch, Robert S. *State and Local Politics: The Great Entanglement*, 6th ed. Upper Saddle River, NJ: Prentice Hall, 2001.

May, A. L. "Swift Boat Vets in 2004: Press Coverage of an Independent Campaign." *First Amendment Law Review* 4 (2005): 66–106.

Mayer, William G. "In Defense of Negative Campaigning." *Political Science Quarterly* 111 (1996): 437–55.

Mayhew, David R. *Congress: The Electoral Connection*, 2nd ed. New Haven, CT: Yale University Press, 2004.

McCombs, Maxwell, and Donald Shaw. "The Agenda-Setting Function of Mass Media." *Public Opinion Quarterly* 36 (1972): 1766–87.

McCroskey, James C. *An Introduction to Rhetorical Communication*, 8th ed. Englewood Cliffs, NJ: Prentice-Hall, 2002.

McDevitt, M. "Ideological Language and the Press: Coverage of Inaugural, State of the Union Addresses." *Mass Communication Review* 13.1 (1986): 18–24.

McKinney, Mitchell S., and Diana B. Carlin. "Political Campaign Debates." In *Handbook of Political Communication Research*, edited by Lynda Lee Kaid, 203–34. Mahwah, NJ: Lawrence Erlbaum Associates, 2004.

McKinney, Mitchell S., Elizabeth Dudash, and Georgine Hodgkinson. "Viewer Reactions to the 2000 Presidential Debates: Learning Issue and Image Information." In *The Millennium Election: Communication in the 2000 Campaign*, edited by Lynda Lee Kaid et al., 43–58. Lanham, MD: Rowman and Littlefield, 2003.

McLeod, Douglas M., and James K. Hertog. "The Manufacture of Public Opinion by Reporters: Informal Cues for Public Perceptions of Protest Groups." *Discourse and Society* 3 (1992): 259–75.

McLuhan, Marshall. *Understanding Media: The Extensions of Man*. New York: McGraw Hill, 1964.

Medhurst, Martin J. "Reconceptualizing Rhetorical History: Eisenhower's Farewell Address." *Quarterly Journal of Speech* 80 (1994): 195–228.

Medvic, Stephen K., and David A. Dulio. "The Media and Public Opinion." In *Media Power, Media Politics*, edited by Mark J. Rozell, 207–33. Lanham, MD: Rowman and Littlefield, 2003.

Miller, Arthur H., and Thomas F. Klobucar. "The Role of Issues in the 2000 U.S. Presidential Election." *Presidential Studies Quarterly* 33.1 (2003): 101–25.

Miller, Matthew "Real White House." *Brill's Content* 3.2 (March 2000): 88–113.

Moyer, Bill. *Doing Democracy: The MAP Model for Organizing Social Movements*. Gabriola Island, BC, Canada: New Society Publishers, 2001.

Murphy, John M. " 'Our Mission and Our Moment': George W. Bush and September 11th." *Rhetoric and Public Affairs* 6 (2003): 607–32.

Neustadt, Richard. *Presidential Power and the Modern Presidents: The Politics of Leadership from Roosevelt to Reagan*. New York: The Free Press, 1991.

"New C-SPAN Study: Congressional Scholars Examine House Television after Twenty-Five Years." April 2004. http://www.cspan.org/C-SPAN25/survey_release.asp.

Nitz, Michael, et al. "Candidates as Comedy: Political Presidential Humor on Late-Night Television Shows." In *The Millennium Election: Communication in the 2000 Campaign*, edited by Lynda Lee Kaid et al., 165–75. Lanham, MD: Rowman and Littlefield, 2003.

O'Mara, Richard. "A Terrorist Is a Guerilla Is a Freedom Fighter: 'Reality' Is a Long and Slippery Slope." *Quill* 78.8 (October 1990): 22–25.

Ostman, Ronald E., and William A. Babcock. "Reagan Inauguration, Hostage Release, or Both?: Publication Time, Ownership and Circulation Size in Daily Newspaper Editorial Decisions." *Newspaper Research Journal* 3.4 (1982): 24–35.

Paletz, David L. *The Media in American Politics: Contents and Consequences*, 2nd ed. New York: Longman, 2002.

Parenti, M. *Make-Believe Media: The Politics of Entertainment*. New York: St. Martin's Press, 1992.

Parry-Giles, Trevor, and Shawn Parry-Giles. "*The West Wing*'s Prime-Time Presidentiality: Mimesis and Catharsis in a Postmodern Romance." *Quarterly Journal of Speech* 88 (2002): 209–27.

Parry-Giles, Trevor, and Shawn Parry-Giles. *The Prime-Time Presidency: The West Wing and U.S. Nationalism*. Urbana: University of Illinois Press, 2006.

Patterson, Thomas. *Out of Order*. New York: Knopf, 1993.

Patterson, Thomas. *The Vanishing Voter*. New York: Knopf, 2002.

Perloff, Richard M. *Political Communication: Politics, Press, and Public in America*. Mahwah, NJ: Lawrence Erlbaum Associates, 1998.

Peterson, Paul E. "The Rise and Fall of Special Interest Politics." *Political Science Quarterly* 105 (1990): 539–56.

Pew Research Center for the People and the Press. "Cable and Internet Loom Large in Fragmented Political News Universe." January 2004. http://people-press.org/reports/display. php3?ReportID=200.

Pew Research Center for the People and the Press. "It's Still the Economy, They Say." August 27, 1998. http://people-press.org/reports/display.php3?ReportID=82.

Pew Research Center for the People and the Press. "New Audiences Increasingly Politicized." June 2004. http://people-press.org/reports/display.php3?PageID=833.

Pew Research Center for the People and the Press. "Popular Policies and Unpopular Press Lift Clinton Ratings." February 6, 1998. http://people-press.org/reports/display.php3?ReportID=96.

Pew Research Center for the People and The Press. "The Dean Activists: Their Profile and Prospects." April 6, 2005. http://people-press.org/reports/display.php3?ReportID=240.

Pew Research Center for the People and the Press. "The Tough Job of Communicating with Voters." January 2000. http://people-press.org/reports/display.php3?ReportID=46.

Pew Research Center for the People and the Press. "Turned off: Public Tuned Out Impeachment." December 21, 1998. http://people-press.org/reports/display.php3?ReportID=73.

Pfau, Michael, et al. "Embedding Journalists in Military Combat Units: Impact on Newspaper Story Frames and Tone." *Journalism and Mass Communication Quarterly* 81.1 (2004): 74–88.

Pitney, John J., Jr. "President Clinton's 1993 Inaugural Address." *Presidential Studies Quarterly* 27.1 (1987): 91–110.

Podhoretz, John. "The Liberal Imagination." In The West Wing: *The American Presidency as Television Drama*, edited by Peter C. Rollins and John E. O'Connor, 222–31. Syracuse, NY: Syracuse University Press, 2003.

Popkin, Samuel L. *The Reasoning Voter: Communication and Persuasion in Presidential Campaigns*, 2nd ed. Chicago: University of Chicago Press, 1994.

Price, Vincent, Lilach Nir, and Joseph N. Cappella. "Framing Public Discussion of Gay Civil Unions." *Public Opinion Quarterly* 69.2 (2005): 179–212.

Project for Excellence in Journalism. "Election Night 2006: An Evening in the Life of the American Media." http://www.journalism.org/node/3015.

Project for Excellence in Journalism. "Embedded Reporters: What Are Americans Getting?" April 3, 2003. http://www.journalism.org/resources/research/reports/war/embed/default.asp.

Project for Excellence in Journalism. "Post Election Headlines Play It Safe." http://www.journalism.org/node/2861.

Racine Group. "White Paper on Televised Political Campaign Debates." *Argumentation and Advocacy* 39 (2002): 199–218.

Rannie, Lee, and John Horrigan. "Election 2006 Online." Pew Internet and American Life Project. http://www.pewinternet.org/PPF/r/199/report_display.asp.

Regan, Allison. "Rhetoric and Political Process in the Hill-Thomas Hearings." *Political Communication* 11.3 (1994): 277–86.

Ricchiardi, Sherry. "Close to the Action." *American Journalism Review* 25.4 (May 2003): 28–35.

Ricchiardi, Sherry. "Preparing for War." *American Journalism Review* 25.2 (March 2003): 29–33.

Rieder, R. "Clinton's Legacy to Journalism." *American Journalism Review* 20.8 (October 1998): 6.

Ritter, Kurt, and David Henry. *Ronald Reagan: The Great Communicator*. Westport, CT: Greenwood, 1992.

Ritter, Kurt, and Martin J. Medhurst, eds. *Presidential Speech-Writing*. College Station: Texas A & M University Press, 2003.

Roper, Jon. "The Contemporary Presidency: George W. Bush and the Myth of Heroic Presidential Leadership." *Presidential Studies Quarterly* 34.1 (2004): 132–43.

Rozell, Mark. "Executive Privilege in the Lewinsky Scandal: Giving a Good Doctrine a Bad Name (Monica Lewinsky)." *Presidential Studies Quarterly* 28.4 (1998): 816–17.

Ruckinski, D. "Rush to Judgment? Fast Reaction Polls in the Anita Hill–Clarence Thomas Controversy." *Public Opinion Quarterly* 57 (1993): 575–92.

Sabato, Larry. *Feeding Frenzy: Attack Journalism and American Politics*. New York: Free Press, 1991.

Selnow, Gary. *Electronic Whistle Stops: The Impact of the Internet on American Politics*. Westport, CT: Praeger, 1998.

Shah, Dhavan V., Mark D. Watts, David Domke, and David P. Fan. "News Framing and Cueing of Issue Regimes: Explaining Clinton's Public Approval in Spite of Scandal." *Public Opinion Quarterly* 66 (2002): 339–70.

Shales, Tom. "The Inauguration: Watching the Watchers: How the Networks Are Covering All the Angles for 75 Million Viewers." *Washington Post*, January 18, 1981, P H1.

Sharkey, J. "The Television War." *American Journalism Review* 25.4 (May 2003): 18–27.

Sheckels, Theodore F. *When Congress Debates: A Bakhtinian Paradigm*. Westport, CT: Praeger, 2000.

Sheckels, Theodore F., and Lauren Cohen Bell. "Character Versus Competence: Evidence from the 2000 Presidential Debates and Election." In *The Millennium Election: Communication in the 2000 Campaign*, edited by Lynda Lee Kaid, et al., 59–71. Lanham, MD: Rowman and Littlefield, 2003.

Shepard, A. C. "A Scandal Unfolds." *American Journalism Review* 20.2 (March 1998): 20–28.

Sillars, Malcolm O. "Defining Social Movements Rhetorically: Casting the Widest Net." *Southern Speech Communication Journal* 46 (1980): 17–32.

Smith, Arthur. *Rhetoric of Black Revolution*. Boston: Allyn and Bacon, 1969.

Smith, Dane, and Dean Barkley. "Diary of an Upset." *Minneapolis Star-Tribune*, November 8, 1998.

Sotirovic, Mira, and Jack McLeod. "Knowledge as Understanding: The Information Processing Approach to Political Learning." In *Handbook of Political Communication Research*, edited by Lynda Lee Kaid, 357–94. Mahwah, NJ: Lawrence Erlbaum Associates, 2004.

Starr, A. "The Man Behind Ventura." *Washington Monthly* 31.6 (1999): 25.

Stewart, Charles J. "A Functional Approach to the Rhetoric of Social Movements." *Central States Speech Journal* 31 (1980): 298–305.

Stewart-Winter, Timothy. "What Was Same-Sex Marriage?" *The Gay and Lesbian Review Worldwide* 13.1 (January-February 2006): 33–36.

Strickler, V. J., and Davis, R. "The Supreme Court and the Press." In *Media Power Media Politics*, edited by M. J. Rozell, 45–73. Lanham, MD: Rowman and Littlefield, 2003.

The American Presidency Project. http://www. presidency. ucsb. edu.

Thomas, Dan, Craig McCoy, and Allan McBride. "Deconstructing the Political Spectacle: Sex, Race, and Subjectivity in Public Response to the Clarence Thomas/Anita Hill 'Sexual Harassment' Hearings." *American Journal of Political Science* 37 (1993): 699–721.

Toulmin, Stephen, Richard Rieke, and Allan Janik. *An Introduction to Reasoning*, 2nd ed. Englewood Cliffs, NJ: Prentice Hall, 1997.

Toulmin, Stephen. *The Uses of Argument*. Cambridge: Cambridge University Press, 1968.

Trent, Judith S., and Robert V. Friedenberg. *Political Campaign Communication: Principles and Practices*, 5th ed. Lanham, MD: Rowman and Littlefield, 2004.

Trent, Judith S., et al. "The Idealized Presidential Candidate: A Vision over Time." *American Behavioral Scientist* 49 (2005): 130–56.

Turner, Paige K., and Patricia Ryden. "How George Bush Silenced Anita Hill: A Derridean View of the Third Persona in Public Argument." *Argumentation and Advocacy* 37.2 (2000): 86–98.

VonStenberg, Bob. "As Vote Nears, Voters Are All Over the Road; From Governor to County Boards, Minnesota's Political Races Couldn't Find Issues to Rev Up the Electorate." *Minneapolis Star-Tribune*, October 28, 1998, A1.

Ware, B. L., and Wil A. Linkugel. "They Spoke in Defense of Themselves: On the Generic Critique of the Apologia." *Quarterly Journal of Speech* 59 (1973): 273–83.

Wattier, Mark J. "The Clinton Factor: The Effects of Clinton's Personal Image in 2000 Presidential Primaries and in the General Election." *White House Studies* 4.4 (2004): 467–89.

Weaver, D. D. Maxwell McComb, and Donald Shaw. "Agenda-Setting Research: Issues, Attributes, and Influences." In *Handbook of Political Communication Research*. Ed. Lynda Lee Kaid. Mahwah, NJ: Lawrence Erlbaum Associates, 2004.

Weiler, Michael, and W. Barnett Pearce. "Ceremonial Discourse: The Rhetorical Ecology of the Reagan Administration." In *Ronald Reagan and Public Discourse in America*, edited by Michael Weiler and W. Barnett Pearce, 11–42. Tuscaloosa: University of Alabama Press, 2006.

West, Darrell M. *Air Wars: Television Advertising in Election Campaigns, 1952–2004*, 4th ed. Washington, DC: Congressional Quarterly Press, 2005.

Wicks, Robert, and Boubacar Souley. "Going Negative: Candidate Usage of Internet Web Sites During the 2000 Presidential Campaign." *Journalism and Mass Communication Quarterly* 80 (2003):128–44.

Wildavsky, Aaron. "The Two Presidencies." In *The Presidency*, edited by Aaron Wildavsky, 23–43. Boston: Little, Brown, 1969.

Williams, Andrew Paul, and John C. Tedesco, ed. *The Internet Election: Perspectives on the Web in Campaign 2004*. Lanham, MD: Rowman and Littlefield, 2006.

Witcover, J. "Where We Went Wrong." *Columbia Journalism Review* 36.6 (March/April, 1998): 19–26.

Yioutas, Julie, and Ivana Segvic. "Revisiting the Clinton/Lewinsky Scandal: The Convergence of Agenda-Setting and Framing." *Journalism and Mass Communication Quarterly* 80.3 (2003): 567–82.

Zelizer, Barbie, and Stuart Allan, eds. *Journalism after September 11*. London: Routledge, 2002.

INDEX